The Search for Peace in Vietnam, 1964–1968

Number Eight:
Foreign Relations and the Presidency
H. W. Brands, General Editor

The Search for Peace in Vietnam, 1964–1968

Edited by
Lloyd C. Gardner and Ted Gittinger

Texas A&M University Press
College Station

Copyright © 2004 by Lloyd C. Gardner and Ted Gittinger
Manufactured in the United States of America
All rights reserved
First edition

The paper used in this book meets the minimum requirements
of the American National Standard for Permanence
of Paper for Printed Library Materials, Z39.48-1984.
Binding materials have been chosen for durability.
∞

Publication of this book was supported by a generous gift from the
Lyndon B. Johnson Foundation.

Library of Congress Cataloging-in-Publication Data

The search for peace in Vietnam, 1964–1968 / edited
by Lloyd C. Gardner and Ted Gittinger.— 1st ed.
    p. cm. — (Foreign relations and the presidency ; no. 8)
  Includes bibliographical references (p.) and index.
  ISBN 1-58544-342-5 (cloth : alk. paper)
  1. Vietnamese Conflict, 1961–1975—Peace. 2. Vietnamese Conflict, 1961–1975
  —Diplomatic history. I. Gardner, Lloyd C., 1934– II. Gittinger, Ted. III. Series.
  DS559.7.S44 2004
  959.704′31—dc22
                                                                2004013319

Contents

THE SEARCH FOR PEACE IN VIETNAM, 1964–1968

Introduction

LLOYD C. GARDNER

The Vietnam War was unusual, perhaps unique, in having so many "peace offers" put forward even as the struggle intensified and American involvement deepened during the Johnson years. Washington's Cold War allies offered their services as interlocutors to get talks started, but so did the Soviet Union's satellites in Eastern Europe. France's Charles de Gaulle, acting from his own agenda, called for the "neutralization" of Vietnam in 1964, not simply as a peace program, but as part of a general realignment in both Asia and Europe that would replace the postwar bipolar structure with a multicentered organization of world affairs. All these crosscurrents make the study of the Vietnam War's peace initiatives essential to those who wish to understand how the conflict was a part of the Cold War, yet called into question basic assumptions about such givens as the Sino-Soviet bloc, and ultimately, as H. W. Brands points out, provided a powerful impetus to détente.

De Gaulle's early insistence upon bringing Communist China into the discussions over Vietnam's future—as the *sine qua non* of any lasting settlement in Southeast Asia—was more than just irksome to American policy makers, as Charles Cogan and Maurice Vaïsse explain so clearly. It posed several difficulties. First, his actions implied that the French experience in Vietnam proved it would be an unwinnable struggle—something that the Americans could not accept. Second, his "meddling" only made matters worse—with both allies and enemies—and delayed success. Third, much of the rationale for U.S. involvement in the postcolonial struggle in Vietnam, after all, had been to block China's expansion dating from the Korean War. Fourth, the domestic political consequences of that war had cost the last Democratic administration dearly, and were a powerful disincentive to consider French proposals, or any others that smacked of appeasement. Again, as H. W. Brands comments in the final chapter of this book, "Communist China still looked like the third rail of U.S. diplomacy: touch it and you die."

As matters stood throughout the Johnson administration, serious negotiations offered only bad outcomes: a quick surrender of the main objective, an independent South Vietnam able to stand on its own; or, at best, a slow surrender and repeat of the prolonged agony of the Korea truce talks to save face. Either possibility was anathema. At the beginning there was the Gulf of Tonkin Resolution, an invocation of national traditions to fulfill the requirement that Vietnam be explained, as Robert Divine points out, as essentially a response "to an attack by others." Having imposed a solemn duty on themselves to see matters through to the end, it would not be easy to accept advice to give it all up and leave Vietnam.

However, fighting limited wars led down ambiguous trails as political leaders wrestled with the contradictions between the need to win and what circumstances permitted. While America fought to maintain credibility with, and for, its Cold War allies, Professor Divine observes, Hanoi's goals were actually the more traditional objectives of warfare: territorial conquest and national unification. "And of course the ultimate irony is that the credibility that both Johnson and Nixon prized so much proved meaningless—other nations, both friend and foe, viewed our devotion to a losing cause as an act of folly, not fidelity."

"In both instances," Korea and Vietnam, Prof. Marilyn Young begins her essay, "policy makers, pundits and, insofar as one can determine this, the public felt the country was mired in Asia; the cold mountains of Korea, like the steamy jungles of Vietnam, had reached up, grabbed the country down, and would not let go." She further points out that the Korean and Vietnam Wars were about China as much as they were about anything else. Credibility meant standing tall against Beijing's efforts to turn history its way. To allow Communist China to shoot its way into the United Nations, John Foster Dulles had once said in words that Johnson-era policy makers reprised about Vietnam, "would confuse American public opinion and weaken support for the President's program looking toward the strengthening of our defenses."

Peace initiatives were not welcome, then, so long as it appeared there was any chance of victory. Moreover, while Secretary of State Dean Rusk consistently argued that Korea had been a major victory for the West in the Cold War, he preferred the Greek civil war as a model for how the fighting would end: with the other fellows fading away in the face of American determination. It would not do, however, to appear unreceptive to overtures for peace. David Kaiser provides us with a study of how the Johnson administration used the Kennedy tactic of welcoming "discussions" in the case of Panama's demands for return of the Canal Zone, to finesse the issue of actual negotiations there and then in Vietnam. The tactic worked for a time. American public opinion was reassured, and the administration could say to the world, as the president did in a speech, that he had done all he could, but "An appeal for unconditional discussion was met with contempt." North Vietnam, of course, was no more open to serious negotiations until the situation changed decisively in its favor. As Kaiser concludes, "neither side allowed third parties to move them into negotiations before they were ready."

Of all the supposed "missed opportunities" for peace, there was one in particular, code-named PENNSYLVANIA, that has drawn the attention of historians. The key player in the Johnson cabinet was Defense Secretary Robert S. McNamara, who in 1967 wished to help Lyndon Johnson extricate himself and the nation from the consequences of political decisions going back perhaps as far as Dwight D. Eisenhower's pledge to extend aid to the first South Vietnamese government. McNamara's efforts produced a change in the American position about bombing the north. Instead of evidence that Hanoi would deescalate its military efforts, the Americans offered to stop bombing North Vietnam if it would lead to "prompt and productive discussions." As Robert Brigham and George Herring reconstruct events, before the offer reached Hanoi, the air force launched a series of intensive raids on the North Vietnamese capital that lasted for two days. "This important incident has never been fully investigated," they conclude, "and some of the key sources remain classified." Yet, despite McNamara's later assertion that it was simply a tragic instance (one of many) of failure to coordinate military and diplomatic actions, these authors instead see PENNSYLVANIA's fate as yet another instance of President Johnson's unwillingness "to run the political risks of angering the military and congressional hawks at a critical juncture in the war at home."

Edwin Moïse further reminds us that PENNSYLVANIA had next to no chance of success in any event. No compromise on the central question of who would rule in Saigon was ever possible. The war, on the American side, was indeed fought on the basis of a miscalculation: that the other side had miscalculated, "and that once they experienced the amount of power being brought against them, they would realize it had been a mistake, and be willing to back out of the struggle if offered the opportunity." The memoranda George Ball presented, Moïse suggests, often cited as offering ways out of the war, were really attempts to ease the other side into a capitulation on American terms.

The American peace movement, like de Gaulle's neutralization schemes, was not offering the kind of opportunity that Johnson and his aides had in mind. The president seemed completely puzzled by what motivated members of his own party in opposing his policies. Did they not see that he was really holding off the Republican right? Actually, as Melvin Small points out, LBJ was too smart to believe some of his own statements about foreign influence on the movement. "Yet, by associating the movement with communists, he could discount its importance as a genuine homegrown response to the increasingly bloody trajectory of the war." The support dovish senator George McGovern received from "hometown" newspapers in South Dakota encouraged him to continue his efforts to dissuade the president from deepening the American involvement. McGovern was always careful to balance his criticisms with high praise for Johnson's domestic policies and achievements. During an audience with the president in the White House in the spring of 1965, Johnson listened to McGovern for a few minutes. Then, writes Thomas Knock, he went back to the designated rationale for the war. "George, you know what they want?" he asked, referring to the Chinese. "They want to take over the world. Vietnam is the very first point. We're not going to let them do it."

McGovern came away more determined than ever about his course; so did Johnson after encounters with the doves. He would not cut and run—from either Ho Chi Minh or Bill Fulbright and his senate supporters. While the president suspected McGovern of being a part of the "Dump Johnson" movement, it was not so. As Knock demonstrates, the South Dakotan understood both the moral complexities of the war and what Johnson meant to the success of the liberal agenda. After LBJ's speech on March 31, 1968, in which he took himself out of the election, McGovern praised the president for taking on "new stature and dignity" by placing peace in Vietnam above his desire for reelection.

Foreign observers who watched the development of the political turmoil in the United States were torn in several directions. De Gaulle's initiatives presented difficulties for them as well, particularly the leaders of West Germany (the Federal Republic of Germany) and Japan. Any movement that threatened to break down the stability of the postwar order posed grave problems for both allies. Both Bonn and Tokyo feared the consequences of America's "hot war" in Southeast Asia, where the issue was clouded and the outcome so uncertain. For them, the question of American credibility was indeed paramount—but not quite in the way Washington policy makers saw the matter. In Germany's case, de Gaulle's insistence that the postwar order be recast in a different mold caused serious anguish. The more deeply the United States became entangled in Vietnam, the more serious was the Gaullist threat to German "security" within the West. French dissent legitimized criticism not only on the Left, but, because de Gaulle voiced it, on the Right as well. As Wilfried Mausbach explains, Germans had sought to reconstruct a new national identity after the final collapse of National Socialism within the framework of the free world, which naturally "implied U.S. leadership and thus inevitably limited French independence." The

Vietnam War became for Germans a divisive question—precisely because it elevated de Gaulle's campaign for a new power center in Europe, with all of its uncertainties compared to the refuge Germany had found in the North Atlantic Treaty Organization (NATO).

German peace efforts thus were largely confined to raising polite questions with American diplomats, leaving to others the more difficult heavy lifting of trying to persuade the combatants to come to the peace table. Moreover, Germany and Japan, facing political dissent at home, had to take into account public opinion. In Tokyo's case, the question of Okinawa's return to Japanese rule loomed large as well. Any Japanese leader who failed to do all that he could to secure that return faced serious problems within his party, as well as from a nation yearning for full sovereignty. Japan sent several "missions" to Vietnam during the war in an effort to sound out the prospects for peace, and even put forward detailed plans for a postwar settlement of the "reunification" problem.

As Prof. Hideki Kan informs us, Premier Eisaku Sato's primary concern was always to bring the postwar era to an end by securing Okinawa's return to Japanese rule. Tokyo attempted to walk a narrow line in Vietnam, taking encouragement from any indications that the United States wanted to assure Hanoi that, once the fighting stopped, Vietnam could work out its own destiny. Hence Sato's efforts to find some sort of connecting point between both sides' "peace programs." As much as it could, Sato suggested to the North Vietnamese, Japan would act as guarantor of the peace terms. These efforts were coupled with several demonstrations of Tokyo's interest in the postwar rehabilitation of Southeast Asia. At times they seemed to be making progress. In reality, however, Hanoi saw Sato's emissaries as simply American messengers. Eventually, therefore, the Japanese foreign office had to concede "All doors seem to be closed to Japanese by North Vietnam." Saigon also closed its doors to Japanese appeals.

Having failed to move the combatants to the peace table, Sato opted for decisive support for Washington's policies. He based his decision on a "calculated" estimate that, like Germany, Japan's security treaty relationship with the United States claimed the highest priority—in part because only in that way could the Okinawa issue be resolved in a timely fashion. Indian peace efforts were likewise determined by extra-Vietnam questions. A member of the International Control Commission (ICC) since 1954, India would have seemed to be in a perfect position to influence the diplomacy of peace negotiations. Yet New Delhi was constrained, as Mark Lawrence notes, by a number of contradictory factors. On one side was China, a very real threat to Indian security; on the other was the United States, fighting a war that was unpopular with both Prime Minister Indira Gandhi and her

Congress Party. India's almost desperate need for food aid, in the form of American wheat shipments, also compromised New Delhi's diplomacy.

Professor Lawrence concludes that recent histories of the Vietnam War place much emphasis upon contingencies—missed opportunities, quirks of personality—to the partial neglect of context. "India's experiences in the 1960s call attention to the glaring lack of any real basis for moderate, neutralist solutions in Asia, no matter how willing the principal Cold War protagonists may have been to bring them about." Canada and Sweden ran into the same difficulties in proposing peace negotiations, even if the constraints on their actions were less binding than those on Germany, Japan or India. Canada, another member of the ICC, chafed at the role Washington envisaged for its diplomats: to deliver the message to Hanoi that "they will be punished" if the war in the south continued. In explaining the Canadian position, Andrew Preston observes that Ottawa saw itself instead in the role not only of ally, but also of intermediary, counselor, and perhaps peace broker. As such, it attempted to engage the North Vietnamese by proposing "talks" that would lead to direct negotiations.

The Canadians suspected that the various American peace "offensives" were designed to undercut serious diplomacy and to place blame for the failure of their efforts (and those of other would-be intermediaries) directly on Hanoi. "It would be a sad ending to our initiative in this matter," Lester Pearson complained, "if we became merely an instrument of U.S. propaganda or putting the DRVN on the spot." On the other hand, Washington resented Canada's assumption that it knew how to find peace. Little wonder, as Preston concludes, that the special missions Canada sent to Vietnam ended in failure, with the added twist that they "convinced the Americans of the necessity of expanding the war; and the North Vietnamese of the necessity of holding fast to their position."

It is a measure of the war's divisive impact that Canada and the United States, the closest of allies in World War II and throughout the Cold War, found themselves suspecting one another of deception and bad faith. Sweden's neutral status, writes Fredrik Logevall, "gave it a special claim to impartiality." Washington officials hoped to use that reputation to send messages to Hanoi like those it had tried to convey through Ottawa. The willingness of Swedish diplomats to pursue efforts to convince their American counterparts that nothing could be accomplished so long as the bombing continued throughout the war, always received a hearing in Washington, despite open opposition to the war by members of the Swedish government and the highly irritating decision that government made in allowing the Bertrand Russell War Crimes Tribunal to be held in Stockholm. Diplomat Torsten Nilsson went into his meetings with Secretary of State Dean Rusk with "high hopes," but always came away discouraged. "Nilsson was far from the only world leader to find Rusk stubborn and unreasonable on Vietnam, someone who demanded more from Ho Chi Minh than he himself was ready to give."

Secretary Rusk held fast to his convictions despite such criticisms. Russian leaders tried to convince Johnson administration officials that the bombing only increased China's leverage in Hanoi—and throughout the third world. Furthermore, writes Ilya Gaiduk, "the problem of credibility haunted the Kremlin no less than the White House in the years of the Vietnam War." In one of the greatest ironies of that conflict, Secretary Rusk himself told the National Security Council (NSC), "The Soviets are paralyzed by U.S. bombing and, as long as it continues, they cannot take any political action without exposing themselves to the criticism that they are not defending a socialist country." Even so, Moscow did what it could to make clear its interest in a peaceful solution, Gaiduk argues, so much so, in fact, that the North Vietnamese came to regard any Soviet move in that direction "with suspicion and disdain."

The ambiguous nature of Eastern bloc efforts to get peace talks started is the subject of James Hershberg's discussion of Czechoslovakian diplomacy, based upon new evidence gleaned from that country's archives. Similarly concerned that only China gained from America's war in Vietnam, Eastern Europeans tried to work around the constraints imposed by Moscow and Washington.

Beijing proved unreceptive to the French leader's overtures, although China in the end proved amenable to Richard Nixon's walk on the Great Wall. As Prof. Qiang Zhai points out below, the Chinese position reflected "Mao's complex calculations of limiting Soviet influence in Indochina, establishing China's leadership position within the third world independence movement, and mobilizing domestic support for his social and political programs." This delicate mixture of concerns characterized Beijing's attitude, although it seemed, as recently released documents reveal, that the Chinese were simply waiting for the one overture that mattered: America's. Suddenly, Vietnam was only a walk on the Great Wall away from settlement and the origins of a détente that favored China's positions equally as much as Russia's. Henry Kissinger thus assured Zhou Enlai in 1971: "What we cannot do is to participate in the overthrow of people with whom we have been allied. . . . If the government is as unpopular as you seem to think, then the quicker our forces are withdrawn the quicker it will be overthrown. And if it is overthrown after we withdraw, we will not intervene."[1]

Kissinger's assurances could have been given to the Chinese much earlier. Indeed, as Herbert Schandler points out, Averell Harriman and Cyrus

Vance—the American delegates to the first peace talks after Johnson's speech on March 31, 1968, announcing a partial halt to the bombing—hoped that they might have an opportunity to say pretty much the same thing to their Vietnamese counterparts in Paris. Johnson's reluctance, even then, to doing anything that might show weakness—either in Vietnam or at home—prevented him from ordering a full bombing halt until a few days before the presidential elections. This stance, of course, made him a prisoner of Saigon's leaders, who held out against the Paris talks as long as they could and then attempted to provide themselves with all the leverage they could by clandestine "negotiations" with go-betweens acting on behalf of Richard Nixon.

South Vietnam's dilemma—how to fight on when its principal ally and source of resources was demanding it participate in peace talks that could only undermine its military and political positions—is the subject of John Prados's essay, "The Shape of the Table." For years, the fight had been about the shape of the table and who would assign the seats. As far as Saigon was concerned, any arrangement that gave the NLF an equal seat symbolically spelled the defeat of America's purpose in creating that regime after the 1954 Geneva conference—and those who had risen to power under Washington's tutelage.

Behind the table, but hardly out of sight of the negotiators, was China. In the closing chapter, H. W. Brands takes us back to the issue of America's relations with Communist China as a starting point for understanding the Vietnam War and the difficulty of making peace. Lyndon Johnson had hoped to finish his presidency with a summit meeting in Moscow that would simultaneously settle the problems in Vietnam and the Middle East and with nuclear weapons. Brands speculates that the Soviet invasion of Czechoslovakia in 1968—which canceled any chance of a Moscow summit—might itself have been a result of concern that the Kremlin "had to demonstrate its resolve on behalf of world socialism, and thus deliver a riposte to Chinese criticism."

However that may be, Lyndon Johnson's final aspiration to link Vietnam to an overarching settlement of Cold War issues was never realized. Richard Nixon claimed that prize, or thought he did, with his overtures to China. However, it was not so much his strategic vision that made such an arrangement possible, as it was that "American vexation with the war had reached a point that made Nixon's audacious move not only possible but desirable—indeed almost necessary." Americans had gone into Vietnam feeling, as Robert Divine suggests, that they once again were in a war to end all wars. If the communist belief in wars of national liberation to further their goals could be refuted here, then the road would be clear ahead. As it turned out,

Vietnam did lead to Charles de Gaulle's hoped-for multipolar reshaping of international politics. Yet, the war's imagined end fulfilled only the expectations of the Vietnamese.

Notes

1. "Beijing, 1971: Oh, to be a Fly on the Great Wall," *New York Times,* Mar. 3, 2002, 7.

Perpetual War for Perpetual Peace

ROBERT DIVINE

THIS BOOK EXAMINES in detail the various aspects of trying to find a peaceful end to the Vietnam conflict. To help place these efforts in context, we need first to compare what happened there with other wars the United States fought in the twentieth century.

The title of this chapter, which I also used for a recent book of essays, stems from two scholars usually dismissed as isolationists: Harry Elmer Barnes and Charles A. Beard. Barnes, who first gained fame, or notoriety, for his revisionist writing on the causes of World War I, used the phrase "perpetual war for perpetual peace" as the title for an anthology of essays by historians critical of American entry into World War II. I was always intrigued by this title, but I only recently discovered that it did not originate with Barnes. Instead, he claims he got it from Charles Beard. Beard, who is best known for his economic interpretation of the framing of the constitution and his magisterial surveys of the American experience, became a bitter critic of Franklin D. Roosevelt, accusing him of lies and deception in leading the United States into World War II. According to Barnes, Beard used the phrase in a conversation in 1947 to sum up twentieth century American foreign policy.[1]

While I do not share the isolationist sentiments of either Barnes or Beard, I do think the phrase captures the essence of American involvement in twentieth century conflicts. We enter each war certain that it will be the last. We appear to be convinced that we are doing the right thing: protecting our national interests and advancing the cause of democracy. By a process of self-hypnosis, we justify our departure from our normally peaceful inclinations by the belief we are taking up arms in a noble cause. Woodrow Wilson set the tone in World War I with his stirring call for Americans to engage in a war to end all wars, to fight to make the world safe for democracy. In the wars that followed, our leaders have used the same idealistic rhetoric to rally the people to the cause—from defending the Four Freedoms in World War II to creating a New World Order in the first Persian Gulf conflict.

The wars we fight, however, rarely achieve the exalted ends we proclaim so confidently at the outset. The Great Crusade of World War I ended in the punitive Treaty of Versailles and the fatally flawed League of Nations. When Americans had to take up arms to wage a second world war within a generation, they did so more realistically, intent only on stopping Hitler's plans for world domination and punishing Japan for its attack on Pearl Harbor. Yet, Americans again saw the war as a noble cause, one that would remove the centers of evil in the world and usher in a new era of lasting peace.

They were destined for disillusionment. World War II led quickly to the Cold War with the Soviet Union. The existence of nuclear weapons made this confrontation particularly dangerous, most notably during the Cuban missile crisis in 1962, but the possibility of total destruction also restrained both sides and kept the Cold War cold.

The campaigns the United States undertook during the era of superpower rivalry in Korea and Vietnam were necessarily limited and hence proved highly unpopular with the American people, who sought total victory over the forces of darkness. Even the last major conflict of the century, the Persian Gulf War in 1991, while ending in a sweeping American military triumph, failed to give the nation lasting satisfaction. Saddam Hussein, the personification of evil for most Americans, survived and for years remained a constant reminder of the nation's inability to solve the world's problems by using force.

The pattern I have outlined reflects the failure of the United States to wage war effectively as an instrument of national policy. We tend to see peace as the normal human condition and war as the exception, failing to perceive the continuity between war and peace. Fighting a war rarely solves any fundamental problem; it simply resolves one set of issues that quickly give rise to others which, in time, cause our leaders to again resort to arms. Each time the American people enter a conflict, they want to believe that it will be their last war—that by defeating the enemy they can be assured of lasting peace and tranquility. Yet, each generation finds itself involved in new crises that give rise to new conflicts.

It is against this background of the continued American cycle of the confident use of force followed inevitably by bleak disillusionment that I want to place the Vietnam conflict. All too often, Vietnam is seen as an aberration, when in reality it has much in common with our experience in the other wars of the twentieth century.

To do so, I will look briefly at three aspects of America's involvement in Vietnam in an effort to show the similarities as well as the contrasts with other American conflicts.

First, let us examine America's entry into the war. Throughout American history there has been a distinctive pattern for going to war. Viewing ourselves as a peaceful democracy, we insist on fighting only in self-defense. It thus was the British who began the Revolutionary War, firing on American minutemen at Lexington and Concord in 1775. In 1846, Mexico began the hostilities by crossing the Rio Grande and attacking Maj. Gen. Zachary Taylor's army, despite the fact that the land Taylor's troops were defending was at best a disputed zone, not American soil. Abraham Lincoln waited for the South to fire on Fort Sumter before beginning the Civil War; William McKinley used the patriotic fervor after the destruction of the battleship *Maine* in Havana harbor to justify war on Spain in 1898. In his 1917 war message, Wilson cited the German U-boat attacks on American shipping, despite the fact that he had drawn the line in 1915 over the questionable issue of American passengers aboard the belligerent *Lusitania*. In 1941, Franklin Roosevelt backed Japan into a corner with financial sanctions and the oil embargo, resulting in the attack on Pearl Harbor.

In Korea, the United States fought ostensibly to defend the 38th Parallel, an artificial dividing line without either historical or ethnographical significance. In 1991, Pres. George H. W. Bush, after failing to warn Saddam Hussein that the United States would defend Kuwait, drew a line in the sand to protect Saudi Arabia and ensure American access to Persian Gulf oil.

It is difficult to cite any one specific event or act leading to American involvement in the Vietnam conflict. As George Herring has so cogently argued, it was America's longest war, with its origins dating back to the policies pursued by Truman and Eisenhower in the 1950s. However, the most intense phase of the conflict, the rapid American escalation in the mid-1960s, offers two examples of the traditional American justification for the use of force.

The first is the Tonkin Gulf episode in the summer of 1964. An American destroyer, the *Maddox*, was conducting electronic surveillance off the coast of North Vietnam while South Vietnamese forces were engaged in guerrilla raids along the same coastline. On August 2, North Vietnam, evidently perceiving the *Maddox* as part of the South Vietnamese raid, sent torpedo boats to attack the American intruder. The *Maddox* successfully beat off the attack, but two days later—joined by a second destroyer, the *Turner Joy*—crewmembers reported another North Vietnamese attack, this time at night, forcing them to rely on sonar echoes rather than actual sightings. The second incident led President Johnson to order retaliatory bombing of North Vietnamese naval bases and to ask Congress to give him a virtual blank check to use force against North Vietnam. After a brief debate, Congress—with only two dissenting votes in the Senate—passed the

Tonkin Gulf resolution, which LBJ used as the legal basis for his later escalation of the war.

We now know that there was no second attack on the American destroyers in the Gulf of Tonkin on August 4, 1964. Why then did Johnson act so precipitately, instead of waiting for evidence to confirm the incident? Some have charged that LBJ was simply waiting for a provocative act by North Vietnam to secure passage of a congressional resolution empowering him to use force in Vietnam—one that had been drafted several months earlier. Others have suggested that Johnson's real motive was political, not strategic. Hoping to outflank Republican candidate Barry Goldwater, Johnson used the Tonkin Gulf resolution to defuse Vietnam as an issue in the fall presidential campaign. Most important, in my judgment, is that LBJ acted in the same way his predecessors had in crisis situations: He used an ambiguous incident to build a case for going to war in self-defense. The broad power to wage war in Vietnam thus met traditional American criteria because the United States was using force only in response to an attack by others.

The second incident that reflects the same national characteristic of going to war in response to the actions of others occurred a year later, in 1965. On February 6, National Liberation Front (NLF) forces attacked the American army barracks at Pleiku and a nearby helicopter base, killing nine Americans and destroying five aircraft. Meanwhile, the situation in South Vietnam had become desperate, as the government in Saigon was near collapse. The Johnson administration had developed two plans to use airpower to try to prevent the fall of South Vietnam. The first, code-named Operation Flaming Dart, called for limited retaliatory air strikes against military targets in both North and South Vietnam. The second, and far more significant operation, Rolling Thunder, was a sustained bombing of North Vietnam designed to compel Hanoi to end its support of the insurgency in the South. President Johnson used the incident at Pleiku as the pretext to begin both air campaigns. Flaming Dart started almost immediately, but was soon replaced by Rolling Thunder, which continued for three years with only brief pauses. During the next few months of 1965, realizing that ground troops were needed to protect U.S. air bases and help defeat the insurgency, LBJ quietly approved the deployment of American marines and soldiers. By late 1968 more than a half-million U.S. troops were in South Vietnam.

Johnson apparently believed he was acting in the best American tradition. He probably felt that his misleading and deceptive resort to force in 1965 was little different than the tactics his mentor, FDR, had used in 1940–41 to align the United States against Nazi Germany with the destroyers-for-bases deal and lend-lease. Johnson's national security adviser, McGeorge Bundy, was more cynical. Questioned as to what the administration would have done if the enemy had not attacked Pleiku, he famously replied that "Pleikus are like streetcars," implying that NLF attacks came along regularly enough to provide the pretext for the Americanization of the war.[2]

Unfortunately for Johnson, critics of the war, whose ranks grew steadily, did not view him as another Franklin D. Roosevelt whose noble goals tended to excuse the deceptive means he used to advance them. Disillusionment with Tonkin Gulf and Pleiku quickly gave rise to the credibility gap. As American casualties mounted and the fighting in Vietnam reached a bloody stalemate, Johnson's popularity plummeted. Yet, his actions as president clearly were in the national tradition of making the enemy fire the first shot, permitting the United States to retaliate with armed force. In this regard, Vietnam does not appear to be different from other American conflicts. To his sorrow, however, LBJ found that the tactics pioneered by Polk and Lincoln in the nineteenth century did not work so well in the far-off jungles of Southeast Asia.

The second comparison I want to make is how Vietnam fits into the traditional American pattern of fighting wars. Here we need to note a shift between the nineteenth century and the twentieth century experience. In its earlier wars, the United States fought for relatively limited and specific goals: independence in the Revolutionary War, neutral rights in the War of 1812, territorial expansion in the War with Mexico (Texas, California, and the New Mexico territory, but not all of Mexico). In the Civil War, Lincoln's goal was to preserve the Union, not end slavery, and in 1898, McKinley went to war for the limited aim of freeing Cuba, although he did not shrink from acquiring the Philippines.

In the two world wars of the twentieth century, however, Americans fought for broader causes. In World War I, Woodrow Wilson refused to make the contest with Germany simply a defense of neutral rights. He instead sent an army of 2 million to Europe to engage in a great crusade for democracy. His goal was to transform the international arena and bring an end to all wars by achieving peace without victory. When the vindictive Treaty of Versailles kept the peace for only two decades, Franklin D. Roosevelt tried to tone down the rhetoric in World War II, calling only for a defense of the Four Freedoms. However, his military objective was total victory, as witnessed at Casablanca by the call for the unconditional surrender of the Axis powers. This demand for a complete triumph over the forces of evil seemed justified in bringing down Hitler's Nazi regime in Europe, but it worked less well in Asia, contributing to Truman's controversial decision to use the atomic bomb to end the war with Japan.

The onset of the Cold War and the realities of the nuclear age forced the United States to reconsider its habit of seeking total victory. In Korea, when

Truman's effort to unite the entire peninsula after Gen. Douglas Mac-Arthur's triumph at Inchon led to Chinese intervention and a humiliating retreat back below the 38th Parallel, the United States finally settled for a truce that left Korea divided. Later, in the first Persian Gulf War, President Bush, although he denounced Saddam Hussein as another Hitler and invited his overthrow, limited the conflict to the one goal on which the international coalition could agree: the liberation of Kuwait. Despite ending in a swift and overwhelming military victory, the war left Saddam Hussein in power, much to the regret of most Americans.

Vietnam fits into the Cold War pattern of fighting to secure limited goals. The objective of American arms was to preserve the government we had installed in Saigon and resist Hanoi's efforts to unify Vietnam under communist rule. The greatest difficulty faced by American military commanders was the lack of a clear strategic goal. At times we appeared to be fighting on behalf of the domino theory, holding back the communist advance into Cambodia, Thailand, and all Southeast Asia. However, we also seemed to be waging a war in behalf of American credibility, struggling to honor our commitment to South Vietnam in order to reassure our other allies of our good faith. In contrast, those in power in North Vietnam suffered no such ambivalence. Hanoi clearly was fighting a war of national liberation to achieve a unified Vietnam.

Much of the tragedy of Vietnam came out of this strategic confusion. William Bundy once described our military effort there as "all-out limited war"—limited in the sense that we did not seek to conquer North Vietnam, but all-out because of our willingness to pour in a half-million troops in a massive effort to defeat the NLF.[3] It was this strategic confusion that led to the bloody stalemate from 1965 to 1968, as the United States sought to wear down the enemy in a war of attrition with search-and-destroy tactics, but succeeded only in losing the support of the American people. For three years, we prevented Hanoi from conquering the South, but we failed to realize that our opponent was content to wait us out, willing to endure heavy casualties until the United States finally gave up out of frustration.

Lyndon Johnson became the victim of his own policies. First college students turned against the war, and then prominent senators, led by a disillusioned William Fulbright, began to voice their dissent. By 1967, LBJ feared to travel across the country lest he face crowds of angry demonstrators. He spoke of being trapped in the White House, "like a jackrabbit hunkered up in a storm."[4]

His wife gave an even more apt description. "A miasma of trouble hangs over everything," Lady Bird Johnson wrote in her diary in early 1967. "The temperament of our people seems to be, 'you must either get excited, get passionate, fight and get it over with, or we must pull out.' It is unbearably hard to fight a limited war."[5]

Revisionist historians, led by Col. Harry Summers, have raised the question, could we have prevailed in Vietnam with a different strategy? If Johnson had opted for all-out, unlimited war, could we have defeated North Vietnam? They argue that the "all-out limited war" approach hamstrung the American military and prevented the United States from taking the war home to the enemy. Had LBJ not chosen a middle course between the hawks and the doves, the revisionists argue, American commanders could have invaded North Vietnam and forced Hanoi to surrender. Fortunately, we never found out whether or not such an all-out military effort would have been successful; political reality prevented it from ever receiving serious consideration. There is one point the revisionists raise, however, that calls for rebuttal: their objection to Johnson's refusal to consider using nuclear weapons in Vietnam. While they do not say we should have, in the words of Gen. Curtis LeMay, bombed North Vietnam "back into the Stone Age," they claim it was a mistake to rule out the use of nuclear weapons.[6] In early 1968, General Westmoreland had begun a secret study of how tactical nuclear warheads might be used to defend the besieged Marine Corps garrison at Khe Sanh, but LBJ ordered him to cancel it. "I felt at the time and even more so now," Westmoreland wrote in his memoirs, "that to fail to consider this alternative was a mistake."[7] Summers argues that America's revulsion at the thought of nuclear war "cost us a major strategic advantage . . . the ability to pose a threat to the enemy to raise the level of warfare beyond his ability (or willingness) to respond."[8]

Lyndon Johnson made many mistakes in Vietnam, but he must be given credit for resisting the temptation to use nuclear weapons to make up for his strategic errors. From the outset, he insisted on keeping the war limited, both by refraining from bombing targets too close to China and by ruling out any possibility of using weapons of mass destruction. Intent on keeping China and the Soviet Union out of the conflict, Johnson made it clear to his generals that "all-out limited war" did not include nuclear weapons.

In retrospect, it is clear why America lost in Vietnam. The United States failed to bring its ends and means into a reasonable balance. We tried to use virtually unlimited means to achieve the limited end of preserving a separate and independent South Vietnam. In view of Hanoi's determination to fight on until it had unified Vietnam under its rule, this goal was unrealistic. The strategic confusion in Vietnam, however, was not unique. It proved to be similar to two other limited wars America fought in the twentieth century: Korea, where we tried to achieve forcible unification of a divided nation with only limited means, and the Persian Gulf conflict, where the United States hoped that a war fought to liberate Kuwait would somehow lead to the downfall of Saddam Hussein. Lyndon Johnson thus proved to be as poor a strategist as Harry Truman and George Bush.

My last comparison relates to the way the United States has ended its wars. A brief survey of our past conflicts indicates that we had even greater trouble ending wars than fighting them. There is an old folk saying that sums up our national experience: "the United States always wins the war and loses the peace." This homily suggests a flattering self-image of heroic exploits by American soldiers on the battlefield being undermined by wily Old World diplomats at the peace table. In fact, America's homespun diplomats proved quite adept at peacemaking in the eighteenth and nineteenth centuries. Witness Benjamin Franklin winning such generous boundaries for the new nation in the Treaty of Paris of 1783, John Quincy Adams at Ghent preventing any loss of territory to Britain (in this case, one could argue that the United States lost the war but won the peace), and even the much maligned Nicholas Trist fulfilling manifest destiny with the Treaty of Guadalupe-Hidalgo in 1848. Both Lincoln and McKinley succeeded in achieving their wartime goals: preservation of the Union and qualified freedom for Cuba.

It was the twentieth century experience with peacemaking that seemed to give new life to the old cry of "losing the peace." For all his efforts at the Paris Peace Conference, Wilson was unable to prevent our European allies from claiming the spoils of war and punishing Germany with reparations and the war-guilt clause. In World War II, FDR's policy of unconditional surrender contributed to the onset of the Cold War, as the Soviet Union filled the vacuums of power in Europe and Asia left by the total defeat of Germany and Japan. After both world wars, the American people felt disillusioned with the outcome—their dreams of a lasting peace led only to new and more serious confrontations abroad.

In Korea and the Persian Gulf, our experience with ending conflict was little better. Under Truman, peace negotiations began at Panmunjom in 1951, but a deadlock over forcible repatriation of prisoners of war prolonged the fighting for two more years. Eisenhower finally succeeded in negotiating a truce, partly with a veiled threat of nuclear retaliation and partly as the result of the uncertainty in the communist world created by the death of Stalin in March, 1953. The truce in Korea, however, left two hostile regimes locked in bitter rivalry for the next five decades, and even today North Korea is viewed as a rogue nation whose missiles threaten our Pacific allies.

Even the last conflict of the century, the Persian Gulf War in 1991, while ending in a sweeping American military triumph, failed to give the nation lasting satisfaction. Saddam Hussein, the personification of evil, remained in power for twelve more years. Even his capture after the war with Iraq in 2003 failed to quell the armed insurgency there that served as a reminder of the difficulty in using force to solve the world's problems.

The peacemaking effort in Vietnam, which the following chapters explore in detail, offers an equally discouraging picture of American failure. In this case, it was not a question of translating battlefield success into permanent political gains. Rather, the outcome revises the folk saying, for in Vietnam, the United States not only lost the peace, but the war as well.

I do not want to tread on ground that other contributors will be covering much more intensively in their chapters. I would, however, like to raise one general question in an effort to continue the comparison between Vietnam and other American wars.

Why did it take the United States more than four years—from the time of Lyndon Johnson's March 31, 1968, speech that began the peace process, to January 27, 1973, when the Paris peace accords were finally signed—to end American participation in the Vietnam War? The blame must be shared by both LBJ and his successor, Richard Nixon. Despite his initial offer on March 31, Johnson dragged his feet throughout the summer and fall of 1968, as Lloyd Gardner has so clearly shown. Still unwilling to admit that the United States had been defeated on the battlefield, Johnson sought to preserve an independent South Vietnam at the peace table.

Richard Nixon proved even more reluctant to accept the inevitable. In the 1968 campaign, he hinted at a solution to the Vietnam dilemma without ever offering a formula for peace, beyond his vague political promise "to end the war and win the peace."[9] When Nixon took office, the sticking point in the Paris peace negotiations was the American refusal to accept Hanoi's insistence that North Vietnamese troops remain in place in the South. The issue clearly was whether or not the United States was willing to abandon South Vietnam. Nixon, like Johnson before him, believed that American credibility was at stake and would not budge. "If we were to lose in Vietnam," he told an associate, "there would have been no respect for the American President . . . because we had the power and didn't use it . . . We must be credible."[10]

Four years later—after withdrawing the bulk of American forces from South Vietnam, invading Cambodia, raiding Laos, and battering Hanoi with massive air strikes—Nixon finally accepted the terms that had been available since 1969: the withdrawal of all remaining American troops in exchange for the return of our prisoners of war. The South Vietnamese government would remain in power in Saigon, but with North Vietnam in control of much of the countryside, it was only a matter of time before Hanoi would claim complete victory. Two years later, triumphant communist forces captured Saigon and finally brought the long war to an end.

The American failure to make peace in Vietnam reveals the same problem we faced in ending our other, more successful military conflicts. We failed to realize that war is but another way to advance the national interest, that the goal of fighting is always political. Winning or losing a war on the battlefield by itself does not necessarily advance or endanger the national interest. We won the first Persian Gulf War, protecting our access to the region's vast oil reserves, but we failed to curb Saddam Hussein's power—leaving him to be dealt with by the next Bush generation. In Korea, we fought to a stalemate, unable to achieve our goal of a united, peaceful Korean peninsula. In Vietnam, lacking a clear strategic objective beyond preserving our own credibility, we would have been well-advised to negotiate for withdrawal in 1969, rather than prolong the conflict four more years, with the loss of twenty thousand more American lives as well as more than a half-million Vietnamese. The ultimate irony is that the credibility Johnson and Nixon prized so highly proved meaningless. Other nations, both friend and foe, viewed our devotion to a losing cause as an act of folly, not fidelity. Staying the course in Vietnam served only to tarnish our international reputation, not enhance it. Vietnam, then, has much in common with other American wars: In making peace, we once again miscalculated the underlying political realities.

In conclusion, I reiterate my contention that the Vietnam War, while distinctive in many ways, is not as unique as it is often portrayed. How the United States became involved, the way we fought the conflict, and our efforts to end it all reflect common patterns of national behavior. Despite the preaching of George Kennan and Hans Morgenthau, as well as the realpolitik expounded by Henry Kissinger, American foreign policy still reflects an essentially Wilsonian belief that American power can and should be used to reform the world, not simply protect the national interest. In that sense, Vietnam has much in common with our other wars. We fought out of a misguided sense of democratic mission, only this time the disillusionment came during the war, not with its aftermath. As long as we are guided by a missionary impulse to save the world, we will continue to be engaged in perpetual war for perpetual peace.

Notes

1. Harry Elmer Barnes, ed., *Perpetual War for Perpetual Peace* (Caldwell, Idaho: Caxton, 1953), p. viii.

2. George C. Herring, *America's Longest War: The United States and Vietnam, 1950–1975* (3d ed., New York: McGraw-Hill, 1996), p. 144.

3. George C. Herring, *LBJ and Vietnam: A Different Kind of War* (Austin: University of Texas Press, 1994), p. 20.

4. Eric F. Goldman, *The Tragedy of Lyndon Johnson* (New York: Dell, 1974), p. 491.

5. Herring, *LBJ and Vietnam,* p. 140.

6. Lewis L. Gould, *1968: The Election That Changed America* (Chicago: Ivan R. Dee, 1993), p. 148.

7. William C. Westmoreland, *A Soldier Reports* (New York: Dell, 1980), p. 445.

8. Harry G. Summers Jr., *On Strategy: A Critical Analysis of the Vietnam War* (New York: Dell, 1984), p. 105.

9. Melvin Small, *The Presidency of Richard Nixon* (Lawrence: University Press of Kansas, 1999), p. 28.

10. Herring, *America's Longest War,* p. 273.

Fighting While Negotiating

MARILYN YOUNG

General de Lattre spoke at length about the importance of the war in Indochina. He said that every day he asks those whom he meets in the United States if Indochina and Korea are not one war. The answer is always "Yes."
—Record of Pentagon meeting with
Jean de Lattre de Tassigny, September 20, 1951

If there must be war, let it be Asians against Asians. America must avoid the kind of bungling that got us into Korea. Young farm boys must stay on their farms; the students stay in school.
—Dwight D. Eisenhower, September 22, 1952

DAVID HALBERSTAM had it wrong in 1964 when he warned against the quagmire of Vietnam as if it were newly made. In fact, the bog had been there for more than a decade. From early June, 1951, when the subject of truce talks was broached, until July, 1953, when an armistice was finally achieved, the United States seemed as relentlessly stuck in Korea as, eleven years later, Lyndon Johnson felt himself to be in Vietnam. In both instances policy makers, pundits, and, insofar as one can determine this, the public believed the country was mired in Asia. The cold mountains of Korea, like the steamy jungles of Vietnam, had reached up, pulled the country down, and would not let go. Thus did negotiations in Korea foretell those in Paris some twenty years later. In between, moreover, the Geneva Conference of 1954, which had been convened to work out a political settlement for the Korean War, was used instead to negotiate a cease-fire between the Democratic Republic of Vietnam and the French, a cease-fire which itself contributed to the next war in Indochina. General de Lattre was right in more senses than he knew.

Thinking of both wars at once, the Vietnam War seems like Korea in slow motion. In Korea, as in Vietnam, the U.S. government chose war—

all the while insisting the choice was not theirs, but that of their enemy. In both, the resistance of a weak and unstable ally, in whose name the war was being fought, created unanticipated difficulties for American negotiators. In both, a marginal issue, prisoners of war (POWs), assumed surprising centrality. Both were fought—in one case literally, in the other rhetorically—against the People's Republic of China. In both wars, the United States deployed its massive firepower against technologically inferior forces, directed that firepower against civilian as well as military objectives, and used weapons and tactics whose cruelty raised questions among its European allies. In both, the United States claimed to be saving countries it effectively destroyed. Both were deeply unpopular with the public that paid for them even though only in Vietnam did that unpopularity have a significant public voice.

What is perhaps most surprising is that after the Korean War there ever was a Vietnam War. Yet, we are all of us familiar with the limited lessons history seems to offer the state, whatever it may teach its citizens. Moreover, I have begun to think that the way the Korean War ended may explain why it took so long for the United States to accept defeat in Vietnam. Unsatisfactory at the time, a stalemate that felt like a loss, the Korean War nevertheless provided a model, however misleading, for the way a limited war could come to at least a temporary halt, bringing with it certain permanent gains. In another, more obvious sense, the Korean War made the Vietnam War possible, if not especially desirable: it was the matrix in which the military-industrial-scientific complex, whose essential elements were laid down in World War II, was forged and flourished, allowing for visions of guns and butter to entice all succeeding administrations. It contributed to the articulation of a global anticommunist crusade that could be packaged and marketed at home and abroad; it allowed for the development and perfection of weapons systems and combat tactics; and it offered a broad field on which private and official psychological warriors could play. All of these elements were necessary if not sufficient building blocks for the American enterprise in Vietnam.

I know of only one analyst who has undertaken a systematic comparison between the Korean and Vietnam Wars. However, Yuen Foong Khong, in his book *Analogies at War: Korea, Munich, Dien Bien Phu, and the Vietnam Decisions of 1965,* is at least as interested in how analogies work as he is in the decisions themselves.[1] Leaving aside his acronyms (AE=Analogical Explanation), tables, formulae, and charts, Khong's argument is straightforward enough. Whatever people at the time thought of the stalemate in which the Korean War ended, by the 1960s it was counted a victory. Communist aggression and expansionism had been dealt a severe blow, Red China branded by the UN as an aggressor, South Korea preserved, and American arms and willpower demonstrated. By 1958, all Chinese troops had been withdrawn from the Korean peninsula, whereas American troops remain there to this day. Nor were Chinese hopes of a larger political settlement emerging from the war satisfied. It took the Vietnam War itself to bring the issues China had hoped to deal with in 1954 (entry into the UN, the status of Taiwan) to any resolution.

Khong demonstrates the degree to which Korea framed policy makers' understanding of events in Vietnam. With the exception of George Ball, whose acute analysis of Vietnam was not, however, matched by his take on Korea, no one in the Vietnam War administrations thought of either conflict as a civil war. Both were understood as acts of aggression and challenges to U.S. authority. Dean Rusk, who had played a significant role in Korean decisions, "was convinced that what we had done in Korea was a good thing to do and we had finally won in Korea and therefore by applying enough effort and enough time we should be able to prevail in Vietnam as we had in Korea."[2] As early as 1949, Rusk had seen Korea and Indochina as aspects of the same problem, dictating the same solution. In a memo to Secretary of State Dean Acheson, Rusk outlined an "action program" for East Asia: refusal to recognize the Communist regime in China, aid to the French effort in Indochina, and prevention of the spread of communism in Asia.[3] It was Rusk who helped stiffen the spine of the Joint Chiefs of Staff (JCS) when they urged complete withdrawal from Korea in the wake of Chinese victories in November, 1950. "Rusk," Acheson recalled, "said that the military men were too dejected. They needed some of the do-or-die spirit that had led the British in two world wars to hang on against overwhelming odds and with no visible hope of success."[4] "Unfortunately," Thomas Zeiler laconically comments in his biography of Rusk, "hanging on in Korea set a historical precedent for staying the course in Vietnam fifteen years later."[5]

Robert McNamara, new to government service, did not bring a fresh perspective. Years later, explaining why "like most Americans," he saw the communist world as "monolithic," Defense Secretary McNamara admonished readers not to forget that "Mao Zedong had aligned China to fight with Korea against the West in 1953."[6] Colonel Herbert Schandler summarized the wisdom the military had extracted from its three years in Korea: "The general outlook of U.S. Army doctrine was that revolution could not be instigated or be successful without the support of an external sponsoring power. Experience in Korea taught that guerrillas were the early warning of crossborder conventional attacks."[7]

Lyndon Johnson also remembered Korea. Indeed, in the early months of his presidency he seems to have been haunted by it. His memories certainly were bleaker than those of Dean Rusk. To Robert Kennedy he expressed his concern about congressional resistance to any increase in American participation in the Vietnam conflict. Even in Korea, he pointed out, when the United States had the full backing of the UN, "we had a very divided country and a lot of hell, and we finally really lost—the Democrats did—on the Korea thing."[8] In May and June of 1964, Johnson and his friend Sen. Richard Russell of Georgia had Korea very much in mind as, for hours, they tossed the Vietnam question back and forth. The danger was evident to Russell: "It's a mess. And it's going to get worse. And I don't think the American people are quite ready to send our troops in there to do the fighting." Russell was convinced sending U.S. troops would bring in the Chinese. He went on to point out, with a kind of casual racism, "we'd do them a favor every time we killed a coolie, whereas when one of our people got killed it would be a real loss to us."[9] Johnson complained that all of his advisers— Rusk, McNamara, Bundy, Harriman and Vance—wanted to "show some power and some force . . . they're kinda like MacArthur in Korea—they don't believe the Chinese Communists will come into this thing."

Moreover, Johnson complained to Russell that Nixon, Rockefeller, and Goldwater wanted to take the war north. "Bomb the North and kill old men, women, and children?" Russell asked. No, Johnson reassured him, just "selected targets, watch this trail they're coming down." But Russell's recollection of events in Korea was sharper than that of Johnson's other advisers: "We tried it in Korea. We even got a lot of old B-29s to increase the bomb load and sent 'em over there and just dropped millions and millions of bombs, day and night . . . they would knock out the road at night . . . the damn people would be back traveling over it. . . . We never could actually interdict all their lines of communication although we had absolute control of the seas and the air, and we never did stop them. And you ain't gonna stop these people either." Johnson refused to join Russell in this sort of reminiscing. Instead, he insisted that he would be impeached if he ran from Vietnam. When Russell suggested the possibility that a South Vietnamese president could be induced to invite the United States to leave, Johnson deflected the idea. "That's right, but you can't do that. . . . Wouldn't that pretty well fix us in the eyes of the world though and make it look mighty bad?" To which Russell, laughing, responded: "I don't know. We don't look too good right now." And then, ironically: "You'd look pretty good, I guess, going in there with all the troops and sending them all in there, but I tell you it'll be the most expensive venture this country ever went into." Hanging up on Russell, Johnson immediately called McGeorge Bundy, choosing, however, to repeat only the senator's fears about Chinese intervention: "[I]t looks to me like we're getting into another Korea. It just worries the hell out of me. . . . I believe that the Chinese Communists are coming into it. I don't think that we can fight them ten thousand miles away from home. . . . I don't think it's worth fighting for and I don't think that we can get out."[10]

Johnson listened more closely to his Texan intimate A. W. Moursund than he did to either Russell or his own doubts. Moursund also saw Korea as the touchstone. The conversation worried Johnson, who repeated it to Russell. "Goddamn," Moursund had told him, "there's not anything that'll destroy you as quick as pulling out, pulling up stakes and running. America wants, by God, prestige and power." When Johnson expressed his reluctance to "kill these folks," Moursund replied: "I don't give a damn. I didn't want to kill 'em in Korea, but if you don't stand up for America . . . [the fellows in Johnson City or Georgia or any other place] they'll forgive you for anything except being weak." Russell was not impressed. What Moursund urged would take a half-million men and the country would be bogged down for the next ten years. Sobering, Johnson agreed: "We never did clear up Korea yet." "We're right where we started," Russell pointed out, "except for 70,000 of 'em buried over there." Although he agreed that it was hard to see a way out of Vietnam ("as a practical matter, we're in there and I don't know how the hell you can tell the American people you're coming out . . . they'll think that you've been whipped, you've been mined, you're scared, it would be disastrous"), Russell insisted that the American people were not "so opposed to coming out. I don't think the American people want to stay there."[11]

The main lesson Johnson drew, despite his sense that "killing these folks" had not done much good in Korea and might not in Vietnam, was the danger of getting trapped in a war against China. From this point of view, as Russell repeatedly urged, early withdrawal was much the best policy. Right-wing Democrats and Republicans drew another lesson, however. As McNamara informed Johnson after Congress passed the Tonkin Gulf resolution, this group "didn't want a 'no-win' policy and another Korea." The lesson they drew was to hit hard and fast; to deliver the knockout blow denied the United States in Korea. The larger sense of the futility of the Korean War that Russell so fleetingly recalled did not weigh very heavily with either group.

Korea was Nixon's teacher, too, as he explained in 1968. "How do you bring a war to a conclusion?" he asked delegates at the Republican convention in Miami. "I'll tell you how Korea was ended. We got in there and had this messy war on our hands. Eisenhower . . . let the word go out diplomatically to the Chinese and the North [Koreans] that we would not tolerate this continual ground war of attrition. And within a matter of months, they negotiated."[12] The notion that the threat of nuclear bombs had brought the Chinese to heel in Korea was, as Jeffrey Kimball has observed, "part of Republican historical doctrine." Nixon not only believed it, he incorporated its principles into his "madman" approach to negotiations in Vietnam.[13] On China itself, Nixon was more interesting than his predecessors. Rather than "keep China out," he hoped to bring China in on the U.S. side, trading a seat in the UN and normalization of relations for Chinese pressure on Hanoi to end the war on American terms. Nixon also learned a great deal about the political usefulness of POWs from Korea, a subject I shall return to later in this chapter.

One immediate problem posed by later administrations' reflections on Korea was confusion about exactly what needed to be negotiated. Johnson, for example, imagined that Eisenhower had negotiated his way to a secure separation of the country, retaining South Korea as a separate, hopefully secure, anticommunist bastion. "We've got to try to find some proposal, some way, like Eisenhower worked out in Korea," Johnson told Russell. This was a serious problem of historical misunderstanding: what Eisenhower achieved in July, 1953, had been an available possibility as early as July, 1950. Instead, the decision was made to overthrow the North Korean regime and unify the country on American terms. The effort failed. Two years later, the war ended where it had begun: with a divided Korea. There was no North Vietnamese invasion of the South at the time Johnson was using Korea as a model, no uniformed army that could be forced to fold its tents and march home. The Eisenhower-like proposal that Johnson imagined might have settled the war in Vietnam was tantamount to a call for the NLF and Hanoi to surrender unconditionally.

In Korea, as in Vietnam, early possibilities of disengagement were firmly rejected. Barely a month after the initiation of the war, when UN forces seemed in danger of imminent defeat, the Soviet Union, responding to an appeal by the Indian government, suggested a quid pro quo: admission of the People's Republic of China into the UN in exchange for the resolution of the Korean War by a newly constituted Security Council on the basis of a cease-fire, North Korean withdrawal from the south, and a five-power conference on unification that would include representatives of both South and North Korea. Only George Kennan thought the offer worth exploring; no one else in the high councils of government agreed.[14]

Despite the rejection of the Soviets' July offer, the Indian government in August, 1950, continued to press for a settlement, urging a cease-fire, North Korean troop withdrawal, and the search for a more permanent settlement by a UN commission composed of the nonpermanent members of the Security Council. That effort, and others like it in September and October,

1950, by the Dutch, the Soviet Union and, briefly, the People's Republic of China, all failed. On July 17, Kennan had urged the possibility at the regular meeting of State Department and Defense officials with the secretary of state (he had been excluded from meetings with the president). Why not allow the UN issue to come to a vote? The United States could abstain and "leave the question entirely to the judgment of the international community." He thought, he noted in his diary, "that in this way we might get the question removed from the area of discussion, so that Stalin could no longer exploit it as an excuse for not facing up to the situation in Korea." What difference did it make, after all? Entry into the UN did not mean the United States would recognize the country. It was a "minor issue, on which we should never have allowed ourselves to get hooked in the first place." Nonetheless, he was "shouted down on this."[15]

John Foster Dulles, present in the councils of the Truman administration because of his work on the Japanese peace treaty, insisted such a move would look "as though we were retreating on the Chinese Communist issue in the belief that we were thereby buying some Russian concessions on Korea." The public would feel the country had been "tricked into giving up something for nothing." Kennan, defeated, confided to his diary: "I hope that some day history will record this as an instance of the damage done to the conduct of our foreign policy by the irresponsible and bigoted interference of the China lobby and its friends in Congress."[16]

He returned to the struggle the following week, but found himself "for the most part in a lonely position of single opposition to the views of my associates." Seating China, he urged, would "constitute no new reality of any great significance. The significant reality was created when the Chinese Communists overran the mainland of China." Nor could it harm U.S. interests or change the character of the UN—after all, "two vetoes were not stronger than one." China, to be sure, disagreed with the majority of the membership on the subject of Korea. However, the Chinese had not been party to the UN action, so all their disagreement amounted to was "a conflict of interest, founded in bitter strategic and political realities." It was not, Kennan insisted, "a moral issue." He repeated earlier arguments: the United States could abstain from the vote, need not recognize the government, and could continue to criticize, in the harshest terms, China's "offensive and childish" international behavior. Once more Dulles objected, "primarily on the ground that it would confuse American public opinion and weaken support for the President's program looking toward the strengthening of our defenses." Given Dulles's goals, widely shared in the Truman administration, public "confusion" was indeed a danger.[17]

Acheson supported Dulles, which brought an end to the discussion—but not before Kennan summarized the implications of the decision. First, that the government did not believe it could persuade the public except by "working [the people] up into an emotional state, and this emotional state . . . would then have to be the determinant of our action." Second, that the UN "would not be universal" but rather an "alliance against Russia." Finally, that U.S. policy in Asia "from here on out would be an emotional anticommunism which would ignore the value to ourselves of a possible balance between the existing forces on the Asiatic continent, would force everyone to declare himself either for us (and incidentally for Chiang Kai-shek) or against us; that this would break the unity not only of the non-Communist countries in Asia but also of the non-Communist community in general, and would be beyond our military capacity to support."[18]

To his diary, Kennan observed that while Dulles's views were firmly pegged to public opinion, others of his colleagues, including Dean Rusk, had a "real sense of moral indignation about the Chinese Communists" that he attributed to a general American conviction of its own singular righteousness. "In our participation on the international scene," he wrote, "we are only one of a number of contenders for the privilege of leading a national existence on a portion of the territory of the world." We had enemies, of course, "But let us recognize the legitimacy of differences of interest and philosophy between groups of men and not pretend that they can be made to disappear behind some common philosophical concept." Two days later, Kennan learned that after the meeting Dulles had confided to a journalist that while he had once "thought highly" of Kennan, "he had now concluded that he was a very dangerous man: that he was advocating the admission of the Chinese Communists to the United Nations and a cessation of US military action at the 38th parallel."[19]

All through the summer, Kennan wrote years later, he had the feeling "that the situation was slipping away not only from the control but from the influence of people like myself." Rather than serious analysis of Soviet intentions, the focus was solely on their capabilities and it was always "safer to give [the enemy] the benefit of every doubt in matters of strength and to credit him indiscriminately with *all* aggressive designs." He felt himself surrounded by "willful personalities and poorly schooled minds" while "utter confusion" governed the public mind. No one, as far as he was concerned, understood U.S. foreign policy—not the president, nor Congress, nor the people, nor the press. "They all wander around in a labyrinth of ignorance and error and conjecture, in which truth is intermingled with fiction at a hundred points, in which unjustified assumptions have attained the validity of premises."[20] In December, 1950, in a mood of "near despair," Kennan wrote his friend Chip Bohlen: "You may blame me for not having done more . . . but remember that there is a real ceiling on the usefulness of any one of us, and that is the point at which he becomes so importunate in his views that they cease to be listened to with any respect at all."[21]

An early peace in Korea had little to recommend it. There was simply too much left to do: maintain and enhance the defense budget; demonstrate American willpower and strength; blunt the attack of those who insisted the Truman administration had misplaced China; implement Washington's version of collective security; shore up those who wavered on European or Japanese rearmament; build a model nation in a reunified Korea. In sum, though barely acknowledged, a swift end to hostilities would have shaken the elaborate structure of the national security state which intervention in Korea promised to make possible. Nor did an early peace in Vietnam win many fans. As Fredrik Logevall has summarized it: "From January 1961 to November 1963, the [Kennedy] administration adhered firmly to the position that the insurgency in the South had to be defeated and that no diplomacy should be undertaken until that result was ensured. Negotiations should be entered into only when there was nothing to negotiate." Not only did officials resist negotiations, they "were downright fearful" of them. At issue for the Kennedy administration, Logevall argues, was its credibility, both domestically and internationally.[22]

However, it was not only a hasty negotiated peace that worried the Truman administration; even victory was unattractive. Frank Pace recalled Secretary of Defense George Marshall's response to General MacArthur's happy tidings in October, 1950, that victory was in sight. "Well, he said, 'Pace, that's troublesome.'" Pace was surprised and repeated the good news: "Well, I said, 'Sir, you must not have heard me, I said, the war would be over by Thanksgiving and the troops home by Christmas.' He said, 'I heard you, but,' he said, 'to precipitate an end to the war would not permit us to have a full understanding of the problems that we face ahead of us.'" Pace protested. Surely the public had by this time grasped the "full implications of the cold war." Marshall demurred: "you didn't live through the end of World War II the way I did, and watch people rush back to their civilian jobs and leave the tanks to rot in the Pacific and the military strength that was built up to fade away."[23] Meanwhile, Truman fretted to the National Security Council in November, on the eve of full-scale Chinese intervention, "if the Chinese Communist threat evaporates, [he] questions that you could go through with the $45 Billion [defense] program."[24]

For a time, prolonged war in Korea offered some decided benefits to the military. Marshall summarized them for a May, 1951, meeting of the National Security Council: liaison between the services had improved; the new policy of rotating troops served as a "school of arms" for the America's young men; and the United States was building a "practical and hardened soldiery." All in all it was a lot like the "experience of the British fleet during the Napoleonic wars. At sea during the entire conflict, the British fleet ended by establishing its mastery of the seas."[25] Until the spring of 1951, the Truman administration was able to resist the pressure from its allies to open negotiations, and from the public and Congress to end the war one way or another. As in Vietnam, the demand was one of "in or out." If the Soviet Union or China were the real enemy, then they should take the war there and finish it once and for all. If not, they should bring the boys home.

Any too peremptory a demand for negotiations on the part of America's allies was met with the threat that to yield to such pressure would enrage both the American public and the Congress, inciting them to a vengeful "isolationism" that would result in a retreat not only from Asia but from Europe itself.[26] Public insistence on ending the war—expressed in polls and letters to the press, the president, and Congress—was answered by conjuring the horrors of the global war that would ensue from either expansion of the fighting, which could lead to nuclear war, or withdrawal, which would only whet the enemy's appetite for renewed aggression. Like Wayne Morse, Ernest Gruening and, more circumspectly, Mike Mansfield and Gaylord Nelson in the 1960s, some members of Congress, fearless of labels, called for a principled end to the fighting. In May, 1951, Edwin "Big Ed" Johnson (D-Colorado) introduced a cease-fire resolution in the Senate:

> Whereas to permit civilization to be destroyed by World War III is
> utter insanity and unworthy of the men of this century; and
> Whereas the Korean war has every appearance of being a hopeless
> conflict of attrition and indecisiveness and a breeder of racial ha-
> treds; and . . . Whereas the North and South Koreans, the Chinese
> and the UN have suffered more than 1,000,000 casualties, with the
> only tangible result so far the indescribable misery which has been
> heaped upon the Korean people . . . and Whereas by slaughtering
> additional millions of humans an uneasy peace might in time be
> forced upon the vanquished; and . . . Whereas it has long been the
> policy of the American people that no nation should seek to extend
> its form of government over any other nation or people, but that as
> an inherent right every people should be left free to determine its
> own form of government and its own way of life, unhindered, un-
> threatened, unafraid—the little along with the great and powerful;
> and Whereas the traditional policy and desire of the people of the
> United States of America is now and has been a just and enduring

peace; and Whereas it is never too early for God-fearing and peace-loving peoples to earnestly endeavor to stop needless human slaughter: Now, therefore, be it *Resolved,* That it is the sense of the Senate that the United Nations call upon all nations and all groups now engaged in the war in Korea to cease fire and declare an armistice at 4 am (Korean time) June 25, 1951; and that prior thereto the United Nations forces restore to points south and the opposing forces retire to points north of the thirty-eighth parallel; and that before December 31, 1951, all prisoners of the Korean war shall be exchanged and all non-Korean persons, military and nonmilitary (except for ordinary diplomatic representatives), shall depart from North and South Korea.

A week after his speech, Johnson was interviewed on the popular radio program *Pro and Con.* Most of the press, he pointed out had "shied away" from any discussion of his resolution and some had accused him of being "a defeatist, an isolationist, an appeaser," but the response from his constituents had been overwhelmingly positive. When asked if he were troubled that the Soviet press had praised his resolution, Johnson responded that it was "good news. Peace is not a one-way street. There can be no peace in the world unless Russia agrees to it. . . . So if Russia is interested in establishing peace in Korea, the battle is half won." Was not this appeasement? Johnson, unimpressed, said that all his resolution did was "turn Korea back to the Koreans. Under its terms every people other than the Koreans get out by next New Year's Day. . . . Korea is a testing ground for negotiating peace. . . . If we wait for an unconditional surrender before we start developing peace terms, we better start preparing for a hundred year's war." To be sure, the result would be a divided country. "The United States Government created the thirty-eighth parallel. Now the Koreans are stuck with it and only the Koreans can eliminate it. Even bad eggs cannot be unscrambled. We created the same botched-up misfortune for Germany. . . . Perhaps time, patience and good will may eliminate these wicked and arbitrary divisions of peoples and states."[27] Predictably, the Republican Right attacked, with Sen. William Knowland leading the charge. However, Johnson's speech represented an eloquent version of an increasingly popular position. The deep rejection of the Korean War, reflected in qualitative and quantitative poll data, easily matched the public disaffection with the Vietnam War. The difference is that over time the public's disaffection with Vietnam inspired a movement, whereas the public registered only passive, sullen disbelief toward the conflict in Korea.

It was an article of fixed belief in Washington that negotiations could not begin until the military situation had put the United States in a position of decided strength. A move toward peace would otherwise signal only weakness. Once the war was joined, the Chinese were in full accord with this view and turned down a UN proposal (endorsed by Acheson only out of his certainty the Chinese would reject it) in January, 1951. By the end of May, 1951, however, after the defeat of a major Chinese offensive in April, Mao Zedong was ready to entertain a new strategy: "fighting while at the same time negotiating." Given an absolute lack of trust in U.S. motives, Chinese policy looked to the possibility of a prolonged war, for which they would continue to prepare, while simultaneously striving "to end the war through peace negotiations."[28] Kim Il Sung was not pleased but, given the circumstances, could only acquiesce. Chinese terms were simple: the withdrawal of all non-Korean forces from the peninsula, restoration of the border at the 38th Parallel, and the establishment of a demilitarized zone between North and South Korea. Earlier demands for UN membership and a settlement of the Taiwan issue were dropped entirely. In June, Mao asked the Soviet Union to explore the possibility of talks. Washington, too, bowing at last to what Truman called the "popular clamor" for peace and the pressure of its allies, approached Moscow, through George Kennan (recalled to service for this purpose), about arranging a cease-fire.

The Soviet response was positive and took the public form of a speech by its ambassador to the UN. On June 23, Jacob Malik, the Soviet UN ambassador, practiced his first radio address to the American public with his language tutor, Lillian Seidel. "*The Soviet Union threatens no one,*" Malik read from his text, only to have Seidel stop him. "'If you really mean that . . . ' I said. 'What do you mean *if* I really mean it?'" Malik interrupted angrily. Seidel explained that whatever the words, it sounded "as though you were just about to shoot someone. I'm only suggesting that you say it with less hostility." No matter what tone of voice he used, Malik's offer was simplicity itself: "*The Soviet peoples believe that, as a first step, discussions should be started between the belligerents for a cease-fire and an armistice providing for the mutual withdrawal of forces from the Thirty-eighth Parallel.*"[29] The following month, talks, to be conducted by the military with an agenda strictly limited to a military cease-fire, opened in Kaesong.

If, at least until mid-1951, the wars and the avoidance of an early peace were similar, the ultimate outcomes were radically divergent. Although in both the agendas was a military cease-fire with as few political implications for the future as possible, the talks in Korea were conducted, on the American side, entirely by the military and, albeit with stringent press censorship, in public. The Vietnam talks were conducted by high-ranking civilians in both public and secret meetings, giving the Nixon administration more room to maneuver than was the case in Korea. The struggle between the Pentagon and the State Department, which marked the endgame in Korea, was largely absent in Vietnam. Nor did Nixon have to contend with trying to keep America's European allies in line, or deal with powerful senators seeking to expand the role of one of their favorites, Chiang Kai-shek, and protect a second, Syngman Rhee. On the other hand, neither Truman nor Eisenhower ever faced a Congress ready to use its budgetary powers to hamper military operations.[30]

In Korea, however intent the United States may have been on achieving propaganda victories, the effort to destroy the North Korean regime had been abandoned and no one was up for a major war with China. What was sought was a return to the *status quo ante*. In Vietnam, the *status quo ante* was what the war had been about to begin with; there could be no peace on the basis of an anticommunist South Vietnamese state. By acting as though U.S. goals in Korea had always and only been about repelling North Korean aggression—conveniently forgetting that in August, 1950, or even earlier, war aims had shifted to military unification of the country—a successful cease-fire in Korea more or less on the 38th Parallel could be sold as a kind of victory. This was impossible in Vietnam, where the Nixon administration faced the problem of satisfying mounting domestic demands for disengagement without actually conceding defeat.

Bargaining in Korea initially focused on whether the cease-fire line should be at the 38th Parallel, as the North Koreans and Chinese insisted, or farther north; on the rehabilitation of North Korean airfields; and on the forms of prisoner exchange. The organization of Rhee's regime in the South was never at issue (except when American officials, impatient with his efforts to disrupt the armistice, contemplated getting rid of him), and the possible unification of the country—along with the withdrawal of American (but not Chinese) troops from the peninsula—was postponed for discussion at a later date. In Vietnam, negotiations over the organization of the South Vietnamese government after a cease-fire was agreed upon could not be avoided. Moreover, in counterpoint to Korea, American forces ultimately withdrew while North Vietnam's remained in place.

In both sets of negotiations, however, the attitudes of American negotiators toward their opposite numbers were similar. Henry Kissinger would have sympathized with Gen. Matthew Ridgway's assessment of the Chinese and North Koreans. To sit down with them, Ridgway wrote in a letter to the JCS, and deal with them "as representatives of an enlightened and civilized people is to deride one's own dignity and to invite the disaster their treachery will inevitably bring upon us." They were "treacherous savages" who must be spoken to in language they could not misunderstand.[31] Other senior officers in Korea called them "common criminals," "talking animals," and "sons of bitches . . . outside the pale of normal gentlemanly humanity."[32] Kissinger, for his part, thought the Vietnamese "fanatics" and "a bunch of shits. Tawdry, filthy shits."[33] In Korea, as in Vietnam, punishing, albeit limited, military actions accompanied resistance to U.S. terms. Bombing restrictions previously in force were lifted in an effort to extract concessions and demonstrate, to friends at least as much as foes, Washington's ongoing determination and its nearly absolute indifference to civilian loss of life. In both wars, Washington persuaded itself that such actions yielded positive gains, though all one can say with any certainty is that the United States had, in Michael Sherry's excellent phrase, bombed itself back to the table.

Between July, 1951, and January, 1952, all of the issues on the negotiating agenda had been resolved save one: the exchange of POWs. From January, 1952, until July, 1953, this issue alone prevented the conclusion of a cease-fire agreement. Despite its violation of the Geneva Convention of 1949, despite the military's resistance, despite the fact that it would prolong the captivity of U.S. and UN soldiers, despite the mounting U.S./UN casualty toll, despite the bad publicity prisoner uprisings in UN camps occasioned, and despite the near certainty that failure to conclude an armistice would cost the Democratic Party the 1952 presidential election, Truman held firm to the principle of voluntary (modified later to nonforcible) repatriation of POWs. The origins of the policy were multiple. According to Rosemary Foot, Brig. Gen. Robert McClure, in charge of the army's psychological warfare program, raised it first. He argued partly on humanitarian lines concerning the fate of returning prisoners who might be punished by the Chinese and North Koreans, as had prisoners returning to the Soviet Union after World War II. More important were the "adverse effects upon future U.S. psychological warfare operations."[34] For thousands of prisoners to refuse repatriation to communism would be an immediate propaganda victory. It also held out even greater promise for the future in terms of encouraging defections not only in Asia but also in Eastern Europe—indeed, in the Soviet Union itself.

Paul Nitze recalled that his own position was influenced by Chip Bohlen, who had been so horrified by the Soviet treatment of POWs returning from Germany that he was determined "that this shouldn't happen again."[35] Until Bohlen raised the issue, U. Alexis Johnson told an interviewer years later, "at the end of hostilities you sent all prisoners back, period. And this was an assumption under which everybody was working. The military in particular—I don't say just the military, but in particular I say our military—naturally thinking in terms of doing the maximum to get our men back, also thought in terms of everybody being returned from both sides. And they did not in general take very kindly to anybody even questioning the principle." Only Truman could resolve the dispute and it was put to him, Johnson continued, very clearly: "If he did not insist on voluntary repatriation, we probably could get an armistice fairly quickly and end the Korean war. But if he continued to insist on voluntary repatriation, it would not be possible to achieve an armistice, probably, prior to the election. I may be oversimplifying a little bit, but not much. It emerged very, very clearly." Johnson remembers there being a "vigorous" debate, ended by Truman's "clear, unequivocal decision that he expressed to everybody there, that we were going to stand for voluntary repatriation, because that was the moral and the right thing to do. I have cited this sometimes as the greatest act of political courage by a President that I witnessed while I have been in the employ of the Government. And it's one thing above all for which I remember President Truman."[36]

The newly organized Psychological Strategy Board turned the POW issue into a small cottage industry, producing thousands and thousands of pages of analysis and recommendations on the best way to "exploit" it. One thing was clear: to anyone who asked, "Why is the United States in Korea?" there was now an answer: to preserve the right of individuals to choose freedom. Any compromise, Acheson declared, would "constitute an abandonment of the principles fundamental to this country and the United Nations. We shall not trade in the lives of men. We shall not forcibly deliver human beings into Communist hands."[37] Brigadier General Haydon Boatner, who supervised the largest POW camp, caustically observed that there was something odd about a country which restricted immigration in peacetime, "when men are relatively free," but took great pride on the "conversion of our erstwhile enemies. . . . Especially when they were in fact in our prisons, subject to our indoctrination and therefore not free to make a 'free choice.'"[38] But he kept his observations to himself until after the war.

Several members of the Policy Planning Staff found the psychological warfare arguments unconvincing. Frank Stelle, for example, argued that defections were always "local" and stories about Korean POWs were unlikely to have much impact in the Balkans. Moreover, the morality of the U.S. positions left something to be desired. There was little possibility of an honest screening of prisoners to discover their preferences since the camps were "violently totalitarian" and the "thugs who run them are the people, aside from our own U.S. prisoners, that are the actual objects of concern in the POW issue." Stelle urged that the "only truly important element in [the] maintenance of our stand on the POW issue, would appear to be . . . not the moral or practical merits of our position itself, but the cumulative effects which withdrawal from any position we have once adopted may have on the negotiating appetite of the enemy." Should a concession on the prisoners be followed by an immediate armistice, the issue "would be so buried in more important matters, that I doubt if the effect on domestic, allied, or communist opinion would be anything but salutary."[39] Another member of the staff, C. B. Marshall, strongly disagreed. The POW issue, he wrote, "gets at the heart of the contention between Communism and the tradition we live by. It bears on the rights of men to make choices and to claim protection. . . . [The enemy] has not defeated us . . . and there is no reason why we should yield to him on an issue that cuts the heart out of our case. Rather than do that, we should prepare to hang on in Korea and to increase our effort in whatever measure necessary to compel the enemy rather than ourselves to do the yielding on the fundamental issues."[40] The actual conditions in the camps, the extent to which anything resembling either free choice or protection existed, played no role in Marshall's argument.

As peace talks continued to stall on the single issue of POW repatriation, an analyst in the Office of Intelligence and Research prepared a lengthy memorandum for Paul Nitze, urging that the subject be entirely rethought. Henry Owen began his discussion with a pithy paragraph on World War I. He noted the way in which the powers of the day "allowed their preoccupation with the need for keeping one step ahead of each other in day-to-day preparations for war to foreclose certain possibilities for resolving the Serbian issue by negotiation." Their obsessions had little to do with their actual security interests, since war would be a disaster for all of them. Owen gently suggested that Washington suffered from a "similar myopia" in its pursuit of the Cold War.

In particular, the handling of the POW issue worried Owen. Discrete decisions on potentially fruitful approaches to the issue foundered on the question of which side might score the biggest propaganda victory. He recognized that a U.S. concession on prisoners might mean a propaganda setback; but it might also yield a truce, which was far more important. Perhaps the communists would conduct a "propaganda circus," but so what? "It would probably not spur the Communists to achievements of which they would otherwise be incapable." In any case, the communists would find "something to beat us over the head with" no matter what the United States did or did not do and while some people would believe them, neither the people of the world, nor their governments "will determine their national policies on grounds other than (if not more sensible than) what *l'Humanite* . . . says about us. . . . The trouble is that we have now created a vast propaganda bureaucracy which has no other function than to engage in this PW chess game with their Soviet opposite members."[41]

Advocates of the policy were delighted to be given the opportunity to defend it before Congress. John M. Allison, assistant secretary of state for the

Far East, appeared before the House Committee on Foreign Affairs in May, 1952. The occasion was an inquiry into the behavior of the commander of the Koje-do POW camp, who had been held hostage by prisoners demanding an improvement in camp conditions and an end to forced screening. The uprising was suppressed with maximal force, and it raised the policy of nonforcible repatration itself. "If we are fighting for anything," Allison told the committee, "we are fighting for a moral principle on this thing, and the fact that you do not throw people back." It would be tragic if more Americans had to die to uphold the principle, Allison concluded philosophically, but "war itself is a tragedy."[42] Representative Walter Judd welcomed Allison's remarks and applied them broadly. "The commies stand by their people and you can count on them. I think that this is one of the strongest psychological weapons in this whole world struggle, the fear the neutrals have, those on the fence, that the United States is too soft." Another committee member called the communists "scientific savages" who lacked even the "basic scruples" of the Germans. They took advantage of "our chivalry, our decency, to win their biggest victories. . . . We have been fighting them as if they were nice westernized people."[43]

Truman was adamant on the question, although his reasoning is a little hard to follow. Rather than the high moral ground ascribed to him by Alexis Johnson, Truman seemed more concerned with the negative impact, domestically and internationally, of compromise as such. At a late-September, 1952, meeting of the National Security Council, he insisted that the United States must not yield on its prisoner proposal simply to get an armistice. The whole point to an armistice was peace in the Pacific, but not "under conditions which may later enable the Communists to take over Japan or elsewhere." Public pressure for withdrawal from Korea in the event of an armistice was a real danger: "If and when the armistice is signed," Truman said, "we will find ourselves in the same position as on September 2, 1945, when we accepted the surrender of Japan and then tore up our military machine. . . . We cannot sit down now with the doors open and no military machine to protect us—we must build up our military strength." The time had come to present a package proposal, give the Chinese ten days to accept it, and, if they did not, then the talks should be recessed and military pressure applied. General Omar Bradley agreed. Holding firm on the prisoner issue would, he thought, "deter the coming of World War III because the Communists would be unwilling to take the chance of mass surrender movements induced by the knowledge that we would not forcibly return them." Truman "repeated that he had been trying to prevent World War III and he would hate to end his political career by bringing it on, but we cannot give in on principles."[44]

The principle involved was not particularly popular with the public. Pearl Tupper Henrickson, for example, wanted her son home. "You seem to be more concerned over what happens to the Red P. O. W.'s," she wrote Truman, "than you do the P. O. W.'s the Reds have of our own boys. . . . If you had a son, would you trade him for a Chinaman or North Korean? I think that one GI is worth more than all the Red prisoners that we hold." Mrs. William Platz wanted to know why the "whims and begging of a few Chinese are more important than the American boys who are prisoners? . . . What kind of war is this?"[45]

The House Un-American Activities Committee subsequently investigated the families of Korean War POWs who organized in an attempt to pressure the government to negotiate a quick truce and the release of their sons. Two decades later, Richard Nixon also stood on principle, but with the Mrs. Platz's and Henrickson's in mind, he reversed the field. At the opening of the public talks in Paris, Henry Cabot Lodge was instructed to call for the "early release of prisoners on both sides."[46] The Nixon administration mobilized POW families itself and orchestrated a skillful propaganda campaign that gave the impression the war continued solely in order to free captured Americans. Jeffrey Kimball summarized Nixon's motives, which included "the diversion of public attention from the Saigon government's mistreatment of political and military prisoners in South Vietnam by drawing attention to enemy cruelties; the establishment of a 'public record' of having tried to win the release of the POWs; [and] the creation of a propaganda counterweight to the antiwar message of the American peace movement." It was a campaign designed to win "the hearts, if not the minds, of many Americans"—and it worked.[47] The obstacle the POW issue presented in the Paris talks was differently configured than during the Korean War, focusing on the status of political prisoners held by the Saigon government rather than nonforcible repatriation. Nevertheless, the combination of ultimata and coercive bombing, of actions undertaken for purposes of propaganda rather than substantive gains, do recall Panmunjom.

Rosemary Foot concludes that in the Korean case, the United States "could claim to have obtained certain satisfactions at the conference table—some of a material and some of an ideological kind—and these could serve to demonstrate its power and to uphold the notion of the near universality of its interests." The POW issue allowed the United States to display its readiness to sacrifice lives for a principle, demonstrated the illegitimacy of communist claims to the loyalty of their citizens, created anxiety in the Soviet Union about troop defections in any future war, and, with the Eisenhower administration's claim that nuclear threats finally forced

Chinese capitulation, "the resolution of this item could be projected as that winning combination of military power in the service of moral rectitude."[48]

Yet the distinction Foot makes between material and ideological gain is misleading. Ideological gains *were* substantive for Truman, Eisenhower, and all the Vietnam presidents. The problem both wars posed for the administrations that fought them is that limited wars, by definition, must end in compromise, mutual concession, and less-than-total victory. How then to display toughness, draw the line between American virtue and enemy vice, and use the force that was, all agreed, the only language communists of any nationality understood? How, most especially, to persuade a doubting public that the war had been about something, that the stakes really mattered, that the deaths of U.S. soldiers had meaning?

Neither war could boast clear battlefield victories, but an inflexible posture in negotiations, combined with ongoing punishment of the enemy and a cooperative press, could yield victory in the struggle to win American hearts and minds. In Korea, refusal to compromise on nonforcible repatriation, a State Department analysis concluded, left "no shadow of doubt in anyone's mind that our will has been imposed on the enemy."[49] The case was more difficult to make in Vietnam, but the Christmas bombing and the extravaganza of Operation Homecoming, Nixon had reason to hope, conveyed the same message. In neither war did it really work. Samuel Lubell, polling the country before the 1952 elections, found people cursing at the very mention of Truman's name. Public reaction to Korea, he wrote, punctured the myth that "'the people only have to be told the facts to do what is expected of them.' The expression 'We don't know what the War is all about' was voiced most frequently by persons with sons or husbands in Korea. Clearly they did not lack information; but emotion had stopped their ears to all explanations of why we were fighting in Korea."[50]

Lubell predicted that the era of limited war was over, that the 1952 election amounted to a public repudiation of such policies. "The same dread that the American people might not support a prolonged attrition," he wrote in 1956, "which would prompt our politicians to try to avoid involvement could be expected to spur them to get any war over with quickly once we were engaged."[51] It would take the Vietnam War to fulfill his prediction and the 1991 Persian Gulf War to implement it.

Contemplating Nixon's trip to China, a friend once remarked: "Sometimes only the bad can do good." Richard Rovere put it a little differently in his analysis of what Eisenhower had achieved in Korea: "if a Democratic administration were in power, and if it attempted to negotiate a truce on these terms, there would be neither praise nor silence; on the contrary, mere anticipation of the noise and excoriation would in all likelihood have effectively restrained a Democratic administration from even seeking to get approval for the kind of settlement that is now in the process of being made." One of the "neater ironies of the moment," Rovere observed, "is that the party considered to be the unbending one in its view of the national interest is, by very virtue of its reputation for inflexibility, able in this matter to pursue the more flexible policy."[52] It was an irony that President Johnson, had he been in a savoring mood, might have appreciated.

Notes

1. Yuen Foong Khong, *Analogies at War: Korea, Munich, Dien Bien Phu, and the Vietnam Decisions of 1965* (Princeton, N.J.: Princeton University Press, 1992).

2. Ibid., p. 111.

3. Bruce Cumings, *The Origins of the Korean War*, vol. 2, *The Roaring of the Cataract, 1947–1950* (Princeton, N.J.: Princeton University Press), p. 162.

4. Dean Acheson, *Present at the Creation: My Years in the State Department* (1969; reprint, New York: W. W. Norton, 1987), p. 476.

5. Thomas W. Zeiler, *Dean Rusk: Defending the American Mission Abroad* (Wilmington, Del.: Scholarly Resources, 2000), p. 27.

6. Robert S. McNamara, James G. Blight, and Robert K. Brigham, *Argument Without End: In Search of Answers to the Vietnam Tragedy* (New York: Public Affairs, 1999), p. 41.

7. Ibid., p. 321.

8. Michael Beschloss, *Taking Charge: The Johnson White House Tapes, 1963–1964* (New York: Simon and Schuster, 1997), p. 390.

9. Ibid., p. 363–64.

10. Ibid., p. 370.

11. Ibid., pp. 401–402.

12. Jeffrey Kimball, *Nixon's Vietnam War* (Lawrence: University Press of Kansas, 1998), p. 83.

13. Ibid., p. 82.

14. Rosemary Foot, *A Substitute for Victory: The Politics of Peacemaking at the Korean Armistice Talks* (Ithaca, N.Y.: Cornell University Press, 1990), pp: 21–23.

15. Kennan's initial position firmly supported sending American troops to repel the North Korean invasion. Additionally, he urged action to "assure that Formosa did not fall into Communist hands." However, throughout the crisis, he held firm against any move against North Korea itself. See Wilson D. Miscamble, *George F. Kennan and the Making of American Foreign Policy, 1947–1950* (Princeton, N.J.: Princeton University Press, 1992), pp. 319 ff. Quote is from George F. Kennan, *Memoirs*, vol. 1, *1925–1950* (Boston: Little, Brown, 1967), pp.492–93.

16. Kennan, *Memoirs*, pp. 1:492–93.

17. Ibid., p. 1:485. As late as February, 1951, well after China's punishing intervention might have been expected to solidify anti-Chinese sentiments, 57 percent of those polled by the *New York Times* said they would favor China's entry into the UN if it meant peace in Korea. See Hugh Garland Wood, "American Reaction to Limited War in Asia: Korea and Vietnam" (Ph.D. diss., University of Colorado, 1974), p. 141.

18. Kennan, *Memoirs*, p. 1:495.

19. Ibid., pp. 1:493–96.

20. Ibid., pp. 1:499–500.

21. George F. Kennan, *Memoirs,* vol. 2, *1950–1963* (Boston: Little, Brown, 1972), p. 34.

22. Fredrik Logevall, *Choosing War: The Lost Chance for Peace and the Escalation of the War in Vietnam* (Berkeley: University of California Press), p. 21.

23. Frank Pace Oral History, Harry S. Truman Library, Independence, Mo. (hereafter Truman Library). I am grateful to Curt Cardwell for access to this and other documents from the Truman Library collected by the late Frank Kofsky.

24. Thomas J. Christensen, "Threats, Assurances, and the Last Chance for Peace: The Lessons of Mao's Korean War Telegrams," *International Security* 17 (summer, 1992): pp. 130–31 n 2.

25. Meeting of the NSC, May 3, 1951, Truman Library.

26. Foot, *Substitute for Victory,* p. 6.

27. *Congressional Record,* 82d Cong., 1st sess., May 17, June 27, 1951, vol. 97, pt. 4 and 5, pp. 5424, 7192.

28. Chen Jian, "Mao's China and the Cold War" (MS in author's possession), pp. 129–30.

29. Lillian Seidel, "Was Malik Surprised?" *New Yorker,* February 9, 1952.

30. D. Clayton James offers a good a summary of civilian-military differences with respect to a cease-fire in Korea. See *Refighting the Last War: Command and Crisis in Korea, 1950–1953* (New York: Free Press, 1993), chap. 10.

31. Quoted in Ernest May, "Introduction," Herbert Goldhainer, *The 1951 Korean Armistice Conference: A Personal Memoir* (Santa Monica, Calif.: RAND Corporation, 1994), p. xix.

32. Foot, *Substitute for Victory,* p. 11.

33. Richard Nixon, *RN: The Memoirs of Richard Nixon* (New York: Grosset and Dunlap, 1978), pp. 599, 733.

34. Foot, *Substitute for Victory,* pp. 87, 88. For a discussion of the importance of psychological warfare to the Truman administration, see Gregory Mitrovich, *Undermining the Kremlin: America's Strategy to Subvert the Soviet Bloc, 1947–1956* (Ithaca, N.Y.: Cornell University Press, 2000).

35. Paul Nitze Oral History, Truman Library.

36. Ibid.

37. Foot, *Substitute for Victory,* p. 150.

38. Quoted in Barton J. Bernstein, "The Struggle over the Korean Armistice: Prisoners of Repatriation?" in *Child of Conflict: The Korean-American Relationship 1943–1953,* ed. Bruce Cumings (Seattle: University of Washington Press, 1983), p. 286.

39. Policy Planning Staff, Country File, Jan. 24, 1952, Truman Library.

40. Ibid., Jan. 28, 1952.

41. Ibid., May 29, 1952.

42. "Koje-do Prisoner Mutiny and its Impact on Cease-Fire Negotiations," Hearings before the House of Representatives Committee on Foreign Affairs, May 19, 1953, in *U.S. Policy in the Far East,* part I (Washington D.C.: GPO, 1980), p. 177.

43. Ibid., p. 203.

44. Meeting of the NSC, Sept. 24 1952, Truman Library.

45. Letters to the President, Truman Library. I am grateful to Ron Robin for these documents.

46. Kimball, *Nixon's War,* p. 167.

47. Ibid., pp.166–67.

48. Foot, *Substitute for Victory,* pp. 206–207.

49. Ibid., p. 221.

50. Samuel Lubell, *Revolt of the Moderates* (New York: Harper Brothers, 1956), p. 265 n 5.

51. Ibid., pp.45–46.

52. Letter from Washington, *New Yorker,* June 20, 1953, p. 84.

Discussions, Not Negotiations

*The Johnson Administration's Diplomacy
at the Outset of the Vietnam War*

DAVID KAISER

During the Cold War, within which the Vietnam War took place, American diplomacy was frequently based upon visions of what the world should be, rather than upon what it was. Thus, in Europe, successive administrations refused in various ways to recognize the political consequences of the Second World War, including the imposition of communist regimes in Eastern Europe, while in Asia the United States refused for more than twenty years to recognize the Communist Chinese regime. From time to time, however, various administrations found it necessary to express an interest in the peaceful resolution of diplomatic disputes, even though they had no intention of legitimizing the status quo. As a result, the State Department developed techniques for avoiding serious negotiations on difficult subjects while claiming to favor them.

This approach characterized the Eisenhower administration's stance on all-Vietnam elections after the conclusion of the Geneva Accords in 1954. More importantly for our purposes, it also characterized the Johnson administration's initial statements on peace talks to settle the Vietnam War, specifically during 1965. Although the Johnson administration certainly desired a favorable peace in the long run, it had committed itself to objectives that would require a tremendous improvement in the situation on the ground to secure. These objectives also contravened the Geneva Accords of 1954, which theoretically still governed the status of South Vietnam. In addition, as we shall see, the Saigon government resolutely opposed negotiations in the near and medium term, and the American embassy in Saigon supported that stance. On the other hand, the American people clearly hoped that the war would not last very long. Washington also faced important international pressure from adversaries, allies, and the UN secretary general to begin serious talks as soon as possible. Drawing on precedents from the Cold War and a more recent crisis in Latin America, President Johnson tried to square the circle on April 7 when he offered Hanoi "unconditional discussions" but avoided the word "negotiations." In the short run, this strategy served its political purpose very well. In the long run, however, it contributed to popular disillusion with the war when three years of fighting failed to show any real progress. The administration did not abandon this strategy until the waning months of LBJ's presidency.

The American government's tactic of theoretically endorsing but actually avoiding negotiations to which it had committed itself in principle or which appealed to important international constituencies seems to have emerged first in Europe, specifically with respect to the German problem. Committed to four-power resolution of the German question by the Potsdam agreement, the United States had definitely decided by 1949 to abandon that framework in favor of a two- or three-power approach (including the United States, Britain, and eventually France) designed to rebuild Germany's western zones and create a West German state friendly to, and eventually integrated within, the western alliance. Whether or not this decision was correct—and, history now seems to have vindicated it—it required the United States to reject Soviet initiatives designed to reopen four-power talks on Germany's future. In his commendably frank memoirs, former secretary of state Dean Acheson explained, for example, how the United States in the spring of 1951 managed to block any serious four-power talks on Germany in Paris by stringing out an argument over the agenda. A year later, the Soviet note of March 10, 1952, struck him merely as a Soviet attempt to undo the western powers' progress in replacing the occupation agreements with contractual arrangements between Washington, London, and Paris on one hand, and Bonn on the other. Acheson may well have been right, but the note, as he recognized, had been cleverly drafted to appeal to European and West German opinion, and therefore required some kind of positive response. Thus, an agreed western response issued on March 26 demanded an investigation of conditions throughout Germany—including East Germany—to ascertain whether "free conditions prerequisite to free elections" existed as a first step toward any settlement. The Soviets failed to agree.[1]

The Eisenhower administration maintained this demand in new controversies over Germany's future, and introduced it into its diplomacy toward Vietnam in 1955, when the issue of the 1956 all-Vietnam elections called for by the Geneva Accords was becoming acute. "Our proposal," Secretary of State John Foster Dulles explained to the American embassy in Saigon on April 6, 1955, "is based on [Anthony] Eden's plan put forward at [the] Berlin Conference for all-German elections and already approved by France for use [in] Germany and rejected by the Communists. [The] basic principle is that Free Viet-Nam will insist to [the] Viet Minh that unless agreement is first reached by the latter's acceptance of safeguards . . . no further discussions are possible regarding the type of elections, the issues to be voted on or any other factors."

The supervisory body—which in Eden's proposal would have come from the United Nations—was to "have full powers to act to ensure free elections" and to guarantee "freedom of movement; freedom of presentation of candidates; immunity of candidates; freedom from arbitrary arrest or victimization; freedom of association and political meetings; freedom of expression for all; freedom of the press, radio, and free circulation of newspapers, etc."[2]

Taking an even harder line, prime minister and later president Ngo Dinh Diem of South Vietnam refused to acknowledge the authority of the Geneva Accords at all. Nonetheless, Dulles's position remained the official U.S. line on any future elections in South Vietnam throughout the 1950s. In the fall of 1961, during intense deliberations over Laos and South Vietnam inside the new Kennedy administration, Amb. W. Averell Harriman suggested that the United States might propose a discussion of means to implement the 1954 accords effectively, adding, "We should not preclude a restudy of the possibility of elections as a matter of strategy." President John F. Kennedy asked that these proposals be studied further on November 14, 1961, but no one ever followed up on this request.[3] Instead, the Kennedy administration began a new advisory effort designed to help the South Vietnamese fight the guerrilla war against the Vietcong (VC) more effectively while violating several important military restrictions embodied in the 1954 accords.

During the first four months of its existence, from December, 1963, through March, 1964, the Johnson administration decided to prepare for war in Southeast Asia and began defining its objectives. After Defense Secretary Robert S. McNamara visited Saigon in December and returned with a new and very alarming assessment of the situation, the president quickly approved covert actions against North Vietnam. In March, William Bundy, who was just moving from the Pentagon to the State Department as the new assistant secretary for Far Eastern Affairs, prepared several draft reports of yet another McNamara visit that laid out possible military action against the North. In his second draft, Bundy specifically addressed the issue of negotiations in terms that foreshadowed the administration's subsequent positions. Acknowledging that the American and South Vietnamese position was currently too weak for negotiations, he argued that eventual talks would have to improve the provisions of the 1954 accords to remove all numerical and qualitative restrictions on outside military assistance, provide for effective policing of South Vietnam's borders, and drop the provision for all-Vietnam elections. Bundy's final report of McNamara's trip (which the secretary took from March 9 through March 12, 1964) became the basis for National Security Council (NSC) action memorandum 288 dated March 17.

While it dropped the specific discussion of revising the terms of the Geneva Accords, it committed the United States to the objective of "an independent, non-Communist South Vietnam . . . free to accept outside assistance as required to maintain its security." This remained the official statement of American objectives at least through the Johnson administration. It effectively ruled out any talks until the military and political situation within South Vietnam had substantially improved.[4] President Johnson, however, decided to defer the announcement and execution of this policy—including attacks on North Vietnam—until after the November presidential election.

Meanwhile, a crisis in Latin America had led the new president to revive and make public a diplomatic distinction of considerable future significance for Vietnam. United States–Panamanian relations had encountered several problems since the 1950s. The Panamanians sought economic concessions and some acknowledgement of their sovereignty over the Canal Zone, and Pres. Dwight D. Eisenhower had tried to meet these demands despite vociferous congressional opposition. In a June, 1962, meeting with Panamanian president Roberto Chiari, President Kennedy had agreed to "discussions" of problems that had arisen in relations between Panama and the Canal Zone, but had rejected renegotiating the 1903 treaty that had leased the Canal Zone "in perpetuity" until the United States and Panama first agreed on a new sea-level canal.[5] Kennedy made clear that he wanted to satisfy some of the Panamanians' more symbolic concerns and to increase economic aid, as indeed he did, without embarking upon a renegotiation of the 1903 treaty. In the spring of 1963, however, President Chiari decided to recess ongoing discussions during the coming Panamanian election campaign because their results had disappointed his countrymen.[6]

Meanwhile, the "Zonians"—Americans living in the Canal Zone—resented assertions of Panamanian sovereignty. In January, 1964, angry Zonians took down the Panamanian flag from a Canal Zone high school. When Panamanians responded with demonstrations outside the school, the Zonians began a riot. A much larger Panamanian demonstration across the border led to exchanges of rifle fire. Panamanians sacked American buildings in Panama City during more than three days of rioting, and on January 10 President Chiari broke off diplomatic relations with the United States. American officials immediately pledged to respect the existing agreement to fly the Panamanian flag, but added somewhat gratuitously that communists had been behind the riots.[7]

President Johnson showed genuine resentment of Panamanian tactics in several long telephone conversations about the crisis. Using the same language that Kennedy had used privately, he expressed willingness to "discuss all problems" between the two countries, but immediately bridled when President Chiari claimed that Johnson had agreed to renegotiate the 1903 treaty. The crisis eased in March, 1964, when both sides found a new formula (they would "review every issue" dividing them), but the distinction between "discussions" and "negotiations" had become part of the administration's public diplomacy. After the November election—during which the president had feared that too soft a stance would play into his opponent's hands—Johnson graciously reversed course and agreed in principle to make a new treaty that would set a time limit on American control of the canal. He did not, however, alter his determination to maintain an independent, noncommunist South Vietnam.

Indeed, a new interdepartmental working group began preparing fresh recommendations for Vietnam in the week following Johnson's overwhelming election. By then the situation had deteriorated further and one senior policy maker, Undersecretary of State George Ball, had raised serious questions about the wisdom of fighting for American objectives in South Vietnam. Thus, in preparing three options for senior policy makers, two key second-level figures—William Bundy and John McNaughton, the assistant secretary of defense for International Security Affairs—prepared a preferred Option C that foresaw settling for something less than a secure, independent, noncommunist South Vietnam. Bundy's original Option C had proposed some significant American military actions against North Vietnam, but expected them to lead to pressure for a new Geneva conference, which the United States would have to accept. In that case, he speculated, "we might judo our way to a settlement that might involve some modifications [of our terms] but would give South Vietnam a fair chance to survive and get going." McNaughton drafted a similar proposal, and the final Option C—drafted by Bundy on November 21, 1964—also suggested that the United States might have to settle for much less than its preferred terms. However, when the NSC's Executive Committee met on November 24—without the president—Secretary of State Dean Rusk in particular rejected this option out of hand. According to the *Pentagon Papers,* Rusk "did not accept the Working Group's rationale that we would obtain international credit merely for trying. In his view, the harder we tried and then failed, the worse our situation would be."[8]

Thus, the Working Group's final recommendations, which President Johnson approved on December 7 and which became the basis for American policy and strategy in the Vietnam War, stated an unequivocal set of American objectives: to remove North Vietnamese support and direction of the Vietcong; to "re-establish [*sic*] an independent and secure South Vietnam with appropriate international safeguards, including the freedom to accept US and other external assistance as required;" and to insure the full observance of the 1962 Geneva Accords on Laos. It also committed the United States to a gradual but entirely open-ended program of military action, during which Washington "would be alert to any sign of yielding by Hanoi, and would be prepared to explore negotiated solutions that attain US objectives in an acceptable manner." In short, the official definition of American goals for the war on which the United States was about to embark left no room for negotiations on anything less than the United States' own terms—terms that went well beyond the Geneva Accords of 1954.[9]

After intense discussions between Saigon and Washington beginning in the last week of December, 1964, and concluding in the first week of February, 1965, the bombing of North Vietnam began with a single strike on February 7. Further controversies in Washington and political turmoil in South Vietnam delayed both the beginning of the Rolling Thunder campaign and the deployment of marines to Da Nang until the first week in March. Washington by that time had already come under significant pressure to begin immediate negotiations from at least two major sources—UN secretary general U Thant and British prime minister Harold Wilson—and had developed its private response.

On February 16, U Thant told U.S. ambassador Adlai Stevenson that he had been urging bilateral talks between the United States and North Vietnam for more than a year, and that in December the Soviets had told him that the North Vietnamese would be willing to meet U.S. representatives in Rangoon. U Thant alternatively proposed a meeting of the two Vietnams, the Communist Chinese, and the non-Chinese permanent members of the Security Council. Stevenson endorsed this suggestion in a letter to President Johnson the next day, and pointed out that the British, Soviets, and several other interested parties also favored talks. On February 19, McGeorge Bundy told Johnson that such a conference would be "weighted against" the United States and cautioned him that America could not appear to be "hunting negotiations." A week later, U Thant publicly suggested that the United States was avoiding a chance for peace. Dean Rusk telephoned him and said "bilateral talks were out of the question, particularly since there were no indications they would be fruitful." Rusk implied that the United States needed a "real indication" of Hanoi's "willingness to stop the aggression."[10] Washington took the same line when U Thant publicly called for a seven-power conference and a three-month cease-fire on March 8.[11]

Subsequent instructions from Rusk to Stevenson on February 27 elaborated Rusk's view. "None of the important political negotiations of modern times," they read, "would have been successful if there had not already been some advance indications that both sides wanted to 'talk turkey' and work out some reasonable accommodation." Rusk cited as examples the talks that ended the Berlin blockade, the Korean armistice, the Cuban missile crisis settlement, and the nuclear test-ban treaty. Stevenson replied on March 1 that Rusk's analogies were not relevant. In each of those cases, the communists clearly had no means of getting their way, whereas in the present case the United States might not be able to stop them. Stevenson also favored early talks, but Rusk was not interested.[12]

The British government felt a special responsibility to promote peace since it remained the cochair (with the Soviets) of the adjourned Geneva conference. However, Rusk told British ambassador Lord Harlech that the United States would not allow the cochairmen to "impose a unilateral cease fire on us," and apparently managed to prevent Prime Minister Wilson from making a statement calling for a cease-fire and talks in early March.[13] The French government, meanwhile, continued to reject American policy and call for immediate negotiations.

Faced with similar calls for negotiation by columnist Walter Lippmann and editorial writer Robert Kleiman of the *New York Times,* President Johnson issued a statement of his own on March 25. The problem in South Vietnam, he said, was "aggression by Communist totalitarians against their independent neighbors." The United States, he continued, "will never be second in seeking a settlement in Vietnam that is based on an end of Communist aggression. As I have said in every part of the Union, I am ready to go anywhere at any time, and meet with anyone whenever there is promise of progress toward an honorable peace. We have said many times—to all who are interested in our principles for honorable negotiation—that we seek no more than a return to the essentials of the Agreements of 1954—a reliable arrangement to guarantee the independence and security of all in southeast Asia."[14]

This carefully drafted formula in effect reinterpreted the Geneva Accords of 1954 to call for the establishment of secure, internationally recognized borders between the North and South while ignoring their provisions regarding all-Vietnam elections and reunification, and leaving an escape hatch to finesse their restrictions on Saigon's freedom to accept assistance.

Johnson had now scheduled a major speech at Johns Hopkins University on April 7, and he decided to use it to reply to an April 1 appeal by seventeen nonaligned nations meeting in Belgrade for immediate negotiations without preconditions. Pledging the United States to fight indefinitely to stop aggression, Johnson responded favorably. However, borrowing from his experience in the Panama crisis a year earlier, he made one key word change:

peace demands an independent South Vietnam—securely guaranteed and able to shape its own relationships to all others—free from outside interference—tied to no alliance—a military base for no other country.

These are the essentials of any final settlement.

Johnson's attempt to combine some key provisions of the Geneva Accords with key elements of U.S. objectives was rather contradictory, since South Vietnam might for the sake of its own security decide to make an alliance or accept the presence of foreign military forces. He continued:

We will never be second in the search for such a peaceful settlement in Vietnam.

There may be many ways to this kind of peace: in *discussion or* negotiation with the governments concerned; in large groups or in small ones; in the reaffirmation of old agreements or their strengthening with new ones.

We have stated this position over and over again, fifty times and more, to friend and foe alike. And we remain ready, with this purpose, for *unconditional discussions.*[15]

"Unconditional discussions," as opposed to negotiations, meant two things. First, they meant no cease-fire, which the United States was determined to reject until it had a clear military advantage and evidence of Hanoi's willingness to meet American terms. Second, they meant no immediate agreement to do anything but exchange views. Johnson had managed to express a willingness to *talk* without indicating any willingness to *negotiate,* much less to abandon, any of his objectives. Yet, in the short run, the speech served its most important purpose: to reassure American and allied opinion. U Thant and the British and French governments welcomed it, the *New York Times* hailed the president's "willingness to negotiate," and Senate Majority Leader Mike Mansfield—a frequent administration critic—added his praise. Such optimistic interpretations probably reflected both the enormous prestige Johnson continued to enjoy, and the universally shared hope that the conflict might come to a relatively quick end.

Hanoi, indeed, had replied to Johnson's statement on April 13 with its own Four Points. These included the recognition of the rights of the Vietnamese people to unity, sovereignty, and territorial integrity, and the withdrawal of American forces and the cessation of American military activity in Vietnam; the observance of the military provisions of the 1954 accords, pending the "peaceful reunification of Vietnam;" the settlement of the internal affairs of the South according to the program of the National Liberation Front (NLF), that is, by the creation of a coalition government; and the peaceful reunification of the country on terms agreed upon by the Vietnamese themselves. These remained the North Vietnamese demands throughout the conflict, and they secured most of them in principle in the eventual 1973 Paris Accord with the United States. For the time being, however, they insisted that these were the only possible bases for a settlement— and since Hanoi was no more able to impose its terms on the United States than Washington was to force Hanoi to give in, the contrast between the two positions meant that no talks would take place any time soon.

The Johnson administration had settled on the strategy that it stuck to until the spring of 1968: to emphasize its interest in peace and imply the possibility of imminent negotiations with public statements and bombing halts, while *rejecting* actual negotiations until the North Vietnamese gave clear signals that they were willing to meet American terms. This led the administration into more diplomatic gymnastics regarding a new British initiative. In April, Prime Minister Wilson sent Patrick Gordon Walker, his erstwhile foreign secretary, to the Far East to suggest a Geneva conference on Cambodian neutrality. When the U.S. ambassador to Thailand, Graham Martin, reported Thai and South Vietnamese opposition to such a step, William Bundy drafted a revealing reply: "Without questioning your negative judgment of the initial attitudes of the Thai and Vietnamese governments, I want to stress that we simply cannot afford to get into a clear negative position on this proposal if we are to maintain the world, and even the domestic support we require to keep pressure on Hanoi."[16]

Similarly, Bundy wrote Rusk on April 21 that Taylor should inform South Vietnamese prime minister Phan Huy Quat that while the United States "is not enthusiastic about such a conference in itself," it "cannot well be negative when the Communist side has agreed and we have taken the position of favoring 'unconditional discussions' on Vietnam."[17] As it happened, the proposal was not accepted because Hanoi—equally intransigent and militarily stronger—insisted that the NLF represent South Vietnam at such a conference.

George Ball was now emerging as the leader of organized opposition to escalation within the administration. In early May, he recruited former secretary of state Dean Acheson to submit a joint peace plan suggesting that the Saigon government announce a halt to its operations and offer the Vietcong amnesty and elections provided that they laid down their arms. Ball submitted the plan on May 13, in the midst of a brief bombing halt that the administration had ordered to coincide with the Buddha's birthday on May 12, and discussed it with President Johnson on May 16. Johnson on that day indicated that the halt was simply a gesture to Senator Mansfield and Sen. J. William Fulbright, but Rusk agreed to forward the plan to Saigon. The Soviet government refused to deliver a message to the North Vietnamese embassy in Moscow regarding the halt. Ball's assistant, Thomas Ehrlich, hand-carried his plan to Saigon, where Amb. Maxwell Taylor and Deputy Chief of Mission U. Alexis Johnson replied on May 20 that the present South Vietnamese government—as it turned out, the last civilian government South Vietnam ever had—was too weak to offer anything convincing to the Vietcong or to neutrals, and would therefore have to reject it.[18] The opposition of successive South Vietnamese governments remained another obstacle to negotiations for the rest of the Johnson administration.

The same game of international peace moves, administration dissent, the fears of the Saigon embassy, and the basic American commitment to maximum objectives went through another iteration between June 7, when Gen. William C. Westmoreland asked for forty-four battalions, and July 28, when President Johnson publicly (if guardedly) announced his assent. On June 22, both Ambassador Taylor and General Westmoreland expressed concerns about pressure for a cease-fire from the British Commonwealth and other sources, and Westmoreland made clear that the American and South Vietnamese position was much too weak for talks.[19] On June 24, McGeorge Bundy gave President Johnson a memo rejecting Sen. Wayne Morse's careful argument for turning the Vietnam problem over to the United Nations because the South Vietnamese would not like it and the Soviets would take the enemy's position.[20] Nevertheless, the president remained determined to publicize a willingness for peace, albeit on American terms. On June 25, in a speech in San Francisco commemorating the founding of the United Nations, LBJ used the passive voice to produce an account of the process that Hanoi might have been willing to endorse:

> The processes of peaceful settlement today are blocked by willful aggressors contemptuous of the opinion and the will of mankind. Bilateral diplomacy has yielded no result. . . .
> The efforts of the distinguished Secretary General have been rebuffed.
> An appeal for unconditional discussion was met with contempt.
> A pause in bombing operations was called an insult.
> The concern for peace of the Commonwealth Prime Ministers has received little and very disappointing results.[21]

Meanwhile, the administration's internal deliberations enabled William Bundy, who still seems to have been unconvinced as to the wisdom of

American objectives, to propose secret American contacts with the NLF or the Democratic Republic of Vietnam (DRV) in early July. On July 5, however, Ambassador Taylor replied that such approaches were premature "now or in any short term future," that any leak would have a very "dangerous" effect on the Saigon government, and that "overeagerness to negotiate" would "nullify our past and present efforts to convince the VC/DRV that we have the will and determination to turn the tide against them sooner or later—so that they had better come to terms sooner rather than later."[22] McNamara, in his July 20 report on his trip to Vietnam recommending Westmoreland's new deployments, finessed this question by arguing that the new troops would be necessary to reach *any* satisfactory settlement.[23] The report endorsed secret contacts with Hanoi and the NLF, while noting that Taylor, U. Alexis Johnson, and Ambassador-designate Henry Cabot Lodge all opposed them. In the end, the administration secretly exchanged views with a North Vietnamese representative in Paris later that year, but it never contacted the NLF.

In a July 26 draft of an official statement publicly announcing the deployments, Washington appeared to take a further step toward the North Vietnamese proposal, not only endorsing "the purposes in essence" of the 1954 Geneva Accords, but adding that American principles for a settlement implied and included "the use of free election under international supervision" to decide upon reunification of the country, "just as soon as the end of aggression permits." However, Air Marshal Nguyen Cao Ky and Gen. Nguyen Van Thieu—the new leaders of South Vietnam—objected to the endorsement of the Geneva Accords, which they argued could not bind them. What they did accept, according to Taylor, was the "fact that Communists never have accepted international supervision of elections and can be expected to oppose in future," and he asked that the phrase "as soon as the situation permits" be dropped. The administration essentially was sticking to the elections stratagem that the Truman administration had invented for Germany and that Dulles had adapted to Vietnam ten years earlier. In fact, the whole statement became somewhat more vague when, on July 28, Johnson reiterated his willingness to begin "unconditional discussions with any government, at any place, at any time." Responding to a question on another troublesome issue—that of Vietcong representation at potential peace talks—Johnson stated, "The Viet Cong would have no difficulty in being represented and having their views presented if Hanoi for a moment decides she wants to cease aggression"—thus declining to accord them any official status in possible talks.[24]

Developments during the remainder of 1965 confirmed and refined the administration's basic approach. On August 6, 13, 18, and September 1, former ambassador Edmund Gullion had four discussions with Mai Van Bo, a North Vietnamese representative, in Paris.[25] Putting the administration line into practice, Gullion inquired about reconvening a Geneva conference without preconditions, but Bo demanded a halt to American bombing and acceptance of the Four Points as the basis for a settlement. In the August 13 meeting, Gullion asked Bo to "reflect on the devastation which might be unleashed if the war escalated. No one who had not seen U.S. power could imagine its full potential." (Asked in 1996 if the words he had used referred to nuclear weapons, Gullion replied, "Not to me.") Washington and Hanoi clearly remained far apart.

Meanwhile, a new administration split emerged, as Arthur J. Goldberg, who had stepped down from the Supreme Court to replace the late Adlai Stevenson at the United Nations in July, recommended responding positively to new proposals from U Thant for a "return to the essentials of the 1954 Geneva Agreements," including the withdrawal of foreign forces and elections supervised by the International Control Commission (ICC). The State Department replied on August 27, offering its own interpretation of those agreements, demanding the withdrawal of North Vietnamese forces from the South, and denying that those agreements were "directly applicable to the resolution of the internal problems of either North Vietnam or South Vietnam separately, pending procedures for re-unification"—including elections as called for in numerous American statements.[26] Goldberg's initiative drew a rejoinder from Ambassador Lodge on August 31 that came close to rejecting the whole idea of negotiations or a settlement with the enemy. The United States, he indicated, had to help the South Vietnamese government secure control over the South Vietnamese population in the Mekong Delta and along the coastal plain—surely an enormous task—and when those goals had been achieved, a settlement would be unnecessary. When Goldberg publicly called for negotiations as the only way to peace, Lodge on September 15 advised him that offers of negotiations could play into the hands of the communists if the United States had not yet secured its objectives.[27] The new prime minister, Air Marshal Ky, who had overthrown South Vietnam's last civilian government in July, continued to argue that the South was not yet ready for negotiations and not yet capable of dealing with the Vietcong on the ground.[28]

As 1965 came to an end, the administration, led by McNamara, reached the conclusion that large new deployments of forces and heavier bombing of North Vietnam would be necessary in 1966. In making these recommendations, McNamara also pushed for a bombing halt. In a memo dated November 3, he once again considered and rejected adjusting American objectives downward, but recommended a pause before going ahead with a new phase of deployments. The pause would give the North and the Vietcong a chance to seek a settlement, should they be so inclined, while at the same time demonstrating "to domestic and international critics that our efforts to settle the war are genuine." Despite determined opposition from the Joint Chiefs of Staff and Rusk, McGeorge Bundy in late November also endorsed the bombing pause, stressing the need for a vast increase in Defense appropriations to pay for further escalation and the corresponding need to convince the American public and the world that the administration wanted peace. Johnson agreed on December 17, and the pause began on December 24 and continued until January 31.[29] It produced no result, but its supporters had not really expected that it would.

The administration's tactics had little or no independent bearing on the course of events. Given its objectives and the military and political situation within Vietnam, it could not yet enter into serious negotiations. It took nearly three years of combat for the administration to reluctantly conclude that it could escalate the war no further. Even then, in 1968, two of the president's three most senior advisers remained committed to achieving a military victory. Indeed, as George Herring has shown, the only reason they accepted peace negotiations later that year was that they assumed such a victory was at last at hand.[30] Meanwhile, the North Vietnamese had staked out a maximum position themselves, one which they were very slow to alter—although it is fair to say that their determination was largely rewarded when the Four Points eventually became the basis for the 1973 Paris agreements.

The objectives of the two sides, rather than their negotiating positions, prolonged the war. Hanoi's intransigence was more absolute, and perhaps more remarkable, than Washington's, and neither side allowed third parties to move them into negotiations before they were ready. The Johnson administration's inability to secure a military victory led to the failure of its policies, but it was the administration's attempt to convince American and world opinion that talks might begin at any moment that undoubtedly helped undermine its credibility when the Tet Offensive convinced so many Americans that no real progress had been made.

Notes

1. Dean Acheson, *Present At the Creation: My Years at the State Department* (New York: W. W. Norton, 1969), pp. 554–55, 629–31.

2. *Foreign Relations of the United States* (*FRUS*), *Vietnam 1955–57*, vol. 1 (Washington, D.C.: GPO, 1985), pp. 102–103.

3. David Kaiser, *American Tragedy: Kennedy, Johnson, and the Origins of the Vietnam War* (Cambridge, Mass.: Harvard University Press, 2000), pp. 114–15.

4. Ibid., pp. 305–307, 538 n 80.

5. Document no. 405 (conversation of June 12, 1962), *FRUS, 1961–63,* vol. 12, *American Republics* (Washington, D.C.: GPO, 1996).

6. Ibid., Document nos. 406, 410.

7. Walter LaFeber, *The Panama Canal: The Crisis in Historical Perspective* (New York: Oxford University Press, 1978), pp. 108–11.

8. Ibid., pp. 358–70; see also *The Pentagon Papers: The Defense Department History of United States Decisionmaking on Vietnam,* Senator Gravel ed., vol. 3 (Boston: Beacon Press, 1972), pp. 237–38.

9. Kaiser, *American Tragedy,* pp. 373–74.

10. Memorandum of conversation, Adlai Stevenson and U Thant, Feb. 16, 1965, Lyndon B. Johnson Library (hereafter LBJL), Gibbons Papers, II/16; Stevenson to Johnson, Feb. 17, ibid., II/17; LBJL, NSF, memos to the President, VIII/6, Feb. 19; telephone conversation of Feb. 24, LBJL, Gibbons Papers, II/23.

11. Kaiser, *American Tragedy,* p. 422.

12. Papers of Adlai Stevenson, Walter Johnson, ed., vol. 8 (Boston: Little, Brown and Company, 1979), pp. 722–24.

13. LBJL, NSF, VN, NODIS/LOR I(B) 64, Feb. 21, 1965; ibid., I(B)/57, Mar. 8.

14. *Public Papers of the Presidents of the United States: Lyndon B. Johnson,* vol. 1, *1965* (Washington, D.C.: GPO, 1966), p. 319.

15. Ibid., p. 1:396. (Emphasis added.)

16. LBJL, NSF, VN, NODIS/LOR II(B)/125, Deptel 2363, Apr. 19, 1965.

17. *FRUS,* vol. 27, Document no. 154.

18. Kaiser, *American Tragedy,* pp. 434–35.

19. Westmoreland papers, LBJL, HB (History Backup) XVI/76, June 22.

20. *FRUS, Vietnam, July–December 1965,* vol. 3, Document nos. 18, 19.

21. *Public Papers of the Presidents of the United States: Lyndon B. Johnson,* vol. 2, *1965* (Washington, D.C.: GPO, 1966), p. 704.

22. *FRUS,* vol. 3, Document nos. 46, 47, 50.

23. Ibid., no. 67.

24. Ibid., nos. 89, 91; *Public Papers: Johnson, 1965,* pp. 2:796–97.

25. *FRUS,* vol. 3, Document nos. 113, 120, 122, 133; Gullion and Bo are referred to as X and Rupert, respectively.

26. Ibid., pp. 119, 129.

27. Ibid., pp. 131, 143.

28. Ibid., p. 172 (conversation of October 20).

29. Ibid., pp. 189, 208, 231.

30. George Herring, *LBJ and Vietnam: A Different Kind of War* (Austin: University of Texas Press, 1994), p. 173.

The PENNSYLVANIA Peace Initiative

June–October, 1967

ROBERT K. BRIGHAM AND GEORGE C. HERRING

PENNSYLVANIA WAS THE LAST of the major peace initiatives before the Tet Offensive. It was given its "tag," its name, because Pennsylvania was the home state of State Department executive secretary Benjamin Read, who oversaw and named most of the initiatives. It took place between June and October, 1967, the most intensive activity coming in July and August. It remains among the most complex and mysterious of the many complicated and confusing peace "feelers" between 1964 and 1968. American and Vietnamese participants and scholars still sharply disagree on why it failed, whether and how it was significant, and to what extent it may have represented a lost opportunity for serious peace negotiations.

The PENNSYLVANIA initiative came at the end of a long period of diplomatic maneuvering between the United States and North Vietnam. Even before Pres. Lyndon Baines Johnson escalated the war in 1965, Hanoi and Washington had begun to offer—sometimes on their own initiative, other times responding to third parties, sometimes publicly, sometimes secretly—a series of complex and intricate proposals and counterproposals for starting negotiations to terminate hostilities. While each side undoubtedly saw in these peace moves possible ways to end the war, they also used them to probe their adversary's bargaining position and win points in the competition for world and U.S. public opinion. The crucial issue for getting negotiations started was the U.S. bombing of North Vietnam. Hanoi insisted that the bombing must be stopped unconditionally before negotiations could begin; the United States demanded that the North Vietnamese, in return for a cessation of the bombing, must take steps of mutual de-escalation such as ending or at least reducing the infiltration of men and supplies into South Vietnam. Although several of these initiatives seemed tantalizingly close to success, all of them eventually broke down, with the result that, up to mid-1967, the secret search for peace had produced nothing of substance. On several occasions, the United States had suffered serious embarrassment by diplomatic bungling, most recently in December, 1966, when U.S. aircraft bombed Hanoi at a most delicate stage in the so-called MARIGOLD contact, in which Poland had served as intermediary, thus apparently destroying a possibly promising opportunity to begin talks.[1]

PENNSYLVANIA took place during an especially difficult period as far as the United States was concerned. During the spring and summer of 1967, the U.S. military command in Saigon and the Joint Chiefs of Staff (JCS) in Washington, backed by restless "hawks" in Congress, pressed Johnson relentlessly to win the war by expanding the bombing of North Vietnam, increasing the number of ground troops, and taking the war into North Vietnam and its Cambodian and Laotian sanctuaries. In June, hawkish Mississippi senator John Stennis announced the intention of his Senate Preparedness Subcommittee to hold hearings on the conduct of the air war. Increasingly certain that the war could not be won, on the other hand, opponents of the war and congressional "doves" pushed the administration to stop the bombing and do whatever was necessary to negotiate a settlement. On July 31, dovish senator J. William Fulbright introduced a nonbinding resolution declaring that it was unconstitutional for the executive branch to enter into overseas commitments without congressional approval.[2]

Whipsawed between hawk and dove, a beleaguered LBJ clung precariously to the steadily shrinking middle ground he had staked out at the start of the war, making some concessions to hawks and doves but refusing to align himself with either. Talk in the press that the war had bogged down into a stalemate especially troubled him, and in the summer of 1967 he launched a public relations campaign to persuade a skeptical nation that the war was being won.[3]

PENNSYLVANIA emerged, as had many previous peace moves, from the intervention of third parties. At a June, 1967, meeting in Paris of the so-called Pugwash Group—an international assemblage of scientists committed to working for world peace—French microbiologist Herbert Marcovitch proposed to Harvard professor Henry A. Kissinger, a member of the group, that Raymond Aubrac, a French scientist working with the UN's Food and Agriculture Organization and an old friend of Ho Chi Minh, might serve as a go-between to promote negotiations between the United States and North Vietnam. Aubrac agreed in late June to undertake such a mission to Hanoi with Marcovitch. Kissinger in turn referred the proposal to Secretary of State Dean Rusk, with a copy to Defense Secretary Robert S. McNamara.[4]

Ironically and significantly, it was the defense secretary who took the lead in the diplomacy of what soon came to be called PENNSYLVANIA. As early as 1965, McNamara had concluded that the war could not be won. Prompted by loyalty to his chief and recognizing LBJ's reluctance to admit failure, he sought various expedients to end the war—or at least wage it at less cost—by pushing for bombing pauses in an effort to get negotiations started and by promoting a shift of military emphasis from search-and-destroy operations to "pacification" to reduce U.S. casualties. In May, 1967, the defense secretary prepared for Johnson a draft presidential memorandum the authors of the *Pentagon Papers* have rightly labeled "radical." In it, he proposed an end to military escalation, scaling back U.S. war aims, and a negotiated settlement.[5]

Already deeply committed to finding a way out of Vietnam, McNamara learned of Kissinger's proposal in mid-June, 1967, and pushed it vigorously at a subsequent Tuesday lunch meeting with Johnson and his key advisers. Rusk and Johnson were skeptical, McNamara later recalled, dismissing the Kissinger letter as "just another of those blind alleys that lead nowhere. We've been down them before. Forget it." The defense secretary persisted, however, and persuaded the group to let him pursue the lead, promising—curiously—to do so in a way that would not embarrass the United States. In early July, it was agreed that Aubrac and Marcovitch should go to Hanoi and present to the North Vietnamese the so-called Phase A, Phase B proposal that had been offered during MARIGOLD. The United States would stop the bombing in return for confidential assurances that North Vietnam would stop infiltration into key areas of South Vietnam within a reasonable period. Once Hanoi acted, the United States would freeze its combat forces at existing levels and peace talks could begin.[6]

The primary U.S. instrument for the PENNSYLVANIA initiative was Kissinger. The then relatively obscure Harvard professor had picked up the suggestion in Paris and delivered it to Washington. When the initiative subsequently took shape, he became the intermediary between Washington and Aubrac and Marcovitch. It was his maiden voyage in the perilous seas of high-level international diplomacy. Johnson fretted that Kissinger might be a closet dove. National security adviser and leading administration hawk Walt Rostow feared he might "go a little soft when you get down to the crunch."[7] Despite their reservations, McNamara succeeded in persuading the president to try it. In fact, Kissinger turned out to be a valuable and reliable intermediary, although Aubrac later complained that he could be "a bit peremptory and very professorial" and that, as the effort went on, he seemed to become "invested in some sort of mission, as if armored by the authorities."[8]

The initial results appeared promising. After some delays, Aubrac and Marcovitch arrived in Hanoi on July 24, 1967, and met with Ho Chi Minh and Premier Pham Van Dong. The legendary revolutionary leader was no longer involved in the day-to-day details of government, so Ho's visit with the two Frenchmen was largely ceremonial. The meeting with Pham Van

Dong, on the other hand, was substantive and seemed productive. Dong continued to insist that North Vietnam could not negotiate while it was being bombed, but he also indicated that the United States need not announce publicly that it had stopped the bombing; a de facto cessation would be enough. When asked if there would be a delay between the end of the bombing and the beginning of negotiations, which was a matter of concern to the United States, Dong vowed that this would not be a problem. He went on to affirm that both parties could agree on the channel to be used and that the initial negotiations would involve only the United States and North Vietnam, not their South Vietnamese and National Liberation Front allies. He concluded with soothing and seductive words: "You may think your travels are useless. In fact, you have given us much to think about. I will see you again and we will talk again." Aubrac and Marcovitch returned home on July 28 and immediately briefed Kissinger. He promptly wrote up his notes and presented them to Chester Cooper, a top aide to W. Averell Harriman, the presidential adviser who was responsible for matters relating to negotiations.[9]

By the time the message got back to Washington, McNamara was even more eager to get negotiations going. July, 1967, was an especially difficult time for the defense secretary. Already exhausted from the war and increasingly troubled by his inability to extricate the United States from a situation he found hopeless, he also had to deal with difficult personal problems. His wife was admitted to the hospital with a bleeding ulcer, an affliction he believed had been caused by the stress he was under and should, he often commented, have been his. On July 19, his friend and closest adviser, John McNaughton, also a closet dove, was killed in a plane crash. There seemed to be no escape from the war for the beleaguered defense secretary. During a brief vacation in Colorado, protestors surrounded his residence and chanted antiwar slogans. Johnson is said to have worried that a stressed-out McNamara might go the route of one of his predecessors, James Forrestal, who had leaped to his death from a Bethesda Naval Hospital window in 1949.[10]

McNamara was also increasingly alarmed by the threat of a major escalation of the war. He and Undersecretary of State Nicholas Katzenbach, a fellow dove, made a fact-finding visit to Saigon in early July. McNamara was persuaded that the war was going better—there was no stalemate—but he was also concerned with Gen. William C. Westmoreland's renewed request for an additional two hundred thousand troops and growing pressures from hawks such as Senator Stennis to expand the war. Seeing in PENNSYLVANIA "the most interesting message on the matter of negotiations we have ever had," he took it up with a new passion and made it the centerpiece of what would be a last-ditch effort to extricate the United States from the war. It would be his swan song as a key presidential adviser.[11]

With McNamara in the lead, the United States used the apparent North Vietnamese overture to set forth a new scheme to get negotiations started. Aubrac and Marcovitch's report seemed sufficiently enticing to keep the channel open, and, under McNamara's close supervision, the administration in early August significantly modified the Phase A, Phase B proposal. Abandoning its longstanding insistence on mutual de-escalation, the United States promised to stop the bombing with the understanding that it would lead to "prompt and productive discussions" and that North Vietnam would not take military advantage of the U.S. de-escalation. Eager to avoid past mistakes and desperate to get things moving, McNamara took great care in developing and presenting the proposal. He assured the North Vietnamese the United States would keep the offer confidential and urged Hanoi to do the same. Without apologizing, he explained that the recent bombing of dikes in North Vietnam had been accidental and not a deliberate act of escalation. McNamara arranged to have Cooper accompany Kissinger to Paris to indicate to Aubrac and Marcovitch—and the North Vietnamese—that the United States was serious.[12]

At the urging of the two Frenchmen, the administration went still further. Perhaps seeking to avoid the fate of the Polish initiative, they had specifically requested that the United States suspend the bombing of Hanoi for a ten-day period covering the time they were to be in Hanoi. At McNamara's urging, Johnson on August 19 authorized Kissinger to inform the intermediaries that "effective August 24 there would be a noticeable change in the bombing pattern in the vicinity of Hanoi to guarantee their personal safety and as a token of our good will." Such orders, it was added, were generally good for ten days.[13]

Despite McNamara's close supervision, the initiative aborted much as previous efforts had. On August 20, shortly before Aubrac and Marcovitch were to leave for Hanoi, U.S. planes struck the North Vietnamese capital in a series of intensive bombing raids. On that day alone, U.S. aircraft flew more than 200 sorties, more than on any previous day of the war, and there was especially heavy bombing near Hanoi, Haiphong, and the Chinese border. The bombing continued for the next two days.

This important incident has never been fully investigated by historians, and some of the key sources remain classified. The official explanation, as in MARIGOLD, was that the raids had been scheduled to take place earlier but were delayed because of bad weather. Once the weather broke on August 20, they were conducted in accordance with standard operating procedures and without regard to the impending peace mission. "Once again, we had failed miserably to coordinate our diplomatic and military actions," Mc-Namara lamented nearly thirty years later.[14]

The evidence does not support such an argument. Throughout the war, to be sure, the coordination of diplomatic and military moves was bad, and the convoluted system under which the war was managed, with the bombing campaign being run by the commander in chief of U.S. forces in the Pacific out of Honolulu, left ample room for snafus. Outside of the JCS chairman, Gen. Earle G. Wheeler, moreover, no military officials were aware of the PENNSYLVANIA initiative. In this instance, however, McNamara's explanation simply does not hold up. On the evening of August 18, Johnson, Rusk, McNamara, Wheeler, and Rostow discussed at great length the bombing targets to be struck before the August 24 suspension went into effect. They considered the possibility of civilian casualties and generally agreed that it was necessary to get authorized targets "out of the way" before the raids were halted. The president even approved one target on the grounds that if talks should materialize he would not want to approve it later. Administration officials may have felt that since the promised restrictions would not be imposed for almost a week, bombing prior to that was perfectly acceptable. They did not even discuss the possible impact on the North Vietnamese, perhaps believing that since they had already made a major concession that was enough. Even after the MARIGOLD fiasco, they failed to see what now appears all too obvious: an apparent escalation of the bombing on the eve of a possible peace mission was not a formula for diplomatic success.[15]

To understand why this second major "mistake" took place, it is also necessary to appreciate the larger political context in which it occurred. Just as he had used this latest peace initiative to keep the doves at bay, so also Johnson had expanded the bombing in the summer of 1967 to appease the hawks. On July 20, keenly aware of the approaching Stennis Committee hearings on the air war, the president approved a Rolling Thunder 57 "package" that included sixteen new targets in the Hanoi-Haiphong area. The only restriction was to limit the number of strikes to three targets per day, thus trying to avoid the *appearance* of a major escalation of the bombing. On August 9, the day the Stennis hearings began with testimony from Adm. U.S. Grant Sharp, commander in chief of U.S. forces in the Pacific, the president added twelve new targets to the Hanoi list, including two major bridges and a thermal power plant. Unaware of the PENNSYLVANIA initiative, frustrated by bad weather, and angered when Johnson on August 19 ordered that the bombing of Hanoi be restricted beginning August 24, military leaders sought to use the slight window of opportunity available to them to inflict the maximum possible damage in the minimum time.[16]

Even had Johnson admitted the possibility of a conflict between his diplomatic and military moves, he might not have intervened to stop the bombing. He had never taken the PENNSYLVANIA initiative that seriously, and he might very well have been unwilling to run the political risks of angering military and congressional hawks at a critical juncture in the war at home.

Whatever the reason behind it, this new round of especially intensive bombing attacks doomed a second Aubrac-Marcovitch visit to Hanoi. Little is known of the decision-making process in Hanoi at this time. Quite possibly, as some writers have suggested, North Vietnamese hawks were able to use the air attacks as an excuse to squelch any move toward negotiations, thus significantly weakening the doves' position. Whether hawk or dove, North Vietnamese must have been infuriated by this latest round of U.S. bombing and more determined than ever to stop it. Whatever the case, Hanoi informed the two French intermediaries they should not come to Hanoi for fear of their own safety. Allowing them to come under such circumstances, North Vietnamese officials added, would also have "discredited us and ultimately you."[17]

The U.S. proposal was instead submitted on August 25 to Mai Van Bo, the Vietnamese commercial agent in Paris and a frequent and often mysterious player in the peace process.[18]

Throughout the next month, there was frantic diplomatic maneuvering on at least two continents to try to get some kind of talks going. Aubrac and Marcovitch met regularly with Bo in Paris, renewing their request for a visa to travel to Hanoi and seeking to arrange a face-to-face meeting between Kissinger and Bo. Experienced in the arcane ways of secret U.S.–North Vietnamese discussions, Bo likely recognized the significance of the change in the American bargaining position. He did what was necessary to keep the channel open, hinting that "something could happen" if the bombing was halted. Eager to keep the initiative alive, to promote peace, and undoubtedly to further his own ambitions, Kissinger pleaded with Washington for additional patience and restraint. In a manner that would become his trademark as a high-level negotiator, he sought to use his skill with words to rephrase the U.S. proposal in ways that narrowed the differences between the two sides.[19]

In Washington, McNamara and Katzenbach, occasionally with help from Rusk, did everything in their power to persuade a skeptical LBJ to keep the channel open. When Bo hinted that prolonging the suspension of air attacks on Hanoi might help, the doves pounced on it. McNamara went further, pushing for an unconditional bombing halt to demonstrate good faith to the North Vietnamese and get negotiations started. Katzenbach professed to see in North Vietnamese communications a "less strident tone" and an "important dramatic change of attitude." He further informed the president: "The significance of the Paris-Kissinger exercise lies in the fact that it is the closest thing we have had yet to establishing a dialogue with North Vietnam." Admitting that "serious discussions" were still unlikely, he insisted that stopping the bombing would not be a high price to pay for the chance of peace and as a way of muting domestic protests against the war.[20]

The doves made some limited progress with a frustrated and divided LBJ. On September 1, certain that the North Vietnamese were "playing us for suckers," he reluctantly approved a temporary extension of the bombing halt around Hanoi and subsequently extended it indefinitely. To try to win points among the doves at home and perhaps to help blunt a massive antiwar protest scheduled for mid-October, he publicly revealed in a major speech in San Antonio on September 29 the no-advantage formula offered to the North Vietnamese earlier.[21]

At the same time, he once again felt compelled to deflect pressure from the hawks. The Stennis hearings lasted nearly three weeks, from August 9–28. McNamara's dramatic testimony on August 25 dismissed the air war as ineffective and therefore expendable (perhaps to prepare the way for a bombing halt), exposing beyond doubt the civilian-military conflict the president had struggled to keep hidden. On the other hand, some military witnesses insisted that it was the restrictions imposed on the air war that had hobbled its effectiveness.[22] The committee's report, released on August 31, generally agreed with the uniformed experts, castigating the administration's restrictive and gradualist air campaign that defied "the best military judgment," and charging that the civilians had "shackled the true potential of airpower," thus dragging out the war unnecessarily and costing countless American lives.[23] Meanwhile, General Wheeler pushed relentlessly for the authority to strike bridges and power plants in Hanoi authorized in the Rolling Thunder 57 package. The president rebuffed Wheeler, keeping the Hanoi restrictions in effect, but on August 30 and September 5 he authorized new targets around Haiphong. On September 10, heavy air strikes were launched against targets authorized earlier at the lesser North Vietnamese ports of Cam Pha and Hon Gay.[24]

Not surprisingly, the September efforts produced no breakthrough. Bo rejected Aubrac and Marcovitch's second request for a visa as well as their proposal for him to agree to direct discussions with Kissinger. On September 11 (the day after U.S. aircraft struck Cam Pha), he delivered the official North Vietnamese response to the U.S. proposal of August 25. The American message had been communicated after an "escalation of the attacks against Hanoi and under the threat of continuation of the attacks against Hanoi. It is clear that this constitutes an ultimatum to the Vietnamese people."[25] On September 21 and 23, he accused the Americans of "playing a double game—on the one hand they are offering us peace; on the other they increase their bombing." He also charged that the bombing of Cam Pha and Haiphong had caused "extermination and systematic destruction." At the same time, he seemed to indicate a wish to keep the channel open. His response also hinted at a slightly veiled concession that might make it easier for the United States to accept a coalition government in South Vietnam.[26]

For three more weeks, the would-be peacemakers struggled to keep the PENNSYLVANIA channel open and the prospects for negotiations alive. Aubrac and Marcovitch continued meeting with Bo and pleaded for direct talks with Kissinger. Meanwhile, Kissinger continued to try to narrow the semantic, if not the substantive, gap between the positions staked out by both sides. He assured Bo through Aubrac and Marcovitch that the recent attacks on Hanoi, Haiphong, and Cam Pha were not part of a deliberate, two-faced policy on the part of the United States but had resulted from the "extreme secrecy" with which the initiative was being conducted.[27] In Washington, Katzenbach and McNamara continued to urge the president to keep the channel open, maintain the restrictions on bombing Hanoi, and approve a full bombing halt to get negotiations going.

Nothing of substance resulted. Bo remained as coy as ever. He adamantly refused to see Kissinger while urging that his discussions with Aubrac and Marcovitch continue. A major U.S. concern was whether negotiations would start promptly if it stopped the bombing campaign. In January, 1967, North Vietnamese foreign minister Nguyen Duy Trinh had affirmed that after the unconditional cessation of bombing and other acts of war against North Vietnam "there could be talks between the DRV [Democratic Republic of Vietnam] and the U.S." At one point, Bo referred to the Trinh statement as a "solemn engagement" on the part of North Vietnam, only to later deny having said it. He rejected all U.S. proposals as conditional and therefore unacceptable. On October 17, he again charged the United States with escalation and denounced its "double-faced" policies. "At a time when the U.S. is pursuing a policy of escalation we cannot receive Kissinger, nor comment on the American proposals transmitted through this channel. The position of the DRV is perfectly clear: it is only when the U.S. has ended without condition the bombardment that discussions *can* take place."[28]

The doves in Washington had only a little more success with LBJ. By this time weary and even more wary, the president expressed anger that the United States had held back on the bombing "just because two professors are meeting." He was absolutely certain that the bombing was hurting North Vietnam, and he yearned to "pour the steel on" in order to get his enemy down and keep him down.[29] In mid-October, the president grudgingly agreed to another Kissinger rephrasing of the U.S. proposal, but hedged it with a frightful (if perhaps metaphorical) threat. "I'm going to give it one more try," he snarled in what must have been for Kissinger an especially unnerving telephone conversation, "and if it doesn't work I'm going to come up to Cambridge and cut off your balls."[30]

Johnson and his top advisers hashed the issue out one last time at a tense two-hour meeting on the evening of October 18. According to informal presidential adviser and future defense secretary Clark Clifford, who was there, the major participants were exhausted, the discussion rambling and muddled. He believed too much attention was being paid to "a minor and ineffectual channel of communication." Kissinger pushed to keep the channel open and urged linking it with a bombing pause. Katzenbach and McNamara backed him, the latter insisting that he could prove that the bombing did not significantly affect North Vietnam's capacity to make war in the South. Talks, they assured LBJ, would begin once the bombing stopped.

On the other side, Rusk, as always, was skeptical. Clifford insisted that the Kissinger contact had brought no real progress and warned that a bombing halt would make "the possibility of peace much more remote." PENNSYLVANIA should be closed down. Johnson remained the key skeptic. McNamara's testimony before the Stennis Committee had enraged him, opening wider the rift with his defense secretary and leading in time to McNamara's departure from the cabinet. The president was still convinced that the North Vietnamese were trying to trick him into stopping the bombing. "I know if they were hitting my bridges and railroads and highways, I would be delighted to try out discussions through an intermediary for a restriction on the bombing. It hasn't cost him [Ho Chi Minh] one bit. The net of it is that he has a sanctuary in Hanoi in return for having his consul talk with two scientists who talked with an American citizen." Johnson would go no further than permitting Kissinger to return to Paris and meet with Aubrac and Marcovitch, thereby perhaps keeping the channel alive. He was not, however, willing to approve a bombing halt without firmer assurances of the North Vietnamese response.[31] Finally, on October 6, he responded to mounting pressure from the JCS by approving seven new bombing targets around Haiphong.

With this decision, PENNSYLVANIA for all practical purposes came to an end. Kissinger returned to Paris on October 20, and Aubrac and Marcovitch again requested a meeting with Bo. This time the response was blunt and unequivocal. The "situation is worsening," Bo said, there was no reason to talk again. He responded to their pleas by effectively terminating the channel. "Our position is perfectly clear. We stand on the Trinh interview . . . of January 28. There is nothing new to say."[32] With the reason for restraint no longer operative, Johnson once again escalated the bombing. On October 24 he authorized air attacks on the Phuc Yen airfield, a target he had long denied, and lifted the suspension on bombing Hanoi imposed during the early days of PENNSYLVANIA. Over the next five days, the United States mounted heavy attacks on the North Vietnamese capital, striking major bridges and a thermal power plant.[33]

What should we make of PENNSYLVANIA more than three decades after the events? Like most of the other peace initiatives, this one has been a source of controversy. Participants such as Lyndon Johnson and Clark Clifford dismissed it at the time as unimportant and some scholars have agreed, viewing it as just another episode in that extended and intricate diplomatic mating dance between two parties whose negotiating positions were far apart and who lacked the military advantage necessary to impose terms. More recently, Robert McNamara and some Vietnamese participants and scholars have countered that the summer-fall, 1967, peace feelers were indeed quite significant, a missed opportunity foiled only by misperception on both sides. This continuing controversy raises the fundamental questions of how PENNSYLVANIA was significant, why it failed, and whether it did in fact represent a missed opportunity for serious negotiations and a possible settlement.[34]

The failed initiative of late 1967 appears, in retrospect, to have been more significant than its critics argued. It produced a major new U.S. proposal, an important departure in that it did not require the North Vietnamese to match U.S. de-escalation. There is clear evidence that the North Vietnamese recognized the significance of this U.S. concession and took it seriously. Although it ultimately failed, the PENNSYLVANIA initiative appears to have persuaded some North Vietnamese officials that talks might be imminent.

Like so many earlier efforts, PENNSYLVANIA was aborted. Moreover, misperception played a part in bringing about its demise. The North Vietnamese could not but have misread the escalation of the bombing in August and September, 1967, as a crude effort, directly connected to concurrent peace moves, to bludgeon them into discussing peace on U.S. terms—the mailed fist behind the velvet glove. North Vietnamese participants and scholars have also recently suggested that the comparatively soft tone of Hanoi's rejection of talks in late 1967 constituted a signal that the Americans missed or chose to ignore.[35]

The escalation of the U.S. bombing campaign in August, 1967, coupled with Lyndon Johnson's steadfast refusal to offer an unconditional bombing halt, contributed to PENNSYLVANIA's failure. Intensification of the bombing was not directly connected to the peace move, as the North Vietnamese believed. Nor was it exactly a "mistake," as McNamara and other Americans have claimed. As shown here, the escalation of the bombing was a result of Johnson's calculated effort to appease his own military and hawks in Congress. Stopping the bombing at that time would have tested North Vietnam's sincerity and willingness to discuss serious peace terms. Yet it seems inconceivable, in the context of events in the summer and fall of 1967, that LBJ would have done this as long as he was still persuaded that the United States could get what it wanted by military pressure and as long as he was under pressure from hawks in the Pentagon and Congress. He was not willing to pay the domestic political price required for talks that seemed to him unlikely to produce results he could accept.

Even if Johnson had stopped the bombing and North Vietnam had agreed to peace talks, it seems unlikely that there would have been serious negotiations leading to a settlement. The key issue, of course, was South Vietnam's political future—and here there was some slight movement during PENNSYLVANIA. McNamara, Katzenbach, and Harriman had concluded that the United States must accept some sort of coalition government to extricate itself from the war.[36] There were signs from Hanoi during the PENNSYLVANIA discussions that North Vietnam was willing to make this concession easier for the United States. However, there are few indications that a settlement of this sort was likely, much less possible. Johnson, Rusk, and Rostow were not prepared to accept a coalition government. Indeed, the United States in early September had sponsored nationwide elections in South Vietnam, underscoring its commitment to the Saigon regime. It showed no willingness to concede on this issue even when formal negotiations began after the Tet Offensive in 1968. Short of such an agreement, there was little possibility of meaningful negotiations.

In a more subtle sense, the significance of PENNSYLVANIA seems to be that it was an important step along the path to substantive negotiations. By abandoning its insistence on mutual de-escalation and opting for the San Antonio "no advantage" formula, the United States took a major step toward meeting North Vietnamese conditions for negotiations. Interestingly and significantly, Vietnamese diplomats and scholars have recently suggested that the Paris initiative and the San Antonio formula persuaded at least some North Vietnamese officials that "talks between the United States and Vietnam were now possible" and could "take place in the near future." They thus began serious preparations for negotiations. They also recalled that the indirect discussions "gave tremendous support and encouragement to those of us who were at that moment working on a negotiating strategy."[37]

These people have also testified, however, that while they saw PENNSYLVANIA as an important breakthrough, they still did not believe the time was opportune for serious peace talks. Until the "aggressive will" of the United States had been broken, there was no chance of negotiations. For that reason and in an effort to break the costly stalemate that the war had become, Hanoi decided even before PENNSYLVANIA had begun to launch a major military offensive in late 1967 or early 1968. For that reason, they also more or less closed down the Paris channel in October, 1967, just as the first phase of what would become the Tet Offensive began. At the same time, to create the possibility of talks when the situation appeared more appropriate, Foreign Minister Trinh in December, 1967, on the heels of PENNSYLVANIA, modified his earlier statement to indicate that when the U.S. unconditionally stopped the bombing, "talks will begin." The Tet Offensive eventually produced what PENNSYLVANIA had failed to accomplish: the opening of direct talks between the United States and North Vietnam in Paris in May, 1968. However, the complexity of the problem and the continuing rigidity of positions on both sides were such that not even that could bring about an agreement. It took five more years and thousands more deaths to bring the American phase of the war to an end.

Notes

1. The best analysis of MARIGOLD is James G. Hershberg, Who Murdered "Marigold"? New Evidence on the Mysterious Failure of Poland's Secret Initiative to Start U.S.–North Vietnamese Peace Talks, 1966 (Washington, D.C.: 2000). A brief account of the various peace initiatives can be found in George C. Herring, *LBJ and Vietnam: A Different Kind of War* (Austin: University of Texas Press, 1994), pp. 89–120. For more detailed coverage along with important documents see George C. Herring, ed., *The Secret Diplomacy of the Vietnam War: The Negotiating Volumes of the Pentagon Papers* (Austin: University of Texas Press, 1983).

2. The summer of 1967 is covered in Herring, *LBJ and Vietnam*, pp. 51–57.

3. See ibid., pp. 141–46.

4. Herring, ed., *Secret Diplomacy*, pp. 717–18; Raymond Aubrac, *Ou La Memoire S'Atarde* (Paris: Cold War International History Project, 1996), translation of PENNSYLVANIA section in authors' possession.

5. McNamara's May 19 draft presidential memorandum is in Neil Sheehan et al., *The Pentagon Papers as Published by the New York Times* (New York: Times Books, 1971), pp. 577–85.

6. Robert S. McNamara, *In Retrospect: The Tragedy and Lessons of Vietnam* (New York: Times Books, 1995), pp. 295–96.

7. Tom Johnson, notes on meeting, Aug. 8, 1967, Tom Johnson Notes on Meetings, Box 1, Lyndon B. Johnson Library, Austin, Tex. (hereafter LBJL).

8. Aubrac, *Ou La Memoire.*

9. Herring, ed., *Secret Diplomacy,* pp. 720–25.

10. McNamara discusses some of these events in *In Retrospect,* pp. 297–98, 313.

11. Ibid., pp. 283–84, 298.

12. Herring, ed., *Secret Diplomacy,* pp. 729–31.

13. Ibid., 729.

14. McNamara, *In Retrospect,* p. 299.

15. Record of meeting, Aug. 18, 1967, Meeting Notes File, Box 2, Lyndon Baines Johnson Papers, LBJL.

16. Historical Division, Joint Secretariat, Joint Chiefs of Staff Historical Files, "The History of the Joint Chiefs of Staff—The Joint Chiefs of Staff and Vietnam, 1960–1968," unpublished MS, chap. 44, pp. 1–19. (Copy in possession of the author.)

17. Herring, ed., *Secret Diplomacy,* p. 745.

18. Mai Van Bo's equally mysterious role in an abortive 1965 peace initiative is recounted in Herring, ed., *Secret Diplomacy,* pp. 75–115.

19. Walter Isaacson, *Kissinger: A Biography* (New York: Simon and Schuster, 1992), 122.

20. McNamara, *In Retrospect,* p. 301.

21. Herring, *LBJ and Vietnam,* pp. 117–18.

22. For the Stennis Hearings, see Charles W. Hartford, "Senate Sanctuary: The Stennis Hearings of 1967, the President, the Joint Chiefs of Staff, and the War in Vietnam," M. A. thesis, University of Kentucky, 1999.

23. *The Pentagon Papers: The Defense Department History of United States Decisionmaking on Vietnam,* Senator Gravel ed., 4 vols. (Boston: Beacon Press, 1971–72), pp. 4:203–204.

24. "History of the Joint Chiefs of Staff," chap. 44, p. 5.

25. Herring, ed., *Secret Diplomacy,* p. 737.

26. Ibid., pp. 749–51.

27. Ibid., p. 753.

28. Ibid., p. 766. (Emphasis in original.)

29. Tom Johnson, notes on meetings, Sept. 26 and Oct. 4, 5, and 16, 1967, Tom Johnson Notes on Meetings, Box 1, LBJL.

30. Isaacson, *Kissinger,* p. 122.

31. Ibid., p. 123; Clark Clifford, *Counsel to the President* (New York: Random House, 1991), pp. 453–54; Tom Johnson, notes on meeting, Oct. 18, 1967, Tom Johnson Notes on Meetings, Box 1, LBJL.

32. Herring, ed., *Secret Diplomacy,* p. 769.

33. "History of the Joint Chiefs of Staff," chap. 44, pp. 11–12.

34. Robert S. McNamara et al., *Argument Without End: In Search of Answers to the Vietnam Tragedy* (New York: Public Affairs, 1999), pp. 308–309.

35. Transcript, Critical Oral History Project on the Vietnam War, June, 1997, Thomas J. Watson Institute, Brown University, Providence, R. I. See also McNamara, *Argument Without End,* p. 298.

36. W. Averell Harriman, memorandum of conversation with Robert S. McNamara, Aug. 22, 1967, Box 486, W. Averell Harriman Papers, Manuscript Division, Library of Congress.

37. Transcript, Critical Oral History Project. See also McNamara, *Argument Without End,* pp. 300–301.

The Mirage of Negotiations

EDWIN E. MOÏSE

THE ODDS FOR A diplomatic settlement of the Vietnam War were never good. It is not an accident that when serious peace negotiations finally occurred, they failed to settle the war. Four years of the Paris negotiations could produce nothing better than the Paris Agreements of 1973, a spurious settlement that neither side signed in good faith. Diplomacy having failed, as it had almost inevitably been going to fail, the war was finally resolved on the battlefield in 1975.

The reason there had never been much possibility of a diplomatic settlement of the war was that there had never been any possibility—and please note that I am saying absolutely no possibility whatever—of a genuine compromise settlement. And where no genuine compromise is possible, diplomacy is very difficult.

The war was really about the question of who would rule South Vietnam. Somebody was going to end up in control. Two groups—the communists and the anticommunist leaders, mostly ARVN officers, who dominated the Saigon government—were determined to control South Vietnam. If either side ever gained a clear upper hand, it would use that power in the way the Saigon government had in fact used it when it had the upper hand from 1955 to 1958: by erasing its opponent's political and military power as completely as it was able. Any agreement between the two sides stating that they would coexist within South Vietnam was necessarily going to be a farce. While they might perhaps sign such an agreement, neither side would abide by it in good faith, partly because neither side would expect the other to abide by it. Each side knew that the only way to avoid suffering an unmitigated defeat in the struggle for control of South Vietnam was to inflict one.

In theory, one might consider the possibility of a third force coming into power, but this possibility was not very relevant to the question of a negotiated settlement during the Johnson administration. In the short term, a solution to the war had to be based on the political forces that existed at the time (see the comment on Robert Kennedy, below). No potential "third force"—the Buddhists, for example—had a fraction of the power that would have been required to push aside both the Army of the Republic of Vietnam (ARVN) and the communists.

The logic I am describing is a brutal and ugly logic. It is not surprising that there were, during the years of Lyndon Johnson's presidency, many Americans who looked for some alternative, some method other than force for settling the conflict. Some people in the antiwar movement wanted the United States simply to abandon the struggle and allow the communists to win it. Such an idea was, however, so far out of the American mainstream that it had essentially no influence in the corridors of power during the Johnson administration. The advocates of negotiations who had a voice in policy, the ones whose ideas and actions have been a major topic for historians, were those who proposed negotiations as something other than a way of ratifying a communist victory in the war. Some of them sometimes seemed to be hinting that the United States would simply have to accept a communist victory in the war, but if so, they knew they could not afford to make such a proposal explicitly.

Some of them did not really have a proposal for a settlement of the war; they simply hoped that if negotiations occurred, a settlement of some sort would emerge. We thus have Senate Majority Leader Mike Mansfield's plea that the Saigon government sit down and talk with the National Liberation Front (NLF): "Perhaps among themselves they can come up with a solution."[1] This chapter, however, will focus mainly on the people who gave at least some vague indication of what sort of settlement they thought could be achieved once negotiations began. These fall into two broad categories: the ones who hoped for a peace settlement embodying the main American war objectives—in other words, victory at the conference table—and the ones who believed in what I have been saying was impossible: a genuine compromise peace.

Victory at the conference table was naturally the more attractive option. In November, 1963, James Reston wrote a column headlined "Why a Truce in Korea and Not in Vietnam?" asking why the United States seemed unwilling to negotiate a settlement of the war. He suggested trying for a settlement similar to the one that had ended the Korean War. This would have meant leaving South Vietnam firmly under the control of anticommunist forces; in other words, an acceptance of defeat by the communist forces in the war being waged for control of South Vietnam. Reston did not say why he thought the communists might be willing to surrender at the conference table everything they had won on the battlefield.[2] Slightly more than two years later, Robert Kennedy proposed that the United States try to negotiate a peace settlement based on the hope that the communists might be willing "to lay down their arms and return the area and people now under their control to the central government" in return for a promise of political rights under the rule of the Saigon government.[3] Kennedy, however, offered an explanation of why he thought the communists might abandon their struggle: he hoped that they could be persuaded the struggle was hopeless, that they could not win.

This was actually a reasonable hope. The discrepancy in size, wealth, and power between the United States and Vietnam was such that one did not have to be a fool to think that the Vietnamese communists' effort to fight the United States was hopeless and could soon come to be seen as hopeless. Many Americans believed that the Vietnamese communists had gotten into a war with the United States by mistake and that, after experiencing the amount of power being brought against them, they would realize it had been a mistake and be willing to back out of the struggle if offered the opportunity.

When Robert Kennedy stopped believing the communists might be ready to agree to something approaching surrender, he proposed sidestepping the problem of finding some other basis for peace between the communists and the Saigon government headed by Gen. Nguyen Van Thieu and Air Marshal Nguyen Cao Ky. He suggested the United States try to arrange the replacement of Thieu and Ky by "a civilian government, far more effective than the military rule which exists at present—one willing and able to take effective part in a negotiated settlement."[4] He did not, however, claim to know of any particular civilian politicians capable of filling this rather optimistic prescription.

The belief that the communists had no hope of victory was probably the main factor behind almost all suggestions that they could be persuaded to surrender at the conference table. In April, 1965, Lyndon Johnson offered an economic development program that would embrace North Vietnam if Hanoi would abandon the war.[5] However, I think his hope that Hanoi would accept this offer was based not just on expectations of North Vietnamese greed for economic development, but also on the presumption that Hanoi had nothing to gain from continuing the war and could be persuaded to see that it had nothing to gain.

Three months later, as it became apparent that the United States was getting into a land war in Vietnam, The *New York Times* editorialized that Hanoi was unlikely to "give in" anytime soon, so the United States should plan on years of war "until . . . negotiations on honorable terms become possible."[6] Apparently, honorable terms meant that the communists had to concede.

George Ball is generally regarded as having been the house dove in the Johnson administration. He was appalled by the deepening American involvement in what he eventually came to call "an immoral and unwinnable war."[7] In 1965 he wrote a series of papers, some with input from Dean Acheson and others, urging an attempt to negotiate a settlement of the war. If Lyndon Johnson had given serious consideration to any advocate of negotiation in 1965, it probably would have been Ball.

The February 13, 1965, draft said it was unrealistic to hope for a settlement requiring Hanoi to call off the insurgency and deliver the whole of South Vietnam to government control. Nevertheless, a settlement might be attainable that would end North Vietnamese support for the insurgency, after which the United States and the Saigon government would have a reasonable chance of defeating the Vietcong (VC). In effect, he was suggesting that the war be settled on the battlefield after a peace agreement had created the conditions for an anticommunist victory. He did not say why he thought the communist leaders in North Vietnam might be willing to abandon the war in this fashion.[8]

Elsewhere in this book, Andrew Preston quotes a statement George Ball made in an oral history interview in 1971 indicating that U.S. negotiating proposals, though sincere, had been "foredoomed efforts, because we weren't prepared to make any real concessions. Negotiation at that time still consisted pretty much of saying to Hanoi, 'Look, let's work out a deal under which you will capitulate.'"[9] In his oral history, Ball said that "each" of the memos he wrote during this period had said the United States could not win in Vietnam, and concluded, "Therefore we should cut our losses."[10] Yet of the available texts, only a couple toward the end of the series even came close to matching that description. In most of his memos, Ball did what he later criticized others for having done: he suggested that Hanoi be asked to capitulate at the conference table.

The version Ball sent to President Johnson April 21, 1965, was longer than the February 13 draft, and substantially different: it proposed a negotiated settlement that actually settled the conflict. Internationally supervised free elections would follow in South Vietnam, with communists permitted to campaign as candidates. That such elections could happen only after the communists withdrew their armed forces from the South and handed over to the Saigon government all of the territory they currently controlled, was not explicitly stated in the paragraphs discussing the proposed settlement, but was clearly indicated in the paragraphs describing the negotiating process that would produce it. The talks were to start with an intermediary approaching Hanoi and asking "would the North Vietnamese be prepared to call off the fighting in the South and disband the Viet Cong as a military force on the understanding that those South Vietnamese–born members would be permitted to remain in civilian life in South Viet-Nam and to participate peaceably in the political life of the country?"[11] Why Ball thought Ho Chi Minh and his colleagues might accept such a deal after having been burned with a promise of elections under international supervision in the Geneva Accords of 1954 was not explained.

The next draft, dated May 13, 1965, also made it clear that the Vietcong were to disband their armed forces as the price of being admitted to peaceful politics in South Vietnam.[12] American troops might begin to withdraw "when the insurgency stops and the Government has effectively extended its authority throughout the country" or might perhaps begin withdrawing when the insurgency had only stopped in most areas.[13] In either case, the American withdrawal was not to be completed until the ARVN were able to move freely throughout the country. There was no provision for international supervision of the elections. Indeed, the promise that communists who behaved peacefully would be permitted to participate in them was not to be embodied in any formal agreement between the Saigon government and the communists. Ball did not want to ask the South to compromise "the posture that it was not 'negotiating' with the North or with the National Liberation Front."[14]

To make any sense of Ball's plan, one had to suppose that the communists were doomed to defeat if they fought and were well aware of that fact. It is hard to see how anyone could otherwise have taken seriously the notion that the Vietcong might lay down their weapons and allow Saigon to extend its military control throughout South Vietnam in return for a promise that the Saigon government would then respect their political rights, even if such a promise had been embodied in a formal treaty. Yet Ball was suggesting the communists might do just that in response to informal assurances from a government whose hatred of them was the reason it was unwilling to sign a formal agreement with them. Ball, however, did not base his presentation on an assumption of communist despair; instead, he said the communists might think his proposal offered them a reasonable chance of winning full control of South Vietnam.

The communists, of course, *did* win the war, and I think it is apparent that the dominant element in the ranks of their leadership always believed, at the very least, that they had a good chance of victory. American hopes that the communists might be about to give up hope were mistaken. Moreover, if they failed to abandon hope, the notion that they might have accepted a plan such as Ball's would have been absurd. What Ball was proposing would have worked out de facto as a total surrender by the communists. That was why even Walt Rostow, one of the leading hawks, felt comfortable proposing pretty much the same thing the following year.[15]

Ball's recollection, as he wrote it years later, was that his plan had been rejected after Maxwell Taylor, the U.S. ambassador to Saigon, denounced it as "a giveaway program of the worst sort."[16] This is not, however, what the record shows. Taylor in fact said quite reasonably that it was "hard to see why" the communists, who believed they could win the war, would want to shift to the political arena in the fashion Ball was proposing. Taylor also noted that it would be difficult to persuade the Saigon government to allow the communists the sort of political rights contemplated by Ball's plan.[17]

On June 28, Ball finally sent a truly pessimistic memo to a few other top officials. It was based "on the premise that we are losing the war in Vietnam," and argued that instead of trying to turn the situation around by expanding the bombing of North Vietnam, sending more troops to the South, or both, the United States should think in terms of cutting its losses. This might involve withdrawing from Vietnam, but if so, the withdrawal should not be quick or precipitate. He envisaged prolonged negotiations, with U.S. troops remaining in Vietnam to ensure adequate leverage in the talks. He said nothing about what sort of settlement might emerge from such negotiations. He clearly believed that communist rule in South Vietnam was the likeliest result of his proposals, but he could not bring himself to say explicitly even that it was a possible outcome.[18] The memo, which was discussed on June 29 at a meeting in the State Department, was firmly rejected by those present. Ball then produced a revised draft sent to the White House on July 1. This version started out just as pessimistically, saying that the war was being lost and that if the United States made a major commitment of military force to try to turn the situation around, the probable outcome would be humiliating failure.[19] Rather than follow a course likely to prove disastrous, Ball proposed that the United States accept a "compromise." He used the word over and over; indeed, the memo was titled "A Compromise Solution for South Viet-Nam." However, the closest he came to describing an actual proposed compromise was a passage in which he said the United States could inject into peace talks "the concept of self-determination that would permit the Viet Cong some hope of achieving some of their political objectives through local elections or some other device."[20] This implied a return to his previous formula of asking the Vietcong to lay down their arms in return for permission to participate in politics within a framework dominated by the Saigon government.

The idea of "national reconciliation" achieved through allowing the communists to participate in elections held by the Republic of Vietnam popped up repeatedly in later discussions of U.S. diplomatic strategy. Late in 1966, when second-level officials were discussing how to give such proposals credibility, W. Averell Harriman worried that the current Saigon government intended to include a clause in the Republic of Vietnam's new constitution forbidding communist participation in politics. The State Department's Daniel Davidson said it would be hard to deter Premier Nguyen Cao Ky and Pres. Nguyen Van Thieu from putting such a clause in the constitution. "We should realize that when Ky and Thieu spoke of national reconciliation they were thinking in terms of defections from the NLF/VC not of the NLF/VC itself playing a political role in South Vietnam."[21] When the constitution was formally enacted in 1967, article 4, paragraph (2) stated, "Every activity designed to propagate or implement Communism is prohibited."[22]

What about the proponents of a genuine compromise peace? Some of these defined their goal vaguely or not at all. Walter Cronkite, in his famous documentary on the Tet Offensive, predicted that the Vietnam War would end in a "stalemate" and said that negotiations—genuine negotiations, "not the dictation of peace terms"—would represent the only rational response to the situation. He clearly believed the negotiations would have to lead to some sort of genuine compromise, but he did not describe what he thought it should include.[23]

Those who did say something about their goals often spoke of neutralizing South Vietnam, all of Vietnam, or an even wider area. Senator Albert Gore Sr., for example, proposed the neutralization of all Southeast Asia.[24] The word was very ambiguous, with a number of sharply divergent possible meanings of "neutralization" as applied to Vietnam.

First, there was the possibility of Vietnam under a communist government modeled on Tito's Yugoslavia that was "neutral" in the sense that it was not allied with the Soviet Union or China, and thus not a threat to the United States. I will not try to argue that this was inherently impossible, since it is what Vietnam has actually become in recent years. It is what I would have tried for had I been a top official in the 1960s. Nevertheless, people like me, people who could endorse such a policy, were not rising to positions of power in the United States in that era. I do not think it would have been possible to persuade the U.S. government at that time to trust the communists to keep a promise that a communist Vietnam would refrain from functioning as an ally of the larger communist states.

Second, one might suppose South Vietnam under a noncommunist government that was "neutral" in the sense that it was not allied with the United States, and thus not a threat to the communists—on the model of India, Burma, and Sweden. The problem is the phrase "not a threat to the communists." Which communists? A noncommunist government in South Vietnam that was not allied with the United States might not be a threat to China or the Soviet Union, but it would be a quite serious threat to Communist Party organizations in South Vietnam.

Third, South Vietnam could become "neutral" by forming a coalition in which power was shared between communist and anticommunist forces. The problem with this option was that the communist and anticommunist forces in South Vietnam simply were not going to coalesce.

The Geneva Accords of 1962 had attempted to create a neutral Laos using a hybrid government combining the second and third of these models. Prince Souvanna Phouma, a neutralist statesman who was neither communist nor anticommunist, headed a government that was a coalition containing communists and anticommunists as well as neutralists. The accords were negotiated essentially between the United States and the Soviet Union. In the worldwide framework of the Cold War, neutralizing Laos made excellent sense. The United States and the Soviet Union, wanting to avoid a conflict over Laos, were both quite willing to forgo control of the country provided it became genuinely neutral and was not controlled by the other side. A solution that made sense from a global-strategic viewpoint, however, could not be made to work unless it were compatible with the local power relationships. A truly neutral Laos would have been a disaster for the Vietnamese communists because it would have meant closing down the Ho Chi Minh Trail. The bottom line was that a neutralized Laos could not be made to work without the cooperation of Vietnamese communists.

Almost all proposals for the neutralizing of Vietnam suffered from the same problem. Their proponents shaped them in such a way that they were acceptable in a global-strategic context, but failed to consider how to make them acceptable to the contending parties in Vietnam.

In a column quoted above—"Why a Truce in Korea and Not in Vietnam?"—James Reston, writing shortly after the overthrow of Ngo Dinh Diem, suggested that both North and South Vietnam might be neutralized. Although he did not explain what this entailed, Reston probably meant it was to be a neutral communist North Vietnam and a neutral noncommunist South Vietnam.[25] On May 21, 1964, the lead editorial in the *New York Times* stated: "We must confront the Communists with options short of unacceptable defeat." It then went on to explain that this meant "a political settlement based, of course, on a non-Communist South Vietnam, independent, neutral—free of Communist guerrillas as well as of foreign troops and bases—and guaranteed by the Great Powers."[26] One wonders which communists the editors had in mind, when they suggested that "the Communists" could be persuaded not to see an unacceptable defeat in a settlement that blocked the reunification of Vietnam and placed the South solidly under the control of a noncommunist government.

It was much easier to believe in a genuine possibility of a neutral South Vietnam if one doubted, as many Americans did during the Johnson administration, that the National Liberation Front was a communist organization. If the NLF had been a genuine united front in which communist and noncommunist forces shared power, it would have opened up a serious possibility that a neutral government in which communists and noncommunists shared power could be created by a peace settlement. Unfortunately, the united front was largely a sham: the noncommunist leaders in the NLF were there more as window dressing than as genuine power sharers.

There was no possibility of a peace based on genuine power sharing between the communists and the ARVN generals who ruled the Republic of Vietnam. The struggle between them was not going to end without one of these groups disappearing from South Vietnam. In order for a peace agreement to settle the war and not simply set the stage for continued fighting (like the Paris Agreements of 1973), it had to condemn one side or the other to the destruction of its political and military power in South Vietnam. If it had ever become apparent to one side that it had lost and that there was no real prospect of turning the defeat around, then that side might have been willing to negotiate a peace in which it acknowledged the other side's victory. However, at no time during Lyndon Johnson's administration did either side even come close to feeling that its situation was so hopeless. There thus was no lost opportunity for peace.

Notes

1. *Congressional Record,* 90th Cong., 1st sess., Nov. 20, 1967, pp. 33130–31.

2. *New York Times,* Nov. 6, 1963, p. 40.

3. "Senator Robert Kennedy Explains His Position," *U.S. News & World Report,* Mar. 14, 1966, p. 68. Kennedy was clarifying a statement dated February 19, text in the *Congressional Record,* Mar. 14, 1966, pp. 5617–19.

4. *Congressional Record,* 90th Cong., 1st sess., Mar. 2, 1967, p. 5283.

5. Address at Johns Hopkins University, Apr. 7, 1965, in *Public Papers of the Presidents: Lyndon B. Johnson,* vol. 1, *1965* (Washington, D.C.: GPO, 1966), pp. 394–99.

6. "At War in Vietnam," *New York Times,* July 14, 1965, p. 36.

7. George Ball, "Present After the Creation," *New York Review of Books,* Dec. 17, 1992, p. 11.

8. Ball to President Johnson, Feb. 13, 1965, in *Foreign Relations of the United States, 1964–1968,* vol. 2, *Vietnam January–June 1965* (Washington, D.C.: GPO, 1996), pp. 252–61, esp. 258–59.

9. George Ball, Oral History Interview 1, July 8, 1971, Lyndon B. Johnson Library, Austin, Tex., p. 39.

10. Ibid., p. 18.

11. Ball to President Johnson, in *FRUS, 1964–1968,* pp. 2:583–92, esp. 590–91. (Emphasis in original.)

12. "A Plan for a Political Resolution in South Viet-Nam", in ibid., pp. 652–60.

13. Ibid., p. 658.

14. Ibid., p. 657.

15. Rostow to President Johnson, Nov. 17, 1966, in *Foreign Relations of the United States, 1964–1968,* vol. 4, *Vietnam, 1966* (Washington, D.C.: GPO, 1998), pp. 853–56.

16. Ball, "Present After the Creation," p. 14.

17. Maxwell Taylor and U. Alexis Johnson, "Questions and Comments Relating to 'A Plan for a Political Resolution in South Viet-Nam,'" May 20, 1965, in *FRUS, 1964–1968,* pp. 2:676, 678.

18. George Ball, "Cutting Our Losses in South Viet-Nam," n.d., text in *Foreign Relations of the United States, 1964–1968,* vol. 3, *Vietnam June–December, 1965* (Washington, D.C.: GPO, 1996), pp. 62–66.

19. George Ball, "A Compromise Solution for South Viet-Nam," in ibid., pp. 106–107.

20. Ibid., p. 109.

21. Memorandum of meeting, Nov. 10, 1966, in *FRUS, 1964–1968,* pp. 4:824–26.

22. Constitution of the Republic of Vietnam, Apr. 1, 1967, in Senate Foreign Relations Committee, *Background Information Relating to Southeast Asia and Vietnam* (Washington, D.C.: GPO, 1969), p. 239.

23. "Who, What, When, Where, Why: Report from Vietnam by Walter Cronkite," CBS Television, Feb. 27, 1968, in Peter Braestrup, *Big Story* (Boulder, Colo.: Westview, 1977), p. 2:188.

24. *Congressional Record,* 90th Cong., 1st sess., Oct. 24, 1967, pp. 29801–806.

25. *New York Times,* Nov. 6, 1963, 40.

26. "New Phase in Vietnam," *New York Times,* May 21, 1964, p. 34.

Who Gave Peace a Chance?

LBJ and the Antiwar Movement

MELVIN SMALL

T HE AMERICAN ANTI–VIETNAM WAR movement was the largest and most sustained antiwar movement in the nation's history. However one may evaluate the wisdom of its opposition to American involvement in the wars in Southeast Asia, there is no doubt that it had an impact on the public, the media, the Johnson and Nixon administrations, Congress, and Hanoi. Most of the scholarly and journalistic attention has revolved around the question of its effectiveness in ending the war, with opinions ranging from those who maintain the movement prolonged the war by encouraging the North Vietnamese, to those who suggest that it foreclosed more forceful military options and influenced U.S. diplomatic strategies.[1] Few observers have *directly* examined the relationship between Lyndon Johnson's attempts to open diplomatic negotiations with the communists and the activities of the antiwar movement.

This is an important issue. Both the doves and the president contended that their policies and actions would result in a just resolution of the conflict. Yet, from March, 1965—when the mass antiwar movement was launched as a response to the bombing of North Vietnam—through March 31, 1968—when the president made his fateful decisions—they often appeared, from the administration's perspective, to be working at cross-purposes. Indeed, while the movement played a major role during those three years in affecting the national debate over the war, its existence and growing strength made it more difficult for the administration to pursue diplomatic and related military options that some believed might have led to a more speedy termination of the war. As we shall see, that was not the movement's fault.

The relationship between the antiwar movement and the president was largely defined by the way LBJ viewed those who took to the streets to oppose his Southeast Asia policies. Johnson was a strong-willed politician who, like many of his breed, did not take kindly to criticism, especially when that criticism came from within his own party.[2] Most of the participants and many of the leaders of the amorphous movement were liberals who should have championed the greatest Democratic reformer since Franklin D. Roosevelt. Instead, they were ingrates who publicly took issue with U.S. involvement in the war and, because of the issue, threatened to tear the party apart. When Sen. Frank Church (D-Idaho) criticized the president's Vietnam policy in early 1965, LBJ allegedly told him, "Okay, Frank, next time you need a dam in Idaho, ask Walter Lippmann for one."[3]

Johnson could live with expected assaults from Republican right-wingers who called for escalation. He could not tolerate calls from the Left for appeasement, particularly since he was convinced that not only was he doing all he could to bring the war to a speedy and honorable conclusion, but that he was holding off the Right. The Right, according to Undersecretary of State George Ball, whose demands for the employment of all possible military options could have led to World War III, was the "Great Beast to be feared."[4]

Like all presidents, LBJ did not want to appear weak. He did not want either his foreign enemies or his allies to suspect that he could be affected by the crowds in the streets or the handful of critics on Capitol Hill. "I don't want to back out—and look like I'm reacting to the Fulbrights," he explained while contemplating ending a bombing pause in January, 1966.[5] In part, this was the personal reaction of a stubborn and proud man. However, it also reflected his perception of how Hanoi interpreted his responses to the growing antiwar movement. As Lady Bird Johnson confided to her diary in February, 1966, the movement was "giving our enemies the wrong idea of the will of this country to fight." Echoing the same theme, Johnson aide Jack Valenti told the president, "Every student anti-U.S. policy demonstration is priceless gold for the Viet Cong."[6] Of course, as we shall see, Johnson's responses to the movement occasionally encouraged Hanoi. At several important junctures, it appeared that he *was* reacting to the Fulbrights and the movement.

In fact, not only did the president believe that the doves were aiding and abetting the communists, he also appeared to be convinced that they were given their marching orders by the Comintern. In 1967, he complained that "Most of the protests are Communist-led," including the October Pentagon demonstration that was "basically organized by international communism."[7] Here his paranoia was fed by an FBI only too happy to find communists behind the antiwar movement and by aides like John Roche, a former head of the Americans for Democratic Action, who explained why Martin Luther King Jr., came out forcefully against the war in April, 1967, "King—in desperate search of a constituency—has thrown in with the commies."[8]

In the broadest sense, organizations and individuals with communist, socialist, or Marxist affiliations often appeared in leadership roles in the large, ephemeral coalitions that organized mass demonstrations. Most prominent was the Socialist Workers' Party, a Trotskyite group that was especially skillful at the arcane political maneuvering needed to seize control of the coalitions. Moreover, its longtime rival, the American Communist Party was welcomed, if not always very warmly, under the big tent of the antiwar movement. Finally, quite a few of the pacifist leaders and organizations had communist or fellow-traveling affiliations. All the same, the CIA was unable to discover the movement's *foreign* communist connections, even after making several exhaustive investigations requested by both Johnson and Richard Nixon. Neither president was satisfied with the results of those investigations. In fact, in 1970, Nixon considered establishing his own intelligence service under the Huston Plan—in part because of the alleged counterintelligence failures of his official agencies.

Johnson's conversations were littered with references not only to the communists in the antiwar movement, but also to the communists who, directed by Moscow, manipulated the flow of opinion in the United States. He told biographer Doris Kearns, "Then the communists stepped in. They control the three networks, you know, and the forty major outlets of communication."[9] Lyndon Johnson was given to hyperbole. He was too intelligent to believe some of his more outlandish statements about the way foreign communists influenced and even directed domestic antiwar activities. Yet, by associating the movement with communists, he could discount its importance as a genuine homegrown response to the war's increasingly bloody trajectory. Furthermore, believing that Moscow and Hanoi were behind the movement, he could more easily dismiss the dovish negotiating strategies. He did not want to show that they were winning the battle for the hearts and minds of Americans.

Finally, whether or not the movement was made up of communists, like most presidents, LBJ was confident that he and his advisers knew much more about international affairs than the crowds in the streets. As he asked Kearns rhetorically after he left the presidency, "Why should I listen to all those student peaceniks marching up and down the streets? They were barely in their cradles in the dark days of World War II. . . . They simply don't understand the world the way I do." That also applied to the professors who "believe you can get peace by being soft and acting nice."[10]

Nonetheless, while he derided the protesters and other critics, they did have an impact on his interrelated military options and peace overtures. For example, when the mass antiwar movement first burst on the scene with the celebrated "teach-in" at the University of Michigan in late March, 1965, Johnson took note. In fact, several aides who were not entirely pleased with LBJ's bombing decision the previous month hoped that the teach-in might serve to discourage further escalation.[11] Paradoxically, in a somewhat convoluted way, one might also argue that the teach-ins did not help the cause of peace because National Security Adviser McGeorge Bundy's participation in a debate spawned by the teach-in movement in June, 1965, earned Johnson's disfavor and ultimately contributed to the reasons for his leaving government service in March, 1966. Walt Whitman Rostow, who was more hawkish than his predecessor, replaced Bundy.

If Johnson thought he might be able to bomb the communists to the peace table, then the existence of a growing protest movement was one of the factors that restrained him. From 1965 through 1967, as he contemplated measures that might bring about negotiations faster than the incremental bombing escalations seemed to be doing, he had to be concerned about the reaction of the movement and its allies in both the media and Congress. He no doubt was concerned about international reaction, particularly from China and the Soviet Union, but his domestic antiwar critics also worried him. One thus could make the argument that the movement helped to keep the president from employing more forceful military actions that might have brought the communists to the peace table. According to this line of reasoning, the movement worked at cross-purposes with an administration trying to end the war through more brutal military tactics that it hoped would lead to a peace on U.S. terms. Needless to say, the suggestion that more brutal tactics could have brought Hanoi to the peace table is a debatable one.

In a related vein, as the antiwar movement grew and as draft resistance became one of its tactics, another one of Johnson's escalatory options was weakened. Valenti told him in August, 1966: "I have talked with enough people to know that mothers and fathers of draft-age sons are totally blind to reason and logic. They just don't want their sons to go to Vietnam."[12] Johnson himself believed that the draft was one of the main causes of the growth of the antiwar movement, although he did not go quite as far as Richard Nixon, who claimed that students joined the movement "to keep from getting their asses shot off."[13] President Eisenhower had earlier warned that "sending conscripted troops to Vietnam would cause a major public-relations problem."[14]

Although constantly confronted by the need for more troops for the ground-combat struggle, Johnson feared ending the graduate student deferment until 1968. In addition, although he could have resolved the problem as other presidents had done in other wars by calling up the reserves or the National Guard, he refrained from doing so because they had become popular refuges for middle-class young people who enlisted before they could be drafted by the regular armed services and sent to Vietnam.[15]

Again, that perverse argument: if Johnson thought he could bring the other side to the peace table with exponential rather than linear escalatory strategies, he was hamstrung in part by the unpopularity of the draft among increasingly antiwar young people and their parents.

By 1967, with the formation of "The Resistance" and other antidraft organizations, legal and illegal assaults against the Selective Service System began to trouble the administration. In addition, with the insubordination in 1966 of the "Fort Hood Three" and Dr. Howard Levy, the Pentagon began to confront the problem of antiwar dissent in the military itself. In 1967, in the first of many such instances, a former draft resister, Pvt. Andy Stapp—demanding that he be allowed to exercise his First Amendment rights—organized a soldiers' union and an underground newspaper at Fort Sill, Oklahoma. It soon became evident that the dependability of the pool of draftees available for the ever-escalating war of attrition in Vietnam had become questionable.

More important than helping to limit the president's military options, of course, is the positive way the antiwar movement and congressional antiwar critics influenced LBJ's peace overtures. The first instance was the Johns Hopkins speech, delivered two weeks after the Michigan teach-in, which promised a generous development plan for all of Vietnam once the war was over. According to the president's press secretary, George Reedy, and George Ball, the speech was in good measure a response to the harsh criticism that the February bombing decision had elicited.[16] Similarly, Johnson accepted Defense Secretary Robert S. McNamara's suggestion to pause the bombing of North Vietnam from May 13–18, 1965, primarily to quiet liberal intellectuals and members of Congress.[17] Although McNamara does not credit the antiwar movement with this impact, there is no doubt that liberal intellectuals and members of Congress, particularly Democrats, were affected by antiwar activities and arguments. Much of this had to do with the fact that a good portion of antiwar activism took place on the campuses of the elite schools attended by their children and those of their friends and relatives. As McNamara himself pointed out, "What disturbed me most during my campus visits was the realization that opposition to the administration's Vietnam policy increased with the institution's prestige and the educational attainment of its students."[18] The head of the Selective Service, Gen. Lewis B. Hershey, inadvertently echoed this theme when he reported that he encountered little trouble with the draft on the campuses of all but fifty or so institutions. Those fifty included Harvard, Yale, Columbia, and most of the nation's other top-ranked universities.[19]

It is likely that LBJ timed a peaceful message to compete with the First International Days of Protest in October, 1965. Two months later, he announced and then extended another bombing pause from Christmas through January because of mounting antiwar criticism. Reflecting the public relations aspect of the overture, Secretary of State Dean Rusk noted, "We do not, quite frankly, anticipate that Hanoi will respond in any significant way."[20] Of course, this could work both ways, with, for example, Johnson being careful not to offer any new peaceful overture or media offensive on the eve of the National Committe for a Safe Nuclear Policy (SANE)–led November 27, 1965, Washington demonstration because Hanoi might conclude that he was worried about the protestors.[21] He was concerned that too much of a direct correlation between a peaceful pronouncement and an antiwar demonstration would give the communists the idea that the home front was weakening and lead the demonstrators to think they were influencing him.

One can see these how these two themes were linked in the speech Johnson delivered in San Antonio on September 29, 1967. The president softened his terms for the opening of negotiations, in part as a preemptive strike against the doves, who were planning a major demonstration in Washington on October 21 that evolved into the famous "siege" at the Pentagon. At the same time, amid relatively conciliatory talk, he warned the communists not to "mistake dissent for disloyalty" and not to think "that the protests will produce surrender."[22]

As with other links between peace overtures and the antiwar movement, it is difficult to demonstrate that the president would not have made them in the absence of domestic criticism. After all, he did want to end the war as quickly as possible. Nonetheless, he was continually feeling pressure from new antiwar activities and organizations, particularly those with a moderate bent, to make what appeared to be a more sincere effort to get to the peace table. For example, in 1967 he had to confront not only the Washington demonstration that fall, but also Martin Luther King Jr.'s dramatic break with the administration earlier in the spring and the formation of "Negotiations Now!" The latter was an organization whose leaders included King, John Kenneth Galbraith, Victor Reuther, Reinhold Niebuhr, Arthur Schlesinger, and Joseph Rauh. Negotiations Now! seemed rather reasonable in its call for an end to the bombing, reduced levels of fighting in South Vietnam, and internationally supervised elections. Earlier that year, administration officials had expressed concern about the lobbying visit to Washington of theologians from a group known as Clergy and Laymen Concerned About Vietnam. Its members were, according to the State Department's William Jorden, "leading church figures and theologians, not irresponsible agitators."[23] They did not especially trouble Johnson at the time, but the fact that the clerics deeply affected Sen. Eugene McCarthy (D-Minnesota) would certainly be important later in the year.[24]

Although LBJ's many peace initiatives should have kept moderate doves happy, when word occasionally leaked out about their failures attributed to the administration's clumsy tactics or rigid positions, it convinced critics that the president was not doing all that he could to end the war, despite his protestations. Botched peace plans enhanced the movement's arguments. Such was the case following the controversy surrounding the U Thant peace probe, as well as the more significant MARIGOLD schemes.[25]

Sometimes, antiwar critics learned of negotiating positions directly from the communists. During Johnson's years in office, as many as seventy Americans traveled to North Vietnam to tour the countryside and to meet with ordinary citizens and government officials to discuss ways to end the war.[26] Indeed, one reflection of how important the North Vietnamese considered the propaganda value of those Americans was the fact that a surprising number met with Premier Pham Van Dong, the country's number-two leader. One American who made the trip commented that although she could not get an interview with her own congressman to discuss the war, she was able to meet with the North Vietnamese premier.[27]

The communists, who had access to American newspapers and magazines, did not think the visitors and the movement they represented enjoyed the support of a majority of their compatriots. When, as late as September, 1967, Mary Clarke of the Women Strike for Peace warned Foreign Minister Nguyen Duy Trinh not to count on the American peace movement to dramatically affect Johnson's policies, he replied that while he was encouraged by the movement, North Vietnam would have to rely on its own resources to achieve its goals.[28]

Nevertheless, the Americans' visits to Hanoi did serve their purposes— particularly encouraging the citizens of North Vietnam, who saw with their own eyes that many Americans were making common cause with them. Alice Herz, the antiwar Detroiter who immolated herself in March, 1965, was an obscure figure at home but a famous heroine to the North Vietnamese, who named a street after her. Hanoi offered similar recognition to Norman Morrison, the Quaker who burned himself to death outside the Pentagon that November.[29]

Reports of the peaceful villagers and even more peaceful leaders brought back by those who went to Vietnam made LBJ's life more difficult. In one of the most celebrated missions, Tom Hayden, Staughton Lynd, and Herbert Aptheker traveled in North Vietnam in late December, 1965, and early January, 1966. Pham Van Dong told them that all his country was fighting for was a broad national democratic coalition administration, including, but not run by, the National Liberation Front. Moreover, he told the three Americans that Washington did not have to pull out its troops before talks could start, it only had to withdraw some of the new units that had recently arrived.[30] The story of the interview and the rest of the trip immediately made its way into print to embarrass the administration, first in newspapers and then in a book.[31] This was precisely what the seemingly conciliatory North Vietnamese had hoped for when they offered American doves so much attention.

What made matters worse was that in most cases, administration officials refused to meet with the envoys who claimed they were carrying exciting new peace initiatives from Hanoi. Dean Rusk scoffed at those who returned from North Vietnam eight months pregnant with peace, but who never had anything serious to offer.[32] In 1967, after Sanford Gottlieb, the head of SANE, and antiwar activist Father Philip Berrigan tried unsuccessfully to obtain State Department support for a trip to North Vietnam to help the peace process with private diplomacy, the State Department's Chester Cooper commented on such emissaries, that though they might have been "very, very good people—nice people. . . . Their discretion was suspect; their judgment was suspect; their emotional biases were suspect. They could not be used as confidential channels."[33]

In April, 1968, the president himself ordered his people to have no contact with American peace tourists who went to Hanoi, because such contacts might "result in a posture of quasi-negotiation which misleads Hanoi and undercuts our position at home."[34] There were occasional quiet briefings, as was the case when Hayden and David Dellinger met with W. Averell Harriman after their return from a trip to Hanoi in November, 1967, but most of the time, the administration did not think they had much to offer to help bring the communists to the peace table.[35] Johnson did meet with Jim Jackson, one of the three prisoners of war (POWs) Hayden and Dellinger brought back with them after their visit to Hanoi. Representatives of the peace movement were able to secure the release of three other POWs in February, 1968, and three more five months later. Such humanitarian successes for the movement helped to undercut the administration's claims that it alone was capable of conducting an effective policy in Southeast Asia.

What was surprising was how gently the administration treated the visitors to Hanoi, who after all, had traveled to an enemy capital during "wartime," and even engaged in diplomatic conversations that appeared to violate the Logan Act. Although the State Department seized the passports of several such travelers when they returned to the United States, a U.S. Court of Appeals ruled in December, 1967, that passports could be seized only if they had been brought into a country on the proscribed list. Most of the travelers to North Vietnam made certain not to bring their passports into the country, or at least, not have them stamped by their hosts.

The visibility of the antiwar movement and its arguments, as well as its ties to the worldwide antiwar movement, helped to undercut the administration's positions abroad as well. By January, 1968, for example, 87 percent of British people polled thought that their country's chief role in Southeast Asia was to help get the peace talks started, rather than simply supporting the United States. Four months later, 53 percent told pollsters the United States should accept North Vietnam's terms for opening negotiations. At the same time, the British people split evenly in their responses to questions about whether the United States was doing enough to make peace.[36] Ironically, it was citizens of the European nation generally most supportive of Washington's policies who expressed these opinions.

The antiwar movement abroad often borrowed slogans and tactics from its American counterpart. This was especially true in Canada, where the infusion of U.S. draft resisters and political refugees contributed to the growth and vitality of the movement there. As the war continued and peace marchers in allied nations took to the streets, governments in Ottawa, Bonn, Rome, Amsterdam, Tokyo, and elsewhere felt the pressure. Such pressure helped to explain why they were not especially supportive of the administration's political and military actions in Vietnam and also why they went to such extraordinary lengths to serve as intermediaries to assist the president in his attempts to engage in peace talks with the communists. As for the enemy camp, the Soviet Union embarrassed the United States in 1966 when it canceled the popular annual joint track meet allegedly because of the antiwar sentiment among the athletes.

The administration no doubt thought that the North Vietnamese maintained their perceived hard-line position on negotiations because of the growing strength of the American and international peace movement. Defense Department aide Alain Enthoven advised Secretary McNamara and his colleagues in the spring of 1967 that Ho Chi Minh was biding his time until the antiwar forces compelled the United States to come to the peace table from a position of weakness.[37] Years later, Dean Rusk expressed his frustrations about trying to deal with the North Vietnamese. "One of our problems was that they could see two hundred thousand people marching on the Pentagon. And it was difficult trying to set up negotiations with those who are quoting your own senators back at them," he complained. The doves "in effect said to Hanoi, 'now just hang in there fellows, and you will get what you want politically even though you won't win it militarily.'" Rusk was convinced that if the United States had "maintained solidarity on the home front," it would have been in a stronger diplomatic and military position.[38] He contended that the antiwar movement affected him little, but instead impacted primarily on Hanoi, "which had no real incentive to negotiate."[39] Rusk and his colleagues were convinced the North Vietnamese would have been more accommodating had it not been for the antiwar movement and its impact on American leaders, media, and public opinion in general.

Presidents Johnson and Nixon and many of their key aides maintained during the war that the antiwar movement never influenced their policies. However, by admitting that it influenced Hanoi's policies, they also were admitting that it influenced their policies since they had to take into account the movement's impact on communist strategies as they developed their military and diplomatic responses.

Hanoi presumed that the war of attrition the United States was waging in South Vietnam would be paralleled by a war of attrition for the hearts and minds of Americans back home. That had been the case in their eight-year war with the French. For them, the general weakening of the American people's support for a war with no apparent end, brought about primarily by the alienation of important American opinion makers, would lead to eventual victory. If anything, the North Vietnamese may have been disappointed by how long it took the war's opponents to reach a critical mass in the United States.[40] Whatever the case, there was a clear connection between the growth of the antiwar movement and the alienation of important American leaders.

By the fall of 1967, more and more American political and civic leaders, journalists, and editors had become disheartened by the way the war was tearing the nation apart. The spectacle of thousands of young "hippies" confronting young soldiers in front of the Pentagon on the weekend of October 21–22 was troubling.[41] The unprecedented disruptions and violence, often at elite colleges where members of the establishment sent their children, was even more troubling on a personal level to policy makers. There were seventy-one major antiwar demonstrations on sixty-two campuses during the first half of the 1967–68 academic year. There were 221 such demonstrations on 101 campuses during the second half.[42]

By 1967, the college and national demonstrations had become more rowdy and uncivil and more and more of the protestors had adopted hippie garb and countercultural lifestyles. It may well be that the scruffy peaceniks featured prominently by journalists always searching for the most colorful picture or sound bite helped to buy the president more time. In the wake of the Pentagon siege, McGeorge Bundy took solace in the "public distaste for the violent doves."[43] Many Americans who were on the fence concluded that if the bizarre and crude people they saw on television were against the war, then they must be for it, or at least supportive of their beleaguered president. On the other hand, since the young people protesting the war and the "establishment" were disproportionately from the upper and upper-middle classes, their parents may well have concluded that ending the war would inspire their children to clip their hair, start taking baths again, and apply for law school.

Whatever the ultimate impact of the many demonstrations in 1967, the administration was responding to what it perceived to be a domestic crisis when, at a meeting of the "Wise Men" on November 1, McGeorge Bundy called for an emphasis on "the light at the end of the tunnel" to combat the growing opposition to the war.[44] So it was that Gen. William Westmoreland and Amb. Ellsworth Bunker came home that month to deliver pep talks to the nation about how well things were going in Vietnam. Their boasts about the progress being made in Southeast Asia would be remembered by an even more skeptical population when Vietcong sappers who had infiltrated the U.S. embassy compound on the first day of the Tet Offensive appeared on their television screens little more than two months later.

When Lyndon Johnson made his concessions to the North Vietnamese in his momentous March 31, 1968, speech, it was clear that the growth of antiwar opinion, fueled in part by the antiwar movement, figured prominently in his decisions. This was set in motion in part by the credibility problem created by the upbeat public-relations campaign of the previous November in response to the increasingly violent protests. Moreover, among the options he faced as he and his advisers evaluated their Vietnam policies was further escalation that involved as many as two hundred thousand new troops, many of whom would have had to come from the reserves or perhaps by ending undergraduate student deferments. By the spring of 1968, the adverse political fallout from threatening to send more middle-class young people to Vietnam weighed heavily on the president. With the well-publicized proclamation by 158 Selective Service opponents the previous September of their support for "A Call to Resist Illegitimate Authority," the prospect of better organized and more militant draft resistance also troubled him. In addition, when the Wise Men turned against further escalation in late March, 1968, they may not been reacting directly to the antiwar movement, but they clearly were reacting to the state of public opinion in the nation—which had to have been affected in part by the movement and perhaps, even more important, by the perceived societal instability it and its hippie allies had created. Finally, the Democratic Party began splitting apart after antiwar activists convinced senators Eugene McCarthy and Robert F. Kennedy (D-New York) to enter the primaries. The relatively obscure and uncharismatic McCarthy finished a very close second in New Hampshire. In the end then, the antiwar movement did contribute dramatically to the search for peace in Vietnam by making it difficult if not impossible for the president to escalate again. According to Joseph Califano, LBJ had "misjudged the eventual power of the Left in American society, particularly its influence on the formation of American public opinion."[45]

The movement did, however, retard the chances for peace in Vietnam in 1968 in one other way. The Democrats and their presidential candidate, Vice Pres. Hubert H. Humphrey, were dealt a severe blow by the violent riots at their national convention in Chicago in August. The riots were precipitated, in part, by the antiwar Democrats' failure to nominate an antiwar candidate or even to obtain a suitable peace plank in the party platform. When many liberal Democrats sat out the election campaign and refused to work for the party or turned to third-party candidates in November, they helped elect Richard Nixon, who though running on a platform to end the war, took four years to do so. Had Humphrey won the election, he most likely would have ended American involvement in the war more quickly than did Nixon, for whom the way the United States left Vietnam was central to his approach to Great Power relations.

Who then did give peace a chance? In the long run, there is no doubt that the antiwar movement and its leaders and supporters in Congress and the media ultimately played a role in Johnson's March 31, 1968, decisions. Through 1967, however, one could make a case that the activities of his critics—both within the movement and in the population at large—may have made it unlikely that the stubborn president would adopt a more conciliatory posture toward the North Vietnamese. He dug in his heels, convinced that the ragtag bunch of hippies, professors, and ungrateful liberals were at least misguided and at worst communist-inspired. From 1965 through 1967, he was fearful of antagonizing the Soviets, China, and domestic doves by adopting the hard military policies advocated by the Right and, for a variety of political and personal reasons, was resistant to the Left's arguments for deescalation, negotiation, and withdrawal. Thus, as he searched for ways to end the war, he found himself in the middle: a "dawk" rejecting what he saw were two dangerous extreme positions. The middle, however, proved not to be the best place from which to launch a successful peace offensive.

Notes

1. Adam Garfinkle, *Telltale Hearts: The Origins and Impact of the Vietnam Antiwar Movement* (New York: St. Martin's, 1995), makes the most forceful case for the ineffectiveness of the movement, while Melvin Small, *Johnson, Nixon, and the Doves* (New Brunswick: Rutgers University Press, 1988) and Tom Wells, *The War Within: America's Battle Over Vietnam* (Berkeley: University of California Press, 1994) offer examples of its relative effectiveness.

2. Robert Dallek, *Flawed Giant: Lyndon Johnson and his Times, 1961–1973* (New York: Oxford University Press, 1998), p. 258.

3. Thomas Powers, *The War at Home: Vietnam and the American People, 1964–1968* (New York: Grossman, 1973), p. 48.

4. Meeting Notes, Dec. 17, 1965, Box 2, Lyndon B. Johnson Library (hereafter, LBJL), Austin, Texas.

5. Ibid., Jan. 27, 1966.

6. Lady Bird Johnson, *A White House Diary* (New York: Holt, Rinehart, 1970), p. 360; Dallek, *Flawed Giant,* p.280. See also U.S. Grant Sharp, *Strategy for Defeat: Vietnam in Retrospect* (San Rafael, Calif.: Presidio Press,),), p. 74.

7. Dallek, *Flawed Giant,* pp. 467, 490. See also, ibid, pp. 366, 367.

8. Marvin Watson to Johnson, Apr. 16, 1967, Box 54, HU 4 Freedoms, confidential, LBJL; Dallek, *Flawed Giant,* p. 467.

9. Doris Kearns, *Lyndon Johnson and the American Dream* (New York: Signet, 1976), p. 331.

10. Ibid., pp. 327, 328. Dean Rusk often talked about the naive and uninformed Oxford University students he encountered in the thirties who adopted pacifist postures in the face of the fascist threat. As for professors, Rusk derided those "who know about enzymes" but were uninformed about international relations (Small, *Johnson, Nixon, and the Doves,* pp. 44, 113).

11. Small, *Johnson, Nixon, and the Doves,* p. 36.

12. Charles De Benedetti, with Charles Chatfield, *An American Ordeal: The Antiwar Movement of the Vietnam Era* (Syracuse: Syracuse University Press, 1990), p. 165.

13. George Q. Flynn, *The Draft: 1940–1973* (Lawrence: University Press of Kansas, 1993), p. 214; Curt Smith, *Long Time Gone: The Years of Turmoil Remembered* (South Bend: Icarus Press, 1982), p. 217.

14. Flynn, *Draft,* p. 167.

15. Concerns about the draft pool led McNamara in 1966 to launch Project 100,000, which lowered the minimum intelligence-test requirements for recruits.

16. Small, *Johnson, Nixon, and the Doves,* p. 40.

17. Robert S. McNamara, with Brian Van De Mark, *In Retrospect: The Tragedy and Lessons of Vietnam* (New York: Times Books, 1995), p. 185.

18. Ibid., p. 253.

19. Lewis Hershey, oral history, LBJL, pp. 43–45.

20. Wells, *War Within,* pp. 56, 64. It was true, however, that letters supportive of Vietnam policy sent to the White House in 1965 generally increased after each major demonstration. Moreover, unlike during the Nixon administration, these letters were spontaneous. See Melvin Small, *Covering Dissent: The Media and the Antiwar Movement* (New Brunswick: Rutgers University Press, 1994), pp. 41, 45, 47.

21. Wells, *War Within,* p. 61.

22. *Department of State Bulletin,* Oct. 23, 1967, p. 522; Small, *Johnson, Nixon, and the Doves,* p. 111; George C. Herring, *LBJ and Vietnam: A Different Kind of War* (Austin: University of Texas Press, 1994), p. 141.

23. Mitchell K. Hall, *Because of Their Faith: CALCAV and Religious Opposition to the Vietnam War* (New York: Columbia University Press, 1990), p. 37.

24. Wells, *War Within,* pp. 120–21.

25. See Herring, *LBJ and Vietnam,* pp. 89–120.

26. For a complete listing, see James W. Clinton, *The Loyal Opposition: Americans in North Vietnam, 1965–1972* (Niwot: University of Colorado Press, 1995).

27. Ibid., p. 142.

28. Mary Hershberger, *Traveling to Vietnam: American Peace Activists and the War* (Syracuse, N.Y.: Syracuse University Press, 1998), p. 97. See also Jeffrey Kimball's perceptive comments, based on interviews with Vietnamese officials, in *Nixon's Vietnam War* (Lawrence: University Press of Kansas, 1998), p. 46.

29. Hershberger, *Traveling to North Vietnam,* pp. 42–44.

30. Tom Hayden, *Reunion: A Memoir* (New York: Random House, 1988), p. 193.

31. Staughton Lynd and Thomas Hayden, *The Other Side* (New York: Signet, 1966). Aptheker wrote his own, less-celebrated account: *Mission to Hanoi* (New York: International, 1966).

32. Small, *Johnson, Nixon, and the Doves,* p. 88.

33. De Benedetti, *An American Ordeal,* p. 170.

34. Hershberger, *Traveling to Vietnam,* p. 101.

35. Clinton, *The Loyal Opposition,* p. 59.

36. Caroline Page, *U.S. Official Propaganda During the Vietnam War, 1965–1973: The Limits of Persuasion* (London: Leicester University Press, 1996), pp. 217–19.

37. Enthoven memo, Apr. 28 1967; Enthoven to McNamara, May 1, 1967, in *The Pentagon Papers: The Defense Department History of United States Decisionmaking on Vietnam,* Senator Gravel ed., vol. 4 (Boston: Beacon Press, 1971), pp. 456–57, 463–64.

38. Dean Rusk, *As I Saw It* (New York: Norton, 1990), pp. 472, 493.

39. Small, *Johnson, Nixon, and the Doves,* p. 87.

40. Ibid., p. 88. If anything, Hanoi thought that the antiwar movement was more potent under Nixon because it restrained him from escalating.

41. For Johnson's interest in and concern about the Pentagon demonstration, see Joseph Califano to Johnson, Oct. 21, 1967, Office File of Matthew Nimitz, Box 14, LBJL, as well as other documents in that file.

42. Rhodri Jeffreys-Jones, *Peace Now! American Society and the Ending of the Vietnam War* (New Haven, Conn.: Yale University Press), p. 72. See also, ibid., pp. 54–55.

43. Bundy to Johnson, Nov. 10, 1967, President's Appointment File, Diary Backup, LBJL.

44. Jim Jones to Johnson, Nov. 2, 1967, Meeting Notes, Box 2, LBJL. Earlier that year, according to one of General Westmoreland's aides, "As the antiwar movement grew there was a growing need to demonstrate success" (Small, *Johnson, Nixon, and the Doves,* p. 109).

45. Joseph Califano, *A Presidential Nation* (New York: Norton, 1975), p. 220.

George McGovern and Mr. Johnson's War

A Liberal Democrat Dissents

Thomas J. Knock

T HE CHAMBER was nearly empty on the afternoon of September 24, 1963, when George McGovern, a forty-one-year-old South Dakotan some eight months into his first Senate term, rose to deliver a remarkable address. Although he was a Democrat and a protégé of the president, his message was not calculated to please the Kennedy White House. His main subject was the arms race—a proposal to cut pending defense appropriations by 10 percent, which, at $53.6 billion, then accounted for well over half of the entire federal budget. He made a good case for pruning. With thousands of nuclear weapons at the ready, he observed, the United States and Soviet Union together had amassed in their lethal stockpiles the equivalent of from forty to sixty billion tons of TNT, or a ten- to twenty-ton bomb for every human being on the face of the earth. In the light of such "overkill capacity," he wondered, "what possible advantage" could accrue from providing "additional billions of dollars to build more missiles and bombs"? The threat of annihilation was one thing, but the size of this appropriation was so immense, he feared that "we are to a considerable degree determining the priorities of our national life." For what, in this instance, could his proposed $5 billion savings mean? It could "build a $1 million school in every one of the nation's 3,000 counties, plus 500 hospitals costing $1 million apiece, plus college scholarships worth $5,000 each to 100,000 students—and still permit a tax reduction of a billion dollars."

These items, of course, composed only part of an unfinished domestic agenda that languished, he said, because of the obsession with military power in the struggle to contain communism—a strategy that both failed to apprehend "the limitations of military power" and neglected other "important aspects of the international challenge." "The current dilemma in Vietnam," he went on, was "a clear demonstration" of what he meant. The $50 billion arms budget had proved useless in coping "with a ragged band of illiterate guerrillas fighting with homemade weapons." Even worse, in Saigon, the United States was financing a government that tyrannized its own citizens. Alas, Pres. John F. Kennedy's course was scarcely one of victory—or even stalemate. It was, rather, "a policy of moral debacle and political defeat" in which American resources were being "used to suppress the very liberties we went in to defend." The senator closed with a warning: "the failure in Vietnam will not remain confined to Vietnam. The trap we have fallen into there will haunt us in every corner of this revolutionary world if we do not properly appraise its lessons . . . [and] rely less on armaments and more on the economic, political, and moral sources of our strength."[1]

In retrospect, this speech was at least a minor historic occasion—the earliest trenchant commentary by any senator on the nation's growing entanglement in Southeast Asia. Moreover, McGovern had on one hand called into question the basic assumptions that had guided American foreign policy since the onset of the Cold War; on the other, he had implied that its architects grievously ignored serious material and spiritual inadequacies in the lives of millions of Americans. Coming at a time when "Vital Center" liberalism was approaching high tide, it was an unusual indictment—a portent that the Center might not hold—that anticipated the clash between himself (along with several other liberal Democrats) and a president who in other circumstances would have enjoyed his undivided fealty. Whereas Lyndon Johnson presumed that in order to conduct his "War on Poverty" he must also fight communism in Vietnam, McGovern believed that in order to achieve a "Great Society" the United States must refrain from, or curtail, military interventionism in the name of anticommunism.

McGovern's coupling of the pursuit of peace and progressive change was not only premonitory. The propositions that he asked his fellow citizens to consider had long roots in his past and in his own understanding of America's Progressive tradition. In this respect, one may discover in his efforts at least as much wisdom as in those of any Cold War president. Indeed, as Johnson himself once allowed (even after the South Dakotan had helped to drive him from office), George McGovern's life composes "a dramatic and inspiring story of what America is."[2]

The son of a conservative Methodist minister, McGovern was born on July 19, 1922, and grew up in Mitchell, South Dakota, during the Great Depression. At Mitchell High School, a gifted history teacher spurred his decision to major in history at Dakota Wesleyan University, where he enrolled in the fall of 1940 and became a star debater.[3] He interrupted his studies in 1942 to train as a pilot in the Army Air Forces. The young aviator subsequently flew thirty-five combat missions in four-engine B-24 Liberator heavy bombers over Germany, Italy, and Austria. The courage and skill he displayed during his tour of duty—most conspicuously for making a perilous emergency landing on a tiny island in the Adriatic and another that required him to bring in his disabled plane on only one tire—earned him the Distinguished Flying Cross with three oak leaf clusters.[4]

McGovern had gone overseas inspired "by the vision of Roosevelt and Churchill and . . . the United Nations," he recalled. Returning home in 1945 imbued with confidence in America's future, he felt as if he was about "to participate in the launching of a new day in world affairs."[5] His wartime experiences rekindled his desire to study American history and international relations. With the help of the GI Bill, he entered the doctoral program at Northwestern University in the autumn of 1947. His professors included Ray Allen Billington, the eminent historian of the American frontier; Richard Leopold, one of the early "deans" of diplomatic history; and L. S. Stavrianos, a specialist in Eastern European history. Above all, there was the young Arthur S. Link, who became his dissertation supervisor and lifelong friend. Link's devotion to the subjects of Woodrow Wilson, Progressive reform, and internationalism influenced his student in both subtle and conclusive ways.[6] McGovern, however, was equally impressed with the works of the Progressive historians of the previous generation—practitioners such as Vernon L. Parrington and Charles Beard—who emphasized not consensus (as Link did), but the role that conflict played in bringing about change in American history.[7] In this regard, McGovern's dissertation topic, "The Colorado Coal Strike of 1913–14," is instructive. Through the process of becoming a historian and of rendering labor's struggle in the great coalfield war, his view of politics and social conflict began to crystallize— and thus so the intellectual context in which he would embrace, for example, the cause of civil rights and the antiwar movement.[8]

As for foreign policy, McGovern's reading included Owen Lattimore, E. H. Carr, Edwin Reischauer, and John K. Fairbank. Their writings made it impossible for him to regard Harry Truman and Dean Acheson with anything but skepticism. ("There would have been no American intervention in Vietnam," he later wrote, "if the views of Lattimore and other competent Asia scholars had been heeded."[9]) Like many of his peers and professors, he supported Henry Wallace in 1948. However, he came away from the Progressive Party convention disturbed by the fanatical elements among Wallace's left-wing adherents and did not vote for any presidential candidate that year.[10] Nonetheless, by the summer of 1950 he had reached the conclusion that the Cold War was a two-way street—the result, as he put it in a letter to Arthur Link, "of U.S. blundering and allegiance to reactionary regimes on the one hand and Soviet stubbornness and opportunism on the other hand."[11] Indeed, America's course had been basically flawed since the death of Franklin Roosevelt, he wrote his mentor, in September, 1950. "I somehow feel that Russia has understood and exploited the forces of nationalism and socialism which are convulsing Asia . . . whereas we are engaged in a hopeless process of sitting on the lid in the tension centers of the world." What with the onset of McCarthyism, he feared that if Truman allowed the conflict in Korea to blow up into a bigger war, it "would mean the death blow to what ever liberalism remains in the United States."[12] Thus, long before he ever ran for office, McGovern had found his compass; and, if not quite revealing the final destination, it pointed in an unmistakable direction.

By 1953, McGovern had earned his doctorate and was in his third year of full-time teaching at Dakota Wesleyan. Politics, however, had become an irresistible attraction. In 1954 he astonished his academic friends by resigning from a tenure-track position in order to reorganize South Dakota's then-moribund Democratic Party. ("What a loss to history!" Arthur Link exclaimed when he heard the news.) Yet, in 1956, and again in 1958, McGovern won election to the House of Representatives. As a congressman, he distinguished himself in the fields of agriculture and education and gained renown for superb constituency work. By 1960, he was ready to challenge red-baiter Karl Mundt for his Senate seat; but the combination of the latter's incumbency, constant reminders of McGovern's sympathy for Henry Wallace, and the issue of John F. Kennedy's Catholicism precluded an upset.[13]

The following January, President Kennedy appointed McGovern to serve as the director of Food for Peace. The program was established in 1954 under Public Law 480 primarily to alleviate the burden of America's huge grain surpluses by distributing them abroad. Dwight Eisenhower's critics called it a "dumping" program. In contrast, Kennedy's charge to his special assistant was to make "the most vigorous and constructive use possible" of America's agricultural abundance in order to narrow the gap between the haves and the have-nots.[14]

The assignment was well-nigh perfect for McGovern. Under his direction, Food for Peace underwent a vast expansion and public-relations makeover molded both by earnest humanitarian impulses and New Frontier anticommunism. For two years he traveled constantly, overseeing allotments of hundreds of thousands of tons of food and fiber that would be used to fuel labor-intensive economic development projects. In twenty-one third-world countries, Food for Peace provided partial wage payments for about seven hundred thousand workers engaged in land clearance, reforestation, irrigation, and reclamation and in the construction of bridges, dams, roads, schools, and hospitals. For McGovern, this was the way to fight the Cold War. "American food," he liked to say, "has done more to prevent communism than all the military hardware we have shipped around the world."[15]

Dearest to his heart, however, was the overseas school-lunch program, which he had worked extremely hard to revitalize. It resulted in dramatic improvements in school attendance and in the health of legions of children. By 1962–63, the children at the Food for Peace table numbered 1 million in Peru, 2 million in Korea, 3.5 million in Egypt, 4.5 million in Brazil, 9 million in India, and more than 10 million in Southeast Asia.[16] McGovern thus had superintended arguably the single greatest humanitarian achievement of the Kennedy-Johnson era. The experience would have a lasting impact on his thinking about the ways powerful nations, for weal or for woe, might figure in the life of weaker nations.

Despite his success, McGovern still longed to be a senator. With Kennedy's blessings, he entered the South Dakota race in 1962 and won.[17] His inaugural floor speech was appropriately informed by his previous assignment. Entitled "Our Castro Fixation vs. the Alliance for Progress," it demonstrated the critical perspective on American foreign policy for which McGovern would become famous. It also annoyed the president. Although the speech defended the administration against right-wing attacks for its apparent disinclination to overthrow the Cuban dictator after the missile crisis, the senator also characterized as a "tragic mistake" Kennedy's own trespasses against Cuba. The United States, he said, would do better to refrain from ill-advised military interventionism in the name of anticommunism and instead "point the way to a better life for the hemisphere and, indeed, for all mankind." If his fellow citizens intended to fulfill "their promise both at home and around the globe," then rather than dissipating their energies "in a senseless fixation on Castro," they should put their shoulders to the wheel of domestic reform.[18]

It is important to note that the initial stage of McGovern's Senate apprenticeship occurred during the interlude between the Cuban missile crisis and the expansion of the war in Vietnam. The prevailing state of international relations, he believed, held the possibility both of curbing the nuclear arms race and of at least partially dismantling America's colossal military-industrial complex—this by way of a gradual, orderly shift in the nation's economy toward more pacific industrial enterprises.

Motivated by the conviction that it was "no longer possible to separate America's domestic health from our position in world affairs,"[19] the senator introduced legislation that was extraordinary for its time to serve those ends. To begin, in the late summer of 1963, he proposed the aforementioned $5 billion cut in defense spending for fiscal 1964.[20] This, however, was only the half of it. Not far from his mind was Eisenhower's theretofore uncelebrated farewell address, which served as a major consideration behind another initiative entitled the National Economic Conversion Act, introduced in October, 1963.[21] Counseling a coordinated effort between industry and government, the bill called for a presidential commission to formulate systematic plans to ease the coming transition to a peacetime economy.[22] McGovern explained in considerable detail how this would at once relieve the anxieties of all concerned who had grown dependent upon the "gigantic WPA [Works Progress Administration]" that the Pentagon had become; how it would "add new force to disarmament discussions by removing fear of the economic consequences;" and how it could "cause a boom, rather than a drag on our economy." Apart from everything else, he made a reordering of priorities seem like a matter of common sense.[23]

Mainly owing to Vietnam, McGovern's perception of a "peace dividend" was fleeting. Nevertheless, he always contended that the Cold War could not be won by military means. Thus, even before Kennedy's assassination (as we have seen), he had begun to worry about Vietnam. In August, 1964, he listened attentively to Wayne Morse's and Ernest Gruening's admonitions concerning the "incident" in the Gulf of Tonkin. He suspected the two lone naysayers might be right.[24] Yet the chairman of the Senate Foreign Relations Committee claimed otherwise. The Tonkin Gulf resolution, Sen. J. William Fulbright assured his interlocutors, "doesn't mean anything"—except to take the issue of Vietnam out of politics and foil Barry Goldwater.[25]

Like other skeptics, McGovern himself believed (or wanted to believe) that President Johnson "was more interested in domestic policy and that he did not quite know how to liquidate the Kennedy policy in Vietnam before the election."[26] He cast his vote in favor of the resolution—for the sake of a Great Society, but nonetheless with great misgivings. The following day, he explained his vote. "This resolution is designed to make perfectly clear that the President has the support of the Congress and the American people in meeting the recent aggression," but nothing more than that, he said. "In my judgment an indefinite continuance of the military conflict in South Vietnam is a hopeless course that will lead in the end to the defeat or entanglement in the kind of major war which we are ill prepared to fight in Asia. Let us seek a political settlement as soon as possible for a problem that is basically political."[27] Within weeks of Johnson's electoral triumph, McGovern would begin his ascent to a position of central importance among critics within the liberal establishment that had itself conceived the war.[28]

Shortly before Christmas, 1964, McGovern engaged Vice Pres.–elect Hubert Humphrey in conversation in the Senate cloakroom. The subject was Vietnam. "I think this is a disaster. We just have to wind this thing up," he said to his dear friend and political mentor. Humphrey was impatient. "We can't just pull out," he retorted, "we're there, we're committed, we've got to see it through . . . we have to respond and take whatever measures are necessary." Their exchange left McGovern uneasy; he construed it, correctly, as clear evidence—"a tip-off," of sorts, he later said—that the Tonkin Gulf resolution was indeed an election-year ploy, and quite a bit more.[29]

The encounter with Humphrey prompted McGovern's first full-fledged policy statement on Southeast Asia, just five days before the inauguration. In it, he appealed to the administration to pursue a negotiated settlement and abstain from escalating the conflict. On January 15, 1965, in an extended historical review of American involvement, he declared on the Senate floor: "We are not winning in South Vietnam. We are backing a government that is incapable of winning a military struggle or of governing its people. . . . South Vietnam is not basically a military problem, but a political one." Indeed, the mission of the United States "should not be military victory, but bringing Ho Chi Minh to the conference table." He then laid out a five-point program for such an endeavor. Once under way, the conference would take measures to bring about, first, a "close association or confederation between North and South Vietnam" ensuring "local autonomy for the South as well as the North"; second, "renewed trade and rail links" to help foster that close association; and, third, cooperative planning to develop the Mekong River to control flooding and produce hydroelectric power for the benefit of all Vietnamese. McGovern's fourth point was the neutralization of North and South Vietnam, "meaning specifically guarantees that foreign troops and military advisers would gradually be eliminated as the situation permits." The final term was somewhat Wilsonian: the introduction of UN peacekeeping forces "to guarantee national borders, to offer protection against external aggression, and insofar as possible to insure fair treatment of tribal and other minorities." In all of this, he said, he recognized the prevailing egregious circumstances in the South. He added that although he was opposed to an increase in the number of American ground troops, he was not advising a withdrawal. Until a negotiated settlement could be effected, he recommended for the immediate future a military policy "of holding the cities while taking whatever attrition is possible of the guerrillas in the countryside."[30]

Informed by personal consultations with Bernard Fall, Charles de Gaulle's proposal for reconvening the Geneva Convention, Lt. Gen. James Gavin's "enclave" theory, and some traces of Woodrow Wilson as well, the speech was the first firm step along a path from which McGovern would rarely stray. It was also part of a new strategy that he and Frank Church of Idaho (his principal kindred spirit in this regard) had devised to put pressure on the president to explore all avenues in the search for peace and, while being careful not to strike at Johnson personally, to make it impossible for him to ignore the counsel of a small but determined minority of fellow Democrats.[31]

McGovern's "Five Points" captured headlines in major newspapers throughout the country. The following month, the *New York Times* filled nearly an entire page of one of its Sunday editions with a debate that it conducted between McGovern and Sen. Gale McGee, a Democratic hawk and former history professor from Wyoming. McGee argued that Vietnam posed "a major threat to the security of the free world because its loss would open the door to an extension of Communist China's power throughout Southeast Asia." Citing such lessons of history as Cuba, Berlin, and Munich, he dismissed negotiation as a sign of weakness and propounded a formula for escalation remarkably similar to the one that would come to pass. In the back-and-forth, McGovern ably refuted his opponent's historical analogies and characterized the struggle as a civil war. He then asserted that a political settlement would serve everyone's interests, arguing that it simply was "not within the power of the United States, or any other combinations of nations, to guarantee a permanently stable political situation in Southeast Asia" by force of arms.[32]

The spotlight was again cast on McGovern a week later when CBS News invited him to join a four-member panel to debate the issue on a live, prime-time "special" entitled, "Vietnam: The Hawks and the Doves." The hawks were McGee and Hanson Baldwin, the *Times*'s military editor, and the doves were McGovern and, curiously, Roger Hilsman. McGee called for "planned escalation." Baldwin contemplated massive bombing and a naval blockade of North Vietnam. If the Chinese intervened, he said, one could rest assured "the upper limit" of America's response would not exceed a million men. As for Hilsman, it was hard to tell where he really stood. "I don't think any number of American troops can win in South Vietnam permanently, at least," he said at one point. However, he then added: "I agree with Mr. Baldwin that we've got to bite this bullet. We've got to make up our minds whether or not we intend to save Southeast Asia." McGovern thus was outnumbered three-to-one in this particular aviary. Yet his mastery of the history of the struggle (far more commanding than that of the others), combined with his spirited case for negotiation, made for an impressive performance. His sharpest exchanges were with Baldwin. In response to the bombing campaign and the kind of ground escalation that the latter entertained, he said in part:

> [E]ven if we could obliterate North Vietnam, with the kind of massive bombing attacks that you suggest, the war would still continue in the South, the guerrillas would continue to fight, the political sit-

uation would continue to deteriorate, and we would have much the same situation in the future that we have today. . . .

I think there will be a staggering loss of life out of all proportion to the stakes involved and I see no guarantee that once we go through that kind of . . . military effort that the situation out there will be any better. In fact, I think that there will be such enormous political instability, such enormous political chaos that indeed we invite a much worse situation than the one that exists. . . .

But it's far better for politicians to take some political risks than for us to risk a course that might cost the lives of hundreds of thousands of our citizens.[33]

McGovern was not only gaining national attention for his reasoned, if impassioned, dissent, he was getting good reviews back home, too. His mail, he said, was running fifteen to one in favor of a cease-fire and a negotiated settlement. The *Mitchell Daily Republic* praised him for a "courageous stand" and characterized "gradual disengagement from the military operations" as the "only sane solution." Even the *Sioux Falls Argus Leader,* South Dakota's largest-circulation newspaper and the senator's leading detractor, opined that, in pressing for a negotiated settlement, he occupied a middle ground between extremes (that is, "an all-out smash or withdrawal") and that "it is well that our minds be kept open." Though doubting that his views would prevail, the Watertown *Public Opinion* said that he had "increased his stature" for having accepted the hazard of challenging "a major policy and commitment of his own party and administration."[34]

Although McGovern recognized that he might be upsetting the commander in chief, he also understood the need to preserve the lines of communication with the White House and appreciated the significance of the president's ongoing legislative accomplishments as well. "[A]s a student of American history, I regard Lyndon Johnson as the most masterful Senate leader in our history," he had remarked when the Texan visited South Dakota to campaign for him in 1960. "[I]f events should bring Senator Johnson into the White House, he [will] go down in history as one of our greatest presidents."[35] Thereafter, McGovern never failed to acknowledge LBJ's historic achievements. For example, he congratulated him on not only his "magnificent civil rights address to the Congress" (calling for the enactment of the Voting Rights Act) but also his "superb" delivery of it. During the *Times*-sponsored debate with McGee, he had praised Johnson for exercising "great restraint" in Vietnam and, in making his case on the CBS broadcast, he had said, "We have in President Johnson not only a great president, but one of the most masterful negotiators of all time."[36]

Johnson no doubt realized that such tributes were offered not entirely without purpose, but they worked well enough. When McGovern requested a private audience to discuss the war, he was accommodated swiftly. The senator arrived at the Oval Office at 7 P.M., on March 26, 1965, armed with a memorandum based on his previous statements. The president listened for about three minutes as his guest recounted the logic of negotiation, the prospect of a Mekong River Tennessee Valley Authority, and so on, before cutting him off. "George, you know what they want?" he asked, referring to the Chinese. "They want to take over the world. Vietnam is the very first point. We're not going to let them do it." McGovern endeavored to refute this Johnsonian article of faith by pointing out that Ho Chi Minh was not a Chinese stooge, that they and the Vietnamese had hated each other for a thousand years, and that Ho might well serve as a very dependable barrier against Chinese expansion. "Goddamn it, George, don't give me another history lesson," Johnson interrupted. "I've got a drawer full of lectures from Mansfield—another professor. I don't have time to be sitting around this desk reading history books." When his half-hour ended, McGovern did not exactly feel comforted by Johnson's reassurances about the personal control he exercised over the bombing campaign, or by his boast of his powers of seduction in reaching up "little Ho Chi Minh's skirt an inch at a time."[37]

A few weeks before the preceding interview, columnist Joseph Kraft had written that McGovern's brief, for all its cogency, was "a case, as W. H. Auden once put it, of 'the right song for the wrong season.'"[38] The president probably agreed, but he evidently could not get the senator's melody out of his mind. On the afternoon he was to deliver his famous address at Johns Hopkins University, he invited both McGovern and Church to his study in the West Wing for a private reading beforehand. The two westerners liked a lot of what they heard; yet they were dubious about what his offer of "unconditional discussions" meant. It was as if he was saying, McGovern later remarked, "I'm giving you what you've been asking for, an offer to negotiate. Now I hope you bastards will shut up."[39]

In the wake of the Johns Hopkins overture, McGovern relented slightly in his criticism of the president's foreign policy after some of the senator's friends, including Hubert Humphrey and Arthur Schlesinger Jr., enjoined him at the administration's behest.[40] However, he could not keep silent when, in July, Johnson announced his fateful decision to escalate. In a Senate speech entitled, "How to Save Lives and Political Face in Vietnam," he spoke grimly of the specter of "a major land war in Asia . . . involving thousands of American casualties, the expenditure of billions of dollars, vast bloodshed and destruction for the Vietnamese people, and an uncertain outcome . . . to say nothing of the impact on our own hopes for a better society." Once again, though, McGovern was cautious. He refrained from calling for withdrawal, reiterating his formula for negotiations instead. Finally, he once again said he believed the president was "searching for a way to peace" and referred to a legislative record "virtually unprecedented in American history." Even so, he admonished LBJ for "preaching that the fate of the human race and the cause of all mankind center in Saigon" and deplored the waste of energy and talent that the administration should have been devoting to "much more important issues related to our national interest, such as the strengthening of the Atlantic Community, the Alliance for Progress, . . . and other steps toward peace that promise a better life for the people of the earth."[41]

McGovern might have added his previous mission to the catalogue of "much more important issues." For, from the beginning, Food for Peace had had a direct bearing on his alarm over Vietnam. Near the end of the Kennedy administration, McGovern had received disturbing information from the American embassy in Saigon. Food for Peace had become "integral" to the feeding of militia trainees in the Strategic Hamlet Program and other counterinsurgency efforts, the chargé d'affaires reported. In order "to maintain a high level of military expenditures for the prosecution of the war," moreover, the proceeds from the sale of the food were being delivered to Ngo Dinh Diem.[42] (Apparently, the chargé thought that the former director would be pleased.)

After 1964, the humanity and good will with which McGovern had imbued Food for Peace would be almost completely subverted. The devolution began in earnest when Johnson decided to turn the program over to the State Department. (There was "no reason to maintain within the White House a bureaucratic structure created primarily to elect George McGovern to the Senate," he reportedly said.) "The free ride is coming to an end," Secretary of State Dean Rusk told the Food for Peace Council in October, 1965. The "Vietnam problem" was "going to [put] a large strain on the Federal Budget," and there was going to be "a sharp reduction in Food For Peace." In fact, there was no "sharp reduction." Commencing in 1965 (and coinciding with the American invasion), it was actually stepped up in Vietnam. What occurred, then, was a raid, a massive diversion of resources to subsidize the Saigon government—by 1966, as much as half of the total program—so that more money would be left over to fight the Vietcong.[43] Food for Peace (or now, "Food for War") thus became yet another of the invisible casualties of America's longest war.

If McGovern had any doubts that he might be mistaken in his manifold apprehensions, the first of the many trips he took to Vietnam—for three weeks in November, 1965—obliterated them. He attended well-orchestrated intelligence briefings in Saigon, where he also met with Amb. Henry Cabot Lodge II and spent a memorably weird evening at the villa of Col. Edward Lansdale. He was moved by all of the young soldiers ("these splendid American servicemen") he encountered. On that score—for his dignity, forthrightness, and dedication to his duty as he saw it—no one impressed McGovern more than Gen. William C. Westmoreland, who accorded him a two-hour parley in his private office.

Nevertheless, most of what he experienced on his journey sickened him. At Tan Son Nhut Air Base he happened upon a convoy of flatbed trucks loaded with row after row of coffins, all addressed to destinations back home. As a veteran bomber pilot he was not unaccustomed to scenes of cruel war, but a visit to an American military hospital shook him to the core: so many fine young men lying there putting on a brave face for him—eighteen-year-old GIs without arms or legs or genitals, a handsome marine lieutenant (with a Purple Heart pinned to his gown) who had lost both feet. As for the enemy, McGovern later recounted for a South Dakota audience, "they are everywhere and nowhere. They are farmers during the day and fighters at night." Flying over the countryside, he beheld the endless jungle terrain and thought, "How are we going to fight in this?"[44]

Back in Washington, he began an escalation of his own, rhetorically, as the war metastasized and began to undermine the Great Society. He continued to pay measured obeisance to LBJ well into 1966, but by then the president would soar to great heights of apoplexy at the mere mention of McGovern's name. "The boss gets wild about him sometimes," Harry McPherson told Joe Califano.[45] Then, in April, 1967, Johnson summoned General Westmoreland home to tell the American people there was light at the end of the tunnel and to spurn the cowards, defeatists, and traitors within the burgeoning antiwar movement and without. The tone and substance of the public relations barrage angered McGovern. He responded on April 25 with a momentous Senate speech that captured perhaps better than any other the depth and range of his thoughts. Published simultaneously in *The Progressive* magazine, "The Lessons of Vietnam" reads, decades later, like the summary chapter of the best scholarly monographs on the subject.

The Vietnam conflict represented the "the most tragic diplomatic and moral failure in our national experience," he began, for it was "degenerating into a defeat for America whether we 'win' or 'lose.'" He reminded his listeners of Douglas MacArthur's remark that "Anyone who commits American forces to a land war in Asia ought to have his head examined" and warned that, if the fighting did not soon abate, the consequences at home and abroad would be severe—"our dreams of a Great Society and a peaceful world will turn to ashes."

Only "by a crude misreading of history and a distortion of our most treasured ideals," he continued, was the administration able to rationalize its actions. He then spoke at length of the warhawks' incessant invocations of Hitler and Munich and the domino theory. "This, I think, is a piece of historical nonsense," McGovern said. "There is no analogy between Munich and Vietnam, and countries are not dominoes." As for Hitler, he was Nguyen Cao Ky's "only political hero." Ho Chi Minh, though a Marxist, was a nationalist, and the struggle he led "grew out of local conditions," for this was "essentially a civil conflict among various groups of Vietnamese." In any case, the challenge of communism could not be met "by forcing an American solution on a people still in search of their own national identity." The United States had "no obligation to play policeman . . . especially in Asia, which is so sensitive to heavy-handed interference by even well-meaning white men." Above all, Americans must learn that "conflicts of this kind have historical dimensions that are essentially political, economic, and psychological; they do not respond readily to military force from the outside." Moreover, "corrupt regimes" like the one in Saigon "do not deserve to be saved by the blood of American boys." Congress, he concluded, "must never again surrender its power under our constitutional system by permitting an ill-advised, undeclared war," thus rendering its function "very largely one of acquiescence." To be sure, dissent recently had been sharp; but, alas, "it has come late in the day."[46]

The speech pretty much signaled an irrevocable break with the administration. Even so, Johnson invited McGovern, along with eleven other of LBJ's Senate tormentors, to an informal stag dinner at the White House in September. Sometime between the presentation of the prime rib and the peach melba, the subject inexorably turned to Vietnam. "He seemed to be almost begging for political advice," McGovern wrote the next morning, "yet, when we would try to interject, he would immediately break in. I think one time—I didn't time him—but he went on for 45 minutes without interruption." When McGovern asked whether the recent formal election of the Thieu-Ky government meant that the United States might now entrust it with greater responsibility for conducting the war instead of sending an additional forty-five thousand American draftees, Johnson lectured incoherently for twenty minutes without answering the question. The senator's follow-up, intimating that the South Vietnamese did not fight with much enthusiasm, hardly improved the atmosphere. "The President is a tortured, confused man—literally tortured by the mess he has gotten into in Vietnam," McGovern recorded in his memorandum. "He is restless, almost like a caged lion, as if some great force has overtaken him."[47]

By the end of the evening, McGovern felt badly for his host and even feared he was going to pieces ("he reacts violently to suggestions that our involvement is immoral, or that he is following the Goldwater line"). For his part, Johnson had resolved, as he had done with Fulbright, to banish the senator from all White House functions. (Not until Gerald Ford's ascension would he be invited back.)[48] As his political fortunes sank lower and lower, the president suspected McGovern of encouraging the "Dump Johnson" sentiment that was taking root. In fact, as of late 1967, McGovern still expected Johnson to win renomination, and he had rebuffed Allard Lowenstein's appeal to him to challenge LBJ in the New Hampshire primary. ("Why don't you go see Lee Metcalf or Gene McCarthy," he had told Lowenstein). In any circumstances, McGovern preferred Johnson at his worst to Richard Nixon at his best. When the president at last withdrew from the race, McGovern threw his support to Robert Kennedy. However, in doing so in a speech at Sioux Falls, he also said, "May I add that President Johnson has taken on new stature and dignity by the magnanimous manner in which he placed the Vietnam issue above his desires for re-election."[49]

During the next electoral cycle, McGovern mounted a "grassroots" primary campaign and went on to capture the Democratic nomination for president himself. Johnson must have relished the irony of it all when the candidate and his running mate, Sargent Shriver, then made a pilgrimage to the Pedernales to secure, if not a ringing endorsement, then at least his tacit approval—which was forthcoming. At the ranch, McGovern and Shriver were mildly shocked by Johnson's appearance. The lines in his face had deepened and he had let his hair grow long. They also noticed that he was smoking cigarettes again, taking little puffs between bites of steak throughout the luncheon as Lady Bird looked on with a pained smile. As for the conversation, McGovern scrupulously heeded the list of "do's" and "don'ts" that Doris Kearns and others had provided in advance: Don't mention Ralph Yarborough or John Connally; do ask him for political advice; don't bring up foreign policy, and so on. It was Johnson himself, however, who raised the sensitive subject. "Well, I know you think I'm crazier than hell on Vietnam. I think you are. So let's omit that," he said at the very start, as if to clear the air.[50]

In a way, it was a rather good summation, although probably only one of the two of them was correct in his perception. McGovern was not crazy on Vietnam, and the former president knew it. If he made him mad, it was because, as Johnson had confessed to an aide back in 1965, McGovern was right.[51] Indeed, in this regard, the South Dakotan fitted better than most historian Fredrik Logevall's classification, in *Choosing War,* of "hero," or, more aptly, "flawed hero" (and in dramatic contrast to the "flawed giant"). McGovern was, to borrow from Logevall's broader observation, one of those "voices who understood already in 1964 the essential futility of what the United States was trying to do in South Vietnam and who believed that Vietnam was in any case not crucial to American or western security."[52]

Yet there was more to it even than that. He always stressed the indivisibility of foreign policy and domestic reform. With Vietnam as his reference point, he argued that the Cold War could no longer be permitted to deplete limited resources that the United States ought more wisely spend on programs for social betterment—whether at home or even in Southeast Asia. What McGovern's campaign amounted to, then, was not only a mission to shut down what was now Mr. Nixon's war, which it was instrumental in doing. More importantly, it was also an extended critical treatise on the so-called American Century, shaped by the former history professor's unrelenting sense of duty to explore alternatives to what he considered the cumulative perversions of containment as well as by his enduring faith in the possibilities for national redemption through authentic internationalism, education, and humanitarianism. That critique held implications for interventionism in the third world; for East-West relations, the armaments race, and the use of force in international relations; for the political economy of the United States relative to other great industrial powers; and, not least of all, for the very nature of the nation's political and social institutions. Thus, in 1972, George McGovern beckoned, "Come Home, America."

Notes

1. "A Proposal to Reverse the Arms Race," in George McGovern, *A Time of War, A Time of Peace* (New York: Random House, 1968), pp. 24–35. See also the container labeled "Speeches and Statements, Sept.-Oct., 1963," in the Papers of George S. McGovern, Seeley Mudd Library, Princeton University, Princeton, N.J. (hereafter McGovern Papers). Presently, the most informative published sources on his life are his *Grassroots: The Autobiography of George McGovern* (New York: Random House, 1977), and an excellent campaign biography by Robert Sam Anson, *McGovern: A Biography* (New York: Holt, Rinehart, and Winston, 1972). However, most of the information presented in this chapter is based on research in the McGovern Papers, and on a series of oral history interviews conducted by the author.

2. As quoted in McGovern, *Grassroots,* p. 228.

3. Ibid., pp. 16–17, and Anson, *McGovern,* pp. 29–31. McGovern met his future wife, Eleanor Stegeberg, when their respective high school teams debated the proposition, "Re-

solved: That Great Britain and the United States should form a permanent alliance." George argued the affirmative while Eleanor argued the negative and won the debate (author's interview with Eleanor Stegeberg McGovern, Oct. 27, 1995). See also, Eleanor McGovern (with Mary Finch Hoyt, *Uphill: A Personal Story* (Boston: Houghton-Mifflin, 1974), pp. 53–55.

4. George S. McGovern, interview by author, Aug. 9, 1991; Kenneth Higgins (member of McGovern's B-24 crew), interview by author, July 27, 1995. See also Stephen E. Ambrose, *The Wild Blue: The Men and Boys Who Flew the B-24s Over Germany, 1944–45* (New York: Simon and Schuster, 2001); a series of syndicated articles on McGovern's war service by Daryl Lembke, published in the *Los Angeles Times* in October, 1972; and McGovern, *Grassroots,* pp. 19–29.

5. McGovern interview, Aug. 9, 1991.

6. McGovern interviews, Aug. 9 and Oct. 1, 1991; William H. Harbaugh, interview by author, Oct. 23, 1995; Alfred F. Young, interview by author, Jan. 9, 2000. See also McGovern, *Grassroots,* pp. 39–41.

7. The writings of Walter Rauschenbusch and Harry Emerson Fosdick on the "Social Gospel" in the 1910s and 1920s also struck a chord (McGovern interviews, Aug. 9 and Oct. 1, 1991; McGovern, *Grassroots,* pp. 34–36).

8. McGovern interview, Oct. 1, 1991; Harbaugh interview. The story that culminated in the infamous "Ludlow Massacre," perpetrated by John D. Rockefeller Jr.'s private army, resonated for McGovern. It reminded him of the travails of organized labor during the Depression, as well as of South Dakota farmers who had struggled against economic forces beyond their control. "The Colorado Coal Strike, 1913–1914" (1953) was the first of thirty-one doctoral dissertations that Link supervised in the course of his career at Northwestern and Princeton.

9. McGovern interview, Oct. 1, 1991; McGovern, *Grassroots,* p. 42.

10. McGovern interview, Oct. 1, 1991; Eleanor McGovern, interview by author, Oct. 27, 1995; McGovern, *Grassroots,* pp. 40–45.

11. McGovern to Link, Aug. 19, 1950, Arthur S. Link Papers, Seeley Mudd Library, Princeton University, Princeton, N.J. (hereafter Link Papers).

12. McGovern to Link, Aug. 19 and Sept. 30, 1950, Link Papers.

13. For details on his teaching career, see Dakota Wesleyan's yearbook, *The Tumbleweed,* for 1952, 1953, and 1955, and various issues of the student newspaper, the *Phreno Cosmian* (in particular, Feb. 13, 1952, and Sept. 16, 1955); for his congressional and senatorial campaigns, see Alan L. Clem, *Prairie State Politics: Popular Democracy in South Dakota* (Washington, D.C.: Public Affairs Press, 1967), pp. 11–15, 38–45, and 118; McGovern, *Grassroots,* pp. 52–83; and Anson, *McGovern,* pp. 63–98. "More than any other figure," Clem wrote, McGovern was "responsible for the existence of both a partisan and an ideological choice in contemporary South Dakota politics" (p. 55). The *Mitchell Daily Republic* and *Sioux Falls Argus Leader,* throughout the summer and fall of 1960, are especially useful for the contest with Mundt. See also Accession no. 67A1819, Box 17, McGovern Papers. Link is quoted in Harbaugh interview, Oct. 23, 1995.

14. Executive Order 10915, Jan. 24, 1961, copy in Richard Reuter Papers, John Fitzgerald Kennedy Library, Boston (hereafter Kennedy Library). This discussion is based on Thomas J. Knock, "Feeding the World and Thwarting the Communists: George McGovern and Food For Peace," in *Architects of the American Century: Individuals and Institutions in Twentieth Century U.S. Foreign Policymaking,* ed. David F. Schmitz and T. Christopher Jespersen (Chicago: Imprint, 2000), pp. 98–120. See also Sen. George S. McGovern, *War Against Want: America's Food for Peace Program* (New York: Walker, 1964). The John F. Kennedy Papers in the Kennedy Library and the McGovern Papers both contain voluminous materials on the Food for Peace Program.

15. Knock, "Feeding the World," pp. 105–107. "I was willing to use some of that rhetoric," he said, "but my own inner sense of the program was that it should not be used in any major way as a Cold War tool" (McGovern interview, Aug. 9, 1991).

16. See McGovern to Kennedy, July 18, 1962, POF, Box 79, Kennedy Papers; Knock, "Feeding the World," pp. 107–109.

17. Knock, "Feeding the World," p. 109. For the plaudits McGovern received, see compilation in James Symington to Anson Yeager, Apr. 27, 1962, Box FFP-5, McGovern Papers. For his resignation and Kennedy's endorsement, see McGovern to Kennedy and Kennedy to McGovern, both July 18, 1962, POF, Box 79, Kennedy Papers. For details on the senatorial campaign, see Anson, *McGovern,* pp. 119–28.

18. "Our Castro Fixation versus the Alliance for Progress," *Congressional Record,* Senate, 88th Cong., 1st sess., Mar. 15, 1963.

19. As he had phrased it in ibid.

20. In addition to the one of September 24, McGovern had introduced a comparable measure on August 2, 1923 (reprinted in McGovern, *Time of War,* pp. 5–22.) He also said it was disheartening that debate grew heated over whether to spend a mere $200 million for the nation's mental health facilities, or $100 million for a youth conservation and training program; yet staggering expenditures for armaments flew through the Senate with hardly a question raised—to the point where the U.S. nuclear arsenal was more than "one and a half million times as powerful as the bomb that wiped out Hiroshima" (ibid., pp. 28–29).

21. "The National Economic Conversion Act," reprinted in ibid., pp. 49–60. See supporting materials in Accession no. 67A1881, Boxes 1 and 3; Accession no. 71A3482, Box 21; and "Speeches and Statements, Sept.–Oct., 1963," McGovern Papers; McGovern interviews, Aug. 7, 1993, and Apr. 4, 1994. In drafting the bill, the senator consulted extensively with Seymour Melman, a professor of industrial engineering at Columbia University, who was an activist in the nuclear disarmament movement.

22. The commission was to be made up of the secretaries of Commerce, Defense, Agriculture, Labor, and the Interior, as well as the chairs of the Atomic Energy Commission and the Council of Economic Advisers, and the directors of the Arms Control and Disarmament Agency and the National Aeronautics and Space Administration.

23. In making the case, he argued that the present level of military spending weakened the competitive position of civilian industries and aggravated the balance of payments problem. Although it once ranked first in machine tool production, the United States had slipped to fifth place. Meanwhile, Japan and Western Europe were modernizing their civilian industrial plant at a far faster rate. Moreover, thousands of public school teachers were failing to meet reasonable teaching standards.

Although thirty-one senators cosponsored the legislation and President Johnson established an exploratory committee, the administration was decidedly cool. Because of the situation in Vietnam, McGovern admitted to a gathering of the United Auto Workers, on February 26, 1965: "I don't think defense spending is going to drop drastically next year or the year after." See "Our Changing Defense Establishment and the Great Society," address to the UAW Aerospace Conference, San Diego, Feb. 26, 1965, along with related materials, in box labeled "Speeches and Statements 1965," McGovern Papers. See also, Jack Raymond, "President Orders Survey on Disarmament Outlook," *New York Times,* Dec. 22, 1963.

24. Four months earlier, on March 10, Senator Gruening had called for the United States to withdraw in what was probably the first extended floor speech of the decade devoted to Vietnam. In light of the political season, McGovern responded cautiously. He quoted from Kennedy's speech during the Dien Bien Phu crisis in 1954, in which the latter had opposed Eisenhower's abortive plan to intervene on behalf of the French. "It is quite ironic," McGovern

remarked, that "the cause was abandoned in French Indochina and for the past decade we have been seeking, with questionable success, to carry on the same policy." See Robert David Johnson, *Ernest Gruening and the American Dissenting Tradition* (Cambridge, Mass.: Harvard University Press, 1998), pp. 241–42, 252–54; for McGovern's remarks, see *Congressional Record,* Senate, 88th Cong., 2d sess., May 10, 1964, vol. 110, p. 4850.

25. According to McGovern, Fulbright would also say to doubting senators, "You pass this thing [and] it doesn't mean anything, but it gives Lyndon a tool in the campaign. Let's pass it and get rid of it. . . . I wouldn't support it if I thought it would lead to any escalation of the war" (McGovern interview, Dec. 29, 1992). See also McGovern, *Grassroots,* pp. 102–104; and esp., Randall Bennett Woods, *Fulbright: A Biography* (New York: Cambridge University Press, 1995), pp. 353–55.

26. McGovern interview, Dec. 29, 1992.

27. See *Congressional Record,* Senate, 88th Cong., 2d sess., Aug. 8, 1964, vol. 110, pp. 18668–70.

28. The historiography on the war is now enormous. However, a good place to start is George C. Herring, *America's Longest War: The United States and Vietnam,* 4th ed. (New York: McGraw-Hill, 2001); Larry Berman, *Planning a Tragedy: The Americanization of the War in Vietnam* (New York: W. W. Norton, 1983); Marilyn Blatt Young, *The Vietnam Wars, 1945–1990* (New York: HarperCollins, 1991); and Lloyd C. Gardner, *Pay Any Price: Lyndon Johnson and the Wars for Vietnam* (Chicago: Ivan R. Dee, 1997). Among the more recent outstanding studies, see Fredrik Logevall, *Choosing War: The Lost Chance for Peace and the Escalation of War in Vietnam* (Berkeley: University of California Press, 1999); David Kaiser, *American Tragedy: Kennedy, Johnson, and the Origins of the Vietnam War* (Cambridge, Mass.: Harvard University Press, 2000); and Robert Mann, *A Grand Delusion: America's Descent into Vietnam* (New York: Basic Books, 2001).

29. Conversation reconstructed by McGovern, interview, Dec. 29, 1992.

30. *Congressional Record,* 89th Cong., 1st sess., Jan. 15, 1965, vol. 111, pp. 784–86. For coverage of the speech, see the *New York Times* and the *Washington Post* for Jan. 16, 1964.

31. Church also spoke that day. For his activities, see LeRoy Ashby and Rod Gramer, *Fighting the Odds: The Life of Senator Frank Church* (Pullman: Washington State University Press, 1994), pp. 183–86, 200–202; David F. Schmitz and Natalie Fousekis, "Senator Frank Church, the Senate, and the Emergence of Dissent on the Vietnam War, 1963–1966," *Pacific Historical Review* 63 (Aug., 1995): pp. 561–81.

32. See "Vietnam: A Debate Over U.S. Role," New York Times, Feb. 28, 1965.

33. See "CBS Special Report: Vietnam: The Hawks and the Doves," Mar. 8, 1965, box labeled "Speeches and Statement 1965," McGovern Papers.

34. See copies of Senate speeches on Feb. 17 and 18, 1965, in "Speeches and Statements 1965" files, McGovern Papers; *Mitchell Daily Republic,* Mar. 5, 1965; *Sioux Falls Argus Leader,* Apr. 25, 1965; *Watertown Public Opinion,* Apr. 19, 1965.

35. McGovern to Johnson, June 3, 1960 (enclosing *Congressional Record,* June 2, 1960, in which McGovern had inserted his own and Johnson's remarks at the event); and Johnson to McGovern, June 8, 1960 (in which Johnson replied, "I hope you know that I want to do everything that I can to reciprocate your warm friendship."). See also McGovern to Johnson, May 27 and Nov. 11, 1960; and Johnson to McGovern, Nov. 19, 1960, all in U.S. Senate, 1949–61, Papers of the Democratic Leader, Box 373, Lyndon B. Johnson Library, Austin, Tex. (hereafter LBJL). McGovern subsequently asked Johnson to campaign for him in 1962. See McGovern to Johnson, May 10, 1962; and Johnson to McGovern, Sept. 29 and Dec. 14, 1962, vice president's files, Box 33, LBJL.

36. McGovern to Johnson, Mar. 23, 1965, Box TK-8, McGovern Papers. In Senate speeches on February 17 and 18, McGovern also expressed support for the retaliatory air strikes that

Johnson ordered on targets in North Vietnam after an attack on American forces at Pleiku and praised his "restraint in the handling of that crisis." As the bombing campaign expanded, however, he also noted, "This is the kind of struggle that is not affected very much by bombings a thousand miles away from the fighting." See copies in "Speeches and Statements 1965" files, McGovern Papers.

37. Conversation reconstructed by McGovern, interview, Dec. 29, 1992. See also, "Statement of Senator George McGovern to President Johnson, Private Conversation at the White House, March 26, 1965," in Horace Busby Office Files, Box 6, LBJL (meeting arranged by Bill Moyers).

38. Joseph Kraft, "Johnson Has the Right Answer—Sit Tight," *Chicago Daily News,* Mar. 1, 1965.

39. McGovern quoted in Anson, *McGovern,* p. 159. See also, Ashby and Gramer, *Fighting the Odds,* pp. 200–202.

40. "A friend of mine in South Dakota . . . expressed concern lest you find yourself being portrayed as opposing the President's policy," Humphrey began, adding, " I know that in the main you have supported what the President has been doing" (Humphrey to McGovern, June 7, 1965, ser. 150.E.47B, Cont. File 1965, Box 846, Papers of Hubert Humphrey, Minnesota Historical Society Library, St. Paul, Minn.). See also Schlesinger to Bill Moyers, May 17, 1965, White House Congressional File, Box 270, LBJL.

41. *Congressional Record,* Senate, 89th Cong., 1st sess., vol. 3, July 27, 1965, pp. 18306–12.

42. William Trueheart to McGovern, Aug. 16, 1963, copies in Accession no. 67A1881, Box 5; and Box FFP-4, McGovern Papers. For a fuller discussion, see Knock, "Feeding the World," pp. 109–12.

43. Johnson and Rusk are quoted in Knock, "Feeding the World," pp. 109, 112, respectively. "[I]f there was some way to use Food for Peace to reduce the budget here at home and also to assist the South Vietnamese budget," McGovern lamented years afterward, "that would take precedence over the Food for Peace program worldwide. I think [Johnson] would have been willing to put the whole thing in South Vietnam, and that became the view of Walt Rostow, [McGeorge] Bundy, and the others" (McGovern interview, Aug. 9, 1991).

44. McGovern interview, Aug. 7, 1993; news report of McGovern's account at town meeting, *Mitchell Daily Republic,* Dec. 17, 1965. See also McGovern, *Grassroots,* p. 107; Anson, *McGovern,* pp. 161–65.

45. McPherson to Califano, Feb. 23, 1966, White House Congressional File (name file "M"), Box 270, LBJL.

46. "The Lessons of Vietnam," *Congressional Record,* Senate, 90th Cong., 1st sess., Apr. 25, 1967, reprinted in McGovern, *Time of War,* pp. 128–45.

47. See memorandum marked "Personal and Confidential," Sept. 22, 1967, Acc. 329–77–64, Box 1a, McGovern Papers. (The guest list included Mike Mansfield, Russell Long, Carl Hayden, Gaylord Nelson, Joe Clark, Frank Church, Warren Magnuson, Mike Monroney, Wayne Morse, and Vice President Humphrey.) A few weeks later, McGovern decided to send the president a last proposal recommending an indefinite bombing halt in North Vietnam on the grounds that all significant military targets had been destroyed; the enlistment of the Soviets to secure a pullback of North Vietnamese forces; replacement of sanguinary "search and destroy" with "clear and hold" operations in the South and the start of American troop withdrawals; and, finally, "that Saigon either assume a greater responsibility for its own defense or else negotiate with the NLF for an end to the war" (Memorandum for the President, Oct. 12, 1967, in ibid).

48. Memo, "Personal and Confidential," Sept. 22, 1967; McGovern interview, Dec. 30, 1997.

49. McGovern interview, Dec. 29, 1992; and the following documents, all in the LBJL: John Lindley to Califano, Jan. 19, 1967, with undated *Argus Leader* editorial ("Subtle Campaign to Oust Johnson Indicated"), in Confidential File FG/RS/PR/18 (1965), Box 16; and memorandum to Johnson, Aug. 3, 1967; Lindley to Humphrey, July 25, 1967; memorandum for Watson from Pierson, Oct. 16, 1967; and Connell to Watson, Dec. 19, 1967, in White House Congressional Files (name file "M"), Box 270. In a memo of a conversation with McGovern, Lloyd Hackler states that McGovern commented "that if Nixon were the Republican nominee, the President would find every dove in the Senate, including McCarthy, campaigning hard for Lyndon B. Johnson" (Hackler to Mike Manatos, Mar. 12, 1968, in ibid.).

50. There are a fair number of documents and news clippings about this event in the postpresidency files, Box 105, LBJL. See also Mollie Parnis Oral History, LBJL. In addition to the Kearns documents, the McGovern Papers (selected correspondence 1972, Box 831) also contains various clippings, memoranda, and letters between McGovern and LBJ. Johnson quoted in McGovern, *Grassroots,* p. 227. Bill Clinton and Taylor Branch were in charge of local arrangements. For an interesting account, see David Maraniss, *First in His Class: A Biography of Bill Clinton* (New York: Simon and Schuster, 1995), pp. 270–73.

51. McGovern was told that Johnson had made this remark more than once (McGovern interview, Aug. 7, 1993).

52. Logevall, *Choosing War,* p. xxii.

Missions Impossible

Canadian Secret Diplomacy and the Quest for Peace in Vietnam

ANDREW PRESTON

THE CANADIAN NATIONAL EXPERIENCE has been shaped inordinately by external, rather than internal, forces. While the bond with Great Britain remained strong into the 1960s, Canadians have always defined themselves and their foreign policy by their relationship with the United States. Even prior to Canadian Confederation in 1867, American territorial expansion, military prowess, and exceptionalist zeal combined to form Canadian reactions. Somewhat paradoxically, Canada also evolved into America's closest ally after World War II, a relationship that survives intact to the present. Thus, with a mixture of disapproval, anxiety, and admiration, Canadian diplomacy has attempted to balance its support for the United States against its frequent disapprobation of American exuberance.[1]

Nowhere was this dilemma more acute than over U.S. policy toward Asia. Culturally, politically, and economically an Atlantic nation at heart, Canadians have faced a difficult task in comprehending what appeared to be unlimited American ambitions in the Pacific. However, because of Canada's close relationship with the United States, remaining prudently neutral during America's Asian crises has proved to be nearly impossible. As early as January, 1941, Lester B. Pearson, then serving at the Canadian High Commission in London, declared to an audience at the University of Nottingham: "It would be, I think, quite impossible for us to remain neutral in any major Pacific conflict in which the United States was engaged."[2] It came as no surprise to Canadians, then, to be fighting communists in Korea alongside their American cousins a decade later. However, Canadian and American perceptions of the conflict in Vietnam diverged so greatly that they became, by 1964, completely incompatible. Since 1954, Canada had represented western, noncommunist interests on the International Control Commission (ICC), a tripartite organization designed to keep the peace in Vietnam; Poland served on behalf of the communist bloc; and India, as both a prominent Asian and nonaligned nation, chaired the body. Canada's role on the ICC afforded it an exhaustive, firsthand look into the Vietnam conflict. Although they agreed with their American counterparts that the

South Vietnamese were suffering from foreign aggression just as the South Koreans had, Canadian officials did not share the view that South Vietnam represented a vital interest worth fighting for. Instead, Ottawa's main priority was to keep the conflict from spreading by helping the United States find a graceful way of exiting from Vietnam.[3] Preventing the spread of communism was always a secondary aim.

Consequently, Ottawa's goals clashed strongly with Washington's. It thus should come as no surprise that American leaders did not appreciate Canada's efforts to secure a peaceful, diplomatic solution to the war through the 1964 Seaborn missions and the 1966 Ronning missions. "There were all sorts of intermediaries through this period: governments, organizations, private citizens, direct contacts between us and Hanoi," Secretary of State Dean Rusk remarked derisively of Canadian diplomacy to journalist Peter Stursberg, "and it looked as though there was a great race on to win the Nobel Peace Prize."[4] It seems that only in retrospect could U.S. officials find any use for Canadian diplomacy. "Hanoi was pushing the war throttle," Lyndon Johnson wrote in his memoirs, but, through the Canadians, "we were trying to put on the brake."[5] More candidly, Undersecretary of State George Ball recalled that the Canadian missions, among others, were "genuine efforts to get discussions going." They were also, however, "foredoomed efforts, because we weren't prepared to make any real concessions. Negotiation at that time still consisted pretty much of saying to Hanoi, 'Look, let's work out a deal under which you will capitulate.'"[6] As we shall see, neither the United States nor the Democratic Republic of Vietnam (DRV) were willing to take the Canadian-sponsored leap of faith and enter into substantive negotiations. Indeed, it was a lesson that Ottawa would learn to its great disillusionment and disappointment.

The BACON Peace Initiative

The assassinations of presidents Ngo Dinh Diem and John F. Kennedy in November, 1963, exposed the reports of progress in the anticommunist war effort in South Vietnam as illusory, even fraudulent. It had become apparent that the United States would need to increase its own military role if a collapse of South Vietnam was to be avoided. Like many other U.S. officials, Henry Cabot Lodge, the ambassador to Saigon, envisioned a new strategy of applying direct military pressure against the North. However, unlike any of the other stratagems floating around Saigon and Washington, Lodge promoted a two-track "stick-and-carrot" approach. The "stick" would encompass private threats to Hanoi, through one or more independent channels, that the United States would bomb the DRV if its support for the National Liberation Front (NLF) in South Vietnam and the Pathet Lao in neighboring Laos continued. The "carrot"—an aspect that, in comparison to the stick, Lodge always left rather ambiguous—included undefined offers of an American military withdrawal from South Vietnam and food aid to the DRV. Although Kennedy had toyed briefly with the idea of using an envoy to Hanoi, possibly in conjunction with the ICC, the concept did not take hold until Lyndon B. Johnson became president.[7] In December, 1963, Lodge outlined the plan to W. Averell Harriman. The "U.S. would like to unload—if terms were right—perhaps leave some economic aid [*sic*], but withdraw troops, provided NVN stops supplying [the] Viet Cong and Pathet Lao and tries for a cease fire. A long-term food agreement might be possible. From another quarter," Lodge continued bluntly, "they could be told that if they don't stop aid to [the NLF and Pathet Lao], they will suffer."[8]

By early 1964, Defense Secretary Robert S. McNamara, the Joint Chiefs of Staff (JCS), Secretary of State Rusk, National Security Adviser McGeorge Bundy, and Saigon all agreed with Lodge that U.S. military measures should be used against the DRV.[9] However, Lodge first needed to convince President Johnson. "I believe various pressures can and should be applied to North Viet Nam to cause them to cease and desist from their murderous intrusion into South Viet Nam," he wrote to a skeptical Johnson in February, 1964. Such a campaign could be initially limited to reprisals for specific communist provocations. "I believe," the ambassador continued, that "North Viet Nam should be told secretly that every terrorist act against Americans in South Viet Nam will provoke swift retaliation against North Viet Nam." An additional benefit of striking the DRV would be an inevitable boost to South Vietnamese morale. In highly emotive language, Lodge stressed that "the South Vietnamese expect us to be brave and that there are big advantages to be gained by not disappointing them."[10]

Based on the model devised by Lodge, in April the Johnson administration prepared to employ a third party to act as an intermediary. Finding a country that could be trusted to deliver faithfully an American message became a high priority. Regardless of who was selected, the intermediary was not to engage in any independent diplomacy. The last thing Washington wanted to do was to entrust its diplomacy to meddlesome or manipulative peacemakers. Lodge had originally thought the Italian ambassador to Saigon, Giovanni D'Orlandi, could be used as a conduit to the Polish representative to the ICC, Mieczyslaw Maneli. In turn, Maneli could use his regularly scheduled visits to Hanoi to meet with DRV leaders and pass along an American message. Lodge, however, did not feel that he could trust either D'Orlandi or Maneli.[11] By the end of the month, immediately before Ottawa was approached, Lodge had rejected as potential intermediaries the United Arab Republic, the United Kingdom, Yugoslavia, and the DRV ambassador to Laos.[12]

Canada seemed to be an ideal choice. In its relations with the United States, particularly over matters of international affairs, Canada had usually practiced "quiet diplomacy," by which disputes between the two allies would be settled privately among politicians and diplomats. Although Canadian officials had been wary of America's military role in Vietnam, particularly after the spring of 1961, their anxieties and admonitions had always been muted and kept out of the public domain. Washington, then, believed that Ottawa could be trusted to deliver faithfully an American message. Moreover, as both a member of the ICC and an intimate ally of the United States, Canada had a regular right of access to North Vietnamese and American officials. Canadian contact with either thus would not seem out of the ordinary and hopefully would go unnoticed. "Canada had [an] obvious attraction if [an] able, discreet individual could be found," Lodge told Rusk and William P. Bundy, the assistant secretary of state for Far Eastern Affairs, at an April 19 meeting in Saigon.[13] Based on these consultations, Johnson decided "that the very best possible Canadian should be assigned to the ICC team in Vietnam with the specific mission of conveying to Hanoi both warnings about its present course and hints of possible rewards in return for a change."[14]

It was now time to broach the subject with the Canadians. On April 30, Rusk flew to Ottawa to meet Prime Minister Lester B. Pearson and Minister for External Affairs Paul Martin and ask them to play the role of messenger. Rusk already had a safe hunch that the Canadians would cooperate. A few days before, Ottawa had readily agreed to undertake a similar project by observing and reporting on Polish behavior on the ICC, particularly in its relations with North Vietnam.[15] It thus was no surprise when Pearson and Martin proved receptive to the idea of playing an intermediary role. Rusk wrote to Lodge and advised him that he had "found our Canadian friends in close concert with the thoughts you and I discussed in Saigon and they assure me that they are most willing to cooperate with us." Pearson and Martin also identified the new Canadian commissioner as J. Blair Seaborn, "an expert in communist affairs" who previously had served in Moscow and Eastern Europe. Rusk presented the initiative as consisting of four facets. First, Seaborn was asked to gauge the temper of North Vietnam's leaders, especially Ho Chi Minh. Second, Rusk stressed that Seaborn "should get across to Ho and his colleagues the full measure of US determination to see this thing through." The third stipulation was that Seaborn "should spread the word that he is puzzled by Hanoi's intentions." Moreover, Rusk continued in what would become a familiar refrain, "If Hanoi would leave its neighbors alone, the US presence in the area would diminish sharply." Finally, in proffering the carrot of trade and food aid, the Johnson administration wanted Hanoi to recognize the fact that the United States could deal with a communist state in Southeast Asia, provided it was not expansionist.[16]

Although this original plan would change slightly, Rusk's guidelines established the basic parameters of the Seaborn missions. For its part, Ottawa gave the initiative the unlikely code name "BACON." On the surface, the BACON initiative was simple: Seaborn would transmit a two-part carrot-and-stick message to Hanoi and Washington would await a response. Deeper down, however, a critical and essentially irreconcilable difference between the American and Canadian perspectives emerged at this time. Neither a search for negotiations nor a diplomatic settlement were ever American aspirations for the Seaborn initiative, although these were precisely the purposes for which the Canadians agreed to participate. Washington viewed the situation far differently. As Lodge had declared to Harriman, "I do not propose a negotiation; I propose that they be told."[17] The purpose of sending an envoy to Hanoi, then, was not to engage in preliminary discussions. "It is," Lodge reiterated to Rusk and William Bundy, "more nearly an ultimatum."[18] With this in mind, the ambassador advised Rusk on May 4 that Seaborn's instructions needed to be toughened significantly by making the threat of U.S. military escalation more explicit.[19]

In general, Johnson and Rusk agreed with Lodge. So much so, that by this time the administration had already formulated a program for bombing the North. McGeorge Bundy explained to Johnson that the "theory of this plan is that we should strike to hurt but not to destroy, and strike for the purpose of changing the North Vietnamese decision on intervention in the South."[20] But the extent to which Lodge saw BACON and a bombing campaign as components of the same imminent plan came as a bit of a shock to the president. A report by an alarmed William H. Sullivan, a State Department official who had recently visited Lodge in Saigon, made a particularly profound impression on Johnson and Rusk.[21] The president subsequently cabled Lodge that he "had not understood that you were proposing that a sequence of actions be initiated in the near future. . . . With respect to the Canadians, I feel it important to know whether you contemplate their being informed of the full range of actions you propose and being advised at this time of the precise nature of the messages you would wish them to convey to the North Vietnamese."[22] Rusk also made his uncertainty known. "On the Canadian matter," he cabled Saigon, "in light of present Canadian attitudes we tend to see real difficulty in approaching [the] Canadians at this time with any message as specific as you suggest, i.e., that Hanoi be told by the Canadians 'that they will be punished.' But," Rusk added portentously, "we are keeping this in mind and will see whether we can go further when we consult them next week" in Ottawa and New York.[23]

Lodge, however, did not share the secretary's sense of diplomatic nuance. "It is not at all necessary that the Canadians either agree or disagree," he responded a few days later. "What is important is that the Canadian transmit the message and be willing to do that and report back accurately what is said. The Canadian is not an intermediary or a go-between, or a broker, or a spokesman, but an interlocutor. Nor is he acting as an ally. If we cannot get an intelligent and willing Canadian," Lodge added caustically, "then there must be other people whom we can and should try."[24] He reemphasized this basic but contentious point the following day: "There is no question whatsoever of consulting the Canadian."[25]

As far as Canadian attitudes were concerned, the trepidations of Johnson, Rusk, and Sullivan were not unfounded. The Canadians perceived their role in precisely the terms—intermediary, go-between, broker, spokesman, ally—eschewed by Lodge. Ottawa accepted the bombing threat as an integral component of the American message to Hanoi, but this did not mean that the Canadians approved of it. Although Canadian officials supported the ultimate American goal of a non-communist South Vietnam, they believed very strongly that the prevention of a wider war was a much more important aim. Memories of fighting in the Korean War, and of the unfettered American exuberance epitomized by Gen. Douglas MacArthur, left them with an uncomfortable sense of déjà vu as they confronted their own Vietnam dilemma in the 1960s.[26] Pearson agreed to the Seaborn mission in the belief that it could plausibly lead to the opening of negotiations.[27] Martin, who was eager for Canada to undertake the mission in order to promote a peaceful settlement, was somewhat skeptical about the Americans' motives.[28] For Ottawa, the worst possible scenario would be if the Johnson administration used BACON to justify a new round of military escalation in Vietnam. "We were willing to do whatever we could to avert a widening of the war," Martin later wrote. However, "In retrospect, I believe . . . that [the United States] was looking for evidence to corroborate [the] view that military action would bring the North to heel."[29]

Sullivan and Chester L. Cooper flew to Ottawa at the end of May for talks with officials of the Department of External Affairs (DEA). Sullivan brought with him a new set of instructions for the Canadians that attempted to bridge the small, but nonetheless significant, gap between

Rusk's original guidelines, delivered personally to Pearson and Martin a month before, and Lodge's insistence that air strikes against the DRV commence immediately. Before leaving for Canada, Sullivan told Rusk that while the revised paper did not include Lodge's preference for the inclusion of an explicit threat, "it does expound upon the massive military power of the United States available in the area and the vulnerability of North Viet Nam should that power be brought into play."[30] The paper Sullivan drafted was tailored to mitigate any potential Canadian objections. Seaborn became, in this rendition, "a political personality who can be dealt with and is not merely an observer who functions as a customs inspector," rather than the passive messenger envisioned by Lodge. The distinction is important, for it is highly doubtful that Pearson and Martin would have consigned one of their most important diplomats to such a minor part in an American exercise in international intimidation. The Sullivan paper also gave Seaborn a wide margin of discretion in discharging his brief. It was essential, nevertheless, for Seaborn to stress to Hanoi that, if faced with a stark choice between war or disengagement, "the Americans would opt for enlarging the military action and escalating direct pressure against North Viet Nam."[31]

In discussions with Sullivan, DEA diplomat Arnold Smith insisted that Seaborn's instructions originate only from Ottawa, a potential sticking point that was quickly conceded.[32] Sullivan met with Paul Martin in a much smaller group the next day. Referring to the Conservative opposition in the House of Commons, Martin was even more concerned than Smith about compromising Canadian independence by merely transmitting American threats.[33] Sullivan wisely reassured the minister on this point and outlined the initiative even more cautiously than he had in the meeting with DEA diplomats the day before.[34] Even so, Sullivan's talking paper, a copy of which the State Department had already provided the Canadians and which formed the basis of Sullivan's briefing, concentrated heavily on the threat of U.S. military power the Americans expected Seaborn to deliver. "This hectoring was quite needless," Martin recalled of the paper, "and I told Sullivan that we would not necessarily convey the entire message to Hanoi."[35] Sullivan, meanwhile, noted in his report that "Foreign Minister Martin seemed a little nervous about the prospect of 'expanding the war.'"[36]

While Sullivan and Cooper briefed Martin and the DEA in Ottawa, Pearson met with Johnson and McGeorge Bundy in New York. Bundy had broached the topic with Pearson beforehand to ensure that the Canadians understood exactly what was expected of them.[37] After the prime minister "made clear his entire readiness to have a Canadian officer play this important role," LBJ underscored his desire to avoid war. The United States, he promised, "was not interested in starting wars, but in keeping peace," while the president himself "was a man of peace, and his Administration was going to be an Administration of peace." Pearson, who had been alarmed by the militaristic rhetoric of Republican presidential candidate Barry Goldwater, eagerly approved of Johnson's message. Indeed, the only objections the prime minister raised concerned the use of nuclear weapons and the need "to have targets carefully defined and sharply delineated."[38] Bundy was less circumspect in a conversation with H. Basil Robinson of the Canadian embassy. "It was not impossible," he told Robinson, "that the United States might feel it necessary to take certain measures against the North Vietnamese, but it would be obviously desirable to ensure that before such measures were taken the North should have a reliable channel for responding if they chose to use it." Robinson "had the impression from Bundy's remarks that all this might develop pretty quickly."[39]

Seaborn, eager to carry out his mission, arrived in Saigon at the beginning of June and traveled to Hanoi on June 15, ostensibly to fulfill his ICC obligations. The Canadian envoy carried with him a letter, written in French, outlining Pearson's guidelines for the mission to present either to Ho Chi Minh or Prime Minister Pham Van Dong. In the letter, Pearson restated that the United States was indelibly committed to South Vietnam; that the United States had no "permanent ambition" in Southeast Asia; and that although Johnson desired a peaceful solution, the Americans would, if provoked, feel compelled to expand the war by striking the DRV. "In such circumstances," Pearson emphasized, "the lack of direct means of communication between governments can become extremely dangerous." In a flagrant breach of the procedures Rusk and Johnson had personally established with him, Pearson instructed Seaborn to "be prepared to transmit to me any commentary or proposition which the Government of the [DRV] may eventually wish to transmit to the United States. I venture to hope that President Ho . . . will interpret your mission as being founded on a genuine desire to ensure the return of peace to Vietnam and to South East Asia."[40] This was exactly the kind of indirect diplomacy Washington had hoped to avoid. It seems that Pearson, who had been awarded the Nobel Peace Prize in 1957 for his efforts to defuse the Suez crisis, could not resist taking advantage of this rare opportunity to try the Canadian hand at peacemaking in Vietnam.

Hanoi also attached great importance to the initiative. Although Ho would not see him, Seaborn conveyed the American message when he met with Pham Van Dong on June 18. Speaking entirely in French, which most DRV officials normally refused to do, Seaborn and Pham engaged in a wide-ranging discussion on the conflict in Vietnam and the U.S. role in it. Seaborn approached his task from three separate, mutually reinforcing angles. First, he presented Pearson's letter as indicative of the official Canadian position, which itself was based predominantly on "our constant detailed and intimate exchange of views with [the] USA which gave us excellent insight into American thinking. On this basis, we were convinced that President Johnson was [a] man of peace, [and] that he would take great pains to avoid and avert situations which could lead to confrontation between major powers. [American] intentions in Southeast Asia were essentially peaceful and USA ambitions were limited, but," he added portentously, the "USA was also determined and its patience was not limitless." Second, Seaborn delivered the American stick-and-carrot message, although he omitted from his remarks an explicit threat. Finally, Seaborn offered his own personal assessment that a peaceful resolution of the conflict was not impossible—provided the North was willing to guarantee the neutralization of South Vietnam and the NLF was willing to participate in a true coalition government.[41]

The DRV prime minister listened attentively and offered Hanoi's perception of the conflict and its potential solutions. "[W]e must learn to coexist," he replied to Seaborn, by finding a "just solution" for all of Indochina. Somewhat confusingly, Pham expounded on what exactly a "just solution" entailed: "[A] USA withdrawal . . . and peace and neutrality for SVN in [the] Cambodian pattern in accordance with [the] programme of [the] Liberation Front which must participate in [the] determination of Vietnam as [a] result of negotiation when SVN [is] ready for negotiation." If the United States continued to increase its military assistance to South Vietnam, the "war will be prolonged and intensified, but our people will go on struggling and resisting. It is impossible for Westerners to understand [the] strength of [the] people's will to resist, to continue, to struggle," Pham declared. "It has astonished us too." In issuing his own warning, the prime minister stated that North Vietnam could not tolerate covert American and South Vietnamese raids against DRV territory or American military activities in Laos. Pham finished his remarks by raising the possibility that many in the United States did not want a war in Southeast Asia and noting sardonically that newspaper columnist Walter Lippmann "sees no light at the end of the tunnel and others speak of [a] new Dien Bien Phu."[42] Seaborn also reported no signs of war weariness in Hanoi, no signs of political division or of an adverse impact from the Sino-Soviet split, and no indications of weakening resolve among the DRV leadership. Although Pham seemed "genuinely grateful for [the] intermediary role Canada was trying to play," Seaborn was struck by North Vietnam's palpable self-confidence.[43]

The American reaction to Seaborn's first mission was muted. Charles Ritchie, the Canadian ambassador to Washington, presented Seaborn's cables to Sullivan and William Bundy, who was succeeding Sullivan as the Johnson administration's coordinator of the initiative. Both were, at best, cautiously optimistic. The mission's limited success, they told Ritchie, stemmed from the fact that a reliable contact with the DRV leadership had been established and "that a worthwhile dialogue might be possible." However, both dismissed the idea, dear to the Canadians, that the Seaborn channel would become regularly used. Bundy immediately qualified his initial praise by also saying that he "had no particular feeling about [the] timing of another visit to Hanoi," while Sullivan admonished Ritchie "that it might be preferable not to show too much eagerness." Moreover, both were extremely doubtful about the desirability of basing a peace settlement for Vietnam on the neutralization of South Vietnam and the participation of the NLF in a coalition government. The "implications of this," a disappointed Ritchie reported to Ottawa, "is that they have as yet nothing new and urgent to say to [the] DRVN."[44] A few days later, Sullivan told the Canadian embassy that "Seaborn's assessment provided a sobering picture. . . . This did not surprise him personally; it just illustrated the size of the job there was to do for SVN and [the] USA." He also reiterated that the NLF could not be dealt with as an independent political entity because it was, in the eyes of the Johnson administration, wholly the creation of the DRV.[45]

The reaction among the American team in Saigon was somewhat more mixed. General Maxwell D. Taylor, who replaced Lodge as ambassador at the end of June, generally agreed with the analyses of Bundy and Sullivan. He advised Rusk that the "ball [is] now in Hanoi's court and their views should be volunteered rather than solicited."[46] Lodge, in characteristically ironic fashion, evinced perhaps the most optimistic American attitude, although it was coupled with his usual penchant for bombing the North. "It seems to me," he wrote to Rusk in one of his last acts as ambassador, "that it is very mildly encouraging." Pham Van Dong's "non-polemic tone . . . and the tone of obvious concern are in contrast with the kind of rough stuff of which Communists are capable." Unlike Sullivan or Bundy, Lodge unequivocally recommended that Seaborn travel to Hanoi by mid-August. Consistent with his advice of the previous eight months, Lodge also suggested that the United States give North Vietnam "a very neat bloody nose" by attacking from the air, possibly to enhance the credibility of the implicit threat conveyed by Seaborn's message.[47]

Ottawa, on the other hand, believed BACON's first installment should not be the last. The Canadians were both encouraged by Pham's hint that a settlement was not impossible and discouraged by the DRV's evident confidence in the face of American military power. Paul Martin's deputy, Undersecretary of State for External Affairs Marcel Cadieux, explained to the minister that "Mr. Seaborn's first and very tentative conclusion is that there may be fewer pressures on the North Vietnamese to reach an accommodation with the United States than the Americans may themselves believe."[48] Ottawa was very much interested in launching the second Seaborn mission immediately. Should the DRV take too long in responding to the American message, Arnold Smith advised Seaborn, "you might have to take [the] initiative and we should be interested in your ideas as to when you could best do so."[49] The Canadians perceived in Seaborn's conversation with Pham Van Dong a small, probably fleeting, opening through which the belligerents could pass in order to secure a peaceful resolution to the conflict.

In terms of peacemaking, the Tonkin Gulf incidents at the beginning of August, 1964, severely reduced BACON's chances of success. The American and North Vietnamese positions would now only harden. Pearson, Martin, and Seaborn were relieved by the limited nature of the U.S. retaliatory bombing—paradoxically, as they believed the reprisal also added credibility to the American threat Seaborn would convey on his next visit to Hanoi. The Canadians hoped the likelihood for a more flexible diplomacy would increase in this atmosphere.[50] Seaborn, who was scheduled to visit Hanoi with the ICC on August 10, went so far as to tell Sullivan that he was "personally delighted" by the bombing raids.[51] Rusk personally briefed Pearson and Martin on the raids, which also helped reassure Ottawa.[52] However, Seaborn's new instructions dispelled any hopes that Washington was interested in using BACON as a means to search for a diplomatic solution to the conflict. Aside from expressing bewilderment at the DRV's provocation and reiterating the same general points from the first mission, the Johnson administration wanted Seaborn to state that the reprisal raids "add credibility" to American statements of resolve; that the Tonkin Gulf resolution, passed by Congress to support LBJ's policy in Vietnam, demonstrated American "unity and determination"; and that "If the DRV persists in its present course, it can expect to continue to suffer the consequences."[53] The new message thus differed little from the old one.

Seaborn traveled to Hanoi on August 10 with the intention of meeting with either Ho Chi Minh or Gen. Vo Nguyen Giap—hopefully both. By the time he left the DRV capital four days later, only Pham Van Dong had agreed to see him—and even that meeting did not come about until the last minute. While Seaborn talked, he noticed that Pham, "who usually maintains [an] equable and even affable exterior . . . was becoming very angry indeed." Seaborn said that he regretted playing the nasty and thankless role of emissary, but that his main purpose was to deliver faithfully the new American message. "Apparently controlling himself with difficulty," an emotional Pham replied that "even to deliver such a message to a PM [Prime Minister] was not very polite, that the message did not merit being listened to and that he would not think to reply to 'these lies.'" After he calmed down, Pham responded officially by providing a mirror image of the American message: the DRV was a victim of foreign aggression; the DRV wished for peace, but the U.S. bombing raids made achieving it more difficult; and the North Vietnamese people's determination would not wane. Moreover, by additionally stressing the inevitable assistance the DRV would receive from other communist countries, and the geographical and military differences between Vietnam and Korea, Pham introduced new points that, like the tautological American messages, served only to reinforce and harden the DRV's position. Nevertheless, Pham did provide some cause for optimism. First, he closed his remarks by requesting that the ICC make a renewed effort "to stabilize [the] situation and seek [a] solution based on [the 1954] Geneva Agreement." This was an important new development, for it appeared to mean the North would temporarily accept two Vietnams, with reunification to follow in the future. Second, Pham apologized to Seaborn "for [the] harsh words he had spoken." When Seaborn asked him if the DRV found the BACON initiative to be useful, Pham "replied without hesitation and with apparent sincerity that he did indeed find it useful and he wanted [the] channel to be kept open."54

Seaborn came away from his second mission unsure of what it had accomplished. Pessimistically, the DRV's stubborn determination revealed nothing new. "I have not compared notes with my Polish and Indian colleagues as to what Pham Van Dong said to them," Seaborn informed Cadieux, "but I doubt whether it varied substantially from his remarks to me."55 Despite the reference to the ICC using the Geneva formula as a basis for peace, Seaborn perceived no signs that Hanoi would yield. "Pham Van Dong gave no indication of being worried by [the] firmness of [the] USA message I delivered," Seaborn reported. "I think [Pham] is genuinely convinced that things are bound to go his way in Indochina and that there is therefore no need to seek compromises."56 Optimistically, however, Pham's willingness to keep the BACON channel open encouraged Seaborn, who told Sullivan of his willingness "to bear US messages, no matter how unpleasant they may be."57 Pearson and Martin also wanted to keep the channel open "in the hope that Washington or Hanoi might communicate something that would help negotiations."58 American officials, however, were less interested in maintaining their Canadian link to Hanoi. Seaborn had, after all, fulfilled the objective of his missions: the DRV had been warned, consistently and accurately, of the probable consequences of continuing the struggle in the South. Seaborn had delivered the U.S. ultimatum and had vaguely hinted at material inducements if the DRV halted the insurgency. Thus, the North Vietnamese had been offered a clear choice between the stick and the carrot. Their decision to bear the brunt of the stick seemed to be categorical. Even so, the declining American interest in the BACON initiative dismayed Canadian officials. Seaborn typified the gloomy mood. "How important do the Americans consider my messenger role, either now or for possible future use?" he asked a colleague. "Can we persuade them to give an honest, not just a polite answer?"[59]

Although Seaborn traveled between Saigon and Hanoi several more times over the next year, he did not undertake any additional missions on behalf of the United States. Throughout the fall of 1964, the DEA continually pestered its embassy in Washington to sound out the State Department about another Seaborn mission, but the Americans showed no interest.[60] Nonetheless, Ottawa still hoped to maintain the initiative for as long as possible. "I am sure you will agree," Cadieux wrote Martin in October, "that the channel is a potentially useful one and that we should take no action which might jeopardize its effective functioning in the future."[61] The Johnson administration, however, did not share Ottawa's view. When Ritchie probed to see whether "Seaborn should take [a] line implying that [the] USA would be interested in eliciting propositions from [the] DRVN," William Bundy answered on behalf of his administration "in [the] emphatic negative."[62] Based on this response, Martin and Seaborn agreed not to ask the North Vietnamese for a meeting with Pham Van Dong or any other high-ranking DRV official.[63] Seaborn repeated virtually identical American messages to lower-echelon DRV officials in March, 1965, and to Foreign Minister Nguyen Duy Trinh in June, but with little impact and no effect.[64] The Canadians were loathe to admit it, but the BACON initiative had been dead, rather than dormant, since August, 1964.

The SMALLBRIDGE Peace Initiative

Seaborn's BACON initiative, which the Canadians generally regarded as a failure, was the primary turning point in Ottawa's transition from backing the United States to seeking peace in Vietnam. Such efforts proved to be in vain, however, when both antagonists escalated the war in February, 1965—the same time that Canada was attempting to stave it off. In April, Pearson delivered a speech at Temple University calling for a unilateral halt to U.S.

bombing in Vietnam, which merely ensured that Canadian concerns about the conflict would fall on deaf ears. The failure of a thirty-seven-day bombing pause over the Christmas holiday, for which Ottawa had pressed vigorously, exacerbated the trend. Nonetheless, partly in an attempt to accumulate political capital for a future run for the leadership of the Liberal Party and partly in keeping with his own foreign policy convictions, Paul Martin decided to try once again for a diplomatic solution. With the twin failures of the Seaborn missions and the Temple speech fresh in his mind, Pearson disavowed the project long before it came to fruition.[65] Martin decided to pursue direct communication with the North Vietnamese of a kind similar to that practiced by Seaborn in 1964. This time, however, Martin, rather than the State Department, would coordinate the process and dictate the message. Martin chose an imperfect messenger for the project, which was given the modest code name "SMALLBRIDGE." Born in China to Lutheran missionary parents, Chester Ronning was renowned as the DEA's foremost Sinologist. However, as a prominent socialist and supporter of the Chinese communists, he was an equally renowned critic of U.S. foreign policy.[66]

As Martin conceived it, Ronning's mission would have up to three destinations—Hanoi and Beijing, and possibly Saigon—but only one purpose. Using SMALLBRIDGE as a response to a January 24 letter from Ho Chi Minh to Pearson, Martin envisioned that Ronning's sole objective would be merely "to sound out attitudes in the two capitals with respect to a settlement of the present conflict." In offering this rationale in a memo to Pearson, the minister for external affairs was being somewhat disingenuous: Ronning was expected to prod, rather than just "sound out" Hanoi and Beijing on negotiations. Martin justified the mission by emphasizing that Washington had always encouraged Ottawa "to help in whatever way [we] can to move the Vietnam problem from the battlefield to the conference table." Contrary to American suspicions, Ronning would not broach the thorny topic of U.S. or UN recognition of the People's Republic of China (PRC).[67] Rather, Martin hoped that the Chinese would tell Ronning about their relations with both the DRV and the NLF, and articulate their position on negotiations or the reconvening of the Geneva conference. Under the dubious assumption that Beijing probably shared Ottawa's goal, Ronning was also to expound the official Canadian position regarding Vietnam: "The Canadian Government sees the promotion of political stability and economic development in [Vietnam] as the primary objectives of its policy."[68] Although he would receive some direction from the State Department, Ronning would not carry any American messages to Hanoi. In this sense, SMALLBRIDGE was not to be a reincarnation of its predecessor, BACON.[69]

The Johnson administration, unsurprisingly, was not thrilled with the Ronning initiative. However, because of the adverse publicity that would inevitably follow any spurned peace initiative, U.S. officials also believed they had no choice but to support SMALLBRIDGE. "Despite our private misgivings as to [Ronning's] personal views," William Bundy explained to the American representatives in Saigon, Hong Kong, and Ottawa, "we have naturally had to say we would have no objection to such a visit and indeed could only welcome any constructive initiative."[70] Rusk was more blunt in providing guidelines to the embassy in Saigon. "If you need to say anything to the South Vietnamese about the Ronning trip," Rusk cabled Lodge, who had returned for a second tour as ambassador the previous August, "you can tell them that he is on no mission for us . . . and that his visit should be considered along with such efforts as have been made by many individuals to have a go at Hanoi. Quite frankly, I attach no importance to his trip and expect nothing out of it."[71] Martin flew to Washington in mid-February to assuage the State Department's concerns. Rusk, who feared that Ronning might disabuse Hanoi of the notion that America's determination had not weakened, told Martin that Ronning should bear in mind that the United States would not shrink from further escalation. "The prospect of greater and sustained losses," Rusk told Martin, "was bound to influence the decision in Hanoi as to negotiations."[72]

Despite positive signals from the North Vietnamese, the mission did not begin auspiciously. Citing Canadian support for U.S. policy in East and Southeast Asia, the Chinese bluntly and unexpectedly denied Ronning permission to enter the country.[73] Beijing undoubtedly did not wish to entertain prominent western visitors while much of China was succumbing to the frenzy and turmoil of the Cultural Revolution, but such explanations generally escaped the attention of the DEA. Instead of deterring the Canadians, the Chinese refusal to admit Ronning reinforced Martin's growing inclination to treat mediation of the conflict as a bilateral affair between the United States and North Vietnam.[74] The DRV's willingness, even eagerness, to discuss matters with Ronning seemed to confirm this. Ronning arrived in Hanoi on March 7 and met with Pham Van Dong three days later. The DRV leadership, including the prime minister, repeated the mixed message they had provided Moore a month before. Using the same alternation of expressions of inexhaustible determination and a conditional willingness to enter into negotiations that he had presented to Seaborn, Pham explained that the pace of American military intervention would determine the DRV's position. On one hand, the North Vietnamese leader boasted "that the greater the escalation of USA troops, the greater would be the ultimate victory." On the other hand, Pham assured Ronning that Hanoi would enter into negotiations if all U.S. military activity north of the 17th Parallel ceased beforehand.[75] Ronning recalled that he "could scarcely believe my ears" at Pham's willingness to negotiate based only on the halt of military activity against the DRV itself. This seemingly new offer appeared tacitly to abandon Hanoi's perpetual insistence—expressed most famously in the "Four Points" issued in April, 1965—on separate representation of the NLF either in negotiations or in a future South Vietnamese government. "This was," Ronning excitedly realized, "too good to be true."[76]

Unfortunately for Canadian diplomacy and the people of both Vietnams, Pham's offer was indeed too good to be true. Canadian reaction was predictably optimistic but prematurely jubilant. Victor Moore, Seaborn's successor as ICC commissioner, was especially enthusiastic. Ronning's "performance was brilliant," he reported to Ottawa in an effort to promote a future installment of SMALLBRIDGE, even if it rendered his own role as commissioner superfluous. "What we have is an indication that [the] DRVN wish to talk . . . and that they have come up with an offer, albeit tenuous."[77] Martin agreed, believing the mission's results to have great promise. Klaus Goldschlag and W. Thomas Delworth, DEA officials who assisted Martin and Cadieux in coordinating the SMALLBRIDGE initiative from Ottawa, were cautiously optimistic.[78] The Canadians intended to present Ronning's discussion with Pham Van Dong—with a dual emphasis on DRV determination and its willingness to enter into talks—as a tentative first step on the road to a peaceful settlement.[79] The Johnson administration, however, viewed SMALLBRIDGE's results very differently.

After returning to Ottawa, Ronning accompanied Ritchie to Washington to discuss the SMALLBRIDGE initiative with William Bundy. Ronning did not elide details of the polemical attacks on the U.S. position, particularly from Foreign Minister Trinh and Ha Van Lau, with which he had been greeted in Hanoi. North Vietnamese officials had also impressed upon Ronning their relentless sense of determination and belief in ultimate victory. Pham's offer of "talks," but not formal negotiations, if the United States stopped all of its military activity against the DRV did not convince the Americans. Bundy pressed Ronning on this point: Did Pham include U.S. and South Vietnamese military activity against the NLF below the 17th Parallel? In return for "talks," would the cessation of military activity against the North imply an acceptance of the DRV's Four Points? Ronning replied that the prime minister had "started to hedge" on these questions, but he nonetheless made it clear that Ronning was "to carry away [to Washington the] impression that [a] cessation of bombing was the only prerequisite; [the] Four Points would apparently be [a] question for discussion in [a] conference."[80] Bundy was mostly noncommittal with the Canadians, but he made it clear that he did not agree with Ronning's basic interpretation. In a brief flash of the cynicism with which the entire administration viewed SMALLBRIDGE, Bundy "observed that the Hanoi ploy was clever; since the bombing question had in the past . . . been linked publicly with the '4 points,' acceptance of the DRV offer implied acceptance of the '4 points.'"[81]

Bundy's reaction revealed the near-unanimous feeling among U.S. officials that Pham Van Dong had told Ronning nothing new. Lodge, who had taken such an intensive interest in the BACON initiative during his previous stint as ambassador, did not even see Ronning after his return from Hanoi. Nor did he discuss the mission's key details with Moore. Lodge only wanted the Canadians' impressions of the psychological and material damage in Hanoi caused by American bombing.[82] Pham's ambiguity; his failure to provide Ronning, as promised, with the offer for talks on paper; and the fact that only Ronning was in a position to decipher the DRV prime minister's true meaning rendered the initiative extremely problematic to Washington. As one State Department official noted to Bundy, "We could hardly respond positively on this; we could, at best, only seek further information."[83] Others believed that Hanoi's ideological rhetoric and Pham Van Dong's seemingly deliberate evasiveness proved definitively that the DRV was not interested in pursuing a diplomatic settlement. "The hardest information we have gotten from Hanoi in some time is contained" in the results of the Ronning mission, NSC executive secretary Bromley K. Smith reported to Johnson. "His report to Prime Minister Pearson will be helpful in destroying illusions still held by some in Ottawa."[84] According to Defense Secretary Robert McNamara, Johnson had, "much to his great annoyance," already humored Ottawa by consenting to the Ronning mission, and he would certainly not embark on another unconditional bombing pause without a firm guarantee of reciprocal concessions by Hanoi.[85]

In retrospect, it is difficult to fault either the Canadians' enthusiasm and hopefulness or the Americans' caution and wariness. Since 1961, Ottawa had watched its closest ally become embroiled in a grisly and increasingly ferocious war in a region of apparently peripheral interest. It is thus unsurprising that Ottawa reacted eagerly to the SMALLBRIDGE initiative's initially promising results. Conversely, the Johnson administration had just endured intense domestic and international criticism—both for being too weak and too inflexible—for the failed 1965 bombing pauses. The United States also sought a way out of the conflict short of a much wider war. However, after nearly two decades of commitment, it was not about to relinquish its main goal of a stable, noncommunist South Vietnam. It is thus hard to imagine the circumstances under which LBJ would accept Pham's vague promise only to talk.

American reluctance stemmed mainly from deep skepticism in Washington that Ronning had actually secured a breakthrough. The State Department waited a month without consulting Ottawa, which infuriated Martin, who wanted Ronning to return immediately to Hanoi.[86] With Moore reporting from Saigon that "it would be embarrassing to return to Hanoi without having something to convey" from the United States,[87] and still having received no word from Washington, Martin telephoned Bundy on April 22 to insist that, if they had something in mind, it was imperative for the Americans to provide Ronning with a response. The Canadians "attached [the] greatest importance to [the] channel which had been opened up by Ronning," the minister reminded Bundy. "In these circumstances it [is] most important that there should be some response to what Ronning had brought back from Hanoi."[88] Martin's fear was closer to the truth than he had imagined. Pham's offer of "talks" was indeed not being considered very seriously in Washington. Nonetheless, despite confessing "We still do not see much in it," Bundy was convinced America's relations with its northern ally were too important not to mollify the Canadians.[89]

He hastily prepared a memo with a new set of instructions for Ronning's next mission to Hanoi. The new instructions, however, did not differ substantially from previous guidelines and did not react favorably to Pham's hint of "talks." The memo reminded Ottawa that during the recent thirty-seven-day Christmas bombing pause, the Johnson administration had established its own contact with the DRV through the U.S. ambassador to Rangoon, Henry A. Byroade, which the North Vietnamese had allowed to lapse. Hanoi's refusal to reciprocate American restraint during the bombing pause was also cited as a reason not to respond positively to the ephemeral signal transmitted via Ronning. "Against this background," the memo continued, the United States "is unable to evaluate the message conveyed to Mr. Ronning as indicating any real 'give' in Hanoi's position. . . . It seems most probable that [the hint at 'talks' for U.S. de-escalation] was still intended to be linked with acceptance of the 'four points,'" although Bundy also admitted "a contrary interpretation is conceivable." Ronning was instructed only to clarify Hanoi's offer, if indeed an offer had been forwarded, to convey the U.S. position that a bombing stoppage would have to be reciprocated by the DRV, and to suggest to Hanoi that the contact with Byroade was a more fruitful method of communicating with the administration.[90]

Working within severely limited constraints, Bundy and the State Department had little choice other than to downplay SMALLBRIDGE's potential. The failure of the previous bombing pauses to produce any tangible progress ensured that an extremely high standard would have to be met before the initiation of a future bombing halt. The Johnson administration had been planning for months to expand air strikes against targets producing petroleum, oil, and lubricants (POL). Ronning's mission in June caused a slight delay in the implementation of the new bombing program.[91] If he found no radical softening in the DRV position, the POL strikes would be launched. The North Vietnamese, who were greatly offended by a May speech in which Pearson had called for reciprocal, simultaneous concessions, did not provide much help. In passing a strongly worded aide-mémoire to the Canadian ICC permanent representative in Hanoi to prepare for Ronning's next visit, the DRV seemed only to confirm Washington's anxieties. North Vietnam "once again affirms that if the USA Government really desires a peaceful settlement it must recognize the Four-Point stand of the DRVN Government, [and] prove this by actual deeds," the paper declared. "[I]t must announce a definitive and unconditional end to its air raids and all other acts of war against the [DRVN]. Only then will it be possible to envisage a political solution to the Vietnam problem."[92] The apparent progress from March had evaporated.

It thus was "with a heavy heart" that Ronning returned to Hanoi on June 14.[93] The Agence France-Presse had just broken the story of the second SMALLBRIDGE mission, which upset both the Americans, who suspected the DRV of leaking the story to sabotage the mission, and the North Vietnamese, who believed it to be futile without the cover of secrecy.[94] Under these circumstances, neither Ho Chi Minh nor Pham Van Dong—both rumored to be out of the country—would grant Ronning an audience. Instead, Vice Foreign Minister Nguyen Co Thach and Vice Prime Minister Nguyen Duy Trinh (who also served as foreign minister) met with Ronning, only to reiterate the now-familiar litany of charges against the United States. Ronning repeated the American position that only a reciprocal de-escalation of military activity could lead to negotiations. As expected, Thach rejected this unequivocally and replied by denouncing the American position as one of "maintaining the logic and view of pirates" and emphasizing that "the Americans instead will suffer a bitter defeat, and not only a defeat in Vietnam but before the whole world." In the face of a greater U.S. commitment, Thach added confidently, the American "defeat will be correspondingly greater."[95] The next day, Trinh repeated his deputy's words. By demanding a reward of negotiations merely for ceasing their own "bad aggression," said Trinh, the Americans were expressing "an attitude which we deem is lacking in goodwill." After thanking the Canadians for their continuing efforts, he said the lack of movement in the U.S. position compelled him to add, "we do not see clearly the usefulness of your desire to show your goodwill." Trinh also wanted Ronning to note that the Americans "just now . . . are nurturing the illusion that they can bring us to our knees." It would be a mistake, he stressed, for the Johnson administration to assume that the continued bombing of the DRV would result in an American victory.[96]

Once again, Ottawa and Washington came to sharply contrasting conclusions on the results of the second Ronning mission. Canadian officials believed, as they had in March, that the Johnson administration had only to halt the bombing unilaterally for talks—which, the Canadians believed, would lead inevitably to productive negotiations—to commence. Moore, who had accompanied Ronning on both visits, revealed as much upon returning to Saigon. "On the day we arrived in Hanoi," the Canadian commissioner reported to the DEA, "it was quite evident . . . that their expectations were high and that they anticipated something of substance." Meanwhile, the North Vietnamese "disappointment was so great, after analyzing our interpretation of the American response," that instead of the amicable Pham Van Dong, "the leadership chose the rigid, doctrinaire [Trinh] to deliver the DRVN reply with suitable bitterness appropriate to him."[97] Ottawa took encouragement, though, from the fact that Hanoi still expressed a keen interest in keeping the SMALLBRIDGE channel open.[98] Even Walt Rostow, a noted hawk who had recently succeeded McGeorge Bundy as national security adviser, thought this interpretation might be correct. "While Hanoi is obviously not prepared to negotiate seriously now," he informed LBJ, "they quite clearly left the door open for the future."[99]

An uneasy and unsettling suspicion grew among Canadian officials that the Americans were not only uninterested in diplomatic solutions, but that they had deliberately sabotaged the June visit. Despite repeated Canadian urgings that secrecy was essential for the mission's success, in early June American officials in Warsaw told representatives from the PRC about their proposal for reciprocal de-escalation. The U.S. position subsequently appeared in the pages of the *New York Times* on June 3, which the Canadians found highly suspect.[100] Referring to the convoluted "peace offensive" that had accompanied the Christmas bombing pause, Moore wrote to Ottawa that "The Americans appear to be putting Hanoi behind the eight-ball again," which would merely repeat "the folly of driving Hanoi into a corner." Like his counterparts in Ottawa, Moore feared the advance publicity of the American position was designed to place the responsibility for the Ronning mission's failure squarely on Hanoi. "I remain convinced," Moore continued, "that such pressure will be counter-productive. Rather, if these tactics raise doubts in even my mind about American sincerity, they will surely convince DRVN leaders of the correctness of their earlier suspicions. We can therefore expect them to withdraw into their corner and foolishly, but doggedly and stubbornly, to continue the war."[101] Moore remonstrated with Lodge on this point: "I hope you Americans are not escalating to a new peace offensive. One thing the Hanoi regime cannot do is to look as though they were giving in to public pressure."[102] Concomitant with this was a suspicion that the Ronning mission's failure had been seized upon to justify further American escalatory measures. Both Martin and Ronning later claimed to have discerned this ulterior American motive.[103] Or, as Pearson put it at the time: "It would be a sad ending to our initiative in this matter if we became merely an instrument of US propaganda or for putting the DRVN on the spot."[104]

Because the Johnson administration had decided long before the second Ronning mission to proceed with the expanded POL air strikes, the Canadian charges seem to be unfounded. Nonetheless, as Rusk outlined to McNamara, American bombs could be more easily defended in the event Ronning returned to Ottawa empty-handed: "If he has a negative report, as we expect, that provides a firmer base for the action we contemplate and would make a difference to people like [British prime minister Harold] Wilson and Pearson."[105] As Rusk's thoughts make clear, American officials did not anticipate any improvement in the DRV's position. Moreover, unlike the Canadians, they did not think it unreasonable to refuse to modify their existing stance on reciprocal de-escalation. Whereas Ottawa detected some room for maneuver in Hanoi's statements, Washington sensed nothing new or encouraging.[106] Finally, American officials may have erroneously gleaned from the Canadians' observations that the U.S. bombing was taking a toll, materially and psychologically, on North Vietnam and that additional air strikes would turn the tide of war in favor of the United States and South Vietnam. Ironically, in trying to nudge the United States toward talks with the DRV, Moore inadvertently conveyed precisely this impression to Lodge.[107] Rostow, in turn, advised LBJ that Moore's report provided "Evidence that the bombing hurts the North—but not enough."[108]

The second and final Ronning mission, then, proved to be as inconclusive as the first. No progress had been achieved on the crucial question of what would happen after another pause in the American air strikes. It was palpably clear that neither the United States nor the Democratic Republic of Vietnam wished to engage in substantive negotiations. As in most wars, both sides were content to let military developments determine a future political scenario, a conclusion that dismayed the Canadians but did not surprise either the Americans or the North Vietnamese. The SMALLBRIDGE peace initiative, designed by Canadian officials to be a proactive attempt to spur negotiations, was therefore no more successful than its more passive predecessor, BACON. Like the 1964 Seaborn missions, the 1966 Ronning missions brought about the polar opposite of what they intended to achieve: instead of bringing the belligerents to the negotiating table, the missions' failures convinced the Americans of the necessity of expanding the war and the North Vietnamese of the necessity of holding fast to their position. In the end, like Lester Pearson and Blair Seaborn before them, Paul Martin and Chester Ronning found themselves completely unable to influence either the course of the Vietnam War or the conduct of their American ally.

Notes

1. On the anti-American tradition in Canada, see J. L. Granatstein, *Yankee Go Home? Canadians and Anti-Americanism* (Toronto: HarperCollins, 1996), esp. pp. 1–11. See also J. L. Granatstein and Norman Hillmer, *For Better or For Worse: Canada and the United States to 1990* (Toronto: Copp Clark Pitman, 1991). Particularly good on the very close Canadian-American relationship are Robert Bothwell, *Canada and the United States: The Politics of Partnership* (Toronto: University of Toronto Press, 1992); and idem., *The Big Chill: Canada and the Cold War* (Toronto: Irwin, 1998). On the fundamental differences, see Lawrence Martin, *The Presidents and the Prime Ministers—Washington and Ottawa Face to Face: The Myth of Bilateral Bliss, 1867–1982* (Toronto: Doubleday Canada, 1982); and Seymour Martin Lipset, *Continental Divide: The Values and Institutions of the United States and Canada* (New York: Routledge, 1990).

2. Lester B. Pearson, *Words and Occasions* (Toronto: University of Toronto Press, 1970), p. 32.

3. See Douglas A. Ross, *In the Interests of Peace: Canada and Vietnam, 1954–1973* (Toronto: University of Toronto Press, 1984), pp. 3–34, 243–81; and Andrew Preston, "Balancing War and Peace: Canadian Diplomacy and the Vietnam War, 1961–1965," *Diplomatic History* 27 (Jan., 2003): 73–111.

4. Peter Stursberg, *Lester Pearson and the American Dilemma* (Toronto: Doubleday Canada, 1980), p. 259.

5. Lyndon Baines Johnson, *The Vantage Point: Perspectives of the Presidency, 1963–1969* (New York: Holt, Reinhart, and Winston, 1971), p. 67.

6. George Ball Interview, July 8, 1971, Oral History Collection, Lyndon B. Johnson Library, Austin, Tex. (hereafter LBJL), p. 39.

7. Michael V. Forrestal, May 2, 1962, "Memo of the President's Instructions at the Laos/Vietnam Briefing," National Security File, Meetings and Memoranda, Staff Memos (Forrestal) Box 320, John Fitzgerald Kennedy Library, Boston, Mass.

8. Paper, Henry Cabot Lodge, "Toward the Neutralization of North Viet-Nam," Oct. 30, 1963, *Foreign Relations of the United States* (*FRUS*), *1961–1963*, vol. 4, *Vietnam, August–December 1963* (Washington, D.C.: GPO, 1991), pp. 657–58; sent to W. Averell Harriman under cover memo, Dec. 3, 1963, ibid., p. 656. Lodge also discussed the concept with Roger Hilsman, the assistant secretary of state for Far Eastern Affairs, and, very briefly, in a meeting with President Johnson shortly after the Kennedy assassination. See memo of conversation, Lodge and Roger Hilsman, Nov. 24, 1963, ibid., pp. 633–34; and memo for the record, drafted by John A. McCone, Nov. 24, 1963, ibid., p. 635.

9. David Kaiser, *American Tragedy: Kennedy, Johnson, and the Origins of the Vietnam War* (Cambridge, Mass.: Harvard University Press, 2000), pp. 295–303, 307–308, 315–18, 322–26.

10. Lodge to Lyndon B. Johnson, Feb. 20, 1964, message, *FRUS, 1964–1968,* vol. 1, *Vietnam, 1964* (Washington, D.C.: GPO, 1992), pp. 94–95.

11. Lodge to Harriman, Dec. 3, 1963, *FRUS, 1961–1963,* p. 4:656. Along with the French ambassador, Roger Lalouette, and the Indian chairman of the ICC, Ram Goburdhun, D'Orlandi had tried a similar gambit before the coup against Diem. Their plan, which never became a reality, was to use Maneli as an intermediary between Diem's brother, Ngo Dinh Nhu, and Hanoi. See Mieczyslaw Maneli, *War of the Vanquished* (New York: Harper and Row, 1971), pp. 117–18. Although Lodge and D'Orlandi were friendly, the Italian's links to the Diem regime doubtless troubled Lodge. The U.S. ambassador had also strenuously objected to French diplomatic efforts simultaneously to secure the neutralization of Indochina and an American military withdrawal from Vietnam, so D'Orlandi's ties to Lalouette would have sown doubt as to the Italian's capacity to deliver faithfully an American threat. On Lodge's antipathy to the French plan, see Anne E. Blair, *Lodge in Vietnam: A Patriot Abroad* (New Haven, Conn.: Yale University Press, 1995), pp. 91–93, 105–106.

12. J. M. Dunn, Apr. 22, 1964, notes of meeting, National Security File (NSF), Country File–Vietnam (CF-VN), vol. 9, Box 4, LBJL; William P. Bundy, Apr. 27, 1964, memorandum for the record, subject: "Discussion of Possible Extended Action in Relation to Vietnam," NSF, CF-VN, vol. 7, Box 3, LBJL. Both documents pertain to a meeting at the U.S. embassy in Saigon held on April 19.

13. William Bundy, "Discussion."

14. McGeorge Bundy to Johnson, Apr. 21, 1964, memorandum, *FRUS, 1964–1968,* p. 1:253.

15. See Preston, "Balancing War and Peace."

16. Rusk to Lodge, May 1, 1964, telegram 1821, *FRUS, 1964–1968,* pp. 1:281–82. For the Seaborn missions and their context within Canadian diplomacy toward the Vietnam War, see Preston, "Balancing War and Peace," 94–102.

17. Lodge, "Toward the Neutralization," 4:657–58.

18. Quoted in Fredrik Logevall, *Choosing War: The Lost Chance for Peace and the Escalation of War in Vietnam* (Berkeley: University of California Press, 1999), p. 155.

19. Lodge to Rusk, May 4, 1964, telegram 2110, NSF, CF-VN, vol. 8, Box 4, LBJL.

20. McGeorge Bundy to Johnson, May 22, 1964, memorandum, *FRUS, 1964–1968,* p. 1:350.

21. Sullivan, May 11, 1964, memorandum of conversation, NSF, CF-VN, vol. 9, Box 4, LBJL.

22. Johnson to Lodge, May 14, 1964, telegram 1942, ibid.

23. Rusk to Lodge, May 22, 1964, telegram 2049, *FRUS, 1964–1968,* p. 1:348.

24. Lodge to Rusk, May 25, 1964, telegram 2305, NSF, CF-VN, vol. 10, Box 5, LBJL.

25. Lodge to Rusk, May 26, 1964, telegram 2318, *FRUS, 1964–1968,* p. 1:349 n 4.

26. Record of Conversation: "Visit of Messrs Sullivan and Cooper to the Department," May 28, 1964, drafted June 3, 1964, vol. 10113, File 20–22-VIET.S-2–1, Record Group 25, Records of the Department of External Affairs (hereafter RG 25), National Archives of Canada, Ottawa, Ont. (hereafter NAC). On Canada's policy of limiting American war aims and methods in the Korean War, which was strikingly similar to Ottawa's diplomacy regarding Vietnam, see Denis Stairs, *The Diplomacy of Constraint: Canada, the Korean War, and the United States* (Toronto: University of Toronto Press, 1974).

27. John English, *The Life of Lester Pearson,* vol. 2, *The Worldly Years, 1949–1972* (Toronto: Knopf Canada, 1992), p. 359. See also Douglas A. Ross, "Canada, Peacemaking, and the Vietnam War: Where Did Ottawa Go Wrong?" in *The Vietnam War as History,* ed. Elizabeth Jane Errington and B. J. C. McKercher (New York: Praeger, 1990), p. 151.

28. Summary Record of Conversation between the Minister and Mr. Sullivan, May 29, 1964, drafted June 3, 1964, vol. 10113, File 20–22-VIET.S-2–1, RG 25, NAC.

29. Paul Martin, *A Very Public Life,* vol. 2, *So Many Worlds* (Toronto: Deneau, 1985), pp. 425, 428.

30. Sullivan to Rusk, May 23, 1963, memorandum, *FRUS, 1964–1968,* p. 1:351.

31. Sullivan, "Talking Paper for Canadians," ibid., pp. 1:352–53.

32. Record of Conversation: "Visit of Messrs Sullivan and Cooper."

33. The nasty and very personal rivalry between Prime Minister Pearson and Conservative leader John G. Diefenbaker personified and drove the animosity between the Liberals and Conservatives throughout the 1960s. On the extremely acrimonious Pearson-Diefenbaker relationship, see English, *Life of Lester Pearson,* pp. 2:200–203, 213–18, 235–66, 291–92, 390; and Denis Smith, *Rogue Tory: The Life and Legend of John G. Diefenbaker* (Toronto: Macfarlane, Walter, and Ross, 1995), pp. 274–98, 407–10, 500–48.

34. Summary Record of Conversation.

35. Martin, *Very Public Life,* p. 2:425.

36. Ball to Lodge, May 30, 1964, telegram 2133, in *The Secret Diplomacy of the Vietnam War: The Negotiating Volumes of the Pentagon Papers,* ed. George C. Herring (Austin: University of Texas Press, 1983), p. 20.

37. "Instructions for McGeorge Bundy's Conversation with Prime Minister Pearson," May 28, 1964, NSF, CF/Canada, Box 165, LBJL.

38. McGeorge Bundy, May 28, 1964, memorandum for the record, *FRUS, 1964–1968,* pp. 1:394–95.

39. Robinson, May 29, 1964, memorandum for the record, vol. 3092, File 29–39–1-2-A, RG 25, NAC.

40. Pearson to Seaborn, May 30, 1964, English trans., vol. 10113, File 20–22-VIET.S-2–1, ibid.

41. Seaborn to Smith, June 20, 1964, telegram 273, ibid.

42. Ibid. Another version of the conversation goes some way to clarify Pham's phraseology: "We want peaceful reunification, without military pressure. We want negotiation round a table. There must be sincere satisfaction with the arrangement for it to be viable. We are in no hurry. We are willing to talk; but we shall wait till SVN is ready." Quoted in Ross, *Interests of Peace,* p. 276.

43. Seaborn to Smith, June 22, 1964, telegram 282, vol. 10113, File 20–22-VIET.S-2–1, RG 25, NAC. Seaborn also met with lower-ranking but more ideologically strident DRV officials who subjected the Canadian "to [the] usual DRVN dissertation on sins of [the] USA and South Vietnam 'lackeys' as [the] root cause of all troubles in Vietnam and Laos" (Seaborn to DEA, June 23, 1964, telegram 286, vol. 10122, File 21–13-VIET-ICSC, pt. 1.2, ibid.).

44. Charles Ritchie to Smith, June 22, 1964, telegram 2250, vol. 10113, File 20–22-VIET.S-2–1, ibid. In early July, Sullivan personally told Seaborn that he "should not appear too eager" to undertake another mission to Hanoi (Telegram 81, Maxwell D. Taylor to Rusk, July 13, 1964, NSF, CF-VN, vol. 13, Box 6, LBJL).

45. Washington, D.C., to Smith, June 24, 1964, telegram 2278, vol. 10113, File 20-22-VIET.S-2-1, RG 25, NAC.

46. Taylor to Rusk, July 11, 1964, telegram 74, NSF, CF-VN, vol. 13, Box 6, LBJL.

47. Lodge to State Department, June 24, 1964, telegram 2567, *FRUS, 1964–1968,* pp. 1:525–26.

48. Marcel Cadieux to Martin, June 24, 1964, memorandum, vol. 10113, File 20-22-VIET.S-2-1, RG 25, NAC.

49. Smith to Seaborn, June 25, 1964, telegram Y-476, vol. 3092, File 29–39–1-2-A, ibid.

50. DEA to Washington, D.C., July 28, 1964, telegram Y-565, vol. 10113, File 20-22-VIET.S-2-1, ibid.; Ritchie to DEA, July 14, 1964, telegram 2527, ibid.; R. L. Rogers to Cadieux, July 31, 1964, memorandum, subject: "Viet Nam–U.S. Intentions," ibid. The oscil-

lating effect of various diplomatic initiatives on the credibility of American policy is examined in Wallace J. Thies, *When Governments Collide: Coercion and Diplomacy in the Vietnam Conflict, 1964–1968* (Berkeley: University of California Press, 1980), pp. 57, 264–65, 270–72, 378, 389.

51. Taylor to Rusk, August 6, 1964, telegram 326, NSF, CF-VN, vol. 15, Box 7, LBJL.

52. Greg Donaghy, "Minding the Minister: Pearson, Martin and American Policy in Asia, 1963–1967," in *Pearson: The Unlikely Gladiator,* ed., Norman Hillmer (Montreal and Kingston, Ont.: McGill-Queen's University Press, 1999), p. 134.

53. State Department to Ottawa, Aug. 8, 1964, telegram 169, *FRUS, 1964–1968,* pp. 1:651–53.

54. Seaborn to Smith, Aug. 15, 1964, telegram 419, vol. 10113, File 20-22-VIET.S-2-1, RG 25, NAC.

55. Seaborn to Cadieux, Aug. 18, 1964, letter no. 312, ibid.

56. Seaborn to Smith, telegram 426, Aug. 17, 1964, ibid.

57. Taylor to Rusk, Aug. 18, 1964, telegram 467, NSF, CF-VN, vol. 16, Box 7, LBJL.

58. Martin, *Very Public Life,* p. 430; English, *Life of Lester Pearson,* p. 2:359.

59. Seaborn to Rogers, Aug. 31, 1964, vol. 10113, File 20-22-VIET.S-2-1, RG 25, NAC.

60. See, e.g., DEA to Washington, D.C., Sept. 23, 1964, telegram Y-689, ibid.; Washington, D.C. to Smith, Oct. 2, 1964, telegram 3513, ibid.; Seaborn to Smith, Oct. 2, 1964, telegram 550, ibid.

61. Cadieux to Martin, Oct. 6, 1964, memorandum, subject: "Seaborn's Special Assignment in Vietnam," ibid.

62. Ritchie to DEA, Dec. 3, 1964, telegram 4190, ibid.

63. DEA to Seaborn, Dec. 4, 1964, telegram Y-883, ibid.; Seaborn to Smith, Dec. 18, 1964, telegram 773, ibid.

64. For the March trip to Hanoi, see Rusk to Ottawa, Feb. 27, 1965, telegram 942, in *Secret Diplomacy,* ed. Herring, pp. 39–40; Taylor to Rusk, Mar. 7, 1965, telegram 2880, ibid., pp. 41–42; William Bundy, Mar. 15, 1965, memorandum for the record, *FRUS, 1964–1968,* vol. 2, *Vietnam, January–June 1965* (Washington, D.C.: GPO, 1996), p. 2:444; and Logevall, *Choosing War,* pp. 366–67. For the June trip, see William Bundy to Ball, May 25, 1965, memorandum, *FRUS, 1964–1968,* pp. 2:689–90; Rusk to Saigon, May 27, 1965, telegram 2718, ibid., pp. 691–93; Taylor to Rusk, May 28, 1965, telegram 3927, in *Secret Diplomacy,* ed. Herring, p. 43; William Bundy to Rusk, June 5, 1965, memorandum, *FRUS, 1964–1968,* p. 2:728; Taylor to State Department, June 6, 1965, telegram 4083, ibid., p. 732; and Thies, *When Governments Collide,* pp. 98–99.

65. Walton Butterworth (Ottawa) to Rusk, Jan. 31, 1966, telegram 981, in *Secret Diplomacy,* ed. Herring, p. 171; English, *Life of Lester Pearson,* pp. 2:371–72; Donaghy, "Minding the Minister," p. 139; comments by Martin and William Bundy in Stursberg, *Lester Pearson,* pp. 272–73.

66. Brian Evans, "Ronning and Recognition: Years of Frustration," in *Reluctant Adversaries: Canada and the People's Republic of China, 1949–1970,* ed. Paul M. Evans and B. Michael Frolic (Toronto: University of Toronto Press, 1991), pp. 148–57; Andrew Preston, "Operation Smallbridge: Chester Ronning, the Second Indochina War, and the Challenge to the United States in Asia," *Pacific Historical Review* 72:3 (Aug., 2003), pp. 353–90. See also Ronning's own account in *A Memoir of China in Revolution: From the Boxer Rebellion to the People's Republic* (New York: Pantheon Books, 1974). Ronning, who was neither virulently nor completely anti-American, had many personal connections to the United States. For example, Ronning's parents came from Iowa, and he studied education at the University of Minnesota after World War I. Moreover, both of his sons-in-law were American: one daughter married a naval officer and the other married journalist Seymour Topping of the *New York Times.* Ronning's anti-

Americanism, for the most part, was confined to U.S. foreign policy, particularly toward East and Southeast Asia.

67. Martin to Pearson, Jan. 20, 1966, memorandum, subject: "Special Visits to Vietnam and China," vol. 9403, File 20-22-VIET.S-2-1-1, RG 25, NAC. The American suspicions are found in telegram 830, Rusk to Ottawa, Jan. 28, 1966, in *Secret Diplomacy*, ed. Herring, p. 171; and Butterworth to Rusk, Jan. 28, 1966, telegram 974, ibid.

68. "Instructions for SMALLBRIDGE, Vietnam: Talking Points for Peking," n.d., vol. 9403, File 20-22-VIET.S-2-1-1, RG 25, NAC.

69. Telegram Y-66, Cadieux to Ritchie, Jan. 27, 1966, ibid. The necessity of preserving secrecy stemmed from the failure of the Italian La Pira peace initiative, which Hanoi quickly abandoned after its details were leaked to the press. See *Secret Diplomacy*, ed. Herring, pp. 166, 834 n 4.

70. Rusk to Saigon, Feb. 4, 1966, telegram 2254, in *Secret Diplomacy*, ed. Herring, p. 172.

71. Rusk to Lodge, Feb. 25, 1966, telegram 2525, ibid., p. 176.

72. Cadieux to Far Eastern Division, Feb. 21, 1966, memorandum, subject: "Mr. Martin's Conversation with Dean Rusk on February 19, 1966," vol. 9403, File 20-22-VIET.S-2-1-1, RG 25, NAC.

73. John English, "Lester Pearson and China," in *Reluctant Adversaries,* ed. Evans and Frolic, p. 142.

74. Martin to Ronning, Hong Kong, Feb. 17, 1966, telegram Y-173, vol. 9403, File 20-22-VIET.S-2-1-1, RG 25, NAC. See also Martin, *Very Public Life,* p. 2:438.

75. Ronning, Saigon, to DEA, Mar. 11, 1966, telegram 184, vol. 9404, File 20-22-VIET.S-2-1-1, pt. 2, RG 25, NAC.

76. Ronning, *Memoir of China,* p. 265.

77. Moore to DEA, Mar. 12, 1966, telegram 188, vol. 9404, File 20-22-VIET.S-2-1-1, pt. 2, RG 25, NAC.

78. Ross, *Interests of Peace,* p. 287.

79. Klaus Goldschlag to Cadieux, Mar. 21, 1966, memorandum and attached talking points for Ronning, vol. 9404, File 20-22-VIET.S-2-1-1, pt. 2, RG 25, NAC.

80. Ritchie to DEA, Mar. 21, 1966, telegram 838, ibid.

81. Memorandum of conversation, Mar. 20, 1966, in *Secret Diplomacy*, ed. Herring, p. 183.

82. Moore to DEA, Mar. 17, 1966, telegram 209, vol. 9404, File 20-22-VIET.S-2-1-1, pt. 2, RG 25, NAC.

83. Harold Jacobson to William Bundy, Mar. 31, 1966, memorandum, in *Secret Diplomacy,* ed. Herring, p. 183.

84. Bromley K. Smith to Johnson, Mar. 16, 1966, memorandum, *FRUS, 1964–1968,* vol. 4, *Vietnam, 1966* (Washington, D.C.: GPO, 1998), p. 287. Smith wrote this in a covering memo for a report on Ronning's views by Oscar Vance Armstrong, the U.S. consul in Hong Kong, who had an opportunity to speak with Ronning while he was en route back to Canada. The Armstrong report, which does not mention Pham's offer of "talks" for a cessation of military action against the DRV, is found in ibid., pp. 4:288–90; and, with drafting information, in Oscar Vance Armstrong to Rusk, Mar. 15, 1966, telegram 1669, in *Secret Diplomacy,* ed. Herring, pp. 177–79.

85. Robert S. McNamara, with Brian VanDeMark, *In Retrospect: The Tragedy and Lessons of Vietnam* (New York: Vintage Books, 1996), pp. 247–48.

86. Ross, *Interests of Peace,* p. 288; Donaghy, "Minding the Minister," p. 141.

87. Moore to DEA, Apr. 7, 1966, telegram 282, vol. 9404, File 20-22-VIET.S-2-1-1, pt. 2, RG 25, NAC.

88. DEA to Ritchie, Apr. 22, 1966, telegram Y-288, ibid.

89. B. M. Moore, Apr. 22, 1966, memorandum for the record, in *Secret Diplomacy,* ed. Herring, p. 184; William Bundy to Rusk, Apr. 22, 1966, memorandum, in ibid., p. 184.

90. Memorandum to the Government of Canada, Apr. 26, 1966, in ibid., pp. 185–86. On the Rangoon contact, code-named PINTA, see ibid., pp. 116–58; and Thies, *When Governments Collide,* pp. 112–22.

91. See Rusk, Brussels to McNamara, June 8, 1966, telegram 87, in *Secret Diplomacy,* ed. Herring, p. 192; and Johnson's comments in summary notes of the 559th NSC meeting, June 17, 1966, *FRUS, 1964–1968,* p. 4:438.

92. Moore to DEA, May 24, 1966, telegram 412, vol. 9404, File 20-22-VIET.S-2-1-1, pt. 2, RG 25, NAC.

93. Ronning, *Memoir of China,* p. 267.

94. Moore to DEA, June 15, 1966, telegram 501, vol. 9404, File 20-22-VIET.S-2-1-1, pt. 3, RG 25, NAC; Goldschlag to Ritchie, June 17, 1966, telegram Y-441, ibid.; excerpt from a Reuters article, London, June 15, 1966, in *Secret Diplomacy,* ed. Herring, p. 195.

95. Moore to DEA, June 18, 1966, telegram 528, vol. 9404, File 20-22-VIET.S-2-1-1, pt. 3, RG 25, NAC.

96. Moore to DEA, June 19, 1966, telegram 527, ibid.

97. Moore to DEA, June 19, 1966, telegram 531, ibid.

98. Ibid.; DEA paper, "Talking Points to be Put to State Department Representative," June 20, 1966, ibid.; Walt W. Rostow to Johnson, June 20, 1966, memorandum, NSF, Memos to the President (MP), Walt W. Rostow Memos (WWRM), vol. 6, Box 8, LBJL.

99. Rostow to Johnson, June 21, 1966, memorandum, NSF, CF/Canada, Box 167, LBJL.

100. DEA to Martin and Cadieux, Brussels, June 6, 1966, telegram Y-405, vol. 9404, File 20-22-VIET.S-2-1-1, pt. 3, RG 25, NAC; Butterworth to Rusk, June 3, 1966, telegram, in *Secret Diplomacy,* ed. Herring, p. 191.

101. Moore to DEA, June 6, 1966, unnumbered telegram, vol. 9404, File 20-22-VIET.S-2-1-1, pt. 3, RG 25, NAC.

102. Lodge, unpublished Vietnam memoir, pt. 4, chap. 7, p. 2, Henry Cabot Lodge II Papers, pt. 8, reel 26, Massachusetts Historical Society, Boston, Mass.

103. Martin, *Very Public Life,* pp. 2:441–42; Ronning, *Memoir of China,* pp. 267–68; Stursberg, *Lester Pearson,* pp. 267–68, 280. Martin hinted to the U.S. embassy in Ottawa that he harbored this suspicion (Ottawa to State Department, June 20, 1966, telegram 1722, NSF, MP, WWRM, vol. 6, Box 8, LBJL.

104. Pearson quoted in Jacques Corbeil to Far Eastern Division, DEA, June 6, 1966, memorandum, vol. 9404, File 20-22-VIET.S-2-1-1, pt. 3, RG 25, NAC.

105. Rusk, Brussels, to McNamara, June 8, 1966, telegram 87, in *Secret Diplomacy,* ed. Herring, p. 192.

106. See, e.g., the American record of the administration's conversations with Martin and Ronning after the second mission in *Secret Diplomacy,* ed. Herring, pp. 197–206.

107. Lodge to Rusk, June 8, 1966, telegram 5379, NSF, CF-VN, Box 46, NODIS vol. 3 (B) Folder, LBJL. Moore, whose name is redacted in the LBJL copy of the telegram, is revealed as Lodge's source in the same, albeit heavily sanitized, telegram in *Secret Diplomacy,* ed. Herring, p. 192.

108. Rostow to Johnson, June 8, 1966, memorandum, NSF, CF-VN, Box 46, NODIS vol. 3 (B) Folder, LBJL.

"How Fuzzy Can One Be?"

The American Reaction to De Gaulle's Proposal for the
Neutralization of (South) Vietnam

CHARLES G. COGAN

THE TIMING of Pres. Charles de Gaulle's initiatives on China and Vietnam—beginning in the late summer of 1963, came shortly after the situation in Vietnam had begun to go badly, which the U.S. ambassador in Saigon, Henry Cabot Lodge, placed as of April, 1963.[1]

The year 1963 had not been an easy one in French-American relations. In spite of pressing blandishments on the part of Pres. John F. Kennedy, the general had refused France's adherence to the Limited Test Ban Treaty, signed on July 25, 1963. Furthermore, the French president—while having abstained from the talks that included the United States, Great Britain, and the Soviet Union—announced four days later, on July 29, 1963, that he intended to call for a conference of the four nuclear powers before the end of the year.[2]

Earlier, in his famous press conference on January 14, 1963, de Gaulle had at one and the same time rejected the Multilateral Force—in turning down an offer of Polaris missiles for France—and denied Britain entry into the Common Market. In trying to interpret this shocking development, which was followed a week later by the signing of the French-German Treaty of Friendship, a gesture President Kennedy clearly viewed as aimed at the United States,[3] the president told the National Security Council's Executive Committee (ExComm) on January 25, 1963: "We should look now at the possibility that de Gaulle had concluded that he would make a deal with the Russians, break up NATO, and push the U.S. out of Europe."[4] He instructed the group to start examining "the contingency of de Gaulle trying to run us out of Europe by means of a deal with the Russians . . . we ought to think now about how we can protect ourselves against actions which de Gaulle might take against us."[5]

All this was done secretly, of course. In the words of McGeorge Bundy, the national security adviser, "Kennedy had reached a conclusion not to pick fights with de Gaulle, and on the public record he was very careful [about this]."[6] Lyndon Johnson chose to follow this same dictum. Notwithstanding, de Gaulle had come to be regarded by the Kennedy administration as a puzzling and serious threat. In the ExComm's meeting on January 31, 1963, Kennedy observed that by signing the Polaris agreement with the British at Nassau in December, "We had narrowly averted a disaster which would have occurred had [Harold] MacMillan decided to join with de Gaulle in a nuclear arrangement. [The president] believed that MacMillan had not understood that de Gaulle was offering the British a French/British nuclear arrangement."[7]

At that same ExComm meeting, Kennedy concluded that de Gaulle apparently "does not want to associate with us."[8] The United States was manifestly uncertain as to how to deal with General de Gaulle. In November, 1963, the RAND Corporation circulated a monograph entitled, "Guesses About de Gaulle." This Defense Department–sponsored study was the work of the late Nathan Leites, a well-known writer in the field of international relations. Moreover, it seemed to reflect a growing apprehension in the United States concerning the French leader's ambitions. At that moment, France's weight was beginning to be felt seriously in Europe. The Algerian problem had been solved the previous year, France was the leading country in the European Economic Community, and the French-German alliance treaty was in force, although it had been watered down at America's urging by a preamble inserted into the treaty by the Bundestag in the spring of 1963.

"In the 1980's," the study begins, "de Gaulle perhaps believes, there will be three world capitals, each reigning over a world zone: Washington, Moscow, Beijing. There may also be a fourth—Paris—dominating a zone comprising Western Europe and parts of Africa. It is to the realization of this possibility that de Gaulle is devoting himself."[9]

The Leites memorandum was quite similar to an assessment made by Thomas Hughes, the director of Intelligence and Research (INR) at the State Department, in which was evoked "The establishment of the kind of Western European bloc [de Gaulle] considers desirable: that is, a bloc of states grouped around France (the one world and nuclear power on the continent) which would be allied on an equal basis with the United States for as long as the Soviet menace makes such an alliance useful to the parties and which would in due course be able to negotiate a settlement or adjustment of European problems with the Soviet Union."[10]

This, then, was the background in the United States when de Gaulle launched his Asian initiative in the summer of 1963. In public, although de Gaulle was recognized as prickly, France was treated both as an ally and as part of the core group of western democracies. In private, there had been such a buildup of suspicion toward de Gaulle that few in official Washington were prepared to consider him an impartial mediator.

De Gaulle's twin and intertwined initiatives on China and Vietnam began on August 29, 1963, when it was announced at the end of a Council of Ministers meeting and in the name of the French chief of state, that France was ready to help in the realization of a Vietnam "independent . . . from the outside, in internal peace and unity and in harmony with [its] neighbors."[11]

Four days after General de Gaulle made this statement, which in effect advocated the neutralization of Vietnam, and which meant, although not directly stated, the neutralization of South Vietnam, CBS's Walter Cronkite interviewed President Kennedy at Hyannisport. Asked what de Gaulle was "up to" with his statement on Vietnam the previous week, Kennedy replied: "General de Gaulle is not our enemy. He is our friend and candid friend—and, there, sometimes difficulty (*sic*)—but he is not the object of our hostility."[12]

Vietnam was the main subject of the interview with Cronkite and in this respect, although the president's words were somewhat equivocal, they did not portend a massive U.S. military effort in Vietnam: "In the final analysis it is the people and the government [of South Vietnam] itself who have to win or lose this struggle. All we can do is help . . . but I don't agree with those who say we should withdraw. . . . I know people don't like Americans to be engaged in this kind of effort. Forty-seven Americans have been killed in combat with the enemy, but this is a very important struggle even though it is far away."[13]

The French president's intentions toward China and Vietnam became an important concern in Washington after his August 29 public declaration. The close connection between the China recognition issue and events in Vietnam was evident—not only from de Gaulle's point of view, but also from the Americans'. The general estimate in Washington was that both France's recognition of China and de Gaulle's neutralization proposal, centered on a new Geneva-type conference, would have an unfortunate effect on the people and government of South Vietnam, possibly even leading to the regime's collapse.

A memorandum issued by the Central Intelligence Agency's Office of National Estimates on October 23, 1963, noted that former prime minister Edgar Faure had arrived in Beijing for a private visit made at General de Gaulle's request. "All things considered," concluded the memorandum, "we believe that de Gaulle is moving toward a more active China policy." The memorandum added: "Finally, and most importantly, French policy toward China is also influenced by its aspirations regarding Indochina. France probably does not have a single, detailed 'master plan' for Indochina. Nevertheless, it seems fairly clear that de Gaulle does have the general aim of reestablishing as much as possible of France's former influence and presence in this area. It seems equally clear that he regards the American presence and influence in the Indochina area as impermanent."[14]

Less than two weeks after the Office of National Estimates memorandum was written, the Vietnamese scene was completely overturned. Diem was overthrown at the beginning of November with U.S. acquiescence and he and his brother Nhu were killed. The fact the United States approved the coup only increased the sense of responsibility that Washington would thenceforth feel toward South Vietnam

Several days later, in a telegram dated November 5, the American ambassador in Paris, Charles E. Bohlen, recounted a conversation he had just had with General de Gaulle. He reported that the French president "gave his view of the future of the present regime [in Saigon] along typically de Gaulle lines. He said the military were in power, the military meant war, this would mean that they would intensify their war efforts and would press us [the United States] for increased assistance, demands which we would find hard to resist."[15]

In less than a month, the political equation again changed drastically with the assassination of President Kennedy on November 22. General de Gaulle and the new president, Lyndon B. Johnson, met briefly during the funeral ceremonies. Their encounter was part of a series of brief meetings LBJ had with foreign dignitaries at the State Department, which was more convenient for this purpose than the White House.[16] After that, Lyndon Johnson and Charles de Gaulle never met again on a bilateral basis. They instead had the dubious distinction of encountering each other only at state funerals: those of Konrad Adenauer and Dwight D. Eisenhower.

This, then, was the backdrop to the French-American relationship at the beginning of 1964. As for relations between Johnson and de Gaulle, in the words of McGeorge Bundy, LBJ's national security adviser, "they didn't amount to anything."[17]

From the beginning, the United States turned a deaf ear to General de Gaulle's repeated calls for an international conference on Southeast Asia, which of course would have to include China. In December, 1963, the United States scotched a separate proposal by Prince Norodom Sihanouk for a conference on Cambodian neutrality on the grounds that it might encourage neutralist sentiment in South Vietnam.[18]

There were several lonely voices that paralleled General de Gaulle's approach. Among them was Sen. Mike Mansfield, the Senate majority leader, who wrote a memorandum to President Johnson on December 7 suggesting the possibility "of an astute diplomatic offensive which would seek to enlist France, Britain, India and, perhaps, even Russia and all other sources of potential use in a bona fide effort to bring an end to the North–South

Vietnamese conflict. A settlement might be on terms which reduced our influence (and costs), provided it also inhibited Chinese domination. France is the key country."[19]

Those in the United States who were not totally wedded to the efficacy of military force echoed the thoughts of de Gaulle and Senator Mansfield. Most prominent among them was Walter Lippmann, who many still considered to be America's leading journalist. Lippmann had a long history of admiration for de Gaulle that the general reciprocated.

Those who thought in terms of relationships of force thought little of de Gaulle's initiative and insisted that de Gaulle lacked influence in the region. From his post in Saigon, Amb. Henry Cabot Lodge observed, "De Gaulle has no real chips to play in Southeast Asia—neither men, nor arms, nor money of any significance."[20]

In the month of January, 1964, there were growing rumors that France intended to recognize Mainland China. This caused disturbances within the ranks of South Vietnam's new leaders because of the likely connection with the idea of neutralizing Southeast Asia, blessed by the major world powers, including China.

On January 8, 1964, in reaction to another memorandum from Senator Mansfield, Secretary of State Dean Rusk, who had a unilinear mind-set on Vietnam not unlike that of Ambassador Lodge, wrote the president that the idea of "neutralization" of Southeast Asia was a "phony": "I have proposed to Gromyko, and he has rejected, the idea that there be a neutralization of both parts of Vietnam, North and South. He said that North Vietnam is a part of the 'socialist camp' and that that cannot be changed."[21]

In a telegram to Ambassador Lodge in Saigon on January 16, W. Averell Harriman, the undersecretary for political affairs, noted that intelligence reports—which Lodge would have seen—suggested that one element in the French negotiations with the Chinese Communists was the latter's agreement to accept the neutralization of Southeast Asia.

Two days later, on January 18, a dispatch from the Agence France-Presse seemed to confirm the intelligence received by Washington. Entitled "The Asian Policy of France," the article suggested that France planned to use its recognition of China to bring about a settlement in Indochina. It equated U.S. actions in South Vietnam with those of North Vietnam and the Vietcong, and called for a cease-fire in South Vietnam.[22]

The new leaders in Saigon were concerned about the article, which appeared to them to be inspired by the Élysée or the Quai d'Orsay. Ambassador Lodge sought to calm their fears, but despite his reassurances, the Saigon leadership reacted to the announcement a week later, on January 27, of the mutual recognition between France and Mainland China. The next day, Gen. Nguyen Khanh, the I Corps commander, confided to his American adviser that he had information to the effect that a coup d'état would be mounted by a group of proneutralist and pro-French officers, possibly as early as January 31. That same day, Lodge suggested the State Department should consider telling General de Gaulle that "[the] U.S. has secret information indicating that there are persons purporting to be under the strong influence of the French Government who are working against U.S. vital interests in Vietnam and requesting him to call off his dogs."[23]

The State Department replied to Lodge the same day, January 28, advising him that "Our relations with de Gaulle at this time are such that [an] approach to him would be fruitless."[24] The following day, General Khanh himself mounted a preemptive coup d'état. He denounced the "neutralists" who wanted to prepare the way for a communist government in South Vietnam and criticized the "colonialists" (the French).[25]

With de Gaulle's recognition of the People's Republic of China, the key point of contention between Washington and Paris shifted to the general's neutralization proposal for Vietnam. In a January 31 press conference in which de Gaulle presented his rationale for recognizing Beijing, he spelled out the link to Southeast Asia: "In fact, there is in Asia no political reality . . . which does not concern or affect China. . . . Thus it would be absolutely impossible to envision, without China, a possible neutrality agreement relating to the Southeast Asian States, in which States for so many reasons, we French feel a very particular and cordial interest—a neutrality which, by definition, must be accepted by all, guaranteed on the international level, and which would exclude both armed agitation supported by any one among them in one or another of the States, and the various forms of external intervention."[26]

The day following President de Gaulle's press conference, the United States took exception to it. "I do not agree with General de Gaulle's proposals," President Johnson stated. "I do not think it would be in the interest of freedom to share his view. . . . I think that the present course we are conducting [in Vietnam] is the only answer. I think that the operations should be stepped up there."[27]

Johnson observed, however, that if the neutralization of both North and South Vietnam could be achieved, this would be considered sympathetically. "You will have to ask General de Gaulle about the details of his proposal," LBJ added. "But as I understand it, the neutralization talk has applied only to South Vietnam and not to the whole of that area of the world. I think that the only thing we need to do to have complete peace in that area of the world now is to stop the invasion of South Vietnam by some of its neighbors and supporters."[28]

But de Gaulle, likely on purpose, had been vague as to where "neutralization" would be applied. On February 2, 1964, Walter Lippmann wrote a column in response to the French president's January 31 press conference. In it, Lippmann made it clear that "we should not confuse ourselves with the notion that General de Gaulle has offered a 'plan' for the neutralization of Southeast Asia which we must accept or reject. We must not be in too much of a hurry. General de Gaulle has not proposed a plan. He has proposed a line of policy and a mode of thinking which we cannot afford to dismiss lightly."[29]

The fact that the general's statements were rather vague had the effect of increasing the anxiety in South Vietnam, according to the State Department.[30] On February 12, during a meeting with the British prime minister, Sir Alec Douglas-Home, Secretary Rusk observed that the United Kingdom and the United States were both using the olive branch and arrows in Southeast Asia, but that de Gaulle was using only the olive branch, and his efforts did not improve the situation.[31]

It is perhaps curious that, during this period of early 1964, David Nes, the new number-two at the American embassy in Saigon, espoused a point of view not far from that of General de Gaulle. In a memorandum to Ambassador Lodge on February 17, Nes offered an analysis of the situation whose salient points were the following: "[R]ecent experiences here lead me to fear that General de Gaulle may be right in his belief that we are faced with the choice between accepting the possible collapse of our counter-insurgency efforts here or the escalation of the conflict toward a direct military confrontation of [North Vietnam] and China by the U.S. . . . [I]t seems to me that de Gaulle has correctly analyzed the Southeast Asia situation if his assumption is correct that we will do no more than continue our present counter-insurgency effort in South Vietnam."[32]

Nes predicted that, in the short-term, "we will be faced with either turning the Southeast Asia ball game over to de Gaulle in the hope that his policy can salvage something from the wreckage or of rapidly escalating our efforts toward a final military showdown with China."[33]

However, Ambassador Lodge's point of view remained unchanged. On February 19, two days after Nes's memo was written but without any reference to it, Lodge averred in a telegram to Washington that the counterinsurgency effort ought to succeed, provided external pressures did not increase. He added that the best thing would be to reduce or even eliminate the pressures coming from Communist China, North Vietnam, Laos, Cambodia, and France.[34]

The following week, Ambassador Lodge suggested anew that General de Gaulle be convinced to issue a brief public statement saying that his earlier calls for neutralization in Southeast Asia did not apply to the present time.[35]

He kept repeating this recommendation during the spring of 1964. Ambassador Bohlen in Paris opposed this approach. In a memorandum dated March 12, Bohlen stated: "Ambassador Lodge had asked some time ago that we endeavor to obtain from General de Gaulle some clarifying statement in regard to French policy toward Vietnam. . . . We should always remember that de Gaulle has stated on a number of occasions directly to American officials, to President Kennedy in May of 1961, and to me, his belief that we could not succeed in the course that we are now pursuing. It is also not clear exactly what type of clarification we desired . . . I . . . [think] . . . that any approach to de Gaulle merely for clarification of French policy would be a very serious mistake."[36]

Ambassador Bohlen further believed that the best way to deal with the French was to go through Foreign Minister Couve de Murville. Going directly to de Gaulle would only produce vague and ambiguous statements by the general and even give him the impression that the United States was throwing itself on his mercy. Besides, de Gaulle had no operational plan for the neutralization of Vietnam and might even be considering communist rule for the whole of Vietnam—which might turn, over time, into a Titoist regime.[37]

The White House, meanwhile, was intent on wringing out of de Gaulle a statement that neutralization did not apply to the present situation but might be appropriate at some point in the future. In other words, the Saigon regime was not a target for "neutralization." The White House was spurred on by a fact-finding report on the Vietnam situation submitted to the president on March 16, 1964. Its authors, Defense Secretary Robert McNamara and Gen. Maxwell Taylor, the chairman of the Joint Chiefs of Staff, stated that General de Gaulle's propositions, given the fact that they recommended a complete American withdrawal from Vietnam, would lead straight to a communist takeover in South Vietnam.[38]

Ambassador Lodge, who at the beginning of the year had downgraded de Gaulle as having neither men, nor arms, nor money of any significance, was forced to admit, in the turmoil of the early months of 1964, that the French leader apparently did have some influence he could bring to bear. On March 23, Lodge wrote: "France has an influence in Vietnam way beyond what it contributes in the way of men, weapons and money. . . . If what is desired is the eventual neutralization of Indochina or of Vietnam, the way not to do it is to create the furor which [the] statements out of Paris create. General de Gaulle is thus a very influential figure in Vietnam and, unwittingly, in a way which is defeating his own stated purpose."[39]

Ambassador Bohlen met with President de Gaulle on April 2, 1964. During their discussion, De Gaulle flatly turned down the idea of his making a statement "clarifying" his neutralization proposal. The most de Gaulle would commit to was that if he "returned" to the subject he would say he did not favor a communist takeover in South Vietnam but would also add that this was the reason he had put forward his neutralization proposal in the first place.[40]

According to the U.S. record, de Gaulle was careful in his meeting with Bohlen not to state openly that the focus of his neutralization initiative was South Vietnam. The closest he came was in this elliptical statement: "[De Gaulle] said that he felt that any military stabilization would only come about with Chinese consent and that with Chinese consent there could be genuine neutrality. He also mentioned that once China had decided in favor of neutrality *he felt sometime in the future the two parts of Vietnam would then come together*."[41]

On April 7, a British diplomatic message from Paris cast further light on the meeting between Bohlen and de Gaulle: "My opposite number in the American Embassy told me yesterday about his Ambassador's conversation with General de Gaulle. . . . Apparently the conversation went even worse than Bohlen told the Ambassador it had gone. Bohlen tried to pin the General down to saying that it was the neutralization of both Vietnams which he had in mind. But the General made it quite plain that he was thinking of South Vietnam. The conversation in fact thereupon turned into something of a wrangle. Bohlen is most anxious that this not become known."[42]

Commenting that it was interesting that de Gaulle should openly admit to the Americans that he was thinking solely of South Vietnam, the author of the message said he thought this was a bad sign as it could mean that de Gaulle would come out in public on the issue.[43]

The message quoted above was related to an earlier message from the British ambassador in Paris, dated February 13, 1964, which made clear the underlying basis of de Gaulle's neutralization proposal: "You will have seen from my telegrams Nos. 96 and 104 that the French aim is to neutralize South Vietnam only. The official instructions are that it is not expedient at the moment to say that this is the French Government's view."[44]

Although de Gaulle's neutralization proposal had indeed been vague, the reasoning behind it, which was summed up by Bohlen at the end of his message on the meeting with the general on April 2, was in fact quite limpid and strikingly congruent with that of Nes:

- The United States cannot win in its current policy of support to the government of South Vietnam.
- Therefore, the best course for the United States is to opt for an immediate policy of neutralization.
- The only alternative would be for the United States to enlarge the war by attacking North Vietnam and probably China as well.[45]

It was a typically French formulation, so much at odds with the Americans' more pragmatic step-by-step approach. For the French, it is in the order of things to find the philosophical framework first, to establish a vision of things, before entering into practical matters. For the Americans, it is necessary first and foremost to be practical and to start by doing what is possible. In the land of Descartes, reality is important, but if there is coherence and beauty in the argument surrounding the reality, this increases its value. This is the serious pendant to the old Washington saw about French negotiators saying, "It works in practice, but does it work in theory?" In short, theory matters.

This epistemological impasse between French and American officials was evident throughout the period under study. In a meeting with French ambassador Hervé Alphand on July 1, 1964, Secretary of State Dean Rusk said, "the fundamental problem was that we did not understand what was meant by a 'political solution.'"[46] Elaborating, Rusk said: "It was distressing that France used the term 'neutralization' without giving it any concrete contents. Used in this manner, the concept becomes negative and creates the impression that France does not really care about the security of the area. The terms 'neutralization' and 'political solution' without concrete contents are merely words, not a policy."[47]

To which the reply was as follows: "Ambassador Alphand felt that these words nevertheless expressed a policy, a direction. He felt that a choice would have to be made, and although he did not wish to exaggerate the importance of the coming [American] elections, he felt that the choice would be reached more easily once the elections are over."[48]

Ever adhering to his official sheet of music, Secretary Rusk "assured Ambassador Alphand that the elections played no role in this."[49]

Fred Logevall, in his book *Choosing War,* points out that the American approach was to parry de Gaulle's proposals and not consider them seriously. In a memorandum to Rusk on June 3, 1964, William Bundy, the assistant secretary of state for Far Eastern Affairs, stated, "We must make another determined effort to get the French not to cut dead across our possible lines of action."[50]

However, some in Washington had a relatively balanced view of what de Gaulle was "up to," notably Thomas Hughes of the State Department's INR, as he shows in this message dated April 20, 1964:

> [De Gaulle's] views are based on the assumptions (or conclusions) that overtly pro-Western regimes cannot be maintained in the area because Communist China is so near, so powerful, and so determined to prevent it, and also because the West cannot defeat the lo-

cal guerrilla forces. This being the case, the only hope of preventing the area from falling under direct Communist Chinese control is to establish regimes which China will suffer to exist but which are not wholly subservient to it. Cambodia is such a regime. De Gaulle would probably not guarantee that such regimes can in fact be established elsewhere in the area, but he would say that however small the chances for this are, they are still greater than those for the success of other policies.[51]

However, throughout official Washington—quite apart from the pervasive distrust of de Gaulle—there was a blanket rejection of comparisons between the earlier French war in Indochina with the developing crisis in South Vietnam in 1963–64. In McGeorge Bundy's view, the two situations were not analogous, as he wrote in the following memorandum on June 30, 1965: "France in 1954 was a colonial power seeking to impose its overseas rule, out of tune with Vietnamese nationalism. . . . The U.S. in 1965 is responding to the call of a people under Communist assault, a people undergoing a non-Communist national revolution; neither our power nor that of our adversaries has been fully engaged as yet."[52]

Others argued that the situations were not analogous because France was not a great power. On June 23, 1965, George Ball observed: "We must judge a decision to withdraw assistance from South Vietnam primarily in terms of its effect on the ability of the United States to maintain its role of world leadership. That role is not an easy one. France could withdraw from Indochina or Algeria without far-ranging consequences since it was not a great power and other nations did not depend on France for their own security."[53]

As Lyndon Johnson himself summed it up to Walter Lippmann at a White House meeting on May 19, 1964: America's power was far greater than that of France and its objectives were more noble.[54] Johnson's view reflected that of the American establishment mainstream: firstly, pride in American power, which meant American military power, so forcefully demonstrated in the way World War II was ended with the totality of atomic weapons and the enemy's unconditional surrender—and along with that pride, a preference for military solutions rather than political ones; and secondly, a perception of the fundamental nobility of American motives and therefore the imperative necessity of accomplishing America's mission in the world. The reinforcement of American national pride emerging from the victory in the extremely dangerous Cuban missile crisis made it all the more difficult for the heirs of the Kennedy administration to, in effect, withdraw from Vietnam.

In June, 1964, the emissary approach was tried on de Gaulle, with Undersecretary of State George Ball as the messenger. This time he carried a signed letter from the president. The meeting took place on June 5. Also present at Ball's meeting at the Élysée Palace were Burin des Roziers, the secretary-general of the Élysée; Ambassador Bohlen; and Roger Vos, an interpreter.

During the meeting, Ball, who was becoming disenchanted with the administration's Vietnam policy, had the impression he was defending a point of view in which he did not believe, and that he was more sympathetic with General de Gaulle's position![55]

According to the American account of this meeting, Ball stated that the U.S. government was in agreement with what it understood to be General de Gaulle's idea: that stabilization in the Southeast Asian area required the agreement and acquiescence of Beijing.[56] There were, however, certain elements of disagreement, one of which was a different appreciation of the phasing of the communist revolution in China. Said Ball: "We see that the Chinese revolution is in a phase reminiscent of the primitive Soviet Communism of 1917 which was both bellicose and expansionist. We do not think that Beijing would accept any arrangement that would limit or prevent the spread of Communism in Southeast Asia or that it would abide by any such arrangement if made."[57]

In reply, the French president said, "I do not believe that you can win in this situation [in Vietnam] even though you have more aircraft, cannons and arms of various kinds." The problem, elaborated the general, was primarily a political and psychological problem. To the people of Vietnam, the United States was a foreign power: "I do not mean that all of the Vietnamese are against you but they regard the U.S. as a foreign power and as a very big foreign power." The general added that the more the United States became involved in the actual conduct of military operations, the more the Vietnamese would turn against the Americans, as would others, in Southeast Asia.[58]

In the margins of the paragraph just cited, someone had written "French experience," meaning what was true for the French was not necessarily so for the Americans. In other parts of the report there are marginal notations such as "Nonsense" and "How fuzzy can one be!" The latter was a reference to the general's proposition for an international conference on Southeast Asia with the participation, besides the United States, of several world powers, including France, India, China, Japan, and the Soviet Union. The Americans could not lead such a gathering alone, the general said, because it would not succeed. A large conference had been attempted in 1954, and although the talks had taken a very long time, that in itself was not a bad thing. If a world conference of the type de Gaulle described could be organized, it would change the state of mind of the Vietnamese people and produce a détente. Furthermore, de Gaulle said, by focusing world public opinion, the conference would have a restraining effect on Ho Chi Minh.[59]

The account of the meeting ended with a comment by Ball, with which Ambassador Bohlen associated himself, to the effect that General de Gaulle probably envisaged that at some time in the not too distant future the United States would begin to consider seriously his suggestion of a conference: "He quite likely assumes that we will then ask the French to take soundings with the Chinese and the North Vietnamese."[60]

Ambassador Lodge's commentary on this account was that the following points should be made to de Gaulle: U.S. objectives in Vietnam were political and not military; military action was designed to reinforce political objectives by providing security; and the Khanh government was the best that South Vietnam could expect under the current circumstances.[61]

However, General de Gaulle, with characteristic consistency, went on pressing his case for the neutralization of Southeast Asia. In a press conference on July 23, 1964—and as pointed out by Thomas Hughes, the director of the INR—de Gaulle went beyond his earlier proposals for the neutralization of Indochina. He proposed that the four powers of France, the Soviet Union, China, and the United States agree "no longer to be committed there."[62] Yet, De Gaulle's statement was in the context of the status quo ante: "[Peace] implies that one return to what had been committed to ten years ago, and that this time one conform to it, in other words that in North and South Vietnam, in Cambodia, and in Laos, no foreign power intervene any more in the affairs of these unfortunate countries."[63]

In thus referring to the Geneva Accords, de Gaulle, without saying so outright, was applying neutralization to South Vietnam only, because the existence of a communist state in North Vietnam had been recognized at Geneva in 1954. De Gaulle made a passing mention of this situation by referring to "the existence of a Communist State installed in Tonkin, from which our troops departed in conformity with the [Geneva] accords."[64]

Hughes, the INR director, estimated that Asian communists' reaction was likely to be more favorable to de Gaulle's position than had been the case at the time of the general's previous press conference in January, 1964, "as indicated by statements from representatives of Hanoi and the Viet Cong. Beijing's attitude remains ambiguous but the regime appears to have taken some steps, especially in the diplomatic sphere, to anticipate this proposal. Soviet reaction is likely to be favorable, if only to keep the proposal alive."[65]

In any event, the United States did not come back to de Gaulle, as George Ball had assumed the general was anticipating. There was no international conference in 1964 or thereafter. This did not prevent France, "as a friend and ally," in the words of one Quai d'Orsay official, from facilitating contacts between North Vietnamese representatives in Paris and the U.S. government, starting with the short-lived "XYZ" contacts in the summer of 1965.[66]

Less than two weeks after the French president's July 23, 1964, press conference, the Tonkin Gulf incident erupted, triggering a chain of events that led to U.S. military intervention in Vietnam, first with the decision to launch a limited but sustained bombing campaign against North Vietnam in February, 1965, and then with the decision—announced by President Johnson on July 28, 1965—to deploy U.S. ground forces in South Vietnam. The net effect, of course, was to lessen even further the chances of a negotiated settlement.

There followed the long parenthesis of the Cultural Revolution in China. Throughout the period following de Gaulle's neutralization proposal at the end of August, 1963, the Chinese, in their contacts with the French, never gave an unequivocal approval to the idea of holding a Geneva-type conference, hewing instead to the rhetoric that the United States should first remove its forces from Southeast Asia. Still, had the United States agreed to a conference, and assuming the willingness of the French, the Soviets, the British, and even the North Vietnamese, who were more flexible on the issue than the Chinese, it probably would have been difficult for the Chinese to refuse to attend—especially since they had been a key participant in the 1954 Geneva conference.

The George Ball–Charles de Gaulle meeting on June 5, 1964, represented the most strenuous attempt by the United States to turn aside de Gaulle's neutralization proposal. Thereafter, with the Tonkin Gulf incident and the subsequent U.S. escalation, it became, for the United States, mainly a question of keeping the French government informed, rather than attempting to change de Gaulle's mind. Arthur Goldberg, the American representative to the United Nations, met with de Gaulle on December 31, 1965, after President Johnson had initiated a bombing pause.[67] De Gaulle described this as having potentially a "good and constructive effect" on world opinion. However, the pause by itself would not be enough for Hanoi to accept President Johnson's offer of "unconditional" negotiations. For Hanoi to accept, said de Gaulle, an agreement to withdraw would have to be made before the negotiations began. This would not, however, require that American troops be withdrawn immediately.[68]

In a memorandum on how the so-called peace offensive associated with the bombing pause was being received, McGeorge Bundy wrote the following on January 3, 1966: "De Gaulle is in a class by himself. He has been fully informed and has expressed his warm appreciation. At the same time he has made clear his conviction that nothing will happen until we announce that we will definitely withdraw at the end of negotiations. His Foreign Minister emphasizes the importance of a recognized role for the NLF [National Liberation Front or Vietcong]. De Gaulle has sneered at our efforts in a private conversation with the British Ambassador. We have not asked the French for anything. This was wise."[69]

The "peace offensive" having not had the desired effect, President Johnson resumed the bombing of the North, announcing his decision in a personal message to General de Gaulle on January 31, 1966. This prompted a reply from de Gaulle on February 5 that McGeorge Bundy described as a "rather tart message . . . that hardly calls for an answer." In it, de Gaulle reiterated his familiar theme that a political solution could only come from negotiations based on the Geneva Agreement; and the only way to start such negotiations was for the United States to announce a decision to withdraw its forces. He repeated the theme of a need to return to the Geneva Accords of 1954 in a press conference on February 21, 1966. Then, as Jean Lacouture described it: "Six months after [the press conference], seemingly echoing the American military escalation, the founder of the Fifth Republic pursued his own verbal and diplomatic escalation—at Phnom Penh, capital of Cambodia, some 300 kilometers from the battlefield in Vietnam."[70]

De Gaulle's September 1, 1966, speech at Phnom Penh evoked "the more and more extended escalation [of the United States] in Asia, closer and closer to China, more and more provocative with regard to the Soviet Union, more and more disapproved by a number of people in Europe, Africa, and Latin America, and, in the final analysis, more and more threatening for the peace of the world."[71]

Averell Harriman, the undersecretary of state for political affairs, characterized the speech as only having made Hanoi more intransigent.[72] And so the dialogue of the deaf between de Gaulle and the Johnson administration continued. The letters exchanged between the two presidents were infrequent and perfunctory. Indeed, the only moment when de Gaulle demonstrated some feeling was when he praised Johnson's "political courage" for having declared a unilateral halt to the bombing in March, 1968.

Curiously, the one U.S. president with whom de Gaulle might have established an effective relationship was Richard Nixon, an avowed admirer of the general. Nixon paid a visit to the French president two months after his inauguration, but that was, unfortunately, only one month before de Gaulle self-destructed politically in the referendum of April, 1969. If de

Gaulle had remained in office, it is possible, though perhaps only remotely, that things might have been different in the Nixon administration's approach to the Vietnam War.

As for George Ball, he became a dissident within the Johnson administration, while still remaining part of the government team. He was the first in a series of persons that would include, before the end of Johnson's tenure, Defense Secretary Robert McNamara himself. Originally, over the summer of 1964, Ball discussed his views with Rusk and McNamara, but after an initial meeting, it was clear that the discussions would go nowhere. Rusk therefore suggested to Ball that he advise the president of his views. Ball proceeded to write eight memoranda between October 5, 1964, two months after the Tonkin Gulf incident, and June 28, 1965, just before the decision for a massive American troop intervention in Vietnam.

Ball argued that the United States, in spite of its many foreign interventions here and there, had never developed, properly speaking, a doctrine of extrication . . . which was manifestly needed in Vietnam. The justification he offered was that since South Vietnam's leaders had not lived up to their commitment with regard to the defense of the country, the United States was released from its own, and that it was time to withdraw American forces.[73]

However, the loyalists in the Johnson administration held to the view exemplified by a remark Secretary Rusk made to Ambassador Alphand on July 1, 1964—words that were sharply contested by the latter: "the security of Asia was as important to us as the security of Europe. To us, the defense of Vietnam has the same significance as the defense of Berlin."[74]

In this same context, one reads with a certain irony the opening lines of an article by Zbigniew Brzezinski in *Foreign Affairs,* published in 1994: "During almost 45 difficult years, the United States pursued a remarkably consistent policy toward the Soviet Union. On the level of grand strategy, this policy was defined as containment of the geopolitical as well as the ideological ambitions of the Soviets. The practical implementation of the policy of containment involved a geostrategic concentration of the United States on the defense of both the western and eastern peripheries of Eurasia."[75]

At the beginning of de Gaulle's neutralization initiative, the choices were stark, as outlined by both David Nes and the French president: to continue on course in South Vietnam was certain to lead to a U.S. defeat, while the only alternative was to expand the war to the North. The Johnson administration chose escalation—"Choosing War," as Fred Logevall has put it—and ten years and fifty-eight thousand American deaths later, the United States finally withdrew completely from Vietnam.

Notes

1. *Foreign Relations of the United States (FRUS), 1964–1968,* vol. 1, *Vietnam, 1964* (Washington, D.C.: GPO, 1992), p. 187.

2. Charles de Gaulle, *Discours et Messages,* vol. 4, *Pour l'effort* (Paris: Plon, 1970), p. 127.

3. *FRUS, 1961–1963,* vol. 13, *West Europe and Canada* (Washington, D.C.: GPO, 1994), p. 162.

4. Ibid., p. 13:491.

5. Ibid., p. 13:487.

6. McGeorge Bundy, interview by author, Jan. 28, 1994, New York City.

7. *FRUS, 1961–1963,* p. 13:161.

8. Ibid., 13:160.

9. Nathan Leites, "Guesses About de Gaulle," memorandum RM-3667ISA, RAND Corporation, Nov., 1963, p. v.

10. "De Gaulle's Foreign Policy, 1964," research memorandum REU-28, RAND Corporation, Apr. 20, 1964, p. 3.

11. *Major Addresses, Statements, and Press Conferences of General Charles de Gaulle, May 19, 1958–January 31, 1964* (New York: French Embassy Press and Information Bureau, 1964), p. 241.

12. *FRUS, 1961–1963,* vol. 4, *Vietnam, August–December 1963,* (Washington, D.C.: GPO, 1992), p. 94.

13. Ibid.

14. Ibid., doc. no. 4a, pp. 4:4–5.

15. Ibid., p. 4:568.

16. Bundy interview.

17. Ibid.

18. *FRUS, 1961–1963,* pp. 4:695–96.

19. Ibid., pp. 4:691–92 (emphasis in original).

20. *FRUS, 1964–1968,* p. 1:33.

21. Ibid., pp. 1:9–10.

22. Ibid., p. 1:30.

23. Ibid., p. 1:38 n 2.

24. Ibid.

25. Ibid., p. 1:43.

26. *Major Addresses,* p. 257.

27. "China: U.S. Policy since 1945," *Congressional Quarterly,* 1980, vol. 8, p. 141.

28. *FRUS, 1964–1968,* p. 1:56.

29. *Washington Post,* Feb. 4, 1964, cited in Fredrik Logevall, *Choosing War: the Lost Chance for Peace and the Escalation of War in Vietnam* (Berkeley: University of California Press, 1999), p. 106.

30. *FRUS, 1964–1968,* p. 1:57.

31. Ibid., p. 1:70.

32. Ibid., pp. 1:90–91.

33. Ibid., p. 1:92.

34. Ibid., pp. 1:92–93.

35. Ibid.

36. Ibid., p. 1:140.

37. Ibid., p. 1:107.

38. Ibid., p. 1:158.

39. Ibid., p. 1:188.

40. Ibid., p. 1:216.

41. Ibid., p. 1:218 (emphasis added).

42. 102141/186/64, British Embassy, Paris, to Foreign Office, London.

43. Ibid.

44. British Embassy, Paris, to Foreign Office, London, Feb. 13, 1964, telegram 118.

45. Ibid., p. 219.

46. *FRUS, 1964–1968*, p. 1:533.

47. Ibid., p. 1:536.

48. Ibid.

49. Ibid.

50. Ibid., p. 445.

51. Memorandum, Apr. 20, 1964, National Security File, Box 169, Lyndon B. Johnson Library, Austin, Tex., p. 17.

52. *FRUS, 1964–1968*, vol. 3, *Vietnam, June–December, 1965* (Washington, D.C.: GPO, 1996), p. 85.

53. Ibid., p. 3:57.

54. Logevall, *Choosing War*, p. 143.

55. George Ball, interview by author, Jan. 28, 1994, Princeton, New Jersey.

56. *FRUS, 1964–1968*, pp. 1:464–70.

57. Ibid., p. 1:466.

58. Ibid., p. 1:467.

59. Ibid., pp. 1:468–69.

60. Ibid., p. 470.

61. Ibid.

62. Ibid., p. 1:573.

63. Charles de Gaulle, *L'esprit de la République* (Paris: Omnibus/Plon, 1993), p. 893.

64. Ibid., p. 892.

65. *FRUS, 1964–1968*, p. 1:573.

66. *FRUS, 1964–1968*, vol. 2, *Vietnam, January–June, 1965* (Washington, D.C.: GPO, 1996), p. 682. The XYZ contacts involved Mai Van Bo, the North Vietnamese representative in Paris, and Edmund Gullion, former deputy chief of mission in Saigon. See *FRUS, 1964–1968*, p. 3:312.

67. Ibid., p. 3:757.

68. Ibid., p. 3:758.

69. *FRUS, 1964–1968*, vol. 4, *Vietnam, 1966* (Washington, D.C.: GPO, 1998), p. 5.

70. Jean Lacouture, *De Gaulle*, vol. 3, *Le Souverain* (Paris: Seuil, 1986), p. 434.

71. Charles G. Cogan, *Charles de Gaulle: a Brief Biography with Documents* (Boston: Bedford Books, a division of St. Martin's Press, 1996), p. 215.

72. FRUS, 1964–1968, p. 4:821.

73. Ball interview.

74. Ibid., pp. 535–36.

75. Zbigniew Brzezinski, "The Premature Partnership," *Foreign Affairs,* Mar.-Apr., 1994, p. 67.

De Gaulle and the Vietnam War

MAURICE VAÏSSE

Opposition to the Vietnam War was virtually unanimous in France.[1] Among students, it was led by the so-called Vietnam committees dominated by the Communist Party, and they organized many protests. There was also an opposition led by the "intellectuals," particularly Jean-Paul Sartre, as well as a political one, led by the president of the Republic himself. De Gaulle had early defined once and for all his general opposition to the war waged by the United States in Vietnam. However, his day-to-day attitude underwent drastic changes from 1963 to 1968, growing increasingly severe toward the Johnson administration's policy.[2]

France proposed neutralization of the Indochina peninsula for two reasons. First, Paris wanted to remain faithful to the Geneva Accords of 1954 concerning the noninterference of foreign powers in the region. Second, it believed that seeking a military solution would lead to an impasse.

This policy had been implemented in Laos and Cambodia. In the view from Paris, the neutrality of Laos and Cambodia necessarily had to serve as a model for all of Indochina. The United States, however, was engaged in a policy that was diametrically opposite, and de Gaulle relentlessly opposed it. After expressing his views privately to presidents Eisenhower and Kennedy, he voiced his disagreement publicly on August 29, 1963—at a time when he was launching a process of establishing diplomatic relations with the People's Republic of China.[3]

The French-American conflict erupted on the occasion of the Southeast Asia Treaty Organization (SEATO) conference in April, 1964, at which France refused to support the Americans.[4] From that point on, the conflict became increasingly aggravated between de Gaulle, who was ever more sharp in expressing his views, and Johnson, who rejected the general's propositions.[5]

When George Ball came to the Élysée Palace to explain American policy, de Gaulle was extremely critical.[6] He told the undersecretary of state that he did not believe America could win, despite its military edge, even if it decided to wage a full-scale war. "Of course you can destroy Hanoi,

Guangzhou, Beijing. Of course you can have Chiang Kai-shek land on Mainland China. But you won't win the war."

At regular intervals, de Gaulle repeated his proposed solution of an international conference, but he did so without any illusions as to the chances of success of this idea, because neither the Americans nor their adversaries were ready to accept it.[7] If France was alone among the major allies of the United States in not providing unreserved support, neither was she prepared to undertake a concerted action with the Soviets.[8] In sum, de Gaulle was preaching in the desert, while adopting the mantle of commander of a moral crusade that served as a cement for those advocates of a "third way."

De Gaulle shared the view of Julius Nyerere of Tanzania in at least one respect. When the French foreign minister, Couve de Murville, met with Ali Bhutto of Pakistan, he stated de Gaulle's apprehensions in this manner: "It's a very bad thing, because it gives the impression that this war is a matter of white people against yellow people."[9]

The year 1966 was decisive. De Gaulle made clear his position: He would not assist with arranging for negotiations unless and until the Americans made a decision regarding the departure of their forces.[10] He linked France's withdrawal from the North Atlantic Treaty Organization to the situation in Vietnam and established contact with Ho Chi Minh through an intermediary, Jean Sainteny.[11] Sainteny had developed an intimate knowledge of the Vietnam and Indochina issues after the Second World War. He also knew Ho Chi Minh well and was appointed as the French representative to North Vietnam after the Geneva conference in 1954. In 1966, de Gaulle asked him to visit the country. Sainteny spent several weeks in Hanoi and met with Ho Chi Minh, who was quite frank with him. "Hanoi wants to get victory at any price," Ho told the French diplomat. "Even through negotiation. The only objective is that Americans quit Vietnam. We don't have any bad intention towards the U.S. We're even ready to take them home with music and flowers. But as you Frenchmen say in slang, let them get off."

Up to this point, de Gaulle had exercised real restraint in both his public speeches and at press conferences. He had not yet publicly criticized U.S. policy in Vietnam, which was why his September 1, 1966, speech in Cambodia was so badly received in Washington.[12] On that date, in a stadium in Phnom Penh, he praised the Cambodians for choosing neutrality and gave his own analysis of the Vietnam War, castigating the United States as solely responsible for its continuation. He ended by calling on the Americans to follow France's example in North Africa and conclude a political agreement that included repatriating their forces within a suitable amount of time.

In a speech at the end of 1966, de Gaulle stigmatized the Vietnam conflict as an "unjust . . . dreadful war." He said it was unjust because it resulted from the illegal U.S. intervention and it was dreadful because it was leading a great nation to crush a small one to death.

A number of efforts were made to end the war in 1967, with the French repeatedly asked to provide information and act as go-betweens. Henry Kissinger, Averell Harriman, and Chester Cooper were in constant touch with Jean Sainteny, asking him to find out how the North Vietnamese would respond to the phasing out of U.S. bombings.[13] De Gaulle, who was not favorable to such a role, asked Sainteny to refrain from becoming a messenger for the United States. At the same time, however, Raymond Aubrac, a well-known icon of the French Resistance, was conducting a mission in North Vietnam with de Gaulle's discreet approval.[14] Meanwhile, at the Quai d'Orsay, Etienne Manac'h, the top public servant responsible for Asia, was in touch with both the Americans and the Vietnamese.[15]

On the occasion of the outbreak of the Middle East crisis in June, 1967, de Gaulle drew a relationship between the Vietnam War and the Arab-Israeli conflict, observing that "one conflict contributes to the start of another."[16] On the other hand, de Gaulle hailed the partial halt of the bombing of North Vietnam on March 31, 1968, "as a first step in the direction of peace and consequently an act of reason and political courage."[17]

Thus it was that Paris, "where all the parties can benefit from equitable and impartial treatment," was chosen as the venue for peace talks. When President Johnson ordered a total bombing halt on October 31, 1968, de Gaulle again lauded his "courageous decisions."[18]

In his relations with the United States and President Johnson, de Gaulle played the card of neutralizing Vietnam, but he seems to have reconciled himself to the fact of a political impasse. It is important to note, however, that de Gaulle did not want to give up on the two nations' long tradition of friendship. When Sartre asked de Gaulle to authorize the informal international criminal court known as the "Russell Court" to sit in Paris, the French president refused, arguing that, in spite of diverging policies, he did not want a friendly state to be judged by an institution that had no legal footing in international law whatsoever.[19] Yet de Gaulle never got out of phase with French public opinion, which was uniformly hostile to the American intervention.

Notes

1. Cf. my book, *La Grandeur, politique étrangère du général de Gaulle 1958–1969* (Paris: Fayard, 1998), which is based on material found in the archives of the Ministry of Foreign Affairs (Archives diplomatiques) and the National Archives. I read through the entire collection of the "Entretiens et Messages" (EM), which record the verbatim meetings of President de Gaulle

with foreign officials in Paris and abroad. The diplomatic documents were published in the *Documents diplomatiques français* (*DDF*) until 1963. Some papers, speeches, and letters were published in Charles de Gaulle, *Lettres, Notes, et Carnets* (*LNC*), *1958–1961, 1961–1963, 1964–1966,* and *1966–1967* (Paris: Plon, 1985, 1986, and 1987); and idem., *Discours et Messages* (*DM*), *1962–1965,* and *1966–1969* (Paris: Plon, 1970). See Jean Lacouture, *De Gaulle,* 3 vols. (Paris: Le Seuil, 1990); and Alain Peyrefitte, *C'était de Gaulle* (Paris: Fayard, 1994, 1997, and 1999).

2. Cf. Philippe Richer, *L'Asie du Sud-Est* (Paris: Imprimerie nationale, 1981); Jean-Luc Domenach and Philippe Richer, *La Chine, 1949–1985* (Paris: Imprimerie nationale, 1989); Philippe Devillers, "De Gaulle et l'Asie," in *De Gaulle et le Tiers Monde* (Paris: Pedone, 1984), pp. 299–329; Philippe Devillers, "De Gaulle et l'Indochine," in *De Gaulle en son siècle,* vol. 6 (Paris: Plon, 1991), pp. 457–71.

3. Meeting with Kennedy, May 31, 1961, *DDF, 1961,* vol. 1; "déclaration au sujet du Vietnam," in de Gaulle, *LNC, 1961–1963,* p. 367; idem., *DM,* vol. 4, *Pour l'effort, Août 1962–Décembre 1965* (Paris: Plon, 1970), pp. 234–37.

4. Cf. *DDF, 1964,* vol. 1, nos. 175 and 177, conference of ministers from SEATO member countries in Manila, Apr. 13–15, 1964.

5. *Foreign Relations of the United States* (*FRUS*), *1964–1968,* vol. 1, *Vietnam, 1964* (Washington, D.C.: GPO, 1992), p. 33; Charles Cogan, "Last Opportunity or Mission Impossible: de Gaulle's Initiatives in China and Vietnam, 1963–1964," in *French Politics and Society* (winter, 1995): pp. 54–77.

6. *FRUS, 1964–1968,* June 4, 1964, docs. 196 and 202; meeting, de Gaulle–Ball, June 5, 1964, EM, 1964; de Gaulle to L. Johnson, June 10, 1964, de Gaulle, *LNC, 1964–1966,* pp. 69–70.

7. Telegram to Norodom Sihanouk, Feb. 13, 1965, de Gaulle, *LNC, 1964–1966,* p. 131; Press conference, Sept. 9, 1965, idem., *DM,* vol. 4, *1962–1965* (Paris: Plon, 1970) , p. 66.

8. Meeting, de Gaulle–Vinogradov (Soviet ambassador in Paris), Feb. 23, 1965, EM, 1965.

9. De Gaulle to Julius Nyerere, Sept. 21, 1965, de Gaulle, *LNC, 1964–1966,* p. 189; meeting, Couve de Murville–Ali Bhutto, May 2, 1965, EM, 1965; meeting, de Gaulle–U Thant, Apr. 30, 1966, EM, 1966.

10. De Gaulle to Lyndon Johnson, Jan. 5, 1966, and Feb. 5, 1966, de Gaulle, *LNC, 1964–1966,* pp. 234 and 249–50.

11. Jean Sainteny, *Face à Hô Chi Minh* (Paris: Seghers, 1970), pp. 187–90; Claude Dulong, *La dernière pagode* (Paris: Grasset, 1989), pp. 258–73. The Sainteny Papers are located in the Fondation nationale des Sciences politiques, Paris (hereafter FNSP).

12. Cf. Lacouture, *De Gaulle,* p. 3:435; meeting, de Gaulle–Sihanouk, Aug. 30, 1966, EM, 1966; the speech is in de Gaulle, *DM,* vol. 5, *1966–1969* (Paris: Plon, 1970), pp. 74–78.

13. Cf. Chester Cooper's and Henry Kissinger's letters in the Sainteny Papers, FNSP; note pour MM. Pompidou et Couve de Murville, Jan. 20, 1967, *LNC, 1966–1969,* p. 66; Dulong, *La dernière pagode,* pp. 173–77.

14. Cf. Raymond Aubrac, *Où la mémoire s'attarde* (Paris: Odile Jacob, 1996), pp. 255–80.

15. Étienne Manac'h, *Mémoires d'extrême Asie* (Paris: Fayard, 1980).

16. Communiqué, June 21, 1967, de Gaulle, *LNC, 1966–1969,* pp. 119–20; meeting, de Gaulle–U Thant, Feb. 14, 1968, EM, 1968.

17. Note pour le Conseil des ministres, Apr. 3, 1968, *de Gaulle, LNC, 1966–1969,* p. 210.

18. French-American meeting, Oct. 9, 1968, in AN, File 5 AG 1; de Gaulle to Lyndon Johnson, Jan. 3, 1969, in de Gaulle, *LNC, 1966–1969,* pp. 273–74.

19. De Gaulle to Jean-Paul Sartre, Apr. 19, 1967, in de Gaulle, *LNC, 1966–1969,* pp. 95–96.

Triangle of Discord

The United States, Germany, and French
Peace Initiatives for Vietnam

WILFRIED MAUSBACH

In the mid-1960s, an American commentator once remarked that Paris "counted in South East Asia for just about as much as did Luxembourg."[1] The gentle reader, reflecting on the topic of this chapter, may be tempted to extend this comparison and ask why anybody would be interested in what the Grand Duchy of Liechtenstein thought of Luxembourg's Southeast Asian policy. Of course, French views carried considerably greater weight than our American commentator believed—and not only in Indochina, but in Europe as well. More important, close relations between Paris and the third actor in the following narrative, the Federal Republic of Germany, were indispensable in keeping the western alliance alive, which in turn represented the cornerstone of America's global predominance. The Vietnam War and French efforts to preempt its escalation put considerable strains on relations between Washington, Bonn, and Paris. These strains derived from different interests rooted in divergent views of both the world and the role each country was destined to play in it. In order to illustrate this point, it might be useful to relate three minor but emblematic episodes that provide a sense of the chemistry within the triangle in which Vietnam struck such a discordant note.

The first episode occurred in the Palais Schaumburg on the occasion of General de Gaulle's visit to Bonn in July, 1964. In the classicist setting of this nineteenth-century building that houses the German chancellery, de Gaulle painted a flamboyant picture of future European greatness anchored in Franco-German cooperation. His opposite, Chancellor Ludwig Erhard, listened with an absent-minded, almost transfixed gaze. When de Gaulle finished, an awkward silence fell over the cabinet room. Erhard looked as if paralyzed by painkillers. Finally, the chancellor spoke. "All right," he said, "let's move on with our agenda."[2]

The second episode occurred shortly before Christmas, 1965. The location was the White House in Washington, D.C. It was almost 11 P.M., and Pres. Lyndon B. Johnson and his guest, Ludwig Erhard, had retired to the West Wing after the state dinner to continue their conversation over what the French would call *digestifs*. However, events would prove to be not easily digestible for Erhard. Congress, the president began, would ask him what other nations were doing in Vietnam. His problems would be more understandable if other nations were involved. He was not asking for combat troops, but rather for a medical unit or a construction battalion. Erhard, after emphasizing that combat troops were out of the question, suggested that construction and medical *teams* might be all right. When Johnson reverted to the question of *battalions,* Erhard responded with talk of legal restrictions. The president exploded. George McGhee, the U.S. ambassador to Germany, who witnessed the encounter, later recalled that LBJ's "tall, rangy figure towered over the comparatively small figure of the chancellor. Gesticulating and speaking in a strong, strident voice, Johnson alternately wheedled and threatened. He put his whole body into his demands. . . . He recounted all we had done for Germany. Now was the time for Germany to pay us back." According to the memorandum recording their conversation, Johnson thundered: "If I can get legislation to put 200,000 more men in Vietnam, surely the Chancellor can get two battalions to Vietnam. If we are going to be partners, we better find out right now." McGhee remembered that Erhard "appeared increasingly uncomfortable, verging on fright." Indeed, the chancellor could think of nothing to say other than to admit meekly, "it isn't fair to take your security in West Berlin and not help you in Vietnam."[3]

The third episode took place at the Élysée Palace in Paris on the occasion of Pres. Richard M. Nixon's visit in early 1969. During a reception, an aide advised Henry Kissinger that de Gaulle wanted to talk to him. Flattered, the professor and newly appointed national security adviser, who had not met *le général* before, walked over to where de Gaulle was standing. As Kissinger approached the French president, "without further introduction or in fact discretion," de Gaulle snapped, "Why don't you get out of Indochina?"[4]

These three episodes delineate the completely different angles from which the United States and its two major European allies viewed the problem of Vietnam. They also reveal the divergent worldviews underlying the allies' respective perspectives. Last but not least, they tell a lot about the different standing each country had within the alliance.

The encounter between Ludwig Erhard and Charles de Gaulle is a classic example of what has been termed the Franco-German "dialogue of the deaf."[5] After World War II, both France and the Federal Republic were, in fact, revisionist powers.[6] Both wanted to undo the results of the war, although admittedly from different positions and in quite different senses. De Gaulle's foreign policy, wrote the German ambassador in Paris, "strives to dissolve the world system that goes back to the Yalta conference . . . and to replace it with a system that will afford individual states—irrespective of their ideology—greater independence and new diplomatic possibilities."[7] Yet, whereas France felt hemmed in by the bipolar system that grew out of the agreements and disagreements after 1945, Germany—in a strangely dialectical fashion—sought to strengthen this very bipolarity in order to overcome its own division. De Gaulle was chiseling away at the dichotomy of the Cold War when he pronounced that France saw itself as belonging to but not being confined to the Western world.[8] The very notion of an entity called the "Free World" implied U.S. leadership and thus inevitably limited French independence. Not only did de Gaulle's extraordinary patriotism disdain such a configuration, his basic frame of reference, shaped before 1914, also stood in stark contrast to it.[9] This frame of reference envisioned a concert of nations, not an American-Soviet duet. As French prime minister Georges Pompidou put it in 1965: "The old division of the world into two monolithic blocs is outdated. Out of this emerges France's role. She is condemned by her geographic situation and her history to represent Europe."[10]

Such a sense of mission had to be utterly alien to any German politician after 1945. In contrast to France, it was impossible after World War II for Germany to aspire to great power status or even to unilaterally articulate its national interests.[11] Postwar Germany was not only a postimperial but also a postnational country. This observation refers not only to the nation's territorial division, but also to the profound lack of orientation experienced by a population that had witnessed the complete military and moral collapse of National Socialism. In trying to reconstruct a national identity, Germans therefore made reference to supranational frameworks. The "Free West" was one such framework. It represented more than a mere geographic landscape. Its demarcation lines were defined by the validity of a specific set of generally accepted values and norms like pluralism, democracy, individualism, and freedom. The conditions of the Cold War made Germans susceptible to this long despised concept of the West. It offered inclusion, refuge and a new sense of belonging. Of course, the western alliance also offered security, especially if one was prepared to lean on the United States. It comes as no surprise, then, that West Germans internalized what Frank Costigliola has called "the Atlantic axioms, a set of beliefs that regarded U.S. leadership of the Western alliance as necessary, democratic, wise, moral, and popular."[12] Contrary to their European partners in Paris, the Germans not only willingly accepted the notion of a holistic Free World, they were also prepared to concede its leadership to Washington. Responding to de Gaulle's 1958 scheme of a Franco-British-American triumvirate, a German

Foreign Office memorandum observed that "the political strength of the present western alliance is based on respect for the equality of each member state . . . , with these member states in turn voluntarily acknowledging the leadership role of the United States."[13] Totally discredited after 1945, Germans could not help but find "the Atlantic Alliance under American domination an egalitarian paradise," as Alfred Grosser observed already in the mid-1960s.[14] A study prepared on behalf of the U.S. government by political scientist Karl W. Deutsch found that German leaders indicated an "emotional attachment to the image of a bipolar world."[15] Thus, de Gaulle's way of thinking could not but appear strange and outlandish to most Germans.[16] Ludwig Erhard, at least, could not make sense of de Gaulle's grand design.

Given the strongly divergent French and German worldviews, it was only to be expected that America's Asian policies would prove to be a burden on the Franco-German partnership as codified in the 1963 Élysée Treaty. At first, however, the impending confrontation between Washington and Paris over Southeast Asia hardly caused a ripple in Bonn. When Charles de Gaulle, having privately cautioned American leaders against wading into the Vietnamese quagmire for more than two years, made public his preference for a unified and neutralized Vietnam in August, 1963, reactions in the West German press were guarded.[17] So were reactions in the German Foreign Office. To be sure, during July and August, 1963, officials in Bonn had assessed the situation in Vietnam anew. This is most apparent in internal discussions about financial aid. In July, the Foreign Office's Southeast Asia Desk had pointed out that it was German policy—a policy strongly advocated by the United States—to support South Vietnam's struggle against communism by quickly realizing a promised loan of 50 million deutschmarks for Saigon. However, this recommendation soon met with opposition on the divisional level. By mid-August, it seemed apparent to Assistant Secretary for Political Affairs Josef Jansen that the Americans had miscalculated in Vietnam. Military aid and military advisers would not solve the conflict. Instead, it was imperative that a strong nationalist government with considerable popular support be established. South Vietnam's president Ngo Dinh Diem, who had not been able to win the people's trust, was in danger of being deposed. Jansen gloomily predicted that the West would have to reckon with the collapse of Diem's regime at any time. He recommended that the Federal Republic not go through with the promised loan and that South Vietnam's request for an additional loan presently under consideration be rejected. Jansen also recommended that Bonn distance itself from events in South Vietnam, that is, from Diem's declaration of martial law and his intransigent reaction to the

Buddhist crisis.[18] This latter recommendation suggests that officials in Bonn were impressed not so much by French criticism of U.S. policy but rather by the crisis in Saigon itself and quite probably also by the first sustained outpouring of critical news coverage from South Vietnam in the American media.[19]

When West Germany temporarily withheld financial aid from Saigon in the summer of 1963, it was neither caused by French insinuations nor did it signal a reorientation away from American wishes and toward Gaullist skepticism. In fact, if the first discordant note within our triangle—struck by de Gaulle's announcement on August 29, 1963—had reverberated particularly in Franco-American relations, the second unpleasant sound emerged from the Franco-German corner after Jansen's prediction came true and Diem fell victim to a coup on November 1, 1963. The next day, according to German officials, Washington asked Bonn to lead the way in recognizing the new government led by Maj. Gen. Duong Van Minh so that an immediate announcement of recognition by the United States—which would have run the risk of corroborating rumors about American involvement in the coup—could be avoided.[20] It might have helped Washington that Ludwig Erhard had by then replaced the aging Konrad Adenauer as chancellor. The latter had not only been the architect of the Franco-German treaty, he also had become increasingly critical of the Kennedy administration. The former, on the other hand, was a strong proponent of close ties with Washington—even at the expense of relations with de Gaulle—and it was believed "that Erhard will be less susceptible to the General's mystique than was the Rhinelander Adenauer."[21] The Germans, at any rate, informed the Quai d'Orsay on November 5, 1963, of their impending recognition of the new regime in Saigon. Although it turned out that actual recognition was not extended until November 8 (one day after the U.S. State Department released a statement of recognition), the French were furious. On November 9, Charles Lucet, the director for political affairs, complained to Karl Hermann Knoke, the German chargé d'affaires, that there had been no need for Bonn to recognize the military leaders in Saigon so quickly. In doing so, the Germans, according to Lucet, had violated the spirit of the Franco-German treaty.[22] The Americans observed that de Gaulle was particularly upset "because he considers the coup a setback to his hopes for neutralizing Viet-Nam." However, German diplomats in Saigon felt little sympathy for de Gaulle. As they pointed out a few months later, it was his policies that had caused the coup. Then, after first postponing recognition for more than two weeks, he had extended it in a way wholly unacceptable to the Minh regime. Finally, in January, 1964, he proposed to send as his new ambassador to Saigon a man who had been a former French deputy governor in Indochina and who was currently serving as ambassador to Cuba—thus, in a certain sense, combining colonialism and communism. German diplomats could not help but think that this affront by a country otherwise famously sensitive to diplomatic nuances had been committed deliberately.[23]

By early 1964, it was the Germans who complained that their Parisian partners were not complying with the Élysée Treaty. The bone of contention was de Gaulle's decision to establish diplomatic relations with Beijing. Since his return to power in 1958, de Gaulle had watched the People's Republic of China with growing fascination. In his view, it was anomalous that France should not have diplomatic relations with the world's most populous country only because the United States disapproved of such relations.[24] In 1963, several developments brought the matter to a head. The Sino-Soviet conflict fractured the eastern bloc. At the same time, the American-Soviet agreement on a nuclear test ban, opposed by Paris, suggested a natural affinity between two medium powers unwilling to adhere to the prescriptions of the superpowers. Moreover, France had just successfully disentangled itself from the Algerian imbroglio and was ready to reassert its claim to be a global power. In its quest to break up the bipolar world, France started to court the so-called third world. Beijing was an obvious candidate with which to begin. Finally, de Gaulle felt strongly that the deteriorating situation in Saigon called for a political solution that he could not imagine without the People's Republic's participation.[25] Explaining his decision to establish diplomatic relations with Beijing, de Gaulle—at a January, 1964, press conference—explicitly referred to his conviction that decisions on either peace or war in Asia were impossible without taking Communist China into account.[26]

De Gaulle seems to have reached this decision in his characteristically secluded fashion. At any rate, when the German embassy in early December, 1963, inquired at the Quai d'Orsay about rumors of an impending announcement of France's recognition of the People's Republic, it was told that the French Foreign Office was not contemplating such a move and that it could not imagine de Gaulle doing so given the damage this would no doubt do to relations with Washington.[27] (To be sure, de Gaulle had already revealed his decision to Edgar Faure more than two weeks earlier.) The Germans thus were caught as much by surprise as the Americans by the French move, notwithstanding that the Franco-German treaty provided for early consultation between the two European countries. The Germans soon learned that Paris had declined to subject its Asian policies to the provisions of the treaty because it regarded Bonn as merely a regional power whereas France was destined to play a global role.[28] The Germans therefore had no right to demand a say in matters not pertaining to European problems or those of the Atlantic alliance.

Receiving Erhard in Paris in February, 1964, de Gaulle explained that his move was intended as a step toward a multipolar world.[29] The chancellor, however, could not comprehend why de Gaulle wanted to transform dualism into pluralism. "The Free World," he told his fellow Christian Democrats back home, "should realize that only a uniform policy can advance our cause."[30]

There were voices in Bonn, to be sure, that were intrigued by the prospect of closer relations with Beijing. Some had their eyes focused on the vast Chinese market, but most simply believed that some form of cooperation with the People's Republic might make Moscow more amenable with regard to the German question and that a trade agreement with Communist China could be used to further isolate the East German regime. Erhard thus hurt himself politically when he ruled out even a goods exchange agreement with Beijing upon departing from Washington in June, 1964. According to one of the chancellor's confidants: "Erhard and the rest of the German party had been impressed by the President's emphasis on the gravity of the situation in Southeast Asia and on the relationship of China to that situation. It was clear to the Germans from these statements that this was not the time to take any new initiative in the area with regard to China."[31] The chancellor's decision was supported in German-American circles, as well as by most politicians in Bonn, who set out to belittle both the economic and the political value of a trade agreement. Members of the American Council on Germany made the point that "obviously a western nation could dump almost everything it produces into . . . Red China. But . . . you could also dump everything in the ocean, and you would get about the same return!" In several editorials, a Bundestag deputy close to Erhard congratulated the chancellor on his decision. He observed that a West German flirtation with Red China, while certainly annoying the Soviets, would never force them to abandon their German policy. On the other hand, Bonn had to avoid anything that might create German-American antagonism. Therefore, "any approach to Beijing must be examined with due consideration to both the endangered Southeast Asian region and our loyalty toward Washington."[32] Although German officials indicated that the subject was not buried forever, their American counterparts warned that, given the strong reaction to be expected in the United States, any such move would "not be worth the candle." Eighteen months later, George McGhee reported from Bonn that "the Chancellor can still be relied on to refrain from any move toward Peiping . . . primarily out of loyalty to the US in its struggle in Viet-Nam."[33]

It was exactly this type of deference to American policies worldwide that angered de Gaulle and damaged the Franco-German relationship. In February, 1964, de Gaulle had explicitly told Erhard that it was necessary to engage Beijing in order to stabilize the volatile situation in Vietnam. De Gaulle thought that a quick solution to the Southeast Asia problem was impossible. The best that could be hoped for was some form of modus vivendi. That, however, required the neutralization of both North and South Vietnam—which, in turn, could not be achieved without Chinese consent. De Gaulle believed that Beijing might have a certain interest in neutralization. At least, one had to try. Such an effort, of course, presupposed diplomatic relations with the communist power.[34]

This analysis illustrates de Gaulle's low regard for ideology. A State Department research memorandum observed the French president believed "that geography and history rather than ideology basically govern political alignments."[35] The prevalence of such national categories over communism suggested that the conflict in Southeast Asia could be resolved by traditional balance of power methods. France wanted Beijing and Washington to agree to a neutral buffer zone in Southeast Asia stretching from Indonesia in the south to India in the west and Taiwan and the Philippines in the east. According to an analysis prepared in the State Department's Policy Planning Council, it was de Gaulle's view that within this neutral buffer zone "the elements of real national strength in Southeast Asia (Sihanouk, Sukarno, and Ho Chi Minh) must be given full rein and latitude to rule the area's destinies, irrespective of their ideological character."[36] Washington's Manichean Cold War approach to Southeast Asia was not compatible with de Gaulle's worldview of a multilateral concert of great powers trying to reconcile their competing interests regardless of ideological preferences. In this regard, it is certainly true, as Anne Sa'adah has aptly observed, that de Gaulle "had a critique of American policy in Indochina even before the United States had a policy in Indochina."[37]

However, whereas traditional great-power politics might have been appropriate for "eternal France," the West German stopgap "nation" was hardly equipped for this kind of game.[38] This is not only revealed by the way Lyndon Johnson pushed Ludwig Erhard around in December, 1965, but even more so by the chancellor's minute distinction between teams and battalions, which a U.S. president could hardly comprehend. Semisovereign at best and tainted by the German past, Bonn needed a supranational framework for its security, its diplomacy, and its psyche. It was just when Germans had come to feel at home in the Free World, that Vietnam became a symbol for the staying power of that very same Free World. In a sense, then, what was threatened in Vietnam was not merely some distant spot in

Southeast Asia, but also the framework of West Germany's nascent identity. It was, therefore, more than a set phrase when Chancellor Erhard declared that there was no country more closely attached to Vietnam than Germany, even if it lay far away geographically.[39] The standard expression to capture this relationship was the analogy between Saigon and Berlin, which U.S. national security adviser McGeorge Bundy carried to extremes when he remarked "that the defense of Berlin, right now, is in Vietnam."[40]

The Berlin-Saigon analogy and the underlying idea of an indivisible freedom adapted Vietnam to the dualistic framework of the Cold War, located it unambiguously on the map of the Free World, and interconnected U.S. policy in Southeast Asia with the most fundamental political experiences of West Germans. It is no surprise, then, that most Germans during the early to mid-1960s approved of U.S. policy in Vietnam and opposed de Gaulle's call for neutralization. Fritz Erler of the opposition Social Democrats, returning from one of the intimate transatlantic Bilderberg conferences, told Dean Rusk that the position taken on the Vietnam problem by the French delegates "could be summarized in five words: 'Save face and lose Viet-Nam.' He said that many people in Germany previously favorable to de Gaulle's policies were becoming disenchanted." That was an all-party view. In October, 1964, the U.S. embassy reported that in both the upper and lower houses of the West German parliament, "there was almost no support for de Gaulle's neutralization plans—most deputies agreed that this is no solution in the present circumstances." The mantra heard over and over again in West German political circles was that in Vietnam neutralization meant "bolshevization." As Ludwig Erhard informed the leadership of the Christian Democrats, the neutralization of Indochina would inevitably lead to its falling prey to communism.[41]

The chancellor also stood his ground in Paris, dutifully and with perhaps some slight exaggeration reporting to U.S. ambassador George McGhee how he had told de Gaulle that neutralization was sheer illusion. However, when McGhee returned to the chancellery asking whether it might not be possible for Erhard to come out publicly against de Gaulle's calls, the Foreign Office balked. Erhard's allegiance to the United States had already severely strained the Franco-German partnership, and German diplomats were reluctant to aggravate the situation any further.[42]

The American attempt to bring the Germans in position against the French on neutralization owed a lot to an increasing nervousness on the banks of the Potomac.[43] The situation in Saigon was extremely volatile after General Khanh's coup in late January, 1964. The press and congressional leaders seemed to become attracted to the notion of neutralization. The State Department's Roger Hilsman complained that "de Gaulle, Lippmann and Mansfield have set the neutralist hares running with self-fulfilling prophecies." President Johnson wanted to order Amb. Henry Cabot Lodge from Saigon into the Paris lion's den "for the purpose of knocking down the idea of neutralization wherever it rears its ugly head."[44] Washington, worried that other European countries might follow de Gaulle's lead, tried to enlist Erhard as an additional knight to slay the dragon. Moreover, reassuring reports on the German government's steadfastness contrasted with alarming signs in the country's press. In the summer of 1964, the United States Information Agency (USIA) reported that "there was less and less comment against negotiations and eventual neutralization of the area, with most of the journals hinting or saying outright that once the American elections are over, the U.S. position on this problem must be changed." Four weeks later, it warned: "the drift toward negotiations and probable eventual neutralization seems even more clear than a month ago."[45]

In fact, Erhard's unequivocal position was not even wholly shared in the Foreign Office. This was mainly due to an assessment of the situation not too dissimilar from de Gaulle's. As early as 1963, German diplomats had reported from Saigon—in a somewhat dated vocabulary—that "final victory" (Endsieg) was nowhere in sight. When it turned out that the military rulers succeeding Diem were equally unable to solve the South's domestic problems, assessments grew even gloomier. German officials questioned whether Washington was at all aware of the grave situation. A continuation of the present course was deemed hopeless.[46] Officials within the Foreign Office were not certain what conclusions should be drawn from this assessment, however. In fact, papers prepared in anticipation of Henry Cabot Lodge's stopover in Bonn during his European tour to drum up support for U.S. policy reflect a decided ambivalence, if not confusion. On August 20, the Political Division sent a memorandum to Undersecretary Rolf Lahr explaining that the United States had been unable to contain the Vietcong in even a single district. Although the Americans were displaying optimism at regaining the South Vietnamese people's trust, events thus far had proven them wrong. The memorandum surmised that the United States now wanted to switch gears and move from what the Germans called "a somewhat chaotic defense" to offensive operations. This change was seen to flow logically from the conviction that neutralization at the present time would inevitably hand the country over to communism, that it was necessary to shore up the Saigon regime, and that for the time being, any solution to the problem would have to be a military one. The memorandum noted that Lodge had been unable to persuade Paris of the wisdom of this course. Nevertheless, it concluded that Bonn should welcome Washington's determination. Four days later, a second memorandum originating in the same office took quite a different tack. It pointed out that the Federal Republic had thus far always faithfully reiterated Washington's stance. However, the talks with Lodge should now be used to convey the Federal Republic's view that it was time to look for a political solution to the Vietnamese conflict. Finally, the memorandum stated, "opportunities for a political solution should also be exploited in order to reconcile the continuing antagonism between the United States and France with regard to Vietnam."[47]

When Cabot Lodge met with German officials the next day, he was asked why the United States would regard the convening of an international conference as a diplomatic defeat. His standard explanation that it would undermine South Vietnamese morale was not challenged. Instead, the Germans navigated a careful middle course that established a pattern for the months and years to come. They signaled understanding of American reluctance to convene a conference right away, but expressed their hope that such a solution would be possible at a later date. Until then, the U.S. policy of strengthening South Vietnam's will to resist was deemed to be plausible.[48] Caught between a rock and a hard place by their two indispensable allies, the Germans in fact wanted to have it both ways. As the Foreign Office's Southeast Asia desk explained in 1965, the Federal Republic approved of the Americans' present policy, while agreeing with the general objective of French policy.[49]

The Foreign Office's more ambivalent attitude toward U.S. policy in Vietnam as compared to Erhard's in the summer of 1964 might well have stemmed from some sharp French criticism. This criticism was triggered by a joint U.S.-German communiqué issued after Erhard's visit to Washington in June stressing Bonn's support for U.S. policy in Vietnam. According to the German ambassador in Paris, de Gaulle had felt this explicit statement to be "a slap in the face." The French expressed their disappointment in no uncertain terms during the semiannual Franco-German summit in July. Erhard's chief of staff, Ludger Westrick, afterward informed McGhee "that the foremost point of irritation on the part of the French . . . during the talks, seemed to be German support of U.S. policy in South Vietnam. Couve characterized German policy as a 'satellite policy.'" De Gaulle no doubt regarded Vietnam in particular as proof of Bonn's vassalage toward the United States.[50] In his July 23 press conference, the French president included it in a long list of grievances against German policies that seemed to disappoint his idea of an independent European policy.[51]

As the German embassy reported from talks in Paris after the general's press conference, the Franco-German relationship was indeed approaching a crisis. It was admitted that there was no way the principal difference between German and French policy—that is, French insistence on independence and German readiness to sacrifice some room for maneuver—could be overcome for the sake of unequivocal security guarantees from Washington. The embassy, however, thought that it was less an unwillingness on de Gaulle's part to accept this basic difference that accounted for the present crisis, but rather the French impression that Bonn had failed to stand up to the United States on each and every issue. Vietnam, the embassy continued, was clearly a case in which de Gaulle considered German interests to be so marginal that it would not have been necessary for Bonn to take sides at all. If Bonn would display at least some independence on issues like this, it might be possible to tolerate the principal difference between French and German policy.[52]

In the weeks and month that followed, both Paris and Washington continued their efforts to impress their views on the Federal Republic. During consultations in December, 1964, the French again stressed that the conflict could not be resolved against Beijing's wishes. China, they said, was ready to negotiate. So was Hanoi, which wanted no more than the neutralization of South Vietnam. French officials explained that both parts of Vietnam had to gradually move closer to one another: The North had to distance itself from Beijing and the South needed to establish a socialist government along Cambodian or Indonesian lines.[53] The Germans, however, remained skeptical, still fearing that negotiations would lead to a communist takeover. The Foreign Office adopted a wait-and-see attitude, primarily out of concern that it would hurt Germany to unequivocally come down on either the French or the American side of the argument.[54] Ludwig Erhard, on the other hand, never refrained from publicly voicing support for U.S. policy in Southeast Asia. All the more so when—after the start of the Rolling Thunder bombing raids on North Vietnam and the American commitment of ground troops in the South—talk of neutralization faded while the U.S. pressured Bonn for a tangible commitment to the cause in Vietnam.

Neither Paris nor Washington fully understood the dilemma created for the Federal Republic when its two indispensable allies each asked for support of their antagonistic strategies in Southeast Asia. In fact, Vietnam was not as peripheral to Germany as de Gaulle believed. Whereas France thought of Vietnam as an American protectorate, West Germany viewed it as a problem of western solidarity[55]—a solidarity that held together the Free World in which West Germans had just found a new home. Frank Costigliola's astute observation that "the Vietnam War had become incorporated into the Germans' structure of meaning" is therefore true even beyond the realm of alliance politics.[56] Certainly, the United States possessed, in the words of the Policy Planning Council, "great assets for leverage on the Federal Republic far outmatching anything de Gaulle can hope to offer"—assets that could "almost certainly assure that Bonn keeps a firm course within the Atlantic Alliance and is not seduced by the sirenic lure of Gaullism."[57] However, when looking at Bonn's Southeast Asia policies we should take into account not only power relationships and alliance theories, but also the role Germany's difficult search for a postwar identity played.

Finally, both French calls for a more independent German policy and American pressure for a German flag in Vietnam were more than any West German government could muster in the 1960s. In the end, Washington's pressure in particular proved to be counterproductive. West Germans, encouraged not least by de Gaulle, increasingly wondered whether America's war in Asia really was in their best interest. After all, if the alliance was mainly concerned with containing Chinese expansionism rather than snatching the eastern part of Germany from the jaws of Soviet communism, then the Berlin-Saigon analogy was of dubious value. Even worse, it tended to turn Berlin, as Frank Ninkovich put it, into "a symbol without any Germanic content."[58] Thus, the American fixation on Vietnam eventually undermined the notion of the Free World as a framework for a West German identity.

Notes

1. Alexander Werth, *De Gaulle: A Political Biography* (New York: Simon and Schuster, 1966), p. 337.

2. Paul Frank, *Entschlüsselte Botschaft: Ein Diplomat macht Inventur,* 2d ed. (Stuttgart: Deutsche Verlags-Anstalt, 1981), pp. 95–96.

3. Meeting in the West Wing, the White House, 10:45 P.M., Monday, Dec. 20, 1965, National Security File (NSF), President's Appointment File (Diary Backup), Box 26, Lyndon B. Johnson Library, Austin, Tex. (hereafter LBJL); George McGhee, *At the Creation of a New Germany: From Adenauer to Brandt, An Ambassador's Account* (New Haven, Conn., and London: Yale University Press, 1989), pp. 184–85.

4. Henry Kissinger, "Dealing with de Gaulle," in *De Gaulle and the United States: A Centennial Appraisal,* ed. Robert O. Paxton and Nicholas Wahl (Oxford and Providence, R. I.: Berg, 1994), pp. 331–41, 331.

5. Frank Costigliola, *France and the United States: The Cold Alliance Since World War II* (New York: Twayne, 1992), p. 149.

6. See Knut Linsel, *Charles de Gaulle und Deutschland, 1914–1969* (Sigmaringen: Jan Thorbecke Verlag, 1998), pp. 157–58.

7. Klaiber to Auswärtiges Amt, Subject: Aspekte der französischen Außenpolitik nach der Rede Couve de Murvilles vom 20. Oktober 1965, Nov. 4, 1965, B 24/559, fol. 168–71, Politisches Archiv des Auswärtigen Amtes, Berlin (hereafter PAAA).

8. See his radio address from the Hotel Matignon, June 13, 1958, in Charles de Gaulle, *Discours et messages* (*DM*), vol. 3, *Avec le renouveau, Mai 1958–Juillet 1962* (Paris: Plon, 1970), p. 18.

9. See Maurice Vaïsse, *La Grandeur: La politique étrangère du général de Gaulle, 1958–1969* (Paris: Fayard, 1998), pp. 22–52; Frank Costigliola, "Kennedy, de Gaulle, and the Challenge of

Consultation," in *De Gaulle and the United States,* ed. Paxton and Wahl, pp. 169–94, esp. 169–70.

10. As quoted by Pierre Mélandri in his comment in *De Gaulle and the United States,* ed. Paxton and Wahl, p. 318. See also de Gaulle's contention in his press conference of July 23, 1964, that "la répartition de l'univers entre deux camps, respectivement menés par Washington et par Moscou, répond de moins en moins à la situation réelle." De Gaulle, *DM,* vol. 4, *Pour l'effort, Août 1962–Décembre 1965* (Paris: Plon, 1970), p. 227.

11. Stephen A. Kocs, *Autonomy or Power? The Franco-German Relationship and Europe's Strategic Choices, 1955–1995* (Westport, Conn., and London: Praeger, 1995), p. 23.

12. Frank Costigliola, "The Vietnam War and the Challenges to American Power in Europe," in *International Perspectives on Vietnam,* ed. Lloyd C. Gardner and Ted Gittinger (College Station: Texas A&M University Press, 2000), pp. 143–53.

13. Memorandum, Subject: Vorschläge de Gaulle's über die Organisation der westlichen Allianz, Nov. 23, 1958, quoted in Linsel, *Charles de Gaulle,* p. 174.

14. Alfred Grosser, "France and Germany: Divergent Outlooks," *Foreign Affairs* 44 (1965): pp. 26–36, 29.

15. Karl W. Deutsch et al., *France, Germany and the Western Alliance: A Study of Elite Attitudes on European Integration and World Politics* (New York: Charles Scribner's Sons, 1967), p. 266. A typescript of the study is in White House Aides Files: Fred Panzer, Box 211, LBJL.

16. Paul Noack, "Er kam und ging als Fremder: Charles de Gaulle in der westdeutschen Einschätzung zwischen 1958 und 1970," in *De Gaulle, Deutschland, und Europa,* ed. Wilfried Loth and Robert Picht (Opladen: Leske und Budrich, 1991), pp. 83–94.

17. Fredrik Logevall, "De Gaulle, Neutralization, and American Involvement in Vietnam, 1963–1964," *Pacific Historical Review* 61 (1992): pp. 69–102, esp. pp. 74–78; USIA, R-185–63(A): Assessment of Reactions to Viet-Nam Crisis, Box 17, Office of Research, Record Group (RG) 306, National Archives and Records Administration, College Park, Md. (hereafter NARA).

18. Fischer-Lossainen, memorandum, subject: Deutsch-vietnamesische Beziehungen, July 11, 1963, B 37/62, PAAA; Jansen, memorandum, subject: Lage in Vietnam, Aug. 22, 1963, ibid.

19. On the Buddhist crisis and its coverage in the American media, see David Kaiser, *American Tragedy: Kennedy, Johnson, and the Origins of the Vietnam War* (Cambridge, Mass., and London: Belknap Press, a division of Harvard University Press, 2000), pp. 213–30.

20. Memorandum, subject: Anerkennung der provisorischen Regierung von Südvietnam, n.d., B 37/62, PAAA. On November 2, Henry Cabot Lodge, the U.S. ambassador in Saigon, welcoming indications from Secretary of State Dean Rusk that Washington was leaning toward prompt recognition, cautioned: "We should not be first to recognize but should assure other friendly Embassies that this is our attitude that we will recognize as soon as a few others have done so." Telegram, Embassy in Vietnam to Department of State, Nov. 2, 1963, in *Foreign Relations of the United States (FRUS), 1961–1963,* vol. 4, *Vietnam, August–December 1963* (Washington, D.C.: GPO, 1991), p. 526. Other evidence from U.S. files suggests that policy makers were much more concerned that an immediate recognition of the military junta would send the wrong signal to Latin America than they were worried about being implicated in the coup against Diem. See Department of State to Embassy in Vietnam, Nov. 1, 1963, telegram, *FRUS, 1961–1963,* p. 4:525; Memorandum for the Record of Discussion at the Daily White House Staff Meeting, Washington, Nov. 4, 1963, 8 A.M., ibid., pp. 4:555–56. On U.S. involvement in the coup, see Kaiser, *American Tragedy,* pp. 248–83.

21. Lampson to Department of State, subject: Current British Foreign Office Thinking about France, Oct. 15, 1963, Bureau of European Affairs, Subject Files (J. Robert Schaetzel), Box 1, RG 59, NARA.

22. Memorandum, subject: Anerkennung der provisorischen Regierung von Südvietnam, n.d. (Nov., 1963), B 37/62, PAAA.

23. Situation Report Prepared in the Department of State for the President, Nov. 23, 1963, *FRUS, 1961–1963*, p. 4:630; Botschaft Saigon to Auswärtiges Amt, subject: Französische Beurteilung der Lage in Vietnam und vietnamesisch-französischen Beziehungen, Aug. 5, 1964, B 37/65, PAAA.

24. See Alain Peyrefitte, *C'était de Gaulle*, vol. 1, *La France redevient la France* (Paris: Fayard, 1994), pp. 314, 319–20.

25. Vaïsse, *La Grandeur*, pp. 514–21; Marianna P. Sullivan, *France's Vietnam Policy: A Study in French-American Relations* (Westport, Conn., and London: Greenwood Press, 1978), pp. 20–23.

26. See de Gaulle, *DM*, pp. 4:178–82.

27. Klaiber to Auswärtiges Amt, Dec. 7, 1963, B 24/479, PAAA.

28. See Paul Frank's comment in *De Gaulle ou l'éternel défi. 56 témoignages recueillis et présentés par Jean Lacouture et Roland Mehl* (Paris: Seuil, 1988), p. 364.

29. See "Gespräch des Bundeskanzlers Erhard mit Staatspräsident de Gaulle in Paris, Feb. 14, 1964," in *Akten zur Auswärtigen Politik der Bundesrepublik Deutschland* (*AAPD*), *1964*, 2 vols., ed. Institut für Zeitgeschichte (Munich: R. Oldenbourg, 1995), pp. 1:203–15.

30. CDU-Bundesvorstand, Feb. 25, 1964, in *Adenauer: "Stetigkeit in der Politik." Die Protokolle des CDU-Bundesvorstands, 1961–1965*, ed. Günter Buchstab (Düsseldorf: Droste, 1998), pp. 607–77, here p. 610.

31. Ackermann and Dunnigan, June 26, 1964, memorandum of conversation, POL 2 GER W, Central Foreign Policy Files, 1964–66 (hereafter CFPF, years covered), Box 2208, RG 59, NARA. See also memorandum of conversation, June 12, 1964, *FRUS, 1964–1968*, vol. 15, *Berlin Crisis, 1962–1963* (Washington, D.C.: GPO, 1994), pp. 119–20; McGhee and Strauss, July 8, 1964, memorandum of conversation, POL 2 GER W, CFPF, 1964–66, Box 2208, RG 59, NARA; Tyler and Knappstein, July 31, memorandum of conversation, 1964, POL 324 GER, CFPF, 1964–66, Box 2195, RG 59, NARA.

32. American Council on Germany, Luncheon Meeting, Dec. 17, 1964, Box 13, Christopher T. Emmet Papers, Hoover Institution Archives, Stanford, Calif.; Ernst Majonica, "Kampf um Südost-Asien," *Passauer Neue Presse*, June 12, 1964, pp. 1–2; idem, "Ein Flirt mit Peking bringt nichts ein," *Rheinischer Merkur*, June 19, 1964, p. 5.

33. Tyler and Blumenfeld, June 18, 1964, memorandum of conversation, POL 324 GER, CFPF, 1964–66, Box 2195, RG 59, NARA; McGhee to SecState, subject: Erhard Visit, no. 6: Eastern Policy and China, Nov. 16, 1965, Box 192, NSF, LBJL.

34. See Gespräch des Bundeskanzlers Erhard mit Staatspräsident de Gaulle in Paris, Feb. 14, 1964, *AAPD, 1964*, pp. 1:203–15, esp. pp. 1:211–12.

35. Hughes to Meloy, subject: Study on Trends of French Foreign Policy, Jan. 8, 1963, Bureau of European Affairs, Subject Files (J. Robert Schaetzel), Box 1, RG 59, NARA.

36. Green to Rostow and Tyler, subject: Some Speculations on de Gaulle's Moves in Asia, Feb. 6, 1964, Records of the Policy Planning Council 1963–64, Box 252, RG 59, NARA. See also André Fontaine, "What is French Policy?" *Foreign Affairs* 45 (1966): pp. 58–76.

37. Anne Sa'adah, "Idées Simples and Idées Fixe: De Gaulle, the United States, and Vietnam," in *De Gaulle and the United States*, ed. Paxton and Wahl, pp. 295–315, here p. 295.

38. See Klaus Hildebrand, "Der provisorische Staat und das ewige Frankreich. Die deutsch-französischen Beziehungen 1963–1969," *Historische Zeitschrift* 240 (1985): pp. 283–311.

39. Gespräch des Bundeskanzlers Erhard mit Präsident Johnson in Washington, June 4, 1965, *AAPD, 1965*, 3 vols. (Munich: R. Oldenbourg, 1996), pp. 2:961–67, here p. 2:962.

40. Congressional Reception, Feb. 12, 1965, Congressional Briefings, Box 1, LBJL.

41. Rusk and Erler, subject: Political Situation in Germany, Mar. 23, 1964, memorandum of conversation, POL 324 GER, CFPF, 1964–66, Box 2195, RG 59, NARA; Sutterlin to Department of State, subject: Proceedings of the West German Bundestag and Bundesrat for the Parliamentary Year 1963–64, Oct. 10, 1964, POL 15–2 GER W, CFPF, 1964–66, Box 2222, RG 59, NARA; Ernst Majonica, "Das State Department und unsere Sorgen," *Rheinischer Merkur,* Apr. 24, 1964; idem, "US-Sorgen und Europa," *Neue Passauer Presse,* Aug. 10, 1964, pp. 1–2; CDU-Bundesvorstand, Feb. 25, 1964, in Buchstab, *Adenauer,* p. 609.

42. Gespräch des Bundeskanzlers Erhard mit dem amerikanischen Botschafter McGhee, Feb. 18, 1964, *AAPD, 1964,* pp. 1:255–63; Aufzeichnung des Staatssekretärs Carstens, Apr. 21, 1964, ibid., pp. 1:447–49; Bundesminister Schröder an Bundeskanzler Erhard, May 17, 1964, ibid., pp. 1:541–42. Erhard nevertheless told those attending a foreign press luncheon in June that there could be no neutralization of Indochina. See USIA, M-488–64: Significant World Press Quotations on Vietnam, July 22, 1964, Office of Research, Research Memoranda 1963–1982, Box 3, RG 306, NARA.

43. Fredrik Logevall, *Choosing War: The Lost Chance for Peace and the Escalation of War in Vietnam* (Berkeley, Los Angeles, and London: University of California Press, 1999), pp. 108–33.

44. Hilsman memorandum, *FRUS, 1964–1968,* vol. 1, *Vietnam, 1964* (Washington, D.C.: GPO, 1992), p. 177; message from the president to the ambassador in Vietnam (Lodge), Mar. 20, 1964, ibid., p. 1:185. See also Lloyd Gardner, "Lyndon Johnson and de Gaulle," in *De Gaulle and the United States,* ed. Paxton and Wahl, pp. 257–78, esp. pp. 265–73; Lloyd C. Gardner, *Pay Any Price: Lyndon Johnson and the Wars for Vietnam* (Chicago: Ivan R. Dee, 1995), pp. 112–17.

45. USIA M-597–64: Free World Reaction to Viet-Nam: Aug., 1964, Sept. 17, 1964; and M-639–64: Free World Reaction to Viet-Nam: Sept., 1964, Oct. 19, 1964, all in Office of Research, Research Memoranda 1963–1982, Box 4, RG 306, NARA.

46. Wendland to Auswärtiges Amt, Betr.: Lage in Süd-Vietnam, Feb. 13, 1963, B 37/60, PAAA; Herrmann to Bundesminister der Verteidigung, Betr.: Die militärische Lage in Süd-Vietnam Ende Februar 1964, Feb. 24, 1964, B 37/66, ibid.; Wendland to Auswärtiges Amt, Betr.: Aktionsprogramm der Republik Vietnam, Mar. 16, 1964, B 37/61, ibid.; Bassler to Ministerbüro, Mar. 16, 1964, ibid.; Aufzeichnung Referat I B 5, Betr.: Südvietnam, n.d. (May, 1964), ibid.

47. Jansen to Lahr, Betr.: Besuch des US-Sonderbotschafters H. Cabot Lodge, Aug. 20, 1964, B 37/65, PAAA; Jansen to Lahr, Betr.: Die Haltung der Bundesregierung zur Südvietnam-Frage, Aug. 24, 1964, B 37/62, ibid.

48. Westrick and Lodge, Aug. 25, 1964, Gesprächsaufzeichnung, B 37/65, PAAA.

49. See Referat I B 5, memorandum, subject: Die Lage in Vietnam, June 26, 1965, B 37/128, ibid.

50. Klaiber to Auswärtiges Amt, July 10, 1964, *AAPD, 1964,* pp. 2:808–11, here p. 2:809; Gespräche des Staatssekretärs Carstens mit Staatspräsident de Gaulle und dem französischen Außenminister Couve de Murville, July 4, 1964, and Gespräch des Bundeskanzlers Erhard mit dem amerikanischen Botschafter McGhee, July 6, 1964, *AAPD, 1964,* pp. 2:766–78, 787–95. Embassy in Germany to Department of State, July 11, 1964, telegram, *FRUS, 1964–1968,* vol. 15, *Germany and Berlin* (Washington, D.C.: GPO, 1999), p. 141.

51. See de Gaulle's press conference held at the Elysée palace, July 23, 1964, de Gaulle, *DM,* pp. 4:222–37, esp. p. 4:230. See also Georges-Henri Soutou, *L'alliance incertaine: Les rapports politico-stratégiques franco-allemands, 1954–1996* (Paris: Fayard, 1996), pp. 272–77; Joachim Scholtyseck, "Frankreich, Westdeutschland und Vietnam 1945 bis 1969," *Revue d'Allemagne et des Pays de langue allemande* 31 (1999): pp. 423–37, esp. pp. 434–35.

52. Jansen to Schröder, subject: Gespräch in Paris über die Pressekonferenz de Gaulles vom 23.7., Aug. 4, 1964, B 24/514, PAAA.

53. Niederschrift über die deutsch-französischen Konsultationen vom 18. Dezember 1964, in Bonn über Süd-und Ostasien, Dec. 23, 1964, B 37/128, ibid.

54. Bassler to Referat L 1, subject: Entwicklung in Südostasien (Ergebnis der Botschafterkonferenz), Feb. 9, 1965, ibid.; Referat I B 5 to von Fröwig, subject: Die Lage in Vietnam. Beitrag anläßlich der deutsch-französischen Konsultation der Leiter der Politischen Abteilungen der beiden Aussenministerien am 25. März 1965, Mar. 22, 1965, ibid.; Referat I B 5, memorandum, subject: Die Lage in Vietnam, Mar. 26, 1965, B 37/161, ibid..

55. See Gespräch des Bundesministers Schröder mit dem französischen Außenminister Couve de Murville, June 8, 1964, *AAPD, 1964,* pp. 2:755–66, esp. p. 763.

56. Costigliola, "Vietnam War," p. 151.

57. Green to Rostow and Tyler, subject: Some Speculations on de Gaulle's Moves in Asia, Feb. 6, 1964, Records of the Policy Planning Council 1963–64, Box 252, RG 59, NARA.

58. Frank A. Ninkovich, *Germany and the United States: The Transformation of the German Question Since 1945,* rev. ed. (New York: Twayne, 1995), 125.

The ASPEN Channel and the Problem of the Bombing

FREDRIK LOGEVALL

The Americans named it ASPEN after the ski resort in Colorado, but no doubt with the cold Swedish winters in mind. A peace initiative undertaken by Sweden during the years of rapid escalation in Vietnam, it featured frequent secret meetings between Swedish officials and North Vietnamese representatives in Warsaw and Hanoi, and between Foreign Minister Torsten Nilsson and Secretary of State Dean Rusk in Washington. The initiative, which lasted from late 1965 to the start of 1968, did not succeed in its aim of bringing about negotiations, but a close look at its history yields important insight into the nature of the war in a crucial period, as well as the reasons why diplomacy failed.

The narrative in this chapter relies extensively on declassified Swedish documents to examine the history of the ASPEN channel.[1] It affirms the generally held view that the initiative (as with others in the period) failed in large measure because neither Washington nor Hanoi were anxious to begin peace negotiations. The prediction by numerous observers in the months before the onset of major combat in 1965—that once the real shooting started and the body counts skyrocketed, both sides would dig in and compromise would become more difficult—proved to be correct. Yet the new evidence also shows that both the Democratic Republic of Vietnam (DRV) and the United States saw real value in maintaining the Swedish channel, even as they rejected opportunities to move toward a diplomatic solution. Both powers deemed the Swedes to be dependable and conscientious and were prepared to accept, at least to a point, that Sweden's neutral status gave it a special claim to impartiality. Even after Swedish leaders made statements and chose policy options that the Johnson administration took to be plainly anti-American and pro-DRV, U.S. officials sought to keep the channel open. To a remarkable extent, these officials were able to keep the secret diplomacy over Vietnam and the growing public tensions with Stockholm separate.

The initiative's history also provides graphic evidence of the global reach of the Vietnam War, of the way it shaped foreign policy decisions and political discourse in countries far removed from the scene of the fighting. The Vietnam War, the Swedish channel reminds us, was a truly international struggle. What is more, the ASPEN story calls attention to something too often forgotten in the scholarship that makes up the so-called New Cold War History: the important role domestic political imperatives played in shaping foreign policy decisions in both large and small nations. Domestic politics helped fashion the Social Democratic government's response to the war from an early point. Moreover, although Prime Minister Tage Erlander and his colleagues worked hard to keep the ASPEN channel secret, they understood very well that the effort, regardless of its success or failure, could ultimately provide a significant boost to their party's standing at home.

None of this should be construed as saying that domestic politics drove the Stockholm government's decision to launch the initiative. The primary determinant was surely the stated one: to act as an intermediary between the warring parties and to help facilitate an end to the bloodshed. As Nilsson later summarized it: "Our ambition was to bring the parties closer together."[2] He and other officials at the Foreign Ministry hoped that Sweden's long tradition of neutrality and nonalignment in world affairs, as well as its reputation as an honest broker on the international stage, might allow it to play a constructive role in terminating the war.

The magnitude of their task quickly became clear. The prospects for an early settlement seemed dim. Both sides were too stubborn and unimaginative, the Swedes reasoned, especially the United States. President Lyndon Johnson's decision to Americanize the war troubled Swedish leaders deeply, all the more so because of their country's close ties to the United States. Sweden in the mid-1960s was perhaps the most Americanized country in Europe—where U.S. consumer goods lined store shelves and *Bonanza* and *Perry Mason* ran on evening television—and the two countries shared a long history as liberal democracies. Swedes admired the dynamism and sense of optimism in American society, while many American observers in midcentury wrote in glowing terms about Sweden's "middle way." True, there had been tensions over Sweden's decision to remain neutral in the early Cold War rather than join the western alliance, but these were overcome. In 1963, while still vice president, Lyndon Johnson said that the "happy and honorable bonds" between the two countries were stronger than ever. Few thought to disagree.[3]

These ties made it all the harder for leaders in Stockholm to understand why Washington insisted on pursuing a military solution in Vietnam. It made no sense to them. Erlander and Nilsson became distraught after viewing images of U.S. aircraft carpet-bombing the Vietnamese countryside and being advised of the massive infusion of American ground forces. As the war ground on through 1966 and 1967, they became convinced that the United States was—as Erlander put it—"squandering its image of goodwill" and its well-deserved reputation as a fair player. American credibility, far from being strengthened, was being drastically undermined. Significantly, many in official Washington had come to agree with this assessment, among them Defense Secretary Robert McNamara, one of the architects of the war. Swedish officials did not know it, but many of the arguments McNamara voiced in late 1966 and 1967 bore a striking similarity to their own. He and they agreed that the U.S. bombing campaign, Operation Rolling Thunder, was not achieving the results American planners had set for it, and that it represented the single biggest obstacle to achieving a negotiated settlement to the war.

Nevertheless, the Swedes believed it was imperative to continue to work for such a settlement. Foreign Ministry officials in Stockholm understood that Washington would be entering the negotiations from a position of weakness, and that the terms of the settlement would be imperfect, but they saw no alternative. Their conviction that there was none drove Nilsson and his colleagues on, right through ASPEN's end. In his final letter to Dean Rusk, on January 25, 1968, Nilsson said he stood ready to do everything in his power to help bring about a peaceful end to the war.[4]

For Nilsson, as for many others in the international community, Vietnam first became the focus of attention in 1964. He spoke about the issue for the first time in September, calling for the great powers to exercise restraint while a solution was sought for the "serious crisis in South Vietnam." Nilsson had received a series of cables from Swedish diplomats in East Asia detailing both the worsening politico-military situation in South Vietnam and the major gains the Vietcong made in 1964, especially in areas close to Saigon. Particularly forceful were those sent by Lennart Petri, Sweden's ambassador in Beijing. Petri became convinced in 1962 that the struggle in Indochina was a nationalist one. Moreover, he believed that the United States—"a very white, very foreign power" in the eyes of most Vietnamese—could never achieve a lasting military victory. It was foolishness, in his opinion, for the Americans to claim that Hanoi took its orders from Beijing. Vietnam was in no way a Chinese puppet, Petri said; his interaction with Chinese officials had made that very clear. Why, then, Petri wondered at several points in 1963 and 1964, were the Americans so resistant to accepting this fact? Ho Chi Minh was a dedicated communist, but he was above all a nationalist, Petri believed, and there was no necessary contradiction between the two. A "national communism" in Vietnam, he wrote in October, 1964, "should not, a priori, be deemed different from the national communism in, for example, Yugoslavia."[5]

Yet Petri got a chilly response in late 1964 and early 1965 when he tried to interest his government in engaging in diplomatic efforts to try to head off large-scale war in Vietnam. Petri had in mind meeting with DRV representatives in Beijing, followed perhaps by his own visit to Hanoi. Such discussions, he suggested, could yield much information about where Ho Chi Minh and his colleagues stood on the question of a negotiated settlement—information that could then be passed on to Washington. Foreign Ministry officials showed scant interest. Indeed, they went so far as to forbid Petri from meeting officially with DRV representatives. Sweden, they reminded him, did not have diplomatic relations with North Vietnam. In a telegram to Petri on February 7, 1965—the very day on which LBJ ordered the first air strikes on North Vietnam—Nilsson gently chided the ambassador for exaggerating what a small neutral state could accomplish in the international arena. Petri could have "limited" contacts with Hanoi diplomats in Beijing, Nilsson said, and he could visit Hanoi "as a tourist," but he could not meet with DRV representatives in an official capacity while there.[6]

Nilsson's perspective changed in the months that followed. Like many in the world community, he had clung to the belief that Lyndon Johnson would ultimately refrain from Americanizing the war. By the spring of 1965, however, a major war seemed imminent. On May 1, Nilsson told a group of labor leaders in Gothenburg that "the ordinary poverty-stricken Vietnamese longs for peace." However, such a peace could be achieved only "if all the parties involved" pledged to take "all opportunities for negotiation and reconciliation."[7]

That summer, with the fighting escalating rapidly and a negotiated settlement seemingly more distant than ever, several analysts at the Swedish Foreign Ministry began batting about ideas for some form of diplomatic initiative. It is here that we find the origin of what later was called ASPEN. In August, Nilsson called the group together for a meeting—included, in addition to Nilsson, were Permanent Undersecretary of State Leif Belfrage, political affairs director Dick Hichens-Bergström, and Jean-Christophe Öberg, the first secretary of political affairs, who had just returned from a diplomatic tour of Djakarta, Bangkok, and Saigon. Öberg had prepared a memorandum for discussion centered on the question of whether there existed some way of breaking the diplomatic deadlock between Washington and Hanoi. Had the time come for a Swedish effort in this direction? Öberg thought it had. He suggested that Stockholm seek contact with one of the National Liberation Front's (NLF) representatives in Europe, in order to

seek an answer to a key question: "Would the NLF agree, without negotiations or a diplomatic settlement, to a mutual suspension of military action
in North as well as South Vietnam?" Such a "freeze" might well interest the
NLF, Öberg reasoned, given its predominant position on the ground, and
would make it possible for Washington to suspend its Rolling Thunder
bombing campaign temporarily without losing face. The parties could then
move toward formal negotiations.

Hichens-Bergström and Belfrage liked the plan immediately. Nilsson
was noncommittal; he told the group he needed to think about it over-
night. After giving his assent the next day so that the initiative could go forward, Nilsson emphasized that the plan should be handled with great
discretion. In particular, the NLF must not be given the impression that the
U.S. government was somehow behind the plan. ASPEN was a Swedish initiative and must be seen as such, Nilsson told his colleagues.[8]

Why the decision to approach the NLF and not go directly to the North
Vietnamese? Öberg did not say. In time, he and his colleagues would alter
their strategy, but in the spring and summer of 1965 they appear to have reasoned that, because Hanoi consistently denied that its troops were fighting
in the South, contact should be made first with the Vietcong. Öberg
thought the American view that Hanoi called all the shots in the insurgency
and completely dominated the Vietcong was simplistic, but the same
charge could be leveled against his own conception of the NLF as the dominant partner. Petri had a much better sense of the complexity of the DRV-
Vietcong relationship, in which there was a constant push and pull but
Hanoi ranked supreme. For the moment, though, the Beijing ambassador's
position remained the minority view.

After an aborted attempt to establish contact with the NLF's Moscow
representative, Stockholm officials arranged a secret meeting in Algiers in
early September between Sweden's ambassador there, Bengt Rabeus, and
the NLF's Algerian representative, Huynh Van Tam. Rabeus had just arrived in Stockholm for a short vacation when he was told to return to Algiers immediately. He met Tam on September 7 and presented the "freeze"
proposal. Tam remained poker-faced throughout. Did the Americans
know of this proposal? he asked. No, Rabeus replied. Did Hanoi? No,
Rabeus repeated. His government had decided that only the NLF should
be informed at the start. Tam said he would pass the proposal on to his superiors and get back to Rabeus when he had a reply.[9]

Tam's answer came a month later, on October 5. He thanked Rabeus for
Sweden's intervention but said the time was not yet ripe for talks. The
United States, he declared, had made this a full-scale war and had sown
"confusion" by massively escalating the fighting while simultaneously offer-

ing to enter talks "without conditions." Before progress could be made on a diplomatic solution, Tam told Rabeus, the Americans had to acknowledge they were the war's initiators (*fateurs de guerre*), accept the 1954 Geneva Accords, disengage from South Vietnam, and accept the NLF as the legitimate representative of the South Vietnamese people.[10]

It was hardly the response the Erlander government wanted, but most officials had not expected concrete results to emerge from an initial meeting. They were sufficiently encouraged by Tam's response—or, more accurately, sufficiently alarmed by the rising level of violence in Vietnam—to press ahead. While Rabeus and Tam continued to meet periodically in Algiers, contacts were also made with NLF representatives in Helsinki, Warsaw, and Moscow. In late 1965, Petri and Åke Sjölin, the ambassador in Bangkok, were recalled to Stockholm. Sjölin also was accredited to South Vietnam. When asked for their assessments of the war, both said the outlook was bleak. The Americans had immense firepower, but the Saigon government lacked popular support and the North Vietnamese were as determined as ever. Both expressed skepticism about further approaches to NLF officials—a waste of time, they believed, since Hanoi made the real decisions—and about the prospects for any kind of cease-fire proposal. The two men asserted that neither the Americans nor the North Vietnamese nor the Vietcong had much desire for such a solution at present.[11]

Nilsson, too, had a dim view of the chances of gaining meaningful negotiations. The reports he received from his diplomats could hardly have been more discouraging. On July 13, 1966, the foreign minister convened a meeting to discuss the Vietnam situation at Hichens-Bergström's home on Blockhusudden in Stockholm. Among those in attendance were the ambassadors to Washington and Moscow, Hubert de Besche and Gunnar Jarring, and China ambassador Petri. De Besche reported that the Johnson administration was uninterested in negotiations at the moment. Jarring said he had the same impression based on his talks with the Russians. He added that the North Vietnamese also appeared to be closed on the subject. Petri agreed. All three men advised against putting forth any kind of concrete Swedish proposal regarding negotiations. Discussions could and should continue, and Stockholm should stand ready to serve as an intermediary between the key parties—Washington and Hanoi, all agreed—but it should not offer its own proposal.[12]

The three ambassadors made an impression on Nilsson. He quietly shelved Jean-Christophe Öberg's freeze proposal, then decided to henceforth give low priority to contacts with NLF representatives in Algiers and elsewhere. From that point on, the aim would be to go directly to representatives of

Washington and Hanoi to see where the two parties stood and to inquire if they desired Sweden to play an intermediary role.

Even before the Blockhusudden decision, the first direct Swedish–North Vietnamese meeting had taken place in Warsaw. On July 2, Öberg had met for three hours with Hoang Hoan Nghinh, the DRV's chargé d'affaires there. Nghinh blasted the United States for its recent bombing of oil depots in Hanoi and Haiphong, saying the action proved Washington sought only a military solution. Nevertheless, negotiations were possible if the United States halted all bombing of North Vietnam. Nghinh emphasized that his government welcomed Sweden's interest in the war and said he hoped there would be more such meetings.[13] Nilsson instructed Öberg to maintain contact with Nghinh. Over the next six months, the Swede made eighteen secret visits to the Polish capital.

In late October, 1966, a more important meeting took place, this time in Hanoi. The parties were Lennart Petri and North Vietnam's foreign minister, Nguyen Duy Trinh. Petri had low expectations for the encounter, which took place on October 28, but Trinh proved to be an engaging and serious-minded host. There could be a political solution, he declared, provided the United States "definitively and unconditionally" stopped bombing North Vietnam and recognized the NLF as the primary (though not necessarily the only) spokesmen for the South Vietnamese people. To achieve a "final settlement," Trinh continued, all U.S. and allied troops would have to leave South Vietnam, a broadly based coalition government would have to rule the South, national elections would have to be held, and preparations made for the future reunification of the country.[14]

To Petri, as well as to policy makers in Stockholm, Trinh's were encouraging words, even if their ultimate import could not yet be determined. They thought it significant that the Soviet ambassador in Hanoi, Ilya S. Shcherbakov, in an earlier conversation with Petri on October 28, had said the DRV was prepared to negotiate—but only if the bombing stopped. The North Vietnamese were concerned about becoming too dependent on Chinese aid, the Russian said, and thus an early settlement held attraction for them.[15] For Nilsson, the time had come to broach the subject directly with Washington. "We must keep in mind how the Americans see the situation," he had told aides that summer. Now he would get his chance to hear from them personally, during meetings in Washington in November, just two weeks after Petri's visit to Hanoi. Nilsson intended to ask Dean Rusk directly what he thought of Trinh's formulation.

On Erlander's advice, Nilsson also sought a meeting with Vice President Hubert H. Humphrey, whose home state of Minnesota had a heavy concentration of Swedish-Americans and who had visited Sweden earlier in the year. Nilsson and Humphrey met in the vice president's office on November 11. Also present were de Besche, Hichens-Bergström, Öberg, and John E. Reilly, Humphrey's foreign-policy assistant.

Nilsson informed Humphrey of Öberg's meetings in Warsaw and the Petri-Trinh encounter in Hanoi. There appeared to be flexibility in the DRV position, Nilsson said. While still adhering ostensibly to the "Four Points" formula laid out by Premier Pham Van Dong in April, 1965, both Nghinh and Trinh spoke of only two conditions to get meaningful talks started: an end to the bombing and Washington's acknowledgment that the NLF was "not the only but the leading" representative for South Vietnam. The ultimate settlement would have to incorporate more elements, Nilsson continued, but these could be addressed during the actual negotiations. The important thing was that Hanoi appeared to be genuinely interested in peace talks.

Humphrey listened attentively. He found especially interesting the differences between what the North Vietnamese had said to the Swedes and what Hanoi had said publicly, notably regarding the issue of the NLF being considered the only voice of the South Vietnamese people. He also said he appreciated Nguyen Duy Trinh's seemingly moderate tone. When Nilsson said he understood that Washington no doubt had many other sources of information regarding the state of mind of leaders in Hanoi, Humphrey nodded but said it was possible the DRV saw neutral Sweden as different, as more impartial and thus better able to accurately convey the North's position. No one could question Sweden's "sincere and honorable neutrality," Humphrey said. The vice president concluded the meeting by saying he would pass on the information the Swedes had provided to both Dean Rusk and Lyndon Johnson. He also expressed a personal desire for an early compromise settlement.[16]

Later in the day, the Swedish team went to Foggy Bottom to meet with Rusk. The session lasted two hours. Undersecretary of State Nicholas Katzenbach and Deputy Assistant Secretary of State Leonard Unger also attended. The change in the atmosphere was striking, Nilsson later wrote. Rusk showed far less interest in what he had to say than the vice president had. It was all well and good to talk of a political solution, Rusk declared, but what would Hanoi do if the United States stopped bombing? The last time there had been a bombing pause the NLF had stepped up its military attacks, not moved toward diplomacy. What if Hanoi said precisely what it would be willing to do in the event of a bombing halt and its offer was acceptable to Washington? Nilsson asked. Could the administration imagine agreeing to an indefinite stop in the bombing? Impossible, Rusk replied.

Rusk went on to say the United States had already let North Vietnam know that it could conceivably accept three of Pham Van Dong's Four Points: recognition of the DRV; peaceful reunification of the country; and the determination of South Vietnam's political arrangements by the Vietnamese themselves. The fourth point—an unconditional American withdrawal—could not be accepted. Nilsson interjected to ask if Trinh's language to Petri could not be considered a softening on this point: Trinh had, after all, avoided mentioning any formal demands regarding how a U.S. withdrawal would be accomplished. Moreover, the Swede continued, this was new information—the meeting in Hanoi had taken place only two weeks earlier.[17]

That evening, Nilsson left Washington for New York City. He replayed the two meetings in his mind and wondered if the Americans really were interested in negotiations. Probably not, he decided. The bombing issue was key, and yet the secretary of state had seemed immovable on the subject. Rusk, Nilsson later wrote, "had throughout given the impression of wanting to demand more and more from his adversaries while not wanting to deliver anything himself."[18]

Meanwhile, in Washington, Rusk instructed Unger to produce a written reply to Nilsson. The document, delivered by Unger to Nilsson at the Hotel Drake in New York City on November 22, said Washington would have a positive attitude if the DRV were prepared to open a discussion channel via Sweden. In order for the United States to halt the bombing, however, Hanoi would have to reduce its infiltration of men and supplies into South Vietnam, reduce the level of military activity in the South, and end the kidnapping of southern officials loyal to the government. Over lunch at the Drake, Unger told Nilsson that Petri should voice support if Nguyen Duy Trinh showed even the slightest interest in receiving a message from the United States. The administration understood very well, he added, that the DRV occupied a difficult position with respect to the risk that China might learn of a contact between Hanoi and Washington.

Nilsson replied that it was too soon to tell if Trinh really was seeking to make use of a Swedish channel. Petri would make another visit to Hanoi soon; perhaps that visit would tell more. Based on everything Stockholm had learned, though, the DRV leaders hardly seemed anxious. According to Petri, for example, the officials he encountered in Hanoi, including Trinh, seemed reasonably satisfied with the situation on the ground in the South. The military picture looked good. North Vietnamese morale, meanwhile, seemed high, thought Petri, and Trinh appeared to believe that time was ultimately in North Vietnam's favor. Maybe so, Unger responded, but American intelligence had picked up signs in recent weeks that Hanoi's optimism may have begun to fade in recent weeks. World opinion in 1966 had not, in fact, turned decisively against the Americans, as Hanoi officials had predicted it would, and U.S. efforts to stabilize the political situation in Saigon had achieved some good results. South Vietnam, Unger said, had "survived the crisis," meaning the time when a wholesale internal collapse seemed possible. As South Vietnam regained its footing, perhaps Hanoi would conclude that its best interests would be served by negotiations. The key, he concluded, would be for Ho Chi Minh's government to show its good faith with some "action on the ground."[19]

Interestingly, neither Humphrey nor Rusk nor Unger made any reference in these November, 1966, discussions to the publicly articulated opposition to U.S. Vietnam policy from some members of the Erlander government. That opposition had been building for more than a year. In mid-1965, a then-obscure young minister of transport and communications named Olof Palme had attacked the Johnson administration's escalation of the war, declaring it "illusory to believe [as the Americans do] that demands for social justice can be met with violence and military force."[20] Erlander and Nilsson quietly encouraged Palme in his condemnation. Moreover, they raised no objections when he and other party members periodically condemned Washington for its actions in the months that followed. At the same time, they were careful to keep largely silent themselves. They much preferred having comparatively minor figures such as Palme express the government's point of view; such an arrangement would allow them to claim—as Erlander did when Hubert Humphrey visited Sweden in June, 1966—that Palme's criticism did not necessarily reflect official opinion. When Nilsson spoke before the UN General Assembly in October, 1966, he refrained from criticizing the Johnson administration directly, stating only that the Vietnamese people wanted peace and that a negotiated settlement based on the 1954 Geneva Accords was the best means by which to achieve an end to the war.[21]

However, this delicate strategy—endorsing in hushed voices the criticisms made by junior colleagues, while at the same time attempting to stay above the fray—suddenly became more difficult at the end of 1966. The crisis in Swedish-American relations that Stockholm had sought to avert threatened to erupt in December, as a result of Erlander's decision to allow Bertrand Russell's International War Crimes Tribunal to be held in the Swedish capital. Russell, who had for several years criticized America's intervention in Southeast Asia, decided at an early stage to organize a tribunal to pass judgment on possible war crimes. At a planning meeting in London in November, 1966, the tribunal—which included such well-known opponents of U.S. policy as Jean-Paul Sartre (president), Isaac Deutscher, Simone de Beauvoir, Stokely Carmichael, Dave Dellinger, and Carl Oglesby—voted to seek to hold the first session in Paris the following spring. When French president Charles de Gaulle refused to allow it to meet in Paris, the tribunal members turned to Stockholm.[22]

Erlander now found himself in a dilemma. He had no interest in bringing the tribunal to Sweden, knowing full well that doing so could harm the good relations with the United States that he was committed to preserving. At the same time, he did not want to go against the age-old Swedish tradition of allowing freedom of assembly and freedom of speech. It thus was with some hesitation that Erlander decided the session could convene in Stockholm.[23]

Did domestic political considerations also influence Erlander's thinking? Perhaps, although probably not decisively. The Swedish public was split on the Vietnam War, but the prime minister surely knew that the Russell tribunal would be seen as overly biased even by many of those opposed to American intervention. Indeed, when the tribunal convened in Stockholm in May, 1967, public opinion polls showed that most Swedes thought the tribunal was unfair and too anti-American. The press also reacted negatively. Liberal *Expressen* delivered the most serious warning, declaring that the "one-sided war crimes tribunal against the U.S. can become a staggering blow to our relations with Washington. The Americans will look upon Sweden as the center for anti-Americanism in Europe. We run the risk of being hurt badly, even at the level of our trade policies."[24]

Still, by the start of 1967 public opinion in Sweden was increasingly opposed to the war. There also is little doubt that the Social Democrats saw the potential electoral benefits of a somewhat stronger antiwar posture. These domestic political imperatives appear to have influenced another decision by the Erlander government in early 1967: to reduce its diplomatic representation in South Vietnam. Torsten Nilsson announced this change at meeting of Stockholm labor union members early in the year; it was made official on April 17. Henceforth, the Swedish ambassador to Bangkok would no longer be accredited to Saigon at the same time, as he had been before. The Swedish government's senior representative in South Vietnam would now be an *honorärkonsul* who was not Swedish but Swiss. There can be no doubt that the move had been accomplished with an eye on the opinion of Swedish elites—many in the Riksdag and in the press had drawn attention to the implied favoritism toward Saigon in the old policy, and had called loudly and repeatedly for a change.[25]

In essence, it constituted a break in relations with South Vietnam. Nilsson denied this, defending the policy by saying that, as Sweden did not have diplomatic relations with North Vietnam either, the new policy merely equalized things. Maybe, but in practice, Stockholm's relations with the DRV would grow closer as Petri continued to make visits to Hanoi, whereas relations with the South Vietnamese government languished. (Two years later, in early 1969, Sweden became the first western nation to extend diplomatic recognition to North Vietnam.)

Washington officials were quick to denounce both the tribunal's decision and the change in relations with Saigon. In late December and again in January, the U.S. embassy informed Swedish officials that the news of Erlander's decision had "disappointed and disturbed" President Johnson. In April, 1967, Walt W. Rostow, Johnson's national security adviser, met with Erlander in Bonn at the time of German chancellor Konrad Adenauer's funeral. In what Erlander later described a "rather animated discussion," Rostow conveyed LBJ's concerns about the Russell Tribunal and warned that Swedish-American relations were bound to suffer if Stockholm did not rescind the invitation. Erlander replied that while he certainly disagreed with the Russell group's one-sided views, and regretted its decision to meet in Sweden, he could not now turn it away. To do so, he said, would not only go against the country's tradition of freedom of speech and assembly; it would also harm Sweden's neutrality by making it appear that U.S. pressure had forced the government to back down. Rostow left the meeting frustrated by his inability to change the prime minister's mind, but he assured Johnson it was not for lack of trying: "Honest, sir, I delivered your message loud and clear. . . . I have no trouble at all being tough when I am carrying out your instructions."[26]

The State Department, meanwhile, condemned the decision to lower the diplomatic presence in Saigon, and instructed the embassy in Stockholm to express strong skepticism regarding Dick Hichens-Bergström's claim to U.S. ambassador J. Graham Parsons that the action would make Hanoi "listen even more closely" to Sweden's views on the war. Far from righting the balance in Sweden's relations with the two Vietnams, Washington officials argued, Stockholm had tilted the scales decisively toward the DRV.[27]

Which raises the following question: To what degree did these Swedish actions—and the verbal attacks on U.S. policy by Palme and many in the Riksdag—affect how Washington viewed the ASPEN channel? Certainly they did nothing to build the enthusiasm of U.S. officials for Stockholm's initiative. As Parsons told Nilsson in early February, 1967, the growth in vocal opposition to U.S. Vietnam policy in Sweden in the month prior was not making the Johnson administration more receptive to the Swedish proposals regarding negotiations.[28] At the same time, it is far from clear that the actions actually made them less receptive. As we shall see, ASPEN-related discussions between Swedish and American officials in 1967 rarely if ever strayed beyond the narrow specifics of the issue at hand—negotiations and the obstacles to getting them started—and Washington policy makers continued to find value in Sweden's secret efforts at taking the pulse in Hanoi.[29] The public row did not need to interfere with the private diplomacy. Thinking counterfactually, if the Russell Tribunal had been denied permission to convene in Sweden, if the diplomatic representation in Saigon had not been reduced, and if Olof Palme had followed his initial instinct to settle in the United States after his graduation from Kenyon College, the administration's attitude toward the Swedish channel might well have been about the same.

The same is likely true of Hanoi. To be sure, the North Vietnamese were delighted with the policy decisions in Stockholm, especially those concerning the Russell Tribunal. In a meeting in Bucharest on May 5, 1967, North Vietnam's ambassador to Romania, Hoang Tu, told Nilsson how pleased his government had been to learn of Erlander's tribunal decision. Later in May, the DRV's Beijing ambassador, Ngo Dinh Loan, expressed the same sentiment to Lennart Petri, saying that Erlander's action on the tribunal was more valuable to Hanoi than shiploads of weapons. On May 28 in Hanoi, Foreign Minister Trinh expressed his thanks in a session with Lennart Petri. When Petri returned to the North Vietnamese capital for three days in late June, he was given a demonstration of some of the materials that had been gathered for the Russell Tribunal, including objects and photographs ostensibly showing evidence of American atrocities. Petri was shaken by what he saw. "Regardless of what the American government's intentions might be," he wrote Stockholm, "its method of warfare against the Vietnamese people both in the North and the South must be seen as extraordinarily barbaric."[30]

Nonetheless, it is doubtful that the Swedish policy decisions in late 1966 and early 1967 significantly altered the DRV's approach to the ASPEN channel. Apply the counterfactual again, and the outcome is about the same. Swedish contacts with DRV officials in Warsaw and Hanoi continued in the spring and summer of 1967 with no real breakthroughs. Petri met with Trinh in Hanoi on several occasions in an effort to get the foreign minister to clarify exactly what Hanoi would do in the event that Washington instituted an unconditional and definitive bombing halt. Trinh remained as noncommittal as before. He professed to understanding that the United States expected some kind of reciprocal action "on the ground," but said he could offer nothing concrete. Stockholm thus had little to report to the Americans regarding this critical point. Trinh did have one message he wished passed on to Washington: He and his colleagues were outraged by the massive escalation of bombing attacks in early 1967, but it did not faze them in the slightest. International and domestic U.S. opinion was turning against Lyndon Johnson's prosecution of the war, Trinh told Petri, and he had never been more confident of ultimate victory. "We are patient," he said in March. "We are patient. We want to negotiate as soon as there is an unconditional and definitive bombing halt, but we are prepared to fight as long as it takes."[31]

Jean-Christophe Öberg received the same message in Warsaw. In February, 1967, Öberg had been "deeply encouraged" by the tone adopted by Hoang Hoan Nghinh in their discussions. He cabled Stockholm that he was "personally convinced after my talks in Warsaw that we have never been closer to a meaningful contact between Hanoi and Washington than during the days surrounding the Vietnamese new year. . . . We must not give up just now."[32] By mid-March, however, following the U.S. escalatory actions after the Tet holiday, Nghinh had changed his tune, and thus so had Öberg. The chances for a Hanoi-Washington contact were much smaller, Öberg wrote Nilsson. "Nghinh's tone is now very bitter." When Nilsson met Hoang Tu in Bucharest in May, Tu said it would be easy to get talks started with Washington; Johnson simply had to stop the bombing. "The U.S. would gain in prestige by doing so" and the war would end. But Tu serenely added that his government was more confident than ever that it would ultimately achieve victory. It should be clear to all, he said, that after centuries of successful struggle against foreign invaders, the Vietnamese people would also defeat the Americans, no matter how large a military commitment Johnson made.[33]

By the late spring of 1967, the principals in Stockholm were despondent about the channel's prospects. A political solution seemed farther away than ever. Both sides were eager to keep the ASPEN channel open as a means of learning what the adversary was thinking, but neither seemed willing to take the steps necessary to break the deadlock. In South Vietnam, the Swedes knew, 1967 was shaping up as the fiercest year of the war, with U.S. ground troops, by then numbering more than four hundred thousand, pushing forward with their search-and-destroy operations. The infusion of American troops since 1965 had prevented the DRV and Vietcong from taking control of the South, but it could not force them to abandon the struggle. Hanoi matched each American infusion of troops with one of its own. The result was stalemate. To the Swedes, the rising number of battlefield deaths would likely only cause both sides to dig in. They reasoned that Johnson, in particular, would feel great personal and political pressure to justify the loss of the thirteen thousand Americans who had died thus far.

Torsten Nilsson was convinced that something had to give. Moreover, Washington would have to initiate the process. The foreign minister could see the logic in the American position—U.S. officials desperately wanted to turn the war in their favor, to avoid negotiations until that change had occurred, and in the meantime keep various secret channels to Hanoi open—even as he disagreed with it. The problem was that all the reports flowing into Stockholm suggested no such military turnaround was going to happen. Hanoi and the Vietcong remained resilient on the ground. Their determination had not slackened. Meanwhile, Johnson faced growing domestic opposition at the same time America's international credibility (its "reputation and as a sensible and fair player," in Nilsson's words) was taking a beating. Nilsson told aides that the United States probably could eventually overpower the DRV, but it would take many years, perhaps decades, and cost hundreds of thousands of lives. He was convinced the only sensible solution was to negotiate a settlement, however imperfect it might be.

Unbeknownst to Nilsson, a top U.S. decision maker, one of the architects of the Americanization of the conflict in 1964–65, had reached the same conclusion. Robert McNamara's doubts regarding a military solution in Vietnam had surfaced early, as early as the first weeks of 1964.[34] However, he had swallowed those doubts and argued forcefully for the escalation that began in earnest the following year. His gloom increased in 1966 because he feared the war was endangering the global security position he had worked so hard to establish after taking office under Kennedy in 1961. The war's destructiveness troubled him deeply, particularly the deaths of civilians, and he increasingly doubted that ultimate victory over the DRV and the Vietcong could ever be achieved. By early 1967 he had concluded that the enemy's morale remained unbroken and that the South Vietnamese were nowhere near achieving political stability. The air war was failing, and had cost the administration mightily in terms of domestic and world opinion. "The picture of the world's greatest superpower killing or seriously injuring 1,000 noncombatants a week, while trying to pound a tiny, backward nation into submission on an issue whose merits are hotly disputed, is not a pretty one," McNamara wrote to Johnson in May.[35] McNamara would have gotten no argument from Nilsson or Lennart Petri, who a few weeks later wrote from Hanoi about America's "extraordinarily barbaric" military measures.

In light of all this, McNamara somewhat hesitantly proposed that America begin scaling down its objectives in the war. Noting that U.S. bombs had succeeded in destroying most of the targets in North Vietnam, he proposed either an unconditional bombing halt or restricting attacks to targets south of the 20th Parallel. He argued that such a move would appease congressional and other domestic critics while at the same time possibly lead to meaningful talks with the North Vietnamese. The eventual settlement would not be perfect. It most likely would not guarantee South Vietnam's long-term survival. Nevertheless, the United States could live with it. Mc-Namara also advocated placing a ceiling on the number of ground troops to be committed to Vietnam and shifting from Gen. William Westmoreland's search-and-destroy strategy to a defensive strategy aimed at "population control."

McNamara appears to have been trying to find a face-saving way for the United States to get out of Vietnam, but LBJ was not yet prepared to entertain such a notion. Nor was McNamara able to obtain support from other current or former senior officials such as Dean Rusk, Walt Rostow, Maxwell Taylor, and McGeorge Bundy. All of them urged staying the course. The president rejected the major expansion of U.S. involvement urged by Westmoreland and the Joint Chiefs of Staff—Westmoreland had asked for an additional two hundred thousand troops, but got only fifty-five thousand—but set no troop ceiling. The search-and-destroy strategy thus remained unchanged. In addition, the scope of the bombing, far from being reduced as McNamara had suggested, was expanded to include formerly restricted areas.

Partly as a result of McNamara's efforts, however, the administration did slightly modify its negotiating posture in the summer of 1967. A peace initiative code-named PENNSYLVANIA, and known in its public phase as the "San Antonio formula," involved backing away from the demand for a firm prior commitment to mutual de-escalation. The United States would stop bombing North Vietnam if given private assurances that this would lead "promptly to productive discussions," and would "assume" that the DRV would not take "military advantage." The North Vietnamese, however, were suspicious. The Americans had increased the number of bombing attacks in August and again in September, which raised doubts in Hanoi as to just how serious Johnson was about seeking a deal.[36]

Moreover, the PENNSYLVANIA initiative took place against the backdrop of Hanoi's preparations for the Tet Offensive, which had begun in the spring of 1967. The first phase of that offensive was by then under way, and it seems likely that the North Vietnamese were not prepared to settle for anything less than an unconditional bombing halt. Indeed, they may have preferred to avoid all negotiations until the Tet Offensive gave them additional advantage. In August, Do Phat Quang, Hanoi's ambassador to Poland, told Öberg in Warsaw that his government remained fully ready to talk to the Americans, provided there was first an unconditional end to the bombing. Öberg, however, detected little sense of urgency in the ambassador's voice. By then, the North Vietnamese leaders were most likely focused on the coming offensive.[37]

The ASPEN channel entered its final phase in the autumn of 1967. On September 27, Nilsson and Rusk met in Washington for a second time. Almost a year had passed since their first meeting, but the conversation was remarkably similar. Nilsson informed Rusk that Swedish meetings with DRV officials had gone on throughout the year in both Warsaw and Hanoi, and he drew attention to the fact that in all of those meetings the North Vietnamese had said they were willing to talk if the bombing stopped "unconditionally and definitively." Nilsson acknowledged that those same officials had carefully avoided stating precisely what steps they were willing to take in response to a bombing halt. Rusk again said that such specifics were necessary if they were to proceed.[38]

Less than a month later, on October 22, Dick Hichens-Bergström, the Foreign Ministry's director of political affairs, traveled to Warsaw for a secret meeting with Do Phat Quang. The Swede came right to the point: Could the United States be assured that Hanoi would take no advantage of a bombing halt to improve its military position? Quang avoided a direct answer and in turn asked how the phrase, "no advantage," should be interpreted. What, he asked, did it mean, precisely? On November 16, Nilsson again called on Rusk in Washington and passed on Quang's question (as well as a subsequent comment from Quang that the intensified bombing around Hanoi in October had harmed the prospects for peace). Rusk asked for time to frame an answer, but he left little doubt as to his thinking. Peace would come only if Hanoi left its neighbors alone, he told Nilsson, repeating a line he had used on countless statesmen over the years. Rusk said he could imagine negotiations going on while the bombing continued, then responded with silence when Nilsson asked him what would happen if the United States withdrew from Vietnam.[39]

The meeting proved to be Nilsson's and Rusk's last. It also marked the end of Sweden's direct contact with Washington concerning the ASPEN channel—or almost the end. On November 18, William P. Bundy, the assistant secretary of state for Far Eastern affairs, asked Hichens-Bergström, who was in New York, to come immediately to Washington in order to discuss what the Swedes could expect to see in Rusk's reply. Bundy thanked Hichens-Bergström for Sweden's emphasis on precision, on exact language, in its dealings with both sides. This was one reason Washington wanted the Swedish contacts to continue, although it was essential that utmost secrecy be maintained. Then Bundy got to the point. "Here's our present position," he said, reading from a prepared script. "First, the U.S. government is prepared for any type of contact at any time without preconditions. Second, The U.S. government is prepared for contacts at any time accompanied by some modest unpublicized reduction in the scope or area of our bombings."

Hichens-Bergström knew that Hanoi would not accept either of those plans. The first was wholly unacceptable, and the second did not go far enough. It would not work, he said, but Bundy held firm.[40] Perhaps granting the Swede's point, however, Rusk's reply to Nilsson, which came via cable on November 23, did not contain Bundy's language. Instead, Rusk asked for clarification on three points. First, "how is a cessation of bombing to be described publicly, and what is to be the private understanding of this term?" It would appear, Rusk wrote, that Hanoi required the cessation to be permanent. Was that, in fact the case? Second, what guarantees would the United States have that North Vietnam would, in fact, come to the table? Also, how soon after the bombing ceased would the talks begin? The third point concerned what Rusk considered central questions surrounding the issue of "no advantage." What would happen to the flow of men and supplies into South Vietnam following a limitation or cessation of the bombing? What about the three North Vietnamese divisions in the Demilitarized Zone (DMZ) that had been employed against U.S. forces south of DMZ? Would they be moved farther south?[41]

On three occasions in the month that followed, Jean-Christophe Öberg met in Warsaw with Hoang Hoan Nghinh, the DRV's chargé d'affaires, to discuss Rusk's three points. Nghinh, after consulting with Hanoi, was able to answer two of them. A bombing halt, he told Öberg on December 21, would not have to be announced publicly nor would it have to be characterized as permanent. Negotiations would take place "within appropriate time" after the halt began, likely within three weeks or less. Nghinh had little to say, however, on the issue of "no advantage" and what the North Vietnamese were prepared to pledge.[42] Nilsson, in a letter to Rusk dated January 25, 1968, declared that the Warsaw talks gave "full evidence that the North Vietnamese Government is prepared to be represented in talks with American representatives, provided the bombing and all other acts of war against North Vietnam cease unconditionally. My conviction is now that such a first contact would take place within three weeks after the cessation of the bombing, maybe earlier."

The foreign minister cautioned Rusk against interpreting the DRV position as a sign of weakness on Hanoi's part. "On the contrary, should negotiations now fail to come about, I fear that the war will be lengthy with obvious risks for peace and security in Asia and the rest of the world. Therefore, I need to repeat that—should you so desire—I am now as before willing to contribute to take advantage of this opportunity for negotiations which now seems to have appeared."[43]

Nilsson's letter took more than a week to reach Rusk. A technical snafu and a miscommunication at the State Department held it up. By the time the secretary of state received it on February 2, the Tet Offensive was under way. The delay probably did not make much difference; Rusk adhered to his hard-line position throughout January, 1968.

This examination of ASPEN shows the centrality of Operation Rolling Thunder to the story of the search for a negotiated settlement in Vietnam in 1965–68. Just as most American officials were certain that the bombing could not be stopped prior to the start of negotiations (the communists surely would take advantage of any lull by making gains on the ground), North Vietnamese and NLF spokesmen insisted it had to be. It is striking how consistent they were on the issue—serious talks just were not in the cards as long as the bombing continued.

Years later, Chester Cooper, a long-time American policy maker during the war, addressed the issue of peace negotiations at a conference of scholars and former U.S. and DRV officials. "There was nothing we could propose until 1968 that would elicit a positive, constructive response in respect to ne-gotiations," he said. Vietnamese diplomat and historian Luu Doan Huynh replied: "Then the Americans are to blame [for the failure of diplomacy]. The Americans!" Cooper's answer: "I can't argue with what you just said."

Cooper, when asked about the rationale for the bombing sometime af-ter that exchange, replied forthrightly that there was none. "We were flail-ing about in frustration," Cooper said.

That was certainly the sense Swedish officials had, and it accounted for their frustration in early 1968. It was also Robert McNamara's view. He, too, questioned whether there was a good rationale for the bombing. Like the Swedes, he had become convinced that the aerial bombardment was actu-ally counterproductive. Although it plainly caused immense destruction to large areas of the DRV, Operation Rolling Thunder appeared to both Mc-Namara and the Swedes to have had the effect of unifying the North Viet-namese people. It encouraged North Vietnamese leaders to prepare creatively for a longer war, and, counterintuitively, made hardships brought on by the war more tolerable for the general populace.

Contrast this with Dean Rusk, a man who must be accorded a central place in any discussion of why diplomacy failed in Vietnam. While the secretaries of defense were advocating a greater attempt at negotiations, the secretary of state continued to press for a military solution. The ASPEN episode showed both the strengths and weaknesses Rusk brought to his office. On the plus side were his maturity and his toleration of opposing views—two attributes often remarked upon by those who worked for him. He did not cut off con-tact when Stockholm began to publicly oppose U.S. Vietnam policy. He also sought to maintain the ASPEN channel even as public criticism grew sharper and more voluble. Torsten Nilsson respected him for that. At the same time, the episode shows with crystal clarity Rusk's aversion to serious Vietnam negotiations. As secretary of state, Rusk was the nation's chief diplomat; it was his business to seek negotiated solutions to international problems. Yet Rusk never showed much interest in diplomacy. He never looked for imaginative ways of getting the United States out of a difficult situation with a minimum of violence and with its prestige largely intact. Nor did he shape his bureaucracy for the purpose of really exploring diplomatic possibilities. Nilsson was far from the only world leader to find Dean Rusk stubborn and unreasonable on Vietnam, someone who demanded more from Ho Chi Minh than he himself was ready to give. It is hard to argue against Nilsson's claim that Rusk must be assigned a large measure of the responsibility for the failure of all negotiating initiatives in the early years of the war.

On February 23, 1968, Lennart Petri flew into Hanoi for three days of meetings with DRV officials. On the last day, February 26, he met for eighty minutes with Premier Pham Van Dong. The premier thanked Petri for the Swedish government's sincere efforts to facilitate a diplomatic solution. He emphasized that North Vietnam was ready for talks. Whether they could be arranged, however, depended entirely on Washington. When Petri replied that there appeared to be divisions within the U.S. government about how to proceed with the war, Pham Van Dong agreed emphatically. "We are very aware of this," he said. "Even if one can't convince Johnson, one can work through other channels, sometimes among people who are close to him, to try to affect the American view of the problem. The Congress is also sensitive to this."

Petri asked how the premier thought reunification of Vietnam would occur. "It is very hard to know how the reunification will happen," Dong responded. "It must be done in a practical way. We have to sit down around a conference table and talk, discuss, and seek to come to a common solution. It will certainly take a long time . . . but you can be certain that it will happen." They would happen, Dong went on, because the Vietnamese people were one. "The Americans made a colossal mistake—and it is their loss—when they thought they would be able to separate us. We will fight until the end. True, there are meaningful differences between South and North, but we stand united, and rest assured that we will together continue the struggle." Dong noted that that he himself was a southerner, and yet here he sat in the north. "I have the southerner's temperament, and I want to keep this disposition," he said. "In the South we are an open people, spontaneous and generous—even when we fight— and that is partly because we live in a generous region. Here in the north it's somewhat different."

The subject turned to negotiations. Petri expressed his government's frustration on the issue and asked the premier what represented the best means to end the diplomatic deadlock. Well, Pham Van Dong replied, it would certainly not be the San Antonio formula. That approach would be impossible, and in reality represented an attempt by the Americans to avoid negotiations. "The San Antonio formula requires that the talks be productive," Dong said. "But that's impossible to mandate in advance. To demand while the fighting is going on that the talks be productive is just plain silly. Moreover, the Americans demand reciprocity. This is completely unthinkable to us. It's that simple. If the Americans were to stop hammering our country, then there would no doubt be talks. It's a matter of common sense but also respect for our honor, for our dignity, for our independence as a state." For the common Vietnamese, Dong added, "it is incomprehensible that we who were attacked should make concessions in order that the attacker will stop attacking us."

Pham Van Dong had a message for Washington: "You Swedes know how [the Americans] have treated us since August 1964, they've dropped more bombs over our land than the combined total dropped over Europe during the Second World War. But it gains them nothing. We don't let ourselves be deterred as a result. The Americans could even increase the bombing, it wouldn't affect us. We are prepared for that. Please tell them so. We repudiate the San Antonio formula point blank."

The meeting neared its end. Petri tried to shift the discussion to another subject, but Pham Van Dong shifted it back. "We will not give up," he declared. "This war is destined to be a lasting one as long as the Americans remain unwilling to change their policy. We have prepared ourselves for all surprises and are ready for the worst. You may not believe this, but the longer the war lasts and the more violent it becomes, the stronger we will be. We're increasing our war-making capacity. We are stronger today than when the war started. . . . I can assure you, this is just the beginning."[44]

For one man in Washington, however, the end loomed. Lyndon Johnson had not wanted this conflict. He was no warmonger. He had possessed early doubts about the whole enterprise, had grasped the weakness of his South Vietnamese ally, had sensed the limits of American power in that part of the world, had known that the odds against success were long, had wondered if the outcome in Vietnam really mattered to U.S. security. Yet he had never seriously considered backing away from the fight. A reluctant warrior he may have been, but he was also a committed one. From the beginning, he had always framed his choices in Vietnam in such a way that standing firm seemed the only reasonable option—it was retreat to Hawaii, bomb the hell out of China, or stay the course. He had walked the middle of the road, but always closer to the escalation side than the withdrawal side. In four-plus years he had never explored imaginative ways out of the war. For him, disengagement without victory constituted humiliation, something to be avoided at almost any cost.

This did not mean Johnson shunned all talk of negotiations. After mid-1965, he constantly pressed George Ball and others for new negotiating ideas. However, as Ball later said, "he really meant merely new channels and pro-cedures." The administration, Ball told his colleagues, was "'following the traditional pattern for negotiating with a mule; just keep hitting him on the head with a two-by-four until he does what you want him to do.' But that was useless with Hanoi; the mule's head was harder than the two-by-four."[45]

In the late winter of 1968, the president in effect conceded the point. Over a period of days in March, Johnson made a decision many had thought unthinkable: he chose not to run for reelection. The weight of the war was too much, the divisions in the country too deep. Instead, he would watch his vice president seek the nomination and the presidency, the same vice president who had warned him in February, 1965, against making Viet-nam an American war. It is never easy to cut your losses, Humphrey had said, but this was the time to do so, before the war escalated. Moreover, dis-engagement was politically possible, given the mood in the country and the smashing election victory the previous November. "Nineteen-sixty-five is the year of minimum political risk for this administration," the vice presi-dent assured him. Johnson had not listened.[46]

On the last day of March, 1968, Lyndon Johnson went before the televi-sion cameras and called for peace in Vietnam. The United States would un-conditionally halt the bombing of North Vietnam, the president announced, with the exception of a small area just north of the DMZ. Even that very lim-ited bombing would end if Hanoi showed similar restraint. "Our purpose in this action," Johnson said, "is to bring about a reduction in the level of vio-lence that now exists. It is to save the lives of brave men—and to save the lives of innocent women and children. It is to permit the contending forces to move closer to a political settlement. . . . I call upon President Ho Chi Minh to respond positively, and favorably, to this new step toward peace."[47]

The negotiations began in Paris on May 12.

Notes

1. The Swedish channel is covered in *The Secret Diplomacy of the Vietnam War: The Nego-tiating Volumes of the Pentagon Papers*, ed. George C. Herring (Austin: University of Texas Press, 1983), pp. 530–31, 654–715; Ulf Bjereld, *Kritiker eller medlare: Sveriges utrikespolitiska roller, 1945–1990* (Stockholm: Carlsson, 1992), pp. 102–31; Torsten Nilsson, *Åter Vietnam:*

Memoarer och reportage (Stockholm: Tidens Förlag, 1981), pp. 65–125; Jean-Christophe Öberg, *Varför Vietnam: Ett kapitel i svensk utrikespolitik, 1965–1970* (Stockholm: Tidens Förlag, 1985), pp. 44–96; Yngve Möller, *Sverige och Vietnamkriget: Ett unikt kapitel i svensk utrikespolitik* (Stockholm: Tidens Förlag, 1992), pp. 65–91.

2. Nilsson, Åter Vietnam, p. 69.

3. Johnson's remarks are in *U.S. Department of State Bulletin* 49 (Oct.–Dec., 1963): p. 583. See also Fredrik Logevall, "The Swedish-American Conflict over Vietnam," *Diplomatic History* 17 (summer, 1993): p. 424. On Swedish-American Relations in the early Cold War, see Charles Silva, *Keep them Strong, Keep them Friendly: Swedish-American Relations and the Pax Americana, 1948–1952* (Stockholm: Akademitryck, 1999).

4. Nilsson to Rusk, Jan. 25 1968, HP1, no. 15, Utrikesdepartementet, Stockholm, Sweden (hereafter UD).

5. Beijing to Utrikesdepartementet, Oct. 15, 1964, HP1, no. 15, UD. Nilsson comment is in *Documents in Swedish Foreign Policy* (*DSFP*), *1964* (Stockholm: Ministry of Foreign Affairs, 1965), p. 44.

6. Utrikesdepartementet to Beijing, Feb. 7, 1965, as cited in Möller, *Sverige och Vietnamkriget*, p. 64.

7. *Dagens Nyheter,* May 2, 1965.

8. Bjereld, *Kritiker eller medlare,* p. 111; Nilsson, Åter Vietnam, pp. 66–67.

9. Utrikesdepartementet to Moscow, Sept. 2, 1965, HP1, no. 15, UD; Öberg, *Varför Vietnam,* pp. 38–39.

10. Algiers to Utrikesdepartementet, Oct. 5, 1965, HP1, no. 15, UD.

11. Möller, *Sverige och Vietnamkriget,* pp. 69–70.

12. Öberg, July 18, 1966, memorandum, HP1, no. 15, UD; Gunnar Jarring, *Utan glasnost och perestroika: Memoarer, 1964–1973* (Stockholm: Bonniers, 1989), pp. 129–31; Öberg, *Varför Vietnam,* p. 50.

13. Warsaw to Utrikesdepartementet, July 2, 1966, HP1, no. 15, UD; Warsaw to UD, July 3, 1966, ibid.; Öberg, July 12, 1966, memorandum, ibid.

14. Bangkok to Utrikesdepartementet (1), Nov. 1, 1966, HP1, no. 15, UD.

15. Bangkok to Utrikesdepartementet (2), ibid.

16. New York to Utrikesdepartementet, Nov. 12, 1966, ibid.; Öberg, Nov. 11, 1966, memorandum, ibid.; Nilsson, Åter Vietnam, pp. 78–88.

17. New York to Utrikesdepartementet, Nov. 12, 1966, HP1, no. 15, UD; *Secret Diplomacy,* ed. Herring, pp. 655–61; Nilsson, Åter Vietnam, pp. 89–105.

18. Nilsson, Åter Vietnam, p. 105.

19. Rusk to Nilsson, Nov. 16, 1966, HP1, no. 15, UD; Nilsson, Åter Vietnam, pp. 105–106.

20. *DSFP, 1965,* pp. 44–50; Parsons to State, Aug. 4, 1965, National Security Files (NSF), Country File (CF)-Sweden, Box 205, Lyndon B. Johnson Library, Austin, Tex. (hereafter LBJL).

21. *DSFP, 1966,* pp. 41–47.

22. Guenter Lewy, *America in Vietnam* (New York: Oxford University Press, 1978), pp. 311–21; "Sartre at 'War Trial,' Terms Rusk a 'Mediocre Functionary,'" *New York Times,* May 5, 1967. See also Bertrand Russell, *War Crimes in Vietnam* (London: Allen & Unwin, 1967).

23. Tage Erlander, *1960-talet, Samtal med Arvid Lagercrantz* (Stockholm: Tidens Förlag, 1982), pp. 110–15.

24. *Expressen,* May 9, 1967.

25. Möller, *Sverige och Vietnamkriget,* pp. 81–82.

26. *Dagens Nyheter,* Dec. 28, 1966; Rostow to LBJ, Apr. 27, 1967, White House CF 277, Sweden, Box 66, LBJL. See also Erlander, *1960-talet,* p. 114.

27. Möller, *Sverige och Vietnamkriget,* p. 82.

28. Utrikesdepartementet to Washington, Feb. 23, 1967, HP1, no. 15, UD.

29. Leonard Unger told Swedish ambassador Hubert de Besche on May 3, 1967, that although Washington was unhappy with the tribunal decision, it did not affect the administration's interest in keeping the Swedish channel open. It was entirely possible, Unger said, to keep the secret ASPEN channel and the public tribunal issue separate (Washington to Utrikesdepartementet, May 5, 1967, ibid.).

30. Utrikesdepartementet to Washington, May 8, 1967, ibid.; and Beijing to Utrikesdepartementet, May 17 and 30, and June 28 1967, ibid.

31. Beijing to Utrikesdepartementet, Mar. 26, 1967, ibid.

32. Warsaw to Utrikesdepartementet, Feb. 15., 1967, ibid.

33. Utrikesdepartementet to Washington, Mar. 13 and May 8, 1967, ibid.

34. See Fredrik Logevall, *Choosing War: The Lost Chance for Peace and the Escalation of War in Vietnam* (Berkeley: University of California Press, 1999), chap. 4.

35. McNamara to LBJ, May 19, 1967, in *The Pentagon Papers,* ed. Neil Sheehan and E. W. Kenworthy (New York: Crown, 1971), p. 580. One of the curiosities about the latter-day McNamara is the degree to which he seems to have forgotten how well informed he was during the key years of escalation, how well he understood the realities of the situation on the ground in Vietnam and in international and domestic U.S. opinion. Today, he expresses astonishment at "revelations" of things that he knew of—and understood—then. See the McNamara-written sections in Robert McNamara, James G. Blight, and Robert Brigham with Thomas J. Biersteker and Herbert Y. Schandler, *Argument Without End: In Search of Answers to the Vietnam Tragedy* (New York: Public Affairs, 1999). Also see the H-DIPLO roundtable review of *Argument Without End* (with essays by David Welch, Lloyd Gardner, Marilyn Young, and myself).

36. *Secret Diplomacy,* ed. Herring, pp. 536–44, 717–71; Lloyd C. Gardner, *Pay Any Price: Lyndon Johnson and the Vietnam Wars* (Chicago: Ivan R. Dee, 1995), pp. 385–94.

37. Warsaw to Utrikesdepartementet, Sept. 8, 1967, HP1, no. 15, UD. See also McNamara et al, *Argument Without End,* p. 296.

38. Nilsson to Rusk, Sept. 27, 1967, HP1, no. 15, UD; New York to UD, Sept. 28, 1967, ibid.; Nilsson, Åter Vietnam, pp. 112–21.

39. Nilsson to Rusk, Nov. 8, 1967, HP1, no. 15, UD; Nilsson, Åter Vietnam, pp. 124–25.

40. New York to Utrikesdepartementet, Nov. 19, 1967, HP1, no. 15, UD.

41. Rusk to Nilsson, Nov. 23, 1967, ibid.; *Secret Diplomacy,* ed. Herring, pp. 706–707.

42. Bjereld, *Kritiker eller medlare,* p. 119; Öberg, *Varför Vietnam,* pp. 88–91.

43. Nilsson to Rusk, Jan. 28, 1968, HP1, no. 15, UD.

44. Beijing to Utrikesdepartementet, Feb. 29, 1968, ibid.

45. George W. Ball, *The Past Has Another Pattern: Memoirs* (New York: Norton, 1982), p. 405.

46. The memorandum is reproduced in Hubert H. Humphrey, *The Education of a Public Man: My Life and Politics* (Garden City, N.Y.: Doubleday, 1976), pp. 320–24.

47. The complete text of the speech is in Marvin E. Gettleman, Jane Franklin, Marilyn B. Young, and H. Bruce Franklin, eds., *Vietnam and America: A Documentary History* (New York: Grove, 1995), pp. 401–409. H. W. Brands makes the important point that what made the speech meaningful regarding Vietnam was Johnson's withdrawal from the presidential race, his "declaration of lame-duckhood." See H. W. Brands, *The Wages of Globalism: Lyndon Johnson and the Limits of American Power* (New York: Oxford University Press, 1995), p. 252.

The Japanese Government's Peace Efforts in the Vietnam War, 1965–1968

HIDEKI KAN

The Japanese government's peace efforts during the Vietnam War roughly corresponded to the administration of Eisaku Sato (November, 1964 to June, 1972). This chapter, therefore, deals with the Sato government's peace efforts.

In examining the Sato government's peace efforts, we should bear in mind two overarching factors that influenced them. First, maintaining close relations between the United States and Japan was a top priority for the postwar Japanese governments led by the conservative Liberal Democratic Party (LDP). The Sato government was no exception. Sato especially regarded close bilateral cooperation as essential. Therefore, even when the escalation of the Vietnam War severely strained relations between the United States and Japan, he steadfastly supported, at first privately and later publicly, U.S. policy in Vietnam. Moreover, both governments faced an important decision in 1970 as to whether their security treaty should be extended, revised or terminated. The Americans wanted to extend it without any revisions. Prime Minister Sato shared this conviction and closely cooperated with Washington, despite mounting public criticism of the treaty during the Vietnam War.

Second, Sato's support for America's Vietnam policy, as well as his cooperative efforts to extend the security treaty beyond 1970, were also designed to promote his primary objective of achieving the reversion of Okinawa. During his bid for premiership in the election of July, 1964, he had made it clear at a press conference that if he won, he would ask the United States to return Okinawa to Japan. Although he lost that election to Hayato Ikeda, the reversion of Okinawa to Japanese control became a fixation for Sato. In January, 1965, while making his first visit to Washington as prime minister, he took up the reversion question with Pres. Lyndon B. Johnson. Then, as a symbolic expression of his strong commitment to the Okinawa question, Sato visited the island on August 19 of that year. No other Japanese prime minister had ever visited Okinawa after World War II. During this visit, Sato proclaimed that bringing the postwar era to an end required the settlement of the territorial question. The fact that Sato made reversion his administration's top priority substantially influenced his attitude toward both the Vietnam War and peace efforts.

Sato's steadfast support for the U.S. war effort as well as his own administration's peace efforts must be examined in this context. He clearly understood that the Japanese government's support for America in Vietnam was essential to achieving the reversion of Okinawa.

The Escalation of the Vietnam War and Japan's Role in Asia

Sato also recognized that as long as the Vietnam War was going on, regaining control of Okinawa would be extremely difficult. American bases in Okinawa played an important role in the U.S. war effort. A squadron of KC-135 jet tankers was used to refuel B-52 bombers during their missions from Guam to targets in Vietnam. The 2d Logistical Command in Okinawa handled about three-quarters of the four hundred thousand tons of goods consumed each month by U.S. troops in Vietnam. In late July, 1965, a fleet of B-52 bombers based in Guam refueled in Okinawa, and then left for a bombing mission to Vietnam.

Restoring peace and stability to Southeast Asia was also necessary for Sato if Japan wanted to play a role in Asia commensurate with its economic achievements. In the early 1960s, Washington began to expect Japan to play a larger role in Asia. Those expectations grew steadily as America's financial burden increased with President Johnson's escalation of the war in Vietnam and with Washington policy makers' observation that Japan's economic achievements in the 1960s had restored the Japanese people's confidence.

Sato welcomed the challenge. The idea of promoting economic and social development in Southeast Asia fitted in with Japan's vision of a larger role in Asia. However, the war in Vietnam made achieving such a role extremely difficult.

In Sato's view, Japan's contribution would be limited to economic and social development in Asia. Because of the restrictions imposed by the peace clause (Article 9) in the Japanese constitution, Japan was in no position to make military contributions. Foreign Minister Takeo Miki, for example, told Secretary of State Dean Rusk on July 6, 1966, that Japan would be able to do more to help in Vietnam "if the stage could be reached in which political and social reconstruction was begun."[1] Sato and Miki believed that the Vietnam War severely limited what Japan could do to meet Washington's expectations. This consideration also motivated them to make peace efforts. With peace and stability restored in Southeast Asia, they reasoned, Japan would be able to play a larger role in the region as desired by both Washington and Tokyo.

The escalation of the Vietnam War in the spring of 1965, however, put the Sato administration in a very difficult situation. The Japanese public and the mass media turned increasingly critical of U.S. policy in Vietnam. America's escalation of the conflict that summer had severely strained bilateral relations. Secretary Rusk attended the luncheon meeting with the Japanese delegation at the fourth meeting of the Joint U.S.-Japan Committee on Trade and Economic Affairs in July, 1965, and observed that "nothing since the security treaty riots of 1960 has so seriously affected American-Japanese relations as our recent actions in Vietnam."[2]

Sato himself thought that the United States relied too much upon military means in the war without fully exploiting avenues of negotiations and talks. When Edwin O. Reischauer, the U.S. ambassador to Japan, met Sato on December 29, 1964, the prime minister stated that the most important problem was "to create civil stability and protect against guerrillas." He further added that it would be much easier for Japan to assist in a United Nations framework, which would allow the Japanese to get involved through technical assistance, the UN Children's Fund, and the World Health Organization.[3]

Consequently, Sato highly welcomed President Johnson's Johns Hopkins University speech on April 4, 1965, in which he announced his intention to promote cooperative efforts in Asia for economic and social development in a regional framework.[4] Sato was so pleased with this speech he himself picked up the phone to call Ambassador Reischauer to inform him of his agreement and satisfaction.[5] The idea of economic and social development in Southeast Asia embodied in Johnson's Baltimore speech was regarded as providing a very good opportunity for the Sato government to make nonmilitary contributions in Asia. Encouraged by the speech, the Japanese government took the initiative, sponsoring a conference of Asian leaders that led to the Southeast Asian Ministerial Conference in April, 1966—the first major postwar international meeting hosted by Japan. The Baltimore speech also stimulated Japan's involvement in the creation of the Asian Development Bank (ADB). When the ADB was finally established in November, 1966, Japan pledged $200 million for the fund, equal to the U.S. capital contribution.

Sato's basic conception of Japan's larger role in Asia, like Foreign Minister Miki's, focused on a broader program of economic and social construction in Indochina states, including Vietnam. In this sense, Japan's peace efforts involved not only an intermediary role but also its contribution to promoting regional economic and social development. Furthermore, it was hoped that economic assistance would contribute to creating conditions that would make clear to North Vietnam and its supporters, particularly Beijing, that they could not win in South Vietnam. Japanese government officials believed that one important means of convincing Hanoi and its supporters that they could not succeed in their ultimate objective was to stabilize and strengthen the Saigon government.[6] Secretary Rusk also found merit in such an approach from a political and psychological standpoint. He expressed such a view to Foreign Minister Etsusaburo Shiina on September 26, 1965, adding that reconstruction efforts need not await the complete pacification of South Vietnam. He went on to say that he hoped many countries would increase their aid to Saigon, "not only to help [the] South," but also "to send a signal to Hanoi and Beijing" that they were not going to succeed in Southeast Asia.[7]

The Sato Administration's Initial Peace Efforts

Before the Sato administration began to take concrete steps in search of peace in Vietnam, both Hanoi and Washington had announced their basic negotiating positions: Hanoi's "Four Points" of April 8, 1965, and Washington's "Fourteen Points" of December 29, 1965. On May 19, 1965, North Vietnam took a further step to make sure that Washington clearly understood Hanoi's thinking on the Four Points. First, the Four Points "were to be considered not prior conditions but rather as working principles for a negotiation." Second, U.S. recognition of the "principles" in the Four Points would open the possibility of a conference modeled on the one held in Geneva in 1954.[8] Subsequent exchanges between Washington and Hanoi revolved mainly around two major issues. First, whether the wording of the third point (the affairs of South Vietnam must be settled "in accordance with the program of the National Liberation Front [NLF]") meant that all other groups, including the Saigon government, were to be excluded or not. Second, Hanoi insisted on the unconditional and immediate cessation of the bombing of North Vietnam, while Washington demanded that Hanoi reciprocate by decreasing or stopping the infiltration of troops and supplies from the North into the South in return for a bombing halt.

Sato's efforts to search for peace in Vietnam began in the fall of 1965. In October, he sent Toshikazu Kase, Japan's former permanent representative to the United Nations, to Saigon and Washington. Kase, who visited Vietnam on "what he characterized as an official mission for PM Sato," showed considerable interest in examining the possibility of separating Hanoi from Beijing and asked if Washington had received any indication that Hanoi was willing to negotiate. Ambassador Henry Cabot Lodge Jr. replied that there were no such signs. Arriving in Washington, Kase pursued this question in his meetings with both William P. Bundy, the assistant secretary for East Asia and Pacific affairs, and Secretary Rusk. Rusk said that Hanoi had not reached that point as yet and suggested that Japan feel out Hanoi's attitude. Kase indicated that unless Hanoi "turned Titoist" and became independent of Beijing, a negotiated settlement would be extremely difficult.[9]

On January 25, 1966, Prime Minister Sato said at a press conference that he was planning to send Masayuki Yokoyama as a special ambassador to Europe and Southeast Asia with the purpose of developing support for a peace conference. His main purpose was to develop a channel of communication with Hanoi. His extensive visits to European and Asian capitals to sound out the prospects for a peaceful settlement of the war in Vietnam produced no tangible results. After returning from the trip, Yokoyama reported in June that no one yet knew how to achieve peace and "there does not appear to be any useful initiative which can be taken now."[10]

The Sato administration also approached various other governments to urge them to make efforts to bring the war to an early conclusion. It soon became apparent, however, that Japan's role as a mediator was handicapped by the U.S.-Japan security treaty ties and the obligations it mandated.[11] It was further compromised when Sato began his vigorous campaign in the fall of 1965 to educate the Japanese public so as to gain their support for the U.S.-Japan security treaty. He began this campaign with a view to extending the treaty beyond its expiration in 1970. The campaign was part and parcel of his objective of achieving the return of Okinawa as well as his belief that Japan should play a larger role in Asia. Previously, his support for America's Vietnam policy had been communicated to the U.S. government privately. The joint communiqué issued in January, 1965, during Sato's first visit to Washington, for example, had made only a brief reference to the effect that "Continued perseverance would be necessary for freedom and independence in South Vietnam." Hence, Sato had carefully avoided any commitment. During and after that campaign, however, he began to express his support for the U.S. war effort more openly. His first such announcement appeared in the *Asahi Shimbun* on May 8, 1965, when he justified the U.S. bombing of North Vietnam on the grounds that it was intended to stop North Vietnam's infiltration of the South.

Sato next approached Moscow. He disclosed to Vice President Hubert Humphrey during his visit in Tokyo in December, 1965, that Foreign Minister Shiina would soon visit Moscow to "explain" to the Soviets the U.S. desire for peace in Vietnam. Sato expressed hope that Ambassador Reischauer would discuss details of the U.S. attitude with Shiina before his departure. Reischauer welcomed the initiative as a hopeful indication of the Sato administration's desire to "do something to help us in Vietnam." He urged Washington to accept it so that it "would help encourage Japan to go on seeking a responsible and useful international role."[12]

Foreign Minister Shiina visited Moscow from January 16–22, 1966. He brought with him a personal letter from Sato to Prime Minister Alexei Kosygin, expressing Sato's hope that the Vietnam question would be discussed. In his meeting with Foreign Minister Andrei Gromyko on January 21, Shiina asked the Soviets to assume a leadership role in bringing the war to an end. Gromyko responded that the United States had violated the Geneva Accords by invading Vietnam and that the Soviet Union could not act as a mediator under such circumstances. Gromyko took the position that Japan, as a U.S. ally, should persuade Washington to stop the "invasion." It was necessary, he reminded the envoy, that Japan should not allow the United States to use its land and resources directly or indirectly for prosecuting the Vietnam War. Shiina countered by saying that Japan was paying careful attention to how the United States used its Japanese bases. It was clear, however, that Gromyko believed Japan should persuade Washington before asking Moscow to mediate anything with Hanoi. When Shiina met with Kosygin the next day, the Soviet premier took a similar line, saying that the Soviet Union had no authority to settle this question and that the United States must withdraw its troops from Vietnam and negotiate directly with the NLF and Hanoi.[13]

Japan's Direct Contacts with Hanoi.

On July 16, 1966, Toru Nakagawa, the Japanese ambassador to the Soviet Union, finally managed to contact Nguyen Van Kinh, North Vietnam's ambassador in Moscow. The North Vietnamese ambassador strongly protested Japan's assistance to the United States and the Saigon government. He said that the Japanese should refrain from such assistance if they wanted to play an intermediary role.[14] Nakagawa met with Kinh a second time on September 15 and urged Hanoi to come to the conference table. Nakagawa, reflecting the U.S. view, said that it would be impossible to make the withdrawal of U.S. troops a precondition and suggested that withdrawing troops should be realized through negotiations. The North Vietnamese ambassador took the same position as before, saying that a solution of the Vietnam question could be achieved only by accepting Hanoi's four conditions. He added that the bombing of North Vietnam violated international law and must be stopped immediately and that Vietnam's independence and territorial integrity was not a subject for negotiations. He also reminded the Japanese ambassador that the United States was fighting the NLF, so there was no other choice but to have the Vietcong participate in negotiations as a representative of South Vietnam. The atmosphere of this second meeting was somewhat improved compared to the first meeting, but Kinh again protested Japan's support for U.S. aggression either directly or indirectly.[15]

Nakagawa and Kinh met a third and fourth time in Moscow on December 23, 1966, and January 11, 1967, respectively. Both meetings deserve close scrutiny because they took place immediately before the Hanoi peace initiative known as the "Trinh signal." On January 28, 1967, North Vietnam's foreign minister, Nguyen Duy Trinh, told Australian journalist Wilfred Burchett that talks could begin immediately if Washington would declare an unconditional bombing halt. The Trinh signal meant that the third of North Vietnam's Four Points was no longer a requirement to start talks; only the cessation of the bombing was required for talks to begin.[16]

In the third meeting, Nakagawa tried to impress on the North Vietnamese ambassador Japan's zeal for peace in Vietnam as well as the value of this channel of communication. He reported that he thought this objective had been "fully attained." He stated that the Japanese government had sounded out U.S. intentions on the three points brought up by the North Vietnamese ambassador at the second meeting, namely, that the NLF should participate in the peace talks; that the United States should issue a declaration stating its respect for the independence and territorial integrity of Vietnam; and that the bombing of North Vietnam should be halted. Having sounded out the Americans' intentions, Nakagawa said that the Japanese government had the impression that the United States would have no difficulty realizing these points. The North Vietnamese ambassador then asked if the channels through which the information had been obtained were "the result of your direct contact with the American side," or had they been obtained "through other routes"? Nakagawa replied that the information had been obtained directly from the Americans "at the highest governmental level." According to Nakagawa, the North Vietnamese ambassador seemed to have been "considerably impressed" by the efforts of the Japanese government.[17]

However, Ambassador Kinh disagreed with Nakagawa's comments that there were no major differences of opinion between the U.S. and Vietnamese governments with respect to the three questions addressed above. First, with regard to the question of a troop withdrawal, he took issue with the U.S. statement that its forces would be withdrawn within six months if

North Vietnamese troops were withdrawn from South Vietnam, and that such a statement was "an excuse for the American forces to stay in South Vietnam permanently" because no North Vietnamese troops were in the South. Withdrawal thus should be accomplished first by the United States. When Nakagawa stated that it was the Japanese government's understanding that a considerable number of personnel from the North had been deployed in the South, Ambassador Kinh reiterated that no North Vietnamese troops were in South Vietnam. However, he admitted that when southerners living in North Vietnam wanted to return to their homeland, Hanoi made no move to prevent them from going since it was their right to do so. Secondly, Ambassador Kinh stated that if America wanted to end the war, Washington should talk directly with the NLF because North Vietnam had no authority whatsoever to settle any problem in the name of the NLF. Third, he stressed that with regard to the question of the independence and territorial integrity of Vietnam, the United States, should recognize these principles, halt the bombing "immediately," and withdraw its forces from South Vietnam. Moreover, with regard to the cessation of the bombing of the North, Kinh stressed that Washington had always attached conditions and that Hanoi would "absolutely never" recognize a bombing halt with preconditions attached. In other words, the United States must halt bombing "unconditionally and permanently."

The contents of the meeting on December 23 were transmitted directly to Secretary Rusk through the Japanese ambassador in Washington. Rusk thereupon expressed his views. First, he said that the United States was ready to halt the bombing of North Vietnam "if the North Vietnam side reciprocated in taking measures to scale down its military action." Second, the secretary of state said that the United States could "absolutely not" be convinced of the Democratic Republic of Vietnam (DRV) ambassador's denial that North Vietnamese Army (NVA) troops were in South Vietnam and that Washington had positive evidence of several divisions of NVA troops in the South. If Hanoi did not recognize this fact, the U.S. government thought any talks between the two would be very difficult. These views were then transmitted to the North Vietnamese ambassador on January 11, 1967.

Clearly, Rusk's views were unacceptable to Hanoi, especially the question of reciprocity with regard to the cessation of bombing. On the first point, Ambassador Kinh again demanded that the United States cease bombing "finally and unconditionally," and expressed the view that attaching conditions was not just. As for the second point, the U.S. pretension that Hanoi had sent troops into South Vietnam was to "libel North Vietnam" and the DRV had nothing more to say on the subject.

The significant outcome achieved through these meetings was the fact that Kinh confirmed the report by Harrison Salisbury of the *New York Times* about Prime Minister Pham Van Dong's assertion of January 2, 1967, that the four points should not be considered as preconditions for holding peace talks, but rather were a basis for negotiation and that these four points could be realized as a result of the discussions. In addition to confirming this understanding, he further stated that if the United States halted the bombing of North Vietnam "finally and unconditionally," and made a proposal to hold a conference, Hanoi would examine and discuss it.

It was clear from these exchanges that the central issue from Hanoi's standpoint was whether the United States would stop the bombing unconditionally and immediately before talks commenced. Washington, however, demanded that Hanoi reciprocate by scaling down its military action. Washington's two separate phases of a mutual de-escalation proposal that later became known as the "Phase A–Phase B formula" was designed so that Hanoi could not have the bombing cessation without also accepting Phase B (execution of all other agreed-upon de-escalatory actions, including reliable information, if possible, regarding the precise steps Hanoi would take in response to a bombing suspension). This question of reciprocity continued to be the major obstacle to getting negotiations started until after the Tet Offensive in January, 1968.

The difference was unresolved again during the talks from February 6 through 13 between Prime Minister Harold Wilson and Soviet Premier Kosygin while the latter was visiting London. During the talks, President Johnson, in response to intelligence reports of Hanoi's stepped-up infiltration efforts, wrote Ho Chi Minh a letter demanding simultaneous de-escalation. Moreover, Johnson reversed the Phase A–Phase B formula and demanded that Hanoi stop its infiltration before Washington ceased bombing. Specifically, the United States would stop bombing North Vietnam "as soon as they were assured that infiltration from North Vietnam has stopped."[18] Ho Chi Minh reacted with considerable bitterness and reasserted that Washington must stop bombing the North before negotiations would begin. At this point, the DRV initiative was practically terminated.

In the meantime, Nakagawa concluded from his first and second meetings with Kinh that Hanoi had begun to "appreciate the usefulness of this channel of contact."[19]

Encouraged by the Nakagawa-Kinh meetings in Moscow, the Japanese Foreign Ministry decided to expand the talks. Tokyo instructed the Japanese ambassadors in Paris, Vientiane, and Phnom Penh to make confidential approaches to North Vietnam's ambassadors in those capitals. They were also authorized to contact NLF representatives in a similar fashion. The Foreign Ministry's official spokesman announced at a news conference on March 16: "We have mobilized all our diplomatic resources to explore every possibility to bring about a peaceful settlement of the Vietnam situation." A Japanese Foreign Ministry officer informed an American embassy officer in Tokyo of these moves on March 17, 1967.[20]

Regrettably, Hanoi's response to the Japanese overtures was negative. After the Kosygin-Wilson mediation effort failed, Hanoi's attitude hardened considerably. North Vietnam's ambassador in Vientiane told Ambassador Wada there that Hanoi had recently sent circular messages instructing all of its ambassadors to avoid formal contacts and conversations with representatives of countries "supporting US Vietnam policy, or friendly or allied to US." On May 12, Ambassador Nakagawa in Moscow requested a meeting with the new North Vietnamese ambassador there to resume the talks begun with his predecessor in mid-1966. However, his request was rejected on the grounds that the United States was waging a "dirty war" against North Vietnam and Japan continued to support Washington. The result of Japan's recent diplomatic efforts, the chief of the Southeast Asia Section of the Japanese Foreign Ministry commented to an American embassy officer, was that "All doors seem to be closed to Japanese by North Vietnam."[21]

Faced with Hanoi's unwillingness to negotiate, the Sato administration's peace efforts seemed to be going nowhere. When Sato met with Rusk in Tokyo in December, 1966, he observed that negotiations were unlikely in the near future.[22] When Sato conferred with Arthur Goldberg, the U.S. ambassador to the UN, during Goldberg's visit to Tokyo in February, 1967, he told Goldberg that Japan had undertaken various efforts to find a way to help, but had thus far been unable to do so. "At this juncture," Sato sadly confessed, "North Vietnam does not appear interested in negotiations and it will be difficult to bring about peace even though the U.S. desires it."[23]

1967: Japan Increasingly Identifies with the Americans and South Vietnamese

By early 1967, the Japanese government's efforts for mediation seemed stalled. Nevertheless, their efforts continued. The *Nihon Keizai Shimbun* published a story on April 25, 1967, describing Japan's efforts to play the role of "honest broker" by conveying both sides' real intentions to each other and stating that the Japanese government supported UN secretary general U Thant's proposals for cease-fire talks and a peace conference. Moreover, this formula also foresaw the neutralization of both North and South Vietnam under an international guarantee with UN peacekeeping forces and the withdrawal of foreign troops from both North and South. The problem of the NLF was to be regarded as part of the South's internal affairs. The future of both North and South Vietnam should be settled in accordance with the principle of self-determination. After a cease-fire was in effect, Japan would offer a conference site to discuss concrete conditions for peace. Furthermore, Japan would be willing to send officers, but not self-defense forces personnel, to be part of an International Control Commission, if such a mechanism was established. In addition, Japan would provide economic aid to assist with postwar reconstruction in both the North and South.

What was notable about this story was that, according to Kiuchi, chief of the Foreign Ministry's Southeast Asia Section, the newspaper article represented the "general line of thinking" of Foreign Minister Miki, who had replaced Shiina in December, 1966. Miki himself had discussed these ideas with Sato. This proposal was drafted as Sato and Miki had asked the Foreign Ministry to "staff out positions" along those lines.[24] In this sense, it was the first concrete proposal formulated by the Japanese government.

The Japanese proposal reported in the *Nihon Keizai Shimbun* was formulated in connection with Miki's forthcoming visit to Moscow, Eastern Europe, and West Germany. The Japanese government, in this regard, also asked Washington to clearly define the U.S. posture on peace negotiations. On July 15, William Bundy gave Japanese ambassador Takeso Shimoda in Washington a thorough rundown of the past records on negotiations. Bundy reiterated that the United States needed "substantial information from [a] reliable source" of Hanoi's assurance that the DRV would take appropriate reciprocal action in return for the cessation of bombing. Shimoda was also informed of the two separate phases of a mutual de-escalation proposal (the Phase A–Phase B formula). Simply stated, the Phase A–Phase B formula contained the condition of reciprocity as the basis for beginning negotiations. Bundy said that the formula had been conveyed indirectly to Hanoi through the Soviet Union late in the preceding year, but Washington had received no reaction to it from either Moscow or Hanoi. Bundy, however, hoped that Miki would probe what actions or initiatives the Soviets would be willing to take in getting negotiations started.[25]

After hearing several such briefings, the prospect for Miki's talks with Soviet leaders in Moscow July 21–23 seemed dim. Kosygin maintained a hard line on Vietnam throughout the talks. The Soviet premier, referring to the fact that the Glassboro Summit talks between himself and President Johnson had made no progress, reiterated that he had told President Johnson the Soviets could not negotiate on behalf of the Vietnamese people. When

Miki called Kosygin's attention to the Americans' difficulty with accepting unconditional and immediate withdrawal without reciprocal action by the other side, the premier replied that the Soviets were in no position to convey peace proposals to Hanoi. He also added that the unilateral withdrawal of U.S. troops was the only way out. Ambassador Nakagawa in Moscow also tried to contact the North Vietnamese ambassador. After initially refusing, Hanoi's new ambassador announced on July 28 that he would be willing to meet privately. Shimoda informed the State Department of this contact but was told that Washington had nothing to add to the briefings supplied to Miki. Consequently, no progress was expected from this line of communication, either.[26]

After Miki's unsuccessful attempt to persuade the Soviets to mediate between Hanoi and Washington, the Sato administration began to prepare for the Washington summit meeting slated for mid-November. Sato's primary objective was to obtain the president's commitment to return Okinawa to Japanese control within two or three years on terms satisfactory to both Japan and the United States. To achieve this objective, Sato had felt all along the need to express his support for Johnson's policy in Vietnam. The major action taken in this direction was Sato's decision to include Saigon during his tour of Southeast Asia scheduled for that fall. When his decision was made public, the Japanese press criticized Sato for abandoning Japan's neutral position. Foreign Minister Miki tried to justify the trip in the House of Councilors of the Foreign Affairs Committee in the Diet on June 16 and 20 by emphasizing that the purpose of the prime minister's visit to Saigon would be to seek ways to bring peace to Vietnam. Nonetheless, Sato's visit to Saigon was widely regarded within Japanese circles as costing Japan whatever hope it may have had of playing an effective role in achieving a peace settlement.[27]

Sato was quite encouraged, nevertheless, by the results of his Southeast Asia tour. After returning to Japan, he explained to Amb. U. Alexis Johnson that he had found "widespread support for free world efforts to resist communist aggression in Vietnam." He was particularly impressed by these countries' efforts "in a spirit of self-help" to achieve greater welfare and prosperity, noting the encouraging trends among them toward greater regional cooperation. Citing the promising prospects for the Asian Development Bank and its special funds, he emphasized the importance of economic development and the continued need for assistance in their efforts. He also reiterated that Japan was determined to "do all it can in the search for peace." Foreign Minister Miki joined Sato's effort in his speech to the American-Japan Society in Tokyo on October 5, 1967. He stressed that for the United States to halt the of bombing of North Vietnam without some guarantee that Hanoi would begin negotiations would be a "dangerous gamble" and proposed that Hanoi's friends act as guarantors for such talks while America's friends do likewise for the United States.[28] It was clear that Sato and Miki made these remarks bearing in mind their favorable effect on their forthcoming talks with President Johnson in Washington.

A State Department briefing memorandum prepared on November 9 in advance of Sato's visit to Washington noted that the Sato administration had moved to a much stronger public posture on Vietnam in the past few months and cited Sato's visit to Saigon in the face of strong domestic opposition as "making him the first head of government without troops in Vietnam to visit there."[29] Moreover, Johnson's advisers urged the president to take advantage of Sato's strong desire to set a date for the reversion of Okinawa in order to extract a number of concessions from the Japanese. Related to Vietnam among them were Sato's support on such matters as including "public recognition of the importance of American efforts there to Japan's security," "larger economic assistance particularly to small industries," and playing "a major postwar role in economic rehabilitation and in international police-keeping." Rusk's memorandum for the president regarded these as "the most helpful steps Japan can take on Vietnam."[30]

During their meeting in Washington, Secretary Rusk remarked to Prime Minister Sato that the American people wanted to know why Japan, India, and Western Europe did not believe it important to contribute to the U.S. effort in Vietnam. Sato said that although there were some elements in Japan critical of the bombing of North Vietnam, this feeling was confined to "a very small group." He said he felt "guilty about this sentiment," especially because Washington was "making such sacrifices." Rusk also expressed his great appreciation for Sato's visit to Saigon on October 21, praising it as "a courageous act." He said he thought it would help convince the American people that Japan associated itself with the U.S. effort, which he regarded as "an invaluable step."[31]

Sato, who felt "guilty about" the antiwar sentiment in Japan, decided to embark upon a more vigorous campaign to educate the Japanese public. Returning from Washington, he started to arrange for port calls by nuclear-powered surface vessels to overcome the strong antinuclear feelings among the public. Sato's effort culminated in the USS *Enterprise*'s entry into Sasebo on January 19, 1968, sparking massive protests at the time. He also announced in his speech to the Diet on December 5 that further efforts for Japan's self-defense program would contribute to an early reversion of Okinawa. Ambassador Shimoda also delivered a speech at the Japan-America Society in Washington on December 1 in which he defended the U.S. war effort in Vietnam. A majority of the Japanese realized, he said, that America was fighting in South Vietnam "upon request from its government" to counteract the "infiltration and aggression from the North." He then justified the bombing of the North as "a measure necessary to cut off the flow of reinforcements into South Vietnam." He also expressed a strong desire for Japan to continue its "patient efforts" to act as an intermediary to help get early negotiations started. William Bundy sent a note to Rusk drawing his attention to the fact that Shimoda's speech was "quite extraordinarily frank and forthcoming" and urged the secretary to express appreciation for it. Rusk agreed and sent a letter to Shimoda in which he voiced particular appreciation for the support Shimoda had expressed "for the efforts and goals of the United States in Vietnam."[32]

American officials appreciated the Japanese government's efforts to "voice publicly" its support for U.S. efforts in Vietnam, but these cooperative efforts in turn further compromised Japan's role as an intermediary to bring about a negotiated settlement in Vietnam. This was especially so after Ambassador Shimoda's speech described North Vietnam's action as "aggression from the North" and justified the U.S. bombing as necessary to prevent reinforcements from moving into South Vietnam. Such a position clearly defied Hanoi's principle assertion that the U.S. bombing of North Vietnam was a serious violation of its sovereignty. The fact that Tokyo had always accepted the U.S. demand for reciprocity for the cessation of the bombing also made Japan's role as an intermediary that much harder for Hanoi to accept because the cessation of the bombing was not something negotiable to the DRV's leaders.

The American embassy in Saigon noted the negative consequences of Sato's visit to South Vietnam by reporting Hanoi's reaction, which had appeared in the Communist Party newspaper *Nhan Dan*. The *Nhan Dan* article called the visit a "criminal" and "hostile act against the Vietnamese people." Thus, the article implied, according to the embassy cable, that Hanoi "considers Sato's visit as eliminating any potential mediatory role [the] Sato government may have been able to play in settlement of war." A Soviet government note sent on January 29, 1968, in addition to referring to Sato's visit to Saigon, also accused the Japanese government of "collusion with the U.S." with respect to U.S. military procurements in Japan and calls on Japanese ports by U.S. warships. A research memo prepared for Rusk on December 8 within the State Department noted Sato's and Miki's increased backing for U.S. policy in Vietnam over the past few months, stressing support for U.S. attempts to achieve "a just and equitable settlement" as well as the need for reciprocal action by Hanoi in return for a cessation of the bombing of North Vietnam. The same document also pointed out, however, that Japanese effectiveness in acting as an intermediary "is limited by its increasing identification with the US/GVN side as well as the apparent reluctance on Hanoi's part to negotiate at all."[33]

The Japanese Foreign Ministry was well aware that Japan's increased backing of U.S. policy in Vietnam would result in compromising its role as a go-between. A document drafted by the Southeast Asia Section of the Foreign Ministry on July 15, 1967, commented that finding ways to achieve a settlement was very difficult. Japan had no diplomatic relations with Hanoi, but it did have an alliance with the United States. Consequently, Japan "cannot act," the drafters admitted, "as a go-between from a purely neutral position." The communist side saw Tokyo and Washington as "a monolith, with the former providing bases for supporting the U.S. conduct of the war in Vietnam." Nonetheless, the document stressed the need to maintain and explore avenues of communication with Hanoi while continuing to press for cooperation from other countries.[34]

Both Sato and Miki nevertheless took an increasingly forthright stand in support of U.S. war efforts even in the face of strong domestic criticism. In this sense, Sato's visit to Saigon, as well as other concerted efforts within the Japanese government to support U.S. policy in Vietnam, was a calculated effort by these Japanese politicians and government officials to achieve an early return of Okinawa as well as to strengthen U.S.-Japan relations by extending the security treaty beyond 1970. After the November summit in Washington, the fact that Sato and Miki accelerated their campaign to enhance the Japanese people's defense consciousness as well as provide more vigorous support for U.S. policy in Vietnam clearly demonstrated that they were willing to sacrifice Japan's intermediary role to achieve those central objectives.

The Tet Offensive, the Johnson "Shock," and Japan's Post-Vietnam Planning for Peace

During the Washington summit meeting, Sato was asked not only to support America's Vietnam policy publicly, but also to continue to seek a basis for peace. So the Sato government continued to search for peace. Foreign Minister Miki's "guarantor scheme" for peace in Vietnam was another such effort.[35] However, with Hanoi's and Washington's approaches still far apart, and given Hanoi's increasingly suspicious view of Japan as a "neutral" intermediary, it soon became apparent that Miki's guarantor scheme would go nowhere. Deputy Vice Minister of Foreign Affairs Shinichi Kondo, after spending three weeks in Vietnam, told the American embassy in Vientiane during his brief visit to Laos in early May, 1968, that Miki's plan for "guarantors" as an aid to negotiations was "definitely shelved."[36]

Under such circumstances, the Japanese government began to emphasize Japan's contribution "in the non-military aspects of organizing peace." Japan's contribution to Asia's social and economic development as a crucial element of Japanese diplomacy had been developed in the postwar years mainly under the country's constitutional restraints as well as the strong pacifist sentiments of the Japanese people. It was based on their belief that effective aid could strengthen the capacity of Southeast Asia countries to resist communism. Miki said during his talk with Rusk in September, 1967, that "Communism, like water, flows down hill." It thus was essential, said Miki, to "build up the low spots of a social and economic nature." With respect to the Vietnam situation, Miki stressed that both "military and political efforts" must be combined. From his standpoint, then, the problem was the government of South Vietnam, and the solution was developing an effective civilian government with broad popular support. It seemed to him that this might in fact be "a more practical manner of influencing Hanoi." Although Secretary Rusk agreed "in general," he thought that "in any combination of military and political factors," the military aspect was "most important."[37]

There was an important difference in emphasis in their attitude toward how best to contribute to peace and stability in the region. Nevertheless, Rusk also recognized the importance of the political aspects of Japan's contribution to the social and economic development of Asia. Specifically, "although ASPAC and ASEAN were not conceived as security arrangements," the secretary stated, "they have nonetheless a security result as an expression of common interest and international cooperation." He even asked Japan to "give some thought to her marginal and insignificant trade with North Vietnam." "The economic benefits are small," he continued, "but the political consequences are great."[38]

Rusk's appreciation of the nonmilitary aspects of Japan's contribution in Asia encouraged Tokyo to renew its effort to provide more economic assistance. At the same time, Japan began to place more emphasis on a postwar role in economic rehabilitation and international peacekeeping. The mid-November summit meeting in this context provided a timely opportunity for Sato because the U.S. participants, including President Johnson, variously emphasized the need for Japan to make a greater political and economic role in the region. Such an emphasis on Japan's nonmilitary role was welcomed as an encouraging message for both Sato and Miki. Thus, Ambassador Shimoda's speech, delivered less than three weeks after the summit, stressed that "a majority of Japanese agree with most Asians," that "military means alone" would not solve Vietnam's problems, and that "a political settlement by negotiation would be the only alternative."

When U.S.-Japan planning talks were held in Tokyo a week after Shimoda's speech, the Japanese participants stated that while they wanted to give economic assistance to South Vietnam, they were handicapped by opposition in Japan "while the war continues." Accordingly, Japan's peace effort had to shift its emphasis from mediation to economic assistance and rehabilitation. Japan's increasing identification with the U.S. side necessitated a similar shift of emphasis. Japanese participants at the planning talks emphasized, throughout the discussions, the usefulness of the various regional organizations—particularly the Ministerial Conference on Southeast Asian Economic Development—in "organizing the peace in Asia." It should be noted that the Japanese side, according to the record of discussions, "emphasized strongly" the importance it attached to the pledge of the Johnson-Sato joint communiqué of November 15 to provide increased economic assistance to Southeast Asia.[39]

Beginning in late December, 1967, and early 1968, the Japanese government's peace effort began to emphasize postwar economic rehabilitation and peacekeeping activities in Southeast Asia. Two events in early 1968 affected the changing context of Japan's peace efforts, reinforcing such an orientation within Japanese government circles. The Tet Offensive, unleashed by the NLF on January 30, shattered the illusion of military success in Vietnam and dramatically altered American opinion. Ambassador Johnson in Tokyo reported to Washington on February 23 that both Miki and Sato were "privately taking a more and more bearish attitude on our prospects in Vietnam." Sato believed that he had "very much hitched his wagon to our star, especially in Vietnam."[40] Then, on March 31, President Johnson announced his decision to reduce air attacks against North Vietnam and enter into direct talks. Simultaneously, he also decided not to seek reelection. The president's speech stunned the Japanese and further heightened Sato's anxiety. Sato told Ambassador Johnson that it would be fatal if the United States should withdraw completely from Vietnam and asked whether the president's March 31 announcement might presage a change in its policy toward China. He wished to send a special envoy to Washington to discuss "thoroughly the implications of all the recent developments involving Vietnam and beyond." He thought it "very important" to discuss whatever policy changes might take place in the period following a peaceful settlement in Vietnam, particularly with respect to China. The ambassador had to assure Sato that such possibilities would not develop "before the conclusion of talks on Vietnam," and that the president's decision "did not represent a reversal of policy, or a surrender in Vietnam."[41]

The growing concern with a post-Vietnam situation among Japanese officials was reflected in the conference of Japanese embassies held in

Bangkok on March 30. The meeting focused primarily on postwar planning for Southeast Asia. The ambassadors discussed Japan's role in a posthostilities Vietnam and recommended a major economic rehabilitation program and Japan's role in an international supervisory commission. They thought Japanese participants in such a commission should come from the Japanese Self-Defense Forces rather than the police. On another occasion, Miki readily supported the idea of Japan's participation in an enlarged International Control Commission or other supervisory arrangement except that he thought Japanese participation should be restricted only to civilian personnel. He also expressed Japan's willingness to help in the economic development of Southeast Asia. During his European tour in mid-July, 1968, he emphasized to the French the importance of the North-South problem. Calling their attention to the increasing trend toward greater regional cooperation in Asia, Miki advocated "his scheme of Asia-Pacific Regional Cooperation" as an important pillar of Japan's post-Vietnam policy.[42]

President Johnson's March 31 announcement of a partial bombing halt against North Vietnam led Hanoi to agree to meet with U.S. officials in Paris, and face-to-face talks between representatives from Hanoi and Washington began on May 13. The Paris talks continued until Richard Nixon was elected president in November.[43] While the Paris talks were going on, U.S. officials were concerned that Hanoi would get the wrong message. Ambassador Johnson, for example, suspected that Hanoi was not yet prepared to negotiate seriously and was still hoping domestic and international pressures would force a reversal of U.S. policy. Therefore, from his standpoint, "anything Japan could do to disabuse Hanoi of this notion was the biggest contribution Japan could now make to peace." Miki mentioned that Japan did not want any settlement that would result in a communist South Vietnam and that any settlement should be based on the principles of the 1954 Geneva Accords, beginning with the mutual withdrawal of North Vietnamese and American forces. The ambassador quickly suggested that Japan announce this publicly. Miki accepted that it be conveyed by the Japanese ambassador in Vientiane to the North Vietnamese ambassador there. According to Ambassador Johnson, Japan could contribute to the Paris peace talks by not giving Hanoi the impression that Tokyo was urging Washington to make peace at any price.[44]

The Japanese government continued throughout 1968 to try to develop closer contacts with Hanoi so that it could help mediate, but Hanoi repeatedly rebuffed such efforts. On November 9, a North Vietnamese chargé in Vientiane rejected the suggestion of periodic private dinners with Amb. Yoshito Shimoda, "on instructions from Hanoi." In early August, 1968, the

North Vietnamese ambassador in Vientiane agreed to the idea of informal contacts but declined to comment on Miki's formula of "guarantors." Foreign Minister Miki, during his European tour in mid-July, asked for an appointment with the North Vietnamese delegation in Paris but his request was turned down. Etienne Manac'h, the director of Asian affairs at the French Foreign Ministry, who had sounded out the North Vietnamese, said he thought the "real reason is [the] Japanese government's open support for US Vietnam policy." The Soviet Union likewise continued to point out the contradictory attitude of Japan with respect to Vietnam. During Transportion Minister Yosuhiro Nakasone's talks in Moscow with Andrei Kosygin, the Soviet premier said that on one hand Japan was crying for peace while on the other Japanese companies were profiting from orders from South Vietnam and the United States and also allowing "U.S. submarines to use Japanese ports."[45]

Conclusions

Japan's intermediary role in the Vietnam War during the Sato administration was burdened from the very beginning by its security treaty ties with Washington. The U.S.-Japan security treaty allowed the United States to use its bases in Japan "for the international peace and security in the Far East." As Ambassador Johnson acknowledged, "Japan was vital to our effort in Vietnam." It provided ports and supply dumps, repaired and rebuilt facilities, and provided stopover points for aircraft and hospitals for badly wounded soldiers.[46] When these facts were brought up by either Hanoi or Moscow, Sato and other Japanese political leaders rebutted by saying that the United States was allowed to use bases and facilities in Japan under the terms of the security treaty and that there were no legal prohibitions against U.S. purchases of supplies in Japan. However, justifications based on legal grounds made little sense from the communist standpoint.

The Sato administration's peace efforts were also substantially defined by two overarching factors: the prime minister's determination to maintain close cooperation between Japan and the United States with the extension of the security treaty in 1970 and his more immediate objective of achieving the reversion of Okinawa while he was in office. The strategy of achieving these two objectives invariably influenced Japan's peace efforts, as it meant Japan's increasing identification with the United States against China and the Soviet Union, as well as its support for South Vietnam against North Vietnam. Consequently, Hanoi and its supporters naturally tended to view Japan's intermediary role as not neutral, making it difficult for Tokyo to persuade Hanoi to engage in peace talks. The Soviet Union basically saw Japan in the same light and was often cool to Japanese overtures.

Despite these constraints, Sato's support for U.S policy in Vietnam was more privately than publicly carried out until a few months before the Sato-Johnson November summit in Washington. A State Department briefing paper prepared for the president in November, 1967, accurately summarizes the principal components of Japan's policy toward Vietnam before the summit: (a) the use of military bases in Japan "without publicity" for logistical and other support of U.S. forces in Vietnam; (b) stress in public statements and diplomatic efforts the desire for peace, "but on terms acceptable to the U.S."; (c) provide relatively modest economic assistance to South Vietnam; and (d) offer "private expressions" of full support for U.S. Vietnam policy.[47]

However, Japan's "leaning" toward Washington and Saigon became even more visible as the Sato-Johnson summit approached. The Sato administration assumed a much stronger public posture on Vietnam beginning with the prime minister's visit to Saigon on October 21, 1967. These moves reflected Sato's deliberate effort to impress Washington in the hope that the reversion of Okinawa to Japanese control would be facilitated. These moves in turn further compromised Japan's position as a neutral intermediary and Hanoi's attitude toward Tokyo hardened thereafter. The North Vietnamese openly said that Japan's position was one-sided and expressed their opposition to Japanese participation in peacekeeping activities or in an international supervisory arrangement.

Japan's effort to search for peace was not limited to an intermediary role. Sato, Miki, and the Foreign Ministry all believed that Japan could contribute to peace and stability in Southeast Asia through nonmilitary means. Sato and Miki thus stressed that the strengthening of the Saigon government through Japan's economic assistance would supplement and reinforce Washington's efforts to achieve peace through negotiations. They hoped that leaders in Hanoi could somehow be convinced that they could not succeed by continuing to fight. Only then, they believed, would there be a role for Japan to play in bringing about a negotiated peace settlement. The Johnson administration basically agreed. Officials in the United States recognized that Japanese military contributions were barred both by Japan's constitution and the strong antiwar sentiments of the Japanese people. Washington thus sought three things from Sato with respect to Japan's support for Vietnam: (a) Japan should publicly voice its support for U.S. efforts there as well as its public recognition of the importance of U.S. efforts in Vietnam to Japan's security, (b) Japan's larger economic assistance, and (c) a major postwar role in economic rehabilitation and international peace-keeping.

The importance of the second and third points increased in 1968 not only for the Sato government but also for the U.S. government. In this connection, the Tet Offensive in late January and President Johnson's March 31 announcement became a turning point in the sense that the new U.S. policy of "Vietnamization" and the deterioration of the military situation in Southeast Asia made it clear to the Japanese government that the war would sooner or later come to an end. If a cease-fire agreement were reached, Japan could play a larger role in making the settlement stick through its economic assistance and, in the next stage, contribute to peace and stability by providing aid and assistance for rehabilitation and reconstruction in Southeast Asia.

The U.S. government both welcomed and encouraged such a role for Japan. In this sense, the Japanese government's effort to search for peace in the Vietnam War was not limited to its intermediary role. Sato and Miki, as evidenced by their intentions and efforts, believed that they could contribute to peace and stability in the region through economic and technical assistance as well.

Notes

1. Memorandum of conversation, "Miki-Rusk talks," Tokyo, July 6, 1966, Central Foreign Policy Files, 1964–66 (hereafter CFPF, years covered), Box 2377, Record Group 59, General Records of the Department of State (hereafter RG 59), National Archives and Records Administration, Washington, D.C. (hereafter NARA); American embassy, Tokyo, to Sec State, "Secretary's meeting with PM Sato: Vietnam," Dec. 6, 1966, cables, vol. 5, Jan., 1966–Feb., 1967, Country File (CF)-Japan, Box 251, National Security File (NSF), Lyndon B. Johnson Library, Austin, Tex. (hereafter LBJL).

2. Rusk, memorandum for the president, July 10, 1965, memos, vol. 3, Sept., 1964–Oct., 1965, CF-Japan, NSF, Box 250, LBJL.

3. American embassy, Tokyo, to Rusk, cable 2058, Dec. 29, 1964, Sato's Visit, memos and cables (1of 2), CF-Japan, NSF, Box 253, LBJL.

4. *Public Papers of the Presidents of the United States: Lyndon B. Johnson,* vol. 1, *1965* (Washington, D.C.: GPO, 1966), pp. 394–99. For an analysis of U.S.-Japan relations in the 1960s in the context of emerging regionalism in Asia and the Vietnam War, see Hideki Kan, "U.S.-Japan Relations in the 1960s and U.S. Policy toward the Emerging Regionalism in Asia," *Hosei Kenkyu* (*Journal of Law and Politics*) 66 (July, 1999): pp. 786–804. For a fascinating analysis of the relationship between President Johnson's Johns Hopkins speech and his vision of transforming Vietnam (the Mekong Delta) into a "Tennessee Valley," see Lloyd C. Gardner, *Pay Any Price: Lyndon Johnson and the Wars for Vietnam* (Chicago: Ivan R. Dee, 1995), pp. 189–97.

5. Reischauer to Rusk, cable 3185, Apr. 7, 1965, cables (2 of 2), vol. 3, Sept., 1964–Oct., 1965, CF-Japan, NSF, Box 250, LBJL; memorandum of conversation, Apr. 13, 1965, memos (1 of 2), ibid.

6. Department of Defense to American embassy, Tokyo, telegram 584, Aug. 27, 1965, CFPF, 1964–66, Box 2383, RG 59, NARA.

7. "Rusk-Shiina meeting September 26," USUN New York to Sec State, telegram Secto 6, Sept. 27, 1965, ibid.

8. *The Secret Diplomacy of the Vietnam War: The Negotiating Volumes of the Pentagon Papers,* ed. George C. Herring (Austin: University of Texas Press, 1983), pp. 78, 98.

9. American embassy, Saigon, to Sec State, telegram 1173, Oct. 5, 1965; memorandum of conversation, Oct. 28, 1965, "Mr. Kase's call on the Secretary"; and memorandum of conversation, Oct. 26, 1965, "Call by Mr. Toshikazu Kase," all in CFPF, 1964–66, Box 2376, RG 59, NARA.

10. American embassy, Tokyo, to Sec State, Jan. 27, 1966, telegram 2614; telegram 2883, Feb. 17, 1966; and American embassy, Tokyo, to Sec State, Feb. 21, 1966, Airgram A-1009, all in CFPF, 1964–66, Box 2377, ibid.

11. For an early indication of Japan's handicaps as a mediator, see, e.g., Foreign Minister Subandorio's remark to Vice President Shojiro Kawashima during his visit to Indonesia, that Japan would not give the impression that it was "in the service of an imperialist's interests" in the Vietnam War. See "Kawashima Fukusosai Indoneshia Hoomon," Aug., 1965, Gaiko Shiryokan, Tokyo (Diplomatic Record Office, Japanese Foreign Office; hereafter DRO).

12. American embassy, Tokyo, to Sec State, Dec. 29, 1965, CFPF, 1964–66, Box 2376, RG 59, NARA.

13. "Shiina Gaisho Ooshu Homon," Jan., 1966, DRO; American embassy, Tokyo, to Department of State, Feb. 3, 1966, Airgram A-920, "Japanese Foreign Minister's Visit to USSR," CFPF, 1964–66, Box 2377, RG 59, NARA.

14. Department of State to American embassy, Tokyo, Jan. 14, 1967, telegram 118870, and attached report regarding Nakagawa-Kinh conversation of Dec. 23, 1966, dated Jan. 3, 1967, Embassy of Japan, Washington D.C., CFPF, 1967–69, Box 2251, RG 59, NARA (hereafter, "Gist of conversation").

15. "Mosuko (Moscow) ni okeru Nakagawa Taishi/hokuetsu Taishi no Sesshoku," July (undated) and Sept. 15, 1966, DRO.

16. Robert S. McNamara et al., *Argument Without End: In Search of Answers to the Vietnam Tragedy* (New York: Public Affairs, 1999), p. 282.

17. For details of the third meeting, see "Gist of conversation." The following four paragraphs are drawn from the same source.

18. McNamara et al., *Argument Without End,* p. 285; *Secret Diplomacy,* ed., Herring, pp. 397–98; Lyndon B. Johnson, *The Vantage Point* (New York: Popular Library, 1971), pp. 592–95.

19. "Gist of conversation."

20. American embassy, Tokyo, to Sec State, Mar. 17, 1967, telegram 6627, CFPF, 1967–69, Box 2251, RG 59, NARA; Department of State to American embassy, Tokyo, Mar. 17, 1967, telegram 157616 (regarding the *Washington Post* article by Richard Halloran), ibid. The *Asahi Shimbun* published a story on March 15 to the effect that Japanese embassies around the world had been ordered to establish contacts with North Vietnamese in order to assist the Japanese government in determining what role Japan could play in bringing peace to Vietnam. See also Richard Halloran, "Japan Launches Vietnam Peace Effort," *Washington Post* Mar. 17, 1967.

21. Department of State to American embassy, Tokyo, Mar. 17, 1967, telegram 158080, CFPF, 1967–69, Box 2251, RG 59, NARA; Department of State to American embassy, Tokyo, May 25, 1967, telegram 202577, ibid.; American embassy, Tokyo, to Sec State, June 20, 1967, telegram 9015D, ibid.

22. American embassy, Tokyo, to Sec State, Nov. 18, 1966, telegram 3737, CFPF, 1964–66, Box 2377, RG 59, NARA; "Matsuno Nouso Tonan Ajia Homon," Nov., 1966, DRO; Ameri-

can embassy, Tokyo, to Sec State, "Secretary's meeting with PM Sato: Vietnam," Dec. 12, 1966, Lyndon Baines Johnson Papers, 1963–69 (hereafter LBJ Papers), LBJL.

23. American embassy, Tokyo, to Sec State, "Goldberg-Sato conversation," Feb. 27, 1967, telegram 6061, cables, vol. 5, Sept., 1966–Feb., 1967, Box 251, CF-Japan, NSF, LBJ Papers, LBJL.

24. American embassy, Tokyo, to Sec State, Apr. 28, 1967, telegram 7877, CFPF, 1967–69, Box 2246, RG 59, NARA.

25. Department of State to American embassy, Tokyo, "Briefing of GOJ for Miki Visit to Moscow," July 15, 1967, telegram 7570, cables, vol. 6, Feb., 1967–Oct., 1967, CF-Japan, NSF, Box 251, LBJ Papers, LJBL; William P. Bundy to Mr. Kohler, "Your meeting with Ambassador Shimoda," July 17, 1967, CFPF, 1967–69, Box 2250, RG 59, NARA.

26. Department of State to American embassy, Tokyo, July 28, 1967, telegram 13999, CFPF, 1967–69, Box 2251, RG 59, NARA; Department of State to American embassy, Tokyo, July 28, 1967, telegram 13790, Box 2243, ibid.

27. American embassy, Tokyo, to Sec State, "Sato Plan to Visit South Vietnam Draws Fire," June 23, 1967, telegram 9116, Box 2243, ibid.

28. American embassy, Tokyo, to Sec State, Oct. 21, 1967, telegram 6976, cables, vol. 5., Jan., 1966–Feb., 1967, Box 251, CF-Japan, NSF, LBJ Papers, LBJL; Director of Intelligence and Research, Department of State, to Sec State, Oct. 6, 1967, CFPF, 1967–69, Box 2246, RG 59, NARA.

29. "Visit of PM Sato, November 14–15, 1967," Visit of Prime Minister Sato—Briefing Book, CF-Japan, NSF, Box 253, LBJ Papers, LBJL.

30. Rusk, memorandum for the president, "Your Meeting with PM Sato, Nov. 14 & 15," Nov. 10, 1967, ibid.

31. Memorandum of conversation, Nov. 15, 1967, Visit of PM Sato, Nov. 14–15, 1967, ibid.

32. Rusk to Ambassador Shimoda, Dec. 5, 1967, CFPF, 1967–69, Box 2250, RG 59, NARA; William P. Bundy, note to Sec State, Dec. 2, 1967, ibid.; William P. Bundy to Sec State, concerning Ambassador Shimoda's speech of Dec. 1, Dec. 4, 1967, ibid.

33. American embassy, Saigon, to Sec State, "Sato's Visit to Saigon," Oct. 26, 1967, telegram 9650, CFPF, 1967–69, Box 2243, RG 59, NARA; American embassy, Tokyo, to Sec State, Feb. 13, 1968, Airgram A-1060, Box 2251, ibid.; American embassy, Moscow, to Sec State, Jan. 30, 1968, telegram 2635, ibid.; Director of Intelligence and Research, Department of State, research memo to Sec State, "Current Problems Facing the Japanese Government," REA-54, Dec. 8, 1967, Box 2246, ibid.

34. "Vietnam mondai" (Tonanajia Ka, Kaimusho), July 15, 1967, DRO.

35. According to this scheme, Washington would cease bombing Hanoi and withdraw within six months after an agreed settlement, while Hanoi would reciprocate by guaranteeing the cessation of its infiltration and assistance to communist forces in South Vietnam within a reasonable period after the U.S. bombing halt. Japan, Canada, India, Poland and Rumania would act as guarantors of this scheme (Memorandum of conversation, Office of the Assistant Secretary of Defense, Nov. 18, 1967, NSF country file, Japan, Box 253, Visit of PM Sato, LBJL). See also American embassy, Tokyo, to Sec State, Nov. 10, 1969, telegram 3222, CFPF, 1967–69, Box 2244, RG 59, NARA; William P. Bundy, briefing memorandum for Rusk, Nov. 11, 1967, Visit of PM Sato—Briefing Book, CF-Japan, NSF, Box 253, LBJ Papers, LBJL.

36. American embassy, Vientiane, to Sec State, May 9, 1968, telegram 8397, CFPF, 1967–69, Box 2244, RG 59, NARA.

37. Memorandum of conversation, Secretary's Office, Sept. 14, 1967, "Security and Regional Development," pt. 2 of 5, ibid.; memorandum of conversation, Secretary's Office, Sept. 14, 1967, "Vietnam," pt. 5 of 5, Box 2249, ibid.

38. Ibid, pt. 5 of 5.

39. Henry Owen, Policy Planning Council chairman, to Sec State, "US-Japan Planning Talks," Dec. 12, 1967, memos, vol. 7, Oct., 1967–Dec., 1968, CF-Japan, NSF, Box 252, LBJ Papers, LBJL.

40. American embassy, Tokyo, to Sec State, Feb. 23, 1968, telegram 5848, CFPF, 1967–69, Box 2249, RG 59, NARA. In a cable dated April 4, Ambassador Johnson described Sato as "under heavy attack in both press and Diet for having too closely tied GOJ [Government of Japan] to a highly unpredictable USG [U.S. Government], which is now abandoning policy to which Sato had given so much support" (American embassy, Tokyo, to Sec State, Apr. 4, 1968, telegram 7136, cables, vol. 7, Oct., 1967–Dec., 1968, CF-Japan, NSF, Box 252, LBJ Papers, LBJL).

41. Memorandum of conversation, American embassy, Tokyo, "Ambassador's Meeting with PM Sato," Apr. 7, 1968, CFPF, 1967–69, Box 2249, RG 59, NARA. See also, U. Alexis Johnson, *The Right Hand of Power* (Englewood Cliffs, N.J.: Prentice Hall, 1984), pp. 499–501.

42. Department of State to American embassy, Tokyo, July 18, 1968, CFPF, 1967–69, Box 2247, RG 59, NARA; American embassy, Paris, to Sec State, July 20, 1968, telegram 18277, Box 2244, ibid.; "Nichi Futsu Kaidan, Miki Hatsugen Yoryo, Miki Gaisho Oushuu Homon," July, 1968, DRO.

43. Allan E. Goodman, *The Lost Peace: America's Search for a Negotiated Settlement of the Vietnam War* (Stanford, Calif.: Hoover Institution Press, 1978), pp. 65–73.

44. American embassy, Tokyo, to Sec State, Aug. 21, 1968, telegram 11300, CFPF, 1967–69, Box 2249, RG 59, NARA.

45. American embassy, Vientiane, to Sec State, "NVN Charge Cool to Japanese Overtures," Nov. 29, 1967, Airgram A-131, Box 2251, ibid.; American embassy, Vientiane, to Sec State, Aug. 13, 1968, telegram 8434, ibid.; telegram 8388, ibid.; Aug. 12, 1968, ibid.; American embassy, Paris, to Sec State, July 15, 1968, telegram 18009, Box 2244, ibid.; American embassy, Moscow, to Sec State, "Soviet Government Statement to Japan," Jan. 30, 1968, telegram 2635, American embassy, Tokyo, to Sec State, Feb. 13, 1968, Airgram A-1060, Box 2251, ibid.; telegram 13417, ibid.; Oct. 30, 1968, Box 2244, ibid.

46. Johnson, *Right Hand of Power,* pp. 444–45.

47. "Japanese Foreign Policy," Nov. 9, 1967, Visit of PM Sato—Briefing Book, Box 253, LBJ Papers, LBJL.

The Limits of Peacemaking

India and the Vietnam War, 1962–1968

MARK A. LAWRENCE

New Delhi buzzed with diplomatic intrigue in the first days of 1967. Indian officials had been aware for some time of a possible softening in North Vietnam's position on the war in Vietnam. Then, on January 4, Nguyen Hoa, Hanoi's consul general in Delhi, made explicit what had previously come secondhand. In a meeting with Tikki Kaul, the secretary of India's Ministry of External Affairs, the consul stated that if the United States stopped bombing North Vietnam "unconditionally and indefinitely," the gesture would lead to "cessation of hostilities and other steps" in the South. Optimistic about a possible breakthrough toward a negotiated settlement of the war, the Indian ambassador in Washington urgently relayed the message to Secretary of State Dean Rusk. The North Vietnamese demarche was, the Indian insisted, "more than a whisper." Though skeptical of the vague proposal, Rusk asserted that Washington was "most interested" in pursuing the matter further. He asked the Indians to meet again with Nguyen Hoa to obtain more precise information about what Hanoi had in mind.[1] American officials felt confident enough about the new channel of communication with North Vietnam to assign it a code name for easy reference: NIRVANA.

Within a few weeks, however, NIRVANA was dead. The North Vietnamese consul had backed away from his initially encouraging tone, and the Americans saw no reason to pursue the matter further. Some Indian diplomats believed that press leaks in New Delhi had ruined the initiative, while others suspected that hawks in Hanoi had squelched it. The circumstances surrounding NIRVANA's failure are not especially important. As numerous historians have argued, neither Hanoi nor Washington, whatever their willingness to entertain feelers, was in any mood for a negotiated settlement in 1967.[2] The failure of the much more elaborate MARIGOLD and SUNFLOWER peace initiatives around the same time suggests that NIRVANA, a relatively tentative and fleeting affair, had no real prospect of success. The episode is nevertheless worthy of inquiry if approached from a different angle, for it prompts a question whose answer is both elusive and illuminating: Why was the NIRVANA channel the best that India could manage to promote a peaceful resolution to the Vietnam War?

On the face of it, India was well positioned to play a constructive peace-making role in Indochina. Under the 1954 Geneva Accords, the Indian government chaired the International Control Commission (ICC), the three-nation body responsible for monitoring the cease-fire that ended the First Indochina War. The ICC retained its formal responsibilities throughout the American war, and Indian peace monitors, along with their Canadian and Polish counterparts, remained stationed in Vietnam as the fighting worsened. Yet India's qualifications as a peacemaker went beyond its ICC role. Delhi nurtured close ties with both the United States and the Soviet Union, maintained a diplomatic presence in both Saigon and Hanoi, and enjoyed a reputation as a leader among nonaligned states and as a country singularly devoted to the cause of international peace. Most importantly, the Indian government aspired to play a significant diplomatic role in settling the Vietnam issue. "The Foreign Office in Delhi was forever trying to mediate the conflict," Braj Kumar Nehru, India's ambassador in Washington during much of the 1960s, recalled in his memoirs. "Every other day," he wrote with some exaggeration, "I used to get a telegram making some proposal or other for peace in Vietnam and invariably asking me to take up the matter 'at the highest level.'"[3]

Nonetheless, India played at best a marginal role in the diplomacy of the Vietnam War, lagging behind Poland, Canada, Sweden, Britain, the Soviet Union, and other governments that became deeply involved at various times in efforts to arrange peace talks. The Indian government's enthusiasm for its ICC responsibilities waned so dramatically that in 1965, as American troops poured into Vietnam, Prime Minister Lal Bahadur Shastri told U.S. diplomats that India was "embarrassed by its role" and wished it "could get out of it."[4] Nor, despite NIRVANA, did India occupy an especially important place in broader international maneuvering that involved numerous governments and international organizations in the search for peace from 1963 to 1968. Indian initiatives were generally mere rhetorical appeals, lacking substance despite their frequency and the media attention they attracted. Looking back on those years, neither John Kenneth Galbraith, the U.S. ambassador in Delhi from 1961 to 1963, nor Walt Rostow, a senior White House and State Department aide who had close contact with Indian officials throughout the Kennedy and Johnson administrations, could recall a single Indian peace initiative of major significance.[5] The vast scholarship of the Vietnam War has validated this judgment. Only one book, D. R. SarDesai's old study of the period before 1964, explores India's role in

Southeast Asia, and no account of the American war contains more than passing references to India, usually in connection with the ICC's failures or Indian leaders' sniping at U.S. policy after 1965.[6]

This chapter explores some of the reasons for India's ineffectiveness in Vietnam in the belief that dogs that do not bark can be as instructive as those that do. A complete account would depend on the availability of sources that remain beyond the historian's grasp: above all, Indian and North Vietnamese diplomatic records. Fortunately, however, it is possible to write with authority about India on the basis of memoirs, media reports, and above all Western archival materials, which have become increasingly available to researchers in recent years. American, British, and Canadian officials were in constant contact with Indian counterparts, and their voluminous reporting permits insight into Indian calculations with respect to Vietnam. Indian calculations, in turn, shed light on a question of major importance to historians of the Second Indochina War: Why, despite a belief widely shared around the world that Vietnam should be neutralized and international tensions in Southeast Asia reduced, was there no peaceful solution of the conflict? New Delhi's inability to promote a meaningful initiative, despite its apparent qualifications for the job, helps to answer that question by demonstrating the powerful, deeply rooted obstacles to compromise that existed within Asia and the international system more generally during the 1960s.

India's problems were structural and intractable. As the Indian government sought to promote peace in Vietnam during the 1960s, it constantly rediscovered the tight constraints on its ability to act as an assertive and effective broker. All of those constraints stemmed in one way or another from India's struggles—and the struggles of the Asian continent more generally—to create a postcolonial political and social order. India's tense relationships with China and Pakistan, the result of lingering territorial and ideological disputes, limited India's ability to hold an active and independent course in Southeast Asia. Meanwhile, internal political tensions, rooted partly in controversies over economic development and foreign dependency, also dampened the country's scope for effective diplomacy. Finally, Indian reliance on foreign assistance, the result of India's grinding poverty, left it vulnerable to pressure from other governments, including the United States and the Soviet Union. These formidable constraints combined during the course of the 1960s to undermine the peacemaking role the Indian government had charted for itself during the preceding decade and rendered India an embittered onlooker as the war in Vietnam worsened.

India's Indochina Dilemma

Some of the constraints on Indian initiative in Vietnam during the 1960s were already evident during the 1940s and early 1950s, when the new Indian state first confronted the vexing problem of how to respond to conflict in Southeast Asia. During this period, Indian leaders discovered the conflicting priorities that would often, over the years to come, dictate caution, temporization, and inconsistency. On one hand, Jawaharlal Nehru—prime minister, foreign minister, and embodiment of the new Indian state—had good reason to seek a prominent role in ending conflict in Indochina and supporting the establishment of independent states in Vietnam, Cambodia, and Laos. First, the Franco-Vietminh conflict was an opportunity to enhance the new government's claim to a position of major importance in international affairs. An Asian colonial war provided an ideal forum for advancing India's self-appointed role as both anticolonial conscience and champion of peace and nonalignment among states emerging from European control. Second, the Indochina conflict offered Nehru a chance to bolster the domestic political legitimacy of his All-India Congress, whose claim to authority was built largely upon its principled stand against European colonialism. Third, geostrategic considerations called for activism in Indochina. The turmoil in Southeast Asia clearly invited intervention by outside powers such as China, the United States, and the Soviet Union—all of which by 1950 were showing mounting signs of interest in the region. Foreign embroilment promised to diminish Indian influence in the region, undercut the cause of nonalignment in Asia, and possibly even fuel a major war close to India's eastern borders.

On the other hand, various considerations encouraged caution about assuming an active diplomatic role in Indochina. First, Nehru sought close cooperation with Britain and France and was reluctant to antagonize them through advocacy of decolonization in Southeast Asia. The larger reason for Indian caution, however, was Nehru's awareness of Ho Chi Minh's communist affiliation and his fear, especially after the Mao's victory in fall 1949, that the defeat of French policy in Indochina might clear the way for Chinese penetration into Southeast Asia. Mao Zedong's fiery denunciations of Nehru as a Western lackey, as well as high tension along the Sino-Indian border after the Chinese takeover of Tibet in 1950, encouraged the Indian leader's circumspection about any overhasty removal of Western influence. India's geostrategic interests could cut two ways. Indians wished to prevent Southeast Asia from becoming a cockpit of Cold War rivalries, but Nehru, a staunch anticommunist, was equally determined to prevent domination by any single power over the region, especially if that power was Mao's China.[7]

Beset by conflicting priorities, Nehru temporized. Although he sometimes chastised the French government for its repressive behavior in Indochina, he showed little interest in trying to end the war through Indian mediation or an appeal to the United Nations. Not until 1954 did the causes of India's caution drop away sufficiently to free Nehru for the sort of active role in Indochina that his anticolonial principles and peacemaking rhetoric seemed to dictate. By that time, Indian officials had gained a good deal of experience with international mediation, notably as chair of the Neutral Nations Repatriation Commission assembled to implement provisions of the Korean War settlement. However, it was a dramatic thaw in Sino-Indian relations that most altered Indian calculations by removing the most serious impediment—fear of Chinese expansionism in Southeast Asia—that blocked New Delhi from taking any initiative. In a landmark proclamation in April, the Chinese and Indian governments pledged themselves to a new era of peaceful coexistence, not only bilaterally but also in their relations with all of Asia. Increasingly confident that China no longer posed a major threat to Indian interests in Southeast Asia, Nehru signaled that his country would seek a major role in Indochina. In April, Nehru declared to the Lok Sabha, the lower house of India's Parliament, that India had an "earnest desire to assist to resolve some of the difficulties and the deadlocks and to bring about a peaceful settlement."[8]

The Indian government followed through on its new rhetoric of commitment and activism. At an April meeting of five Asian prime ministers in Colombo, Nehru won approval of a comprehensive Indian peace plan for Indochina. Strongly endorsed by the British government, Nehru's plan became the basis for the nine-nation talks on Indochina that got under way in Geneva just as the Colombo meeting was concluding. India, though not a formal party to the Geneva negotiations, performed several crucial tasks in the meetings that brought an end to the First Indochina War and became synonymous with peacemaking in Vietnam. Working behind the scenes, Nehru's emissary, V. K. Krishna Menon, shuttled between the U.S. and Chinese delegations, ultimately producing the understanding that would underpin the Geneva formula. The assembled governments recognized India's status as a principal peace broker in Southeast Asia by appointing it to head the three-nation International Commission for Supervision and Control—commonly referred to as the International Control Commission—responsible for monitoring the cease-fires in Cambodia, Laos, and Vietnam.[9] Britain and the Soviet Union, cochairs of the Geneva conference, would oversee and fund the ICC's work, but the Indian government would set the agenda, head monitoring teams, and submit regular reports on the implementation of the Geneva terms.

New Delhi embraced its ICC responsibilities, dispatching more than a thousand diplomats, clerks, soldiers, and technicians to staff the observer missions set up in various locations throughout Indochina—headquarters offices in Saigon, Hanoi, Vientiane, and Phnom Penh, as well as "fixed teams" scattered in several strategic locations. In August, New Delhi hosted the first high-level meeting with ICC representatives from Poland and Canada, inaugurating a period of optimism and unanimity in ICC deliberations. As SarDesai has chronicled, the ICC enjoyed some notable successes in its first years. In Cambodia, Indian officials were instrumental in preserving the government's neutrality, and in Laos the ICC oversaw the establishment of a neutralist regime under Souvanna Phouma before suspending its activities in 1957 in the mistaken belief that its work was complete. In 1961 and 1962, the Indian government played a central role in new Geneva negotiations that resulted in agreements to neutralize Laos.[10]

In Vietnam, by contrast, the ICC faced enormous problems from the beginning. By mid-1955, South Vietnamese premier Ngo Dinh Diem, encouraged by the United States, made clear that he had no intention of abiding by the Geneva Accords, especially the provisions calling for Vietnam-wide elections in 1956. Although Diem found the ICC to be useful in certain cases—as, for example, when it helped Diem gain a propaganda edge by facilitating the movement of Catholics from north to south—his incentives were mainly to obstruct the organization's work. Diem went so far as to arrange for an anti-ICC riot in 1955 to intimidate officials in Saigon. The departure of French troops and administrators further undercut the Commission's effectiveness by removing the one group that the Indian government could count on for support of the Geneva Accords. France, after all, was a signatory; Diem and the United States were not. For a time, the ICC persevered with its duties. The Polish representative, Mieczyslaw Maneli, later praised the Indians and Canadians for their "loyal cooperation" despite the difficult circumstances under which the ICC labored.[11] Increasingly, however, the strains showed. In early 1962, with the U.S. advisory role escalating in South Vietnam, the Polish representative broke with his Indian and Canadian counterparts and submitted a minority report explicitly condemning American violations of the Geneva Accords. The majority Indo-Canadian report, sticking with the Commission's practice of avoiding direct criticism of either side, refused to allocate blame for the worsening situation. Thus torn by Cold War tensions, the ICC stopped producing its regular reports—there had been ten others since 1955—and avoided any more for three years.

Although hardening divisions between the two Vietnamese governments and mounting tensions between the Indian and Polish ICC delegations had badly damaged the Commission by 1963, it was another development—serious deterioration of the Sino-Indian relationship—that most undercut India's ability to play an effective role in Indochina. During the period of Sino-Indian rapprochement, reinforced by the Bandung meeting of Afro-Asian nations in 1955, the two governments found a good deal of common ground with respect to Indochina's problems, especially a shared opposition to the Southeast Asia Treaty Organization (SEATO) alliance and to the extension of U.S. influence into Southeast Asia. By the end of the decade, however, an upsurge in Chinese criticism of the ICC's performance in Vietnam signaled that this period of relative harmony was drawing to a close. When the Commission indicated at the end of 1961 that it would issue a divided report, the Chinese press responded sharply, attacking the Indian and Canadian delegations for taking an "unjust attitude" and failing to take Washington to task for introducing "large quantities of military equipment and materials in violation of the Geneva agreement."[12]

Such criticism reflected a turn in Sino-Indian relations for reasons extending far beyond Southeast Asia. In 1959, an anti-Chinese rebellion in Tibet ignited new confrontation along the troubled Himalayan border, leading the Indian government two years later to adopt a "forward policy" of occupying disputed areas. Indian activity was intensely provocative and invited a Chinese response. By 1962, Mao was increasingly disposed to act. As historian Qiang Zhai has argued, Mao reoriented Chinese foreign policy for a range of reasons, including his satisfaction with China's economic achievements, his determination to sustain "revolutionary momentum" among his people, and his eagerness to differentiate himself from both Soviet "revisionists" and moderates within his own government.[13] In any case, Mao chose the simmering border dispute with India to demonstrate his new assertiveness. With Washington and Moscow distracted by the Cuban missile crisis in late October, 1962, Chinese forces invaded the disputed territories, overwhelming unprepared Indian defenses. Nehru attempted to rally effective resistance, but his efforts were futile. China humiliated the Indian armed forces and then unilaterally declared a cease-fire on November 21.

Although brief, the war severely damaged Nehru's cherished policy of nonalignment. Not only did the war demonstrate the hollowness of India's claims to occupy a special position outside the international fray, it also drove New Delhi into an uncomfortable reliance upon the United States. During the Chinese invasion, the Soviet government, clearly stung by Chinese accusations of revisionism, reluctantly backed Mao, leaving Nehru little choice but to turn to the United States for assistance. The Kennedy administration responded favorably and rushed equipment for ten mountain divisions to India along with badly needed transport aircraft. Neither ordinary Indians nor the leadership in New Delhi could fail to appreciate that the United States and India now shared the objective of containing reinvigorated Chinese expansionism. Although New Delhi's precise calculations are unknowable, its interest in avoiding overhasty removal of Western influence from Southeast Asia was as clear as it had been before 1954. In many ways, after 1962 the Indian government found itself confronting much the same dilemma it had faced a decade earlier. On one hand, it had good reason to promote peace and noninterventionism in Asia; on the other, it needed to tailor its position on Vietnam in order to discourage Chinese aggression and protect India's security. New Delhi's struggle to balance these competing demands would determine much of India's behavior with regard to Vietnam during the first years of the American war.

India and the Escalation of the American War, 1963–66

Kennedy administration officials hoped that the Sino-Indian war would produce a decisive change in India's attitude toward the whole range of Cold War issues, not least Vietnam. As many historians have chronicled, the new president attached great importance to improving U.S.-Indian relations and sharply increasing American aid.[14] In return, Washington was hopeful that Indian leaders would recognize that their interests in Asia coincided with those of the United States. A State Department appraisal in November, 1961, saw reason for optimism. While the Indian government's growing "experience and maturity" encouraged greater understanding for U.S. policies, the report patronizingly asserted, Washington was showing a "higher tolerance" for India's nonalignment. "These converging trends have produced a growing recognition by the U.S. and India that each shares the same fundamental values and objectives," the report continued.[15] The Sino-Indian war encouraged still more hope. Kennedy's decision to send aid generated unprecedented pro-U.S. sentiment, making the U.S. embassy a scene of wild popularity while Indians hung Mao and Zhou Enlai in effigy.[16] Chester Bowles, who replaced John Kenneth Galbraith just after the war, believed that such sentiments might portend a change in the whole tenor of Indian foreign policy if Washington managed the situation skillfully. The war and the Sino-Soviet rift, Bowles reported from Delhi, "offer us enormous opportunities" for U.S.-Indian cooperation.[17]

As Sino-Indian tensions mounted, Americans detected some signs of positive change in Indian attitudes toward the situation in Vietnam. Years later, Walt Rostow, who served as deputy national security adviser at the time, contended that Nehru totally changed his outlook following the war with China, fully embracing the U.S. position even though old commitments to nonalignment prevented him from saying so in public.[18] While that assertion was probably an exaggeration, it is clear that many Indian officials had a sympathetic view of American policy. As Sino-Indian relations worsened in 1962, Galbraith took pleasure in reporting that high-ranking Indian diplomats seemed increasingly willing to embrace the idea, long propounded by Washington, that North Vietnam sustained the Vietcong and that such sustenance constituted a serious breach of the Geneva Accords. M. J. Desai, a major nationalist figure who would shortly become foreign secretary, was convinced of the Vietcong's dependence upon "leadership as well as weapons from Hanoi," Galbraith reported, noting a significant change in Indian views over the preceding year.[19] Meanwhile, Commonwealth Secretary Yesdezard Dinshaw Gundevia told Galbraith he opposed any U.S. pullout from Vietnam.[20] In Saigon, the British ambassador, Henry Hohler, detected that Sino-Indian tensions were having "repercussions" within the Indian ICC delegation in Vietnam. Although Indian commissioner Ram Goburdhun had previously accepted the need for "positive objectivity" in the ICC's work, Hohler wrote, "he now considers it his duty to use his influence discreetly on the side of the free world—encouraging any activity which favours the Western interests."[21]

American officials worked hard to encourage this trend. In particular, they sought to convince New Delhi to use its ICC powers to validate U.S. policies in Vietnam. Recognizing the potentially powerful propaganda value in Indian backing, the State Department sought to persuade Braj Kumar Nehru, the ambassador in Washington, that India should invigorate and expand the ICC's activities, above all by thoroughly investigating North Vietnamese subversion in the South. American legal experts prepared a paper for the Indian embassy arguing that India should abandon its concern that conflict between the two zones of Vietnam amounted to an "internal" conflict and therefore fell outside the ICC's jurisdiction. On the contrary, the U.S. paper contended the Indian government had a legal obligation to investigate such matters and fully report its findings.[22] Rostow made a similar appeal but grounded his argument in geostrategic rather than legalistic reasoning. "Much of the history of Southeast Asia, Africa, and other areas" depended on India's willingness to use its authority to expose North Vietnamese subversion, Rostow wrote in a letter to the Indian ambassador, "for what is involved is whether or not the international community will declare out of bounds the mounting guerrilla war from outside a sovereign nation, organized, supplied and lead [*sic*] by a foreign power. The alternative to international order in this matter is an extension of the chaos we can observe from Cuba to the 17th parallel."[23]

American hopes that India would accept American logic and use the ICC to promote a pro-Western position in Indochina were disappointed. Indian officials, including Nehru himself during a 1961 visit to Washington, gave repeated assurances that they would step up ICC inspection activities as the U.S. government wished. In practice, however, the Indian government refused to act. Even in Laos, where the Kennedy administration strongly encouraged India to take a leading role during the Geneva talks in 1961 and 1962, Americans were often frustrated by India's performance. To be sure, New Delhi played an instrumental role in bringing about the neutralization accord. But Indian officials sometimes took what American officials considered a shockingly procommunist line. On one occasion, unnamed U.S. officials used the media to lambaste the Indian government for offering proposals that contained "practically every gimmick" favored by the communists and amounted to a "very close replica" of Soviet and Chinese aims.[24]

Indian behavior in this case reflected a determination to maintain the country's nonaligned posture despite the changed strategic situation in Asia. American officials had difficulty understanding how Indians could fail to act on the logic of resisting Chinese expansionism in Southeast Asia. However, two explanations for Indian behavior are now apparent. First, as historian Andrew Rotter has argued, Indian leaders were willing to accept inconsistencies between their approaches to threats along India's borders and to dangers farther afield. Although they were adamant about defending the Himalayan frontier at all costs, they took a relatively nuanced view of the communist danger in Southeast Asia, where communism and anticolonialism were difficult to distinguish.[25] Second, India's national identity and the prestige of its leadership—above all that of Nehru himself—rested on the country's commitment to nonalignment. Many documents remain secret, but it is plain that Nehru had no intention of compromising that position in Vietnam. He would have preferred, he told the Lok Sabha, that India "sank and died" before it became a "camp follower of a military bloc."[26] Thus, instead of pushing India away from nonalignment, the Sino-Indian war reconfirmed it.

Nonalignment also narrowed the options available to Indian leaders as they sought to maintain that course. If the Indian government rebuffed American pressure to compromise its peacemaking role by moving to an explicitly pro-Western position, the alternative course carried just as many risks to India's effectiveness in Southeast Asia. With China eliminated as a partner in India's search for a third way in international politics, the Indian government sought to balance its increasing reliance on the United States against similar support from the Soviet Union, the other major anti-

Chinese power. For the remainder of the 1960s, India's approach to the Vietnam conflict, like its approach to international affairs more generally, would be conditioned by the effort to maintain a balance between Washington and Moscow—a precarious endeavor that required constant adjustments and generated great frustration in both capitals as India tacked one way and then the other, with serious implications for India's potential as a peacemaker. Within the ICC, the need to play to both sides made the Indian government's position even more complicated than it had been before. If New Delhi seemed to act in favor of the United States, it would open itself to Soviet criticism and cheapen its own claims to nonalignment. If it favored North Vietnam, it would risk enhancing China's position in Southeast Asia and alienating Washington.

Indian discomfort was plain. In Saigon, Ambassador Hohler noted in 1962 that Indian ICC officials were "embarrassed" when North Vietnamese propaganda attacked the "Indo-Canadian imperialists" for taking America's side in Vietnam. Far from moving toward the Western position as tensions with China grew, Hohler added, it would likely become "normal practice" for India "to match a favour to one side in the Cold War by a corresponding favour to the other." Western governments, he added, were going to "have to put up with a period during which the Indian Government would not be as helpful as they had been."[27] Under a complicated set of conflicting pressures, the Indian ICC delegation at first retreated into passivity. Some officials even flirted with the idea of closing down the Commission altogether. In a conversation with a British embassy aide in Saigon, Commonwealth Secretary Gundevia confided "en passant" that he wished "his country could only get clear of the embarrassment of chairing the Indo-China commissions."[28] Besides the new political complications, gaining the cooperation of the two Vietnams was not getting any easier. Commission inspections of military operations and cease-fire violations above the 17th Parallel were "totally inhibited by the North." Meanwhile, in South Vietnam, Diem's hostility made it "practically impossible" for ICC teams to function effectively, wrote Hohler, who contributed to a separate British debate around the same time about whether to close down the ICC. Disbanding the Commission was not, however, a serious option since neither London nor New Delhi wished to be responsible for destroying the one existing organization that offered any chance of playing a peacemaking role. For the time being, Goburdhun was inclined to maintain a posture of "masterly inactivity" while "marking time for an indefinite period," Hohler reported.[29]

Passivity generated strong criticism abroad that India was shirking its obligations. Ironically, by 1964 it was not the United States that particularly criticized India in this respect. The rapidly deteriorating situation in Vietnam, as well as declining confidence in the ICC's ability to deal with it, put an end to the brief period of American interest in the Commission during the Kennedy years. The Johnson administration, meanwhile, showed little of the interest that its predecessor had displayed in bolstering the organization. Rostow recalled that by 1965, American officials regarded the ICC as a "ridiculous" organization.[30] By contrast, the Canadian government, easily the closest observer of Indian behavior in Vietnam, sharply criticized its ICC partner. Canadian officials had entertained high hopes for the Commission and were sorely disappointed by India's leadership, which they considered too lethargic and especially too cautious about criticizing Hanoi. Canadian diplomats sent a steady stream of complaints to Ottawa, charging that the Indian chair refused to investigate North Vietnamese violations of the Geneva Accords and declined to bring matters to a vote in the Commission, especially when the communists were likely to be found at fault. By mid-1964, Canadian anger was coming to a head. "Frustration is not . . . a strong enough word," Gordon Cox, the Canadian commissioner in Vietnam, reported to Ottawa. By refusing to move ahead with the Commission's work of investigating subversion and preparing reports, the Indian chair had drawn the ICC into the "'do-nothing' doldrums," Cox wrote. "To follow a course of inactivity . . . simply through acquiescence in India's assessment of her own self-interest is to my mind to put ourselves in [a] potentially embarrassing position," Cox added.[31]

Canadian complaints accomplished little, however. In fact, Canadian officials found even more reason to complain as the United States sharply escalated the war in early 1965. In private, Indian officials offered reassuring words in conversations with U.S. diplomats. Asoka Mehta, a powerful policy maker involved in economic planning, told Bowles in May that "practically all members of the cabinet basically were aware of [the] importance to India of our efforts to keep communists out of Southeast Asia, and it was hoped that this effort would be successful."[32] The new Indian commissioner, M. A. Rahman, also spoke positively of the U.S. role, telling a British diplomat that he was "impressed by American determination to defend South Vietnam" and expected to see a dramatic change in the situation within a few months.[33] At the same time, however, the Indians turned against Washington in the ICC. Most significantly, the Indian commissioner responded to the beginning of the U.S. bombing campaign against North Vietnam in February, 1965, by joining Poland in condemning the United States. The Indo-Polish paper accused the United States of "violations of the Geneva agreement" and asked the British and Soviet governments to issue a general appeal for peace and to take "whatever measures are necessary in order to stem the deteriorating situation." In contrast to the ICC's first split report in 1962, it was the Canadians who now found themselves in the minority. The Canadian paper did not judge the U.S. action except to assert that it was the "direct result of the intensification of the aggressive policy of the Government of North Vietnam."[34]

To the Canadians, the explanation for Indian behavior was increasingly plain. Canadian commissioner J. Blair Seaborn reported that there was a "good deal of truth" in the view that India's Vietnam policy was driven by the country's "imperative requirement for good relations with and tangible assistance from the USSR." Because of the Soviet Union's rivalry with China for influence in Hanoi, Seaborn added, "any condemnation of [North Vietnam] by the [ICC] is not acceptable to Moscow."[35] Understanding did not, however, mean acceptance, and Canadian officials complained privately that Indian sensitivity to Soviet needs was embarrassing Canada and ruining any chance the Commission might have of playing a significant role in bringing about new peace talks. In March, 1965, Paul Martin, the Canadian minister of external affairs, sent a lengthy memorandum to his Indian counterpart, Swaran Singh, listing some of Ottawa's grievances against Indian leadership. "My concern," Martin wrote, "relates to an apparent willingness on the part of Indian representatives to have the Commission react promptly and in certain circumstances, publicly, to complaints from the North, while complaints from the South, which are no less urgent in terms of their seriousness, are generally handled in such a way as to result in delays and inconclusive results."[36] In internal correspondence, Seaborn even floated the idea of Canada withdrawing from the ICC.[37] That idea was rejected for much the same reason that India and Britain had rejected it previously: the belief that the ICC's existence might be discouraging violence in some small way and the assumption that, under sharply changed circumstances, the Commission might yet help find a settlement. Nevertheless, Canadian exasperation continued to mount in 1966. "The Canadians," a British diplomat wrote after consulting with the latest Canadian commissioner, Victor Moore, "understood and sympathized with the reason behind the present Indian attitude—viz. their desire to avoid giving offence to the Russians—but . . . they did not believe that this made it necessary for the Indians to adopt such a one sided attitude in the Commission. No one imagined that Indo-Russian relations would be fatally compromised if the Commission came out with one or two condemnations of North Vietnam, particularly since this would be primarily objectionable to Hanoi and, by extension, to Peking."[38]

By that time, however, disputes about the ICC were irrelevant to much more than Canadian pride. Indian vacillation and bald Cold War conflicts between the Polish and Canadian delegations had badly weakened the Commission, but it was the North Vietnamese government that dealt the coup de grace. After the start of sustained U.S. bombing in February, 1965, Hanoi evicted the six fixed ICC teams operating in North Vietnam, offering as a pretext that it could no longer assure their safety. Rahman insisted that Commission officials were willing to accept certain risks to stay at their posts, but Hanoi refused to back down. The expulsion left only the ICC headquarters in Hanoi to carry out the Commission's work. The action sparked a flurry of U.S. interest in the ICC as Secretary of State Dean Rusk took a personal interest in extracting maximum propaganda value from such an overt indication of Hanoi's belligerence.[39] Nonetheless, American interest faded when the incident passed. For its part, the Indian government avoided public protest, accepting yet another blow to the Commission's role.

The escalation of the American war and the ICC's slide into near-total irrelevance did not, however, signal the end of India's involvement in Indochina. On the contrary, powerful incentives remained for New Delhi to stay active in the search for peace in Vietnam. The governing party's legitimacy continued to rest in part on the country's adherence to a nonaligned position in world affairs, even more so after Jawaharlal Nehru's sudden death in May, 1964. The new prime minister, Lal Bahadur Shastri, a far less charismatic individual, had strong reason to tie himself to Nehru's legacy. India's standing at the head of the nonaligned group of states also demanded an active voice on the Vietnam issue. Moreover, Indian officials continued to worry that prolonged war in Southeast Asia could harm their country's security. As the fighting escalated, that danger seemed to grow more serious and the need for peacemaking more urgent. At the end of 1965, Rahman asserted what was becoming conventional wisdom among Indian officials: a long war would only increase North Vietnam's dependence on China, while it might also encourage the Chinese and Soviet governments to set aside their differences—a nightmare scenario from India's point of view.[40]

Such considerations gave rise to a new period of assertiveness and creativity as the Indian government under Shastri sought to reanimate its peacemaking role. During 1965, India's professional diplomats sought with renewed energy to promote better understanding between Hanoi and Washington. Indian officials frequently informed their American counterparts of observations by Indian diplomats in Hanoi and Beijing. Diplomats also occasionally served as go-betweens, conveying information to Washington and, presumably, Hanoi in an effort to generate progress toward a new Geneva-type meeting. In March, for instance, Morarji Desai informed

Chester Bowles of Soviet suggestions that Washington and Hanoi open face-to-face negotiations in Moscow or Warsaw. Two months later, L. K. Jha, the secretary to the Indian prime minister, told Bowles that the Indian government would make use of "every channel . . . to gauge Hanoi's intentions," including Shastri's upcoming visit to Moscow. Jha gave Bowles a detailed rundown on Shastri's talks with Marshal Tito, as well, and passed along the Yugoslav leader's appraisals of North Vietnamese attitudes. Indian diplomats understood that their effectiveness was limited by Chinese and North Vietnamese hostility to India, but they expressed hope that cooperation with nonaligned leaders more acceptable to those governments, especially Egyptian leader Gamal Abdel Nasser and Ghanaian president Kwame Nkrumah, would enable India to play a mediating role. Jha assured the U.S. embassy that Indian officials "would do their best to exert influence in quarters where they could."[41]

The Indian government also became more active publicly as the war intensified in 1965. On February 8, 1965, just as sustained U.S. bombing got under way, Shastri launched the first of several relatively balanced public appeals New Delhi would make over the course of the year to bring about negotiations. The prime minister called for "immediate suspension of all provocative action" in Vietnam "by all sides" and the convening of a new Geneva conference.[42] A month later, Shastri's government joined a declaration by seventeen nonaligned third world countries blaming "foreign intervention in various forms" for the war and making a new appeal for talks without preconditions. Then, on April 24, Pres. Sarvepalli Radhakrishnan offered the most detailed Indian proposal yet, calling for a cease-fire and the establishment of an Afro-Asian military force to police the demilitarized zone between North and South Vietnam as well as the borders between South Vietnam and its other neighbors, Cambodia and Laos. The proposal stipulated that the present borders of the two Vietnamese states be maintained "as long as the people concerned desire it."[43] In visits to Moscow, Ottawa, and Belgrade later in 1965, Shastri and Radhakrishnan struck similar themes and issued joint communiqués calling for an end to U.S. bombing and a return to the Geneva process.

This spate of Indian activity yielded no results because Hanoi and Washington had scant interest in making them work. With typical venom, Radio Hanoi attacked the Radhakrishnan proposal, for example, as a violation of the Geneva Accords and "a new plot to use the Afro-Asian countries to serve the U.S. aggression against Vietnam."[44] Although Washington was far less categorical and even publicly welcomed the seventeen-nation and Radhakrishnan proposals, U.S. officials mainly regarded the Indian initiatives as opportunities to reiterate the president's much-proclaimed willingness to negotiate and as occasions to point out contrasts between U.S. expressions of interest and Hanoi's hostile rebuffs. The Johnson administration never gave Indian diplomats serious encouragement to pursue the proposals. Lack of interest in Washington and Hanoi may account for the demise of the Indian proposals in mid-1965, but it fails to explain why the Indian government's flurry of peacemaking activity faded away toward the end of the year, by which time other governments and international organizations were becoming deeply involved in promoting negotiations. To understand why Indian activity and effectiveness waned after 1965 it is necessary to consider the conflicting interests that continued to pull Indian policy makers in different directions and encouraged the same inconsistent pattern that had characterized Indian behavior since at least 1962.

Many Indian officials continued to give Washington quiet support. On a few occasions, the Indian government even shared detailed information about North Vietnamese military preparations. One such report—written in March, 1965—conveyed information about air-raid precautions being taken in North Vietnam and the locations of air bases from which Soviet aircraft were operating.[45] In August, Bowles reported to Washington that many Indian leaders privately sympathized with U.S. policy in Vietnam. Bowles asserted that Shastri was "anxious not to offend" the United States more than the Indian government had already done.[46] At the end of the year, Bowles reported even more favorably on the Indian attitude toward American exertions in Vietnam. "Shastri and his associates would view with great alarm a U.S. setback and much more a U.S. withdrawal from South Vietnam, Laos and Thailand," the ambassador wrote. While Shastri would likely criticize American bombing of North Vietnam, Bowles observed, he nevertheless seemed to accept the "sincerity" of the Johnson administration's repeated appeals for negotiations. Bowles also asserted that Shastri was "embarrassed" by India's performance as ICC chair and wished his country "could get out of it," implying that the Indian leader felt hemmed in by the expectation of neutrality and unable to act in the pro-Western manner that he really favored. All in all, Bowles reckoned that Indian leaders were "likely to do better by [the] U.S. in the future" and that Shastri even hoped that within a decade India could begin to "carry more responsibility for the general containment of China in Asia." In the short term, Bowles believed that the Indian government might respond positively to American requests that New Delhi send a token force—most likely an ambulance corps—to South Vietnam. Although the ambassador rated the odds at less than fifty-fifty, such a move would have carried enormous symbolic value at a time when the Johnson administration was making strenuous efforts to convince other governments to contribute forces to fight alongside Americans.[47] In any case, Washington had Indian assurances that New Delhi had turned down Soviet requests to ship weapons to North Vietnam through Indian territory.[48]

At the same time, competing pressures led Indian officials to avoid any hint of siding with the United States and encouraged some to single out the Americans for special criticism. With the exception of the Radhakrishnan proposal, the steady drumbeat of Indian pronouncements nearly always identified the U.S. bombing campaign as a particular impediment to peace. Meanwhile, Indira Gandhi, the minister of broadcasting and information, began speaking out sharply against the United States. In June, 1965, Gandhi, the daughter of Jawaharlal Nehru, denounced U.S. "intervention" during a speech in Madras state. The "whole world" was against the United States, Gandhi stated, adding that U.S. action was only inviting further Chinese involvement in Southeast Asia, a trend that threatened Indian security.[49] Such comments, coupled with the frequency of Indian pronouncements, prompted Johnson to protest to the Indian ambassador. In a July meeting, the president wondered aloud why the Indian government "seemed compelled to comment so often on Vietnam" and sarcastically demanded Indian wisdom on the best way to end the war. "If Shastri knew how to settle Vietnam, we wished he would tell us," Johnson said, according to the U.S. record of the conversation.[50] Joseph N. Greene, the U.S. deputy chief of mission in New Delhi, made the same point when meeting with Indian officials. Employing more diplomatic language, Greene told Shastri on one occasion that LBJ had declared American honor to be at stake in Vietnam and that "in such circumstances, the U.S. cares a great deal both about what happens and what people say."[51]

Pressure by the United States may have helped mute Shastri over the second half of 1965, but Indian criticism of the United States reached new heights during the year that followed. As before, shifting Indian attitudes toward Vietnam resulted from changing international circumstances. This time, however, domestic developments also contributed in a powerful way. The most obvious reason for a more critical Indian approach was Shastri's sudden death in January, 1966, coupled with Indira Gandhi's ascension to the position of prime minister. Although relatively inexperienced in politics, Gandhi had a strong political base on the Congress Party's left and a clear stake in her father's commitment to anticolonialism. It was not, however, Gandhi's left-leaning predisposition that drove her to step up criticism of the United States. Indeed, during her first weeks in office, Gandhi was remarkably moderate in her attitude toward U.S. policy in Vietnam, once again displaying India's private acceptance of it. In early February, Gandhi instructed Ambassador Nehru to advise Johnson of her appreciation for

"U.S. peace moves"—specifically the U.S. bombing pause at the end of the year—and to relate "how greatly disappointed she had been at the lack of response" from Hanoi.[52] During a visit to Washington in March, Gandhi made that sentiment public, telling journalists that she was "impressed by the sincerity of the president's desire for a peaceful settlement."[53] American officials were so encouraged that they briefly entertained new hopes that Gandhi might send a "symbolic civil contribution" of some type, perhaps the medical team that they had so long wished for, to assist South Vietnam.[54]

Gandhi's shift to a more critical position stemmed partly from India's growing dependence on the United States and especially an upsurge in political turmoil as the country entered a period of sustained economic crisis. Part of the problem was Washington's willingness to use food aid as a means of applying pressure on India to take a more pro-U.S. position on Indochina. During 1965 and 1966, India faced perpetual crisis from famine because of population growth, agricultural inefficiencies, and, above all, drought. Throughout the Kennedy and early Johnson years, the United States had sharply increased food assistance, along with military and other kinds of aid. With famine looming in 1965, Washington again increased its assistance. As it had during the 1962 border war, the United States offered a uniquely generous response that set it apart from other donors. The numbers were staggering: By the end of 1967, America had shipped 14 million tons of wheat to feed about 90 million Indians.[55] The extent to which the Johnson administration used this aid as a diplomatic weapon to coerce Indian behavior in connection with Vietnam was controversial at the time and has remained so among historians of U.S.-Indian relations. Newly available documents show that humanitarian motives and the potential gain for U.S. farmers were foremost among American motives. They also show that the U.S. practice of sending food in relatively small increments was aimed primarily at forcing India to adopt badly needed agricultural reforms that would enable the country to meet its long-term food needs.

However, there are innumerable hints in the archival record that Americans expected India to pay a diplomatic price for U.S. relief. American officials repeatedly made clear that they expected India to ease its criticism of the United States in return for American willingness to provide food aid. In mid-1965, for example, Greene, the second-ranking U.S. official in Delhi, told Agriculture Minister S. K. Subramaniam that America's "national honor" was at stake in Vietnam, warning darkly of "the difficulties that can ensue if our friends criticize what we are doing" in such cases.[56] At about the same time, President Johnson told Ambassador Nehru that a congressional committee had just voted against an Indian food request because of exasperation among many members of Congress over Indian criticism of the U.S. role in Vietnam. "The Indians [keep] telling us how to solve Vietnam," the president exclaimed. "This sort of thing certainly affected the vote."[57] Over time, U.S. officials became even more direct in linking food aid to India's public stance on diplomatic matters. In early 1966, Johnson ordered Agriculture Secretary Orville Freeman to "quit giving stuff away" to India and instead extract an unspecified quid pro quo.[58] Vice President Hubert Humphrey was particularly incensed by Indian and Pakistani sniping at U.S. policies at a time when both were receiving tremendous amounts of foreign aid. Meeting with the president and congressional leaders in February, 1966, he said the two governments must "quit throwing dead cats at the U.S. If you disagree," he insisted, "tell us in private."[59] On a trip to India the next month, Humphrey was only a bit more restrained, warning Indian leaders to "be more considerate of our position in the world, particularly in Asia" and to "demonstrate sympathetic understanding of what we are trying to do."[60]

Although these exchanges took place in private, the Indian media suspected Washington of endeavoring to extract a quid pro quo, and Ambassador Bowles struggled to rebut charges that the United State was playing politics with famine relief. There was little he could do, however, at a time when anti-Americanism was a particularly promising political strategy in India. In part, anti-Americanism resonated because of the symbolic role of the United States in fierce, unresolved controversies over the proper path of Indian economic development. The food and economic crises gave new urgency to this debate and radicalized Indian politics between the advocates of free-market reform and proponents of India's state-centered economy. Gandhi's decision to devalue the rupee in June, 1966, was widely viewed as another example of India kowtowing to the United States and set off a new torrent of criticism from within the Congress Party as well as from communists. Anti-Americanism also fed off popular anger over Pakistan's use of U.S.-supplied military equipment during the 1965 war over Kashmir. Ordinary Indians resented Washington's failure to live up to old promises that equipment supplied to Karachi would never be used against India and took pride in their country's success in defeating what one leftist newspaper dubbed "General Patton and his Pakistani corporals."[61] To many ordinary Indians, U.S. behavior in Vietnam seemed yet another indication of American treachery. Although antiwar activism never became widespread, anecdotal evidence suggested strong undercurrents of hostility to American policies in Southeast Asia. In the leftist hotbed of Calcutta, where the street on which the U.S. consulate sits would be renamed for Ho Chi Minh, a theater staged weekly shows of *Invincible Vietnam,* a play that depicted U.S.

servicemen torturing a Vietnamese nurse to death, using napalm and poison gas against defenseless villagers, and burning the Bible and the works of Shakespeare. In Bombay, students burned LBJ in effigy in front of the U.S. Information Agency headquarters.[62]

Against this background, Gandhi came under intense pressure to distance herself and her government from the United States on a whole range of issues, including Vietnam. Members of the Lok Sabha, perhaps looking ahead to parliamentary elections in 1967, stepped up their criticism of Gandhi's leadership. As Gandhi prepared to visit Washington in early 1966, for example, one member accused her of traveling "post haste" in response to a "summons" from President Johnson and succeeded in forcing the government to make public the finance ministry's correspondence with U.S. officials.[63] The government's position was hardly improved when that correspondence revealed that Delhi had accepted a series of American demands for improved fertilizer production and free-market reforms of Indian agriculture. The leftist media also joined in the debate. The mass-circulation weekly *Blitz,* for example, accused the government of "wholesale political and economic surrender to Washington."[64] With the accusations flying, Bowles reported that Gandhi, despite her own left-leaning past, risked being "swept aside" because of a perception that she was an "American stooge."[65]

An obvious method to assuage the government's critics was to step up criticism of the United States, and its prosecution of the Vietnam War was an obvious target. In a condemnatory radio broadcast in mid-1966, Gandhi asserted that there could "be no military solution in Vietnam" and implied that the United States was responsible for a "grave danger of escalation that might embroil the world in a larger conflict."[66] Another solution was to draw closer to the Soviet Union, which Gandhi proceeded to do over the course of 1966. Improving the Soviet-Indian relationship hardly required special effort on Gandhi's part since Moscow and New Delhi had been cooperating closely for at least two years. Beginning in 1964, Moscow agreed to provide India with sophisticated warplanes that the United States refused to sell out of fear of fueling an arms race on the subcontinent. Then, in 1965, the Soviet government offered to help build a huge steel mill at Bokaro, stepping in after the United States refused to contribute to what would be a state-owned plant. In the area of diplomacy, India and Pakistan had turned to the Soviet Union to mediate a solution to the Kashmir issue, and engaged in talks in Tashkent for a period of several weeks.

In a sign of mounting cooperation with Moscow and a desire to distance New Delhi from the United States, Gandhi moved ever closer to embracing the Soviet attitude on Vietnam. In early July, Gandhi launched a peace initiative that U.S. officials considered moderate and helpful. The bid called for mutual de-escalation of the war, followed by a new Geneva conference to seek Vietnam's neutralization. Although State Department officials believed the scheme was full of "bear traps," they nonetheless considered it potentially useful, at least as a propaganda bonus since Hanoi would inevitably reject it.[67] Suddenly, however, Gandhi changed course in a way that raised unprecedented alarm in Washington. During a trip to Moscow in late July, the prime minister joined Soviet leaders in issuing a communiqué that was sharply critical of the United States. After praising Soviet policies on disarmament and international peacekeeping, the statement asserted that the situation in Vietnam posed a growing danger of general war "as a result of aggressive actions of imperialists and other reactionary forces." Bowles immediately assailed the communiqué as a "shocking document" replete with the "familiar language of Soviet propaganda bureaus" and urged Washington to "register vigorous and immediate protest," which it promptly did.[68]

The record of the Moscow meetings between Gandhi and Soviet premier Alexei Kosygin suggests that the Indian delegation bent to the will of the Soviet leadership, which was increasingly exasperated by the war in Vietnam. According to an Australian record of the talks based on an account provided by Indian officials, the Soviet leaders were "very frustrated" by the current state of affairs in Vietnam and seemed to be increasingly inclined toward stronger action to help the North Vietnamese. If U.S. forces crossed the 17th Parallel, Kosygin told the Indians, "that would mean war, since the USSR cannot fail to stand by its ally." Even though the Soviet leader believed that the United States had merely "floundered" into the war on the basis of misguided "idealism," he insisted that Moscow stood ready to give Hanoi "whatever it might ask for in the way of help, in effect . . . a blank cheque." Gandhi was apparently unable or unwilling to resist Soviet pressure for a sharply worded communiqué that took no account of the Indian proposal issued just days earlier calling for mutual de-escalation and a reconvened Geneva conference. In his meeting with Gandhi, Kosygin merely asserted that he could "do nothing without authority from Hanoi" and suggested that Delhi take the matter directly to the North Vietnamese. The apparent lack of Indian insistence on the point was perhaps related to the fact that the Soviets agreed during the summit to contribute a large sum to India's latest five-year plan.[69]

NIRVANA

Much to America's relief, Gandhi pulled back from the strong rhetoric of the Moscow communiqué late in the year, when she held a series of meetings with other Soviet bloc leaders. During those encounters, Gandhi reverted to her earlier pattern: demanding that the United States end the bombing as part of a mutual de-escalation and calling for some sort of return to the bargaining table. The Indian government even grudgingly went along with a Canadian proposal, ultimately vetoed by Poland, calling for the ICC to sponsor a new Geneva-type conference. India played no role, however, in the most important diplomatic activity that took place in the last weeks of 1966 and the first days of 1967, notably the MARIGOLD initiative spearheaded by Poland and the SUNFLOWER peace effort led by Britain and the Soviet Union. In fact, India by that point had dropped far down the list of countries seeking to make peace in Vietnam, often not even registering in State Department papers summarizing the efforts by various third parties to launch peace initiatives. It was all the more surprising, then, when the Indian government suddenly, in the first days of 1967, discovered its best chance to contribute to peace. Although the Indian government did little to bring about the initiative, Indian diplomats responded with enthusiasm, testifying to a lingering eagerness, at least within the foreign-policy bureaucracy, to play a peacemaking role.

On January 2, a Soviet diplomat notified the Indian embassy in Moscow that if the United States would stop bombing North Vietnam, the gesture would "lead to good results." That same day, the Soviet ambassador in New Delhi communicated the same message to Indian foreign secretary Mahommedali Currim Chagla. Two days later, on January 4, an even more significant development took place: the North Vietnamese consul promised that if the United States stopped its bombing campaign "the cessation of hostilities and other steps" would follow. More specifically, the consul stated that North Vietnam would be willing to declare a one-week cease-fire around the Tet holiday at the end of the month on the understanding that the cease-fire would be extended indefinitely. As for a settlement in the South, the United States would have to come to terms directly with the National Liberation Front (NLF).[70]

Ambassador Nehru's optimism encouraged Rusk to agree to pursue the matter, and the secretary of state agreed to ask Kaul to hold another meeting with the North Vietnamese consul to seek clarification of several ambiguous points. On January 28, Nguyen Hoa, following instructions from Hanoi, repeated the North Vietnamese proposal, asserting that as soon as the bombing stopped, Hanoi would be "prepared to enter negotiations with the [U.S. government] to assure peace in Vietnam." Encouraged, C. S. Jha, a high-ranking official in the Indian Ministry of External Affairs, suggested that the Americans secretly contact North Vietnamese diplomats in Cairo, Algiers, Warsaw, or elsewhere to indicate that the message had been received and to ask what steps Hanoi had in mind for starting negotiations.[71] Other developments seemed to confirm that the initiative was genuine and important. G. Parthasarathi, the Indian ambassador to the United Nations, told Arthur Goldberg, his U.S. counterpart, on the same day that the initiative in Delhi seemed "quite significant" and that the time seemed ripe for a bid by Hanoi for meaningful negotiations. In Parthasarathi's view, chaos within China as the Cultural Revolution went forward was having the effect of freeing Hanoi to act more independently, even to gravitate toward the relatively peaceable Soviet line on the war. Secretary General U Thant also believed there were signals that "something was moving" toward negotiations, especially since the North Vietnamese initiative in Delhi seemed to dovetail with similar North Vietnamese statements around that time in Paris, Algiers, and elsewhere.[72]

When Kaul and C. S. Jha met with the North Vietnamese consul again, however, they found a much cooler attitude. In response to questions about the North Vietnamese proposal, Nguyen Hoa gave "a somewhat preemptory reply" in which he referred only to the four-point negotiating position that the North Vietnamese regime had laid out two years earlier, according to a U.S. account. In Jha's view, that account added, "the posture of Hanoi had seemed to stiffen."[73] Given the unavailability of North Vietnamese sources, it is impossible to know what happened after the initial promising meeting. It is possible that a news leak to the Indian press on January 13 might have dampened North Vietnam's enthusiasm for keeping the Delhi channel open. American and Indian officials agreed that doves in Hanoi were likely to be extremely sensitive to any publicity surrounding peace feelers because of a fear of provoking the Chinese government, the NLF, or Hanoi hawks. Indian policy makers in particular were convinced that volatility among competing factions within the Hanoi leadership accounted for the vagueness and inconsistency of North Vietnamese proposals.

NIRVANA, however, was a problematic venture unlikely to produce results for other reasons, as well. On the American side, there was strong skepticism from the outset about the terms that Hanoi seemed to be offering. In Rusk's judgment, the NIRVANA proposal, taken with other North Vietnamese peace feelers around the same time, amounted to "interesting mood music but do not get us very far."[74] As always, Rusk was worried that any suspension of the bombing or a cease-fire in the South would enable North Vietnamese and Vietcong forces to move troops and equipment around the South, as they had done, he was sure, during earlier bombing pauses. The danger, Rusk asserted, was that the United States would make a major concession politically difficult to reverse—ending the bombing—in return for vague promises of reciprocity. Also problematic was the NLF's status. The consul general's proposal, which apparently left it to the United States and the NLF to negotiate a settlement in the South, implied that the NLF operated independently of Hanoi, a pretense that Washington could not accept without abandoning the basic premise of the entire war. Rusk asserted that he was willing to "play games" with the idea for negotiating purposes, but said he had "no illusions whatever that [the NLF] was in fact under Hanoi's direction."[75]

NIRVANA marked the highpoint of India's peacemaking efforts following the demise of the International Control Commission. It also marked the last time India would play any significant role. As it was, American officials expressed skepticism during the NIRVANA episode about India's ability to act effectively as a mediator. American diplomats complained about the uncoordinated mix of views among Indian officials and about New Delhi's unreliability, with some even questioning whether the Indian government was not deliberately exaggerating the importance of the North Vietnamese initiative in order to raise New Delhi's profile on the Vietnam issue.[76] Events later in the year would show that India's potential as a peace broker was entirely used up. In August, Kaul attempted to reestablish an Indian channel for talks after the Indian consul in Hanoi detected interest among North Vietnamese leaders in floating cease-fire ideas. This time, however, U.S. officials showed little interest. Even Chester Bowles, normally India's main champion among U.S. policy makers, expressed doubts. "We have had from Kaul messages from Hanoi before and then been disappointed," wrote Bowles, who suspected that it was the Indians, eager to recover some degree of involvement in peacemaking, who had initiated the contacts in Hanoi, not the North Vietnamese government.[77] The only interest Americans showed in India's role was in improving the ICC's capabilities in Cambodia at a time when Washington had a developing interest in publicizing North Vietnamese incursions. Washington proposed to fund stepped-up ICC activities in Cambodia and to supply helicopters for its use. As always, however, the Indian government refused to buckle to pressure from Washington, insisting that any initiative must come from the Cambodian government.

Indira Gandhi, meanwhile, grew increasingly hostile to the United States during the rest of 1967. In February, the opposition showed its strength by scoring unexpectedly decisive victories over the Congress Party, which managed to hold a slim majority in the Lok Sabha. Pressure from the left undoubtedly helped drive Gandhi to an act that angered U.S. officials almost as much as the Moscow communiqué had the year before. In May, the prime minister sent a message of birthday greetings to Ho Chi Minh, expressing the hope that "the Vietnamese people will have the good fortune of having Ho Chi Minh's wise and dedicated leadership to guide them."

Once again, U.S. officials exploded. "If Mrs. Gandhi thinks," Rusk wrote to Bowles, "that we are just good guys and will take a lot of punishment without reaction, she is underestimating the mood of the American people while we are carrying such heavy burdens. . . . The general mood in this country does not permit us to act like an old cow which continues to give milk, however often one kicks her in the flanks."[78]

The birthday episode epitomized the dysfunctional relationship that had developed between the United States and India with respect to the war in Vietnam. American officials pressured the Indian government to cater to American interests in return for American aid, while the Indian government, beset by unprecedented political challenges, had allowed its peacemaking role to become merely a mechanism for easing its struggles at home. India's twenty-year-old peacemaking role—always fraught with problems and vulnerable to shifting political and strategic winds—was at an end.

Conclusion

Peace eluded Vietnam in the 1960s for many reasons far more important than India's failure to bring it about. Historian George Herring is surely correct in arguing that "peace hinged . . . not on the influence of third parties but on the willingness of the belligerents to compromise."[79] To understand the failure of the innumerable peace initiatives undertaken during the mid-1960s, it is necessary to examine the attitudes and policies of the principal governments involved: those of the United States, China, and the two Vietnams. Nonetheless, examination of the Indian case is instructive in explaining why it was that third parties were so ineffective and, ultimately, unimportant to the main story line of the Vietnam War. In certain respects, no country was as well positioned as India to act as a peacemaker. In 1954, the East and West concurred that India was uniquely qualified to head the International Control Commission, a reflection of India's reputation for international conciliation as well as the belief—widespread among Western governments since the 1940s—that any lasting settlement in Indochina would inevitably involve India. Careful examination of India's performance reveals, however, that the best-placed government was in fact not very well placed at all. Although New Delhi was involved in Vietnam diplomacy for two decades, it performed in a markedly inconsistent manner, often had different public and private positions on the war, and came forward with few proposals for settling the conflict.

Why was India so ineffective? Certainly Washington's lack of cooperation was part of the answer. The Kennedy and Johnson administrations, though more encouraging than the Eisenhower presidency, devoted far more energy to bending India to American purposes than to exploiting India's peace-brokering potential as a means to achieve a lasting settlement. In this regard, examination of the Indian case adds new evidence to sustain the view that U.S. administrations were uninterested in peacemaking before 1968 and proclaimed their interest in negotiations mainly as a means of appealing to domestic and international opinion. Other explanations for Indian ineffectiveness relate to the country's geostrategic and political situation during the 1960s. India's tense relationship with China prevented New Delhi from exercising significant influence in either Beijing or Hanoi, both of which ranged between toleration and outright hostility for Indian peacemaking activities. Moreover, China's hostility toward India drove New Delhi into a fuller dependence on the United States and the Soviet Union for military, political, and economic assistance. Balancing Soviet and U.S. support became New Delhi's top foreign policy priority, and Vietnam diplomacy, like other aspects of India's external affairs, was subordinated to it. The result was inconsistency in Indian behavior as New Delhi at times veered toward Hanoi, and at others toward the United States. There often was a sharp disjunction between what Indian leaders said in public and what they believed in private about where India's interests lay. The country's growing political turbulence in the 1960s only heightened the inconsistency by creating irresistible temptations for Gandhi to use the Vietnam issue to regulate her standing with her many critics.

India's failures merit close attention because they illustrate the impediments woven deeply into the fabric of the international system that prohibited a peaceful resolution to the Indochina crisis during the 1960s. India's experience is especially instructive in light of the recent tendency among historians of the Vietnam War to emphasize personality and contingency in explaining the conflict's escalation. Highly detailed studies of the Western decision-making process have done a great service by illuminating the circumstances surrounding the critical decisions that led the Americans to choose war and eschew negotiation and neutralization.[80] However, they have done so at the risk of overlooking the war's Asian context and ignoring the deep forces that drove conflict—and barred moderation and mediation—in postcolonial Asia. India's experiences in the 1960s call attention to the glaring lack of any real basis for moderate, neutralist solutions in Asia, no matter how willing the principal Cold War protagonists may have been to bring them about. The Indian government thus was constantly rediscovering these impediments to conciliation in Vietnam. A profoundly poor country, India remained highly dependent on foreign assistance and therefore vulnerable to external pressures. Threatened from two directions by bold and militarily powerful states, it had no choice but to adjust its Vietnam policy in ways calculated to improve its strategic position. A country emerging from two centuries of colonial rule, India suffered from fierce political divisions that hindered a consistent and effective foreign policy. In each of these respects, India reflected political and social trends prevalent across Asia—trends that made peace unlikely.

Notes

1. I would like to thank Sumit Ganguly, Anne Foster, Jim Hershberg, Fred Logevall, Gail Minault, Jocelyn Olcott, Mike Parrish, Jon Persoff and Andrew Preston for their invaluable help with this project.
   State Department to New Delhi, Jan. 6, 1967, POL 27–14, Box 2739, Record Group 59, State Department Central Files, 1967–69 (hereafter RG 59, years covered), National Archives and Records Administration, Suitland, Md. (hereafter NARA).

2. See, e.g., George C. Herring, *America's Longest War*, 3d ed. (New York: McGraw-Hill, 1996), pp. 182–86; and Marilyn B. Young, *The Vietnam Wars, 1945–1990* (New York: Harper, 1991), pp. 153–56, 179–83, as well as other chapters in this volume.

3. Braj Kumar Nehru, *Nice Guys Finish Second* (Delhi: Penguin, 1997), p. 438.

4. Bowles to State Department, Dec. 27, 1965, National Security File (NSF), Country File (CF-India), Box 130, Lyndon B. Johnson Library, Austin, Tex. (hereafter LBJL).

5. Author's interviews with Galbraith, Cambridge, Mass., Mar. 12, 2001; and with Rostow, Austin, Tex., Oct. 3, 2000.

6. See D. R. SarDesai, *Indian Foreign Policy in Cambodia, Laos, and Vietnam, 1947–1964* (Berkeley: University of California Press, 1968). The vast scholarship on Indian foreign policy and U.S.-Indian relations contains few references to Vietnam. For the best discussion, see Dennis Kux, *Estranged Democracies: India and the United States, 1941–1991* (Thousand Oaks, Calif.: Sage, 1993).

7. For Indian foreign-policy calculations in the early Cold War, see Kux, *Estranged Democracies;* Robert J. McMahon, *The Cold War on the Periphery: The United States, India, and Pakistan* (New York: Columbia University Press, 1994); Andrew J. Rotter, *Comrades at Odds: India and the United States, 1947–1964* (Ithaca, N.Y.: Cornell University Press, 2000). For a discussion of India's attitude toward Indochina specifically, see SarDesai, *Indian Foreign Policy.*

8. Nehru statement to the Lok Sabha, Apr. 24, 1954, in *Select Documents on India's Foreign Policy and Relations, 1947–1972*, vol. 2, ed. A. Appadorai (Delhi: Oxford University Press, 1985), p. 303.

9. For India's role at Geneva, see SarDesai, *Indian Foreign Policy*, pp. 40–47; and H. W. Brands, *India and the United States: The Cold Peace* (Boston: Twayne, 1990), pp. 78–80.

10. SarDesai, *Indian Foreign Policy*, chaps. 5, 6, and 8. For ICC activities before 1960, see also Robert Bothwell, "The Further Shore: Canada and Vietnam," *International Journal* 61 (winter, 2000–2001): pp. 92–95.

11. Mieczyslaw Maneli, *War of the Vanquished* (New York: Harper and Row, 1971), p. 34.

12. "Chinese Reds Score Vietnam Peace Body," *New York Times*, Dec. 4, 1961.

13. Qiang Zhai, *China and the Vietnam Wars, 1950–1975* (Chapel Hill: University of North Carolina Press, 2000), p. 115.

14. For Kennedy's attitudes about India, see McMahon, *Cold War*, pp. 272–75.

15. Briefing paper, "Prime Minister Nehru's Visit, November 6–10, 1961," President's Office File (POF), Box 118a, John Fitzgerald Kennedy Presidential Library, Boston (hereafter JFKL).

16. Rotter, *Comrades at Odds,* p. 73.

17. Memorandum by Bowles, "Toward a Balance of Political and Military Forces in South Asia," Nov. 12, 1963, POF, Box 118a, JFKL. Bowles had been an eager champion of U.S.-Indian cooperation for many years. As undersecretary of state in 1961, he suggested that the two countries might one day team up to preserve independence and stability in Southeast Asia. In a memo to the president, he invoked the example of U.S.-British cooperation in the Western Hemisphere in earlier decades. He wrote that India could play the U.S. role in Southeast Asia by providing local power and moral guidance, while Washington assumed the British role, standing offshore with overwhelming military power that could be bought to bear if necessary (Bowles to Kennedy, Nov. 3, 1961, NSF, Box 106, JFKL).

18. Rostow interview.

19. Galbraith to State Department, Feb. 28, 1962, NSF, Box 106a, JFKL.

20. John Kenneth Galbraith, *Ambassador's Journal: A Personal Account of the Kennedy Years* (Boston: Houghton Mifflin, 1969), p. 273.

21. Hohler, Saigon, to E. H. Peck, Foreign Office, Jan. 17, 1963, FO371, file 170118, Public Record Office, Kew Gardens, England (hereafter PRO).

22. Salans to McConaughy, "Conversation with Indian Ambassador Nehru Concerning Jurisdiction of the ICC/Viet-Nam," Oct. 27, 1961, NSF, Box 106, JFKL.

23. Rostow to B. K. Nehru, June 1, 1961, ibid.

24. "India's Laos Plan Likened to Reds'," *New York Times,* July 16, 1961.

25. Rotter, *Comrades at Odds,* chap. 1.

26. "Nehru Defends Neutral Policy," *New York Times,* May 15, 1962.

27. Hohler, Saigon, to Foreign Office, Aug. 23, 1962, FO371, File 166734, PRO.

28. R. A. Burrows, Saigon, to F. A. Warner, Foreign Office, Aug. 13, 1963, File 170119, ibid.

29. Hohler, Saigon, to E. H. Peck, Foreign Office, Jan. 17, 1963, File 170118, ibid.

30. Rostow interview.

31. Cox, Saigon, to Ministry of External Affairs, May 4, 1964, File 21–13-VIET-ICSC, pt. 1.2, vol. 10122, Record Group (RG) 25, National Archives of Canada, Ottawa (hereafter NAC).

32. Bowles, Delhi, to State Department, May 20, 1965, POL 7, Box 2283, RG 59, 1964–66, NARA.

33. Gordon Etherington-Smith to J. E. Cable, Dec. 24, 1965, FO371, File 186324, PRO.

34. Report of the International Commission for Supervision and Control, Feb. 13, 1965, File 180573, ibid.

35. Seaborn to Ministry of External Affairs, June 9, 1965, File 21–13-VIET-ICSC-4, pt. 2.2, vol. 10123, RG 25, NAC.

36. Martin to Delhi, March 17, 1965, File 21–13-VIET-ICSC-4, pt. 3.2, ibid.

37. Seaborn to Ministry of External Affairs.

38. Etherington-Smith, Saigon, to D. F. Murray, Foreign Office, May 30, 1966, FO371, File 186335, PRO.

39. Memorandum by J. E. Cable, "Withdrawal of International Commission Teams from North Vietnam," Feb. 22, 1965, File 180573, ibid.

40. Etherington-Smith to Cable.

41. Bowles to State Department, Mar. 15, 1965, NSF, CF, Box 129, LBJL; Bowles to State Department, May 4, 1965, ibid.; Delhi (Greene) to State Department, Aug. 3, 1965, POL 7, Box 2283, RG 59, 1964–66, NARA.

42. State Department to Delhi, Feb. 13, 1965, NSF, CF, Box 129, LBJL.

43. Delhi to State Department, Apr. 26, 1965, ibid.

44. "Negotiating Initiatives on Vietnam," n.d., Box 90, ibid.

45. State Department to Delhi, Mar. 12, 1965, NSF, CF, Box 129, LBJL.

46. Bowles to State Department, Aug. 10, 1965, ibid.

47. Bowles to State Department, Dec. 27, 1965, Box 130, ibid.

48. Rusk to Delhi, Apr. 19, 1965, POL 7, Box 2283, RG 59, 1963–66, NARA.

49. Madras consulate to State Department, July 9, 1965, POL 1, Box 2281, ibid.

50. Memorandum of conversation, July 13, 1965, *Foreign Relations of the United States,* *1964–1968 (FRUS)*, vol. 25, *South Asia* (Washington, D.C.: GPO, 2000), pp. 300–303.

51. Delhi to State Department, July 26, 1965, NSF, CF, Box 129, LBJL.

52. State Department (Ball) to Delhi, Feb. 7, 1966, Box 131, ibid.

53. "Mrs. Gandhi Sympathetic to U.S. Stand in Vietnam," *New York Times,* Mar. 30, 1966.

54. Delhi to State Department, Mar. 9, 1966, POL 7, Box 2283, RG 59, 1964–66, NARA.

55. Kux, *Estranged Democracies,* p. 258.

56. Delhi to State Department, July 20, 1965, NSF, CF, Box 129, LBJL.

57. Memorandum of conversation, July 16, 1965, ibid.

58. Johnson to Komer, Jan. 18, 1966, Box 134, ibid.

59. "Notes of Meeting," 24 Feb. 1966, *FRUS, 1964–68,* vol. 4, *Vietnam, 1966* (Washington, D.C.: GPO, 1998), p. 256.

60. Bowles to State Department, Feb. 17, 1966, NSF, CF, Box 131, LBJL.

61. "No Place for Liars in Government," *Blitz,* July 23, 1966.

62. "Once a Week in a Calcutta Theater: U.S. 'Atrocities' in Vietnam," *New York Times,* Dec. 21, 1966; "Johnson Effigy Burned," *New York Times,* May 5, 1966.

63. "India Needs U.S. Aid—and Honor, Too," *New York Times,* Mar. 6, 1966. For analysis of 1966 events, see Sumit Ganguly, "Of Great Expectations and Bitter Disappointments," *Asian Affairs* 15 (winter, 1988–89): pp. 212–19.

64. "For Freedom—Or Dollars?" *Blitz,* July 23, 1966.

65. Bowles to Johnson, July 5, 1966, POL 1, Box 2281, RG 59, 1964–66, NARA.

66. Quoted in T. V. Kunhi Krishnan, *The Unfriendly Friends: India and America* (New Delhi: Indian Book, 1974), p. 199.

67. State Department to Delhi, July 9, 1966, NSF, CF, Box 131, LBJL.

68. Delhi to State Department, July 18, 1966, POL 7, Box 2284, RG 59, 1964–66, NARA.

69. Moscow to Canberra, cable, July 19, 1966, ibid. This document was immediately passed to the State Department and was the subject of a conversation between U.S. and Australian officials on July 21. See memorandum of conversation, "Indian Visit to Moscow," July 21, 1966, ibid.

70. State Department to Delhi, Jan. 6, 1967, POL 27–14, Box 2739, ibid.

71. Summary of negotiating initiatives, n.d., NSF, CF, 94, LBJL.

72. United Nations to State Department, Jan. 6, 1967, POL 27–14, Box 2739, RG 59, 1967–69, NARA.

73. Delhi to State Department, Feb. 2, 1967, ibid.

74. State Department to Warsaw, Jan. 19, 1967, ibid.

75. State Department to Delhi, Jan. 6, 1967.

76. Delhi to State Department, 2 Feb. 1967.

77. Delhi to State Department, Aug. 19, 1967, NSF, CF, Box 132, LBJL.

78. Rusk to Bowles, May 18, 1967, *FRUS, 1964–1968,* pp. 25:859–60.

79. Herring, *America's Longest War,* p. 169.

80. See esp. David Kaiser, *American Tragedy: Kennedy, Johnson, and the Origins of the Vietnam War* (Cambridge: Harvard University Press, 2000), and Fredrik Logevall, *Choosing War: The Lost Chance for Peace and the Escalation of the War in Vietnam* (Berkeley: University of California Press, 1999).

Peacemaking or Troubleshooting?

The Soviet Role in Peace Initiatives during the Vietnam War

ILYA V. GAIDUK

N*isi utile est quod facimus stulta est gloria.* "If what we are doing is useless, fervor is unwise." It seems that Moscow followed this precept of the Roman fabulist Phaedrus throughout the Vietnam War whenever it had to deal with peace initiatives aimed at ending the conflict. In fact, the Soviets preferred to help others in their efforts to bring peace in Vietnam—rather than strive for the glory of being peacemakers themselves—as long as the prospects of success remained bleak. What considerations, then, did Soviet leaders take into account when they decided to remain mostly behind-the-scenes players in the intriguing and controversial story of the search for peace in Vietnam?[1]

The U.S intervention on the ground in South Vietnam and the beginning of the bombing campaign against the Democratic Republic of Vietnam (DRV) in early 1965 significantly changed the international environment of the Indochina conflict in Moscow's eyes. Before then the Soviet Union could confine itself to purely formal actions concerning the fighting, such as demonstrations of moral support for Hanoi, propaganda campaigns in the press, and recurrent diplomatic initiatives with the purpose of finding a peaceful solution to the problem. However, when a socialist ally found itself under direct attack by an imperialist nation, Moscow had to react to this violation of the status quo. Furthermore, it happened that the first wave of U.S. bombings in February, 1965, coincided with Soviet premier Alexei Kosygin's visit to Hanoi. Soviet ambassador Anatolii Dobrynin described the new situation for Moscow in a conversation with Vice President Hubert Humphrey. "Why did the United States bomb Hanoi while our new Premier was there?" Dobrynin asked. Before Kosygin's visit, the Soviet Union was not committed to heavily supporting North Vietnam, but now it had to be. The USSR, the Soviet ambassador stated, was "morally and ideologically bound to come to the assistance of a sister Socialist State. We can't be a leader and stand by and ignore the bombing of the North Vietnamese."[2] Two years later, in a conversation with the U.S. ambassador, Kosygin himself made it clear that if Washington had consulted him before it started bombing the

DRV, the "Soviet Union would at that time have been willing to do something about North Vietnamese intervention in [the] South."[3]

Once the United States began its armed intervention in Vietnam, two interrelated factors influenced Soviet policy toward the conflict: Moscow's obligations to an ally, and the necessity of proving its leadership of the socialist camp and of the world communist movement. The latter was especially vital for the Soviet leaders because of the Sino-Soviet schism and Beijing's opposition to Moscow's leading role in the revolutionary movement. The Kremlin knew that Mao Zedong, who suspected that Khrushchev's successors had no intention of changing the policy of peaceful coexistence with the United States, would capitalize on any indication of "appeasement" on its part in order to "discredit Moscow and strengthen Beijing's anti-imperialist credentials both within the international Communist movement and among other Third World Countries."[4] The problem of credibility haunted the Kremlin no less than the White House throughout the Vietnam War.

At the same time, Moscow did not desire a confrontation with the United States over Vietnam, which would entail the risk of a major military conflict with unpredictable consequences. Being pragmatic and cautious, the new Soviet leaders were anxious both to avoid an open breach in relations with Washington and to isolate the Vietnam issue from other spheres of Soviet-American relations. According to Dobrynin, the Soviet leaders, though emphasizing the adverse effect of the Vietnam War on relations with the United States, "unanimously recognized" that these relations "were a priority, while Vietnam was not that vital to our national interests."[5] As a result, while publicly accusing the Americans of waging an aggressive war against Vietnam and providing comprehensive assistance to the DRV, Moscow sought to demonstrate its desire to continue its dialogue with Washington.

Foreign Secretary Alexei Gromyko expounded the principles of this "two-track policy" in a memorandum prepared on January 13, 1967, and approved by the Soviet Politburo. Gromyko reaffirmed détente as the *sine qua non* of the Soviet position in the world. The memorandum stated that Moscow "should not avoid agreements with the United States on questions of our interest if such agreements do not contradict our positions of principle in regard to Vietnam." The Kremlin wanted to prevent "a situation where we have to fight on two fronts, that is against China and the United States," and believed that the maintenance of Soviet-American relations was "one of the factors that will help us achieve this objective."[6]

Efficient as it might be, this policy had certain limits that were especially evident when it came to seeking a diplomatic settlement of the conflict in

Vietnam. The same factors that shaped the Soviet attitude toward the Vietnam War profoundly influenced Moscow's role in the search for peace in Indochina. The U.S. bombing of North Vietnamese territory deprived the Soviet leaders of flexibility in their efforts to promote a peaceful solution of the war.[7] They could undertake no step in that direction without evoking suspicion among the North Vietnamese, who initially strongly opposed negotiating with the Americans, and the Chinese, who were waiting for any pretext to accuse Moscow of selling out Vietnam in exchange for the benefits of détente. It is noteworthy that Washington fully understood the precarious situation in which the Soviets found themselves. On March 26, 1965, Secretary of State Dean Rusk told members of the National Security Council, "The Soviets are paralyzed by U.S. bombing and, as long as it continues, they cannot take any political action without exposing themselves to the criticism that they are not defending a socialist country." However, he added that no one could predict what the Soviets would do if the United States stopped bombing North Vietnam.[8]

An opportunity to test Moscow on this score arose during the first bombing pause, which Pres. Lyndon B. Johnson initiated in May, 1965. Along with the temporary cessation of the bombing, Washington, with Moscow's help, launched a series of diplomatic actions aimed at establishing contacts with the North Vietnamese. This operation was given the code name MAYFLOWER and was jointly developed in Moscow and Washington. The details of MAYFLOWER have been analyzed in numerous books.[9] What is of interest to the present study is Moscow's behavior and attitude toward the initiative.

When the decision to initiate MAYFLOWER was made, Secretary of State Rusk contacted Ambassador Dobrynin and gave him a message for the North Vietnamese. The message was also sent to Foy Kohler, the U.S. ambassador in Moscow, for delivery to the DRV embassy there. In his account of the conversation, Rusk noted that Dobrynin "was clearly relieved we [were] not asking them to act as intermediary."[10] Apparently, the ambassador had already been instructed how he should act in such a situation.

That Moscow had indeed taken a noncommittal stance with regard to the U.S. overture became obvious when Ambassador Kohler went to the Soviet Foreign Ministry seeking assistance with delivering President Johnson's message to the North Vietnamese embassy. Deputy foreign minister Nikolai Firyubin rejected Kohler's request to act as intermediary between the United States and the DRV on the grounds that it was "very unusual" in the absence of a similar request from the North Vietnamese. Nevertheless, he accepted Kohler's letter and handed it over to a Foreign Ministry official, Georgii Kornienko, who he instructed to consult with Soviet authorities and also ask for clarification from the North Vietnamese. Kornienko returned later with a written message that Firyubin "carefully read" before informing Kohler that the Soviet government refused to transmit the letter to the North Vietnamese and that it was up to Washington to find "the most convenient way" of passing the message to the DRV. Firyubin brushed aside Kohler's reasons for seeking Soviet assistance, declaring that he was not a postman. Kohler noted, however, that the Soviets made no effort to return the text of the oral communication he had handed them at the outset of the conversation.[11]

A brief conversation between Gromyko and Dean Rusk in Vienna ended the affair when Gromyko flatly stated that the Soviets "will not negotiate about Viet-Nam."[12]

Although these events are generally well known, important details have surfaced thanks to the publication in the United States of complete accounts of the meetings between U.S. and Soviet officials, thus filling in the gaps in the excerpts from the negotiating volumes of the *Pentagon Papers.* First of all, it is worthwhile to note that Firyubin, his declarations against U.S. aggression in Vietnam and his stiff behavior during the meeting with Kohler notwithstanding, was careful to reassure the U.S. ambassador of his government's "support for peaceful solutions of all questions in dispute." At the same time, he briefly outlined conditions in which such solutions could take place. "However peaceful solutions are out of [the] question when negotiations must take place under the gun," he told his counterpart. "They cannot take place under pressure or when one side operates from a position of strength."[13] Although it cannot be confirmed without appropriate documents from Russian and Vietnamese archives, which are still unavailable, it seems probable that Firyubin was spelling out not only Moscow's opinion, but also that of its North Vietnamese friends.

Furthermore, having formally rejected Kohler's request for mediation, Firyubin retained a copy of the American message to the DRV embassy so as to make sure the North Vietnamese eventually obtained it. The Soviets followed the same practice later, during the period of the SUNFLOWER initiative, when Kosygin sent via Moscow the conditions contained in the "Phase A–Phase B" formula with the expectation that Hanoi would pay due attention to it and make a reciprocal gesture of its own.

Harbingers of this Soviet policy also were evident during MAYFLOWER, in the discussions between President Kennedy's press secretary Pierre Salinger and Mikhail Sagatelyan, the former TASS bureau chief in Washington. A Soviet Foreign Ministry official known as "Vasilii Sergeevich" accompanied Sagatelyan. Both Soviets were eager to explain their government's position and to propose a possible course for initiating diplomatic talks between the warring parties.[14] There is no doubt that Sagatelyan, although "protesting he was speaking personally,"[15] had been authorized by his superiors to participate in the meeting. Apparently, the "formula" he offered Salinger for the solution of the Vietnam problem reflected a Soviet approach for achieving a peaceful settlement. "Sergeevich" confirmed this by endorsing the general nature of Sagatelyan's proposal and in turn offering an important suggestion of his own. Having reiterated that the Soviets "could not afford to be [a] middleman" in contacts between Washington and Hanoi, he suggested instead that the "middleman would have to be some Eastern European Socialist country." He refused to specify which country among the Soviet allies would serve as a suitable channel, but he was definite that it should not be Yugoslavia.[16]

Thus, in MAYFLOWER, Moscow seems to have set a pattern: While resolutely opposed to serving as an intermediary, the Soviet leaders made it clear that they favored a negotiated solution to the conflict and were prepared to take certain steps to facilitate contacts between the opposing parties.

Moscow took such a position based on its assessment of the prospects of reaching a political settlement to the Indochina conflict at the time. The Soviets were fully informed about the attitude of their Vietnamese friends toward negotiations with the Americans. Hanoi rejected any possibility of talks as long as the Americans continued to bomb the DRV. This was a pretext, however. In reality, the North Vietnamese leaders were determined to win the war on the battlefield. The twelfth plenum of the Workers' Party of Vietnam (WPV) in March, 1965, adopted a resolution "to inflict a defeat on the aggressive war of American imperialism, to defend the North, to liberate the South, to complete the national-democratic revolution in the whole country."[17] Hanoi thus subordinated political struggle to its military plans. Consequently, the North Vietnamese regarded any Soviet move in favor of a peaceful settlement with suspicion and disdain. Le Duc Tho, a senior member of the Politburo, expressed these feelings in a conversation with a French journalist: "The leaders of the Soviet Union do not believe in our victory and this pushes them to search for a resolution of the Vietnamese question by way of negotiations. We believe conditions for negotiations have not ripened yet."[18]

The North Vietnamese leaders enjoyed support and encouragement from Beijing in their orientation toward the war. The Kremlin was aware that Chinese leaders had undertaken efforts "to channel the development of events [in Vietnam] toward a 'protracted war' and to prevent a political settlement, which is regarded here as a threat to the interests of China."[19] Mao Zedong and Zhou Enlai persistently spoke against peace talks and used every opportunity to persuade the Vietnamese communist leaders of the futility of negotiations with Washington. Zhou Enlai condemned U.S. peace feelers as a hoax. "The very aim of the peace-talks plot hatched by the United States," he claimed at the Vietnamese National Day reception in Beijing on September 2, 1965, "is to bring about negotiations by cajolery so as to consolidate its position in South Vietnam. As long as the United States does not withdraw its troops, it can carry on endless talks with you so that it may hang on there indefinitely."[20]

Moscow also doubted the Americans' sincerity. The Soviet leaders were disappointed by the Johnson administration's pronouncements for peace, so often made as an accompaniment to further escalation of the war. They regarded U.S. bombing pauses as propaganda campaigns aimed at placating critics of the administration at home and abroad, at demonstrating North Vietnamese intransigence, and as part of their strategy to negotiate only from a position of strength. Moscow heard judgments from various sources that Washington believed achieving a military solution in Vietnam was the only possible course of action.[21]

Washington's behavior during the various peace initiatives seemed to confirm this viewpoint. After MARIGOLD's failure, which coincided with American bombing raids in the vicinity of Hanoi at the height of diplomatic contacts, Dobrynin made it clear to Rusk that Moscow saw the attacks as "throwing serious doubt upon the real intentions of the United States."[22] Premier Kosygin reiterated these doubts in a conversation with U.S. ambassador Llewellyn Thompson after the failure of the SUNFLOWER initiative, which in his view resulted from the Americans resuming the bombing campaign before they received Ho Chi Minh's response to President Johnson's letter. As Thompson reported to Washington: "Kosygin said [the] Soviets [are] not confident [that the] US proposal had been very serious. Confidence was most important in this situation."[23]

Lacking confidence in the eventual success of their peace efforts, the Soviet leaders naturally did not want to undertake any decisive, publicized steps in this field. However, they likewise could not afford to keep themselves totally aloof from the search for peace. First of all, Moscow itself was interested in the earliest possible settlement of the Vietnam War, recognizing the danger that it presented to the world in general, and to the Soviet policy of détente in particular. The Soviets also had received encouraging indications from Hanoi that their advocacy of peace talks was not totally futile. In fact, the North Vietnamese leaders had never rejected the *idea* of peaceful negotiations. "In a strange twist of political thinking," according to Robert Brigham, they "supported a Maoist people's war in the South *and* Soviet-sponsored negotiations." Furthermore, by the spring of 1966, Hanoi had decided to promote the Soviet and Chinese lines simultaneously. "We embraced the protracted war and negotiations," one of the Vietnamese Communist Party leaders recently commented, "because these two tracks served our needs best."[24]

There was another factor that discouraged Moscow from adopting a completely noncommittal stance toward negotiating a settlement of the conflict in Vietnam: Soviet leaders had serious misgivings about Chinese intentions to collude with the United States behind their backs. We do not know whether the Kremlin knew about a confidential message Beijing transmitted to the Johnson administration, both through Pakistani president Ayub Khan and the British chargé in Beijing, concerning China's desire to avoid war with the United States as long as the war in Vietnam was not expanded to Chinese territory.[25] If not, Moscow possessed other sources of information that nourished Soviet suspicion about the possible ulterior motives of Chinese policy toward the Indochina conflict. On August 18, 1966, the acting East German consul-general in Cambodia confided to Soviet ambassador Anatolii Ratanov that the Chinese were not going to go to a confrontation with the United States over Vietnam. He warned that it was wise not to exclude the possibility that "the PRC [People's Republic of China] pursues the objective to come to agreement with the United States on the problems of Indochina without the Soviet Union and against the Soviet Union and other socialist countries."[26] It is unclear on what evidence the German based his conclusion, but Soviet allies possessed their own intelligence resources.

All in all, despite the ambiguous situation in which the Soviets found themselves, with the beginning of the U.S. bombing of North Vietnamese territory and their misgivings about the prospects of a peaceful resolution of the Vietnam War, Moscow had enough incentives to continue its behind-the-scenes efforts aimed at bringing the warring parties to the negotiating table.

Soviet tactics were, first, to convince both Washington and Hanoi of the necessity of establishing direct contacts to discuss conditions of a possible settlement; secondly, to stimulate other countries in playing the role of peacemaker; and, finally, to keep open prospects for peace even after all previous mediation attempts had failed.

Moscow's interest in the establishment of direct contacts between the United States and the DRV had been evident almost from the outset. In a conversation with Averell Harriman—who went to Moscow in July, 1965, to urge the Soviet leaders to assist the United States in the resolution of the Vietnam conflict—Soviet premier Kosygin made it clear that, from the Soviet viewpoint, the "only way out in Vietnam is for the U.S. to start talks with the Vietnamese themselves and find a solution for this affair."[27] He hinted to the American envoy that the "Vietnamese comrades would not exclude political settlement, bypassing the Chinese."[28] Later, when Secretary Rusk informed Gromyko that the Johnson administration had followed Kosygin's advice and contacted Hanoi, the Soviet foreign secretary could not conceal his interest and wanted to know "whether contacts with Hanoi had been definitively concluded without result or whether such contacts remained open." Gromyko was evidently relieved when Rusk assured him that "both sides were prepared to renew contact if there was anything interesting to say." According to Rusk, Gromyko's "attitude seemed to indicate a hope that whatever channel that was involved would remain open."[29]

Another problem discussed when Soviet and American officials met was the U.S. bombing campaign. Moscow regarded the continuation of the bombing as the major obstacle to ending the conflict. By persistently invoking this issue in their conversations with members of the U.S. administration, the Soviet leaders were undoubtedly fulfilling the requests of their Vietnamese friends, who made the cessation of bombing the principal condition of possible negotiations. At the same time, they had their own motives for prodding the United States in this direction. For Moscow, stopping the U.S. bombing campaign against the DRV meant the end of American aggression against a fellow socialist country. This would free the Soviets of at least part of their obligation to the DRV and diminish the pressure on Moscow for "proletarian solidarity" and "international duty." Moreover, the cessation of bombing might make it possible for Moscow to assume openly the role of mediator, which it must otherwise try to evade. Gromyko hinted about this when he met with Rusk in September, 1966. "It has been said that if the Soviet Union were to take appropriate action to use its influence in Viet-Nam," Gromyko explained, referring to numerous appeals from Washington to the Kremlin to this effect, "this would bring about a peaceful settlement. But by its actions the United States had severely limited the Soviet Union's possibility and had deprived it of opportunities to take some positive steps."[30] He repeated these words almost verbatim during a subsequent conversation with President Johnson.[31]

One can find ample evidence of the pressure the Soviets applied on Washington to end the bombing. This pressure was one of the reasons why the Johnson administration initiated a thirty-seven-day bombing pause at the end of 1965. On the eve of the pause, Ambassador Dobrynin met with Secretary Rusk and vehemently argued that a better atmosphere would be created if Washington stopped the bombing. He hinted that "the Soviet Union would not try to influence North Viet-Nam while they were being bombed," thus implying that Moscow would obtain more space for maneuver vis-à-vis the North Vietnamese as soon as the American air attacks stopped. If the U.S. administration wanted to finish the war, "Why not begin with the suspension of bombing?" the Soviet ambassador reasoned.[32]

Moscow reiterated this theme, on Hanoi's behalf or on its own, from time to time throughout the period that led up to the start of the peace talks in Paris in 1968. The most dramatic demonstration of the Soviet desire to protect the DRV from the bombing took place during Kosygin's meeting with President Johnson at Glassboro. For the first time, the Soviet leadership took the initiative in an effort to get U.S.–North Vietnamese peace talks started in exchange for the cessation of bombing.

The Johnson administration, however, was not the only object of Soviet background activities. Moscow likewise tried to influence the other side of the conflict, although its actions here were more circumspect and nuanced. Being aware of both Hanoi's resistance to the idea of negotiations with the United States and their own precarious position in the DRV, the Soviets did not want to press the North Vietnamese leaders so hard as to estrange them and thus forfeit Moscow's influence in the country. Nevertheless, the Kremlin did not cease to broach the subject of achieving a peaceful settlement whenever and wherever an opportunity arose, even at the highest levels.

In January, 1966, at the height of the Christmas bombing pause, Moscow sent a secret delegation to Hanoi, headed by Alexander Shelepin, a member of the Soviet Politburo and secretary of the Central Committee. The delegation's purpose was to reach an agreement for further aid to North Vietnam, including military materiel. In addition, the delegation was to examine how the North Vietnamese stored and exploited Soviet weaponry, and how they used military cadres trained in Moscow. The delegation therefore included Dmitrii Ustinov, the Communist Party of the Soviet Union (CPSU) Central Committee secretary responsible for military-industrial matters, and Gen. V. Tolubko, then first deputy commander of the Soviet Strategic Missile Corps.[33] However, the Soviet envoys were not to confine themselves to the issues of aid to the DRV. According to information Gromyko shared with East European diplomats, Shelepin secretly drew the attention of the North Vietnamese to the need to find a political solution to the conflict in Indochina. This approach was rebuffed by the "Vietnamese comrades," who stated that "they will not see the time for negotiations to have come until further military victories have been attained."[34] Several months later, Gen. Nguyen Van Vinh told a gathering of South Vietnamese communist cadres: "Soviet Union's Shelepin, in his visit to our country, seems to have suggested negotiations. Because we have foreseen this, we issued a communiqué containing our determination to fight the U.S. aggressors. Therefore, the revisionists' scheme has failed and they have been advised of our opinion."[35]

Despite this failure, Moscow persisted in its efforts to persuade Hanoi of the necessity for negotiations with the United States. In March, 1966, a North Vietnamese delegation came to Moscow to take part in the Twenty-third CPSU Congress. The head of the delegation, WPV first secretary Le Duan, was greeted at the airport by both Leonid Brezhnev and Kosygin, always a sign of great honor. Brezhnev later met Le Duan privately to discuss the Indochina situation in detail. After making routine pronouncements about solidarity with the heroic people of Vietnam and the USSR's readiness to provide all-out support to the DRV, Brezhnev raised the issue of political struggle: "Perhaps it is necessary, along with military activity, to think over the intensification of political struggle in the international arena. We have talked about this with you and Com[rade] Pham Van Dong. We consider such a line correct. Political struggle is advantageous to our common interests. The Americans will not win the war in South Vietnam, and they know this. Maybe it is necessary to help them leave South Vietnam. Let them preserve their prestige, but leave."[36] Le Duan assured the Soviet leader that Hanoi was going to maintain contact with the Americans, either in Rangoon or in Moscow or in some other place.[37]

While continuing its efforts to persuade the Americans and North Vietnamese of the necessity of a diplomatic settlement of the Indochina conflict, the Kremlin enlisted other countries in the search for peace. As noted earlier, the Soviets proposed during MAYFLOWER that their East European allies serve as peacemakers since they were less sensitive to criticism from Beijing, more independent in their relations with Hanoi, and also enjoyed the Soviets' confidence.

It is possible to state with a fair degree of assurance that Moscow stood behind most of the peace initiatives undertaken by the East European countries. Of course, the full scope and forms of Moscow's involvement in the peace feelers of its satellites can become evident only after the relevant documents from Russian archives are declassified. Yet even now there is sufficient indirect evidence to suggest that the Soviets either urged the Eastern Europeans to play the role of mediators between the United States and North Vietnam, or authorized their actions in this sphere.

Moscow's allies were interested in the early settlement of the Vietnam conflict no less than the Soviets themselves. Besides recognizing the danger this conflict posed for international relations, they must have been jealous that a considerable amount of Soviet resources, which otherwise could be used for their own needs, were being diverted to a protracted conflict in a remote region. Accordingly, they were anxious to contribute to finding a way out of the Vietnam quagmire and did not object to playing the role of peacemakers whenever there was an opportunity.

The Christmas bombing pause was the first such occasion. When the Johnson administration announced a bombing pause beginning December 24, 1965, and sent its envoys around the world to rally support for a major U.S. diplomatic offensive, Moscow, as before, made it clear that it was reluctant to get involved. Dobrynin assured Llewellyn Thompson, the ambassador-at-large, that he would inform his government about the bombing pause but "he was not undertaking to pass this information to Hanoi."[38] As a result, Washington decided to avoid a request for Moscow's assistance and, perhaps keeping Soviet advice in mind, turned instead to the East European countries, primarily Hungary and Poland.

At Secretary Rusk's request, the Hungarians passed the information on the bombing pause and U.S. conditions for a diplomatic settlement of the conflict to a DRV delegation headed by Le Thanh Nghi, which was in Hungary at the time, and then to Hanoi.[39] The Poles sent special envoy Jerzy Michalowski to North Vietnam to deliver the U.S. fourteen-point peace plan, and to persuade the Vietnamese communist leaders to respond favorably to the American peace initiative.[40] The North Vietnamese, however, remained adamant in their refusal to begin negotiations with the United States at a time when the battlefield situation was so hopeful for them.

The Soviets knew what was going on, of course. Gromyko had personally approved Michalowski's mission when the Polish envoy made a stopover in Moscow on his way to Hanoi. Later, at a meeting with the Hungarian and Polish foreign ministers on January 24–25, 1966, he thanked both for their efforts.[41] More than that, the Kremlin's instructions to Shelepin to discuss prospects for a political settlement with the North Vietnamese may have reinforced the efforts of the Hungarians and the Poles.

Moscow followed the same pattern during the MARIGOLD affair, an initiative undertaken by Poland in mid-1966 which, by the end of that year, almost led to talks between American and North Vietnamese representatives in the Polish capital.[42] Without doubt, the Soviets were well informed about Polish ICC member Januscz Lewandowski's approach to the Italian and American ambassadors in Saigon, Giovanni D'Orlandi and Henry Cabot Lodge, with what seemed a new North Vietnamese offer for a political settlement of the conflict. Still, it would be an exaggeration, in relation to MARIGOLD, to speak of the "entry of the Soviet Union into the diplomacy of peacemaking,"[43] because Moscow remained in the background for the most part, approving Polish actions and airing hints and suggestions without active involvement in the process. Only when U.S. bombing raids in the Hanoi region in December threatened MARIGOLD, did they rush to save whatever goodwill might remain on both sides.

Even assuming that the Poles had initiated the operation on their own, they were anxious to get Moscow's approval. When MARIGOLD entered a decisive stage, Polish foreign minister Adam Rapacki flew to Sofia to meet Brezhnev, who was there for a congress of the Bulgarian Communist Party, to brief him on the peace initiative. Brezhnev approved the Polish actions and encouraged Warsaw to proceed.[44] Hanoi also found it expedient to be in contact with the Kremlin concerning its diplomatic steps. Brezhnev told Rapacki that he had already discussed the details of the Lodge-Lewandowski conversations with DRV foreign minister Nguyen Duy Trinh.[45] The Soviets were also notified about Hanoi's intention to cancel the whole affair. As Dobrynin revealed to Rusk two months later, "on the 15th [apparently of December] the DRV Charge had come to the Soviet Foreign Ministry to tell the Soviets that they had told Rapacki to break off his talks with us, on the ground that the US bombing just before that date meant the US thought it could pressure Hanoi to talk, and this they would not do."[46]

Moscow apparently did not limit its support for peace overtures solely to its communist allies; Soviet leaders displayed their readiness to cooperate on this issue with Western countries such as Great Britain as well. In March, 1966, according to Prime Minister Harold Wilson's account, the Soviets helped arrange a meeting of London's envoy, Lord Chalfont, with the North Vietnamese delegation that was in Moscow to participate in the CPSU congress mentioned previously. The conversation went on for six hours but brought no concrete result.[47]

The issue of the Vietnam War was also raised during Anglo-Soviet negotiations in February and July of the same year. Not surprisingly, when efforts to establish U.S.–North Vietnamese contacts in Warsaw got nowhere, Moscow, encouraged by promising signs from Hanoi, decided to explore one more opportunity for initiating peace talks, this time using London as intermediary.[48]

Dobrynin recorded in his memoirs that—on the eve of his official visit to the British Isles in February, 1967—Kosygin received a secret request from Hanoi "to use the government of Prime Minister Harold Wilson, one of Johnson's few European supporters on Vietnam, to put pressure on Washington to reach a peaceful solution in Vietnam."[49] This is corroborated by information contained in Russian archival documents. In his conversation with the Soviet ambassador in Hanoi, Ilya S. Shcherbakov, on January 30, 1967, North Vietnamese premier Pham Van Dong expressed a desire that "the Soviet Union make diplomatic sounding of U.S. intentions so as to find out to what conclusions and decisions the Americans will come to" concerning negotiations with the DRV.[50] The premier's request was relayed to contacts in both the American and North Vietnamese embassies in Moscow developed in the framework of the new initiative called SUNFLOWER.

Kosygin, known for his dislike of the Vietnam War because it diverted Soviet resources intended for economic reforms at home, needed no further urging. Besides, Moscow seems to have been attracted by the opportunity to enlist one of America's closest allies as a mediator. Indeed, Wilson was enthusiastic about the Soviet premier's pronouncements in favor of a settlement of the conflict. He had been able to stir Kosygin's interest in the Phase A–Phase B formula Washington proposed during the contacts with Lewandowski. The Soviet leader became so enthusiastic about the prospects of this formula that he, apparently exceeding his commission, contacted Brezhnev with a recommendation to press Hanoi to accept a compromise in order to start negotiations.[51] "For personal reasons of status," Dobrynin wrote in his memoirs, "Brezhnev was not too happy about Kosygin's initiative, but he let him continue, however unwillingly, lest he be seen as impeding a settlement."[52]

The Soviet premier's efforts were futile, however. Washington's eventual hardening of its conditions for negotiations and Hanoi's unwillingness to modify its four points, as well as the resumption of the U.S. bombing campaign—temporarily suspended for the Tet truce—destroyed the Kosygin-Wilson initiative. While talking to the U.S. ambassador after his return from London, Kosygin could not conceal his disappointment. "[The] Vietnamese had for the first time stated they [were] ready [to] negotiate if bombings were stopped unconditionally," he complained to Ambassador Thompson. Moreover, Kosygin said he supported their proposal "because he had good reason for taking such a step." The Americans, however, did not take this seriously and made a "basic mistake" by resuming the bombing.[53]

It is worthwhile to underline here that in February, 1967, as previously, the Soviets did not abandon their policy of assisting the initiatives of others rather than play the role of mediator themselves. In transmitting his message on the U.S. proposal to Hanoi, Kosygin, according to the authors of the *Pentagon Papers*, "served as a more or less neutral agent," and avoided endorsing it himself.[54] Yet the very fact of Soviet involvement in the affair must have served as a strong indication to the North Vietnamese of the seriousness of the undertaking. After SUNFLOWER failed to bring the warring parties to the negotiating table through the good offices of the Soviets' allies, Moscow apparently decided to try its own hand as intermediary.

The time chosen for the attempt was not propitious. In the aftermath of SUNFLOWER, the North Vietnamese emphasized pursuing a military course to resolve the Vietnam problem.[55] Hanoi's optimism about the prospects of armed struggle in Vietnam made it reluctant to discuss the need for any further negotiations with the Soviets. "After the April [Soviet–North Vietnamese] talks in Moscow," Shcherbakov reported to his superiors, "more than once, during conversations with Pham Van Dong and other leaders we had to listen to monosyllabic responses to the effect that the Soviet comrades' recommendations 'were being studied,' that it was necessary to wait for an appropriate time for a new initiative of the DRV or the [National Liberation] Front in the sphere of diplomatic struggle."[56]

Despite the attitude of their Vietnamese "friends," the Soviet leaders continued to press for peace in Vietnam. They apparently had determined to rely on Soviet prestige as a final incentive to bring about talks.

Using the opportunity of his visit to the United States to attend the UN General Assembly's special session on the Middle East crisis, Kosygin had raised the Vietnam issue with Lyndon Johnson during their summit at Glassboro. He told Johnson that, in anticipation of this meeting, he had contacted Pham Van Dong and asked the North Vietnamese leader's advice on "what he could do . . . to help bring this war to an end." The reply from Hanoi was definitive: "Stop the bombing and they would immediately go to the conference table." The Soviet premier strongly advised his American counterpart to follow up on this proposal. "While he considered North Viet-Nam's proposal to be the President's own business," Kosygin argued, "he emphatically believed that now the President had ample reason to sit down and negotiate with North Viet-Nam."[57]

Although LBJ was not at all enthusiastic about a new approach to the DRV after so many debacles, the fact that the Soviet Union had assumed the role of mediator for the first time influenced his decision. He obviously did not want to discourage Moscow from taking further steps in this capacity in the future. Accordingly, Johnson, on the advice of Secretary Rusk, gave Kosygin a message for transmittal to Hanoi.[58] The president then explained to Kosygin the meaning of his proposal to the DRV, stressing the importance of mutual understanding between the American and Soviet leaders.[59] Kosygin seemed satisfied and promised to inform Washington of the North Vietnamese reaction immediately. A month later, Rusk asked Dobrynin how Hanoi had reacted to the most recent U.S. proposal. The Soviet ambassador explained that the North Vietnamese leaders had rejected it because the Americans continued to send troops to the region.[60]

The failure of Kosygin's GLASSBORO initiative was a serious blow to Soviet ego. Dobrynin wrote that the breakdown of SUNFLOWER "consolidated Moscow's conviction that it was fruitless to meddle in anything between Vietnam and the United States."[61] However, it appears that the Soviet leaders did not reach this conclusion until after GLASSBORO. Never again would the Kremlin openly assume the obligations of an intermediary during the Vietnam War. Even after peace talks began in Paris in May, 1968, Moscow limited its involvement to backstage activities, helping the sides resolve such secondary problems as the shape of the conference table and the speaking order, but leaving all principal issues to the representatives of the opposing parties.

Notes

1. In his introduction to the negotiating volumes of the *Pentagon Papers*, George Herring describes briefly the "enormous controversy" generated by the various peace initiatives during the Vietnam War. See *The Secret Diplomacy of the Vietnam War: The Negotiating Volumes of the Pentagon Papers*, ed. George C. Herring (Austin: University of Texas Press, 1983), p. xxiii.

2. Editorial Note, U.S. Department of State, *Foreign Relations of the United States* (*FRUS*), *1964–1968*, vol. 2, *Vietnam, January–June 1965* (Washington: GPO, 1996), p. 436.

3. U.S. embassy, Moscow, to Secretary of State, Feb. 23, 1967, National Security File (NSF), Country File (CF)–Vietnam (VN), Box 255, Lyndon B. Johnson Library, Austin, Tex. (hereafter LBJL).

4. Qiang Zhai, *China and the Vietnam Wars, 1950–1975* (Chapel Hill: University of North Carolina Press, 2000), p. 167.

5. Anatoly Dobrynin, *In Confidence: Moscow's Ambassador to America's Six Cold War Presidents* (New York: Times Books, 1995), p. 144.

6. Ibid., p. 649–50.

7. For details, see my book *The Soviet Union and the Vietnam War* (Chicago: Ivan Dee, 1996).

8. Summary Notes of the 550th Meeting of the National Security Council, Mar. 26, 1965. *FRUS, 1964–1968*, p. 2:483.

9. See Lloyd C. Gardner, *Pay Any Price: Lyndon Johnson and the Wars for Vietnam* (Chicago: Ivan Dee, 1995); George C. Herring, *LBJ and Vietnam: A Different Kind of War* (Austin: University of Texas Press, 1994); and Brian VanDeMark, *Into the Quagmire: Lyndon Johnson and the Escalation of the Vietnam War* (New York: Oxford University Press, 1991), to cite just a few.

10. State Department to U.S. embassy, Moscow, telegram, May 11, 1965, *FRUS, 1964–1968*, p. 2:639.

11. *Secret Diplomacy*, ed. Herring, pp. 60–64.

12. Ibid., pp. 67–69.

13. Kohler to State Department, May 13, 1965, *FRUS, 1964–1968*, p. 2:650.

14. *Secret Diplomacy*, ed. Herring, pp. 60–64.

15. Kohler to State Department, May 13, 1965, p. 2:661.

16. Kohler to State Department, May 15, 1965, *FRUS, 1964–1968*, p. 2:662.

17. *Boyevoi avangard v'etnamskogo naroda. Istoriia Kommunisticheskoi partii V'etnama* (Militant Vanguard of the Vietnamese People: The History of the Communist Party of Vietnam), trans. from the Vietnamese (Moscow: Politizdat, 1981), p. 141.

18. first secretary of the Soviet embassy in the DRV G. A. Zverev–Ch. Fourgneau, July 6, 1965, memorandum of conversation, fond 5, opis' 50, delo 721, list 181, Rossiiskii Gosu-

darstvennyi Arkhiv Noveishei Istorii (Russian State Archive of Contemporary History), Moscow (hereafter RGANI).

19. Political (Annual) Report of the Soviet Embassy in the People's Republic of China for 1966, Mar. 23, 1967, fond 5, opis' 58, delo 196, list 23, RGANI.

20. Zhai, *China,* p. 162.

21. Among others, the Soviet East European allies provided Moscow with such information. For example, Wendrowski, the head of the Polish delegation to the International Control Commission, argued in his conversation with the Soviet ambassador to Cambodia, Anatolii Ratanov, that "the United States has never wanted peaceful negotiations, and the campaign waged by [the Americans] about their readiness for negotiations was of a purely propaganda character." See Ratanov-Wendrowski, Mar. 17, 1966, memorandum of conversation, fond 5, opis' 50, delo 777, list 104, RGANI. The Hungarians echoed this opinion. They sent information to the Soviets from a Washington correspondent for *Népszabadsag,* the Hungarian Communist Party newspaper. According to this source, the Americans believed that it was necessary to wage the Vietnam War until victory, and military victory was "the only possible exit." See Zoltan Komocsin, secretary of the Central Committee of the Hungarian Socialist Workers Party (HSWP) to Yuri Andropov, secretary of the Central Committee of the CPSU, Nov., 1966, fond 5, opis' 58, delo 203, list 61, RGANI.

22. Rusk-Dobrynin, Jan. 5, 1967, memorandum of conversation, NSF, Memos to the President, Walt Rostow, Box 12, LBJL.

23. U.S. embassy, Moscow, to Secretary of State, Feb. 18, 1967, NSF, CF-VN, Box 255, LBJL. See also *Secret Diplomacy,* ed. *Herring,* p. 485.

24. Robert K. Brigham, "Vietnam at the Center: Patterns of Diplomacy and Resistance," in *International Perspectives on Vietnam,* ed. Lloyd C. Gardner and Ted Gittinger (College Station: Texas A&M University Press, 2000), pp. 102–103. Emphasis in original.

25. This message was first delivered by Zhou Enlai to Ayub Khan when they met in the Chinese capital on April 2, with the request to transmit it to Washington. On May 31, Chinese foreign minister Chen Yi called in British chargé Hopson and delivered the same message, explaining that Ayub's trip to Washington had been postponed and Zhou was concerned that the message had not been transmitted. See Editorial Note, *FRUS, 1964–1968,* p. 2:700.

26. A. P. Ratanov–Kittler, Aug. 18, 1966, memorandum of conversation, fond 5, opis' 58, delo 324, list 145, RGANI.

27. Kosygin-Harriman, July 15, 1965, memorandum of conversation, *FRUS, 1964–1968,* vol. 3, *Vietnam, June–December, 1965* (Washington, D.C.: GPO, 1996), p. 152. For details of Harriman's visit, see Gaiduk, *Soviet Union,* pp. 50–55.

28. Editorial Note, ibid., p. 3:179.

29. Secretary of State Rusk to President Johnson, Sept. 30, 1965, memorandum, ibid., pp. 3:427–28.

30. Rusk-Gromyko, Sept. 24, 1966, memorandum of conversation, *FRUS, 1964–1968,* vol. 4, *Vietnam, 1966* (Washington, D.C.: GPO, 1998), pp. 665–66.

31. Ibid., p. 4:720.

32. Rusk-Dobrynin, Dec. 8, 1965, memorandum of conversation, ibid., pp. 4:626–27.

33. M. S. Kapitza, *Na raznykh parallelyakh. Zapiski diplomata* (On Various Parallels: The Memoirs of a Diplomat) (Moscow: Kniga i bizness, 1996), p. 273.

34. See James G. Hershberg, ed., *Central and East European Documents on the Vietnam War: Sample Materials from Polish, Hungarian, and East German Sources* (Washington, D.C.: Woodrow Wilson International Center for Scholars, 1997).

35. First Viet Cong Cadre Report of Vinh Speech at COSVN Congress, Mar., 1966, Subject File, Box 85, Joseph H. Alsop Papers, Manuscript Division, Library of Congress, Washington, D.C. (hereafter LOC).

36. Secretary General of the CPSU Central Committee L. I. Brezhnev–WPV delegation at the Twenty-third CPSU Congress, Apr. 11, 1966, memorandum of conversation, fond 3, opis' 83, delo 284, list 6–20, Archive of the President of the Russian Federation, in *Istochnik* 3 (1998): p. 128.

37. Ibid., pp. 126–27.

38. Thompson-Dobrynin, Dec. 28, 1965, memorandum of conversation, Special Files: Public Service, Trips and Missions, PINTA, Box 549, H. Averell Harriman Papers, LOC.

39. Hungarian foreign minister Janos Péter's proposal to the Political Committee of the HSWP Central Committee, "Diplomatic Steps Concerning the Vietnam Conflict," Jan. 31, 1966, Magyar Orszagos Levaltar, Budapest, Ministry of Foreign Affairs, XIX-J-1-j, Box 111, in Hershberg, ed., *Central and East European Documents*.

40. Jerzy Michalowski (prepared by Stefan Michalowski), "Polish Secret Peace Initiatives in Vietnam," in *Cold War International History Project Bulletin* nos. 6/7 (winter, 1995–96): pp. 241, 258–59.

41. Ibid., p. 258; Péter's proposal to the Political Committee.

42. For the most recent account of events relating to MARIGOLD based on new evidence, see James G. Hershberg with L. W. Gluchowski, "Who Murdered 'Marigold'? New Evidence on the Mysterious Failure of Poland's Secret Initiative to Start U.S.–North Vietnamese Peace Talks, 1966," Cold War International History Project Working Paper no. 27, Apr., 2000.

43. *Secret Diplomacy*, ed. Herring, p. 211.

44. Michalowski, "Polish Secret Peace Initiatives," p. 259.

45. Hershberg, "Who Murdered 'Marigold,'" p. 16.

46. State Department to U.S. embassy, Moscow, Feb. 24, 1967, NSF, CF-VN, Box 255, LBJL. See also *Secret Diplomacy*, ed. Herring, p. 494.

47. Harold Wilson, *The Labour Government, 1964–1970: A Personal Record* (London: Weidenfeld and Nicolson and Michael Joseph, 1971), p. 213.

48. One such sign was the decision of the thirteenth plenum of the WPV Central Committee (January, 1967) to intensify the diplomatic struggle. Although having emphasized that armed and political forms of struggle remained the principal and decisive factors of communist success on the battlefield, "diplomatic struggle also keeps for itself an important, positive, and independent role." The plenum decided to increase pressure on the United States in the diplomatic sphere, "combining this activity with the military and political offensive." See *Boyevoi avanguard v'etnamskogo naroda*, p. 156.

49. Dobrynin, *In Confidence*, p. 160.

50. Shcherbakov–Pham Van Dong, Jan. 30, 1967, memorandum of conversation, fond 5, opis' 59, delo 327, list 81, RGANI.

51. Chester Cooper, Washington's special envoy to London, informed the State Department: "According to telephone intercept Kosygin called Brezhnev and said 'a great possibility of achieving the aim, if the Vietnamese will understand the present situation that we have passed to them, they will have to decide. All they need to do is to give a confidential declaration'" (U.S. embassy, London, to Secretary of State, Feb. 13, 1967, NSF, CF-VN, Box 256, LBJL).

52. Dobrynin, *In Confidence*, p. 160.

53. U.S. embassy, Moscow, to Secretary of State, Feb. 18, 1967, NSF, CF-VN, Box 255, LBJL.

54. *Secret Diplomacy*, ed. Herring, p. 401.

55. Soviet Foreign Ministry memorandum, "On Some New Aspects of the WPV's Position on the Vietnamese Problem," June 30, 1967, fond 5, opis' 59, delo 327, list 220, RGANI.

56. Political letter from Soviet embassy, Hanoi, "Soviet-Vietnamese Talks on April 1967 and the Subsequent Policy of the WPV Toward Settlement of the Vietnamese Problem," Aug., 1967, list 258, ibid.

57. NSF, CF-USSR, addendum, GLASSBORO Memcons, Box 295, LBJL.

58. See Rusk, memorandum for the president, June 24, 1967, ibid.

59. Johnson-Kosygin, June 25, 1967, memorandum of conversation, ibid.

60. Dobrynin, *In Confidence,* p. 169

61. Ibid., p. 161

China's Response to French Peace Initiatives

QIANG ZHAI

Between 1964 and 1966, French president Charles de Gaulle initiated a number of moves to bring about a political settlement to the conflict in Vietnam. In the end, however, none of his peace proposals bore fruit. Historians have attributed the failure of de Gaulle's peace initiatives to the lack of interest shown by Lyndon B. Johnson's administration.[1] China's response to the French peace moves, on the other hand, has received little scholarly attention. In fact, de Gaulle actively sought Beijing's endorsement of his peace plans, but Mao Zedong turned him down. This chapter examines China's reaction to the French peace initiatives and the effects of Chinese policy on Sino-French relations. Beijing's objection to a peaceful settlement of the war reflected Mao's complex calculations with regard to limiting Soviet influence in Indochina, establishing China's leadership position within the third world independence movement, and mobilizing domestic support for his social and political programs.

The Indochina conflict had been a major obstacle to the improvement of relations between France and the People's Republic of China (PRC) during the early 1950s. Immediately after its establishment in October, 1949, the PRC recognized the Democratic Republic of Vietnam (DRV) and provided advisers and weapons to support Ho Chi Minh's war against France. Chinese leaders made these decisions with the full realization that their actions would incur French hostility. Revolutionary solidarity with the Vietnamese communists carried the day. The thawing of Chinese-French relations did not occur until the 1954 Geneva Conference, when Beijing and Paris cooperated in promoting a peace settlement in Indochina. Shortly after Geneva, the French government began to approach China on the issue of establishing normal relations. However, a number of factors slowed the process: Beijing's resentment at the French reluctance to cut diplomatic ties with Taiwan, Washington's pressure on France not to establish relations with China, as well as Paris's unhappiness with China's support for Egypt during the 1956 Suez crisis and its recognition of the Algerian independence movement from 1958 to 1962.[2]

The conclusion of the war in Algeria in 1962 removed a major sticking point in the improvement of Sino-French relations. By 1963, the Sino-Soviet dispute had reached the point of no return. The signing of the limited nuclear test ban treaty by the United States, the Soviet Union, and Britain in July pushed China and France closer to each other because both opposed superpower domination of international affairs. Beijing denounced Washington and Moscow for colluding to deny nonnuclear states the means to defend their national sovereignty.[3] In January, 1964, France recognized the PRC, delivering a serious blow to American efforts to isolate the Beijing government.[4] The establishment of diplomatic ties between China and France in 1964 represented the convergence of strategic interests between the two countries: the maintenance of their respective influence in the global arena and the creation of a multipolar world.

For de Gaulle, recognition of China could yield additional benefits for his Vietnam diplomacy. He hoped that cooperation with the PRC, when combined with the historic French ties to both Vietnam and the United States, might strengthen his position as a peace broker in the Indochina conflict. De Gaulle saw U.S. military action in Vietnam as a futile and dangerous move, fearing that American escalation of the conflict might trigger a Chinese intervention and eventually lead to the involvement of both France and the Soviet Union. He believed that if the French, with their experience and knowledge of the region, were unable to defeat the communists, then the United States, despite all its power, would also be unable to do so. He thus was anxious to see the United States withdraw its support of the South Vietnamese government.[5]

On August 29, 1963, it was announced during a Council of Ministers meeting presided over by de Gaulle that France was willing to help create a neutral Vietnam that would live in peace and unity and be free from external influences. The announcement marked the beginning of de Gaulle's endeavor to promote an international conference on Southeast Asia with the goal of neutralizing Vietnam on the basis of the 1954 Geneva Accords. Realizing that no international conference on Vietnam would be possible without including China, de Gaulle sought Beijing's participation.[6]

While de Gaulle was calling for the neutralization of Vietnam, Chinese leaders were stepping up their consultations with Communist Party leaders throughout Southeast Asia regarding the promotion of revolution there. In late September, 1963, Zhou Enlai traveled to Conghua, Guangdong Province, to meet with leaders of the Workers' Party of Vietnam (WPV), the Lao People's Party (LPP), and the Indonesian Communist Party (PKI). Present at the meeting were Ho Chi Minh, Le Duan, Muoi Cuc (code name for Nguyen Van Linh), and Nguyen Chi Thanh of the WPV; Kaysone

Phomvihane of the LLP; and D. N. Aidit of the PKI. The conference was held to develop a comprehensive estimate of the existing conditions and future trends in Southeast Asia and to devise a regional strategy. After analyzing Washington's inclination to intervene in Vietnam and Laos, Zhou Enlai pointed out that the United States was overstretched in the world because it had dispatched troops to too many places. Therefore, if the United States started a war in Indochina, it was sure to suffer defeat. The countries of Southeast Asia, Zhou asserted, should establish confidence in their final victory over the Americans. The basic aims for revolution in Southeast Asia, according to Zhou, was anti-imperialism, antifeudalism, and antibureaucratic capitalism. Zhou introduced four methods for achieving these objectives: mobilizing the masses and expanding the united front; going to the rural areas to conduct armed struggle and to establish revolutionary bases; strengthening party leadership over all fronts; and increasing contact between countries and assisting each other in their struggles. Zhou pledged that China would serve as a rear area for the revolutionary movements in Southeast Asia and do its utmost to support the anti-imperialist struggle of Southeast Asian countries. In the end, Zhou also proposed concrete measures for coping with American counterinsurgency warfare.[7] At no time did Zhou suggest compromise or negotiation.

While de Gaulle saw the normalization of relations with China as an asset in his Vietnam diplomacy, Chinese leaders actually perceived it as a liability in their relations with the Vietnamese communists. They feared that rapprochement with France might create an impression among national independence movements in the world, including Vietnam, that China was more interested in improving relations with capitalist countries than in supporting their causes. For this reason, Beijing refrained from engaging in high-level visits with France between 1964 and 1966 despite Paris's strong interest in doing so. In May, 1964, the French Foreign Ministry informed the Chinese embassy that Minister of State André Malraux hoped to visit China. China did not respond at the time primarily because it feared that Malraux's trip might produce a negative impact on the Vietnamese war with the Americans. Beijing declined to accept de Gaulle's invitation for Premier Zhou Enlai to visit France in 1966 for similar reasons.[8]

During a much-publicized press conference in January, 1964, de Gaulle called for the neutralization of all Southeast Asia. Drawing a direct connection between his government's recognition of China and the conflict in Vietnam, he said that "there is no political reality in Asia which does not interest or touch China" and that "it is absolutely inconceivable that without her participation there can be any accord on the eventual neutrality of Southeast Asia."[9] In June, the French president proposed to Chinese ambassador Huang Zheng that the Geneva Conference be reconvened in an effort to restore peace in Indochina. Both China and France had intervened in Indochina, de Gaulle contended, so both countries would have to step back in order for the Geneva Conference to be reconvened. In July, de Gaulle further proposed that China, France, the United States, and the Soviet Union guarantee Indochina's neutrality. Mao responded to de Gaulle's proposal while talking to a group of French legislators on September 10: "You said that we had participated in the intervention in Southeast Asia. So far we have only intervened with empty words to encourage and support Southeast Asian people's war against the United States. A peaceful solution can be found only when the United States no longer wants to fight. The struggle of the Southeast Asian people is targeted at the United States, not at France." Mao asked the French to urge the Americans to stop the fighting in Vietnam. If the Americans wanted to continue the war, Mao concluded, a second Dien Bien Phu was waiting for them.[10] When Mao said that China had only intervened in Indochina with "empty words," he was clearly being disingenuous because the PRC had been providing a substantial amount of military hardware to the DRV since 1962, and in 1964 the Chinese Communist Party (CCP) sent an advisory team to assist the Pathet Lao.[11]

In July, 1965, de Gaulle sent Minister of State André Malraux as his personal envoy to Beijing to seek Chinese endorsement of his peace initiatives. In his meetings with Mao, Liu Shaoqi, and Zhou Enlai, Malraux proposed a "neutralization of Indochina" plan that would redraw Vietnam's boundaries. According to the plan, Vietnam would be divided along the Truong Son Ra Mountain. The area east of the mountain, including Saigon, would belong to the DRV or the National Liberation Front (NLF), while the area west of the mountain—including Laos, Cambodia, and Thailand—would be "neutralized." Malraux also asked the Chinese whether it would be possible to conduct negotiations if the United States "promised" to withdraw troops from Vietnam. Zhou immediately rejected Malraux's "neutralization" plan, claiming that the boundaries of Indochina's countries were long established. Furthermore, the independence and neutrality of Cambodia and Laos should be respected on the basis of the Geneva Accords. As to Washington's intentions, the Chinese premier believed the United States had no desire to leave Vietnam. He told the French visitor that China would firmly support the Vietnamese struggle against the United States.[12]

Despite China's rejection of Malraux's proposal, de Gaulle persisted in seeking Beijing's cooperation. In November he sent Amb. Jean Chauvel as another personal emissary to China. Chauvel broached the subject of Vietnam peace talks in his meeting with Zhou Enlai on November 30. The

Chinese premier reiterated Beijing's support for Hanoi's opposition to the "American peace talk hoax," claiming that "it is the United States that is escalating the war in Vietnam and that the United States, not other countries, must bear the responsibility."[13]

De Gaulle visited Phnom Penh in the summer of 1966. There he met with Prince Norodom Sihanouk; Nguyen Thuong, head of the North Vietnamese diplomatic mission in Cambodia; and Nguyen Van Hieu, the NLF's foreign affairs representative. In a speech before an audience of one hundred thousand in Phnom Penh, de Gaulle referred to the Vietnam War as a national resistance struggle. Citing the French example of ending the Algerian War, he called for an American troop withdrawal as a precondition for a political settlement in Vietnam and insisted that the NLF should be a signatory to the settlement. He again suggested negotiations based on the 1954 Geneva Accords to reestablish peace in Indochina. De Gaulle's statements clearly indicated his sympathy for the North Vietnamese position and his conviction that the United States was primarily responsible for the escalation of the Vietnam conflict.[14] Chinese officials had mixed feelings about de Gaulle's speech. On one hand, they appreciated his call for a U.S. troop withdrawal and his recognition of the NLF. On the other hand, they questioned the usefulness of a political solution. On November 16, 1966, Foreign Minister Chen Yi stated publicly that de Gaulle was correct to demand an American withdrawal and to recognize the NLF, but he added that China did not believe the Geneva Accords were still a useful basis for settling the Vietnam problem because the United States had completely violated them and China no longer trusted American promises.[15]

In July, 1966, de Gaulle also sent Jean Sainteny, a former French colonial official in Indochina who had maintained close ties with Ho Chi Minh, to Hanoi as his personal emissary. Sainteny made stops in Moscow and Beijing, but saw no Chinese during his stay in the Chinese capital. Sainteny later told an American diplomat in Paris "he had already sensed the Chinese were hostile to his trip to Hanoi and therefore for reasons of race he did not ask to see any Chinese."[16] In Hanoi, Sainteny delivered a letter from de Gaulle to Ho Chi Minh and had several conversations with Ho Chi Minh, Pham Van Dong, and other DRV officials.

Frustrated by China's opposition, de Gaulle turned to the Soviet Union for help in bringing about a peaceful settlement of the Vietnam War. Moscow proved to be more receptive to French proposals. Soviet leaders were worried that getting involved in the Vietnam conflict might lead to a direct clash with the United States. Before his ouster from power in October, 1964, Nikita Khrushchev had tried to limit Soviet involvement in Indochina in order to fend off what he perceived as China's attempt to draw the Soviet Union into a conflict with the United States.[17] Although Khrushchev's successors in the Kremlin were more forthcoming in providing assistance to the DRV, they shared their predecessor's estimate that the risk of a superpower conflict over Vietnam was great. To avoid damaging relations with the United States, the Soviet leaders favored a peaceful settlement of the Vietnam War. In addition to urging the North Vietnamese to pay attention to French peace proposals, the Kremlin also launched its own peace initiatives.[18]

Despite China's hostility to peace talks, international efforts to promote negotiations on Vietnam continued, and some mediators bypassed Beijing and concentrated their efforts in other capitals like Paris, New Delhi, and Moscow. In early 1968, United Nations secretary general U Thant met with North Vietnamese representatives in Paris and New Delhi. Upon his return to the United States, Thant informed President Johnson of Hanoi's position insofar as he understood it. On February 25, Thant remarked that Washington could reasonably assume that Hanoi would deal in "good faith" with the issue of ground combat if the United States halted its bombing campaign. The French government endorsed Thant's view three days later. Later, the French offered Paris as a negotiation site, thus breaking the deadlock in DRV-U.S. discussions about a meeting place.[19]

Aware of China's antagonism to a negotiated settlement, Hanoi leaders consulted more with the Soviet Union in pursuing their strategy of "fighting while negotiating" in 1968. In a May 2 meeting with V. Chivilev, Soviet chargé d'affaires in Hanoi, Le Duan, first secretary of the WPV, mentioned that the DRV, after considering Soviet suggestions, planned to propose Paris as a site for the negotiations and asked Moscow to persuade Washington to accept this proposal.[20] When Hanoi announced on May 3 its willingness to talk in Paris, the U.S. government immediately accepted.

Hanoi's decision to begin negotiating with the United States without first consulting Beijing greatly strained Sino-DRV relations. Chinese officials blamed the North Vietnamese for making two major concessions: accepting President Johnson's partial-bombing cessation instead of holding out for a complete end to the bombing before starting negotiations, and abandoning their own preferred negotiation sites of Phnom Penh or Warsaw.[21] In addition, Chinese newspapers criticized France for providing the site for the DRV-U.S. talks. Chinese leaders clearly were disappointed with their inability to shape developments in Indochina. Beijing's uncompromising stand against peace talks had alienated North Vietnam and many other countries interested in a peaceful resolution of the Vietnam conflict. China's intransigence thus diminished its own influence over Indochinese affairs.

Beijing's rigid attitude toward the Vietnam conflict reflected Mao's general militant anti-imperialist foreign policy from 1965 to 1967. Chinese leaders opposed peace talks in Vietnam in order to advance several goals. First, Mao believed that continued fighting in Vietnam would serve as a model war of national liberation that might well demonstrate the correctness of his confrontational approach. Confident in his vision of a socialist linear advance, Mao had few doubts that his political and social formula would improve the world. He presumed to know what was best for humanity and insisted that third-world nations follow the proven path to liberation and progress that the Chinese people had taken. Mao sought to transform the poor and developing countries in Asia, Africa, and Latin America into a revolutionary force capable of challenging and overthrowing the existing international order. These supposedly backward and powerless nations, Mao contended, could be united to form a powerful revolutionary force by adopting the Chinese model as their guide. He envisioned the "rural areas of the world" surrounding the Western "cities of the world."[22]

In the calculations of Mao and his colleagues, a protracted war in Vietnam would mire the United States and exhaust its strength, making it difficult for Washington to dispatch troops to suppress liberation movements elsewhere. In a meeting with Tanzanian president Julius Nyerere on June 4, 1965, Zhou Enlai declared: "the more U.S. forces were tied down in Vietnam, the more beneficial it would be for national independence movements. China is willing to do its utmost to assist the DRV on every front. The U.S. distraction in Vietnam is beneficial to the people of the world. Although the American power is great, it loses its strength when it is divided."[23]

Second, Mao was determined to minimize Soviet influence in Southeast Asia. He reasoned that a peace conference on Vietnam would be controlled by the two superpowers, isolating China. Therefore, a political settlement in Vietnam would constitute a diplomatic triumph for the Soviet Union. He feared that if Moscow and Washington succeeded in working together to solve the Vietnam problem, they might cooperate on other thorny issues in Asia, further diminishing China's influence. The prospect of Soviets and Americans jointly dominating the world was Mao's strategic nightmare. A desire to preserve China's international position and to forestall what he deemed as Soviet-American "collusion" against China may well have been Mao's overriding objective in opposing Vietnam peace talks.

Mao was convinced that Khrushchev's successors had no intention of abandoning the policy of peaceful coexistence with the United States. By downplaying Soviet aid to the DRV and depicting the Soviet Union as opportunistically seeking a bargain with the Americans at the expense of Vietnam, Mao intended to discredit Moscow and strengthen Beijing's anti-imperialist credentials in the international communist movement and among third-world countries. Mao rejected a negotiated settlement in Vietnam because he believed that the present course of the war validated his ideological position on armed revolutionary struggle. In this regard, *Hongqi* (*Red Flag*), the CCP's theoretical journal, published a commentary on February 11, 1966, condemning Soviet motives in Vietnam. It portrayed the Soviet leaders' gesture of support for the DRV as a means "to get more of a say for themselves on the Vietnam question, sow dissension in Sino-Vietnamese relations and help the United States to realize its 'peace talks' plot. In the final analysis, they want to find a way out for U.S. imperialism on the Vietnam question, enable it to occupy South Vietnam permanently and strike a political deal with it."[24]

Finally, Mao found the continued confrontation in Indochina useful for rekindling revolutionary fervor within China and mobilizing domestic support for the Great Cultural Revolution. Since the late 1950s, Mao had become increasingly apprehensive about the direction in which the Chinese revolution was heading. He feared that his life's work had created a political system that would eventually betray his visions and principles, becoming as unjust and exploitative as the one it had replaced. He worried that China's development would succumb to a degeneration similar to that of the Soviet political system and that former U.S. secretary of state John Foster Dulles's strategy would prevail. Mao believed that Dulles's plan to promote "peaceful evolution" within the socialist world was taking effect in the Soviet Union, given Khrushchev's fascination with peaceful coexistence with the West. Mao wanted to prevent that from happening in China.[25]

The problem of succession also preoccupied Mao throughout the first half of the 1960s. His acute awareness of impending death contributed to his sense of urgency. He perceived the emergence of a new ruling elite in China, which, through its centralized control of the economic system, provided little scope for popular participation in the process of development. Mao resented the economic adjustment policy pursued by Liu Shaoqi and Deng Xiaoping in the wake of the Great Leap Forward, viewing them as "taking the capitalist road." While learning from the Great Leap that mass mobilization would not necessarily produce rapid economic growth, Mao retained his faith in popular participation as a tool of ideological renewal, social transformation, and rectification.[26]

The U.S. escalation of the war in Vietnam made Mao all the more eager to put his own house in order. He believed he must stop what he perceived as revisionist tendencies and choose a proper successor. Otherwise, after his death, China would fall into the hands of Soviet-like revisionists who would "change the color" of China, abandon support for national liberation struggles, and appease U.S. imperialism. Mao believed in dialectics. Negative situations could be turned into positive conclusions. The American presence in Indochina threatened the Chinese revolution. Nevertheless, Mao believed that the U.S. threat could become an advantage if he could use it to intensify domestic anti-imperialist feelings and mobilize the population against the revisionists. Mao had successfully employed that strategy against Chiang Kai-shek. Now he hoped to apply it again to prepare the masses for the Great Cultural Revolution. Accordingly, in the wake of the Gulf of Tonkin incident, Mao unleashed a massive "Aid Vietnam and Resist America" campaign across China.[27] By branding American and Soviet peace proposals as a "hoax" and "collusion" and by emphasizing the danger of compromise, Mao reminded the Chinese people that they should not slacken in the class struggle and that the Cultural Revolution was necessary to prevent China from turning revisionist.

Contrary to Mao's wishes, his radical foreign policy undermined rather than enhanced Beijing's position in international affairs. In fact, the period 1965–68 witnessed a general setback in Chinese foreign relations, including relations with France.[28] Mao's policy of encouraging revolution and insurgency in the third world and promoting the Chinese revolutionary model alienated de Gaulle, who was afraid of losing French influence in French-speaking countries in Africa. He urged those countries to strengthen their defenses and coordinate their political and economic development in order to resist the infiltration of Chinese ideology. He asked them not to attend the "second Bandung" Afro-Asian conference in Algiers, which was being actively promoted by China, and not to establish diplomatic relations with Beijing. The French media warned African capitals of the threat of the "yellow peril" and "red dragon" coming from China. The French embassies in Africa sought to limit the influence of visiting Chinese delegations. For instance, they tried to control the number of people going to Chinese dance and acrobatic performances by either limiting the issuance of tickets or announcing wrong dates for the Chinese shows. In April, 1965, a Chinese National People's Congress delegation led by Liu Ningyi visited the Central African Republic. The French embassy in Bangui delivered a note to the Foreign Ministry of the Central African Republic, accusing Liu Ningyi of making a speech that poisoned the friendly atmosphere of the entire diplomatic mission in Bangui.[29] Between 1965 and 1968, six African countries either broke or froze relations with the PRC, and seven expelled New China News Agency correspondents from their soil.[30]

In the meantime, the French government employed a number of measures to downgrade bilateral relations with China: it sent only low-level officials to attend National Day receptions hosted by the Chinese embassy; it increased restrictions on the activities of overseas Chinese in France; it prevented French companies from exporting nickel to China; and it allowed representatives from Taiwan to celebrate the National Day of the Republic of China in Paris. By 1967, official visits between China and France had been halted and mutual charges and protests became the order of the day.[31]

Chinese leaders had hoped that establishing diplomatic relations with France in 1964 would set an example for other Western European countries to recognize the PRC, but it proved to be a false dawn for Beijing. Mao's unavailing search for an anti-American and anti-Soviet united front on Vietnam, the turmoil of the Cultural Revolution, and Washington's pressure against recognition combined to prevent further breakthroughs in China's relations with Western Europe.[32]

Conclusion

To break what he called the "stifling rigidity" of the bipolar confrontation, de Gaulle attempted to bring peace to Indochina. He sought to include China in a new international conference on Vietnam, but Mao turned a deaf ear to his proposals. In fact, from 1964–68, Beijing consistently opposed international efforts to achieve a peaceful settlement of the Vietnam conflict. It did its utmost to sabotage the peace process and to force the DRV to adhere to China's policy. Mao's preoccupation with so-called Soviet revisionism often led him to ignore the interests, priorities, and needs of the Vietnamese communists. His advice to the DRV not to rely on Soviet aid and his disapproval of Hanoi's approach of fighting while talking showed this tendency. Mao's confrontational policy caused not only a setback in Sino-French relations, but also China's further isolation in the world.

Scholars have debated whether de Gaulle's neutralization proposal represented a "lost opportunity" for peace in Vietnam. In retrospect, too many obstacles stood in the way of achieving a permanent peace in Vietnam on the basis of a neutralization scheme. First, Washington opposed de Gaulle's suggestion. Key officials in both the Kennedy and Johnson administrations—including McGeorge Bundy, Walt Rostow, and Robert McNamara—rejected the neutralization of South Vietnam for fear that it might undermine American credibility in Asia. Second, given the past record of distrust and hostility between Ngo Dinh Diem's regime and Hanoi and the conflicting goals of each, it was unlikely that a political settlement could be reached in the fall of 1963. The junta that assumed power after the anti-Diem coup offered a better hope because its members were more noncommunist than anticommunist. They favored a neutral South that would incline toward the West. Although it was possible that they might conclude a temporary settlement with Hanoi, given the WPV's determination to achieve eventual reunification and its commitment to a socialist transformation of Vietnam, it was doubtful it would accept a permanent peaceful coexistence with a neutral South.

Finally, China's intransigence needs to be considered. In the early stages of the American escalation of the war, especially 1964–65, Hanoi leaders still relied heavily on Beijing's assistance and could not afford to alienate the Chinese. During this period, Mao was more interested in fostering revolution in Southeast Asia than in reducing tensions. He was also more inclined to encourage continued fighting in Vietnam than to promote a negotiated settlement. While little Vietnamese evidence is available on Hanoi's response to Chinese policy, third-party observations are plentiful. For instance, both American and British officials believed that Beijing's opposition was a major reason Hanoi did not respond positively to international peace initiatives in 1965. An intelligence estimate prepared on July 23, 1965, by U.S. analysts said that if "the Viet Cong and the DRV at some point wished to move toward negotiations, an important divergence might open up between Hanoi and Peiping. The Chinese are themselves not suffering direct military damage and they fear that negotiations would give the USSR a chance to increase its role in Vietnam. Thus they would exert strong pressures to dissuade the DRV from entering into negotiations."[33] Commenting on Hanoi's reaction to the Commonwealth Peace Mission in July, 1965, Myles Ponsonby, the British consul general in Hanoi, observed that "the North Vietnamese are prisoners of their own propaganda and are fearful of any move that would upset the Chinese."[34] Given North Vietnam's reliance on China's aid and given these third-party observations, it is plausible to argue that Beijing strongly influenced Hanoi's approach to negotiations in 1964–65.

Notes

1. Marilyn B. Young, *The Vietnam Wars, 1945–1990* (New York: HarperPerennial, 1991), p. 107; Charles G. Cogan, *Charles de Gaulle: A Brief Biography with Documents* (Boston: Bedford Books, 1996), pp. 149–50; Fredrik Logevall, *Choosing War: The Lost Chance for Peace and the Escalation of War in Vietnam* (Berkeley: University of California Press, 1999).

2. Pei Jianzhang, chief ed., *Zhonghua renmin gongheguo waijiaoshi, 1949–1956* (Diplomatic of History of the People's Republic of China, 1949–1956) (Beijing: Shijie zhishi chubanshe,

1994), pp. 316–18; Xie Li, "Jianlun Zhou Enlai dui Ouzhou zibenzhuyi didai de waijiao zhan-lue sixiang" (A Brief Analysis of Zhou Enlai's Diplomatic Strategic Thought Concerning the Capitalist Zone in Europe) in *Yanjiu Zhou Enlai: Waijiao sixiang yu shijian* (Studies on Zhou Enlai: Diplomatic Thought and Practice), ed. Diplomatic History Research Office of the PRC Foreign Ministry (Beijing: Shijie zhishi chubanshe, 1989), pp. 239–45.

3. The CCP Central Documentary Research Department, ed., *Zhou Enlai nianpu, 1949–1976* (A Chronicle of Zhou Enlai's Life, 1949–1976), 3 vols. (Beijing: Zhongyang wenxian chubanshe, 1997), p. 2:568. See also Lowell Dittmer, *Sino-Soviet Normalization and Its International Implications, 1945–1990* (Seattle: University of Washington Press, 1992), p. 186; Andrew J. Nathan and Robert S. Ross, *The Great Wall and the Empty Fortress: China's Search for Security* (New York: W. W. Norton, 1997), p. 43.

4. Xie Yixian, ed., *Zhongguo waijiao shi: Zhonghua renmin gongheguo shiqi, 1949–1979* (A Diplomatic History of China: The Period of the People's Republic of China, 1949–1979) (Zhengzhou: Henan renmin chubanshe, 1988), pp. 313–14.

5. Intelligence memorandum, "French Involvement in Vietnam," June 17, 1966, National Security File, Country File: Vietnam, Box 51, "Southeast Asia, Special Intelligence Material, Vol. X(B) 6/66–2/67" Folder, Lyndon B. Johnson Library, Austin, Tex. See also W. W. Kulski, *De Gaulle and the World: The Foreign Policy of the Fifth French Republic* (Syracuse: Syracuse University Press, 1966), p. 317.

6. Cogan, *Charles de Gaulle*, pp. 148–49; George C. Herring, *America's Longest War: The United States and Vietnam, 1950–1975,* 3d ed. (New York: McGraw-Hill, 1996), p. 112; Logevall, *Choosing War*, pp. 1–3; David Kaiser, *American Tragedy: Kennedy, Johnson, and the Origins of the Vietnam War* (Cambridge: Harvard University Press, 2000), p. 241.

7. Tong Xiaopeng, *Fengyu sishinian* (Forty Years of Winds and Rains), 2 vols. (Beijing: Zhongyang wenxian chubanshe, 1994–96), pp. 2:220–21. Tong Xiaopeng was a longtime associate of Zhou Enlai. He participated in the Conghua meeting.

8. Wang Taiping, chief ed., *Zhonghua renmin gongheguo waijiaoshi, dierjuan, 1957–1969* (Diplomatic of History of the People's Republic of China, vol. 2, 1957–1969) (Beijing: Shijie zhishi chubanshe, 1998), pp. 373, 375.

9. Ibid., p. 381; Logevall, *Choosing War*, p. 103. On Washington's reaction to de Gaulle's proposal, see Young, *Vietnam Wars*, p. 107; Logevall, *Choosing War*, pp. 104–106; Frank Costigliola, "The Vietnam War and the Challenges to American Power in Europe," in *International Perspectives on Vietnam*, ed. Lloyd C. Gardner and Ted Gittinger (College Station: Texas A&M University Press, 2000), pp. 143–53.

10. Wang Taiping, chief ed., *Zhonghua renmin*, p. 2:381.

11. For details, see Qiang Zhai, *China and the Vietnam Wars, 1950–1975* (Chapel Hill: University of North Carolina Press, 2000), chap. 5.

12. Chinese Foreign Ministry circular, "Malraux's Visit to China," Aug. 12, 1965, Q 3124, J 123, Jiangsu Provincial Archives, Nanjing. After his return from Asia, Malraux reported that the Chinese did not favor negotiations unless the United States began withdrawing from Vietnam. See Marianna P. Sullivan, *France's Vietnam Policy: A Study in French-American Relations* (Westport, Conn.: Greenwood Press, 1978), p. 101.

For Malraux's account of his visit to China in 1965, see André Malraux, *Anti-memoirs,* (New York: Harcourt Brace, 1968), pp. 325–80. However, the book makes no mention of Malraux's suggestion of redividing Vietnam. In the words of French scholar Jean Lacouture, Malraux's proposal was "the most wildly improbable idea that ever emerged from the brain of a novelist." See Lacouture, *André Malraux,* (New York: Random House, 1975), p. 431.

13. Zhou Enlai's talk with Jean Chauvel, Nov. 30, 1965, in Zhou Enlai nianpu, ed. CCP . . . Department, p. 2:768. Following his Beijing tour, Chauvel visited Hanoi, Phnom Penh, and

Vientiane. After returning to France, a pessimistic Chauvel wrote in *Le Figaro* on January 3, 1966, that negotiations would only be possible "when the Americans will have admitted the futility of the operation they are pursuing. They cannot win this war. No matter how far they push it in the future, they will lose it" (as quoted in Sullivan, *France's Vietnam Policy,* p. 101).

14. Wang Taiping, chief ed., *Zhonghua renmin,* pp. 2:381–82; Sullivan, *France's Vietnam Policy,* pp. 89–91, 99, 101–102; Cogan, *Charles de Gaulle,* p. 148; Jean Lacouture, *De Gaulle: The Ruler, 1945–1970* (London: Harvill, 1991), pp. 403–405. It is interesting to note that when Zhou Enlai urged President Nixon to withdraw from Vietnam in 1972, he also used the Algerian analogy. See the Diplomatic History Research Office of the PRC Foreign Ministry, ed., *Yanjiu Zhou Enlai: Waijiao sixiang yu shijian* (Studies on Zhou Enlai: Diplomatic Thought and Practice) (Beijing: Shijie zhishi chubanshe, 1989), 207; Wang Taiping, chief ed., *Zhonghua renmin gongheguo waijiaoshi, disanjuan, 1970–1978* (Diplomatic of History of the People's Republic of China, vol. 3, 1970–1978) (Beijing: Shijie zhishi chubanshe, 1999), p. 364. See also James Mann, *About Face: A History of America's Curious Relationship with China, from Nixon to Clinton* (New York: Alfred A. Knopf, 1999), p. 45.

15. Wang Taiping, chief ed., *Zhonghua renmin,* p. 2:382.

16. Intelligence memorandum, June 17, 1966; U.S. embassy in France to State Department, July 21, 1966, *Foreign Relations of the United States* (*FRUS*), *1964–1968,* vol. 4, *Vietnam, 1966* (Washington D.C.: GPO, 1998), pp. 508–10.

17. Sergei N. Khrushchev, *Nikita Khrushchev and the Creation of a Superpower* (University Park, Pa.: Penn State University Press, 2000), pp. 695, 716.

18. Ilya Gaiduk, *The Soviet Union and the Vietnam War* (Chicago: Ivan R. Dee, 1996), pp. 77–78; Caroline Kennedy-Pipe, *Russia and the World, 1917–1991* (London: Arnold, 1998), pp. 128–32.

19. Sullivan, *France's Vietnam Policy,* p. 108. On Soviet views of Paris as an ideal venue for negotiations between the United States and North Vietnam, see Gaiduk, *Soviet Union,* pp. 152–53.

20. Gaiduk, *Soviet Union,* p. 154.

21. Zhou Enlai's talks with Pham Van Dong, Apr. 13, 19, 1968, in Odd Arne Westad et al., eds., *77 Conversations between Chinese and Foreign Leaders on the Wars in Indochina, 1964–1977,* Cold War International History Project Working Paper no. 22 (Washington, D.C.: the Woodrow Wilson Center, 1998), pp. 123–29.

22. On the role of the third world in Mao's foreign policy, see Peter Van Ness, "China and the Third World: Patterns of Engagement and Indifference," in *China and the World: Chinese Foreign Policy Faces the New Millennium,* ed. Samuel S. Kim, 4th ed. (Boulder: Westview Press, 1998), pp. 151–168.

23. Zhou Enlai's conversation with Julius Nyerere, June 4, 1965, in *Zhou Enlai waijiao huodong dashiji, 1949–1975* (A Chronicle of Zhou Enlai's Diplomatic Activities, 1949–1975), ed. Diplomatic History Research Office of the PRC Foreign Ministry (Beijing: Shijie zhishi chubanshe, 1993), p. 460.

24. For the English version of the commentary, see *Peking Review,* Feb. 18, 1966, pp. 6–12.

25. On Mao's response to Dulles's policy, see Bo Yibo, *Ruogan zhongda juece yu shijian de huigu* (Recollections of Certain Important Decisions and Events), 2 vols. (Beijing: Zhonggong zhongyang dangxiao chubanshe, 1991–93), pp. 2:1137–57.

26. Kenneth Lieberthal, "The Great Leap Forward and the Split in the Yan'an Leadership, 1958–65," in *The Politics of China, 1949–1989,* ed. Roderick MacFarquhar (Cambridge, UK: Cambridge University Press, 1993), p. 143.

27. Xie Yixian, ed., *Zhongguo waijiao shi,* p. 692.

28. On the failure of China's foreign policy in the mid-1960s, see Thomas Robinson, "China Confronts the Soviet Union: Warfare and Diplomacy on China's Inner Asian Frontiers," in *The Cambridge History of China,* vol. 15, *The People's Republic,* pt. 2, *Revolutions within the Chinese Revolution, 1966–1982,* ed. Roderick MacFarquhar and John K. Fairbank (Cambridge, UK: Cambridge University Press, 1991), pp. 218–36. On the effects of the Cultural Revolution on China's international relations, see Barbara Barnouin and Yu Changgen, *Chinese Foreign Policy during the Cultural Revolution* (London: Kegan Paul International, 1998).

29. Wang Taiping, chief ed., *Zhonghua renmin,* p. 2:382.

30. Burundi, Dahomey, the Central African Republic, and Ghana broke off diplomatic relations. Tunisia closed its embassy in Beijing until 1971; Kenya did likewise until 1978. See Xie Yixian, ed., *Zhongguo waijiao shi,* pp. 385–87; Philip Snow, "China and Africa: Consensus and Camouflage," in *Chinese Foreign Policy: Theory and Practice,* ed. Thomas W. Robinson and David Shambaugh (Oxford, UK: Clarendon Press, 1994), pp. 306–307; Rosemary Foot, *The Practice of Power: US Relations with China since 1949* (Oxford, UK: Clarendon Press, 1995), p. 213.

31. Wang Taiping, chief ed. *Zhonghua renmin,* pp. 2:383–84.

32. Michael B. Yahuda, "China and Europe: The Significance of a Secondary Relationship," in *Chinese Foreign Policy,* ed. Robinson and Shambaugh, p. 268.

33. Special National Intelligence Estimate, July 23, 1965, in *FRUS, 1964–1968,* vol. 3, *Vietnam, June–December, 1965* (Washington, D.C.: GPO, 1996), p. 229.

34. As quoted in Simon Kear, "The British Consulate-General in Hanoi, 1954–73," *Diplomacy & Statecraft* 10 (Mar., 1999): p. 229. Reflecting on his failed attempt to bring about direct talks between the DRV and the United States during 1964–65, Secretary General U Thant wrote in his memoirs that the fear of Beijing's obstruction was the primary reason for his use of Moscow as a channel of communication with Hanoi. See U Thant, *View from the UN* (Garden City, N.Y.: Doubleday, 1978), p. 63.

"A Half-Hearted Overture"

Czechoslovakia, Kissinger, and Vietnam, Autumn, 1966

James G. Hershberg

On September 6, 1966, as the Vietnam War escalated with no movement toward negotiations from either side, the Communist Party of Czechoslovakia Central Committee (CPCz CC) Politburo adopted a resolution approving a plan for a delegation of party and state leaders to visit Hanoi later that month.[1] That action set in motion a short-lived, unsuccessful, and perhaps "half-hearted," yet illuminating, initiative to try to persuade North Vietnam's leaders to engage in peace talks with the United States, or at least add a political-diplomatic track to accompany the military struggle, perhaps using Prague as a mediator to communicate with Washington. The Czechs closely coordinated their actions with their Soviet comrades and also encountered the Chinese—at a time when Moscow and Beijing, already at odds ideologically, differed sharply over the advisability of negotiations.

To apprise American officials of their intentions and probe their reactions, the Czech leadership chose an unusual channel: Henry A. Kissinger, then a professor of government at Harvard University. Reconstructed from declassified materials in both U.S. and Czech archives, the story of this previously unknown initiative sheds light on several interrelated issues at this juncture of the war. These include the diplomatic and political postures of the Soviet Union and its East-Central European allies, Hanoi's position and the perceived influence of the Sino-Soviet rivalry on the Democratic Republic of Vietnam's (DRV) leaders, and—not least, given his later prominence—what was evidently Kissinger's first venture into Vietnam peace-making, an unreported prequel to his involvement in the well-known PENNSYLVANIA initiative the following summer.[2]

In the story of diplomatic attempts to get peace negotiations started between Washington and Hanoi prior to the opening of the Paris peace talks (or "talks about talks") in the spring of 1968, the East-Central European countries occupy a prominent, though still mysterious, position. During the Catch-22 period that followed the start of American bombing raids on North Vietnam in early 1965—with Washington refusing to stop the raids unless assured that fruitful negotiations would commence promptly and

Hanoi insisting that an unconditional halt must precede any direct discussions—U.S. officials frequently saw the East-Central Europeans as potentially important channels through which to probe Hanoi's position, ascertain the impact of U.S. military actions and the Sino-Soviet quarrel on North Vietnam's leaders, and, above all, communicate indirectly with the enemy with a view toward arranging the opening of peace talks and even to sound out terms for ending the war. While myriad would-be peacemakers trooped to and from Hanoi bearing messages and impressions, including Western, Eastern, and neutral government officials, journalists, activists, and private citizens, at least some U.S. officials viewed the East-Central European nations, all Warsaw Pact members, as the most plausible candidates to influence Hanoi or at least accurately appraise the situation there. They did so for several reasons. One, of course, was access—as members of the communist world (and what many still called, with dubious accuracy, the "Sino-Soviet bloc"), they maintained diplomatic as well as interparty ties with the government of the DRV and the Lao Dong (Workers' Party of Vietnam [WPV]) leadership. Second, as Soviet allies, they presumably followed Moscow's position in favoring a political resolution to the war—albeit on Hanoi's terms, if possible—in order to minimize Chinese influence in Southeast Asia and to return Soviet-American relations to an even keel, particularly in Europe (presaging the open move toward détente that would emerge soon afterward). At the same time, they were believed to possess somewhat more freedom to maneuver than Moscow itself, given the Kremlin's reluctance to pressure Hanoi and thus seem to vindicate Chinese charges of "revisionism" and accommodation toward the West. Finally, some U.S. officials gave credence to the possibility that East-Central European agendas diverged from Moscow's, despite their overarching fealty to the Soviet Union, in a fashion that motivated them to promote an end to the war in order to contain Cold War tensions in Europe.

Yet, in virtually every case, senior U.S. officials—above all Pres. Lyndon B. Johnson and Secretary of State Dean Rusk—viewed these East-Central European efforts with considerable skepticism and sometimes distrust, sentiments that often, though not always, intensified when these initiatives invariably ended in failure.[3] In sometimes bitter retrospective accounts, they insinuate or charge outright that these efforts sought less to achieve peace than to string Washington along in order to extend bombing halts and thereby help Hanoi attain military advantages. Moreover, Washington sensed Soviet puppeteers lurking behind the actions of Poland, Czechoslovakia, Hungary, and other East-Central European countries—at a minimum approving and coordinating, and perhaps instigating or controlling the initiatives—yet remained uncertain or divided as to whether the Kremlin truly desired to end the war, and to achieve that end was prepared to rein in Hanoi's ambitions to take over South Vietnam, or, to the contrary, relished Washington's predicament and desired to extend its entanglement in Southeast Asia. To many U.S. officials and Vietnam historians, the true nature, aims, and consequences of Soviet and Soviet-bloc peace-probe diplomacy remain a puzzle.

This chapter stems from an inquiry to reassess several of these initiatives and address some residual mysteries, on the basis of declassified Western archives as well as some early and fragmentary research in the Central and Eastern European archives (plus the hope of eventual hard Vietnamese evidence, which has thus far proved elusive). To the extent that there exists a historiographical literature in this area,[4] it has dealt largely with a few well-known episodes on which East-bloc evidence is now beginning to emerge: (1) Hungarian and Polish activities during the thirty-seven-day bombing "pause" in December, 1965, and January, 1966;[5] (2) Operation MARIGOLD (also known as the Lewandowski Affair) in late 1966, in which Poland attempted to broker the opening of U.S.-DRV contacts;[6] and (3) the PACKERS initiative, involving Romania, in late 1967 and early 1968. To these may now be added, at least as a footnote, what seems to have been Czechoslovakia's one flirtation with Vietnam peacemaking. Of course, a rigorous and comprehensive analysis of Soviet-bloc East-Central European involvement in Vietnam diplomacy naturally requires a focus on the Soviet Union itself. (In October, 1966, when Dean Rusk asked Andrei Gromyko which Eastern European country "had the most reliable contacts" with Hanoi, the Soviet emphatically replied, "Moscow!"[7]) Russian scholar Ilya Gaiduk has made considerable progress in discerning the Kremlin's behavior, but shrinking archival access in Moscow has hampered his efforts.[8] Finally, if one is to really assess East-Central European dealings with the "Vietnamese comrades," as well as evaluate why these initiatives went awry, one requires much harder evidence than is now available from Hanoi's perspective.[9]

Before plunging into these events, I should stress again the *extremely* preliminary and unsystematic nature of the inquiries that have taken place to date in the East-Central European archives regarding Vietnam and, for that matter, the Cold War in Asia. Colleagues in Prague (in particular Oldrich Tuma), working with the cooperation of the Cold War International History Project, located the Czech documents at my request. They managed to obtain a few hundred pages of documents, of which only a handful have thus far been translated. While obviously no substitute for the serious research that needs to be undertaken in these archives by scholars fluent in Czech and conversant with Prague's foreign and domestic policies, it is a start.

The first inkling that the Czechs were up to something came in mid-September, 1966, at the Sixteenth Pugwash Conference, an international gathering of scientists and intellectuals held that year at the Polish seaside resort of Sopot, located just northwest of the port of Gdansk on the Baltic coast. Since the first such meeting in Pugwash, Nova Scotia, in 1957, the periodic conferences had facilitated informal East-West contacts aimed at achieving diplomatic progress, most notably the discussions of Soviet and U.S. physicists seeking to promote the causes of nuclear disarmament and, more pragmatically, a nuclear test-ban treaty.[10] Sopot proved no exception. Despite nominally being devoted to "Disarmament and World Security, Especially in Europe," the conference could not escape the shadow of the escalating Vietnam War, which was the subject both of formal debates and resolutions and of corridor and cocktail-party conversations. Notwithstanding Pugwash's nominally unofficial status, the communist delegates were presumed to represent their party-states. Henry Kissinger, a member of the American delegation, had been a State Department consultant during both the Kennedy and Johnson administrations. A specialist on European history who had first risen to public prominence for his criticism of "massive retaliation" and advocacy of limited nuclear war (in *Nuclear Weapons and Foreign Policy*, published in 1957), Kissinger, the director of Harvard's defense studies program, had advised the Kennedy administration on Berlin but had recently begun to turn his attention to Vietnam. He first visited the region in October, 1965, touring South Vietnam at the invitation of the U.S. ambassador, Henry Cabot Lodge.[11] Evidently he made a good impression. That fall, Lodge advised Washington to dispatch Kissinger to meet privately with congressional critics like Democratic senators Mike Mansfield and William J. Fulbright. Describing him as "extraordinarily well informed and persuasive" on the problems of negotiating with communists as a result of his Berlin experience, Lodge observed that Kissinger "would not be suitable for television but he is very persuasive in private with intelligent, well-informed men."[12] In July, 1966, Kissinger had returned to South Vietnam for a fortnight, following which he reported his impressions to the Johnson administration through Lodge and Harriman.[13]

Kissinger had become a familiar face at Pugwash, having attended four sessions during the previous five years, including the 1964 gathering in Karlovy Vary, Czechoslovakia.[14] While en route to Poland in September, 1966, he stopped in Paris for another bit of "personal" (but precleared in Washington) diplomacy related to Vietnam: a conversation with his old friend Jean Sainteny in line with his urging the State Department to employ the former French Indochina high commissioner as an intermediary with Hanoi. Sainteny, after recent talks with Ho Chi Minh and Pham Van Dong, had reported that the North Vietnamese leaders recognized they would have to pay an "important price" for a U.S. bombing halt, but that a trusted intermediary, possibly an East-European country, was needed to speak to Hanoi.[15] At Sopot, Kissinger told the State Department afterward, he was "the member of the U.S. delegation most active in attempting to thwart the attempts of the Soviet delegation to obtain an all-out condemnation of the United States."[16] His Pugwash presence had already entered the annals of secret Vietnam diplomacy, for it was at Sopot that Kissinger first encountered Herbert Marcovich, the French doctor with whom he would work (along with Marcovich's friend, Raymond Aubrac, an acquaintance of Ho Chi Minh) on the PENNSYLVANIA initiative the following summer.[17] Kissinger also had a series of intriguing conversations on Vietnam with East-bloc representatives at Sopot.[18] The Pugwash plenary debates on Vietnam, he reported, which began on September 13, featured lengthy, "intransigent," "intemperate, highly emotional . . . harangues" against the United States by the Soviets, "supported with much less intensity by the East Europeans." Outside the formal sessions, however, Kissinger found some Soviet delegates far more forthcoming. During a pre-conference cruise in Gdansk harbor, one struck a note that would be frequently, but only privately, repeated by Soviet representatives: China, not the United States, constituted the primary threat to peace. The month before, Mao Zedong had launched his "Great Proletarian Cultural Revolution," with millions of Red Guards rallying in Tiananmen Square and rampaging through various cities. Describing China as "no longer Communist but Fascist," Academician V. S. Emelyanov emphatically endorsed Kissinger's analysis that only Beijing profited from U.S.-Soviet tension over Vietnam. Adopting a moderate tone that sharply contrasted with his anti-American rhetoric in open sessions, Emelyanov asked for patience toward Moscow's hesitancy in urging Hanoi to make peace. The Kremlin, he explained, remained divided because "Stalinists" in the government hoped to exploit the Vietnam conflict "to make a comeback." On September 14, senior Soviet observer V. V. Shustov invited Kissinger for an after-dinner chat and "drew me into a lengthy discussion of Vietnam and the possibilities of a negotiated settlement." Privately, Soviet delegates assured Kissinger that his comments "would be fully reported in Moscow, whatever their actions in open sessions," and that the USSR remained eager to work with Washington on a nuclear nonproliferation treaty. Kissinger also reported that the Soviet delegate he knew best, Gen. N. A. Talensky, not only remained "aloof" from the group's general vilification of the United States during open sessions, but personally stressed to him—in terms reminiscent of those used by U.S. strategists when justifying military intervention in Vietnam in the first place—that China was "the real menace" and the "real problem was to keep Southeast Asia out of Chinese hands."[19]

The conference remained deadlocked on the war, but Soviet-bloc delegates continued to drop hints that they might be helpful in dealing with Hanoi. "Hanoi wants peace," Dobrosielski, a Polish delegate and a former counselor at Warsaw's embassy in Washington, then serving as a member of the Foreign Ministry's policy planning staff, assured Kissinger during a luncheon given by the U.S. ambassador. If Washington gradually reduced and then stopped bombing North Vietnam "without any announcement over a period of two weeks," the Pole hinted, Hanoi would "reciprocate" and halt its infiltration of the South, thus satisfying Washington's key demand. Kissinger reported that Dobrosielski was "evasive" when asked whether he based his prediction on "knowledge or conjecture." Rather than give a firm answer, Dobrosielski (indicating that he belonged to a Foreign Ministry minority favoring Polish mediation despite the negative experience during the "pause") urged that the United States "find out for itself not through official channels but perhaps through private channels."[20]

The most intriguing signals, however, came from Prague's delegates. In the plenary session, Kissinger observed, the Czech position "was so briefly stated and so formal as to amount to a dissociation" from the angry Soviet polemics.[21] The next day, Theodor Nemec, the Czech delegation's secretary, proposed sending a team of "neutral scientists" on a fact-finding mission to Saigon and Hanoi, and impressed Kissinger—who had insisted that the Americans would support the proposal only if it "did not load the dice" against the United States—by keeping "his side of the bargain loyally throughout," including pro- as well as anti-American arguments in the proposed resolution.[22] In fact, Kissinger related, Nemec had agreed during private drafting sessions to a proposal so "weak" as to be unacceptable to the Soviets.[23] In the end, the group adopted a resolution stating simply that, despite "extensive and frank" discussions, it could agree "neither on the causes of the war in Vietnam nor on the means to deal with it."[24]

The notion of a Prague peace initiative was broached to Kissinger by another member of the delegation, Academician Ivan Malek, identified as a CPCz CC member as well as head of the Czech Institute of Biology. Inviting Kissinger to lunch on the fifteenth, Malek stated frankly that his government "desperately wanted the war in Vietnam to end because it could only retard relaxation of tensions in Europe—a major Czech objective." Wanting no part of so distant a conflict, yet compelled to go along out of ideological solidarity (and Soviet-bloc loyalty), he explained, Prague had been "brutally rebuffed" by Hanoi the previous February when it had advocated negotiations. However, he added, Czech leaders might be willing to "undertake another try" if assured that Washington "sincerely wanted peace." After Kissinger (with the usual disclaimer that he lacked official authority) gave the obvious reply—yes, so long as the terms were honorable—Malek, without indicating whether he was under instructions, said that he personally favored another such a "peace effort" and promised to try to arrange meetings for Kissinger with senior Czech officials when the Harvard professor and two other members of the U.S. Pugwash delegation visited Prague the following week for discussions on European questions under the auspices of the Czech Institute for World Politics.[25]

When Kissinger (accompanied by Harvard's Paul Doty and Columbia's Marshall Shulman) flew into Prague on September 19, he found Antonín Snejdárek, director of the Czech Institute of International Affairs, waiting to greet him at the airport. After their first meeting at the 1964 Pugwash Conference (Snejdárek also attended the Sopot conference), Kissinger had reported him to be "fair and reasonable." Kissinger subsequently learned from Central Intelligence Agency (CIA) reports that Snejdárek had been the head of Czech intelligence operations in Germany in the early 1950s after leading a military mission there in the late 1940s, and currently belonged to the Czech Council of Ministers' foreign policy "collegium" as well as the CPCz CC. Snejdárek sought Kissinger out after dinner that evening and informed him that a high-level Czech delegation that included the prime minister (Josef Lenárt), the CPCz CC secretary (Vladimir Koucký), and several deputy prime ministers would leave for Hanoi the next afternoon, stopping in Moscow en route. Koucký, he explained, had authorized him to contact Kissinger as an intermediary so the delegation would be able to tell the North Vietnamese that they "had had no contact with [official] Americans." Kissinger reported that Snejdárek had advised him the delegation would carry to Hanoi several "partially conflicting objectives," including to respond to Soviet and North Vietnamese pressures for increased aid, to "strengthen the Western presence in Hanoi against Communist China," and, most intriguingly, to "press as hard as possible for a peaceful solution." This last aim, Kissinger continued, accounted for the delegation's rank (which bilateral aid talks alone would not require). "Only conversations at the highest level, could, in the Czech judgment, move the Hanoi government towards negotiations."[26]

Nevertheless, Snejdárek confessed, Czech leaders were hardly optimistic about the delegation's prospects in view of the tough stands taken by both Moscow and Hanoi. His candid reflections about the Kremlin's uneasiness are worth noting as they foreshadow the full-blown crisis that would erupt little more than a year later when the "Prague Spring" movement emerged among reformist Czech communists after the retirement of CPCz first secretary Antonín Novotný and his replacement by Alexander Dubcek.

> With respect to the Soviet Union, Snejdarek said that Czechoslovakia could go only so far in risking Soviet displeasure over Vietnam. During the [July, 1966] Warsaw pact meetings in Bucharest, Czechoslovakia had got into difficulties with the USSR by urging restraint over Vietnam. The Czech delegation was stopping in Moscow both coming and going from Hanoi. Anything he told me was subject to a Soviet veto for Czechoslovakia could not risk losing Soviet support in Central Europe over Vietnam. The Czechs were not at all sure that that the Soviets wanted a settlement of the Vietnam war. A relaxation of tensions might bring about a loosening of Soviet control in Central Europe which made the Soviets most uneasy.

To explain Hanoi's hard line, Snejdárek echoed Soviet analyses that cited an ascendant Chinese influence on (and pro-Beijing faction in) the North Vietnamese leadership, at least since the summer of 1966, with Beijing opposing any course other than a military struggle until victory had been achieved. Anticipating resistance to their arguments, he noted, the Czechs had deliberately included in the delegation "many individuals who were personally acquainted with second level Vietnamese leaders who had studied in Prague," and given them "orders to urge the desirability of peace on their Vietnamese contacts."

Snejdárek then said he had been instructed to ask Kissinger three questions and report the answers back to Koucký in the morning: First, was the U.S. "sincere in seeking peace or were the peace offers a smokescreen for continued escalation?" Second, what role, if any, did Washington see for an intermediary? Third, "what were the actual American terms" for ending the war?

Kissinger, after repeating his customary disclaimer that he spoke officially but did not shy away from giving "private impressions," insisted that U.S. officials were "undoubtedly sincere" in seeking peace. However, he stressed that the Czech delegation should take with a grain of salt Hanoi's military claims since the situation was, in fact, "favorable to the United States and improving." Still, he saw a "definite use" for an intermediary, as Hanoi remained "so isolated and so subject to Chinese pressure that the advice of a well-disposed government could be invaluable." As for American terms, Kissinger outlined three "very complex" broad principles he presumed could form the basis for a settlement: an end to U.S. bombing (which would not happen until the North ceased infiltrating troops and supplies into the South), the mutual "withdrawal of troops introduced from outside South Vietnam," and—the point he acknowledged would be the toughest to resolve—an "evolution of political life in South Vietnam on the basis of self-determination." While supporting the emergence of a "broadly based democratic government" in Saigon, Washington remained firmly opposed to the third of Hanoi's "Four Points," which seemed to mandate a reorientation of South Vietnam's politics along the lines of the National Liberation Front's (NLF) program. Kissinger also speculated that the Johnson administration would consider the formation of a coalition government that included the NLF to be "out of the question"—a remark that prompted a reader of his memorandum (Harriman?) to underline it and write a question mark in the margin.

Snejdárek left at that point, but he approached Kissinger again the next morning. He explained that he had been instructed to ask three more questions and report the answers to Koucký immediately, before the delegation's 3 P.M. departure. First, how would a DRV agreement to stop infiltration in exchange for a bombing halt affect the U.S. buildup in South Vietnam? Second, what guarantees (besides a coalition government) could be given to the NLF that its members would not suffer "the fate of the Communist party in Indonesia" (where widespread massacres had taken place since Suharto took power in a military coup the previous fall)? Third, how could Prague best communicate to Washington the results of its soundings in Hanoi? Kissinger, again giving his personal interpretation of the U.S. position, speculated that "resupply and rotation of personnel" would continue in the first scenario, but that limitations on increases in troop numbers could be negotiated. In response to the second question, he confidently asserted that U.S. officials would be "very forthcoming" toward steps to safeguard NLF members. When, in response to the third question, Kissinger suggested simply contacting the U.S. ambassador in Prague, Snejdárek demurred. That would require involving the Foreign Ministry, he explained, whereas the initiative was primarily an affair of the CPCz CC, which eschewed formal contacts with U.S. officials and "wanted these conversations kept to the smallest possible number of people."[27] Snejdárek instead proposed that if there were "anything positive to report" he would wire Kissinger stating he "wished to discuss matters connected with the Central European study group." Kissinger said he would think about it and reply when they met in Vienna at the end of the month at the Institute of Strategic Studies (ISS) annual conference.

After disappearing for three-quarters of an hour (leaving the chairing of a session to a colleague), Snejdárek returned before lunch and, taking

Kissinger aside, told him "that, subject to a Soviet veto, the Central Committee would try to make additional help to Hanoi conditional on a greater flexibility by Hanoi on the issue of negotiations."[28] Because Prague was one of Hanoi's leading military suppliers after the Soviet Union and China, this sounded like a potentially significant step, especially after Novotný's dismissal just one month earlier of a U.S. plea to reduce military aid to North Vietnam.[29]

Kissinger returned to the United States following these discussions. On September 23, he telephoned Daniel I. Davidson, an aide to Assistant Secretary of State for Far Eastern Affairs William P. Bundy and a member of Ambassador Harriman's negotiations team, regarding his exchanges with Snejdàrek. After informing Davidson of the high-level Czech mission to Hanoi, Kissinger emphasized the CPCz CC's determination to "convince Hanoi it should begin negotiations" and the delegation's plans, unless Moscow disapproved, to condition further aid to North Vietnam on increased flexibility toward negotiations.[30] Four days later, Kissinger went to Washington to see Harriman and other State Department officials, present reports on his Sopot and Prague conversations, and seek further instructions. The officials authorized Kissinger to continue his talks with Snejdárek, convey Washington's positive view of the Czech efforts, and in particular assure Snejdárek that U.S. officials stood ready to "explore frankly and sympathetically" the issue of safety for NLF members, in the interests of "national reconciliation of all Vietnamese prepared to forego violence in pursuit of their objectives."[31] Ever ingratiating toward his political patrons, Kissinger implored Harriman to let him use the ambassador's name with the East Europeans because, as Harriman recorded, "he told me that people in Warsaw as well as in Czechoslovakia were very anxious to learn what I thought, because he said they trusted me and felt that if they had word from me it would be real."[32] Afterward, a mildly encouraged William Bundy expressed the belief that the approach "had a plausible ring," and surmised that Moscow had deputized Prague to "carry the ball with Hanoi"—much as it had done with Budapest during the thirty-seven-day bombing pause the previous winter. In his estimation, the Poles continued to be the "wild card in the deck."[33]

Meanwhile, Kissinger and other U.S. officials had no idea whether the Czech delegation to Hanoi had achieved any progress. A September 24 conversation in New York City between Rusk and Gromyko resulted in mixed signals as to whether Moscow might be willing to pressure Hanoi to be more forthcoming. Gromyko had discounted American protestations of a desire for peace in Vietnam by pointing to evidence of further military escalation. He emphasized the need for Washington to stop bombing North

Vietnam as being "a minimum of minimums"—but offered no indication of what Hanoi might do in response. America's actions, Gromyko told Rusk, "had severely limited the Soviet Union's possibilities and had deprived it of opportunities to take some positive steps; this was true not only of the Soviet Union, but of a number of other countries also."[34]

By "other countries" Gromyko may well have been alluding to Soviet allies in East-Central Europe such as Poland, Hungary, and Czechoslovakia, whose delegation had just reached Hanoi the previous day. En route, the Czech delegation had stopped in Moscow, Beijing, and finally Nanning. Only in Moscow, however, did the group have substantive talks, when the Czechs—Lenárt, Koucký, and Prague's envoy to Moscow, Oldrich Pavlovsky—met (probably on September 21) with senior Soviet Communist Party (CPSU) figures Dmitri Polyansky, Mikhail Suslov, and Nikolai Firyubin. According to a brief summary of the discussions in a secret "debriefing report" the delegation presented to the CPCz CC in early October, the Soviets gave a detailed report on Pham Van Dong's recent visit to Moscow, then explained the "suggestions they had put forth on this occasion, and their opinions on the current situation in Vietnam." Although the Czech report does not elaborate on what the Soviets said about these exchanges, the substance can be gathered from a summary of those talks CPSU CC officials gave the Hungarians a week earlier.[35] From that report, it appears that the secret high-level Soviet-DRV talks (only rumors of which reached the West[36]) in the first half of August and again on September 5 left the Soviets exasperated. In conversations with Leonid Brezhnev and Alexei Kosygin, Pham Van Dong, accompanied by fellow WPV Politburo member Vice-Premier Le Thanh Nghi, insisted that the war was going well in both North and South Vietnam and pledged to fight on "until total victory," which would be preceded by a "new Dien Bien Phu" against the Americans. The Soviets, whose data suggested that North Vietnam was suffering far more casualties and disruption than its leaders admitted, contradicted these glowing assessments. They viewed their visitors' military outlook as "unrealistic," seeing a "huge difference" between the French and Americans. On the political front, Pham Van Dong had told the Soviets that "for the very first time," Hanoi desired to solve "flexibly" the problem of achieving its goals (the DRV's Four Points and the NLF's Five Points) through talks. Soviet probing, however, had produced the impression that this statement lacked any "real practical background," and "it remained a mystery what Pham Van Dong meant by flexibility." Beyond these generalities, the DRV leaders had offered no real reply to Soviet criticism that they were losing ground in world public opinion by failing to respond to U.S. initiatives to begin negotiations, even if they were really a deception.[37] Echoing American complaints, the Soviets even believed (though it is not likely they put it so bluntly to Pham Van Dong) that Hanoi's unyielding insistence on the Four Points really constituted an "ultimatum," for if Washington were really to agree to withdraw and recognize the NLF program, what was there left for the North Vietnamese and Americans to talk about? In a further indication of strains, the Soviets reported that the Vietnamese had given evasive responses when asked why Soviet military equipment (especially air defense systems) was not producing positive results (Moscow argued it stemmed from the Vietnamese failure to cooperate with Soviet advisers), why Hanoi had refused to provide immediate access to wreckage of downed American aircraft, why the DRV was seeking some supplies (like aluminum) and training (like nuclear physics related to nuclear weapons) for which it had no evident need (the Kremlin suspected they were trying to get them for China), and why the Chinese were constricting the flow of railway transports of Soviet-bloc supplies headed for Hanoi. Although the Soviets had loyally agreed to most requests for increased aid—Moscow was still contributing the bulk of support for the war—DRV leaders, specifically Pham Van Dong, left the Soviets with the distasteful impression that Hanoi had fallen under China's domination. "Symbolically stated," the Soviets concluded, "the head is in Beijing, and [North] Vietnam is only one of its limbs."

A comparable report to the Czech visitors probably dispelled whatever hope they may have had their quiet peace initiative would have any realistic chance of success when they arrived in Hanoi. The Czechs' own secret report merely noted laconically that their discussions in Moscow were "useful not only in that it provided an opportunity to become acquainted in detail with the Soviets' suggestions, but also because it allowed for early exposure to the reactions and arguments of the Vietnamese side."[38] Informally, however, Kissinger later received from Snejdárek a less favorable assessment of the Soviet reception. On September 30 and October 1, when they conversed during the ISS sessions in Vienna, Snejdárek described the Soviet reaction to Prague's peace initiative as ambivalent and lukewarm. "Moscow gave its grudging O. K. to the Czechs proceeding on their mission," he told Kissinger (in the latter's paraphrase), "but indicated that the mission was foolish and premature since the Americans would sooner or later tire of their efforts in Viet-Nam"—an analysis with which the Czechs disagreed. At the time, Snejdárek had not learned how the delegation had fared in Hanoi—it had not yet returned to Prague—beyond a report that the group had received a "somewhat cool reception which improved later." Given his doubts about the Kremlin's attitude toward the war—he described the Soviet position as "extremely complex" and "extremely confused," unsure whether Moscow "really wanted a relaxation of relations" or, on the contrary, sought to use the war as "a convenient pretext to tighten control over Eastern Europe"—Snejdárek "wondered whether the relatively cool reception the Czech delegation had received in Hanoi was not due to a Soviet attempt to ingratiate themselves with Hanoi by informing them of Czech intentions in advance."[39]

From Moscow, the delegation flew to Beijing, where, given the tense state of Sino-Soviet relations and China's well-known opposition to peace talks in Vietnam, it did not expect—and did not receive— a particularly warm reception. Arriving on the afternoon of September 22, the delegation was greeted at the airport by representatives of the socialist countries (except Albania) and by People's Republic of China (PRC) foreign minister Chen Yi, who also saw the delegation off the next day. However, the Chinese expressed no interest in substantive talks and left the delegation to itself at a government guesthouse. The local press ignored the delegation's stopover. "In Peking, the entire reception and atmosphere was extremely cool," the delegation reported, whereas in the southern city of Nanning, to which, after resting, it next flew to change planes, the members got a "noticeably friendlier" welcome.[40]

The delegation reached Hanoi on Friday afternoon, September 23, and departed on Thursday morning, September 29. In public, as portrayed by North Vietnamese and Czech media, in public speeches, toasts, and statements by both sides, and in their final joint communiqué, the delegation's six-day visit was a paragon of "militant" socialist solidarity against the U.S. "imperialist aggressors."[41] From the bouquets handed the visitors by Hanoi Young Pioneers as they alit from their plane, to the paired Czech and Vietnamese flags and gilt-lettered banners hailing the two nations' unshakable friendship hanging from city lampposts, to the top-level public attention and visibility given the delegation—including several meetings with Ho Chi Minh—the hosts made every effort to give the impression of a warm welcome to the Czechs, as they did that autumn to a succession of Soviet-bloc delegations.[42] For their part, Prague's delegates, led by Lenárt, matched their DRV counterparts in belligerent public rhetoric, denouncing the U.S. "criminal aggression," fulsomely praising Vietnam's "heroic" struggle, and pledging all manner of material aid in a common fight they repeatedly likened to their own battle for liberation from the Nazis. They also fulfilled the requisite ambitious program of symbolic public meetings, banquets, and ceremonies—including a mass meeting with Hanoi residents attended by the diplomatic corps and foreign journalists, visits to an antiaircraft unit (where they received the gift of a piece of wreckage from a downed U.S. F-105 Thunderchief fighter-bomber) an electrochemical plant, an art gallery, and the Vietnam People's Army Museum (where, after hearing a detailed exposition on Dien Bien Phu using a sand model, Lenárt presented a bas relief depicting a battle of Slovak guerrillas against Nazi soldiers), and a tour of a hamlet (Phu Xa) recently hit by B-52 bombers. Ho hosted a farewell "soiree" at the Presidential Palace, and, during a concluding ceremony, Lenárt and Pham Van Dong signed agreements on economic, technical, and military aid. A joint communiqué issued two days after the delegation left implied full and enthusiastic agreement on all issues pertaining to the war.[43]

Of the many public statements made by both sides during the Czechs' visit, the only ones that even slightly raised eyebrows occurred during a September 24 welcoming reception. Observers were watching closely for an authoritative reaction from Hanoi to a fresh statement of American terms given two days earlier by Washington's UN delegate, Arthur J. Goldberg. In a speech to the General Assembly, Goldberg had declared that Washington would halt the bombing of North Vietnam "the moment we are assured, privately or otherwise, that this step will be answered promptly by a corresponding and appropriate de-escalation on the other side," and that the problem of NLF representation in peace talks was not "insurmountable." Echoing DRV press criticism of Goldberg's speech as a sham, Pham Van Dong's welcome to the Czech visitors hardly aroused hopes of a breakthrough. He reiterated that if the U.S. leaders "really want peace" they must recognize the DRV's well-known Four Points and "show their good will by acts," above all, by putting a "definitive and unconditional" halt to bombing North Vietnam and recognizing the NLF as a negotiating partner.[44] Although some foreign observers sensed a possible "softening" in Pham Van Dong's remarks since he did not demand the immediate withdrawal of U.S. forces prior to agreeing to peace talks,[45] U.S. officials saw in them "new formulations" but "no significant concessions."[46] In his own speech, Lenárt expressed firm solidarity with Hanoi's objectives, yet added pointedly that it was "necessary to grasp all possibilities that lead to a realization of these goals"[47]—a passage, implying consideration of political rather than military methods, that "Washington had noted with interest," Kissinger told Snejdárek in Vienna.[48]

After a week of poring through anodyne propaganda blasts, analysts studied the final joint communiqué and found, if anything, a hardening of Hanoi's position from Pham Van Dong's welcoming comments on September 24.[49] Using even more strident language, the two sides also stressed the demand for the withdrawal of Washington's and its allies' forces and liquidation of its bases, condemned the "deceit and perfidy" of American calls for unconditional negotiations while following a "criminal policy of escalation," and even spoke of sending Czech "volunteers" to fight alongside their Vietnamese comrades if Hanoi requested them. Although the communiqué regarded as "particularly useful" the idea of a global "political offensive" that would "thoroughly expose the maneuvers of the U.S. imperialists, isolate them morally and politically, mobilize world opinion against U.S. aggression," and strengthen international support for the DRV and the NLF, the statement expressed no interest in diplomacy and gave no indication that either Prague or Hanoi had any expectation of anything other than a heroic military struggle until "final victory."[50]

Such were the slim pickings from the public record. The *International Yearbook of Communism* summarized the trip in simple terms: "A high-level Czechoslovakian delegation, visiting Hanoi in September, pledged all-around help—moral, political, and material—and affirmed that volunteers for military service would be sent if requested by the North Vietnamese government."[51] That, indeed, was the bottom line. A different story emerges, however, from the secret "debriefing report" prepared by the Czech delegation for its comrades, which recently was obtained from the CPCz CC archives in Prague. The records now available do not include verbatim transcripts of the extensive "political discussions" that the report indicates consumed the bulk of the delegation's visit. Nevertheless, it describes their substance in sufficient detail to reveal clearly the points of contention between the two sides and to hint at a somewhat more contentious atmosphere beneath the public front of militant complete "fraternal mutual understanding."

In combination with the Kissinger-Snejdárek conversation memorandums, the Lenárt delegation's "debriefing report" suggests that the glowing public statements concealed undercurrents of tension and disagreement, exacerbated by divergent assessments of the military situation, the international environment, and the Sino-Soviet split—as during Pham Van Dong's conversations in Moscow—plus an abortive Czech effort to prod Hanoi toward negotiations.

The disagreements began to emerge as soon as the delegations moved to private conversations. These talks began on September 24 and continued for several days in between the public events, with subgroups formed to deal with details of an economic agreement and drafting a joint communiqué. Their report makes clear that Pham Van Dong's lengthy opening presentation did not impress his guests. Not only did his "one-sidedly optimistic" and "noticeably general" "lecture" lack "concrete" or "new information," it "evaluated the current situation unrealistically, both in . . . military considerations [and] international politics." While expecting the Americans to escalate the war further—possibly onto DRV territory—when questioned, the North Vietnamese did not indicate how they would respond. In foreign affairs, Pham Van Dong "indirectly admitted that the situation is unfavorable," expressing the desire for further cooperation and coordination between North Vietnam and socialist states. "Even if nothing can be done to overcome the antagonisms"—a clear allusion to the Sino-Soviet split—the DRV "tries not to do anything to damage the unity of the socialist countries." This delicate comment on a sensitive subject passed without criticism, but the Czechs noted that Pham then "expressed a lack of understanding for the nations of the Third World, whose position he indiscriminately, without any differentiation, referred to as incorrect."

Perhaps anticipating pressure from the Czechs to talk to Washington—as they and other East-Central Europeans had urged during the bombing pause the previous winter—Pham insisted (without giving concrete examples) that "the Vietnamese did not avoid and are not avoiding contacts, and that in the past they had relations with the USA [that] did not lead to anything." Until Washington accepted Hanoi's Four Points, he said, "it is necessary to fight," for generations if need be, although he assured his visitors that he sought to shorten the war and minimize casualties. Clearly aware of Soviet-bloc suspicions that his government leaned toward Beijing, Pham closed his presentation by stressing the DRV's independent foreign policy line and desire to avoid actions that would further strain the divided communist world.

Meanwhile, Lenárt and the Czech delegation saved the toughest issues for last. First they discussed their internal situation and, at the Vietnam side's request, elaborated on Prague's "new system of management." Then came a review of Czech foreign policy, with special attention to countering the purportedly growing threat of West German *revanchism*.[52] It was during the third section of Lenárt's opening presentation, analyzing the international communist movement, that sparks began to fly. The Czech visitors carefully refrained from making explicitly anti-Chinese statements in public, although Lenárt, in his speech on September 24, pointedly praised the Soviet Union as "the first and mightiest socialist country in the world" and the "decisive factor" in the response of the socialist "community" to the U.S. aggression. Less constrained in private, however, Lenárt "openly condemned the [Chinese Communist Party's (CCP)] anti-Soviet platform and factionalist politics," and argued that by its actions the CCP leadership had "isolated itself."

The Vietnamese "reacted rather sharply" to these criticisms. Pham Van Dong interrupted Lenárt, stating, "the Czech delegation expressed opinions about the Communist Party of China which we do not approve." It was improper, he insisted (and an affront to the "movement's purity"), to "speak about a brotherly Party in her absence," adding that in Moscow "we said some things about the Chinese comrades that are misunderstood by the Soviet comrades." Describing the Sino-Soviet split as a "complex problem that would need to be studied as far back as Khrushchev's time," Pham hailed the CCP as an important present, past, and "without doubt" future contributor to the "cause of world revolution," and insisted judiciously that the WPV desired to maintain the "best" ties with both Moscow and Beijing.

Rather than continue the argument, the Czechs declared blandly that each communist party must "contribute actively to the unity of communist and workers' parties," and acknowledged that as the "object of aggression," the WPV had the "highest moral right" to request aid from the socialist fraternity. In addressing the war itself, Lenárt proffered analysis and concrete proposals in three areas: the military situation, coordinating socialist aid, and expanding the "political struggle on an international scale." After reaffirming principled support for Hanoi, the Czech delegation "expressed its disagreement with Comrade Pham Van Dong's one-sided, optimistic evaluation of the [U.S.] force's strength, and voiced a realistic evaluation of the situation." Specifically, the Czechs noted that neither the NLF nor the DRV had achieved the goals they had set for themselves, and warned against underestimating the enemy's "technical and economic resources." The delegation, according to its report, "openly stated that the USA is expecting a prolonged war and that thus far they are preparing for a more active military operation that could create a complicated military situation in Vietnam."

To address problems of coordinating socialist military aid to Hanoi—especially in light of what they saw as a grim military outlook as well as the prevailing chaos in China brought on by the Cultural Revolution (although it is not clear if they explicitly raised the latter consideration)—the Czechs proposed convening a meeting between DRV military specialists and those of other socialist countries "so that they could conceptualize together the questions of defense, preparation of cadres, experts, etc." One problem that needed addressing, they noted, was transport, especially given the limited capacity of Chinese railroads and the danger that shipments sent by sea could easily be cut off by hostile military action. Like Moscow, the Czechs proposed creating a "reloading site" on PRC territory to facilitate ground aid, as well as steps to increase the efficiency of aid shipped via Chinese airports near the Vietnamese border. They also cited the need for improved communications regarding transportation, aid, and the effective use of supplies.

However, it was in the political realm that the Czechs saw the greatest need for change, saying that they judged the present situation to be "unfavorable," with "the initiative not in our hands." To support the armed struggle, they said, it was necessary "also to create a wide, second political front," conducted on a differentiated and flexible basis. "Undoubtedly," they continued, "an effective means of gaining the entire world's public opinion in the political struggle against the maneuvers of the American imperialists would be to propose negotiations during which the Democratic Republic of Vietnam would secure its position expressed in its 4 to 5 points, or a proposal to summon all of the participants of the Geneva Conference, or lastly, a proposal to utilize the services of an intermediary in a probe." The key to enhancing the international political front, the Czechs stressed, was in the DRV leaders' hands.

This, finally, constituted the Czech proposals about which Snejdárek had told Kissinger. Yet there is no indication from the "debriefing report" that Lenárt and his colleagues detailed or argued strongly for these ideas, or even explicitly offered their own services as mediators. Nor, it appears, contrary to the impression Kissinger had initially received from Snejdárek and given the State Department, did the Czechs state or imply that they would condition continued military or economic aid on Hanoi's future "flexibility" on negotiations.[53] When he spoke to Kissinger on September 30, Snejdárek acknowledged that he had been "imprecise" in his statement, clarifying that although Prague "could not stop its aid completely as long as the Soviet Union continued to help," it could "drag its feet in its implementation," especially if Hanoi supplied a suitable technical pretext, and resist new demands.[54]

The Czechs closed their presentation on an upbeat note, expressing satisfaction with bilateral relations, announcing an increase in aid (although not enough to satisfy the DRV's expectations), and inviting Hanoi's leaders to visit Czechoslovakia.

Pham Van Dong's response, while mollifying in tone, did not strike his visitors as especially forthcoming. Regarding actions to enhance the "active unity" of the socialist community, he noted that one must proceed "carefully, wisely, and patiently," remembering all the while that the DRV required its allies' unselfish support. He promised that Hanoi, while not sharing their conclusions, would consider the Czechs' different views of the military situation. The idea of a conference of military experts from the DRV and socialist countries to coordinate support—one sure to arouse Chinese opposition—seemed "interesting" to Pham, but one "whose practical implementation presents many difficulties." He pledged further study on the notions of a "reloading site" on Chinese territory and further use of PRC airports near the Sino-Vietnamese frontier, noting that the Soviets had made similar suggestions to him in Moscow. Vowing to improve communications on aid questions, he expressed understanding of the need to coordinate assistance better, saying they would proceed "as reasonably as possible."

The DRV premier was unwilling to budge more than a little when it came to expanding the political front, however. Although he agreed in principle and promised to give the matter more thought, Pham remarked that the Vietnamese believed that "the situation is not so bad because Johnson is already losing this fight today." Moreover, the debriefing report noted, he expressed no reaction whatsoever to the visitors' call for a meeting of Geneva Conference participants or "the eventual sounding out of a third country as an intermediary"—and there is no indication that the Czechs pressed him any further on the ideas, or explicitly volunteered themselves for the job.

"Overall," the report concluded, "it can be said that the Vietnamese side took a very reserved stand towards Czech suggestions in the realm of politics and international politics as such. None of the suggestions was concretely dismissed, and in fact the Vietnamese side even reacted positively towards some, yet it avoided making any concrete commitments."

The talks on military-economic aid ran reasonably smoothly, although the Czechs resisted or deferred several Vietnamese demands for aid beyond what Prague considered appropriate, reaching a series of a agreements in time for signing at the end of the visit. But negotiations on the joint communiqué, conducted by deputy foreign ministers Karel Kurka and Hoang Van Tiem, were far bumpier. Ignoring a Czech draft, the Vietnamese responded with their own, which "did not adopt even one Czech formulation." Instead, they framed their own more militant statement stressing the "fight against imperialism," coming "very close to the Chinese theses" in the section on "the so-called people's war," and eliminating any discussion of the general international situation and the unity of the international communist movement. "In order to facilitate, or rather, make possible a joint statement during the course of these especially long and complex discussions," the Czechs reported that they firmly opposed "all but the few reasonable Vietnamese formulations," insisted on the elimination of "substantial Chinese theses," pushed to reinsert their own rendition of their position, rather than their hosts', and successfully pressed for a passage on the need for unity of socialist and revolutionary forces. However, they noted, the "unyielding approach" of the Vietnamese marred the working group's proceedings, leaving several "controversial points" to be settled by a direct meeting between Lenárt and Pham Van Dong.

As a "typical example" of these difficult discussions, the Czechs pointed to Vietnamese refusal to include language from Pham's September 24 welcoming speech listing conditions the United States must satisfy to prove it "really wanted peace." Those comments, the Vietnamese explained, had provoked undue international speculation, and were unclear. When the Czechs instead tried to insert comparable language from a January, 1966, message authored by Ho Chi Minh, the Vietnamese first agreed, then "backed away" and rejected its inclusion. In another private meeting, Pham appealed to Koucký not to insist on having the communiqué contain forthcoming language on negotiations, as Hanoi first needed to "research and study the next step in detail." Thus was agreement achieved on language that added tougher conditions (such as a prior U.S. withdrawal) for ending the war. As for broadening the political front, it required long and arduous discussions to reach agreement on a statement that a political offensive "to disclose the maneuvers of the American imperialists to world opinion" would be "especially useful."

In sum, the Czechs left virtually empty-handed. Before the delegation had a chance to report formally to the CPCz CC, a terse handwritten note was circulated to party officials summarizing the trip's results: It had taken place in a "friendly spirit" but "unfortunately [the North Vietnamese] did not accept, will think over" the Czechs' proposal for a second political front (that is, negotiations).[55] Not surprisingly, an internal report prepared by Lenárt's delegation judged the visit to have been "useful"—at least as a show of solidarity with a fraternal ally and for a chance to gain firsthand impressions of the situation in the DRV. The delegation concluded that Beijing's "negative influence" on Hanoi remained "very strong," and "a pro-Chinese group dominates the Central Committee and leadership of the Vietnamese Workers' Party." On the bright side, they noted that Pham Van Dong, while not disavowing "Chinese slander," nevertheless complimented the Czechs as communists and attempted to maintain "some sort of balance," seeking to avoid total dependence on the CCP. It was resolved to continue talks with the Hanoi comrades to "explain different viewpoints, reinforce their efforts at an independent line, and encourage them to think hard about the harmful nature of some of the Chinese leadership's views"— especially since Prague could "go further and voice its opinion more openly than the Soviet comrades."

On their way back to Prague, after an uneventful brief stop in Beijing, members of the Czech delegation had another, more high-level, consultation with Soviet leaders. Lenárt and Koucký reported on their conversations with the Vietnamese to Brezhnev, Kosygin, and others. It all sounded familiar to Brezhnev, who commiserated to the Soviet comrades that DRV officials had made the same inflated claims about military successes, excessive requests for aid that could not help their war effort, and excuses for Chinese conduct that was hampering the common cause. The Vietnamese had promised to investigate the problems and speak to the Chinese, he said with a sigh, but nothing happened. Still, continued dialogue with Hanoi was necessary, so perhaps the Czechs' visit had not been in vain. Brezhnev seemed preoccupied with the Chinese menace, however, and hinted that a meeting in late October of Soviet-bloc allies, among them CPCz CC first secretary Novotný, might further address both the Vietnamese and Chinese dilemmas.[56]

As the Czech delegation traveled homeward, reaching Prague on Sunday, October 2, Kissinger and Snejdárek had conversed over the weekend at the ISS meeting in Vienna, speculating about how Lenárt's group had fared in Hanoi and Moscow. Kissinger's record suggests that their talks continued to be remarkably candid about intracommunist tensions—Sino-Soviet, Soviet-Czech, Czech-Vietnamese, and DRV-NLF.[57] In addition to speculating that the Soviets, wanting to ingratiate themselves with hardline Vietnamese, might even have sabotaged Lenárt's mission before it reached Hanoi, Snejdárek frankly assessed the constraints on Prague's ability to pressure the North Vietnamese to moderate their course: "He said that Czechoslovakia found itself in a very complicated situation. It was most eager for the war in Vietnam to end. The war inhibited the possibility of a relaxation of tensions in Europe which Czechoslovakia required to gain a greater freedom of maneuver. At the same time, Czechoslovakia could not move openly against Soviet wishes because it needed Soviet support against Germany and its economy was geared to Soviet raw materials. He reminded me that even [Czechoslovak President Eduard] Benes had insisted that after the experience of Munich, Czech policy had to rely on the support of Russia."[58]

When talk turned to whether or how communications should continue between American and Czech representatives to follow up on peace efforts, Snejdárek told Kissinger that in light of a common agreement among Eastern European Communist Party Central Committees to eschew official contacts with Americans in light of U.S. actions in Vietnam, the best channel would remain the unofficial one that the two had established during the previous two weeks. However, uncertain as to what had transpired in Hanoi, he told Kissinger that if Lenárt carried news that justified further conversations, he would wire the Harvard professor a telegram expressing a desire to "discuss central European problems with him."

Kissinger telephoned an account of his talks with Snejdárek to a Harriman aide on October 3.[59] Three days later, a coda of sorts to the low-key Czech overture came when Rusk met with Prague's foreign minister, Václav David, during the annual whirlwind of meetings at the UN General Assembly in New York. Had the Czech government had anything to communicate as a result of its delegation's Hanoi conversations, this represented a logical time, place, and level to do so. Instead, David and Rusk engaged in a standard repetition of public, diametrically opposed positions on Vietnam and traded charges of responsibility. David did not volunteer a report on Lenárt's mission, and Rusk did not specifically inquire about it. Their perfunctory tone seemed a world away from that of the candid, collegial chats enjoyed by Kissinger and Snejdárek. Rusk closed the subject by reiterating that Washington remained vitally interested in negotiations, adding "that if the Czech government at any point received any indication of interest that would bring the Viet-Nam issue to the conference table, we would be glad to hear of it."[60]

In late October, Czech documents show, CPCz CC first secretary Novotný also wrote a postscript of sorts to the abortive Prague initiative when he discussed Vietnam during a gathering of Soviet-bloc Communist Party leaders at the Baikonur Cosmodrome in Soviet Central Asia. While not calling for military concessions, the Soviet-bloc leaders agreed (except for Romanian maverick Nicolae Ceausescu, who refused to discuss issues outside the formal agenda) that North Vietnam needed to "wage a battle on the political, propaganda, and diplomatic fronts in support of the defeat of the American aggression," and blamed the Chinese for pressuring Hanoi to reject the opportunities these alternatives offered.[61] When one-by-one the party leaders analyzed the Vietnam situation, Novotný (who was accompanied by Lenárt) acknowledged the recent mission's mixed results. Repeating the delegation's criticism of the DRV leaders for inefficient use of Soviet-bloc military aid, he rebuked them for single-mindedly pursuing a military triumph. "We stated that we are not in favor of terminating the armed struggle, but that it is a shame that we are not taking advantage of fighting on the political front, which would push the United States into a corner," Novotný said. "We openly stated that our hands are tied by the position of our Vietnamese comrades." Egged on by the Chinese, he added, there was a danger that Hanoi's insistence on continuing the war might whet Washington's appetite for aggression elsewhere. "Unfortunately, the Vietnamese comrades do not seem to appreciate that this is not merely about Vietnam, but rather about the wider front of national struggles for peace and a clash of two systems." Although the Czechs would continue to provide aid to Hanoi, Novotný vowed that Prague would try to push the DRV to open a political front "and to get the Vietnamese to hint at their agreement to such a move."[62]

As for Kissinger, though the Czech initiative proved stillborn, he continued to perform semiofficial Vietnam missions for the U.S. government in the year leading up to the PENNSYLVANIA initiative. In mid-October,

1966, at Harriman's behest, he visited Saigon to build support, both in Lodge's embassy and among South Vietnamese leaders, for a national reconciliation and amnesty program Washington was pushing in order to nurture the possibility of NLF defections and, ultimately, negotiations with the central government.[63] Although it was scheduled before the Czech episode, the trip's import was reinforced, U.S. officials believed, by the concerns Snejdárek expressed that NLF cadres not suffer the fate of Indonesian communists were there to be any chance of luring them into a role in a legitimate South Vietnamese political process. After seeing Lodge, Kissinger reported to Harriman via CIA channels that U.S. and South Vietnamese officials "fully" supported the initiative—but the effort later dissipated due to Saigon's foot-dragging.[64] Kissinger's promotion of Sainteny as a backchannel to Hanoi, though cautiously embraced by U.S. officials, likewise came to naught in January, 1967, after Charles de Gaulle vetoed his proposed mission—or any French mediation—on the grounds that such an initiative was "premature" given that Washington "hawks" still hoped for a military victory and predominated over "doves" who favored negotiations.[65]

Kissinger next saw Snejdárek in early 1967, when the Czech said Lenárt "got nowhere" the previous September in prodding Hanoi toward negotiations.[66] In May, 1968, as Kissinger savored the exhilarating "Prague Spring," Snejdárek more fully described the politics behind the abortive approach. He explained that what he had not told Kissinger then was that while Czech leaders "agreed on the desirability of ending the war, Novotný had wanted to gear Czech actions to Moscow's while Lenhart [*sic:* Lenárt] had favored an independent initiative." While in Moscow on the way to Hanoi, Snejdárek said, the Soviet leaders had "made no reply of any kind" on hearing the Czechs relate their plans to propose mediation to Hanoi—a silence that had "confirmed Novotny's doubts" about the initiative's wisdom but which, in retrospect, Snejdárek believed simply "meant that they wanted the Czechs to proceed but also to take the blame if anything went wrong." In any event, "Lenhart had made a half-hearted overture which was dropped when Hanoi reacted very sharply."[67]

At this point, however, as Washington and Hanoi fenced over opening the Paris talks, Snejdárek explained that the Czechs had formally decided again to act as a mediator "if an opportunity presented itself." After adding the caveat that Prague could not act contrary to Hanoi's interests, he suggested that Kissinger communicate with him if a deadlock arose in Paris that required the services of a communist intermediary. There is no indication in the record, so far as I know, that this offer was acted upon. Besides, Czech leaders had far more immediate problems with which to cope in the months to come without taking on a sensitive diplomatic mission involving a far-off conflict.

Conclusions

Though the autumn 1966 Czech peace initiative (if it even deserves the name) never really got off the ground, its conception, brief existence, and rapid demise all point to broader themes present in Eastern European diplomatic efforts on the war. Like the Hungarians and the Poles, it appears, the Czechs acted not necessarily at Moscow's prompting but in the confident belief that prodding the North Vietnamese toward negotiations with the United States and away from full reliance on the Chinese-supported course of seeking military victory fully accorded with Kremlin goals and policy; and, like Budapest and Warsaw, Prague carefully consulted with Soviet leaders to obtain approval and coordinate actions. Moreover, in synch with Moscow, the Czechs, like their Hungarian and Polish comrades, clearly viewed the Chinese as their nemesis, blaming Beijing for pressuring Hanoi to reject peace talks in favor of armed struggle (yet at the same time hindering Soviet-bloc military aid from reaching the DRV), and a militant faction within the Lao Dong leadership for falling sway to Chinese arguments; they also worried that a communist victory in Vietnam would promote an expansion of China's militant ideological influence. With the CPSU loathe to risk Chinese and North Vietnamese anger for open criticism of Hanoi's choice to reject or defer diplomacy, the East-Central European communists felt less constrained, and at least in private counseled the North Vietnamese that adding a negotiating dimension to the military struggle held the best prospect of ultimate victory, and poured cold water on their confidence that revolutionary zeal would suffice to defeat the Americans. And like the other Central European communists, especially the Poles, the Czechs saw a clear connection between the war in Vietnam and the nature of the East-West conflict in their own neighborhood. Further escalation in Southeast Asia risked a sharpening of Cold War tensions and tighter ideological controls, while settling the conflict might improve prospects for a détente in Europe that would permit a loosening of the shackles imposed by their superpower patron. Though not nearly as extensive as other East-Central European diplomatic initiatives, the Czech episode provides further evidence, then, to undercut the more primitive views of the socialist world as a unified monolith by the mid-1960s.

At the same time, however, the East-Central European communists certainly sympathized with the North Vietnamese, favored seeing a defeat for what they regarded as American imperialist aggression, and were loath to imperil their relations with either Moscow or Hanoi—which they firmly regarded as the ultimate moral arbiter of the proper policy—for the sake of promoting peace talks or improving relations with the United States. Therefore, they started from the presumption of unconditional support for the North Vietnamese, who, they reasoned, as those shedding blood, had the ultimate moral right to choose their own strategy. When Hanoi rebuffed advice to consider an alternate course, the East-Central Europeans disagreed but proved unwilling to use economic leverage or express more than the mildest public hint of a different perspective. In one case (the Poles and "Marigold"), they may have come close to achieving at least the minor breakthrough of brokering direct U.S.-DRV contacts, but for the most part they ran up against the same obstacle as the Soviets and everyone else in 1965–67—so long as the North Vietnamese leaders did not judge that the time was right, or the military-political situation ripe, for negotiations or concessions, no one, not even communist comrades, could convince them otherwise. For Henry Kissinger, the failure of his tentative, tantalizing, yet frustrating initial forays into semi-official, indirect diplomacy with the North Vietnamese fleetingly yet accurately foreshadowed the agonizing years of direct negotiating with Hanoi that he would engage in as national security adviser to Richard M. Nixon.

Notes

1. The resolution adopted on September 6, 1966, is cited in the "Debriefing report" on the September 23–29, 1966, CPCz delegation's visit to the Democratic Republic of Vietnam, 705/20, fond 02/1, Svazek 10, Archivna jednotca 11, listú 20, b. 18, Archiv Ustredniho Vyboru Komunisticka strana Ceskoslovenska (Archive of the Central Committee of the Communist Party of Czechoslovakia) (A-ÚV KSC), Statni ustredni archiv (Central State Archive), Prague (SUA) (hereafter, "Debriefing Report"). Like other Czech documents cited in this chapter, it was obtained from the CPCz records in the Central State Archive in Prague and provided to the author by Oldrich Tuma, director of the Institute for Contemporary History, Prague. Tuma also arranged for Francis Raska to translate it into English—with financial support from the Wilson Center's Cold War International History Project (CWIHP). The author thanks Tuma and CWIHP director Christian Ostermann for their cooperation.

2. The standard biography ignores this episode and describes PENNSYLVANIA as "Kissinger's first experience with secret diplomacy and baptism into the difficulties of dealing with the North Vietnamese" (Walter Isaacson, *Kissinger: A Biography* [New York: Simon and Schuster, 1992], p. 121). Kissinger also ignores the Czech episode in his memoirs, while briefly describing his involvement in PENNSYLVANIA. See Henry A. Kissinger, *White House Years* (Boston: Little, Brown, 1979), p. 234, and idem., *Diplomacy* (New York: Simon and Schuster, 1994), pp. 663–64; and Henry A. Kissinger, *Ending the Vietnam War* (New York: Simon and Schuster, 2003), pp. 41–42.

3. An exception was the 1967–68 Romanian mediation effort, which struck U.S. officials as serious, competent, and balanced. Hungarian and Polish efforts in 1965–66, by contrast, ultimately produced as much mistrust as gratitude from senior Johnson administration officials, above all Rusk and LBJ himself.

4. Texts on Vietnam diplomacy addressing Eastern–Central European efforts include David Kraslow and Stuart H. Loory, *The Secret Search for Peace in Vietnam* (New York: Random House, 1968); Wallace J. Thies, *When Governments Collide: Coercion and Diplomacy in the Vietnam Conflict, 1964–1968* (Berkeley: University of California Press, 1980); and *The Secret Diplomacy of the Vietnam War: The Negotiating Volumes of the Pentagon Papers,* ed. George C. Herring, (Austin: University of Texas Press, 1983).

5. For new Polish and Hungarian evidence on this episode, see James G. Hershberg, "Peace Probes and the Bombing Pause: Hungarian and Polish Diplomacy During the Vietnam War, December 1965–January 1966," *Journal of Cold War Studies,* vol. 5, no. 2 (spring, 2003), pp. 32–67.

6. For new Polish evidence, see James G. Hershberg with L. W. Gluchowski, "Who Murdered 'Marigold'? New Evidence on the Mysterious Failure of Poland's Secret Initiative to Start U.S.–North Vietnamese Peace Talks, 1966," Cold War International History Project Working Paper no. 27, Apr., 2000; and Jerzy Michalowski (prepared by Stefan Michalowski), "Polish Secret Peace Initiatives in Vietnam," *Cold War International History Project Bulletin* nos. 6/7 (winter, 1995–96): pp. 241, 258–59.

7. Rusk relayed this comment, "in strict confidence," to British ambassador Patrick Dean. See Sir P. Dean to Foreign Office (FO), no. 2765, Oct. 11, 1966, FO 371, Public Record Office, Kew Gardens, England (hereafter PRO).

8. Ilya V. Gaiduk, *The Soviet Union and the Vietnam War* (Chicago: Ivan R. Dee, 1996); and Gaiduk, "Peacemaking or Troubleshooting? The Soviet Role in Peace Initiatives During the Vietnam War" (paper presented at the "Vietnam: The Search for Peace in the Johnson Years" conference, Apr. 20–22, 2001, Lyndon B. Johnson Library, Austin, Tex. [hereafter LBJL]). Unfortunately, while working on the Vietnam War in Russian archives since 1992, Gaiduk was unable to access many important materials in the presidential, Foreign Ministry, military, and intelligence archives. Moreover, many of the files that he *was* able to review in the former CPSU CC archives in the early 1990s have since been closed.

9. For an assessment of some recent, albeit still preliminary, findings from Vietnamese sources on the war, see Fredrik Logevall, "Bringing in the 'Other Side': New Scholarship on the Vietnam Wars," *Journal of Cold War Studies* 3 (fall, 2001): pp. 77–93.

10. On Pugwash, see Joseph Rotblat, *Scientists in the Quest for Peace: A History of the Pugwash Conference* (Cambridge, Mass.: MIT Press, 1972); and the organization's Web site at http://www.pugwash.org.

11. See *Foreign Relations of the United States* (*FRUS*), *1964–1968,* vol. 3, *Vietnam, June–December, 1965* (Washington, D.C.: GPO, 1996), pp. 460 n 2; and Kissinger, *White House Years,* pp. 231–33. Official State Department memoranda of Kissinger's conversations during his Oct.–Nov. 1965 visit to Vietnam, prepared by the U.S. Embassy in Saigon, can be found in William P. Bundy's official papers. See 'Professor H. Kissinger' folder, box 9, Lot File 85D240, Entry 5408, Subject Files of the Office of the Assistant Secretary of State for East Asian and Pacific Affairs, 1961–1974, Record Group (RG) 59, National Archives (NA) II, College Park, MD (hereafter W. P. Bundy papers, RG 59, NAII).

12. Lodge's comments appear in JCS Chairman (Wheeler) to McNamara, Dec. 21, 1965, *FRUS, 1964–1968,* pp. 3:676–77. Although Kissinger's personal papers at the Library of Congress remain closed to unauthorized researchers, his relationship with Lodge during this period can be partially documented through correspondence in reel 20 of the Henry Cabot Lodge Papers at the Massachusetts Historical Society in Boston [hereafter Lodge Papers].

13. For Kissinger's report to W. Averell Harriman on his July 16–29, 1966, visit to South Vietnam, see Harriman-Kissinger, Aug. 2, 1966, memorandum of conversation, *FRUS, 1964–1968,* vol. 4, *Vietnam, 1966* (Washington, D.C.: GPO, 1998), pp. 543–48. In his memoirs, Kissinger quotes an Aug. 18, 1966, letter to Lodge containing findings and recommendations (including an urgent need for a negotiating "strategy"). See Kissinger, *White House Years,* pp. 233–34. The full document can be found in Reel 20, Lodge Papers. See also documents in "Vietnam, General, Aug.–Sept. 1966" Folder, Box 520, W. Averell Harriman Papers (hereafter Harriman Papers), Manuscripts Division, Library of Congress (hereafter LOC); materials in 'Kissinger 1966' folder, box 9, W. P. Bundy papers, RG 59, NA II; and William Conrad Gibbons, *The U.S> Government and the Vietnam War: Executive and Legislative Roles and Relationships,* Part IV: July 1954–Jan. 1968 (Princeton, NJ: Princeton University Press, 1995), pp. 383–385.

14. Rotblat, *Scientists,* p. 104.

15. See documents in "Vietnam, General" Folders, Box 520, Harriman Papers, LOC, for Aug.–Sept., 1966; for the Sept. 9, 1966, Kissinger-Sainteny memorandum of conversation, see Box 20, Formerly Top Secret Records of the Department of State, 1964–1966, Record Group 59 (hereafter RG 59), National Archives and Records Administration, College Park, Md. (hereafter NARA).

16. Henry A. Kissinger, "Czech Efforts to Induce Hanoi to be More Flexible on Negotiations," Sept. 23, 1966, "Kissinger, Henry" Folder, Box 481, Harriman Papers, LOC.

17. Kraslow and Loory, *Secret Search,* p. 222.

18. This account of Kissinger's activities at Pugwash and his 1966 contacts with Czechs is based mostly on his memoranda found in "Kissinger, Henry" Folder, Box 481, Harriman Papers, LOC. A recent search of the Prague archives produced evidence on Czech talks with the Soviets and North Vietnamese (described below), but no materials on back-channel contacts with Kissinger.

19. Henry A. Kissinger, "Conversation with Soviet participants at Pugwash conference on the subject of Vietnam"; and idem., "Vietnam Resolution at the Pugwash Conference," both dated Sept. 23, 1966, "Kissinger, Henry" Folder, Box 481, Harriman Papers, LOC. On Shustov, see also idem., Sept. 19, 1966, memorandum of conversation, enclosure to Harriman and McNamara to Rusk, Sept. 19, 1966, ibid.

20. For Kissinger's September 17 talk with Dobrosielski, see John A. Gronouski, Sept. 19, 1966, cable (Warsaw 660, confidential); and Henry A. Kissinger, "Conversation with Dobroscelski [*sic*], member of the Policy Planning Staff of the Polish Foreign Ministry," Sept. 23, 1966, both in "Kissinger, Henry" Folder, Box 481, Harriman Papers, LOC.

21. Kissinger, "Conversation with Soviet participants."

22. Kissinger, "Vietnam Resolution at Pugwash Conference."

23. Kissinger, "Czech Efforts."

24. Sixteenth Pugwash Conference, "Final Statement," in Rotblat, *Scientists,* p. 262.

25. Kissinger, "Czech Efforts."

26. The information on Kissinger's conversations with Snejdárek on September 19–20, 1966, in this and succeeding paragraphs is taken from ibid. One former U.S. diplomat stationed in Prague recalls that Snejdárek's "normal function was interaction with foreign-policy-oriented intellectuals," as well as occasionally handling sensitive missions for the government, such as acting as an "unofficial envoy" to Bonn in the normalization of Czech–West German relations in early 1967. See Kenneth N. Skoug Jr., *Czechoslovakia's Lost Fight for Freedom, 1967–1969: An American Embassy Perspective* (Westport, Conn.: Praeger, 1999), pp. 11, 25.

27. Snejdárek also said that the Foreign Ministry was "not informed in detail" regarding the initiative, raising the question of whether the CPCz CC figures pushing the initiative suspected that ministry hard-liners would oppose or undermine it. The delegation also included

Deputy Foreign Minister Karel Kurka and Prague's ambassador to the DRV, Bohumil Mucha, so the Foreign Ministry evidently was not kept completely out of the loop.

28. Kissinger, "Czech Efforts."

29. Skoug, *Czechoslovakia's Lost Fight,* p. 8, citing Jacob D. Beam, *Multiple Exposure: An American Ambassador's Unique Perspective on East-West Issues* (New York: Norton, 1978), pp. 151–52.

30. Daniel I. Davidson, "Czechoslovakian Efforts to Convince Hanoi to Negotiate," Sept. 23, 1966, "Kissinger, Henry" Folder, Box 481, Harriman Papers, LOC.

31. Henry A. Kissinger, "Conversation with A. Snejdárek, Director, Czech Institute of International Affairs," Sept. 30, 1966, ibid.

32. W. Averell Harriman, "Memorandum for Personal Files," Sept. 27, 1966, ibid.

33. Memorandum of meeting, Gov. Harriman's office, 10 A.M., Sept. 29, 1966, top secret-nodis, "Vietnam, General, Aug.–Sept. 1966" Folder, Box 520, Harriman Papers, LOC.

34. Rusk-Gromyko, New York, Sept. 24, 1966, memorandum of conversation, *FRUS, 1964–1968,* pp. 4:662–68 (quotations on pp. 4:665–66). For Harriman and other officials' belief that the Soviets and East Europeans might play a useful role in probing Hanoi's position, see Harriman to Johnson and Rusk, "Negotiations Committee," Sept. 30, 1966, ibid., pp. 4:678–79.

35. This account of Pham Van Dong's conversations with Soviet leaders is from a report by the Hungarian ambassador in Moscow, "Subject: Soviet-Vietnamese talks about Soviet aid," Sept. 21, 1966, 64/1/1966/Sz.t. (strictly confidential), XIX-J-1-j. 1966, 107 doboz (Soviet relations), Magyar Országos Leváltár (MOL; Hungarian National Archives), Budapest, Hungary; located by Csaba Bekes, translated by Aliz Agoston.

36. Thies, *When Governments Collide,* p. 338.

37. In 1973, Brezhnev told Richard Nixon that he had told Pham Van Dong in mid-1966: "Dear friends, to fight is your business. But you must soon negotiate with the U.S." (as quoted in Henry A. Kissinger, memorandum for the president's file, "SUBJECT: Meeting with Leonid I. Brezhnev, General Secretary of the Central Committee, CPSU, on Saturday, June 23, 1973 at 12:22 p.m.," San Clemente, Nixon Presidential Materials, NARA, copy courtesy William Burr, National Security Archive, Washington, D.C.).

38. "Debriefing Report."

39. Kissinger, "Conversation with A. Snejdarek"; Daniel I. Davidson, "Czechoslovakian Efforts to Convince Hanoi to Negotiate," Oct. 3, 1966, "Kissinger, Henry" Folder, Box 481, Harriman Papers, LOC.

40. "Debriefing report"; "Czech Premier Makes Brief Stopover in Peking," Belgrade TANYUG International Service, Sept. 23, 1966, in *Foreign Broadcast Information Service* (*FBIS*) Daily Report, Tuesday, Sept. 27, 1966, Far East, no. 187, 1966, p. BBB 2.

41. Descriptions of the public dimension of the trip are based on North Vietnamese and Czech media coverage translated in the *FBIS* Daily Reports for Monday, Sept. 26, 1966, Far East, no. 186, 1966; Tuesday, Sept. 27, 1966, Far East, no. 187, 1966; Wednesday, Sept. 28, 1966, Far East, no. 188, 1966; Thursday, September 29, 1966, Far East, no. 189, 1966; Friday, Sept. 30, 1966, Far East, no. 190, 1966; and Monday, Oct. 3, 1966, Far East, no. 191, 1966.

42. The British consul-general in Hanoi noted in late November, 1966, that the last few months had "witnessed the arrival here of delegations and political leaders from nearly all the countries of the Bloc: Bulgarian, Czech, Soviet and Cuban delegations have been to Hanoi as well as Monsieur Maurer from Roumania, and possibly the Hungarian Foreign Minister [Janos Peter]," and a Polish delegation was expected "before long" (J. H. R. Colvin to George Brown, Nov. 22, 1966, FO 371/186345, PRO).

43. For the full text (dated Sept. 29, 1966), see *FBIS* Daily Report, Monday, Oct. 3, 1966, pp. jjj 11–16.

44. For Pham Van Dong's Sept. 24, 1966 speech, see *FBIS* Daily Report, Monday, Sept. 26, 1966, pp. jjj 14–19.

45. See, e.g., the Agence France Press (AFP) report by Jean Raffaelli, Hanoi, Oct. 2, 1966, in *FBIS* Daily Report, Monday, Oct. 3, 1966, p. jjj 17.

46. Harriman to Johnson and Rusk, Sept. 30, 1966, FRUS, 1964–1968, 4:679.

47. For Lenárt's speech, see *FBIS* Daily Report, Monday, Sept. 26, 1966, pp. jjj 19–20.

48. Kissinger, "Conversation with A. Snejdarek." Snejdárek told Kissinger that this statement "had been well considered" and "drafted in Prague" before the delegation departed.

49. AFP report by Jean Raffaelli, p. jjj 17.

50. DRV-Czech Communiqué, *FBIS* Daily Report, Monday, Oct. 3, 1966, p. jjj 13.

51. *International Yearbook on Communism, 1966* (Stanford, Calif.: Hoover Institution on War, Revolution, and Peace, 1967), p. 54.

52. The "Debriefing Report" actually does not elaborate on the delegation's private comments on West Germany, but this was a frequent theme of its public remarks.

53. Kissinger, "Czech Efforts."

54. Kissinger, "Conversation with A. Snejdarek."

55. Handwritten cover note (n.d., author unidentified) to "Debriefing Report."

56. "Memorandum on the concluding session of the Central Committee of the Communist Party of the Soviet Union," n.d., but probably describing the Soviet-Czech meeting on Oct. 1, 1966, attached to "Debriefing Report."

57. Kissinger, "Conversation with A. Snejdarek"; Davidson, "Czechoslovakian Efforts," Oct. 3, 1966.

58. Kissinger, "Conversation with A. Snejdarek."

59. Davidson, "Czechoslovakian Efforts," Oct. 3, 1966.

60. Rusk-David, "Subject: Viet-Nam (Part III of III)," New York, Oct. 6, 1966, memorandum of conversation, 21st sess., UN General Assembly, memoranda of conversation vol. 15, Conference Files, Box 423, RG 59, NARA.

61. CPCz delegation (Antonín Novotný, Josef Lenárt, B. Lomsky), "Report on the Visit and Discussions in the USSR between 17 and 21 October 1966," fond 02 11, sv. 12, ar.j. 13, listú 29, b. 13, A-UV KSC, SUA, obtained by Oldrich Tuma, trans. Francis Raska.

62. "A Detailed Report on the Statements of General Secretaries of Communist and Workers' Parties at a Meeting of 21 October 1966," ibid.

63. Previous accounts have left unstated the purpose of Kissinger's short visit (see, e.g., Kissinger, *White House Years*, p. 232), but documents in the Harriman Papers indicate that it was primarily intended to rally support and enhance planning for the national reconciliation and amnesty program.

64. Kissinger to Harriman, Oct. 14, 1966, telegram fm CAS to State Department, "Manila Summit Conference, Meetings, Oct. 24–25, 1966 (2)" Folder, Box 551, Harriman Papers, LOC; see also idem., Dec. 5, 1966, enclosure to Lodge to Kissinger, Nov. 29, 1966, Folder "Lodge, Henry Cabot," Box 484, ibid.

65. See documents in "Vietnam, General" Folders for Aug.–Sept., 1966, Oct.–Dec., 1966, and Jan.–Mar., 1967, Box 520, ibid.

66. Harriman-Kissinger, Feb. 9, 1967, memorandum of conversation, "Kissinger, Henry" Folder, Box 481, ibid.

67. Kissinger-Snejdárek, May 17, 1968, memorandum of conversation, U.S./USSR Conversations, Vietnam and South East Asia Folder 2, Box 2, Papers of Ambassador-at-Large Llewellyn E. Thompson, 1961–1970, RG 59, NARA, copy courtesy William Burr, National Security Archive, Washington, D.C.

The Pentagon and Peace Negotiations after March 31, 1968

HERBERT Y. SCHANDLER

Almost from the beginning of its combat involvement in Vietnam in 1965, the United States sought a negotiated settlement to the war. Various allied and neutral nations presented appeals for peace and arranged private contacts with North Vietnamese officials. Throughout this time, however, there were no direct meetings between high-level North Vietnamese and U.S. officials. Hanoi steadfastly rejected all overtures. Its consistent response was that there could be no talks until the United States unconditionally ceased its bombing of North Vietnam and all acts of war against Democratic Republic of Vietnam (DRV) forces. As far as the Americans were concerned, an unconditional bombing halt would endanger U.S. troops in South Vietnam in exchange for only a vague assurance that talks would begin. American military leaders insisted that the bombing should not be halted without first establishing conditions that would keep the North Vietnamese from taking advantage of such a halt and thereby endanger U.S. troops in the South. Moreover, they believed that Hanoi's offer to begin talks only after the bombs stopped falling was too vague. As far as the Americans were concerned, the North Vietnamese needed to demonstrate a deeper commitment to talks before they would agree to an unconditional bombing halt.[1]

In a dramatic speech on March 31, 1968, Lyndon Johnson once again offered to engage in peace talks with North Vietnam.[2] Largely to satisfy those in the administration who advocated seeking peace negotiations with the North, the president offered several concessions to the North Vietnamese. Many of the concessions were overlooked by the press, which concentrated on the president's dramatic withdrawal from the 1968 presidential campaign. Buried among these concessions was the president's announcement that the United States would halt its bombing campaign except in the vicinity of the demilitarized zone (DMZ) that separated North and South Vietnam, in the hope that negotiations might follow.[3]

The day after the speech, U.S. planes bombed Thanh Hoa, an important transfer point just south of the 20th Parallel and 205 miles north of the

DMZ.[4] The attack thus fell within the unpublicized guidelines established by the president, but just barely. There was an immediate uproar from critics who thought the president had misled them into thinking the bombing would be restricted to a narrow area just north of the DMZ. Senator William Fulbright led the attack in the Congress, even though he had been briefed the day before the speech that the United States would continue attacking targets as far north as the 20th Parallel. On April 1, he angrily charged that, in light of Thanh Hoa, the speech constituted at best a "very limited change in existing policy." Other members of Congress and commentators joined in the attack, although three senators—Mike Mansfield, Richard Russell, and John Stennis—disputed Fulbright's charges.[5]

The president lashed out furiously at Fulbright and other members of Congress "who start attacking us even before the communists do." He bitterly noted that it was "easier to satisfy Ho Chi Minh than Bill Fulbright." To clarify the ambiguous wording of his speech, however, the president instructed Gen. Earle G. Wheeler, chairman of the Joint Chiefs of Staff (JCS), to inform senior commanders in Vietnam to restrict the bombing still further, to the area south of the 19th Parallel instead of the 20th. This self-imposed restriction remained in effect during the remainder of President Johnson's term.[6]

On the morning of April 3, 1968, the debate over the president's speech was swept aside by a stunning event that almost no one in Washington had anticipated: a message from North Vietnam, broadcast over Radio Hanoi. Although it began with a lengthy denunciation of the United States, it contained the following sentence: "However, on its part, the [DRV] government declares its readiness to send its representatives to make contact with U.S. representatives to decide with the U.S. side the unconditional cessation of bombing and all other war acts against the DRV so that talks could begin."[7]

Hanoi's statement did not mention the president's March 31 speech, but it explicitly restricted discussions with the United States to the subject of the "unconditional" cessation of the bombing and all other acts of war against North Vietnam. It did not constitute an agreement to talk about ending the war. Nevertheless, it was the first time Hanoi expressed a willingness to meet with the United States on any basis at all prior to an unconditional bombing halt. For that reason alone, the statement created enormous excitement in Washington.

The message triggered a continuing and profound discussion within the administration over the transcendentally important issue of what the American goal in Vietnam should be during the last ten months of Lyndon Johnson's presidency. After the Tet Offensive, which began on January 31, the president's closest advisers had seemed to split into two factions. In one camp were Dean Rusk, Walt Rostow, Ellsworth Bunker, Maxwell Taylor, and the entire American military command; in the other were Averell Harriman, Cyrus Vance, Nicholas Katzenbach, Paul Nitze, Paul Warnke, and Clark Clifford, the new secretary of defense. Lyndon Johnson found himself at the center of this tug of-war, uncertain of what legacy he wanted to leave in Vietnam.

The roots of the dispute were inherent in his March 31 speech. What had Lyndon Johnson intended? Had he deliberately sacrificed his political career in order to seek an end to the war, or had he put forward a series of half-measures designed to shore up domestic support, at a lower cost, without changing U.S. objectives in Vietnam? Did he know himself what his objective was? How dependent was he upon his closest advisers? Were they in agreement?

His speech had been ambiguous. On one hand, none of his policy announcements were entirely new. Limited bombing halts, for example, had already been tried. On the other hand, the speech's tone and rhetoric, especially coupled with his withdrawal from the campaign, was significantly more moderate than in any of his other recent statements or speeches. Rusk, Bunker, Rostow, and the military believed that the president had moved the United States as far as it needed to go in order to shore up domestic support for the war. They generally did not want to show any additional enthusiasm for negotiations for fear that it would weaken the Saigon government. Clark Clifford, however, has indicated that he wanted the speech to do much more. He thought that it should mark the beginning of an intensive search by the United States for a complete settlement of the war. In short, he wanted to get "our friend [LBJ]" out of this.

The result was an argument—foreshadowing many more along similar lines—among the president's senior advisers over how to respond to Hanoi. Harriman wanted to respond immediately so as to avoid "the public appearance of hesitancy." Rostow suggested that the administration "improve the pace of the negotiations by military means"—which meant increasing the level of American military activity. The president quickly rejected that approach. Rusk favored delaying taking action until the administration had the full agreement of the South Vietnamese. Clifford suggested that the North Vietnamese seemed to be responding to the president's initiative. The president warned against letting the public get its hopes up too high, then said he wanted to respond during the same news cycle, so that the evening television news programs would carry not only Hanoi's offer but also Washington's response. He asked some of his advisers to draft a presidential statement for immediate release, while others prepared diplomatic messages for dispatch to Saigon and the capitals of other U.S. allies in South Vietnam.[8]

Shortly after 5 P.M., the president read a short statement reiterating the administration's readiness "to send its representatives to any forum, at any time to discuss the means of bringing this war to an end." The president then appointed Averell Harriman and Cyrus Vance as the U.S. representatives to any such forum. Less than seventy-two hours had elapsed since he had made his speech from the Oval Office. On April 3, the president approved a message to Hanoi indicating acceptance of the North Vietnamese proposal, and suggesting a meeting in Geneva.[9]

A great national tragedy occurred on April 4: the assassination of Rev. Martin Luther King Jr. Within hours of the announcement of King's death, riots broke out in Washington and other cities across the nation. For a moment, even the Vietnam War seemed to fade into the background. Only two months after the Tet debacle, it seemed as if America was experiencing its own national uprising. President Johnson had planned to fly to Honolulu during the first week of April to consult with Gen. William C. Westmoreland, who was still in command in Vietnam. He canceled that plan as soon as he learned King had been killed and instructed Westmoreland to fly to Washington instead. When the general arrived on April 6, he presented a glowing picture of confidence. "In the negotiations," Westmoreland said, stressing every word, "Governor Harriman will have a hand with four aces and the enemy will have two deuces." Defense Secretary Clifford asked, "Under what conditions would a ceasefire be acceptable?" The general's alarming reply showed the new secretary just how entrenched and unrealistic the U.S. troop commander remained. "I do not see any acceptable ceasefire," Westmoreland stated. "We would just like the North Vietnamese to go home and turn in their weapons."[10] That was a "wish" not likely to be forced by American arms.

On April 9, Rusk, Wheeler, Clifford, Harriman, Vance, William Bundy, and Ellsworth Bunker, who had just arrived from Saigon, flew to join the president at Camp David. Bunker told the president that the pacification programs had been badly hurt by the Tet Offensive, although not nearly so badly as reported by the press. Like Westmoreland, he thought the press had badly misreported the outcome of the battle. "In fact," he said, "we go into the negotiations from a position of strength." He stated that Pres. Nguyen Van Thieu was expecting another enemy offensive between May and October, an accurate prediction, as it turned out, of the offensive that took place in May. In a less accurate assessment, Bunker was also upbeat about Thieu, who he said had begun "acting like a leader." Finally, Bunker said the United States should move as slowly as possible in the negotiations.

"Saigon is not at all ready," he said. Supporting Bunker and agreeing with his report, Rusk said what was clearly obvious: Hanoi's objective was to end all of the bombing of the DRV. He predicted the first phase of the talks would be very tough: "We have to hang in there. Either get them to make concessions or get them to take the responsibility for breaking off the talks."

"What happens if they are just fooling around with us?" the president inquired. Clifford was ready for that question. "In that case," the defense secretary replied, "Bus Wheeler [the chairman of the Joint Chiefs of Staff] and I will have some choice targets in the North ready for you."[11]

Rusk reported that the group affirmed America's basic but ambitious negotiating position. Other than wanting the North Vietnamese to move promptly to substantive talks, he stated, the goal should be to get the North Vietnamese to agree to a cease-fire, accept the South Vietnamese government at the conference table, negotiate a mutual withdrawal of American and North Vietnamese forces, respect the demilitarized zone, stop attacking South Vietnamese cities, release American prisoners of war, and comply with the Laos Accords of 1962.

There was one immediate problem: The United States and North Vietnam still had not agreed on a negotiating site. On April 4, the president had proposed that talks begin in Geneva on April 8. At almost exactly the same time, Hanoi sent a message proposing that contacts begin at the ambassadorial level in Phnom Penh, the capital of Cambodia. The United States had no embassy or representation in Cambodia, which left the U.S. leaders confronting a dilemma. The president's oft-repeated pledge to go "anywhere, anytime" to meet with Hanoi's representatives was proving to be an increasing embarrassment as public pressure built for LBJ to fulfill his pledge. The result was an international tap dance that went on for more than a month as the two sides bickered over where the peace talks should be held.

A grand total of fifteen cities—as well as an Indonesian warship—were eventually thrown into the discussion. The United States kept one obvious choice, Paris, a city familiar to the Vietnamese leadership and with a large Vietnamese overseas colony, off the list, hoping that Hanoi might eventually propose meeting there. This hope was fulfilled when, after a month of sterile exchanges, the North Vietnamese on May 3 proposed to meet in Paris. Although Lyndon Johnson was not enthusiastic about Paris because he feared Charles de Gaulle's hostile attitude toward the war might negatively influence the talks, he listened to his advisers and the next morning announced America's acceptance of the agreement.[12]

On May 8, the president met with Harriman and Vance to go over his instructions. After some bureaucratic battles between the State and Defense

Departments, a reasonable opening position had been produced for the U.S. negotiators. Harriman and Vance were given four objectives: First, "prompt and serious substantive talks looking toward peace in Vietnam, in the course of which an understanding may be reached on a cessation of bombing in the North under circumstances which would not be militarily disadvantageous;" second, the creation of a control mechanism with which to oversee any peace or cease-fire; third, the reestablishment of the DMZ as a genuine boundary; and fourth, the full involvement of the government of the Republic of Vietnam in any talks on the future of South Vietnam.[13]

During the meeting, yet another argument over the bombing broke out between the secretary of defense and the secretary of state. Rusk wanted to resume air strikes between the 19th and 20th Parallels. Clifford, on the other hand, opposed this on the grounds that it would be wrong to escalate military activity on the eve of the Paris talks. The president agreed with Clifford, but the issue was hardly dead. A week later, at the regular Tuesday Lunch, Rostow and Wheeler joined Rusk in raising the issue. Clifford again stood his ground, arguing that it made no sense to increase the bombing just as the Paris talks were beginning. Again the president rejected Rusk's proposal, but he was upset that such a strong argument still persisted between his two top cabinet members so soon after negotiations had begun.[14]

Johnson might have been more upset had he known of the argument between his negotiator, Averell Harriman, and the JCS representative to the peace talks, Gen. Andrew Goodpaster, while they were flying to Paris. Harriman told his team it was their job to end the war. The old "cold warrior" had chafed at the strict instructions the president had given him. General Goodpaster disagreed. "That's not my understanding," he stated. The Joint Chiefs had their own negotiating terms: the delegation was to negotiate with the North Vietnamese, but it was in no way to compromise the maximum pressure being exerted on the battlefield.[15]

The Harriman-Goodpaster argument reflected the president's unwillingness at that time to challenge the military directly by allowing the delegation to go beyond questions concerning a bombing halt. Hanoi had sent a delegation to discuss that issue and the JCS wanted to make certain that nothing more than that was discussed.

The arguments within the Johnson administration reflected a fundamental and unresolved question: What was America's objective in Vietnam? Rusk and Clifford seemed to differ profoundly as to what the goal should be in the limited time the administration had left. Clifford had concluded that the objective should be to extract the United States from Vietnam before the end of the year. Rusk did not agree. To him, the Paris talks were simply another chapter in the long twilight struggle with communism throughout the world. He was unwilling to consider even as a possibility what Clifford viewed as a fact: that the war was not an integral part of that worldwide struggle and that the administration's obsession with Vietnam was weakening the United States in other parts of the world. Rusk believed that politics played too large a role in Clifford's position, whereas Clifford saw domestic politics as a legitimate and unavoidable part of a successful policy toward Vietnam.[16]

Clifford described the Tuesday Lunch session on May 21 as grim. Rusk suggested, as he had before, that the United States resume bombing targets as far north as the 20th Parallel in view of North Vietnam's intransigence in Paris and in view of the communists' stepped-up attacks in the South. Clifford, meanwhile, continued to argue strongly against expanding the bombing campaign. "If we escalate again," he argued, "it will diminish the chance of success in Paris, and it would be catastrophic if Paris broke up and we had to go back to a purely military policy." The president looked at him quizzically. "Why is that so bad?" Johnson asked. "It's bad because we will lose more boys than ever before," Clifford replied slowly, "and because I don't think we can win the war by military means." The president seemed annoyed. "What do you mean?" he asked.

Clifford—arguing in front of three powerful opponents: Rusk, Rostow, and Wheeler—replied:

> With the limitations now placed on our military—which I do not oppose—no invasion of the North, no mining of the harbors, no invasion of the sanctuaries—we have no real plans or chance to win the war. Our hopes must go to Paris. . . . In the fall of 1967, the North Vietnamese decided that their earlier plans were no good. They put in their stack; that was Tet. They didn't win but they can still control the situation in the South: they can hit and run, they can attack the cities, they can control the level of casualties. Now, they may have concluded it is a good time to have a political settlement. They can't win the war militarily. But we can't win the war militarily.

"I disagree," said the president. Rusk, showing greater emotion than he ever had before, stated: "We ought to keep North Vietnam from overtaking South Vietnam with force. We have succeeded. We win when they know they can't win." Clifford, determined not to yield, replied: "Hanoi cannot win the war militarily—they know that, we know that. But that doesn't mean we can win it. If Paris does not come off, we will be back where we were before. . . . Can anybody here tell me what our plan is if the Paris talks fail? If Paris fails, we have no alternative but to turn back to the military—and they have no plan to bring it to an end." Listening somewhat wearily to these arguments between his two advisers, the president once again said that, against his better judgment, he would put off the bombing.[17]

Despite all the talk, no progress was being made in Paris. The two sides met each Thursday and read polemical statements to each other. There were no actual negotiations. In Vietnam, the communists launched a second wave of attacks that was quickly dubbed the "mini-Tet Offensive." American casualties in Vietnam reached a new high during the second week in May, increasing the pressure to resume attacks on targets north of the 19th Parallel.

The president called Cyrus Vance back from Paris in order to hear his views. He arrived in Washington on May 27 and was extremely negative about expanding the bombing campaign. Vance's calm, unemotional style had an enormous effect on the discussions, visibly cooling down the "hawks" around the table. For the first time in almost two months, Clark Clifford had an influential ally. Vance, backed by a cable from Harriman, succeeded in persuading the president to postpone making a decision on the question of resuming air strikes on targets as far north as the 20th Parallel, but the issue was far from resolved in the president's mind.

On June 4, the same day that presidential candidate Robert F. Kennedy was assassinated, Johnson received a private message from Soviet premier Alexei Kosygin urging the United States to stop bombing North Vietnam. "My colleagues and I believe, and have grounds to believe" that if the United States stopped the bombing it would lead to a breakthrough and produce *prospects* for peace" (emphasis added). Harriman and Vance were excited. They were certain the Soviet Union, which was giving Hanoi vast amounts of aid, could help bring about a negotiated settlement. Harriman had engaged in private talks with Valerian Zorin, the Soviet ambassador in Paris, hoping to encourage the Soviets to intervene in bringing Hanoi around. He delivered a personal warning to Zorin that if the president were forced to resume the bombing campaign, he would be intensely pressured to remove all previous restraints.

Defense Secretary Clifford favored a positive gesture that would put Moscow "on the spot" to produce results. He said the United States should just "assume it means what we want it to mean." Clifford proposed that the United States take action in Vietnam—perhaps by reducing the number of bombing attacks on targets in the North, for example—based directly on the Soviet message. At the same time, he said the administration should make it clear to both Moscow and Hanoi that the U.S. action would be terminated if the North Vietnamese took no corresponding action. Two months had passed since the president's speech and there had been no movement in Paris. In the meantime, many more deaths had occurred on the battlefield.[18]

Rusk and Rostow, on the other hand, thought the message lacked clarity. They urged that Kosygin be asked for a specific explanation of what Hanoi would do to reciprocate. They wanted an explicit understanding in advance—not only from Moscow, but also from Hanoi—as to what would happen if the United States stopped bombing targets in North Vietnam. The president, once again caught between his top advisers, wavered. He wound up sending a noncommittal message to Kosygin asking what assurances could be given that a positive U.S. action would result in de-escalating the war. Neither Moscow nor Hanoi responded. Instead of a low-cost test of the prospects for peace, there had only been, to Clifford's mind, a sterile exchange of telegrams with Moscow concerning the meaning of Kosygin's message. He believed that Kosygin's initiative had not received a true test and that they might never know if it had meant something or not.[19]

Although the dissension within the administration was, for the most part, unknown to the public—and heatedly denied whenever it became the subject of media speculation—it had become a well-established fact. The distrust between the secretary of state and the secretary of defense, as well as their supporters, reached such a high level that Kosygin's message to Johnson was withheld from the defense secretary for almost a full day. Clifford mentioned this to Rusk at the end of a meeting at the State Department on June 7. The secretary of state apologized and promised it would not happen again. In early June, Rostow had told the State Department executive secretary, Benjamin H. Read—who controlled the distribution of many of the most sensitive telegrams within the government—not to send the Pentagon any of the sensitive telegrams from the Paris negotiating team. Read, who was one of the most respected officials in the government and who was close to Dean Rusk, was also deeply committed to the search for a way out of the war. Read told Rusk that the defense secretary could not do his job properly if he did not receive the telegrams from the negotiating team. Rusk, who firmly believed government should function according to certain rules of rational and civilized behavior, agreed with Read. Without telling Rostow, Read set up a private messenger service through the secretary's military assistant, Col. Robert Pursley, to keep Clifford fully informed of events in Paris from that time forward.[20]

The differences within the administration persisted. Clark Clifford and his supporters continued to be dismayed that the president—having, in his own words, ended his political career in order to devote himself to the pursuit of peace—continued instead to pursue a military victory, seemingly convinced that the war was going so well that he should not lessen his terms for a settlement.

Early in the evening on June 26, Cyrus Vance slipped out through a side door in the American embassy in Paris, eased himself carefully into an unmarked sedan, and traveled by a circuitous route to a "safe house" in the suburbs for a secret meeting with the second-ranking North Vietnamese representative in Paris, Ha Van Lau. After an intense argument within the administration, Vance had been instructed to tell the North Vietnamese that the United States would stop the bombing on three conditions: that it lead to "prompt and productive" talks involving the Saigon government, that the DRV respect the sanctity of the DMZ, and that the communists refrain from launching rocket attacks on major South Vietnamese cities. The North Vietnamese immediately rejected the proposal, stating that they would never accept any conditions regarding the cessation of bombing. Nonetheless, the United States had finally opened a serious secret channel of discussion with Hanoi.[21]

The summer months had seen a significant drop in the level of fighting in South Vietnam as the communists regrouped after suffering heavy losses in their two offensives earlier in the year. Most intelligence analysts concluded that the lull foreshadowed another offensive in September or October. There was little doubt the enemy's strategic goal was to influence the American election campaign. In mid-June, the president asked Defense Secretary Clifford to go to Vietnam to assess the situation, then fly to Honolulu and join LBJ for a summit conference with President Thieu scheduled for late July.[22]

On Sunday, July 14, 1968, Clifford flew into Saigon, which, in anticipation of the predicted enemy offensive, had been turned into a gigantic armed camp surrounded by a ring of allied troops on full alert. American B-52s were flying missions against communist strongholds north and west of Saigon as Clifford arrived, and a brigade of the U.S. 9th Infantry Division was engaged in a fierce firefight with North Vietnamese troops in Phouc Vinh Province.

The highlight, if that is the right word, of Clifford's trip to Vietnam was two meetings held in Saigon, one with President Thieu and Premier Ky, the other with Ambassador Bunker. Both were blunt, no subject-barred sessions. The first convinced Clifford that the South Vietnamese leaders did not really want a settlement with Hanoi; the second confirmed his worst fears about the American embassy's attitude and role in encouraging that attitude. Clifford met with Thieu and Ky at the Presidential Palace, which was ringed with South Vietnamese rangers. After listening to a long presentation by the Vietnamese, he began a frank discussion of the American commitment to the war. Flanked by Bunker, Generals Wheeler and Creighton Abrams, Bill Bundy, and Col. Bob Pursley, Clifford told the Vietnamese leaders that, in the absence of visible progress, the American public simply would not support the war effort much longer. If the United States could not achieve a settlement in Paris, the South Vietnamese would gradually have to take over the war.

Bunker was shocked at Clifford's bluntness, but Clifford seemed convinced that the gentle and dignified ambassador had failed to make Thieu and Ky sufficiently aware of the degree of impatience and frustration felt by both the president and the American public. As the outsider from Washington, he thought he could speak more frankly than a resident ambassador.

Saigon's weakness was the major cause of the American dilemma, and Clifford saw no reason to indulge it. Bunker may have perceived growing stability in the government and discovered "statesmanlike" qualities in Nguyen Van Thieu, but Clifford—looking at the situation from Washington's point of view—saw a group of squabbling and corrupt generals, selfishly maneuvering for their own advantage while Americans and Vietnamese continued to die in combat.

Clifford subsequently met with Bunker, accompanied by Deputy Amb. Samuel Berger and Bill Bundy. In what became a somewhat emotional meeting, Clifford told the two ambassadors that they all would be derelict in their duty if they failed to make use of the six months the Johnson administration had left to seek an honorable end to the war. Bunker and Berger were startled by his vehemence and unalterably opposed to his suggestions. Bunker considered it heresy to suggest that Saigon should bend a little to help get negotiations started. Clifford expressed concern that Saigon appeared to oppose any agreement with Hanoi.

Clifford was convinced that his was an isolated voice among the senior people in the administration. Moreover, the Saigon trip only increased his conviction that the war was drifting along out of control. He sent the president a message asking for a private meeting with him, Rusk, and Rostow as soon as he arrived in Honolulu. When they landed, Bunker immediately rushed to Rusk and alerted him to the tone Clifford was going to take with the president.[23]

During his meeting with LBJ, Rusk, and Rostow, Clifford made three points. First, he was more certain than ever that the United States could not win the war militarily. His second point shocked the president and visibly disturbed and offended Rusk. He stated that he was "absolutely certain" the South Vietnamese government did not want the war to end—not while they were being protected by more than half a million U.S. troops and were the recipients of a "golden flow of money." Thieu and Ky clearly feared the loss of American support the moment the war ended. Moreover, Clifford stated, the entire American-Vietnamese relationship was riddled with corruption. The senior civilian in the government, Prime Minister Tran Van Huong, had put it well: corruption was the "national cancer."

Finally, Clifford urged the president to inform the Vietnamese that the United States would make an all-out effort to settle the war during the next six months. He suggested that the president explain to Thieu that the next president, whether Nixon or Humphrey, would have a strong national mandate to end the war—which meant Thieu would have less bargaining power and less influence in Washington. He pointed out that every candidate, with the exception of George Wallace, was making statements that suggested moving away from support of the war. (For example, Richard Nixon, the most likely Republican nominee, had referred to "phasing out" the American troop presence in South Vietnam. The Republican platform contained similar language.)

After Clifford finished, Rusk said he disagreed with all three of his points, and repeated his familiar arguments. President Johnson, only a few hours away from his scheduled meeting with the South Vietnamese president, was clearly made uncomfortable by the fundamental rift between his top two cabinet officers. At the appointed time, the two presidents began their summit with a forty-five-minute private meeting. Afterward, LBJ pulled Clifford aside and told him that he had been impressed with his three points and had raised all of them with Thieu.[24]

The United States had given its word that it would not participate in serious talks on the future of South Vietnam without a Saigon representative present as a full participant. In Honolulu, however, Thieu sought a further commitment from Johnson: that he would not stop the bombing until all North Vietnamese troops had been withdrawn from the South. This would have constituted a major hardening of the U.S. position. However, the Paris talks seemed far away from Honolulu, and no one present wanted a confrontation with Thieu over what appeared to be a theoretical point. The U.S. representatives thus chose to treat his efforts as a propaganda ploy rather than an indication of serious trouble to come. They should have taken Thieu's views more seriously and recognized that he and Ky (as Clifford had told the president and Rusk) opposed making any settlement.

However, given the president's refusal to resolve the internal conflict within his administration, it was impossible to formulate a coordinated position, even as a contingency, for dealing with Saigon. As a result of the delicate balance within the administration over how to deal with Saigon, it was given to the man on the ground, Ambassador Bunker, to cast the deciding vote.

All factors considered, the Honolulu summit proved to be a misguided venture that set back U.S. negotiating efforts in Paris without advancing the nation's military objectives in Vietnam. The big winner seemed to be Nguyen Van Thieu. He had failed to obtain his primary objective, but his rigid positions, which Bunker supported, stiffened the American position. The United States had gained nothing in return, not even a vague acceptance of the need for greater flexibility in Paris. Bunker returned to Saigon satisfied. Clifford returned to Washington determined to continue the fight for the president's heart and mind—where the final decisions would be made.[25]

The invasion of Czechoslovakia took place on the eve of the Democratic convention in Chicago, but the Democrats barely paused to notice it as they battled fiercely over the Vietnam section of the platform. It was now clear that the Democrats, having lost Bobby Kennedy and not wishing to embrace Eugene McCarthy, were going to nominate Hubert Humphrey. As vice president, he had loyally supported a Vietnam policy he had played no role in creating. Now he found himself trapped between his natural liberal constituency and the man to whom he owed his job. During the summer, he considered issuing a limited declaration of independence from the administration on the war. It was inevitable that word of this should reach the president—and equally inevitable that he would react furiously. At times, he branded Humphrey weak and "disloyal." More importantly, however, the possibility of Humphrey's defection stiffened the president's resolve not to make concessions to Hanoi and made him determined to obtain the Democratic Party's backing for his Vietnam policy at the convention.

Humphrey had decided to try to bridge the split within the Democratic Party by offering the "doves" an olive branch with conciliatory language in the platform. There was historical irony in the fact that Hubert Humphrey, who had risen to prominence in 1948 by refusing to agree to a platform compromise on civil rights, would pay such a heavy price for his efforts at a platform compromise in 1968. Humphrey's success depended on the president accepting a platform that differed, at least slightly, from that of the administration. However, this was asking too much of Lyndon Johnson, who was feeling beleaguered and betrayed, and had decided to fight back.

The next two weeks were a nightmare for the vice president, who was actively searching for a position that would satisfy both the liberals and the president. Humphrey and his advisers actually achieved this seemingly impossible feat with a carefully worded draft statement that was accepted by

Dean Rusk and Walt Rostow, on one hand, and the moderate liberals, on the other. On the eve of the convention, however, in a fateful telephone call, the president told Humphrey he could not accept the compromise plank. Humphrey then made a critical decision: He acceded to the demands of his president and supported a plank that was unacceptable to the liberals, thus ensuring that there would be an up-down vote on the platform.

President Johnson's platform victory was a disaster for Humphrey. At a moment when he should have been pulling the party back together to prepare for the battle against Republican Richard Nixon, Humphrey had been bludgeoned into a position that had further split the party and given more evidence of his own weakness. There was worse yet to come: the battle of Chicago, one of the low points in the history of American politics, was about to unfold. As the convention got under way, televised scenes of police officers in riot gear using tear gas and clubbing young demonstrators senseless drove a dagger into the heart of the Democratic Party and its candidate.[26]

On July 29, Averell Harriman and Cyrus Vance boldly proposed that, after consultations with Saigon and other U.S. allies, the president announce his intention to stop the bombing on the assumption that the North Vietnamese would not take advantage of the halt. "If [these] assumptions are invalidated," they said in a cable to Washington, "we would resume the bombing." It was the right proposal at the wrong time. The president would have none of it. He called the telegram "mush," and said it was part of a conspiracy designed to force him to stop the bombing. "The enemy is using my own people as dupes," he said bitterly.[27]

As September began and Election Day neared, Clifford hoped the president might become more flexible. Johnson was clearly relieved that both parties had adopted platforms supporting the administration's position in Vietnam. However, he was beginning to smart under Nixon's attack on his domestic programs. Perhaps the fact that the election was proceeding without him was beginning to sink in on the old campaigner. At one point, LBJ said: "Look, I want the Vice President to win. I want the Democratic party to win. They are better for the country. I have told the Cabinet not to let the records of their departments be distorted by the Republicans. I want the Cabinet to do whatever is appropriate to help the Vice President. Where I help depends on where the Vice President wants me to help. Humphrey wants space. In his heart he is with us, but he thinks it is politically wise to keep space."[28]

Clifford was encouraged by this declaration of support for Humphrey. He knew that Humphrey, in his heart, was against the war, but the defense secretary still thought it was necessary to stick with the president.

On the weekend of September 14–15, a three-thousand-word telegram from Harriman and Vance arrived. They had just finished the first significant private conversation with Le Duc Tho and Xuan Thuy, the North Vietnamese negotiators. For the first time, they said, they were ready to begin serious discussions immediately after the bombing stopped. The telegram had arrived at a fortuitous moment. Even the president seemed impressed with the news of the first break in Paris. Nevertheless, the president adamantly refused to announce an unconditional bombing halt without receiving some form of advance public commitment from the North Vietnamese.[29]

American presidential elections affect people throughout the world, and other governments have preferences, expressed or otherwise, among the candidates. However, no other election in U.S. history had ever seen, or probably will ever see, as much overt involvement by foreign governments as that of 1968. One of those governments, the Republic of Vietnam, actually succeeded in affecting the outcome. As *New York Times* columnist William Safire stated, "Given the narrow margin of Nixon's victory it seems clear that the outcome of the 1968 election, and with it, the shape of politics in America for the next generation, was decided by the events of October."[30]

As that decisive month began, it was clear that it was too late for LBJ to negotiate an end to the long war in Vietnam—but it was not too late to engage in significant negotiations. If such talks were to begin before November 5, they no doubt would help Humphrey. The final four weeks of the campaign thus were played out against a backdrop of almost unbelievable pressure and drama in Paris, Washington, and Saigon—and quite possibly Moscow and Hanoi as well.

Ambassador Harriman returned to Washington on September 17 and met with the president. The old Cold War negotiator told Johnson that he was convinced the North Vietnamese clearly understood the U.S. position regarding violations of the demilitarized zone or the conduct of significant attacks on South Vietnamese cities during a total bombing halt. He doubted, however, that they would ever enter into a formal agreement, because they wished to claim a bombing halt was "unconditional." Cyrus Vance, America's second principal negotiator, met with the president on October 3. He repeated Harriman's perceptions and indicated to the president that he and Harriman would continue emphasizing the three points LBJ insisted on in order to ensure there was no misunderstanding.[31]

The secret talks in Paris suddenly seemed to accelerate. Meeting with Harriman and Vance in the Paris suburbs on October 11, the North Vietnamese envoys asked whether the United States would stop the bombing if it had a clear answer concerning the Saigon government's participation in the talks. The next day, Vance's counterpart at the Soviet embassy in Paris delivered an urgent message from Moscow. Using language deliberately identical to Kosygin's June 5 letter to the president, he told Vance that if the United States stopped bombing North Vietnam, Hanoi would agree to the Saigon government's participation in the ensuing negotiations.

Bunker and Abrams cabled that they would support an end to the bombing of the North if there were prior understandings on the sanctity of the DMZ, no shelling of the South's major cities, "serious talks," and, of course, full participation by Saigon. Bunker predicted that Thieu would "find these instructions acceptable," but that he "must be given time to inform" Vice President Ky, Prime Minister Huong, and others.[32]

That same day, unbeknownst to anyone in the Johnson administration, Henry Kissinger secretly informed Nixon's campaign manager, John Mitchell, that there was a strong probability the administration would stop bombing North Vietnam before the election. Kissinger had met privately in Paris with Harriman, Vance, and other members of the delegation in mid-September, just before the first Harriman-Vance secret meeting with the North Vietnamese, and they had shared with him their frustration and brought him up to date on the state of the negotiations.[33]

While Harriman and Vance waited in Paris for instructions on how to answer Hanoi, Bunker obtained, or thought he had obtained, Thieu's agreement with the American negotiating position. "Thieu concurs in instructions to be given Harriman-Vance," he cabled Washington. The next day, October 14, he sent a more detailed report that included this passage: "Thieu then said so long as we are going to press the offensive in the South and in Laos, and so long as we are prepared to resume the bombing if they violate the DMZ or attack the main cities, he is ready to go along. 'After all,' he said, 'the main problem is not to stop the bombing but to stop the war, and we must try this path to see if they are serious.' I thought this a statesman's view." After receiving this message, officials in Washington were certain Thieu had committed himself and his government to the U.S. negotiating position, as Ambassador Bunker had reported. Bunker's personal comment at the end of his report, Clifford thought, revealed yet again his excessive regard for Thieu.[34]

The president needed to send Harriman and Vance their instructions, but, as he had in March, he wanted to meet with the Joint Chiefs of Staff before making any final decisions. He even asked Westmoreland, who was in the hospital undergoing tests, to attend. Johnson wanted to ensure that the former Vietnam commander supported the policy. One by one, the chiefs, including a reluctant Westmoreland, said they agreed with the new instructions to Harriman and Vance as long as aerial reconnaissance over the North continued and the bombing would resume if Hanoi violated the understanding. Westmoreland later stated that he thought Clifford's attitude had gone "beyond dovishness." The defense secretary's indecision, Westmoreland charged, helped prolong the war. The president concluded the meeting with the following statement: "I know I will be charged with doing this to influence the election. Nixon will be disappointed. The doves will criticize us for not doing this earlier. The hawks will say I shouldn't have done it at all. I don't have much confidence in the Soviets or the North Vietnamese. I don't think they will accept this. And if they accept, I don't think they will honor it. But if this doesn't work, I don't think I will have another opportunity."[35]

That evening, the president's advisers assembled again. It was their third meeting of the day. This time, only the president, Rusk, Rostow, Wheeler, Tom Johnson, and Clifford were present. The president pledged them to total secrecy before asking each of them, rather formally, if they agreed with the instructions to move forward with the North Vietnamese. After everyone concurred, he told Rusk to send the message to Paris that would trigger a full bombing halt and formal negotiations on ending the war. It seemed that the United States was at last prepared to stop the bombing campaign.

However, just when it seemed that the key players in the Johnson administration were at last in agreement, Rusk and Rostow obtained presidential approval for a new condition. In order to show the world that the United States had "gotten something" in return for calling a halt to the bombing of North Vietnam, Harriman and Vance were instructed to tell Hanoi that negotiations must begin within twenty-four hours after the last bomb fell. The next day, October 15, Ambassador Bunker reported from Saigon that President Thieu wanted Washington to delay its response to Hanoi while he conferred with his own government.[36]

Within hours, a message from Hanoi matched the delay request from Saigon. The "next day requirement" amounted to a new condition, Thuy said. He told Vance that, while Hanoi would be ready to meet with American negotiators the day after the bombing stopped, the North Vietnamese could not guarantee the presence of representatives of the National Liberation Front, the political organization of the Vietcong, within such a short time. Harriman and Vance strongly recommended that the United States proceed with the bombing halt even if it did not know when the NLF representatives would show up. Clifford reluctantly disagreed with his colleagues in Paris. He took the position that America should not stop the bombing until it knew when the four-party talks would begin. However, he saw no reason to insist on a meeting within twenty-four hours after the bombing stopped; he thought that any reasonable "date certain" for the first meeting should be sufficient, and said so. The president and Rusk, agreeing with Clifford's position, relayed the word to Paris.[37]

On October 16, the president placed a conference call to all three presidential candidates, including the independent, George Wallace, to bring them up to date on the situation. Nixon promised he would make no statement that might undercut the negotiations. Rumors that something big was about to happen in Paris began to spread through the world press. Carefully worded and technically accurate denials kept the story under control, just barely, but the rumors put everyone, especially the Republicans, on full alert.[38]

However, just as the administration reached accord in Paris, its agreement with the South Vietnamese began to fall apart. Calling Bunker to his office on October 17, Thieu now raised a series of specific objections to the agreement the United States had reached with Hanoi. He said he was concerned that the NLF would be treated as a "separate government" in the Paris talks, with its own flag and other attributes of sovereignty. It was clear, said Thieu, that the Americans sought different objectives from a bombing halt: they wanted only to ensure that it did not lead to increased deaths of American and South Vietnamese soldiers, whereas Thieu sought to prevent the NLF from gaining political advantage by obtaining recognition as a separate delegation at the negotiations. Bunker reported that Thieu's concerns were minor problems that would be cleared up quickly. The result was that Washington failed to pay them sufficient attention.

Thieu, in an emotional session with Bunker on October, once again stiffened his position. He stated that the NLF should not participate in the Paris talks unless it was as part of the North Vietnamese delegation. Whatever the logic in this proposal from Saigon's point of view, Thieu had never previously suggested anything like it in more than five months of detailed discussions. Thieu knew Hanoi would never accept his condition; to introduce it at this point would surely result in a protracted delay in the start of the negotiations.

Near the end of a five-hour marathon meeting in Paris on October 26, Xuan Thuy told Harriman and Vance that if the United States would stop the bombing the next day, the first meeting could occur on November 2, a five-day interval. Acting on instructions from Washington, Harriman and Vance replied that no more than a three-day gap was agreeable. On October 27, the next to last Sunday before the U.S. election, Harriman and Vance met again with Xuan Thuy. Thuy proposed that the United States stop the bombing on October 30. He could not promise that the NLF representatives would be ready for the first meeting on November 2, but said they had agreed to join in "as early as possible." Hanoi's latest concession met almost of the American conditions. If acted on, it meant the bombing would stop on Tuesday, only two days hence, with the first plenary meeting in Paris on Saturday. Cyrus Vance called the White House from Paris. "We have now got everything we have asked for," he said.[39]

When the president's advisers convened at the White House at 7:30 P.M. to consider this issue, the president began with a simple question: "What do you think we should do?" Dean Rusk was the first to respond. "We should go ahead," he said. "I smell vodka and caviar in this proposal. The Soviets have moved into this negotiation." Clifford was encouraged. It seemed that he and Rusk finally were on the same side. "Why do we have to yield now?" the president asked. "If ten steps once separated us, they have taken eight and we have taken two," Clifford replied. "I would say it is even nine to one in our favor," Rusk added. "I still think this is a political move to affect this election," the president said, still conflicted. Rusk responded with unusual strength: "Even if this were so, Mr. President, it is in our interests to do so." The president continued to express reluctance. "I think we are being herded into this under pressure," he said. "I want Soviet assurances on the DMZ and the cities. November 2 is a bad date, a dangerous date. Nearly everyone will think it is connected to the campaign."

"You have a good story to tell." Clifford said, "For five months we have told Hanoi we couldn't go ahead without Saigon present. Finally, they changed their position. They chose the time, not us. We wanted substantive discussions. They capitulated." The president replied, "I would rather be viewed as stubborn and adamant than be seen as a tricky, slick politician. Everyone will think we're working toward electing Humphrey by doing this. But this is not what motivates us. I want to take it slow."

Clifford and Walt Rostow were puzzled by Johnson's adamant refusal to go ahead promptly now that the North Vietnamese had gone so far. Even General Wheeler indicated that the military agreed the administration had achieved all of its negotiating objectives with Hanoi. Finally, the president said that he needed another discussion with General Abrams before he would agree to anything. "Abrams has the color of the field commander," he said. "Senator Russell tells me Abrams would be the most effective in selling a bombing halt. Let's get him back."

Why did the president take such a negative position? Clifford concluded that with the election only nine days away, he was determined not to let anyone conclude he was acting to help Humphrey. The president justified his position rather ingenuously, stating: "I had deliberately taken myself out of political contention in order to devote all my energy to the urgent tasks that remained. I had done this to remove any doubt about political motivations or ambitions regarding any action I felt had to be taken." Clifford pointed out to him that, at this stage of the campaign, either action or inaction would benefit one candidate and hurt the other. What did it matter if a bombing halt helped Humphrey? Continued bombing would help Nixon. The president should focus on the search for peace and not worry about its effect on the election. It would be irresponsible to pass up an opportunity for negotiations that might not be there after Election Day.

At about the same time, a new and potentially explosive factor entered the picture: the discovery, through intelligence channels, of a plot—there seems to be no other word for it—to help Nixon win the election by flagrant interference in the negotiations. Two people played key roles in electing Richard Nixon in 1968: Bui Diem, South Vietnam's ambassador in Washington, and Anna Chennault, the Chinese-born widow of Maj. Gen. Claire Chennault, the commander of the famed Flying Tigers in Burma and China during World War II. A small, intense, and energetic woman, Mrs. Chennault was chairwoman of Republican Women for Nixon in 1968. Early in the year, she took Bui Diem to New York to meet Nixon. When Diem alerted his closest friend in the administration, Bill Bundy, of the meeting, Bundy raised no objections. It was quite appropriate for an ambassador to meet with a former vice president. Diem, however, neglected to mention to Bundy that he had, at Nixon's request, opened a secret personal channel to John Mitchell and other senior members of the Nixon team through Chennault and John Tower, the Republican senator from Texas.

There were few people in Washington as well informed as the popular and affable Bui Diem. The State Department kept him informed of the negotiations in Paris, his own government sent him reports on the Bunker-Thieu talks in Saigon, and he maintained close relations with many prominent Americans, especially Republican conservatives in Congress. It was not difficult for Ambassador Diem to pass information to Anna Chennault, who was, she later said, in contact with John Mitchell "at least once a day." Even more important, Diem could convey advice from the Nixon camp to Thieu.[40]

In his memoirs, Diem claims he sent only two "relevant messages" to Saigon during October. Although "they constituted circumstantial evidence for anybody ready to assume the worst," he wrote, "they certainly did not mean that I had arranged a deal with the Republicans." Some of Diem's messages to Saigon later became public. On October 23, he cabled Thieu: "Many Republican friends have contacted me and encouraged us to stand firm. They were alarmed by press reports to the effect that you had already softened your position." Four days later, on October 27, he cabled: "The longer the present situation continues, the more we are favored. . . . I am regularly in touch with the Nixon entourage." In his book, as well as in a recent conversation, Diem admits sending those cables but adds that he made no deal with the Republicans. There are, he states, "uncomfortable ambiguities" in the situation.[41]

Diem was not Anna Chennault's only channel to Saigon. "My impression was that she might have played her own game in encouraging both the South Vietnamese and the Republicans," he later wrote. She took seriously Nixon's request that she act as "the sole representative between the Vietnamese government and the Nixon campaign headquarters," and she certainly found other routes for communicating with President Thieu—including the South Vietnamese ambassador to Taiwan, who happened to be Thieu's brother. What was conveyed to Thieu through the Chennault channel may never be fully known, but there was no doubt that she conveyed a simple and authoritative message from the Nixon camp that was probably decisive in convincing President Thieu to defy President Johnson—thus delaying the negotiations and prolonging the war. Rather proudly, she recounted one specific message she received from John Mitchell in the last few days of the campaign: "Anna," she quotes him as saying, "I'm speaking on behalf of Mr. Nixon. It's very important that our Vietnamese friends understand our Republican position and I hope you have made that clear to them."[42]

The activities of the Nixon team went far beyond the bounds of justifiable political combat. It constituted direct interference in an international negotiation and the administration's responsibilities to negotiate on behalf of the nation. The Nixon campaign's activities constituted what probably was illegal interference in the nation's security affairs by private individuals.

The Johnson administration first became aware of these activities through the normal operations of the intelligence community in the weeks prior to the election. Gradually, the president and his advisers began to realize that President Thieu's growing resistance to meetings in Paris was being encouraged, indeed stimulated, by the Republicans, especially Anna Chennault, whom they referred to as the "Little Flower."

In total privacy—and, at the president's direction, without consulting Humphrey—the president, Rusk, Rostow, and Clifford discussed what to do about the Republican attempt to thwart the negotiations. It was an extraordinary dilemma. On one hand, the administration had positive evidence that Mrs. Chennault and other people speaking for the Republican candidate were encouraging President Thieu to delay the negotiations, to keep the war going for political reasons. On the other, the information had been derived from extremely sensitive intelligence gathering operations of the Federal Bureau of Investigation, the Central Intelligence Agency, and the National Security Agency that included surveillance of the ambassador of a U.S. ally and an American citizen with strong political ties to the Republican Party. In a decision filled with consequences for both the election and history—and acting on the advice of Secretary of State Rusk—President Johnson, although furious at Mrs. Chennault, never used the information or made it public in any way.[43]

All this raises a critical question: What did Richard Nixon know, and when did he know it? In the terminology of the Watergate era, no "smoking gun" has ever turned up linking Nixon directly to the secret messages to Thieu. There are no self-incriminating tapes from the campaign, no documentary proof. The whole incident has been relegated to the status of an unsolved mystery. On the other hand, the chain of events described undeniably began in Richard Nixon's apartment in New York. Moreover, his closest adviser, John Mitchell, personally ran the Chennault channel—with full understanding of its sensitivity. Given the importance of these events, it is reasonable to assume that Mitchell told Nixon about them, and that Nixon knew, and approved, of what was going on in his name.

In the middle of October, the whole negotiation, so painfully developed over so much time, began to unravel not only in Saigon and in Paris, but also in Washington. As the week began, General Abrams secretly boarded a C-141 transport jet in Saigon to return to Washington. Bunker met with Thieu in Saigon to go over the agreement negotiated in Paris. He reported that Thieu stated, "I don't see how we can ask for anything more." Kosygin again weighed in with a strongly worded message, this time stating that any "doubts with regard to the position of the [North] Vietnamese side are without foundation."

Early that evening, LBJ met with his advisers to discuss their next steps. The president continued to withhold his final decision, pending a discussion with Abrams, who was due to land at Andrews Air Force Base around 2 A.M. Clifford argued that Hanoi had met every one of the original U.S. conditions, and that the administration could not keep adding new ones. Rusk agreed. "The record is as hard as it can be short of a contract," he said. As the president adjourned the meeting, he asked everyone present to return to the White House later that night for a meeting with Abrams.

At 2:30 A.M., LBJ's advisers reassembled at the White House. The president began the meeting with a long review of the negotiations. Everyone in the room except Abrams had witnessed these events—they all understood that the review was for the field commander's benefit. It was, Clifford thought, a sort of dress rehearsal for the public defense of the president's actions if he should ever be accused of stopping the bombing for political purposes.

The president began interrogating Abrams. "I am going to put more weight on your judgment than that of anyone else," he said. Rusk and Clifford listened in silence for nearly an hour. They knew the general's answers could still derail a bombing halt, and, although General Wheeler had reassured Clifford that Abrams understood the situation, he was not entirely sure how the general would respond. The defense secretary listened intently to the president's questions and Abrams's replies:

"General, do you think they will violate the DMZ and the cities?"

"I think they will abide by it on the DMZ, Mr. President. On the cities, I am not so sure. I am concerned about Saigon."

"If the enemy honors our agreement, will this be an advantage militarily for us?"

"Yes, Mr. President."

"Will it compensate for lack of bombing north of the 19th parallel?"

"Yes, sir, it will."

"Can we return to full-scale bombing easily if they attack?"

"Yes, sir, very easily."

"In August you said that stopping the bombing would increase enemy capability several fold. Why can we stop the bombing now?"

"First, our interdiction in the panhandle [of North Vietnam] has been successful. Second, they haven't replaced their losses in the region. He cannot cause the mischief he could have caused in August."

Abrams's answer gave Clifford a private sense of vindication after his long dispute with Rostow and the president over the effectiveness of the restricted bombing.

"Can we do this without additional casualties?" the president asked.

"Yes, sir, we can."

"If you were President, would you do it?"

"I have no reservations about doing it, even though I know it is stepping into a cesspool of comment. It is the proper thing to do."

Clifford later stated that it was at that point in the exchange between LBJ and his combat commander that he remembered thinking: "Abrams has carried the ball across the goal line."

The president solemnly polled his senior advisers one by one, although he already knew where they stood on the matter. First Rusk, then Clifford, and then Wheeler urged him to proceed. He asked Rusk, special counselor Harry McPherson, and Clifford to start drafting a speech immediately.[44]

While the president and his advisers met with Abrams, Bunker was with Thieu in an effort to gain his final approval. "When do we hear from Bunker?" the president asked. Rusk replied that they were waiting for a telephone call and a "flash" message. As they waited, they received an intelligence report stating that an NLF delegation had left Hanoi for Paris. Wheeler and Clifford returned to the Pentagon where they began preparing the orders to halt the bombing. Shortly after 6 A.M., Rusk called with terrible news: Thieu had reneged on everything to which he had previously agreed. Johnson immediately reconvened his cabinet officials. They were all, by this time, weary, angry, and depressed. According to Bunker's cable, Thieu had decided that November 2 was "too soon" for the first meeting, ignoring the fact that it was Washington and Saigon that had insisted on the shortest possible time frame between the cessation of bombing and the first meeting. Thieu said he needed to consult with the South Vietnamese National Security Council again. Bunker reported that he had told Thieu there was no reason for any further delay, but he ended his cable with a comment that suggested to Clifford that he was neither sufficiently forceful nor committed to bringing the South Vietnamese president around: "We have put Thieu under such constraints of secrecy, which he has observed, that he feels he needs more time to bring [his National Security Council] and others along. I think that they can be brought around to a joint announcement tomorrow or next day if we could offer them a short postponement of the meeting date."

It was a shattering message, an unexpected disaster. Clifford was furious.

"They can get a man to Paris in twenty-four hours," Bunker's cable continued. "They could use their Ambassador in Paris. . . . Their objection does not have merit. It seems to me they are playing extraordinary games. . . . It seems reprehensible and utterly without merit. We must force them to Paris."[45]

The president immediately concurred. He attributed Thieu's intransigence to the secret channels operating on Nixon's behalf. "It would rock the world if it were said that Thieu was conniving with the Republicans," LBJ speculated. "Can you imagine what people would say if it were to be known that Hanoi has met all these conditions and then Nixon's conniving with them kept us from getting it?"

Rusk wavered between wanting to confront Thieu and agreeing to Bunker's request for a "short" delay, but gradually moved toward Bunker's position. He did not want to have an open break with Saigon. "Let's not give the orders to stop the bombing until we get one more bounce back with Thieu out there," he said.

Clifford was fed up with Saigon, and ready for the break: "We have two courses. One, we can wait another day to see what Thieu says. Two, we can tell Thieu that this is the plan we agreed to, and it is too late to turn back, that it is the will of the president and the American people. I much prefer the second."

Rusk, believing the United States could not make an ally act against its will, tried to take the long view: "President Kennedy said we would make a battle there to save South Vietnam. That set us on course. We lost 29,000 men killed and invested $75 billion to keep South Vietnam from being overrun. We must be careful not to flush all this down the drain. But we do have a right to expect cooperation from the South Vietnamese. . . . If the problem in Saigon is only a matter of timing, we should set a time convenient to them."

Clifford saw this background as being irrelevant. If Thieu refused to honor agreements he had made with the United States, Clifford believed that Washington would have to go it alone. He stated that Saigon had wanted to be at the talks and that North Vietnam had finally agreed to that. He pointed out that the South Vietnamese had had five months to select their Paris representative; they were putting Bunker off, making it difficult for him to talk to them; and they were letting U.S. domestic politics sway them. "I consider this an issue of good faith," the defense secretary said. There was no reason, in his estimation, to share Bunker's belief that Thieu might come around if given another day.

Harriman and Vance were up in arms. Harriman was particularly bitter and angry with Bunker. He blistered his old Yale schoolmate in a conversation over the secure telephone. Looking at what might be his last days of public service, Harriman wanted to force Thieu to bend to America's will. Unfortunately, there was no way the United States could physically force its South Vietnamese ally to send a delegation to Paris. In truth, the United States now had only two choices: either go it alone or allow Thieu to sink the negotiations in Paris.

Within hours the presidential advisers met again, this time for their regularly scheduled Tuesday Lunch. Rusk indicated that the administration could not let Thieu's refusal sabotage the Paris talks. Already having agreed to expanded talks, he stated, they would have to proceed even though the South Vietnamese were unwilling to send a delegation to Paris. Clifford expressed his disgust with the Saigon government. He said he was sure they were stalling. General Abrams shared his anger. The Pentagon was united on the issue of halting the bombing of North Vietnam and proceeding with negotiations to end the war. The president thanked Abrams for making the long and tiring flight, then suggested he immediately return to Saigon. As Abrams left, Clifford congratulated him warmly and told him he had performed magnificently.[46]

345

Despite their unanimity, the president's advisers were still unable to convince LBJ of the need to press on with the talks. During the afternoon, more bad news arrived from Bunker. Thieu had refused to see him again, and Foreign Minister Thanh had said that a plenary session of Parliament was needed to authorize the government to send a delegation to Paris. The South Vietnamese government, Thanh said, would need "materially more time" to prepare. Bunker's reply to this negative message from the foreign minister seemed to most of the president's advisers to be weak and inadequate. Bunker's report concluded: "I pressed Thanh again to say whether I should report to Washington that the GVN [Government of (South) Vietnam] is not going to cooperate with Pres Johnson's request, and again he said it was only a matter of time and clarification. . . . I then said I regretted very much to conclude from our conversation that I had to report that the GVN is not prepared to cooperate with us in ending bombing and scheduling negotiations on the basis that we had proposed."

To Washington's amazement, Bunker then suggested giving Thieu another twenty-four-hour delay so that members of his government could "pull themselves together." Clifford indicated that he was appalled at the tone of Bunker's message. Where was the anger that should be shown when an ambassador receives a message he thinks is insulting to the president and the nation? Rusk and Clifford, prior to a subsequent meeting at the White House, were now in agreement and came to a common course of action they both would recommend. They said it seemed self-evident that Saigon's delays were caused by the South Vietnamese leaders' preference for Nixon over Humphrey and not by substantive concerns. Clifford stated their recommendation: "Bunker should tell Thieu that either he comes with us or we go it alone. Although sometimes doing nothing is the best course, this is not such a time. I feel it is inappropriate for us, after bearing these burdens for so many years, to turn this war over to Thieu and a new Administration in this manner."

President Johnson, however, was once again uncertain as to how to proceed. He told his advisers:

> We don't want to tear ourselves to pieces over this. Doing it before
> the election would be interpreted as political. The Nixon forces have
> been working on South Vietnam. We must reassess this. We can't
> walk out, quit, split—we have to hold together. Sure, we must tell
> Saigon we won't stand for their vetoing this deal but . . . you see the
> reasons for Saigon's concern. It may be better to wait until after the
> election. . . . I don't feel good about a quickie before the election.
> Let's not go it alone. I know what forces are at work. I would be

willing to agree to a postponement for a day or two before I broke up the alliance with South Vietnam. . . . Thieu and the others are voting for a man they see as the one who will stick with it—Nixon. . . . I think we have to give Thieu some more time.

The president said he wanted to postpone the starting date of the Paris talks until November 4, as Bunker and Rusk had previously suggested. He asked that a strong message be sent to Bunker to deliver to Thieu, warning him that the United States might go it alone if he did not join in those talks. The long day, which had started with Abrams's enthusiastic support for the bombing halt, had ended dismally, as far as Defense Secretary Clifford was concerned. That same day, President Johnson sent President Thieu a personal message urging him to join the Americans in Paris under the arrangements already worked out.[47]

Bunker's next report arrived early in the morning on October 30. He had delivered a strong message to Thieu, whose answer amounted to a refusal to participate in any talks with Hanoi prior to Election Day. He said he needed a week between the cessation of bombing and the opening session of the talks. He would give a formal answer later that evening, but it seemed clear what that answer would be: Hoping for a Nixon victory, Thieu would stall. Nonetheless, Bunker still held out hope. If Thieu did not agree to the U.S. position in Paris, Bunker recommended they go ahead and halt the bombing on October 31, but agree to a one-week delay before the first meeting in Paris. It was the first time Bunker had recommended a break, even a small one, with Saigon.

Shortly before noon, the president received Thieu's answer to his personal message. Although the reply was friendly and expressed deep appreciation for everything the United States had done to help South Vietnam survive, it made clear that Thieu would not accept the U.S. proposal unless certain conditions were met. Realizing that the conditions Thieu sought were impossible to achieve, LBJ decided to go forward with his plans.[48]

Later that morning, Clifford received a call from the president, who expressed his significant change of heart about the negotiations. He asked the defense secretary to return at once to the White House. "We have to act, with or without Saigon," LBJ said. "Let's start all over again, and see if a different approach will give us some sort of result." The president quickly took over the White House meeting. "Tell Bunker we are ready to go tonight," he told Rusk. The United States would stop the bombing on the following day, October 31, and wished to schedule the first plenary meeting for Wednesday, November 6, the day after the election. This would leave the United States, as Johnson put it, "a hundred and sixty-eight hours until next Wednesday" to persuade Saigon to send someone to Paris, as Bunker had suggested. The president said he wanted to announce the complete cessation of the bombing to the nation the following day.

Near the end of the meeting, LBJ disclosed another reason for his change of heart: "There are two things that caused me to make my decision. One was the constant harassing and persuasive and eloquent argument of a fellow named Clifford. . . . The second thing is General [Abrams] saying here in this room what the other generals said to me—that this bombing halt does not hurt our men and really helps them."[49]

There is no doubt that Clifford had raised doubts in the president's mind concerning the policies that continued to be advocated and defended by his other close and trusted advisers. As was his way, Johnson, who sought consensus among his advisers, had finally achieved that consensus in a dramatic fashion with his field commander. The American people—indeed, most of the government bureaucracy—heard only faint echoes of this policy debate within the administration. The president, to a large extent, was isolated from the public on this issue; his decisions were personal decisions.

Defense Secretary Clifford awoke on October 31 believing it was the day the United States was finally going to stop bombing North Vietnam. However, understanding that he had walked up this mountain several times in the last two weeks, only to be disappointed each time, Clifford had a feeling that Bunker would ask for another delay before the day was over. Later that morning, Clifford received a call from Ben Read in the State Department. "Thieu is acting very badly," he said, sounding worried. He said that while they were sleeping, Bunker had held separate meetings with Thieu, Ky, and Thanh to make sure they understood that the United States was going to proceed with or without them. The South Vietnamese National Security Council was still in session and still objecting to U.S. actions. Despite his own reports, Bunker, to everyone's amazement, still thought Thieu was "coming around," and said there was a better than fifty-fifty chance the South Vietnamese government would go along with the Americans. Clifford was furious, but not surprised.

Clifford's next call was from the president. He had just received, in response to his request, a written statement from the Joint Chiefs of Staff stating that stopping the bombing "constitutes a perfectly acceptable military risk." Johnson wanted a stronger statement of support from the armed forces' top officers. "They are weaseling out," he said. Clifford almost begged him to forget about the chiefs. Their letter was sufficient, he said. In any case, it was the most the defense secretary could get in writing from them. The president's closest advisers met at the White House midday to help draft the final portion of LBJ's speech.[50]

As they reviewed the draft, the president said he was still worried that he might be making a mistake and asked Clifford whether Hanoi's concessions might not be an indication that they were "washed up militarily." Clifford responded that, in his opinion, although the enemy had been hurt, they retained the capability to fight on indefinitely.

In Saigon, Bunker had completed a painful, seven-hour marathon session with Thieu that had been punctuated by outbursts of anger by the South Vietnamese. The two men failed to agree on a position that would satisfy both the United States and South Vietnam. The die was finally and irrevocably cast. The president instructed Bunker to inform Thieu that the United States believed it had no choice but to proceed with a unilateral announcement. At 6 P.M., LBJ placed a conference call to the three presidential candidates to inform them of his speech. He made one particular allusion to the Chennault-Thieu channel: "Some old China hands are going around and implying to some of the Embassies and some others that they might get a better deal out of somebody that was not involved in this. Now that's made it difficult and it's held up things a bit, and I know that none of you candidates are aware of it or responsible for it."

Nixon wrote in his memoirs that he was not surprised at the news of the bombing halt. He had been kept informed through "a highly unusual channel," Henry Kissinger, who "continued to have entree into the Administration's foreign policy inner circles." He added that his real reaction to Johnson's decision to stop the bombing was "anger and frustration." However, ignoring the veiled allusion to the Chennault channel, Nixon told Johnson he would support the decision completely.[51]

At 8 P.M., the order went out to the air force and the navy to halt all aerial bombing of North Vietnam as soon as possible, and within twelve hours at the latest. The president spoke to the American people on television that evening. He announced that he had "ordered all air, naval and artillery bombardment of North Vietnam to cease as of 8:00 a.m. Washington time, Friday morning." He indicated that a regular session of the peace talks would be held the following week and that "representatives of the government of South Vietnam are free to participate." The president also indicated that NLF representatives would also be present, but emphasized that their presence did not indicate recognition of the Vietcong in any way. The president stated that events had reached the stage where "productive talks can begin." He also warned the American people that the beginning of talks did not mean that peace had come to Southeast Asia. "There may be hard fighting ahead," the president said.[52]

On November 2, the last weekend before the election, Thieu played the single best card he had left to help Nixon: he announced flatly and publicly that he would not send anyone to the November 6 talks in Paris. It was a final blow to the administration and to Hubert Humphrey's candidacy. Bunker, who had misread Thieu at every step, was powerless to stop him. So was the entire Johnson administration. In growing fury at the Chennault-Thieu connection, Johnson told Sen. Everett Dirksen, the Republican Senate minority leader, on November 3 that he knew all about Anna Chennault's activities. Dirksen, the man who probably came closest to being a true friend of both Johnson and Nixon (and who also knew Chennault well), immediately informed Nixon of Johnson's fury and warned that Johnson might make the connection public. Nixon called the president, who was at the LBJ Ranch awaiting the Humphreys's arrival. Sensitive to Johnson's mood, Nixon realized the danger to his floundering campaign if he failed to placate the president and the secret channel to Saigon became public. Anna Chennault and Bui Diem, at John Mitchell's suggestion, had convinced Thieu to boycott the November 6 meeting in Paris. Now Nixon had to persuade Johnson that these activities were not of his doing. The candidate succeeded; Johnson again decided not to go public.[53]

On Tuesday, November 5, the victory went to Richard Nixon, but the war and the negotiations continued. A week after the election, on November 12, South Vietnamese information minister Ton That Thien announced that the Johnson administration had halted the bombing of North Vietnam and had agreed to participate in the Paris talks without Saigon's approval. The next day, in a press conference, Defense Secretary Clifford, deliberately angry, responded to media queries in strong language that the United States had had the Saigon government's full agreement until the last minute—at which time the South Vietnamese suddenly decided not to join U.S. representatives in Paris. He indicated that the president "owed it to the American people to go ahead with the talks." Ambassador Bui Diem subsequently described the actions of both Senator Dirksen and syndicated columnist Stewart Alsop, who delivered messages to him on November 9 to send to Saigon, saying that both the president and the president-elect wanted Thieu to send a South Vietnamese delegation to Paris "before it was too late." Diem promptly flew to Saigon to convey their requests to President Thieu.[54]

Nearly four weeks went by before the South Vietnamese government decided to send a delegation to Paris. The head of the delegation did not arrive in Paris until December 8. On January 18, agreement was reached on all procedural issues concerning the Paris meetings. Thus, only two days before Lyndon Johnson left office, the stage was finally set for "substantive discussions" for peace in Vietnam. The first of the new meetings, which were to drag on for almost four years, was held five days later, on January 25.[55]

Negotiations with the North Vietnamese during the last year of the Johnson administration had centered on the one constant North Vietnamese demand: that the United States "unconditionally" halt the bombing of North Vietnam before serious negotiations could begin. The Pentagon, particularly the new defense secretary, Clark Clifford, was convinced that the North Vietnamese conditions should be met so that serious negotiations could begin. Military officers in the Pentagon and Secretary of State Dean Rusk initially opposed Clifford strongly in this regard. They were convinced that the United States should receive something in return from the North Vietnamese in exchange for a bombing halt, and that the South Vietnamese government should be included in the negotiations. The problem was that the South Vietnamese knew their government was too weak to survive without the U.S. presence; too weak to outlast the North in any compromise with the more popular and organized communists. They therefore calculated that they must avoid negotiations at all cost.

As the negotiations dragged on, they were overtaken and influenced by political considerations in the United States. In a presidential election year, it seems that Richard Nixon's campaign, through secret channels, had little difficulty convincing members of the South Vietnamese government, especially Pres. Nguyen Van Thieu, that they would fare better under a Republican administration than under a Democratic administration that seemed on the verge of deserting them in favor of negotiations with the North. Defense Secretary Clifford was able to bring the Joint Chiefs of Staff and General Abrams around to his point of view: that a bombing halt would not be a threat to South Vietnam or to American forces in Vietnam. The South Vietnamese, however, held out. They feared that a negotiated settlement would leave them defenseless. Nixon's campaign advisers, it seemed, had worked to undermine the negotiations and continue the war in the South in order to assist Nixon's election campaign. By the time President Johnson finally agreed to break with Thieu and order a complete bombing halt, it was too late to keep Nixon from winning the presidency.

Throughout this ten-month period, we see the actions of a defense secretary convinced that American participation in the war in South Vietnam should end as quickly as possible, through negotiations, as well as those of a secretary of state opposed to negotiations and willing to indulge a weak and hapless ally in the military pursuit of containment.

The struggle within the administration raises many questions. Why was the president so reluctant to stop the bombing "unconditionally"—especially after he became convinced that it would pose no danger to American forces, and that it would help Hubert Humphrey's campaign for president? Did he want to stay aloof from the political battle? Did he really believe that a complete bombing halt would threaten U.S. troops in Vietnam? Was he convinced America could win the war militarily? Johnson was ambiguous at best about Humphrey's ability to perform as president. Moreover, he feared the Republicans would accuse him of playing politics with soldiers' lives if he ordered a complete bombing halt. In reality, however, it was Nixon's campaign—by influencing the South Vietnamese not to agree to negotiations and by keeping the war going at least until the election was over—that was playing politics with soldiers' lives.

In the end, the Johnson administration had established "substantive negotiations" directed toward ending the war in Vietnam. Yet, as Dean Rusk pointed out, two things the administration could not turn over to Richard Nixon were a unified Congress and a unified people. Although some hope for South Vietnam's survival existed at the end of 1968, Rusk said that the simple truth was that the American people were tiring of the war. Unfortunately, it seems the Nixon administration failed to learn from experience. Exactly four years later, just before the 1972 election, President Thieu defied the Nixon administration (and Ellsworth Bunker, who was still ambassador) in a similar manner and for similar reasons, refusing to sign the cease-fire agreement Henry Kissinger had negotiated, even though they had previously agreed to each stage of the talks and after Kissinger had announced that "peace was at hand." This led directly to a U.S. attempt to revise the cease-fire terms, Hanoi's refusal to do so, and to the 1972 Christmas bombing attacks that followed. After Hanoi returned to the negotiating table, the Saigon government was pressured to accept the agreement or the United States would be forced to proceed on its own. The agreement ending hostilities was signed on January 23, 1973.

During the nine months following the 1968 Tet Offensive, while the Johnson administration tried desperately to negotiate a halt to the bombing and the Nixon campaign sought to keep South Vietnam from agreeing to any such halt, American and Vietnamese forces suffered their heaviest losses of the war.[56]

Notes

1. Robert S. McNamara, et al., *Argument Without End: In Search of Answers to the Vietnam Tragedy* (New York: Public Affairs Press, 1999, p. 212.

2. Lyndon B. Johnson, *The Vantage Point: Perspectives of the Presidency, 1963–1969* (New York: Holt, Rinehart, and Winston, 1978), pp. 493–94.

3. Harry McPherson, *A Political Education* (Boston: Atlantic Monthly, Little, Brown, 1971), p. 435.

4. "U.S. Jets Hit Deep in North Vietnam: Bomb Targets 259 Miles Above DMZ," *Washington Post,* Apr. 2, 1968, p. A1.

5. *Congressional Record,* vol. 114, 90th Cong., 2d Sess., pp. 8,569, 4,869–77.

6. Johnson, *Vantage Point,* pp. 493–95.

7. *Public Papers of the Presidents: Lyndon B. Johnson, 1968–1969,* vol. 1 (Washington, D.C.: GPO, 1970) p. 492. See also Paul W. Ward, "Hanoi Gives U.S. Reply on Parley Bid," *Baltimore Sun,* Apr. 9, 1968, p. A1.

8. Herbert Y. Schandler, *The Unmaking of a President: Lyndon Johnson and Vietnam* (Princeton, N.J.: Princeton University Press, 1977), pp. 290–319.

9. Johnson, *Vantage Point,* p. 498.

10. Clark Clifford, *Counsel to the President: A Memoir* (New York: Random House, 1991), p. 529.

11. Ibid., p. 529.

12. Johnson, *Vantage Point,* pp. 500–501.

13. Ibid., p. 501.

14. Ibid., pp. 501–505.

15. Lloyd C. Gardner, *Pay Any Price: Lyndon Johnson and the Wars for Vietnam* (Chicago: Ivan R. Dee, 1995), p. 469.

16. Ibid., pp. 540–41.

17. Ibid., pp. 546–46; Johnson, *Vantage Point,* p. 510.

18. Gardner, *Pay Any Price,* pp. 547–48.

19. Ibid., p. 547.

20. Ibid., pp. 547–48.

21. Ibid., pp. 549–50.

22. Johnson, *Vantage Point,* p. 511

23. Clifford, *Counsel,* pp. 550–51.

24. Johnson, *Vantage Point,* pp. 511–12; Clifford, *Counsel,* pp. 551–52

25. Clifford, *Counsel,* pp. 552–53.

26. Ibid., pp. 562–66. See also Hubert H. Humphrey, *The Education of a Public Man: My Life and Politics* (Garden City, N.Y.: Doubleday, 1976), pp. 383–87.

27. Johnson, *Vantage Point,* pp. 514–15; Clifford, *Counsel,* p. 566.

28. Clifford, *Counsel,* pp. 569–70.

29. Ibid., p. 570; Johnson, *Vantage Point,* pp. 514–15.

30. William Safire, *Before the Fall: An Inside View of the Pre-Watergate White House* (Garden City, N.Y.: Doubleday, 1975), p. 88.

31. Johnson, *Vantage Point,* pp. 514–15.

32. Ibid., pp. 515–16.

33. Clifford, *Counsel,* p. 574.

34. Ibid., p. 575.

35. Ibid., p. 576.

36. Ibid., pp. 576–77.

37. Ibid., p. 577.

38. Johnson, *Vantage Point,* pp. 525–26.

39. Ibid., pp. 516–18.

40. Anna Chennault, *The Education of Anna* (New York: Times Books, 1980), p. 174.

41. Bui Diem with David Chernoff, *In the Jaws of History* (Boston: Houghton Mifflin, 1987), pp. 235–45.

42. Chennault, *Education of Anna,* p. 190.

43. Clifford, *Counsel,* pp. 583–84.

44. Johnson, *Vantage Point,* pp. 520–21.

45. Clifford, *Counsel,* p. 587.

46. Johnson, *Vantage Point,* pp. 522–23; Clifford, *Counsel,* pp. 588–89.

47. Johnson, *Vantage Point,* p. 524.

48. Ibid., p. 524; Clifford, *Counsel,* pp. 589–91.

49. Clifford, *Counsel,* pp. 591–92.

50. Ibid., pp. 592–93.

51. Johnson, *Vantage Point,* p. 526; Clifford, *Counsel,* p. 593.

52. *Public Papers,* pp. 469–76; Johnson, *Vantage Point,* pp. 528–29.

53. Clifford, *Counsel,* p. 594.

54. Diem, *In the Jaws,* pp. 245–46.

55. Clifford, *Counsel,* p. 601.

56. Ronald Spector, *After Tet: The Bloodiest Year in Vietnam* (New York: Free Press, 1993), p. 25.

In preparing this chapter, I also examined the personal notes of George Elsey and Tom Johnson of the Office of History, Department of Defense, Washington, D.C.

The following works also offer insights on this subject: George Ball, *The Past Has Another Pattern: Memoirs* (New York: W. W. Norton, 1982); Phil C. Goulding, *Confirm or Deny: Informing the People on National Security* (New York: Harper and Row, 1970); Henry J. Graff, *The Tuesday Cabinet* (Englewood Cliffs, N.J.: Prentice Hall, 1970); David Halberstam, *The Best and the Brightest* (New York: Random House, 1972); Stanley Karnow, *Vietnam: A History* (New York: Viking, 1983); Henry A. Kissinger, *White House Years* (Boston: Little, Brown, 1979); David Kraslow and Stewart Loory, *The Secret Search for Peace in Vietnam* (New York: Vintage Books, 1968); Walt W. Rostow, *The Diffusion of Power: An Essay in Recent History* (New York: Macmillan, 1972); Willard J. Webb, *The Joint Chiefs of Staff and the War in Vietnam, 1969–1970* (Washington, D.C.: GPO, 2001); Dean Rusk, as told to Richard Rusk, *As I See It* (New York: W. W. Norton, 1990); Taylor, General Maxwell D. Taylor, *Swords and Plowshares* (New York: W. W. Norton, 1972); Cyrus Vance, *Hard Choices: Critical Years in America's Foreign Policy* (New York: Simon and Schuster, 1983); and Gen. William C. Westmoreland, *A Soldier Reports* (Garden City, N.Y: Doubleday, 1976).

The Shape of the Table

Nguyen Van Thieu and Negotiations to End the Conflict

JOHN PRADOS

Almost all analyses of efforts to begin negotiations on ending the Vietnam War—as well as of the Paris peace talks that eventually took place—lack a critical dimension: coverage of South Vietnam's interests and objectives. This is problematical in American historiography since it was for South Vietnam that the United States was ostensibly fighting the war. It is also a problem in analysis given that South Vietnam would ultimately have to carry out whatever peace agreement negotiators achieved. Finally, it is a problem in the history of the events since the United States would be obliged to tender any prospective accord to both Saigon and Hanoi to secure their governments' agreement. Indeed, breaking the barriers to negotiation with Hanoi would be only part of making talks work, the other piece would be bringing along the South Vietnamese. What evolved could in many ways be characterized as triangular diplomacy, a simultaneous game among Washington, Hanoi, and Saigon.

My purpose in this chapter is to supply a view of the missing dimension in the Vietnam negotiations brew. Because power in Saigon was concentrated in the hands of Pres. Nguyen Van Thieu, this story is really about the South Vietnamese leader's attitude toward talks and subsequently his negotiating position. Other than the account of Thieu's background, this analysis is based primarily on the record of the South Vietnamese leader's direct exchanges with American diplomats. Some of the exchanges took place during the Johnson administration era of seeking to jump-start diplomacy. Most occurred during the Nixon years, when American officials sought to inform the Saigon government of the negotiations being carried on in its name. On the South Vietnamese side, at least, the peace negotiations can only be understood as a single continuum from the Johnson years to the 1973 Paris peace accord.

The Advent of Nguyen Van Thieu

Nguyen Van Thieu, like so many other South Vietnamese political leaders, had been a military man. As was also common among the Vietnamese,

Thieu had connections on both sides of the revolution. A product of central Vietnam, Thieu, born on April 5, 1923, in a village near Phan Rang, had sided with the anti-French nationalists in the August Revolution of 1945. The revolutionary leadership, largely drawn from communist circles, was highly popular among Vietnamese, Thieu included. He became a district leader in the revolutionary movement despite being the son of a relatively well-off farmer who was rich enough to send his brother Hieu to Paris for university and law studies. After his return from Europe, Hieu became a minor French official. Swept away by the passions of the August Revolution, Nguyen Van Thieu apparently responded to mainstream political sentiments in Vietnam. This is one key to his character.

As communist leaders turned the newly created Democratic Republic of Vietnam toward that political perspective, Thieu soured on the revolution and left it behind in 1946. The following year he enlisted in the merchant marine, but transferred to the Vietnamese National Military Academy at Dalat in 1948, when the French were frantically trying to create a Vietnamese army as a token of the independence they claimed to have already accorded Vietnam. As a young officer, Thieu studied in France in 1949, then returned to his homeland to lead infantrymen. He rose steadily through the ranks, benefiting from the rapid expansion of the Vietnamese armed forces serving under the French flag. He acquired a reputation for caution, probably enhanced by service in 1953 as the operations staff officer for the Hung Yen sector of the Red River Delta in Tonkin, one of the areas most heavily infiltrated by the Vietminh adversary. Thieu commanded an infantry battalion in central Vietnam the following year and resorted to artillery and mortar fire to drive the Vietminh out of his own ancestral home and village. The combination of caution and determination would also be central to Thieu's character.

Thieu remained in the South Vietnamese army following the acceptance of the 1954 Geneva Accords. Promoted to command a regiment in central Vietnam, then to deputy commander of the military region headquartered at Hue, Thieu became superintendent of the Dalat academy in 1955. He thus had the good fortune to be outside the military chain of command that year, when Prime Minister Ngo Dinh Diem used the military to consolidate a set of political maneuvers that made him president of the newly created Republic of Vietnam (really still only South Vietnam, as distinguished from "North" Vietnam, the *Democratic* Republic of Vietnam), and made political loyalty a litmus test for promotion. Where Diem was an ardent Roman Catholic, Thieu described himself as a moderate Catholic, although he hailed from an area of Vietnam noted for animistic worship and was married to a Buddhist. Diem outlawed political parties other than his own and suspected Thieu of connections with the Dai Viet (Greater Vietnam) nationalist party, which may have led to Thieu's transfer from the army's Field Command. Colonel Thieu traveled to the United States in 1958 for a special weapons course at Fort Bliss, Texas. American intelligence analyst George W. Allen, who saw Thieu managing the luggage of the senior officers on this trip, decided that he was the "ultimate 'survivor.'"[1]

In 1962, Colonel Thieu was transferred from Hue to command the 5th Infantry Division, headquartered a little north of Saigon. Coincidentally or not, Thieu had recently joined the political party of Ngo Dinh Diem's brother Nhu. Less than a year later, the South Vietnamese army overthrew Diem in a coup. Thieu was given the mission of isolating the barracks of Diem's presidential guard, but his regiments were an hour or two late getting on the road—leading some of the coup plotters to suspect that Thieu had hung back to see which way the wind was blowing. Once again the image he portrayed was that of an officer with a streak of opportunism.

Promoted to brigadier general after the coup, Thieu became a member of the Armed Forces Council, a group of generals that stood behind the Saigon government for the next four years. It was Thieu's first overtly political role. In September, 1964, he also took command of the IV Corps in the Mekong Delta. When the generals mounted another coup—this time against military strong man Gen. Nguyen Khanh in January, 1965—Thieu sided with the plotters anew. He subsequently left his military command to serve as deputy prime minister. In June, Thieu became the chief of state in a reorganization masterminded by air force commander Nguyen Cao Ky, who became prime minister. This combination, Nguyen Van Thieu and Nguyen Cao Ky, remained in control of the Saigon government until 1971.

Politics in Saigon during this period was dominated by a struggle for primacy between Thieu and Ky. With a new constitution adopted by Saigon in 1966, and presidential elections held in 1967 and again in 1971, political posturing remained important. Nguyen Cao Ky began this competition in the top spot, only to be eclipsed gradually by Thieu, who was less controversial and more focused than his rival. The U.S. role in convincing Ky to accept the vice-president slot, with Thieu as presidential candidate, in the 1967 election, has hardly been noted but emerges clearly from cable traffic.[2] The Thieu-Ky ticket handily won the election, but Ky's political allies were widely dispersed throughout the Saigon government, which forced Thieu to proceed very slowly. Another turning point occurred in May, 1968, during the second wave of the Tet Offensive, when a number of Ky's allies were wounded or killed in an accidental air attack during fighting in Saigon. Thieu allies replaced Ky people in the national police, the customs service, and vital defense ministry posts. Thieu also appointed Tran Van Huong, a nationalist figure allied with the former Armed Forces Council (in which Thieu had prevailed earlier and isolated Ky), as prime minister. Some observers credit this maneuver with destroying the last vestiges of Ky's faction,[3] although the political endgame with Nguyen Cao Ky continued to play out through 1971.

American initiatives to begin peace negotiations with Hanoi must be viewed in the context of these South Vietnamese political developments. For example, in 1966 there were a series of proposals for "reconciliation," a political opening to the Vietcong. American officials were confident that political concessions by the Saigon government would open a fissure in the National Liberation Front (NLF)–North Vietnamese axis. Thieu, however, proved unrelenting in his antipathy for dealings with the NLF. Ky, who at that time still enjoyed political primacy, could not afford to be seen as any less tough than his colleague. While Vietnamese leaders promised U.S. officials action on a reconciliation declaration more than once, none eventuated. In its actual public form, "reconciliation" became nothing more than another appeal calling for Vietcong loyalists to surrender.[4]

It was in the wake of Tet, in April, 1968, that Washington and Hanoi finally agreed to begin negotiating. This event came just as Thieu was moving to consolidate his political power. With characteristic caution, Thieu did nothing at first to support the negotiations. When the Saigon government finally took formal notice of them, it was to demand that it, too, be included in the forum. That situation continued until October, 1968, when political maneuvers in the United States (covered elsewhere in this volume) afforded Thieu an opportunity to affect the American counterparts with whom he would have to deal for the next four, or possibly eight, years. Thieu seized the opportunity and used arcane consultative provisions in Saigon political procedures to obstruct and delay the response Lyndon Johnson needed to initiate formal peace talks. From November through January, Saigon disputed the forum for negotiations and even the shape of the table around which delegations would sit in order to exclude the NLF.

Thieu's Peace Positions, 1968–73

There can be no doubt that, at least in Nguyen Van Thieu's mind, the Vietnam peace negotiations were bound up with prosecution of the war. This is nicely framed by the date April 4, 1968. That day, while Washington announced that it and Hanoi had agreed to seek negotiations, President Thieu met in Saigon with the American commander in Vietnam, Gen. William C. Westmoreland, to formalize his approval of increased force levels for the South Vietnamese armed forces. The South Vietnamese new force levels would be for 1969, just when the impending peace negotiations had gotten under way. Thieu wished to have an American plan anticipated to take fifteen months completed in twelve, and he, Ky, and the Saigon government cabinet talked of full mobilization. According to the Central Intelligence Agency, "The only positive decision to emerge thus far is that the government of Vietnam (GVN) should immediately take steps to show the people of South Vietnam and the world that it is determined to resist communist aggression. The step most often discussed has been full mobilization since this would indicate that the GVN was preparing to carry on alone if need be."[5]

Subsequent cabinet meetings of the Saigon government repeatedly covered questions of force increases—and Thieu promulgated a mobilization law. Thieu also created a restricted body called the "war cabinet," and both this and the larger group adopted the principle that Saigon would reject any peace agreement that obliged it to participate in a coalition with the NLF. On June 4, in a talk with visiting U.S. ambassador Kenneth T. Young, Thieu declared that "many Vietnamese are afraid of an American abandonment of Vietnam or a sell-out in Paris" where negotiations were beginning. Again acting in the name of the Vietnamese people, Thieu asked why the United States had failed to set a deadline for the North Vietnamese to stop sending supplies and troops to the South. Thieu insisted South Vietnamese forces were dominant on the battlefield and again warned against an agreement calling for a coalition government.[6]

The essential elements of a South Vietnamese peace position existed in outline form by June, 1968, a point at which negotiations had barely begun and had yet to delve into substance. Thieu rejected any coalition solution, which meant the NLF would have to accept a settlement with no concessions—in other words, defeat. Hanoi was supposed to stop infiltrating troops and supplies into South Vietnam, from which it was only a short step to the final form of the Saigon postulate: that Hanoi withdraw all of its forces from South Vietnam. Although South Vietnamese forces supported by their American allies had never been able to impel the enemy to either of these conditions, Thieu believed Saigon's war mobilization could carry it to victory in the absence of an agreement.

On October 14, with the Paris talks seeming to have acquired momentum, U.S. ambassador Ellsworth Bunker visited President Thieu to reveal the possibilities for serious negotiations. Thieu used the moment to ask, according to the U.S. record, "why we did not make infiltration an issue." Thieu said he was ready to go along with negotiations so long as the United States continued to press the offensive in South Vietnam and Laos and was prepared to resume bombing North Vietnam if Hanoi violated the De-militarized Zone or attacked cities in the South. As already seen, however, President Thieu dragged his feet as the U.S. election approached and the moment came to move forward with this commitment.[7]

In a conversation with Ambassador Bunker on December 28, 1968, Thieu's negotiating position emerged full blown. There were two separate obstacles to peace in Saigon's view. The first was Hanoi's "invasion" of the South, which would have to be met by a withdrawal of North Vietnamese forces, both reg-ular units and individual soldiers who had been incorporated into the NLF. The second problem would be the NLF's situation before and after Hanoi's withdrawal. No coalition would be accepted, but Thieu announced his willingness to advance national elections from 1970 to 1971 and permit the NLF to create its own legal political party. Of course, since the South Vietnamese constitution explicitly outlawed communism and commu-nist political parties, creating a "legal" political party really meant the NLF would have to renounce its political beliefs. President Thieu had used the moment of the U.S. election to make his best deal with what turned out to be the incoming Nixon administration, then cautiously fashioned his position for talks. As shall be seen that position remained rather consistent.[8]

The first open airing of Saigon's approach to peace in Vietnam did not occur until March 25, 1969, when Thieu offered in a speech to hold his own talks with the NLF, shortly to reconstitute itself as the Provisional Revolu-tionary Government (PRG). However, it would not be until July 11 that Thieu, in another speech, presented the details of a peace plan. Thieu pro-posed elections, the timing of which could be discussed, to be supervised by an electoral commission on which the NLF/PRG could be represented. This was, in fact, the same plan Thieu had postulated to Bunker in De-cember, 1968. To get this chance, the NLF/PRG would first have to lay down their arms and renounce communism. There was little chance the adversary would accept such a plan.[9]

Meanwhile, it fell to the Nixon administration to conduct the Paris peace talks. Aware of Thieu's concerns, when Richard Nixon met the Sai-gon leader at a summit on Midway Island on June 8, 1969, Nixon declared that the press was trying to drive a wedge between the United States and South Vietnam, that public speculation regarding U.S. pressures on Saigon to agree to a coalition government was entirely unfounded. When the U.S. side asked whether Thieu intended to go beyond his March 25 speech, the Saigon leader reverted to his characteristic caution and replied, "We must not be put into the position of always making new proposals." He did not want to be pushed from one position to another, "as was the case with the 'shape-of-the-table' issue." Moreover, Thieu wanted the United States to give assurances that *it* would not use each Saigon concession as a signal for a new demand either, "there must be an end to it." Saigon's bottom line: "Thieu replied that if there were a withdrawal of [North Vietnamese] forces and an end of terrorism, the GVN could consider the NLF as another party in elections."10

Nixon next saw Thieu in Saigon on July 30, during the American president's only visit to South Vietnam. It is instructive that with Nixon about to send his national security adviser, Henry A. Kissinger, on the first of a series of trips to secretly negotiate with Hanoi's representatives, in the Saigon meeting Nixon made only the most elliptical of references to this initiative (Kissinger was to meet with the other side just four days hence, on August 4): Nixon said he felt it "highly desirable" to issue a warning to Hanoi in the near future, and that "this will be done in an unorthodox way."11 Nixon did not consult Thieu on negotiations or indeed explicitly inform Saigon the United States was about to break the deadlock on the public Paris talks using the secret meetings.

The United States did, however, inform Saigon of the secret meeting after it had taken place. In December, 1969, Thieu went out of his way to ask Ellsworth Bunker if there had been any secret U.S. meetings of which he had not been informed. He was given appropriate assurances. Then, from February through April, 1970, Kissinger and the North Vietnamese engaged in another series of secret meetings in which the United States proposed a phased mutual withdrawal of American and North Vietnamese forces from South Vietnam. Hanoi rejected the formula. Ellsworth Bunker's cables reported that Thieu had been especially interested in these discussions when he was subsequently informed of them.12

Hanoi's rejection of mutual withdrawal in April, 1970, is especially significant because of Saigon's position. Not that there had ever been much real chance of acceptance of a mutual withdrawal formula—Hanoi's view continued to be that it had no forces in a foreign country, sometimes even claiming that none of its forces were in South Vietnam—but the rejection ended any hope for Saigon to attain one of Thieu's main demands. When the United States proposed a new formula in October, 1970, it was for a cease-fire in place. By definition, that formula left North Vietnamese troops in South Vietnam. When President Thieu probed meanings here, he would be told the North Vietnamese would be removed by virtual attrition, that is, a prohibition of further infiltration and a clause reaffirming the inviolability of the Demilitarized Zone between the two Vietnams would leave the northern troops in the South to wither on the vine. In later years Henry Kissinger, his deputy Alexander M. Haig, and Bunker's deputy Charles S.

Whitehouse would claim that Thieu had explicitly agreed to every peace maneuver they carried out during the Vietnam negotiations. This was, in fact, not true. The divergence between the United States and Saigon began with the shift to a cease-fire in place in October, 1970.[13]

Meanwhile, President Thieu continued to be cautious in advancing actual proposals on Saigon's behalf. Although Thieu told American reporter Osborn Elliott in May, 1970: "We will negotiate. We are negotiating," he had said nothing openly since offering his July, 1969, plan for what amounted to an NLF/PRG surrender. From the time of the U.S. cease-fire in place proposal of October, 1970, Washington began to press Saigon for a fresh political initiative. When U.S. defense secretary Melvin R. Laird visited Saigon in early 1971, Thieu agreed in principle to propose such an initiative. On January 8, 1971, he told Ambassador Bunker that he had been giving the idea much thought, but "there were limitations on how much more he could say." When the United States backed a South Vietnamese invasion of Laos that started in February, Thieu said he would refrain from making proposals during the operation because they might suggest weakness. On April 17, after the South Vietnamese had been routed and driven out of Laos, Thieu told Bunker "it is too soon after" the invasion to offer anything. Two days later he told Bunker that his staff was "still studying" an amplification of his July, 1969, offer, but added that he did not see how he could "take the initiative now." Even a projected South Vietnamese gesture of repatriating sick and wounded prisoners from North Vietnam, planned early in 1971 and painfully agreed upon by Washington and Saigon, was never permitted to come to fruition.[14]

Washington continued its own secret meetings with Hanoi's diplomats. By the summer of 1971 it was only a United States withdrawal that was being negotiated, coupled with a standstill cease-fire and respect for the 1954 Geneva Accords. The sticking points revolved around the return of American prisoners held in North Vietnam. The United States still wished to field a joint proposal with Saigon and continued to press Thieu. In language for a possible joint draft on August 10, 1971, Thieu inserted: "Among the problems that should be settled is the implementation of the principle that all armed forces of the countries of Indochina must remain within their national frontiers." He also insisted on language prohibiting infiltration. Months after the North defeated South Vietnam's greatest offensive military effort, Nguyen Van Thieu continued to attempt by diplomacy to force Hanoi to withdraw its troops from South Vietnam.[15]

American–South Vietnamese contacts for the purpose of evolving a joint negotiating proposal continued through early 1972. Thieu announced the joint proposal in a speech on January 26 (Nixon's speech on January 25, in which he also revealed Henry Kissinger's secret meetings with the North Vietnamese, is better known to Americans). Elements of the proposal included the withdrawal of all U.S. and allied troops, a standstill cease-fire with provisions on infiltration, a prisoner exchange, a reaffirmation of the 1954 and 1962 Geneva Accords, international supervision, and an understanding that Southeast Asian countries would settle their own political problems.[16]

Two points are noteworthy concerning the January, 1972, proposal. The first is that Thieu and Saigon continued to demand that the infiltration provision provide for *no* new forces to be permitted to enter the South. Kissinger finessed the issue with Saigon, but in his negotiation with Hanoi agreed to one-for-one replacement, sanctioning an open replacement route along the Ho Chi Minh Trail. The second point is that the January, 1972, proposal was silent on the question of a North Vietnamese withdrawal, upon which Thieu had insisted vociferously. Thieu may have gone along with the proposal thinking there would not be any agreement, or he may have been prevailed upon in a moment of weakness, or he may have been misled, or withdrawal may have been deliberately left out, but Saigon would not remain long on the reservation, and, as shall be seen, presently began to back away from the joint proposal. In the meantime, it had taken Saigon thirty months—since July, 1969—to table this new position.

Further private negotiations between Kissinger and the North Vietnamese eventually followed. Hanoi invited Kissinger to a luncheon meeting in March, but the event was first postponed and then canceled when North Vietnam opened a massive conventional offensive in the South. A meeting finally took place in Paris on May 2, with North Vietnam offended in turn when the United States mined Haiphong Harbor and resumed bombing targets in the North on May 8. Negotiations did not resume until July 13, with the talks being characterized by vagueness. Suddenly, on August 1, both the United States and North Vietnam tabled detailed proposals. Conversations proceeded so rapidly that by August 14 there were draft agreements. Henry Kissinger flew to Saigon to present the provisions in detail to the South Vietnamese, meeting with President Thieu and other officials from August 16 to 18. During these crucial sessions, Thieu objected that the United States seemed to have dropped the demand for mutual withdrawal. Kissinger responded that Hanoi would never accept such a provision.[17] It is suggestive that Kissinger was essentially considered an undesirable in Saigon after his August, 1972, visit, after which Nixon relied exclusively on Al Haig as the U.S. emissary to Thieu.

Meanwhile, Henry Kissinger went to Paris for more meetings with Hanoi's diplomats in September. At the beginning of October, General

Haig saw President Thieu and presented the latest North Vietnamese proposal. On October 2, Haig outlined the contents of the proposals; two days later he met with Thieu to hear Saigon's reactions. Thieu said he believed that Hanoi had "ambushed" Kissinger. He added that the Committee of National Reconciliation established in the agreement would substitute for the Saigon government, and he complained that Hanoi had demanded a U.S. withdrawal "while North Vietnam has obligated itself to do nothing in return." The Saigon government's proposals had been embodied in a September 13 memorandum to the United States, to which Haig replied that Saigon's counterproposal "in all probability would have broken up the talks." Ambassador Bunker came back the next day. He informed Thieu that the Nixon administration intended to go ahead with a planned negotiating session whether or not Saigon agreed, and said that an open dispute between the United States and Saigon "would lead to complete disaster." Nixon did undertake to try obtaining assurances of withdrawals from Laos, Cambodia, and South Vietnam, but Bunker advised, "we do not expect the meeting to succeed."[18]

Shortly thereafter, the Americans met with the North Vietnamese and finalized a draft agreement and timetable for signing it. Kissinger, meanwhile, planned a trip to Saigon and Hanoi to have the agreement initialed. President Nixon sent President Thieu a letter on October 16 making it clear that the talks were in the final stages and reassuring him that Saigon's political concerns were being safeguarded (Thieu's military concerns were not specifically addressed). Meanwhile, Thieu's answer had, in effect, already been made: it appeared in a column in that day's edition of the *New York Times*. In a reprint of a recent speech, President Thieu asserted: "North Vietnam is the aggressor . . . it has the duty to end all acts of aggression in the South and withdraw all of its tools of aggression to the North." Later in the column Thieu again declared, "All foreign countries must withdraw their armies back to their territories." He then demanded that an international conference be convened to make that happen.[19]

During the days that followed, Saigon's opposition repeatedly forced Kissinger to postpone his planned Southeast Asian trip—to the point that Hanoi realized the peace agreement was coming unstuck. On October 26, Hanoi went public with an account of the talks and released the draft agreement. Kissinger countered on October 28 with a press conference in which he attempted to put the blame on Hanoi's intransigence. Saigon released its own commentary, claiming it had not been informed of trips, signings, letters, and so on, but specifically objecting that it had insisted all along that North Vietnamese troops must withdraw, that the Demilitarized Zone must be defined (that is, made impermeable to the passage of North Vietnamese troops), and that political solutions must be left to the South Vietnamese people themselves. Richard Nixon responded to the commentary by sending Thieu another letter promising that Kissinger would make an effort to get "the maximum number of changes reflecting the views expressed to him during his visit to Saigon."[20]

Nguyen Van Thieu, however, called the proposed agreement a surrender document. His government delivered a detailed analysis on November 3. Among many other points, the strongest were about the Committee on National Reconciliation and the military issues. For example, "the problems of the total withdrawal of the North Vietnamese army from South Vietnam into North Vietnam and the four Indochinese countries should be stated clearly. Likewise the basic principle of the 1954 Geneva Agreements that there are two zones North and South Vietnam which cannot invade each other and interfere in each other [*sic*] internal political affairs, and that there is a Demilitarized Zone, should be respected." Several pages later, the document again makes the withdrawal and Demilitarized Zone demands, and a few pages after that the South Vietnamese included language that could be inserted in the draft peace agreement. Elsewhere, by referring to *four* Southeast Asian nations (instead of merely Laos, Cambodia, and Vietnam), South Vietnam made an attempt to promote itself to nation status, which was explicitly precluded in the 1954 Geneva Accords and which the impending international agreement was intended to restore. Ambassador Bunker, reporting home after his meeting with Thieu on the substance of Saigon's objections, said it had seemed the withdrawal of North Vietnamese forces was the most crucial.[21]

The final acts of this long tale concern desperate maneuvers by Washington and Saigon over the agreement virtually finalized in October. Kissinger held new rounds of negotiation with the North Vietnamese in November and December, 1972. Nixon simultaneously moved to reassure Thieu. At the end of November, Saigon envoy Nguyen Phu Duc went to Washington with a personal letter from Thieu to Nixon. The November 26 letter once again reiterated Thieu's concerns about the Committee on National Reconciliation and repeated his demand that North Vietnam withdraw all of its forces from South Vietnam. In a series of meetings between Nixon and Duc, as well as Kissinger and Duc, the United States sought to make clear that it intended to go ahead with an agreement after one more round of bargaining—whether or not Saigon was prepared to sign. Nixon also put Thieu on notice that if South Vietnam did *not* sign, Congress would cut off aid to that erstwhile ally, and the perceptions Nixon was attempting to structure so as to enable him to intervene anew in Vietnam against Hanoi's violations of the agreement would not be created. With a view toward ensuring that Thieu did not decide Saigon could make a better deal elsewhere, Nixon emphasized that Kissinger spoke for him and that there were no differences between them.[22]

The importance of the meetings with Nguyen Phu Duc to the Vietnam peace process cannot be overstated. According to Kissinger's preparatory memo to Richard Nixon, "The purpose of this crucial meeting is to convince an almost psychopathically [sic] distrustful Thieu, through a key member of his Palace inner circle, to close ranks with us this week on the Paris Agreement."[23] At the November 29 meeting Nixon explicitly said: "There should be no illusions. The total withdrawal of North Vietnamese forces was out of the question." When Nguyen Phu Duc tried to frame the issue in terms of selling an agreement to the South Vietnamese people, Kissinger agreed to try to get some appropriate language approved by Hanoi, but warned that he had spent three hours on this very question with the North Vietnamese at the last round of talks without getting anywhere.

President Thieu was not satisfied with these exchanges. He appeared before South Vietnam's National Assembly on December 12 and gave a speech asserting that the North Vietnamese must completely withdraw and that the reconciliation committee was a disguised coalition government. So familiar had the refrains become that in reporting these declarations to Nixon, Alexander Haig termed them "standard [GVN] arguments."[24]

Meanwhile, Henry Kissinger continued to converse with North Vietnamese diplomats. However, as predicted, he received no concessions. The Nixon administration followed these talks with a massive air campaign against North Vietnam that has come to be known as the "Christmas Bombing." This aerial offensive has been described in detail in memoirs by Kissinger, Nixon, and others as an effort to force Hanoi into making concessions in Paris.[25] Those claims have served to obscure the Nixon administration's equally, if not more vital, objective of assuring South Vietnam that the United States could make good on Nixon's promise of a forceful intervention should anything go wrong with the Paris talks—just as Nixon's people had calculated would happen.

President Thieu ultimately capitulated and decided to go along with the agreement, but not before yet another exchange of letters with President Nixon. There were several other expressions familiar to American ears. On December 30, *after* the Christmas Bombing campaign ended, the South Vietnamese ambassador in Paris had U.S. diplomat William H. Sullivan over for lunch to deliver the message that Thieu "could never sign an agreement which failed to provide for withdrawal." That same day, Ambassador Bunker reported from Saigon on yet another face-to-face meeting with the South Vietnamese president: "Thieu has continued his efforts to develop support for his position concentrating largely on the issue of [North Vietnamese] troops remaining in South Vietnam." It seemed that Thieu had begun focusing more on the legal principle, which Bunker thought indicated he now "realizes the difficulty of securing an actual withdrawal." Yet, in the final analysis, the Saigon leader never gave up the demands he had first made in 1968.[26]

As for Hanoi, a comparison of the agreement signed in Paris in January, 1973, with the October, 1972, draft reveals changes regarding the National Committee on Reconciliation and Concord as well as cosmetic changes on other matters. There was no recognition of national status for South Vietnam, no provision requiring North Vietnam to withdraw, no change to the standstill cease-fire or the provision for one-for-one replacement of troops and equipment (that is, infiltration would continue), and a clause covering the Demilitarized Zone that was *somewhat more favorable to Hanoi* than the previous one.[27]

At the End of the Day

Steadfast in his quest to preserve South Vietnam, Nguyen Van Thieu, the general turned president, settled very early on negotiating objectives that might lead him to success in that endeavor. He held to those goals with characteristic stubbornness and conservatism and throughout remained reluctant to present fresh proposals that could have facilitated the negotiation process. He also consistently rejected any course of action that conveyed any degree of legitimacy to the National Liberation Front, the communist guerrilla adversary in the South, and sought to establish the Saigon government as the sole legitimate political authority in South Vietnam. During the 1968 U.S. presidential campaign, President Thieu made an opportunistic calculation as to which potential American leader offered a more dependable avenue to his desired outcome. Thieu cast his lot with Richard Nixon and then maintained the negotiating position outlined in this chapter.

Opening the Saigon political process to the NLF on the basis of the Vietcong laying down their arms was a political ploy that had little possibility for success. Provisions in the Saigon constitution called for the NLF to renounce its own political program in addition to disarming itself, a combination that amounted to surrender. Military pacification programs never succeeded to the extent that the Liberation Front's leaders perceived their acceptance of the Thieu formula might be preferable to continuing the war. No political advantage for the NLF was evident in the Saigon position, either. From the standpoint of nationalism, the Liberation Front would have been discrediting itself to accept the formula. From the point of view of the degree to which Hanoi really controlled the NLF, the Liberation Front also would never have been permitted to accept the Thieu formula even had it desired to do so. As the talks progressed, Thieu eventually accepted the impossibility of this outcome and shifted to a position of no coalition government with the NLF. He actually achieved this outcome, in large measure, with the agreement made in Paris in January, 1973, owing to Saigon's ability to ensure that the National Committee for Reconciliation and Concord and the four-power military committee created by the agreement would remain moribund.

President Thieu's other key goal was to oblige Hanoi to withdraw its military forces from South Vietnam and, by prohibiting infiltration, ensure that they would never be replaced. As has been seen, this goal was formulated at the beginning of the Vietnam peace talks and never abandoned, even on the eve of signing the final agreement. Given this position, the Nixon administration's move to a settlement necessarily had to involve an element of blandishments to and coercion of Saigon. Such a maneuver by Washington duly took place in November, 1972, and afterward.

The realism of the South Vietnamese proposals must also be questioned. In effect, President Thieu demanded that the negotiating process achieve what South Vietnamese forces, even when backed by the United States, had not been able to accomplish on the battlefield. Neither Hanoi nor the NLF had any incentive to agree, given these circumstances. Moreover, Hanoi's perspective could only be that the progressive withdrawal of the United States from the conflict, made obligatory by the lack of support at home for the war, would gradually cripple Saigon's military potential. Saigon made a major error by not actively seeking the best deal it could make while its bargaining power was at its peak.

Explanation has to be speculative, but the most logical one is that Nguyen Van Thieu believed South Vietnam would achieve victory or, short of that, secure an agreement that would force the United States to renew its intervention in Vietnam. We have briefly seen—and the evidence has been presented at much greater length elsewhere[28]—that the Nixon administration made exactly that kind of promise. The agreement was to be structured so as to force Hanoi to commit violations that would furnish new justification for fighting in Vietnam. However, Richard Nixon miscalculated the readiness of Americans for yet another round of war in Vietnam. At the same time, the Watergate debacle robbed his administration of the ability to take the initiative in Southeast Asia. Of such stuff are the ends of wars made.

Notes

1. *Current Biography, 1968* (New York: H. W. Wilson, 1968), pp. 397–400; George W. Allen, *None So Blind* (Chicago: Ivan R. Dee, 2001), p. 110. This profile of Thieu is also drawn from author's notes compiled over many years.

2. Bunker to Rusk, cable (Saigon 23667), April 21, 1967, Lyndon B. Johnson Library, National Security File (hereafter cited as LBJL, NSF), Memos to the President series, box 15, file "Rostow, v. 26." Memo, Jorden-Rostow, April 21, 1967, ibid. Cable, Bunker to Rusk (Saigon 28218), June 16, 1967, ibid. Library of Congress, W. Averell Harriman Papers, Subject series, box 250, file "Vietnam: General, April–June 1967"; Memo, Harriman-Ball, June 16, 1967, ibid.

3. Richard Critchfield, *The Long Charade* (New York: Harcourt, Brace, and World, 1968), pp. 385–86.

4. Department of State, "National Reconciliation in South Vietnam," *Vietnam Information Notes,* no. 8, July, 1967; in *Foreign Relations of the United States, 1964–1968,* vol. 4, *Vietnam, 1966* (Washington, D.C.: GPO, 1998), pp. 502–504, 640–41, 660–61, 698, 762–63, 825–26, 862–64, 895, 926, 929–30, 951.

5. Bunker to Rusk, cable (Saigon 23958), Apr. 4, 1968, LBJL, NSF; "Central Intelligence Agency Report, 051656Z April 1968," "VN2G Manpower Mobilization 7/67–12/68" Folder, Central File–Vietnam (CF-VN), NSF, Box 75, LBJL; "VN6(G)3 Talks with Hanoi 4/1–10/68," Box 95–96, ibid.

6. Young to Rusk, cable (Saigon 29468), June 8, 1968, MPS, "Rostow, v.81" Folder, NSF, Box 35, LBJL.

7. Bunker to Rusk, cable (Saigon 40178), Oct. 14, 1968, "Memos to the President re Bombing Halt, v.1" Folder, CF-VN, NSF, Box 137, LBJL.

8. Bunker to Rusk, cable (Saigon 45710), Dec. 28, 1968, "Memos re Bombing Halt, v.7" Folder, CF-VN, NSF, Box 138, LBJL.

9. U.S. Congress, 93d Cong., 2d sess., Senate Foreign Relations Committee, *Report: Background Data Relating to Southeast Asia and Vietnam,* 7th rev. ed. (Washington, D.C.: GPO, 1975), pp. 354–56.

10. Nixon and Thieu at Midway Island, June 8, 1969, memorandum of conversation, "Beginning June 1, 1969" Folder, President's Office Files (POF), White House Central File (WHCF), Box 1, Nixon Library Project (NLP), National Archives and Records Administration (NARA), College Park, MD.

11. Nixon and Thieu at Independence Palace, July 30, 1969, memorandum of Conversation, West Wing Office File Series, "Vietnamese War: Secret Peace Talks [Mr. "S" File] (3)" Folder, National Security Adviser's Files (NSAF), Box 34, Gerald R. Ford Library, Ann Arbor, Mich. (hereafter GRFL).

12. Bunker to Kissinger, cable (WHS-010), Mar. 21, 1970, NSC Convenience File (NSCCF), Saigon Embassy Series (SES), "Saigon to Washington, 12/15/69–12/16/71" Folder, NASF, Box 1, GRFL.

13. On the negotiations in general see Jeffrey Kimball, *Nixon's Vietnam War* (Lawrence: University Press of Kansas, 1998). For claims by Kissinger, Haig, and Charles Whitehouse, see the transcript of the conference sponsored by the Nixon Center on April 24, 1998, marking the anniversary of the Paris Peace Accord, broadcast by C-SPAN.

14. Bunker to Rogers, cable (Saigon 0314), Jan. 8, 1971, NSC Files, Paris Talks Series (PTS), "Paris Talks (NODIS/Plus) August 1970" Folder, Box 189, NLP, NARA; Bunker to Kissinger, cable (Saigon 0270), Apr. 17, 1971, NSCCF, SES, "Saigon to Washington, 12/15/69–12/16/71" Folder, NSAF, Box 1, GRFL; Bunker to Rogers, cable (Saigon 5834), Apr. 19, 1971, NSC Files, PTS, "Paris Talks (NODIS/Plus) August 1970" Folder, Box 189, NLP, NARA.

15. Joint U.S.–Government of Vietnam document, "Draft Agreed Statement of Principles for a Negotiated Settlement of Indochina," Aug. 10, 1971, NSCCF, SES, "Saigon to Washington, 12/15/69–12/16/71" Folder, NSAF, Box 1, GRFL.

16. Nixon Presidential Address, Jan. 25, 1972, Public Papers of the Presidents; Richard M. Nixon, Washington, D.C., 1977) vol. 1972, p. 100. Thieu Address to the Nation, Jan. 26, 1972, Gram Martin Series (GMS), "Saigon to Washington, Jan. 3–28, 1972 (4)" Folder, NSAF, Box 1, GRFL.

17. Kimball, *Nixon's Vietnam War*, pp. 330–31.

18. Haig and Thieu, Oct. 4, 1972, memorandum of conversation, copy provided to author by Larry Berman; Ellsworth Bunker, "Talking Points for Meeting with President Thieu," Oct. 5, 1972, NSCCF, SES, "Memos, Speeches, Correspondence 7/26/72–11/11/72" Folder, NSAF, Box 7, GRFL.

19. Nixon to Thieu, Oct. 16. 1972, Richard Cheney Files (RCF), "Vietnam, Correspondence from Nixon to Thieu" Folder, Box 13, GRFL; Nguyen Van Thieu, "Mr. Thieu Calls for a Bandung-like Conference of Asian Nations to Find Peace," *New York Times,* Oct. 17, 1972.

20. Nixon to Thieu, Oct. 29, 1972, RCF, "Vietnam, Correspondence from Nixon to Thieu" Folder, Box 13, GRFL.

21. Government of Vietnam Foreign Ministry, "Memorandum of November 3, 1972 Outlining the Points Raised by the Government of the Republic of Vietnam on the Draft Agreement Dated October 17, 1972," NSCCF, SES, "Memos, Speeches, Correspondence 7/26/72–11/11/72" Folder, NSAF, Box 7, GRFL; Bunker and Thieu, Nov. 3, 1972, memorandum of conversation, ibid.

22. Thieu to Nixon, Nov. 26, 1972, NSC Files, PTS, "Paris Talks, July 1972–1973" Folder, Box 192, NLP, NARA; Kissinger and Duc, Nov. 29, 1972 (5:30 P.M.), memorandum of conversation; Nixon, Kissinger, and Duc, Nov. 29, 1972 (3:05 P.M.), memorandum of conversation, Prisoner of War–Missing in Action Files, NLP, NARA, copies provided to author by Larry Berman.

23. Kissinger to Nixon (annotated by Nixon), Nov. 28, 1972, memorandum, NSC Files, PTS, "Paris Talks, July 1972–1973" Folder, Box 192, NLP, NARA.

24. Haig to Nixon, Dec. 12, 1972, memorandum, provided to author by Larry Berman; Bunker to Rogers, cable (Saigon 17552), Dec. 14, 1972, National Security Archives, "Vietnam—Ceasefire, 1973," Folder, Box 1, George Washington University, Washington, D.C.

25. Henry A. Kissinger, *White House Years* (Boston: Little, Brown, 1979), pp. 1430–55; Richard M. Nixon, *RN: The Memoirs of Richard Nixon* (New York: Grosset and Dunlap), pp. 733–36.

26. Bunker to Kissinger, cable (Saigon 0313), Dec. 30, 1972, GMS, "Saigon to Washington, 12/26/72–1/15/73 (1)" Folder, NSAF, Box 3, GRFL; Rogers to Porter, cable (State 233994), Dec. 30, 1972, NSC Files, PTS, "Paris Talks (NODIS/Plus) August 1970" Folder, Box 189, NLP, NARA.

27. John Prados, "Fighting to a Finish: The Christmas Bombing of 1972," *VVA Veteran,* Dec., 1998–Jan., 1999, pp. 23–25.

28. Larry Berman, *No Peace, No Honor* (New York: Simon and Shuster, 2001), pp. 197–204, 216–17, 256–63.

Vietnam and the Origins of Détente

H. W. Brands

Without the Vietnam War, détente would have come sooner than it did, but it would have come less decisively. Moreover, its author would have been Lyndon Johnson rather than Richard Nixon.

This is the thesis I would like to test here—partly for its own sake, but partly as a way of demonstrating how thoroughly the war in Vietnam was an aspect of international history. It was Vietnam's war, first and foremost. It was America's war by America's decision. However, it was also the Soviet Union's war, and China's war. As a result, getting from war to peace required reconfiguring relations not simply between the two Vietnams, nor between the Vietnams and the United States, but among the United States, the two Vietnams, and the two communist great powers.

The evidence for testing my thesis will consist of primary American documents, published and unpublished; the work of other scholars, including several who have participated in earlier sessions of Lloyd Gardner's and Ted Gittinger's ongoing seminar; and—unavoidably, since this falls in the category of counterfactual history—some commonsense conjecture (at least I hope it will seem common sense). My analysis today will also include a surprise—not a surprise to historians, exactly, since they know it happened (although, out of context, some may have forgotten it), but a surprise to most of the historical actors at the time it happened, including Lyndon Johnson, who was on the verge of a diplomatic breakthrough that would have changed the course of history, and certainly changed our historical perception of him.[1]

The idea of détente had been around for a decade at the time Johnson took office. However, when first put forward it had nothing to do with Vietnam, which hardly registered on the radar of those hoping for an accommodation between the superpowers and a lessening of the combination of ideological confrontation and geopolitical jockeying that constituted the Cold War. After Joseph Stalin's death in 1953, various spokesmen in the West floated the idea of a meeting between the new Cold War leaders—Dwight

Eisenhower for the Americans, and whoever surfaced in the Soviet Union. The meeting took time to organize, but eventually was held in Geneva in the summer of 1955. The Geneva conference, being the first summit since before the Cold War, raised real hopes for settlement of one sort or another among many on both sides. However, as Gunter Bischof, Saki Dockrill, and the contributors to their new book on the subject demonstrate, the Geneva conference was burdened with all manner of issues besides relations between the United States and the Soviet Union. As a result, nothing of lasting importance came of it.[2]

The "spirit of Geneva," such as it was, dissipated under the strain of the Suez and Hungary crises of 1956, the Berlin crisis of 1958–61, the Bay of Pigs invasion and the Cuban missile crisis of 1962, and the sundry other irritations that made the last years of Eisenhower's administration and the first years of John Kennedy's peculiarly difficult in superpower relations. Yet the same period was similarly difficult in relations between the Soviet Union and China, and the possibility of a falling-out between Moscow and Beijing led American policy makers to consider the possibility of a falling-in, so to speak, between Moscow and Washington.[3]

Three months after Kennedy became president, analysts at the Central Intelligence Agency (CIA) assessed the state of Sino-Soviet relations:

> The present Soviet leaders have, since Stalin's death, come to recognize the complexities of the world scene. Since that time, they have become increasingly aware of tactical variety, the uses of diplomacy, exploitable differences among the imperialists and even among the new nations, levels of risk, the political assets and liabilities of their main antagonists. In pursuing the opportunities opened up by these insights, they have become increasingly subtle and increasingly disposed, sometimes out of necessity, to consider a wider set of variables.
>
> To the Chinese, still possessed by a much simpler, black-and-white world, this signifies that the USSR is becoming increasingly enmeshed in conventional international politics at the expense of world revolution and Chinese national interests.
>
> Given the depth of each side's views, and the fact that each has committed its prestige, neither is likely to win the other over by rational argument. A common goal and a common enemy will remain. But a common policy for combating this enemy, and reaching this goal, will be increasingly difficult to preserve.[4]

The CIA analysts were not saying that the Soviet Union had abandoned, or even materially modified, its attachment to world revolution and the overthrow of Western capitalism—although that is what the Chinese were saying about the "revisionists" in the Kremlin. The intelligence-gathering agency was merely pointing out that some tactical space had opened up between the Marxist-Leninist-Stalinists in Moscow and the Marxist-Leninist-Stalinist-Maoists in Beijing. Nor were the American analysts drawing any policy conclusions at this point—partly because no one asked them to, and partly because they remembered the fate during the McCarthy years of those who had drawn policy conclusions about the potential for division among the communists. Even so, this memo—dated April 1, 1961—revealed that Washington, or at least an important agency of the executive branch, appreciated the rift that was developing between the China and the Soviet Union.

During the rest of Kennedy's presidency, American officials observed the maneuvering between Moscow and Beijing with growing interest. A National Intelligence Estimate (NIE) made in August, 1961—produced at the height of the final, acute phase of the Berlin crisis—sized up the theoretical and practical elements of relations between the major communist powers. Theoretically, important differences between the communist powers should have been impossible, the abolition of classes in the communist countries having eradicated the contradictions that gave rise to struggles within and among the bourgeois powers. In practice, however, the unity of the communist movement during the early years of the Cold War had resulted far less from theoretical unanimity than from what the NIE analysts—representing the CIA, the State Department, the FBI, the Joint Staff, and the Army, Navy, and Air Force Departments—characterized as "the overwhelming authority exercised by Moscow." The Soviet Union was the oldest and best-established communist power; its economic and military power far overshadowed that of China or any other communist country; its leadership—Stalin until his death—enjoyed a preeminence among communists not approached by any rival.[5]

However, this was bound to change—and it had. China pulled itself together after its long and bitter civil war. In Eastern Europe, dissidents challenged orthodox communist rule in East Germany, Poland, and Hungary. Yugoslavia broke out of Moscow's sphere entirely. When Stalin died, his successors came nowhere near matching the man of steel's ruthless authority. As the world revolution rolled into Asia and Africa, China supplied a more credible role model than Russia.

The NIE paper précised these developments and then asserted that such changes would inescapably have "profound significance for the security and interests of the West." Should recent trends continue, these changes might "considerably diminish the effectiveness of the Communist movement as a whole. This would give the West opportunities for maneuver and influence which could provide important advantages in the world struggle." The NIE analysts ventured to say that "in the long run, Chinese power, assertiveness, and self-interest might increase so far as greatly to impair the common policy with the USSR, and even lead the Soviets to believe that they had more in common with the ideological enemy than they have today." This was the long term—about which kibbitzing was comparatively safe. "For some time to come, however, the most likely prospect is that the USSR and China will maintain their relationship in something like its present form. It will be an alliance which is from time to time troubled and inharmonious, but which nevertheless preserves sufficient unity to act in concert against the West, particularly in times of major challenge."[6]

With the advantage of hindsight, it might seem obvious that America's policy should have been directed toward exploiting the differences between the two primary threats to American security. It did not seem so obvious at the time, however. Communist China still looked like the third rail of U.S. diplomacy: touch it and you die. The China lobby—that is, the Taiwan lobby—had lost little of its influence; and largely because Communist China's economy remained so undeveloped, no countervailing Communist China lobby had developed. (In time—for example, by the time the Clinton administration engineered permanent normal trade relations for China—it would develop, and it would be even more effective than the Taiwan lobby.) Although diplomacy pointed toward making gestures to Beijing, politics pointed in the opposite direction. Not for the first time, nor the last, politics trumped diplomacy.

A few intrepid voices in the Kennedy administration advocated exploiting the new communist reality. Robert Komer of the White House staff urged a reconsideration of the policy of treating Chiang Kai-shek's regime on Taiwan as the one true representative of the Chinese people. "For a decade we've successfully prevented Peiping from consolidating its international position," Komer told McGeorge Bundy, his boss and Kennedy's national security adviser. "But the sands are running out on our ability to do so—and if we go down with flags flying instead of adjusting gracefully, our prestige and position will take an even greater pasting than otherwise." The current pressing issue was representation in the United Nations, which Taipei had and Beijing wanted. Washington sided with Taipei, but Komer did not think it should, or could, much longer. "We can't ever afford to forget that we are bucking a fundamentally adverse trend," he explained. "Our China's [that is, Taiwan's] international position is already seriously eroded and with each succeeding UN session will become weaker still. Thus this Administration faces the painful task of adjusting to this reality. While probably able to postpone a disaster this year, we must bear in mind that sooner or later we will have to take our lumps. True, as the President says, anything can happen between this year and next. But the odds are that whatever happens will be bad rather than good."

Komer acknowledged that political considerations in the United States seriously constrained the administration's policy choices. "Therefore, we must maneuver so as to permit a gradual retreat from our present position." The cover Komer proposed for the retreat was Chiang's "intransigence"— something never in short supply. Komer recommended admitting Beijing to the UN, while keeping Taipei there as well. This was currently anathema to Taipei and its lobbyists in America. Komer, however, believed it was in the interest of the United States. "No matter how we twist and turn, we can't avoid the fact that a Two Chinas policy is fundamentally in our interest." The most telling evidence supporting this view, Komer thought, was that Beijing was dead set against a two-Chinas policy. If the United States could shift the appearance of intransigence from Chiang to Mao, such a shift would suit American purposes. The administration could not wait forever, though. "The longer we postpone the inevitable, and the more isolated we become on such issues as Chirep [Chinese representation in the UN], the harder it will be to get Two Chinas accepted."[7]

Komer's remained a minority viewpoint. Kennedy had no stomach to force an unacceptable policy change on Chiang Kai-shek, a course that— especially after the Castro revolution in Cuba—almost certainly would have unleashed the dogs that had chased Harry Truman and Dean Acheson from office not that many years before. At one point, the president sent McGeorge Bundy to Taiwan to sound out Chiang, who gave the national security adviser an earful. "The Generalissimo made it abundantly clear that for the past thirteen years his sole purpose, and that of the GRC [Government of the Republic of China], had been to prepare for a victorious return to the mainland," Bundy cabled home. "To this end he had created on Taiwan a government which represented Free China, built a military machine capable of exploiting the deterioration of Communist control on the mainland, worked to create an expectation of deliverance among the Chinese people now under Communist rule, and maintained faith in ultimate victory among his adherents on Taiwan." Far from readying the retreat Robert Komer advocated, Chiang was preparing to reopen the war. Writing in June, 1962, Bundy related that Chiang told him that an offensive had originally been scheduled for the past April or May, but had been postponed for six months out of deference to American wishes. Yet Chiang said he could not delay much longer. He and his lieutenants must be "fully prepared to act in October."[8]

Bundy could not tell how serious Chiang was about reopening the civil war, but with the help of CIA director John McCone, Bundy got the generalissimo to agree to consult Washington before launching his invasion. Even if Chiang were merely making a point, however, that point was that Taiwan was not about to go gently into the night of second-class status in the United Nations or elsewhere.

Unwilling to buck Chiang, Kennedy confined American policy toward the mainland to the passivity of watchful waiting. There was much to watch. Chiang was not entirely wrong about the deteriorating conditions on the mainland. The "Great Leap Forward" had proved a disaster—a disaster compounded by bad weather and the suspension of Soviet economic and technical cooperation. "The combination of these factors has brought economic chaos to the country," declared Kennedy's NIE team. "Malnutrition is widespread, foreign trade is down, and industrial production and development have dropped sharply. No quick recovery from the regime's economic troubles is in sight." Yet even though the NIE team acknowledged "widespread disillusionment and disaffection" among the Chinese masses, it did not mean much. "We believe that widespread organized resistance to the regime is unlikely to develop. In any case, the regime's monopoly on arms, organization, and communications is probably sufficient to crush any incipient uprising."[9]

The administration's phlegmatic attitude was put to the test several months after the Cuban missile crisis. A fresh war scare developed in the American press, this time regarding what certain influential columnists considered the Chinese Communists' cavalier attitude toward nuclear war. Joseph Alsop asserted, "The Chinese evidently wish to reduce the world to smoking ruins, in the desperate expectation that among the ruins China would at last find her proper, predominant place." Walter Lippmann chimed, "The Red Chinese who profess to regard nuclear war as so tolerable that it need not be avoided, so desirable that it might profitably be provoked, have not yet been able to understand the actual nature and the revolutionary consequences of nuclear weapons."[10]

Kennedy, who could not ignore what Alsop and Lippmann were saying, gave the State Department the task of finding out what was behind the fevered language. The department's Bureau of Intelligence and Research assured the White House that the impassioned punditry "greatly oversimplifies and distorts Peiping's actual position," and noted that the Chinese Communist government had issued a statement flatly denying that Mao had ever advocated nuclear war. "We believe that the Chinese are cold-blooded but not irrational," the State Department analysts explained, "that their judgment is not always well-based or accurate, but that it is formed in terms of what the Chinese believe to be their self-interest." The evidence adduced to support the alleged Chinese inclination toward general war was threefold: Mao's notorious 1956 remark that even after a nuclear war China would still have a population of 300 million and be a great power, a 1960 statement by *Red Flag* that a new and more beautiful communist society would rise upon the ruins of imperialism after a nuclear war, and a recent statement by the Soviet Central Committee alleging that the Chinese had attempted to provoke a major war between the United States and the Soviet Union. The State Department analysts placed the Mao and *Red Flag* statements in the realm of brave polemic; as to the Soviet charge, it had to be weighed according to its source. "The Soviets may well believe that the courses of action proposed by the Chinese might have led to war between the US and the USSR and [that] this may even have been Peiping's object. Peiping's suggested policies might indeed have led to war." This was not the aim, however, nor would it be. "We believe they are unlikely to deliberately invite nuclear disaster upon the world or themselves." That having been said, complacency was hardly the appropriate course. "This does not, however, eliminate the element of miscalculation in Chinese Communist thinking, much less remove their intention to push aggressively wherever their estimate of the risks, political as well as military, seems adequately low."[11]

Yet the costs of miscalculation appeared to increase after the Chinese tested a nuclear device in the autumn of 1964. Although not a complete surprise by the time it happened, the Chinese test had not been expected so soon. As recently as 1962, Kennedy's intelligence experts had spoken of a limited Chinese nuclear capability "by the end of the decade." Assorted reports and intelligence tidbits in the first half of 1963 pushed the test date possibly forward—but only possibly. In July of that year, a State Department memo declared, "While there is some uncertainty surrounding the status of a Chinese nuclear program, it is tentatively estimated that a first device might be tested in early 1964, but that such a test might not occur until late 1964, 1965, or even later."[12]

By the time the first Chinese test occurred in October, 1964, Lyndon Johnson was president. However, events elsewhere in Asia—in Vietnam, to be precise—were complicating the question of U.S. relations with the communist great powers. Vietnam had been an issue among the Americans, Soviets, and Chinese since the early 1950s, of course. Great power pressure at the Geneva Conference in 1954 had produced the interim settlement that split Vietnam and, at several years' remove, provoked the war that was being waged more bitterly than ever during the mid-1960s. Until the 1960s, however, Vietnam had counted for relatively little in American diplomatic and political planning. When Robert Komer advocated a two-China policy as a way of easing tension in East Asia, he gave little thought to what such a policy would do to, or for, the situation in Vietnam—or vice versa.

By 1964, however, Vietnam had grown much larger in American thinking. American involvement, and American responsibility for Saigon's fate, had expanded exponentially in the decade since the Geneva Conference. With the increased involvement came the perception among American leaders that America's credibility required a victory in Vietnam. The recent overthrow of Diem, with Washington's complicity, added a certain moral element to the calculations; South Vietnam was now America's baby, to save or see destroyed. The United States still had interests regarding China and the Soviet Union that were distinct from Vietnam—interests that included, most pressingly, curtailing the spread of nuclear weapons. However, it became increasingly difficult for American leaders to separate those interests from Vietnam.

Meanwhile—to a degree American officials rarely appreciated—China and the Soviet Union had their own credibility problems regarding Vietnam. Ilya Gaiduk, Xiaoming Zhang, Robert Brigham, and Qiang Zhai have ably illuminated the contest that developed between Beijing and Moscow toward Hanoi. Both sides wished to maximize their influence with their Vietnamese comrades, while minimizing the burden of fighting Hanoi's war. Each side desired to portray itself as the leader of the socialist revolution, and therefore the pole toward which revolutionaries in other countries ought to gravitate. In certain respects, Moscow's and Beijing's Vietnam problems were greater than those of Washington. Washington simply had to try to win the war. Moscow and Beijing had to win the war, but at the same time keep each other from getting the credit for doing so. On top of this, the broader struggle between China and the Soviet Union was growing deeper and more intense—and, with the detonation of China's first nuclear bomb, much more alarming.[13]

Officials of the Johnson administration were unaware of much of the communist maneuvering over Vietnam, but they saw enough to pique their curiosity. In April, 1964, CIA director John McCone remarked at a National Security Council meeting that Chinese rhetoric regarding Russia had taken an unusually insulting turn. "Even the person of Khrushchev is now attacked by the Chinese Communists," McCone said. He added that certain intelligence sources (revealed to the president and the rest of the NSC but excised from the documentary record when it was declassified) "make it clear that the differences between the USSR and Communist China are even greater than those which have been made public."[14]

At the same meeting, Secretary of State Dean Rusk mused on the possibility of a permanent split between the two great communist powers.

Should such a split occur, Rusk said, it would produce a "revolutionary change in world affairs." For one thing—of particular importance as the United States moved farther into Vietnam—the Chinese would not be able to count on Soviet support if they sent troops to Vietnam.[15]

The possibility, and stakes, of a Sino-Soviet split seemed to increase when Beijing detonated its nuclear bomb a few months later. Johnson immediately convened the NSC to consider what this most recent development portended. John McCone pointed out that while China posed no nuclear threat to the United States—because it lacked intercontinental bombers and missiles—it did pose a threat to its neighbors, including the Soviet Union, which could be targeted by the Il-28 bombers already in China's arsenal.[16]

Carl Rowan, director of the U.S. Information Agency during the Johnson administration, thought the fallout would be psychological and political as well as military. Rowan predicted that the Chinese test would have a "major effect" in Africa, where the Chinese and the Soviets were vying for the favors of the newly emerging countries. Many Africans found the Chinese version of revolution more compelling than that of the Soviets, but Soviet strategic power had been hard to argue with prior to that time. By getting the bomb, the Chinese had gone far toward neutralizing the Soviet advantage on that score.

Dean Rusk saw a perhaps even more unsettling effect in Asia. India and Japan would have to pay attention to China's new status, not least because China's medium-range rockets could reach their territories.

Rusk was never the gambling type. Where others in the administration—Robert Komer, for example—might have seen this as an opportunity to press for a new relationship with Beijing, the secretary of state concluded just the opposite. "Now is no time for a new policy toward Communist China," he advised LBJ.

The president endorsed Rusk's caution. He told the NSC to prepare a "study in depth of Chinese Communist nuclear capabilities," but otherwise he stood pat.[17]

Johnson had two reasons for doing so, beyond those inherent in relations with China. The first was that, with the presidential election a mere three weeks away, he had no desire to derail what was shaping up as a major victory over the hawkish Barry Goldwater. China would simply have to wait.

The second reason was that, despite the administration's dovish sounds on Vietnam, LBJ was weighing a major escalation of the war there. Two months earlier, the president had requested, and duly received, congressional authorization for the use of American military forces in Indochina. The Tonkin Gulf resolution proved to be exceedingly elastic, stretching to cover a far larger war than any but the most pessimistic legislators had envisioned. Johnson, however, envisioning a much larger conflict, had no desire to complicate things by innovating with respect to China.

Within a month, Johnson's first reason for caution with respect to China—the 1964 election—was successfully liquidated. Meanwhile, the second reason grew more pressing. As Johnson approved the escalation in Vietnam, China's specter haunted his thinking. "If we come in with hundreds of thousands of men and billions of dollars, won't this cause them to come in?" the president demanded of Gen. Harold K. Johnson, the army chief of staff, who was requesting precisely those hundreds of thousands of men and billions of dollars. When the general replied, "I don't think they will," the president snapped, "MacArthur didn't think they would come in either." Suppose the Chinese did enter the war, the president mused, what would that mean? General Johnson thought for several moments and said, "If so, we have another ball game." To which President Johnson rejoined, "I have to take into account they will."[18]

Robert McNamara understood the president's worries and attempted to alleviate them. "So long as no US or GVN [South Vietnamese] troops invade North Vietnam, and so long as no US or GVN aircraft attack Chinese territory," the defense secretary said, "the Chinese probably will not send regular ground forces or aircraft into the war." Yet, as careful as Washington might be, McNamara recognized that the elbowing between Beijing and Moscow might provoke the Chinese to react to American actions in a way the United States could neither predict nor control. "The possibility of a more active Soviet involvement in North Vietnam might precipitate a Chinese introduction of land forces, probably dubbed volunteers, to preclude the Soviets' taking a pre-eminent position in North Vietnam."[19]

When LBJ agreed to send the first hundred thousand troops, he did so in a way designed to minimize the likelihood that China—and the Soviet Union—would feel required to respond in kind. The president's decision to cloak the escalation by announcing only the dispatch of the initial fifty thousand troops, and deferring announcement of the second fifty thousand, is typically interpreted in terms of American domestic politics. As far as it goes, this interpretation is correct. Yet Johnson's caution—which shaded over into prevarication—had a foreign audience as well. He revealed his thinking to the NSC when he ordered, "We will neither brag about what we are doing nor thunder at the Chinese Communists and the Russians."[20]

Johnson's fear of prodding the Chinese or the Soviets to overtly intervene in the war led him to set an outer limit on the use of American forces. During the first half of 1966, when the generals sought permission to bomb petroleum facilities in the Hanoi-Haiphong area and to mine Haiphong's harbor, Johnson expressed skepticism. "Do you think this will involve the Chinese Communists and the Soviets?" he demanded of Gen. Earle G. Wheeler. "No, sir," the chairman of the Joint Chiefs of Staff replied. "Are you more sure than MacArthur was?" the president pressed. "This is different," Wheeler explained. "We had ground forces moving to the Yalu." Johnson granted permission for the bombing, but refused to authorize the harbor mining. More importantly, he never even entertained the equivalent of sending troops to the Yalu—that is, invading North Vietnam.[21]

The war in Vietnam involved the Johnson administration in a number of ironies. Of these, the first was that even though the purpose of the war was to contain the expansion of Chinese influence, the Johnson administration in large part allowed the Chinese to dictate what means might be applied to effect that containment. Critics then and later have alleged that American forces failed in Vietnam because they were forced to fight with one hand tied behind their back. So they were, but the one doing the tying was the Chinese. Johnson could never know exactly how the Chinese would respond to particular provocations, but once they revealed that they had nuclear weapons he would have been foolish not to prepare for the worst.

A second irony—one clearly recognized by American officials at the time—was that even cautious conduct of the war played into China's hands in critical ways. "Peiping now appears to be seeking a decisive and humiliating defeat for the US," asserted a National Intelligence Estimate of mid-1965. No surprise there. What was less obvious, however, was that the mere presence of the United States in Vietnam contributed to Beijing's anti-Soviet offensive. The Chinese had been preaching the necessity of "wars of liberation" against the West while the Soviets were counseling "peaceful coexistence." American intervention in Vietnam appeared to bolster the Chinese position, at least in the thinking of that large part of the world that still considered colonialism the principal problem.[22]

The NIE authors stated their current assessment of China's view of its erstwhile patron:

> Peiping now sees Moscow as a rival for leadership of the world Communist movement, as a dangerously degenerate force which threatens to lead the movement into a revisionist, neo-bourgeois dead end, and as an unfaithful ally who refuses to lend proper support to legitimate Chinese objectives. The Chinese leaders are also well-imbued with traditional anti-Russian feeling; they are acutely conscious of Tsarist territorial grabs, resentful of numerous indigni-

ties perpetrated by the Communist Russians, nervously aware of their long common boundary, and on guard against Russian subversion of China's border tribes. The bitter rivalry with the USSR sometimes diverts Chinese energies from their focus on the US, but often the same course of action can serve both anti-US and anti-Soviet ends, as it does in Vietnam.

The NIE analysts laid out what they saw as China's principal policy objectives during the next few years:

1. to eject the West, especially the US, from Asia and to diminish US and Western influence throughout the world;
2. to increase the influence of Communist China in Asia;
3. to increase the influence of Communist China throughout the underdeveloped areas of the world;
4. and to supplant the influence of the USSR in the world at large, especially in the presently disunited Communist movement.

The first three items on the list were entirely unexceptional; it was the last that bore attention. The NIE authors underlined their point by rephrasing it: "The USSR has come increasingly to rival the US as a dominant problem for Chinese foreign policy."[23]

This development was what held out the promise of détente. From the time he assumed office, and for reasons largely independent of Vietnam, Johnson had hoped for better relations with the Soviet Union. The Cuban missile crisis had put the fear of nuclear Armageddon into everyone, and anything that would reduce the risk of general war was welcome. When the Chinese detonated their bomb in 1964, the doomsday clock jumped several minutes closer to midnight, not simply because another unfriendly country now had nuclear weapons, but because the Chinese broke the industrial-power barrier that seemed to have separated the nuclear haves from the have-nots. If China could get the bomb, so could five or ten or twenty other countries. The thought was enough to steal the sleep of any American president.[24]

The escalation of the war in Vietnam added to Johnson's incentives for détente. His war strategy had one aim: to convince the Vietnamese communists they could not win. One prong of this strategy was to strengthen South Vietnam's defense; that was the purpose of the American buildup. Another prong was to diminish North Vietnam's offensive capacity; that was where détente could most help. If the Soviets could be persuaded to cut back their assistance to Hanoi, the war might be measurably shortened.

A similar strategy had worked twice before. In 1954, Moscow and Beijing had imposed their will on Ho Chi Minh at Geneva. The success achieved there was not complete, as the war now continuing demonstrated. It had, however, forced France out of Indochina. It also gave the South Vietnamese several years of breathing room. Johnson would have been happy for another such success. More recently, the communist powers had collaborated in a settlement of the Vietnam-like civil war in Laos. Although it was no resounding victory for the West, Johnson was realistic enough to appreciate that resounding victories in Southeast Asia simply were not in the cards. Something that preserved the status quo for a time, and gave Saigon a chance to get on its feet—with continued American help, to be sure—would be more than welcome.[25]

Yet if Vietnam made détente more attractive to the United States, it also made détente more difficult to achieve. As noted, both the Soviets and the Chinese had their own credibility issues in Vietnam. The Vietnamese communists had accepted the Geneva Accords of 1954 only grudgingly; stronger now, they were unlikely to accept dictation from their communist comrades. Furthermore, the growing division between Moscow and Beijing made the cooperation of those two regimes increasingly unlikely. Absent such cooperation, neither regime separately would be inclined to push the North Vietnamese to the peace table, lest the other accuse it of capitulating to the capitalists.

Johnson nonetheless pressed forward on the issues that would form the centerpiece of détente. His first focus was a treaty to constrain the spread of nuclear weapons. The Chinese nuclear test in 1964 caused nonproliferation to move several rungs up the ladder of American priorities. Their test of a hydrogen device in June, 1967, made nonproliferation appear even more imperative. The 1967 war in the Middle East, which occurred in the same month as the Chinese H-bomb test, underscored the need for containing nuclear weapons by making the U.S. government confront more squarely the issue of Israel's capacity for producing such weapons. ("Don't you be the first power to introduce nuclear weapons into the Middle East," Dean Rusk warned Israeli foreign minister Abba Eban. "No," answered Eban, "but we won't be the second.")[26]

Johnson got his chance to pitch nonproliferation, and to treat other issues in U.S.-Soviet relations, at the unlikely venue of Glassboro, New Jersey. In the wake of the Middle East war, Soviet premier Alexei Kosygin came to the United Nations to profess Moscow's abiding interest in world peace. The president aimed to catch Kosygin en route and profess his own interest in peace, as well as in such substantive issues as nonproliferation. Glassboro turned out to be an acceptably neutral site, being roughly midway between the Soviet mission at the UN and the White House.

Johnson did not expect to accomplish much concrete at the meeting, following the advice of Averell Harriman, the veteran diplomat and Soviet-interlocutor. "With Russians," Harriman said, "it takes three meetings to make a deal: the first, courteous; the second, rough; the third, the deal is made." Still, the president hoped at least to make a start. He asserted his and Kosygin's responsibility for keeping order in the Middle East, explaining that the superpowers ought to act as "older brothers" to their friends and allies in the region and provide them "proper guidance." Johnson may or may not have known that Ho Chi Minh commonly referred to the Soviet Union and China as Vietnam's "big brother and big sister." If he did, it was a nice touch to use on the Soviet premier.[27]

From the Middle East, discussion turned to a question related more directly to the Cold War heart of U.S.-Soviet relations. Both sides were contemplating the construction of antiballistic missile (ABM) systems. Johnson and his advisers, especially Robert McNamara, feared an arms race in defensive weapons similar to that already under way in offensive weapons. The ABMs would be very expensive, administration officials guessed; moreover they would destabilize the nuclear balance. At Glassboro, Johnson and McNamara urged Kosygin to accept an agreement to forgo ABMs. Kosygin was skeptical, saying that the argument from the expense of the new systems represented "a commercial approach to a moral problem." He added, "When I have trouble sleeping, it's because of your offensive missiles, not your defensive missiles."[28]

Johnson made more progress on nuclear nonproliferation. The Soviets had hoped China could have been prevented from acquiring nuclear weapons, but there was nothing to be done on that score now. Moscow's primary concern was West Germany. Although the Germans showed little present interest in nuclear weapons, they might not always be so diffident, and the Soviets wanted to lock Bonn into a nonnuclear position. The United States was less worried about the Germans than about countries like India, Pakistan, Israel, and South Africa—any of which might feel obliged to obtain nuclear weapons out of fear of their neighbors. At Glassboro, neither Johnson nor Kosygin committed his country to anything specific, but the discussions indicated that the superpowers saw the situation complementarily, if not similarly. Johnson authorized his spokesman to report "definite headway" on the nonproliferation issue; a confidential administration memo asserted of the Russians, "It is perfectly clear that they want a non-proliferation treaty if they can get one."[29]

The two leaders also talked about Vietnam. Johnson delineated the American position that South Vietnam, as an independent nation, had every right to request American help in its defense, and that the United

States had every right to supply such help. Kosygin held to the Soviet line that "the Vietnam problem must be solved by the Vietnamese people themselves." Kosygin went on to assert that if Johnson stopped the bombing of Vietnam, peace talks could begin. This got Johnson's attention. He asked the Soviet leader if this were really so. Kosygin reiterated that it was. Kosygin added that Vietnam had disrupted relations between the Soviet Union and the United States, and had afforded China "a chance to raise its head, with consequent great danger for the peace of the entire world."[30]

On the general subject of superpower relations, Kosygin called himself "somewhat perplexed" at a statement Johnson made between sessions suggesting that tensions must always exist between socialist and capitalist systems. Johnson diplomatically declared that he was misquoted. On the contrary, he said, he believed that the two sides could work toward "mutually acceptable solutions to outstanding problems."[31]

The talks, which were hardly congenial, produced nothing like a breakthrough. "Meetings like this do not themselves make peace in the world," Johnson told the American people afterward. Yet the president refused to be discouraged. "It does help to sit down and look at a man right in the eye and try to reason with him, especially if he is trying to reason with you. We may have difficulties and differences ahead, but I think they will be lessened, and not increased, by our new knowledge of each other."[32]

In the months following the Glassboro summit, Johnson pressed ahead on several fronts. American and Soviet negotiators converted the agreement-in-principle that nuclear nonproliferation made superpower sense into a document to which the two parties could affix their signatures. The president pushed the Kremlin on the ABM issue. Historian John Prados has suggested that what has commonly been interpreted as a slip of the Johnson tongue—an earlier statement in which he admitted that American reconnaissance satellites allowed U.S. intelligence to count Soviet missiles—may in fact have been deliberate, a way to reassure Americans that he knew what he was doing on the arms-control question. Whether canny or careless, Johnson during the latter half of 1967 piggybacked the ABM issue, and the related question of caps on offensive systems, onto nonproliferation, with the result that when the nonproliferation treaty was opened for signatures in July, 1968, the United States and the Soviet Union announced their agreement "to enter in the nearest future into talks on limitation and reduction of offensive strategic nuclear weapons delivery systems as well as systems of defense against ballistic missiles."[33]

Meanwhile, of course, the war in Vietnam was going badly. The Tet Offensive prompted Johnson to suspend the largest part of the bombing of North Vietnam and—having thereby fulfilled most of the precondition

Kosygin had identified at Glassboro—to seek negotiations with Hanoi. Just hours before the speech in which he announced the suspension, Johnson spoke with Soviet ambassador Anatolii Dobrynin. He told Dobrynin that the bombing halt signified not weakness but a sincere desire for peace. Many Americans wanted him to widen the war, but he did not wish to follow this advice because a wider war would damage the interests of both the United States and the Soviet Union. He needed help, however—Soviet help. It was the responsibility of both superpowers, LBJ said, "to end the war soon and prevent hostilities from spreading."[34]

As matters transpired, the Russians were slow in bringing Hanoi to the bargaining table. Johnson had inferred some of Moscow's difficulties regarding Vietnam; now he experienced them directly. Hanoi held out for a complete bombing halt, and Moscow was reluctant to push its protégé—its "little brother"—to accept less. Not until October, 1968, did the North Vietnamese consent to formal negotiations, at which point Johnson was on the verge of a complete bombing halt for reasons relating primarily to the American election. (To be fair to the communist side, America's little brother—South Vietnam—was raising objections of its own.) A bitter Dean Rusk thereupon told the Russians to put up or shut up: "Now, I am also saying to all of those who have said, oh, things will be wonderful if you stop the bombing, we are saying to them, all right, get busy, get busy. See what you can do. We have made our move, now you make yours."[35]

Moscow's failure to help on Vietnam made Johnson's quest for détente more difficult but not—in the president's view—impossible. At Glassboro he had said he would send his top people to Moscow to get the arms-control process moving. "I'll have Robert McNamara in Moscow next Wednesday morning at nine o'clock," he told Kosygin. "Will you see him?" Now he indicated a determination to go to Russia himself. The Kremlin agreed to another summit, and a joint statement announcing an October visit was scheduled for August 20.[36]

Before the announcement was made, however, Johnson encountered a rude surprise. On the morning of August 20 the White House received word that Soviet armor had invaded Czechoslovakia to suppress the reform movement there.

The crushing of the "Prague spring" had immediate implications for Johnson's incipient détente. "Obviously the Soviet leaders were prepared to jeopardize their relationship with us . . . ," Clark Clifford told Johnson, "in order to shape the Czechoslovakian internal situation more to their liking." Johnson himself wondered aloud, "Can we talk now, after this?" Dean Rusk thought talks might yet be possible. "Soviet action against Czechoslovakia has not eliminated many major world strategic problems involving the U.S.S.R. and the U.S.," the secretary of state said.[37]

Johnson briefly hoped that the planned summit could be salvaged and the momentum toward détente preserved. However, by the time the furor over Czechoslovakia had died down, Richard Nixon had been elected president and the Kremlin saw no point in extending itself for a lame duck.[38]

At the beginning of this chapter I claimed that in the absence of the Vietnam War, détente would have come sooner than it did. As I near the end, it is time to substantiate this claim.

In the first place, as the evidence cited on China demonstrates, American officials, starting early in the Kennedy administration, were fully aware of the troubles developing between the Chinese and the Soviets. They were cautious about acting on this knowledge, although some (Dean Rusk, for instance) were more cautious than others (Robert Komer et al.). Yet the cautious and the bold alike understood that the rift in the communist camp created new opportunities for the United States, as Beijing learned to vilify Moscow in the same breath as Washington, if not quite in the same terms. The United States had originally committed to defend South Vietnam in order to contain China, at a time when the Soviet Union had no particular interest in China being contained. By the mid-1960s, however, Moscow had begun to see the benefits of a China-containment policy and could be expected to contribute to that end.

Any anti-China accommodation between the United States and the Soviet Union would begin geopolitically, as a straightforward exercise in realpolitik. It could not, however, help having ideological ramifications. Since the late 1940s American policy had been based on an assumption of immoral equivalency: all communists were essentially the same: basically evil. To accommodate the Soviets in the interest of corralling the Chinese would require modifying that view by accepting the idea that some communists were less evil than others. From this to a form of ideological agnosticism—communists could be good or evil, depending on their actions vis-à-vis American interests—might be but a short step.

The Vietnam War, however, blocked the accommodation both sides sought. As the war expanded, it became the touchstone for nearly every aspect of U.S. foreign policy. If the Soviet Union could not deliver Hanoi to the bargaining table, then Johnson could not afford to take significant steps in Moscow's direction. The Kremlin operated under similar constraints. Its credibility—vis-à-vis China and the rest of the second and third worlds—required supporting the Vietnamese communists against the American imperialists, even if that delayed or prevented actions otherwise in Soviet interests. (It would be interesting to know to what extent the Soviet decision to invade Czechoslovakia—the move that cost Johnson his Moscow trip and froze progress toward détente—reflected a Vietnam-exacerbated sense in the Kremlin that it had to demonstrate its resolve on behalf of world socialism, and thus deliver a riposte to Chinese criticism.)

I also said at the beginning that if détente had arrived during Johnson's presidency, it would have been less decisive than it actually proved to be. This is where conjecture comes into play. Richard Nixon was initially more cautious than LBJ in the matter of relations with the communists. He insisted on implementing his new policy with respect to the Vietnam War— the policy of "Vietnamization"—before turning his attention to the communist great powers. Yet, when he did deal with Moscow and Beijing, Nixon did so more boldly than Johnson had ever thought of doing. To some degree this reflected his larger strategic vision: of a new structure of international relations, based on three (or more) pillars, rather than the two pillars of the Cold War. Johnson had vision, but it related almost entirely to domestic affairs. Nixon's boldness, on the other hand, reflected what quickly became conventional wisdom: that it took an old red-baiter like Nixon to go to China. Johnson, or any other representative of the party of Truman and Acheson, would have had a far harder time pulling off such a coup.

Finally, Nixon's détente reflected the four additional years of the Vietnam War that separated 1972 from 1968. By the later date, America's vexation with the war had reached the point that Nixon's audacious move was not only possible, but also desirable—indeed, almost necessary. Vietnam had been a festering sore during Johnson's presidency; by the end of Nixon's first term, it had become a raging boil that had to be lanced by the most drastic means available.[39]

Notes

1. The Gardner-Gittinger seminar has produced two volumes to date: *Vietnam: The Early Decisions* (Austin: University of Texas Press, 1997), and *International Perspectives on Vietnam* (College Station: Texas A&M University Press, 2000), both edited by Lloyd C. Gardner and Ted Gittinger.

2. Gunter Bischof and Saki Dockrill, *Cold War Respite: The Geneva Summit of 1955* (Baton Rouge: Louisiana State University Press, 2000).

3. The course of the Cold War in the late 1950s and early 1960s can be followed in any standard treatment, including Walter LaFeber, *America, Russia, and the Cold War, 1945–1996* (New York: McGraw-Hill, 1997); and John Lewis Gaddis, *Russia, the Soviet Union, and the United States: An Interpretive History* (New York: McGraw-Hill, 1990). A recent account of Sino-Soviet problems is Odd Arne Westad, ed., *Brothers in Arms: The Rise and Fall of the Sino-Soviet*

Alliance, 1945–1963 (Washington, D.C., and Stanford, Calif.: Woodrow Wilson Center Press and Stanford University Press, 1998). The most succinct account of the Sino-Soviet–American triangle is Gordon Chang, *Friends and Enemies: The United States, China, and the Soviet Union, 1948–1972* (Stanford, Calif.: Stanford University Press, 1990).

4. "The Sino-Soviet Dispute and Its Significance," Apr. 1, 1961, National Security File (NSF), Box 24, John F. Kennedy Presidential Library, Boston, Mass. (hereafter JFKL).

5. NIE 10–61, "Authority and Control in the Communist Movement," Aug. 8, 1961, *Foreign Relations of the United States (FRUS), 1961–1963,* vol. 22, *Northeast Asia* (Washington, D.C.: GPO, 1996), pp. 114–18.

6. Ibid.

7. Komer to Bundy, Oct. 19, 1961, Box 22, NSF, JFKL.

8. Bundy to Kennedy, June 7, 1962, Box 22–24 addenda, ibid.

9. NIE 13–4-62, "Prospects for Communist China," May 2, 1962, *FRUS, 1961–1963,* pp. 22:221–23. On the Great Leap Forward and its aftermath, see Roderick MacFarquhar, *The Great Leap Forward, 1958–1960* (New York: Columbia University Press, 1983); and Alfred L. Chan, *Mao's Crusade: Politics and Policy Implementation in China's Great Leap Forward* (New York: Oxford University Press, 2001).

10. Alsop and Lippmann quoted in research memorandum RFE-64, "Is Peiping Trying to Trigger World War III?" forwarded in George C. Denney Jr. to Dean Rusk, July 22, 1963, NSF, Box 22–24 addenda, JFKL.

11. Ibid.

12. NIE 13–4-62, *FRUS, 1961–1963,* p. 22:222; Robert H. Johnson to Walt Rostow, July 19, 1963, NSF, Box 22–24 addenda, JFKL.

13. Ilya V. Gaiduk, "Containing the Warriors: Soviet Policy toward the Indochina Conflict, 1960–65"; Xiaoming Zhang, "Communist Powers Divided: China, the Soviet Union, and the Vietnam War"; Robert K. Brigham, "Vietnam at the Center: Patterns of Diplomacy and Resistance"; and Qiang Zhai, "An Uneasy Relationship: China and the DRV during the Vietnam War"—all in *International Perspectives on Vietnam,* ed. Gardner and Gittinger. On the nuclear angle in the Sino-Soviet rivalry, see McGeorge Bundy, *Danger and Survival: Choices about the Bomb in the First Fifty Years* (New York: Random House, 1988), pp. 525–35.

14. Notes of meeting, Apr. 2, 1964, NSC Meetings File, Box 1, Lyndon B. Johnson Library, Austin, Tex. (hereafter LBJL).

15. Ibid.

16. Notes of meeting, Oct. 17, 1964, ibid.

17. Ibid.

18. Notes of meeting, July 22, 1965, ibid.

19. McNamara to Johnson, June 26, 1965, (revised July 1, 1965), ibid.

20. Notes of meeting, July 27, 1965, ibid.

21. Notes of meeting, June 22, 1966, NSC Meetings File, Box 2, LBJL.

22. NIE 13–9-65, May 5, 1965, NIE File, Box 4, LBJL.

23. Ibid.

24. On Johnson's policy toward the Soviet Union, see Vladislav M. Zubok, "Unwrapping the Enigma: What was Behind the Soviet Challenge in the 1960s?" in *The Diplomacy of the Crucial Decade,* ed. Diane B. Kunz (New York: Columbia University Press, 1994); and John Prados, "Prague Spring and SALT: Arms Limitations Setback in 1968," in *The Foreign Policies of Lyndon Johnson: Beyond Vietnam,* ed. H. W. Brands (College Station: Texas A&M University Press, 1999).

25. On the Soviet role in brokering a settlement for Laos, see Gaiduk, "Containing the Warriors," pp. 65–70.

26. Rusk and Eban in Douglas Little, "A Fool's Errand: America and the Middle East, 1961–1969," in *Diplomacy*, ed. Kunz, p. 306.

27. Harriman in Rostow to Johnson, June 24, 1967, Country File, Box 229, LBJL. On the GLASSBORO summit, see H. W. Brands, *The Wages of Globalism: Lyndon Johnson and the Limits of American Power* (New York: Oxford University Press, 1995), pp. 215–18; and Robert Dallek, *Flawed Giant: Lyndon Johnson and His Times, 1961–1973* (New York: Oxford University Press, 1998), pp. 432–38. Dallek's is the most thorough and judicious account of Johnson's presidency. The memoranda of the GLASSBORO conversations, dated June 23 and 25, 1967, can be found in Declassified and Sanitized Documents from Unprocessed Files (DUSDUF) File, Box 1, LBJL. The quote from Ho is in Xiaoming Zhang, "Communist Powers Divided," p. 83. Regarding the sibling metaphor, Lloyd Gardner observes, "Probably not since FDR welcomed Stalin to the 'family circle' at Tehran had there been so much talk about older brothers and the rest of the world" ("Fighting Vietnam: The Russian-American Conundrum," in *International Perspectives on Vietnam*, ed. Gardner and Gittinger, p. 48). Gardner provides another account of the GLASSBORO summit.

28. Memoranda of conversation, June 23 and 27, 1967, DUSDUF File, Box 1, LBJL; Brands, *Wages of Globalism*, p. 217; Dallek, *Flawed Giant*, p. 436. The best accounts of Johnson's arms-control policies are Prados, "Prague Spring," and Robert A. Divine, "Lyndon Johnson and Strategic Arms Limitation," in *The Johnson Years*, vol. 3, *LBJ at Home and Abroad*, ed. Robert A. Divine (Lawrence: University Press of Kansas, 1994).

29. Dallek, *Flawed Giant*, p. 436. On the nonproliferation issue, a good starting point is Bundy, *Danger and Survival*, pp. 513ff.

30. Memoranda of conversation, June 23 and 27, 1967, DUSDUF File, Box 1, LBJL; Brands, *Wages of Globalism*, p. 217; Gardner, "Fighting Vietnam," pp. 49–50.

31. Dallek, *Flawed Giant*, pp. 436–37. Johnson's statements on the talks are in vol. 1 of *Public Papers of the Presidents: Lyndon Baines Johnson, 1967* (Washington, D.C.: Government Printing Office, 1968), pp. 650–52.

32. Johnson's statement of June 25, 1967, in ibid., p. 652.

33. Prados, "Prague Spring," p. 23; U.S.-Soviet statement, ibid., p. 24.

34. Johnson quoted in Gardner, "Fighting Vietnam," p. 53.

35. Ibid., 56. For a fuller treatment of this and many other matters relating to Vietnam, see Lloyd C. Gardner, *Pay Any Price: Lyndon Johnson and the Wars for Vietnam* (Chicago: Ivan R. Dee, 1995).

36. Dean Rusk, as told to Richard Rusk, *As I Saw It* (New York: Norton, 1990), p. 293.

37. Clifford to Johnson, Aug. 24, 1968, Memos to the President File, Box 39, LBJL; notes of meeting, Sept. 4, 1968, NSC Meetings File, Box 2, LBJL.

38. Prados, "Prague Spring," is the best summary of the connection between the invasion of Czechoslovakia and the collapse of the planned summit.

39. By far the most thorough account of détente is Raymond L. Garthoff, *Détente and Confrontation: American-Soviet Relations from Nixon to Reagan* (Washington, D.C.: Brookings Institution, 1994).

Contributors

H. W. Brands is distinguished professor of history and Ralph R. Thomas Class of '21 professor in liberal arts at Texas A&M University. He is the author of *The Wages of Globalism: Lyndon Johnson and the Limits of American Power; What America Owes the World: The Struggle for the Soul of Foreign Policy*, and other books.

Robert K. Brigham is an associate professor of history at Vassar College in Poughkeepsie, New York. He is the author of *Guerrilla Diplomacy: The NLF's Foreign Relations and the Vietnam War; Ending a Deadly Conflict: Why the Vietnam Peace Process Failed, and its Lessons for the 21st Century* (with James G. Blight, pending), and "Vietnamese-American Peace Negotiations: The Failed 1965 Initiatives," in the *Journal of American-East Asian Relations.*

Charles G. Cogan is a senior research associate at the John F. Kennedy School of Government, and an affiliate at the John M. Olin Institute for Strategic Studies and the Center for European Studies, Harvard University in Cambridge, Massachusetts. He spent thirty-seven years in the Central Intelligence Agency. From mid-1979 to mid-1984 he was chief of the Near East and South Asia Division in the Directorate of Operations at CIA headquarters. From September, 1984–September, 1989, he was the CIA chief in Paris. He has published articles in *Cahiers de la Fondation Charles de Gaulle; French Politics and Society; Centre d'Etudes d'Histoire de la Défense;* and the *Cold War International History Project.*

Robert A. Divine is Littlefield Professor Emeritus of History at the University of Texas at Austin, where he taught American diplomatic history for forty-two years. His primary interest is in twentieth-century American foreign policy and the presidency. He has written and edited books on three presidents—Franklin D. Roosevelt, Dwight D. Eisenhower, and Lyndon B. Johnson. Professor Divine has also written about nuclear testing and the American response to *Sputnik*. His latest book, *Perpetual War for Perpetual Peace*, is a comparative analysis of America's twentieth-century wars.

ILYA V. GAIDUK is a senior research fellow at the Institute of World History, Russian Academy of Science in Moscow. He is interested in the history of Soviet foreign policy and Russian (Soviet)-American relations. For a number of years he has made a special study of Soviet policy toward the Vietnam War. He is the author of *The Soviet Union and the Vietnam War* and currently is at work on another book on Soviet policy toward the Indochina conflict in the period 1954–63.

LLOYD C. GARDNER has been at Rutgers University, New Jersey, since 1963, where he is the Charles and Mary Beard Professor of History. He has published widely on U.S. foreign policy, including *Approaching Vietnam: From World War II to Dien Bien Phu* and *A Covenant With Power: America and World Order From Wilson to Reagan*.

GEORGE C. HERRING of the University of Kentucky edited *The Secret Diplomacy of the Vietnam War: The Negotiating Volumes of the Pentagon Papers* and is the author of *America's Longest War: The United States and Vietnam, 1950–1975*. He has been a visiting professor at the United States Military Academy, is past editor of the journal *Diplomatic History*, and a Guggenheim Fellow.

JAMES G. HERSHBERG is an associate professor of history and international affairs at George Washington University; the author of *James B. Conant: Harvard to Hiroshima and the Making of the Nuclear Age;* and CWIHP Working Paper no. 27 (April, 2000), "Who Murdered 'Marigold'? New Evidence on the Mysterious Failure of Poland's Secret Initiative to Start U.S.–North Vietnamese Peace Talks, 1966."

DAVID KAISER is a professor in the Strategy Department at the Naval War College in Providence, Rhode Island. He is the author of *American Tragedy: Kennedy, Johnson, and the Origins of the Vietnam War* and "Men and Policies, 1961–69," in *The Crucial Decade: Foreign Policy in the Kennedy-Johnson Years,* ed. Diane B. Kunz.

HIDEKI KAN, of the Graduate School of Social and Cultural Studies at Kyushu University, Japan, is currently working on U.S.-Japanese security relations in the 1960s and 1970s, the Vietnam War, and international relations. He has published articles on these topics in the *Journal of Law and*

Politics, the *Japanese Journal of American Studies,* the (Japanese) *Journal of International Relations,* and the (Japanese) *Journal of Western History.*

THOMAS J. KNOCK is an associate professor of history at Southern Methodist University in Dallas. He is the author of *To End All Wars: Woodrow Wilson and the Quest for a New World Order* and is currently writing a political biography of George McGovern.

MARK LAWRENCE is an assistant professor of history at the University of Texas, Austin. A specialist in the history of U.S. foreign relations, Lawrence is revising a book-length study of the relationship between the United States, France, and Great Britain with respect to Indochina between 1944 and 1950 for the University of California Press. The book is entitled *Embracing Vietnam: The United States, Europe, and the Making of the Cold War Consensus in Indochina.*

FREDRIK LOGEVALL is an associate professor of history and codirector of the Cold War History Group at the University of California at Santa Barbara. He is the author of *Choosing War: The Lost Chance for Peace and the Escalation of War in Vietnam.* Logevall is presently at work on an international history of the struggle for Indochina from 1945–65 and is coeditor in chief of the forthcoming *Encyclopedia of American Foreign Policy.*

WILFRIED MAUSBACH is a research fellow in the Department of History at the University of Heidelberg. He is the author of *The United States and Germany in the Era of the Cold War 1945–1990;* coeditor of *America's War and the World: Vietnam in International and Comparative Perspectives* (forthcoming); and currently is at work on a book tentatively titled *Vietnam in Germany: The Impact of America's War on West German Politics and Society, 1963–1975.*

EDWIN E. MOÏSE is a professor of history at Clemson University in South Carolina. His main current research interest is the Vietnam War. He is the author of *Tonkin Gulf and the Escalation of the Vietnam War; Modern China: A History;* and *Land Reform in China and North Vietnam.*

JOHN PRADOS is an independent scholar and director of the Vietnam Documentation Project at the National Security Archive in Washington, D.C. He is the author of *The Blood Road: The Ho Chi Minh Trail and the Vietnam War; Valley of Decision: The Siege of Khe Sanh,* and many other works. He is also a prize-winning designer of strategic games.

ANDREW PRESTON is a Canadian in the final year of his doctoral work in history at Cambridge University (Sidney Sussex College). His dissertation is titled "The Little State Department: McGeorge Bundy, the NSC Staff, and the Escalation of the Vietnam War, 1961–66." He is a graduate of the University of Toronto and has an MA from the London School of Economics. He was a Fox International Fellow at Yale University, and has presented papers on Canada and the Vietnam War at Society of Historians of American Foreign Relations and American Historical Association annual conferences.

HERBERT Y. SCHANDLER is a qualified Special Forces officer who served two tours in Vietnam. He earned his doctorate at Harvard University and has served on the faculties of the U.S. Military Academy and National War College. He is the author of *The Unmaking of a President: Lyndon Johnson and Vietnam* and contributed a chapter to Robert McNamara's *Argument Without End: In Search of Answers to the Vietnam Tragedy.*

MELVIN SMALL is a professor of history at Wayne State University in Detroit. A former president of the Peace History Society, he is the author of *Johnson, Nixon, and the Doves; Covering Dissent: The Media and the Anti-Vietnam War Movement;* and *Democracy and Diplomacy: The Impact of Domestic Politics on U.S. Foreign Policy, 1789–1994.*

MAURICE VAÏSSE is director of the Center for Defense History Studies, Château de Vincennes, Paris, and university professor at the Institut d'études politiques de Paris. His works include *Diplomatie et outil militaire, 1871–1991,* and *La Grandeur: politique étrangère du général de Gaulle, 1958–1969.*

MARILYN YOUNG is a professor of history at New York University and director of NYU's Center for Advanced Studies, which is currently focusing on the Cold War. Her most recent work is *The Vietnam Wars, 1945–1990.* She currently holds a Guggenheim Foundation fellowship and is working on a book on the Korean War.

QIANG ZHAI is a professor of history at Auburn University at Montgomery, Alabama. He is the author of *The Dragon, the Lion, and the Eagle: Chinese-British-American Relations, 1949–1958,* and *China and the Vietnam Wars, 1950–1975.*

Index

ISBN 1-58544-342-5

90000